The
Sociology
of Law

The Sociology of Law

A Social–Structural Perspective

Edited by
WILLIAM M. EVAN
University of Pennsylvania

THE FREE PRESS
A Division of Macmillan Publishing Co., Inc.
NEW YORK

Collier Macmillan Publishers
LONDON

Copyright © 1980 by The Free Press
    A Division of Macmillan Publishing Co., Inc.

The Free Press
A Division of Macmillan Publishing Co., Inc.
866 Third Avenue, New York, N.Y. 10022

Collier Macmillan Canada, Ltd.

Library of Congress Catalog Card Number: 78-24669

Printed in the United States of America

printing number
1 2 3 4 5 6 7 8 9 10

Library of Congress Cataloging in Publication Data

Main entry under title:

Sociology of law.

    1. Sociological jurisprudence--Addresses,
essays, lectures. I. Evan, William M.
K376.S65   340'.115   78-24669
ISBN 0-02-909760-6

To the next generation
of sociologists of law

Contents

PART V: SOCIAL-STRUCTURAL THEORY OF LAW: ORGANIZATIONAL ANALYSIS

Appendix III: Legal Documents

PART VI: SOCIAL-STRUCTURAL THEORY OF LAW: INTERINSTITUTIONAL ANALYSIS

Preface

The sociology of law is in a state of ferment. A variety of theoretical approaches have been formulated in recent years, and a multitude of empirical studies have been undertaken. Under the circumstances, a book purporting to encompass this growing field must be highly selective. Six major theoretical perspectives have been chosen for consideration: behavioralist theory, jurisprudential theory, functionalist theory, conflict theory, socialization theory, and systems theory. For some time to come, these alternative paradigms will be the subject of analysis and controversy as well as a source of ideas for different styles of inquiry in this field. It is my judgment, however, that in the course of the next decade one or another version of a systems theory of law*—integrating several of the key concepts and propositions of competing theories—will be developed.

This book is divided into seven parts. In Part I the question of defining the subject matter of the sociology of law is addressed. Part II surveys alternative theoretical orientations, concluding with a systems theory perspective. Since a systems theory of law is still in embryonic form, a social-structural model of law—based on some ideas of systems theory combined with some elements of Parsons's theory—provides the organizing framework for the book. This model consists of four interrelated elements: values, norms, roles, organizations, and the derivative concepts of institutions and interinstitutional relations. Each of these structural components is treated, in turn, in Parts III, IV, V, and VI. Part VII analyzes several failures of legal systems and examines the role of law in planned social change.

Apart from the diverse theoretical contributions by sociologists, anthropologists, political scientists, and social psychologists, the reader will discover a rich assortment of empirical studies dealing with different societies: United States, Czechoslovakia, Communist China, West Germany, Britain, France, and India. In addition, the five legal appendices, a distinctive feature of the book, present sets of legal documents that will give the reader a further appreciation of the nature of legal decision-making, legal reasoning, and legal process as these are shaped by social institutions. Although most of the legal documents in the appendices are drawn from the American legal

*See my paper "Systems Theory and the Sociology of Law," presented at the Ninth World Congress of Sociology in Uppsala, Sweden, August 1978 (to appear in my forthcoming book *Law and Social Structure*).

xv

system, one pertains to the Japanese legal system and several refer to international law.

This book is intended for students, teachers, and researchers with an interest in the relationship between law and society. It is designed to introduce the student—undergraduate, graduate, and law student— to a research specialty within sociology that is bound to grow at an even faster rate in the years ahead than in the past decade. Whether the student is interested in pursuing a career in law or in increasing his knowledge of the workings of the legal system in its various social settings, he will find this book of forty carefully selected and arranged readings instructive and provocative.

Instructors may wish to use this book in a one-semester or a two-semester course. In the latter case, students can be asked to undertake library investigations or empirical studies on any of the topics in the book. In the introductions to each part, several unsolved problems are identified, which students may wish to explore. Likewise, the introductions to the five legal appendices pose a variety of questions for further study.

When I first offered a course in the sociology of law at Columbia University in 1958, I had the good fortune of having several outstanding students, among them Vernon Dibble, Ezra Levin, and Mildred A. Schwartz. All three of these highly gifted students, who are now distinguished professionals, helped me clarify some perplexing questions in this field. Once again I would like to record my indebtedness to a friend and a teacher, Thomas A. Cowan, a legal scholar of singular originality, grace, and wisdom. I should also like to thank several of my recent students at the University of Pennsylvania: Deborah Baskin, Albert Crawford, Laura Farmelo, Roman Koropey, David Labaree, Charles McClure, and Michael Nussbaum. In the final stages of editing this book, Albert Crawford and Laura Farmelo made several invaluable suggestions, for which I am very grateful indeed.

Finally, I would like to express my sincere gratitude to Charles E. Smith, Assistant Vice President of Macmillan Publishing Company, and to Gladys Topkis, Sociology Editor of The Free Press, for their counsel in publishing a book that will in effect replace my 1962 *Law and Sociology* volume, which has long since been out of print. At the rate the sociology of law is likely to grow in the coming years, a new edition will probably be necessary within four or five years.

This book is dedicated to the next generation of sociologists of law whose research efforts, aided by more powerful theory and more rigorous methodology, are bound to produce new insights into the functioning of law in society.

Philadelphia, Pennsylvania   William M. Evan

PART I

Defining the Sociology of Law

The subject matter of a discipline or a subdiscipline is seldom defined by an individual scientist or scholar. Barring the appearance of an exceptional genius such as a Newton, a Freud, or an Einstein, a discipline, or a specialty thereof, tends to be defined collectively and progressively. Common concepts arise through the cumulative development of a body of knowledge and lead to a series of redefinitions of the subject matter.

In the case of the sociology of law, there has been a temptation to define it as a branch of general sociology that draws on the theory and methodology of the discipline as a whole. This has been the view of a number of European sociologists of law, notably Geiger, Segerstedt, and Aubert (Blegvad, 1966; Podgórecki, 1974: 32–51). The drawback in such a view is that the field of general sociology is still so ill defined itself and there is such a diversity of conceptions as to the substance and scope of general sociological theory and methodology that it is not at all clear what particular perspective general sociology brings to bear on the law.

In the selection by Campbell and Wiles, two contrasting views of the subject are articulated: the "sociology of law," as a specialty within general sociology that seeks to illuminate the relationship between the legal order and the social order, is differentiated from "socio-legal studies," with its focus on problems of justice and law reform. Are these two approaches to the subject as mutually incompatible as Campbell and Wiles suggest? Or do these views represent alternative research strategies, with one functioning as a means to the attainment of the end posited by the other?

1

Just in case the foregoing questions are not sufficiently perplexing, the reading by Cotterrell opens up a Pandora's box of questions. Can or should the sociology of law ignore the questions raised by the field of jurisprudence in the course of millennia of inquiry concerning the nature of law and legal concepts, the sources of law, the grounds for the validity of law, the nature of justice, etc.? Cotterrell contends that the sociology of law cannot ignore the heritage of jurisprudence, in this respect echoing the views of Selznick (1961) and others. If Cotterrell's conception of the subject matter of the sociology of law is accepted, wherein does its distinctive contribution lie? Is it in the explication of the social sources and consequences of legal norms and values? Is it in particular theories and methodologies?

Perhaps least problematic is the view advanced in the selection by Bohannan, who is not directly or even indirectly concerned with defining the subject of the sociology of law. However, in formulating his concept of "double institutionalization," Bohannan has identified a fundamental process of concern to the sociology of law: Under what circumstances do nonlegal norms and values articulated in one or another nonlegal institution become "doubly institutionalized," that is, reinforced within the legal institutions of a society? Are literate or modern societies more likely to exhibit the process of double institutionalization than nonliterate or traditional societies? Does Bohannan's concept imply that legal institutions must of necessity follow the lead of other social institutions, that they cannot *initiate* new forms of institutionalization of norms and values that are not already grounded in custom? He does acknowledge that a legal system can perform an innovative function, institutionalizing a norm that is not already incorporated in a nonlegal institution. Under what circumstances does this occur? Perhaps a potentially significant contribution of the sociology of law lies in the description and explanation of this innovative function.

Thus, with the aid of Bohannan's concept, we may now formulate an even more general problem for the sociology of law: Under what circumstances are legal norms *institutionalized* and *de-institutionalized* in a society?

References

Blegvad, B. -M. (1966). "The Systematic Position of Sociology of Law in Current Scandinavian Research." *Acta Sociologica*, 10: 2-19.

Podgórecki, A. (1974). *Law and Society*. London: Routledge & Kegan Paul.

Selznick, P. (1961). "Sociology and Natural Law." *Natural Law Forum*, 6: 84-108.

1

Law and Legal Institutions
Paul Bohannan

More scholarship has probably gone into defining and explaining the concept of "law" than into any other concept still in central use in the social sciences. Efforts to delimit the subject matter of law—like efforts to define it—usually fall into one of several traps that are more easily seen than avoided. The most naive beg the question and use "law" in what they believe to be its common-sense, dictionary definition—apparently without looking into a dictionary to discover that the word "law" has six entries in Webster's second edition, of which the first alone has 13 separate meanings, followed by five columns of the word used in combinations. German and French have even more complex ambiguities, since their comparable words (*Recht*, *droit*) include some dimensions for which English uses other words. . . .

In the effort to define "law," some modern scholars like Hart (1954) conclude that there are three "basic issues": (1) How is law

Excerpt from "Law and Legal Institutions," *International Encyclopedia of the Social Sciences*, Volume 9 (New York: Macmillan Company, Free Press, 1968), pp. 73–78, by permission of author and publisher.

related to the maintenance of social order? (2) What is the relation between legal obligation and moral obligation? (3) What are rules and to what extent is law an affair of rules? Others (Stone 1966) describe several sets of attributes that are usually found associated with law. Accordingly, law is (1) a complex whole, (2) which always includes social norms that regulate human behavior. These norms are (3) social in character, and they form (4) a complex whole that is "orderly." The order is (5) characteristically coercive and (6) institutionalized. Law has (7) a degree of effectiveness sufficient to maintain itself. Anthropological studies of law in the non-Western world have followed a similar course. To cite one of the most vivid and orderly presentations, Pospisil (1958) examined several attributes of the law— the attribute of authority, that of intention of universal application, that of *obligatio* (the right—obligation cluster), and that of sanction. In his view, the "legal" comprises a field in which custom, political decision, and the various attributes overlap, though each may be found extended outside that overlapping field, and there is no firm line, but rather a "zone of transition," between that which is unquestionably legal and that which is not.

It was Kantorowicz (1958) who pointed out that there are many subjects, including some of a nonlegal nature, that employ a concept of law. He perceived that each needs a different definition of "law" if it is to achieve its purposes. . . . Kantorowicz's method in jurisprudence is very like Pospisil's in anthropology. Instead of trying to find points for definition of law, Kantorowicz examined some characteristics of law that are vital to one or more of the specific definitions. Law is thus characterized by having a body of rules that prescribe external conduct (it makes little immediate difference to the law how one feels about it—the law deals in deeds). These rules must be stated in such a way that the courts or other adjudging bodies can deal with them. Each of the rules contains a moralizing or "ought" element—and Kantorowicz fully recognized that this "ought" element is culturally determined and may change from society to society and from era to era. Normative rules of this sort must, obviously, also be distinguished from the real uniformities by which men (sometimes with and sometimes without the help of courts and lawyers) govern their daily round of activity. Law is one of the devices by means of which men can reconcile their actual activities and behavior with the ideal principles that they have come to accept, and can do it in a way that is not too painful or revolting to their sensibilities and in a way which allows ordered (which is to say predictable) social life to continue. No act is wholly bad if it is "within the law"; no law is wholly good if it condones "immoral" action.

Rules

Custom is a body of more or less overt rules which express "ought" aspects of relationships between human beings and which are actually followed in practice much of the time. Law has an additional characteristic: it must be what Kantorowicz calls "justiciable," by which he means that the rules must be capable of reinterpretation, and be actually reinterpreted, by one of the legal institutions of society so that the conflicts within nonlegal institutions can be adjusted by an outside "authority."

It is widely realized that many peoples of the world can state more or less precise "rules" which are, in fact, the ideals in accordance with which they think they ought to judge their conduct. In all societies there are allowable lapses from rules, and in most there are more or less precise rules (sometimes legal ones) for breaking rules.

Legal Institutions

In order to make the distinction between law and other rules, it has been necessary to introduce furtively the word "institution." We must now make an honest term of it. A social institution can be defined as a group of people who are united (and hence organized) for some purpose; who have the material and technical means of achieving that purpose or at least of making rational attempts at it; who support a value system, ethics, and beliefs validating that purpose; and who repeat more or less predictable activities and events in the carrying out of the purpose (Malinowski 1945). With this rubric, all human activity can be viewed either as institutionalized or as random (and the degree of random behavior may be the most diagnostic feature of any society). It need hardly be added that "institutionalized" does not necessarily mean "approved" by the people who participate in the institutions.

With these ideas it is possible to distinguish legal institutions from nonlegal ones. A legal institution is one by means of which the people of a society settle disputes that arise between one another and counteract any gross and flagrant abuses of the rules of the other institutions of society. Every ongoing society has legal institutions in this sense, as well as a wide variety of nonlegal institutions.

It can be pointed out that some nonlegal institutions—the priestly, the psychiatric, and the like—serve the function of settling disputes. To make the distinction between legal and nonlegal, social scientists generally invoke the doctrine of coercion and use of force. Such a settlement is sensible because the legal institutions with which modern Western lawyers deal are usually associated with a political unit of which the state is one type. A political organization *ipso facto* supplies theorists with a "sovereign" of Austinian type and the "enforcement" predicated by Holmes and others. From this point of view, then, legal institutions must have two defining criteria: (1) they must settle the disputes that arise in other (nonlegal) institutions, and (2) they must be associated with (or even constitute) some sort of political organization. Obviously, for some purposes—particularly in the study of less-developed legal systems—the second criterion can and must be dropped; for most purposes of Western jurisprudence, just as obviously, it is probably necessary to retain it.

In carrying out the task of settling difficulties in the nonlegal institutions, legal institutions must have specific ways to (1) disengage the difficulties from the institutions of origin which they now threaten, (2) handle the difficulties within the framework of the legal institution, and (3) set the new solutions back within the processes of the nonlegal institutions from which they emerged. Indeed, the presence of such characteristics is a vivid index of the presence of a political organization.

There are, thus, at least two aspects of legal institutions that are not shared with other institutions of society. First, legal institutions alone must have some regularized way to interfere in the malfunctioning (and, perhaps, the functioning as well) of the nonlegal institutions in order to disengage the trouble case. Second, there must be two kinds of rules in the legal institutions—those which govern the activities of the legal institution itself (called "adjectival law" by Austin and "procedure" by most modern lawyers) and those which are substitutes for, or modifications or restatements of, the rules of the nonlegal institution that has been invaded (called "substantive law"). The above are only the minimal aspects that are shared by all known legal institutions.

Seen in this light, the distinction between law and custom is fairly simple. Customs are rules (more or less strict and with greater or less support of moral, ethical, or even physical coercion) about the ways in which people must behave if social institutions are to perform their tasks and society is to endure. All institutions (including legal institutions) develop customs. Some customs in some societies are *re*institutionalized at another level: they are restated for the more precise purposes of legal institutions. When this happens, therefore, law may be regarded as a custom that has been restated in order to make it amenable to the activities of the legal institutions. In this sense one of the most characteristic attributes of legal institutions is that some of these "laws" are about the legal institutions themselves, although most are about the other institutions of society, such as the familial, economic, political, and ritual.

Malinowski, by his little book *Crime and Custom in Savage Society* (1926), has widely influenced lawyers with a faulty mode of distinguishing law from nonlaw. His idea was a good one; he claimed that law is "a body of binding obligations regarded as right by one party and acknowledged as the duty by the other, kept in force by the specific mechanism of reciprocity and publicity inherent in the structure of . . . society." His error was in equating what he had defined with the law. It is not law that is "kept in force by . . . reciprocity and publicity" ([1926] 1961, p. 58). It is custom as we have defined it here. Law is better thought of as "a body of binding obligations regarded as right by one party and acknowledged as the duty by the other" *which has been reinstitutionalized within the legal institution so that society can continue to function in an orderly manner on the basis of rules so maintained.* In short, reciprocity is the basis of custom; but the law rests on the basis of this double institutionalization.

Rights

One of the best ways to perceive the doubly institutionalized norms, or "laws," is to examine the smaller components as they attach to persons (either human individuals or corporate groups) and so to work in terms of "rights" and their reciprocal "obligations." In the framework of rights and duties, the relationships between law and custom, law and morals, law and anything else can be seen in a new light. Whether in the realm of kinship or contract, citizenship or property rights, the relationships between people can be reduced to a series of prescriptions with the obligations and the correlative rights which emanate from these prescriptions. In fact, thinking in terms of rights and obligations of persons (or role players) is a convenient and fruitful way of investigating much of the custom of many institutions. Legal rights are only those rights which attach to norms that have been doubly institutionalized; they provide a means for seeing the legal institutions from the standpoint of the persons engaged in them.

The phenomenon of double institutionalization of norms and therefore of legal rights has been recognized for a long time, but analysis of it has been only partially successful. Legal rights have their material origins in the customs of nonlegal institutions but must be *overtly restated* for the specific purpose of enabling the legal institutions to perform their tasks.

Sanctions

. . . Sanction is generally understood to mean what the law itself says will or may happen to one found guilty of having transgressed a legal rule. The word is often used in common parlance to mean "the teeth in the law." When it is used as a verb, its true ambivalence becomes apparent. "To sanction" something is in ordinary usage not to interfere with someone's doing it; yet jurists also use it to mean "visit an evil on doing it," and social scientists have extended the word "sanction" far beyond its technical meaning for modern law. Radcliffe-Brown (1934) described positive and negative sanctions for behavior, embracing not only penalization of nonconformity but also rewarding of conformity—and all this without specifying precisely who confers rewards or inflicts punishments.

The problem of sanction would seem to be better summarized in terms of legal institutions which, in some situations, apply specific types of correction to adjudged breaches of law. That is, the "sanction" is the body of rules according to which legal institutions interpose themselves for the purpose of maintenance of a social system so that living in it can be comfortable and predictable.

Law and Social Science

It is apparent that we must examine two further factors. First, what sort of definitions of law may be needed by the social sciences? Second, and related to this, how can social scientists go about investigating the legal institutions and the legalization of rights in any specific culture or in any concatenation of cultures?

The kernel of the social scientist's concept of law must be found, I believe, in the phenomenon of double institutionalization of rights: once within customary institutions, then again within the legal institutions. Therefore he is required absolutely to study both the legal institutions and the social institutions on which they feed—and only in this way can he ever make any progress with the thorny problem of the relationship between law and society.

The social scientist studying law is quite right when he considers the law a type of social superstructure to be judged by criteria or values of the social sciences. He is, however, quite wrong if he extends this position to mean that he need not consider what is known about the law on its own ground. The determining variables of the law may be considered as part of a social field; but equally so, the social field must be considered by jurisprudence. In short, what is required is a sort of stereoscopic vision, looking at data with the lens of jurisprudence in one eye and the lens of social science in the other.

Seen thus stereoscopically, a legal right (and, with it, a law) is the restatement, for the purpose of maintaining peaceful and just operation of the institutions of society, of some but never all of the recognized claims of persons within those institutions; the restatement must be made in such a way that these claims can be more or less assured by the total community or its representatives. Only by so viewing legal rights can the moral, religious, political, and economic implications of law be fully explored.

In fact, a primary problem of all legal studies may be the intersecting of the law and the other institutions of society. This relationship is no mere reflection of society in the law: it must be realized, rather, that the law is always out of phase with society, specifically because of the duality of the statement and restatement of rights. Indeed, the more highly developed the legal institutions, the greater the lack of phase, which not only results from the constant reorientation of the primary institutions but is magnified by the very dynamics of the legal institutions themselves (Stone 1964, chapter 1, sec. 1).

Thus, it is the very nature of law and its capacity to "do something about" the primary social institutions that create the lack of phase. Moreover, even if one could assume perfect legal institutionalization, change within the primary institutions would soon jar the system out of phase again. What is less obvious is that if there were ever to be perfect phase between law and society, then society could never repair itself, grow and change, flourish or wane. It is the fertile dilemma of law that it must always be out of step with society but that people must always (because they work better with fewer contradictions, if for no other reason) attempt to reduce the lack of phase. Custom must either grow to fit the law or it must actively reject it; law must either grow to fit the custom or it must ignore or suppress it. It is in these interstices that social growth and social decay take place.

Social catastrophe and social indignation and resultant changes in custom are sources of much new law. With technical and moral change new situations appear that must be "legalized." This truth has particular and somewhat different applications to developed and to less highly developed legal systems. In developed municipal systems of law, in which means for institutionalizing behavior on a legal level are already traditionally concentrated in political decision-making groups such as legislatures, there is a tendency for the legal institution not to reflect custom so much as to shape it. As developed nations put more faith in their legislatures, nonlegal social institutions sometimes take a very long time to catch up with the law. On the other hand, in less-developed legal systems, it may be that little or no popular demand is made on the legal institutions, and therefore little real contact exists or can be made to exist between them and the primary institutions (Stone 1966, chapter 2, sec. 17). Law can become one of the major sources of innovation in society.

The social scientist's first task, then, is the analysis of the legal institutions to be found and their interrelationships with the nonlegal institutions of society. There may be courts as in some parts of indigenous Africa or indigenous Europe; there may be self-help, oracles, moots, town meetings, contests, and certain types of feuds (although most feuds do not correct the difficulty and feed the corrected situation back into the nonlegal institutions of society). The social scientist can examine the particular types of customs that are legalized in any particular society. He can begin the process of comparing the customs of mating and child rearing with the laws of marriage; the customs of trading with the laws of contract; the customs of interpersonal relations with the law of tort; the customs of approved behavior with criminal law.

And what will he find? He will find that the practice of law is a force by itself, a force for preserving and molding society that both has its roots irrevocably in social institutions and must supersede any particular historicoethnographic phase of them.

The social scientist's next task is the reporting and comparison of legal institutions *in the terms of the people who participate in those institutions* and the subsequent comparison of those terms with the terms in which other people live in analogous or similar institutions.

His third task is the exposition of what Hoebel (1954) has called the "postulates" of that people's law: the assumptions held about the "natural" ways of the world, most often without even a possibility of overt statement, by the people who live by a custom and a law. These postulates lie behind the law as they lie behind every other aspect of that people's activity. They are those "values," or unquestioned premises, on which a people bases not merely its behavior (including law) but its moral evaluation of behavior (including ethics). The postulates behind a legal system are congruent with the postulates behind the accompanying economic or religious system. What may seem blatant discrepancies and contradictions and, indeed, hypocrisies (as between Sunday school and the market place) are in fact no more than inadequate analyses of the postulates. A postulate lying behind Anglo-American law is that the human body is inviolably private unless marriage or certain contracts have been entered into; a postulate behind Eskimo law is that life is hard and that kinship, amity, or love between individuals cannot be allowed to override the welfare of the society. The postulates underlying a people's law also underlie the rest of its culture. Law cases provide one of the best mechanisms by which the ethnographer can capture these postulates and make them overt. . . .

Author's 1978 Addendum

Today I would change only one aspect of this piece. The term "double institutionalization" says what I mean, but I would drop the term "*re*institutionalization," because the "re" has led some critics to overlook my overt recognition that legal institutions (both judicial and legislative) may be a primary source of innovation. Changes can be initiated, obviously, in either the customary or the legal institutions. The struggle to reduce the lack of phase between principles in the two contexts—the double institutionalization— remains the primary problem of students of law and social science. A creative example is to be found in Lenore J. Weitzman's "Legal Regulation of Marriage: Tradition and Change" (62 *California Law Review* 1169 [1974]).

References

Hart, H. L. A. (1954). Definition and Theory in Jurisprudence. *Law Quarterly Review* 70: 30–60.

Hoebel, E. Adamson. (1954). *The Law of Primitive Man: A Study in Comparative Legal Dynamics.* Cambridge, Mass.: Harvard University Press.

Kantorowicz, Hermann (1958). *Definition of Law.* Edited by A. H. Campbell. Cambridge University Press. Published posthumously.

Malinowski, Bronislaw. (1926) (1961). *Crime and Custom in Savage Society.* London: Routledge. A paperback edition was published in 1959 by Littlefield.

Malinowski, Bronislaw. (1945). *The Dynamics of Culture Change: An Inquiry Into Race Relations in Africa.* New Haven: Yale University Press. A paperback edition was published in 1961.

Pospisil, Leopold. (1958). *Kapauku Papuans and Their Law.* Yale University Publications in Anthropology, No. 54. New Haven: Yale University, Department of Anthropology.

Radcliffe-Brown, A. R. (1934). Sanction, Social. Volume 13, pages 531–534 in *Encyclopaedia of the Social Sciences.* New York: Macmillan. Reprinted in the author's *Structure and Function in Primitive Society.*

Stone, Julius. (1964). *Legal System and Lawyers' Reasonings.* Stanford, Calif.: Stanford University Press.

Stone, Julius. (1966). *Social Dimensions of Law and Justice.* Stanford, Calif.: Stanford University Press.

2

The Study
of Law
in Society
C.M. Campbell and Paul Wiles

In recent years two novel phrases have been heard in departments of law and in departments of social science in British universities.[1] These are "socio-legal studies" and "sociology of law". A casual observer might regard these phrases as synonyms or simply verbal preferences, which indicate that there has been an increase of interest in using the methods and theories of the social sciences to resolve problems about the nature and operation of law. As always with conclusions which are drawn at the expense of eradicating subtle linguistic distinctions, such a superficial view is valid only at a level of generality which masks the gulf which separates these two phrases. For while there has been a growing recognition that the social sciences and the law need somehow to be conjoined, there have been fierce disagreements as to how this should be achieved and for what purpose. The two phrases have been flown as standards in the battle for whatever resources and intellectual or practical prestige might be at stake. Behind the standard of the "sociology of law" ranged those who denigrated the other side as antitheoretical, concerned with social engineering through the existing legal order, and not with ex-

Excerpt from "The Study of Law in Society in Britain," *Law and Society Review* 10 (Summer 1976), pp. 547–555. Copyright © 1976 by the Law and Society Association. Reprinted by permission of authors and publishers.

plaining that order or transcending it by critique. The word "sociology" was emblazoned in gold on their banner because it signified a claim to greater theoretical sophistication. Under the ensign of "socio-legal studies" encamped those who chastised the other side as abstract theoreticians, whose speculations were divorced from reality and lacked practical relevance. Law, lawyers and the legal system were taken as they were found, and their interrelations with real people were examined and evaluated.

To understand the present state of law and society research in Britain, it is necessary to look behind such slogans and rhetoric if we are to do more than merely reiterate the prejudices and ideologies of the debates. The two sides are caricatured in our account, but the caricatures are neither original nor without effect. As in many good battles each side has propagated in its attacks a crude distorted picture of the other. Since both have been reasonably successful, a pronounced bifurcation of the field has developed. While examining this bifurcation, we attempt to relate arguments within the field to debates in the social sciences and jurisprudence, and thus endeavor to separate what is genuinely new from what is merely a controversial reformulation of the familiar.

Socio-Legal Studies

Socio-legal studies have been proclaimed as radically different from the work previously done in law departments in general, and by jurisprudential scholars in particular. The emergence of socio-legal studies in Britain was welcomed therefore by some commentators (e.g., Willock, 1974; Twining, 1974) as an innovative, novel and exciting departure for the study of law. Thus it is claimed that in utilizing social research methods and in recognizing the empirical nature of many disputes in jurisprudence previously assumed to be of a conceptual nature, socio-legal work is significantly different and important. Departing as it does from the focal concerns of much prior legal theory, it is seen as new activity which is *relevant* because it deals with the *actual* operation of law and its effects on people—with access to legal services, with the treatment afforded to defendants in court, with welfare and poverty issues. Such a view of socio-legal research has, we suggest, considerable force as long as it is borne in mind that the touchstone is research activity by legal scholars or within law departments. Compared with the conventional research concerns and procedures of academic lawyers, the differences are sufficiently real to have produced strains and tensions in law departments. The new socio-legal approach is regarded as subversive by some law teachers, and others believe it represents the indulgence of those who do not understand what is truly entailed in the study of law. To these critics the proper domain of the law teacher is "hard law" or "black letter law"—the careful analysis and exposition of positive or written law. Their resistance to possible encroachments from socio-legal researchers who wish "to broaden the study of law from within," or to teach "contextual law," is reinforced by suspicions that socio-legal work is too much concerned with the policy of the law, and sometimes even with the politics of the law. The current arguments among lawyers about the legitimacy and desirability of socio-legal work have revealed the existence of competing conceptions of the function of law departments, and socio-legal researchers have become involved in larger disputes, for example, about the importance of legal reform as against the vocational training of students.

Yet if we move from the specific context of law departments, the difference between socio-legal work and traditional legal scholarship seems exaggerated and over-emphasized. There is a congruence between socio-legal work and jurisprudence in other, probably more important, respects. (Campbell, 1974; cf. Black, 1973; Shklar, 1964). Although the use of social research methods in studying law may be new, many of the questions posed are familiar ones. For example, the concentration of effort by socio-legal researchers on the activities of the legal profession, the administration of criminal justice and; in particular, court procedures, and on the provision of legal services exhibits a fascination with the extent to which prevailing legal norms are reflected in reality or are implemented as mandated by written law.[2] But this concern is underpinned by an assumption (logical and often moral as well), that the ideal prescriptions contained in the law ought to be directly mirrored in reality.[3] On the basis of this assumption, should there prove to be a divergence between the law and empirical reality, it is convenient and easy to reach one of two conclusions. *Either* there is something wrong with the substance of the law and it should be changed; *or* there is nothing wrong with the substance of the law but the mechanisms or procedures to implement it are inadequate in some way. These conclusions in turn suggest calls for the reform of the substantive law, or for the improvement of legal procedures, and one characteristic of socio-legal studies in Britain has been interest in such reforms.

This socio-legal approach may be illustrated by recent work on the provision of legal services. In such work the proclaimed ideal of equality before the law is accepted as meaningful and worthwhile, but, since research has revealed that there is inadequate access to the legal system among some sections of the community, a problem clearly exists. Researchers have responded to the problem in slightly different ways: some argue for changing the provisions of the state legal aid scheme (Zander, 1969; White, 1975); some promote the establishment of law centers (Abel-Smith *et al.*, 1973; Zander, 1969); others suggest the geographical resiting of lawyers' offices to better serve the community at large (cf. Foster, 1973; White 1975); and yet others call for the improvement of publicity services so that the public may be better informed about available legal remedies and the services lawyers provide (Bridges *et al;* 1975). The contours of the "problem" identified by socio-legal researchers are clearly revealed in this array of proposals. Disjunctions between the prescriptions of written law and reality are explored on the assumption that they result from accidental or contingent effects in particular discrete areas. The problem is, therefore, one of how to implement in the most efficient way the ideal of quality before the law by *legal* reform. Thus posed the problem does not require consideration of the general relationship between the legal order and the social order.

Combined with and indeed allied to this orientation to the legal order in general, is a concern about "justice" which runs as a *leitmotif* through socio-legal studies. It is not *merely* that the law sometimes does not operate as it should, or as it promises. In socio-legal work there is a concern about poor people, about the bias in the law, the abuse of discretion, the prevalence of discrimination and partiality. Researchers press for greater justice for a previously disenfranchised community. As conscious advocates of liberalism and radicalism, many socio-legal researchers advocate reform of the legal structure to provide justice for those for whom they speak (e.g., Abel-Smith *et al.*, 1973; Adler and Bradley, 1976). Such motivation is no doubt praiseworthy and may prove of value, but, to be understood in the context of socio-legal research two riders are necessary. First, although justice is an important concern, it does not seem to require any conceptual clarification nor to entail discussions as to the nature of justice or of different philosophies of justice. Rather, quite concrete demands and claims are pressed on the law. Second, the claims that are made seem of a narrowly circumscribed nature. Even though socio-legal studies are most often regarded as novel because of their concentration on policy matters and on reform, it can be argued that what is new is not the interest in policy nor reform but rather the direction or type of reform which is proposed. Law teachers have consistently shown interest in legal reform and the amendment of the law to eradicate anomalies or to take account of changes in society. Socio-legal research, resting as it does on empirical evidence, dwells on the interests and problems of social groupings or social classes that were previously ignored or seen as marginal. To match interest in the reform of property or fiscal laws we now have concern about poverty and welfare law.[4] Just as amendment of positive law was previously the goal so it is now; the relevance of legal determinations and legal procedures is taken for granted. Underpinning this reformism is the idea that proper legal regulation is the panacea for all the iniquities identified by socio-legal research.

The problems posed by socio-legal studies are clearly suited to empirical research methods, and the traditional range of social surveys, questionnaires, formal interviews and standard quantitative techniques are widely employed. Probably because theoretical or more abstract questions are so rarely raised these methods are sometimes employed in a crude positivist fashion with the result that alternatives to empiricism are not considered, and even discussion of alternatives is regarded as of dubious, if any, relevance. This may be understood if it is appreciated that the research carried out typically demonstrates what was previously known, what could be plausibly guessed, or what might prove of practical utility in suggesting reform. Indeed on occasion public demonstration seems to be the goal rather than new information. Research is descriptive, it focuses on particular legal agencies or discrete legal institutions, and it operates within the framework of the assumptions mentioned above. Given the interest in justice, in reform and the improvement of the legal system, social science methods are seen as useful in precisely identifying the optimum means to achieve the ends in view. Social scientists are regarded as intellectual subcontractors, or, as Willock, (1972: 3) put it, "they should be on tap, not on top." (cf. Willock, 1974).

Socio-legal research in Britain may then be said to have developed into a coherent field of activity possessing at least the following general characteristics. First, the hegemony of law is accepted and furthered, even though some of the particular provisions of the law may be thought to require change. Second, the nature of the legal order is treated as unproblematic, especially in its relationship to the rest of the social world. Equally the general functions of law in society tend to be taken for granted or are assumed to involve the balancing and regulating of different social groups and their interests. Such a perspective assigns high priority to ensuring that the law is informed by liberal and reformist sentiments. Research is unambiguously utilitarian and pragmatic in orientation, and the suggestions for reform which flow from it tend to be limited in scope and of a legalistic nature.

Sociology of Law

Academics who profess sociology of law adopt different stances on most of these issues, and as a result their research is of a different kind. The focus is no longer on the legal system, known and accepted, but on understanding the nature of social order through a study of law. Insofar as law is scrutinized it is from a perspective that attempts to be exogenous to the existing legal system. The goal is not primarily to improve the legal system, but rather to construct a theoretical understanding of that legal system in terms of the wider social structure. The law, legal prescriptions and legal definitions are not assumed or accepted, but their emergence, articulation and purpose are themselves treated as problematic and worthy of study. Reform of the legal system is not, as such, the goal even though an adequate theory of law may entail a consideration of the relationship of law to social change. Even for those sociologists of law who are committed to a methodology which demands a link between research and action (e.g., the Marxist notion of "praxis"), the purpose of action is not circumscribed by the technical and legal considerations that hold sway in socio-legal studies. There is much less reliance on empirical examination of the working of particular legal procedures or provisions than in socio-legal studies. Where such inquiry is undertaken, it tends to stem from a broader theoretical concern and to focus on particular procedures for heuristic purposes.

Compared with socio-legal studies the subject matter for research in sociology of law is markedly different. For example instead of (or prior to) research into the implementation of legislative provisions there is considerable interest in the processes by which law emerged or was created. Historical research is undertaken into the context and configurations which allowed or promoted the passing of legislation. (Carson, 1974(a); Paulus, 1975). The "official versions" of the intentions and purposes of particular statutes are not granted automatic respect but are instead challenged and subject to critical scrutiny (Winkler, 1975): so too are the conventional justifications of court procedures (Carlen, 1976) and the legal representation of clients (Mungham, 1974; cf. Bankowski and Mungham, 1976). Sometimes the contrast with socio-legal perspectives is explicitly drawn; discussing the socio-legal preoccupation with the problems of the poor and the provision of legal services, Cain (1975: 51) has argued that greater attention should be paid to "rich man's law." Inquiry in this area, she argues, is likely to lead to greater advances of our understanding of the operation of the law in British society, as well as portraying the true dimensions of the problems of the poor and the possibility of solving them through extending the provision of legal services. (cf. Morris, 1973).

We have drawn the contrast between socio-legal studies and sociology of law in stark terms, and deliberately so. But it is important to add that the examples we have given of perspectives and research concerns in sociology of law, are illustrative only. As a field of inquiry sociology of law is not marked by any special unity or internal coherence, and for this reason we have expressed the contrast with socio-legal work in relatively negative terms. If the comparison is extended to the methodology employed, the same point must be repeated. In sociology of law there is no orthodoxy in methodology and discussions include concern with the most basic philosophical questions of social science methodology such as, for example the epistemological status of alternative research procedures. There are therefore debates about the possibility of making claims to knowledge on the basis of this mode of theorizing, that type of procedure, this form of comparison, or that sort of inference. Altogether the conceptual apparatuses used in sociology of law are various, theoretical insights and perspectives from many other of the social sciences are adopted or discarded in studies, historical and cross-cultural research often remote from "the law in action" is regarded as relevant. This variety may be understood if it is appreciated that the elementary commitment of sociologists of law is different from that of socio-legal researchers; it is not to law departments, the law or reform of the law, but to furthering knowledge and understanding of the law in terms of the wider social order. . . .

References

Abel, Richard L. (1973). "Law Books and Books about Law." Review of M. Rheinstein: *Marriage, Stability, Divorce and Law* (1972) University of Chicago Press. 26 *Stanford Law Review*, 175.

Abel-Smith, Brian and Robert Stevens (1967). *Lawyers and the Courts*. London: Heineman.

—— (1968). *In Search of Justice*. London: Alan Lane.

Abel-Smith, Brian, Michael Zander and Rosalinde Brooke (1973). *Legal Problems and the Citizen*. London: Heineman Educational Books.

Adler, Michael and Anthony Bradley (eds.) (1976). *Justice, Discretion and Poverty*. London: Professional Books.

Bankowski, Z. and G. Mungham (1976). *Images of Law*. London: Routledge & Kegan Paul.

Black, Donald (1973). "The Boundaries of Legal Sociology" in D. Black and M. Mileski (eds.), *The Social Organization of Law*. New York: Seminar Press.

Blom-Cooper, L. J. and G. Drewry (1972). *The Final Appeal: A Study of the House of Lords in its judicial capacity*. Oxford: Clarendon Press.

Bottoms, A. E. and J. D. McClean (1976). *Defendants in the Criminal Process*. London: Routledge & Kegan Paul.

Bridges, Lee, Brenda Sufrin, Jim Whetton and Richard White (1975). *Legal Services in Birmingham*. Birmingham: Institute of Judicial Administration, University of Birmingham.

Byles, A. and P. Morris (1975). *Unmet Need: The case of the neighbourhood law centre.* London: Legal Advice Research Unit (mimeo).

Cain, Maureen (1975). "Rich Man's Law or Poor Man's Law?" 2 *British Journal of Law and Society* 61.

Campbell, C. M. (1974). "Legal Thought and Juristic Values." 1 *British Journal of Law and Society* 13.

Carlen, Pat (1976). *Magistrates Courts.* London: Martin Robertson.

Carson, W. G. (1974). "Symbolic and Instrumental Dimensions of early Factory Legislation: A case study in the social origins of legislation" in R. G. Hood (ed.), *Crime, Criminology and Public Policy.* London: Heineman.

Elston, Elizabeth, Jane Fuller and Mervyn Murch (1975). "Judicial Hearings of undefended divorce petitions." 38 *Modern Law Review* 609.

Foster, Ken (1973). "The Location of Solicitors." 36 *Modern Law Review* 153.

Frost A. and C. Milton (1975). *Representation at Administrative Tribunals.* London: Legal Advice Research Unit (mimeo).

Galanter, Marc (1973). "Notes on the Future of Social Research on Law." Unpublished paper presented to Conference on Developments in Law and Social Science Research, University of North Carolina (April).

McCabe, Sarah and Robert Purves (1972a). *Bypassing the Jury.* Oxford: Basil Blackwell.

—— (1972b). *The Jury at Work.* Oxford: Basil Blackwell.

—— (1974). *The Shadow Jury at Work.* Oxford: Basil Blackwell.

McGregor, O. R., L. J. Blom-Cooper and C. Gibson (1970). *Separated Spouses: A study of the matrimonial jurisdiction of Magistrates Court.* London: Duckworths.

Morris, Pauline (1973). "A Sociological Approach to Research in Legal Services," in P. Morris, R. White and P. Lewis, *Social Needs and Legal Action.* London: Martin Robertson.

Mungham, G. (1974). "Legal Services, The Poor and the Politics of the English Legal Profession: A Study of Present Attempts to Bring Law to the People." Unpublished paper presented to the Socio-Legal Group Conference, Manchester, England (January).

Paulus, Ingeborg (1975). *The Search for Pure Food.* London: Martin Robertson.

Shklar, Judith (1964). *Legalism.* Cambridge: Harvard University Press.

Twining, W. (1974). "Some Jobs for Jurisprudence," 1 *British Journal of Law and Society* 149.

White, Richard (1975). "The Distasteful Character of Litigation for Poor Persons." *Juridical Review* 233.

Willock, I. D. (1972). "Getting On with Social Scientists." Unpublished paper presented to the Socio-Legal Group conference, Manchester, England (December).

—— (1974). "Getting On with Sociologists." 1 *British Journal of Law and Society* 3.

Winkler, J. T. (1975). "Law, State and Economy: The Industry Act 1975 in Context." 2 *British Journal of Law in Society* 103.

Zander, Michael (1968). *Lawyers and the Public Interest.* London: Weidenfeld & Nicholson.

—— (1969). "The Legal Profession and the Poor." 20 *Northern Ireland Legal Quarterly* 109.

Notes

1. In Britain, university legal education takes place in "Law Departments" or "Law Faculties"—the difference merely reflecting the internal administrative structure of particular universities. "Law Schools" in the American usage is less common in Britain but may be used generically to refer to both Departments and Faculties. To avoid transatlantic misunderstanding, we refer to "department" throughout. It is worth noting that legal education in Britain is at undergraduate level, with the numerically small exceptions of research postgraduate courses and taught Masters courses.

2. Research effort in these areas encompasses the vast bulk of socio-legal work in Britain. More specific treatment of the research is provided below, but representative published material includes the following: Abel-Smith & Stevens: *Lawyers and the Courts* (1967), and *In Search of Justice* (1968); Zander: *Lawyers and the Public Interest* (1968); Blom-Cooper & Drewry: *The Final Appeal* (1972); McGregor, Blom-Cooper & Gibson: *Separated Spouses* (1970); Bottoms & McClean: *Defendants in the Criminal Process* (1976); McCabe & Purves: *Bypassing the Jury* (1972), *The Jury at Work* (1972), *The Shadow Jury at Work* (1974), Adler & Bradley: *Justice, Discretion and Poverty* (1976), Abel-Smith, Zander and Brooke: *Legal Problems and the Citizen* (1973); Bridges, Sufrin, Whetton and White: *Legal Services in Birmingham* (1975); Byles & Morris: *Unmet Need* (1975); Elston, Fuller & Murch: "Judicial Hearings of Undefended Divorce Petitions" (1975); Frost & Milton: *Representation at Administrative Tribunals* (1975).

3. Apparently this parallels, in some respects at least, the situation that prevails in analogous work in America, at least judging by Abel (1973), Black (1973), Galanter (1973).

4. Law teachers who enter the socio-legal field are "encouraged" to work in such areas. Disadvantaged and deviant groups have always been the easiest targets for social research, and, in Britain, there is a developed sociology of working class communities and life-styles, but very little on the middle class.

3

Jurisprudence
and
Sociology
of Law
R.B.M. Cotterrell

The sociological study of law is by no means a recent development. Nor is it one that has been exclusively or even predominantly the work of professional sociologists. For as long as researchers and speculators have recognized and sought to explore the social functions and mechanisms of law, attempts have been made to locate "the law" in its place in the social and political structure, and to predict, or at least speculate on, the effects of particular laws on behavior patterns. The techniques of wise legislation demand nothing less.

Growth of Sociology of Law

But it is only in recent decades that widespread attempts have been made to link the disparate problems associated with law's social control functions into the subject matter of a coherent "sociology of

Excerpt from "Direction and Development in Anglo-American Jurisprudence and Sociology of Law," *Anglo-American Law Review* 4 (1975), pp. 386-411, by permission of the author and publisher.

law." In the Anglo-American context a number of pioneer works by European writers such as Ehrlich, Gurvitch, and Timasheff, available to or written for an English-speaking public, took the "sociology of law" as their title and made isolated but valuable early contributions toward the development of a clearly identifiable discipline. But while powerful modern influences from both sociology and the law have fostered a wealth of "sociolegal" study, supported by grants, engaging both lawyers and sociologists and often geared toward the solving of pressing problems of social control through law, the growth of a "sociology of law" deserving the name has become possible only through a careful assessment of objectives and a widening of perspectives among leading workers in the field.

In this nebulous realm of inquiry, the aptness of the term "sociology of law" when applied to a cluster of sociolegal researches and developments in a particular geographical context can probably be measured only in terms of the degree to which empirical researches are directed by and organized around established theoretical objectives of study, and the degree of coherence and development in the search for knowledge reflected in theory based on empirical research. By this test it seems that sociology of law in the United States is more firmly established and better developed than elsewhere.[1]

The attempt to clarify objectives of study and to establish the sociology of law as a coherent focus of research has led to far-reaching discussion about, for example, the relationship of sociology of law with its parent discipline, the relative emphasis as between theory and empirical research, the treatment of legal values, and the relationship of the subject with other disciplines, particularly other social sciences.

At least in the United States, sociology of law has developed to the point where its attitude to and relationship with legal theory urgently require clarification. A few sociologists[2] and some jurists have clearly recognized this. Yet, among most, the matter has been shelved or not perceived as crucial in understanding present and future directions and development in both subjects. At first sight this is surprising. The subject matter of jurisprudence and sociology of law is unified by its common focus on "law." Both subjects aim to promote a wider understanding of the law. There must necessarily be considerable overlap in their concerns. Yet beyond these generalities, comparison becomes difficult. At present, the sociology of law is characterized, on the one hand, by a search at high theoretical levels for basic directions of development that would justify its existence as a viable discipline or focus of knowledge and research and, on the other, by a large body of empirical work, developed in piecemeal, pragmatic fashion. The latter has been, for the most part, inspired either by the practical needs of lawyer or legislator or by a desire to test concepts or developments in sociology derived from outside the sphere of its particular interests in law.

Relationship with Legal Theory

In contrast, jurisprudence derives such unity as it possesses from its place within legal education. The majority of influential definitions of the subject stress some aspect of its educational role. It has many functions, only one of which is the systematic gathering and ordering of data about law as a focus of sociological study. It has therefore been correctly stressed by sociologists that much of the literature of jurisprudence views society through a legal prism. Legal viewpoints color the perceptions of reality, as well as the ethical questions with which legal philosophy concerns itself. Rational justification is undertaken from "within the law." These observations have, however, resulted in two false conclusions sometimes being drawn. One is that legal theory is, thus, of interest solely in illustrating the rarefied thoughtways of the legal profession. Such a conclusion greatly underestimates the importance of legal thought as a means of "mentally ordering" the world. The recognition of the importance of legal concepts and symbols in the thinking of people at all levels of society has been indicated by influential jurists[3] to be a prerequisite of an adequate understanding of the role of law as a social institution and of the mechanisms by which it directs behavior. The second misconception is that legal thought and rationalization within jurisprudence are in some way a "distortion of reality," that the realistic study of law as a sociological institution will progress farther and quicker if these "distortions" can be avoided or replaced with tested sociological concepts. This misconception, reflected also within jurisprudence in the writings of some American Realist legal theorists, is based on the assumption that unless legal concepts have some counterpart in sociological fact they either have no significance or else are "wrong" and therefore dangerous. More fundamentally, this misconception implies that the link between the abstract, conceptual world of the law and the observable, behavioral world of legal activities is so close that observation of the latter should be capable of fully explaining the former. The fallacy of such an assumption has long been recognized within legal theory.

Observing the development of modern sociology of law in the light of the unwieldy and daunting literature of jurisprudence, it is not difficult to conclude that some present imbalances in the direction of energies and the formulation of priorities in sociology of law might be remedied through a closer collaboration with legal theory. At present such collaboration is minimal. Some legal sociologists have explored particular areas of legal theory and adapted them to their purposes. Some, such as Philip Selznick, have plotted out an extensive program for sociology of law but in doing so have tied it to a particular theoretical preference, which is the subject of bitter jurisprudential debate and seems a controversial foundation for objective, empirical study. Defensive insularity and misconceptions militate against more widespread and fruitful collaboration. On the jurists' part there has been a frequent acceptance of the amazingly simplistic Kelsenian assumption that a division between normative and factual spheres pinpoints the different concerns of jurist and sociologist. Thus jurists have often failed to appreciate fully the extent to which sociological theory contributes to the analysis of normative phenomena and, most important, the extent to which assumptions and objectives underlying large areas of jurisprudential writing are themselves seen as problematic from the perspectives of sociologists. On the sociologists' side there has, I think, often been a failure to observe that jurisprudence today extends far beyond the mere rationalization and justification of legal concepts and doctrines. Thus, within the rarefied and sometimes distorting educational environment in which it flourishes, a significant and large body of modern and not-so-modern jurisprudential literature seeks to explain law as a social phenomenon and a purposeful enterprise within which values and ideals are organized, balanced and symbolized.[4]

It is no doubt tempting for a sociologist faced with the bewildering bulk of legal theory to attempt to brush it aside with the charge that it merely represents lawyers' thoughts on the law, an insider's view, which cannot stand as a substitute for objective research. But in lining up the sociology of law alongside the sociology of other institutions—for example medicine, education, industry—there is a danger of losing sight of the pervasiveness of law. Apart from the tiny minority who are incapable not only of living according to social rules but even of understanding them in any form, legal thought in some form is a part of the life of all. Legal ideas may be used in widely differing ways, and legal reasoning may exhibit varying degrees of complexity, detail, and rationality in different contexts and within different sections of a society. It may reflect patterns of social stratification and be affected by other factors of social differentiation. Nevertheless, the key concepts of the law pervade societies having stable, responsive legal systems.

As one legal theorist puts it:

> The fundamental legal concepts are not exclusive professional tools for the jurists. They belong to the common stock of concepts that everybody needs

for his contacts with his fellow-men. Expressly or implicitly we are using them in everyday life, buying things, taking a room in an hotel, or paying debts. In this connection they are vehicles for attaining practical ends. But they are also essential ingredients in our view of the community in which we are living, and of the world at large. When we speak of governments, of elections, of state officials, of new laws and new taxes, of trials and punishments, of peace and war, we are using legal concepts . . . they are necessary means of conveying information as to what is going on in the world.[5]

I believe that it is the widespread neglect of this fundamental point among legal sociologists which, in spite of the powerful influence of Weber, has so far prevented the study of legal thought and legal symbols and concepts from occupying a central place in the sociology of law. In turn this situation helps to explain the lack of recognition among legal sociologists of the importance of legal theory as a storehouse of knowledge and analysis on various aspects of legal thought.

Obstacles to Collaboration

Immense difficulties hamper fruitful collaboration between jurisprudence and the emergent sociology of law. The most important is the sheer size and complexity of the subject of study which loosely links both. The literature of jurisprudence boasts examples of theories of the nature of law which, despite their attempts at generality and comprehensiveness, hardly meet at any point when compared side by side. Yet the conclusion to be drawn from such examples is not simply, as Thurman Arnold has suggested, that jurisprudence is the pursuit of a "priesthood" offering sermons on the rationality of the law from various viewpoints.[6] No doubt the literature of jurisprudence contains many such sermons, but the real lesson to be drawn is that the multifaceted phenomenon of law lends itself to fruitful and illuminating study from an immense range of perspectives and emphases. If legal theory has drawn on many diverse disciplines, it has done so, as Julius Stone has stressed, because law cuts across them all, as it cuts across every aspect of social life and helps to shape even our own thought processes and the conceptual apparatus and value systems around which our lives are organized.[7] In the light of this apparently unbounded scope it should not be a matter for surprise that the perspective a sociologist brings to the law may lead to conclusions which appear to have few if any points of contact with those of, say, a linguistic philosopher, an analytical jurist, or a symbolic logician.

Jurisprudence, through the its unique place in legal education, has been in a position to develop a catholicity of approach which, at its best, can illustrate the multifaceted nature of law to law students in a direct and effective way. The only common focus within the diverse material collected into jurisprudence courses is "the law." Frontiers between disciplines and subdisciplines can be crossed at will, and if the student is not bewildered by the frequently changing intellectual landscapes sketched for him, he is likely to attain a greater awareness if not necessarily an understanding of the wider currents of knowledge upon which the study of law impinges. The most obvious danger of this educational approach is that of "collecting insights from other disciplines without asking what they mean, without examining the theoretical structure within which they rest."[8] It is probably a danger that cannot be totally overcome in taught jurisprudence since the present educational objectives of the subject require that a broad and finely balanced collection of diverse materials be pruned and processed to fit within the typical single one-year jurisprudence course.

Leaving aside the specific educational justification for juxtaposing widely differing approaches to the study of law within jurisprudence, it seems to be agreed among legal sociologists and presumably among all who wish to see advance in the systematic study of the nature of law that the concepts, assumptions, and objectives that underlie such study must be explicit, shared, and realistic. Bearing in mind the complexity of the subject matter, the multitude of perspectives possible in relation to it, and a frequent lack of awareness by jurists and legal sociologists of each other's work, prospects are not immediately encouraging. But some important if generalized distinctions in possible areas of study can be drawn. The most obvious of them distinguishes between the two realms of existence of the law. Firstly, there is the abstract, conceptual, or "psychological" realm populated by legal values, symbols, concepts, principles, and rules. From a sociological viewpoint these elements in the world of law comprise the "invisible mechanisms" by which behavior can be directed and controlled. Insofar as these elements are present in the compendium of legal thought of each member of the community, they operate directly as psychological mechanisms of social control. Secondly, there is the behavioral realm of law creation, adjudication, and enforcement; the "law in action," the doings and sayings of officials—judges, police, administrative officials; what might be called the "visible," empirically observable realm of legal activity. That this distinction is obvious should not obscure the fact that comparatively little work in either jurisprudence or sociology of law systematically attempts to relate these two realms at a general level. Jurisprudence has concerned itself almost exclusively with the former and (with the important exception of certain Scandinavian jurists) has rarely attempted systematically to explore the sociological or psychological signifi- cance of legal concepts. American Realist writers and sociological jurists normally contented themselves with pointing out the wide divergence between the two realms. Legal sociologists have concen- trated heavily though not exclusively on the behavioral realm, "law in action". Nevertheless, although these two realms are distinct, in the sense that knowledge of one will not necessarily provide conclu- sions that can be safely applied directly to the other, the relation between them—and specifically the effect of legal ideas on conduct and attitudes—is a central concern for any realistic study of the nature of law.

A second distinction to be drawn is the familiar one between analysis and evaluation. In jurisprudence it is represented as the dis- tinction between "is" and "ought," expository and censorial juris- prudence, a "science of law" and a "science of legislation". It is probably inevitable that lawyers will be drawn toward the "rational justification" of legal principles and concepts, just as sociologists find it difficult to divorce objective studies of social conditions from the advocacy of change or the defense of present social structures. It seems desirable, however, that particularly in the analysis of law a clear distinction should be made between the description of the conceptual and behavioral realms of the law as they are, and the advocacy of policy and the selection of desired ideals and values. It is tempting for those who favor a radical change of attitude to the law and radical changes in its concepts and values to castigate at- tempts to analyze legal thought as it is as the perpetuation of a myth. But the suggestion that an avoidance of legal theory and legal reasoning might be expected on the part of sociologists who dislike what they see[9] is strange indeed. If change is desirable it must be imposed on the law, not wished on it. Jurisprudence has undoubtedly often reflected the ideologies of the legal profession, but a significant amount of the vast literature of legal theory is founded on the assumption that a clarification of the methods of legal reasoning and of the more general mental structures, or "models," that lie behind them can be achieved by a process of generalization and deduction from the raw materials of legal rules, principles, and concepts ex- pressed and explained in legislation and judicial pronouncements.

Conclusion

A final distinction to drawn here is between two approaches to the study of the conceptual realm of the law: on the one hand the search for logical consistency by a process of rationalization of the conceptual structure of the law and of its rules and principles and, on the other hand, the attempt to explain in realistic terms the functional significance of legal concepts, rules, and principles. In essence the distinction here is the familiar one between "validity" and "efficacy" as the central concern of study. It would be tempting to think of it also as the distinction between the view of a detached "outside" observer of legal concepts and reasoning and the view of the citizen living within the legal order who seeks to rationalize legal ideas in order to make use of them with less worry and doubt in regulating his own conduct, carrying out beneficial transactions or at least avoiding unpleasant sanctions. Phrased in this form the distinction would be misleading because a rigid separation cannot be made between the two viewpoints above. Leaving aside the point already made that the distinction between legal insiders and outsiders is relatively unhelpful in the study of any ongoing legal order, each viewpoint presupposes elements of the other. Half a century ago American Realist jurisprudence taught that legal rationalization which ignores the psychological factors influencing the workings of the judicial process will be misleading and sterile. Conversely, any attempt to explain in sociological or psychological terms the effects of legal thought on conduct will not progress far unless it recognizes and examines the powerful pressures exerted by the search for consistency and logical relationships in legal reasoning. Just as for the able "realist" lawyer both a predictive and normative perspective on law must be taken into account in planning legal strategy, so for the realistic study of the conceptual realm of the law, both the rationalizing tendencies fueled by the craving for legal certainty and the psychological significance of the symbols and values of the law in influencing thought and conduct (in rational or irrational ways) are relevant.

Notes

1. See J. Skolnick, "The Sociology of Law in America," in R. Treves and J. F. Glastra van Loon, eds., *Norms and Actions* (1968). M. Rehbinder, "The Development and Present State of Fact Research in Law in the United States" (1972), 24 *Journal of Legal Education* 567, contains an extensive listing of literature and research projects.
2. See *e.g.* the comments of Jack Gibbs, "Book Review" (1968-69), 3 *Law and Society Review* 617; "Book Review" (1969) 62 *Law Library Journal* 118.
3. Particularly the Scandinavian Realist school.
4. *Cf.* N. S. Timasheff, *Introduction to the Sociology of Law* (1939) pp. 49-50. "Despite many misrepresentations, jurisprudence was never merely the study

of the verbal formulae included in positive law or the art of their practical application . . . . the main trend in jurisprudence was not hostile to the study of the facts lying beyond the words of which legal rules consist." See also *e.g.* J. L. Montrose, "Legal Theory for Politicians and Sociologists" (1974), 25 *Northern Ireland Legal Quarterly* 321, arguing that legal theory necessarily involves both a philosophical and a sociological orientation.

5. Karl Olivecrona, *Law as Fact* (1971), p. 135.
6. Thurman Arnold, *The Symbols of Government* (1935).
7. Julius Stone, *Social Dimensions of Law and Justice* (1966), p. 30.
8. See C. M. Campbell, "Book Review" (1974), 13 *Journal of the Society of Public Teachers of Law* (n.s.) 58.
9. C. M. Campbell, "Legal Thought and Juristic Values" (1974), 1 *British Journal of Law & Society* 13 at p. 14.

PART II

Alternative Theoretical Perspectives

In Part II, readings on six theoretical perspectives on the sociology of law are presented. None of the theoretical formulations is sufficiently well developed and crystallized to generate a set of logically inter-related and testable propositions about the functioning of legal systems. Yet each of the six perspectives provides a distinct point of departure for reflection and analysis, if not for systematic empirical research.

The first reading by Black is a vigorous exposition of positivism as it applies to the study of law and society. Espousing a general and "pure" theory of the sociology of law, similar in its emphasis on purity to that of the renowned advocate of legal positivism Hans Kelsen (1945), Black contends that the legal sociologist must focus on legal *behavior* in its multitude of forms and must seek to explain such behavior. Arguing for strict separation of facts and values, Black criticizes much of the literature in this field as dealing with problems of "legal effectiveness" or with the social impact of legal policy decisions; because of the tacit or avowed commitment to particular values on the part of the authors of such studies, he concludes that they have no scientific merit.

What does Black mean when he says, "A pure sociology of law does not study humans in the usual sense. It studies law as a system of behavior"? Why does he exclude legal rules or "lawyer's law" from his definition of law as behavior? Because of his emphasis on studying legal behavior, I have referred to his theory as "behavior-alist," a term also used by political scientists such as Becker (1964)

31

and Nagel (1969). Although Black's theory should not be confused with "behaviorism" in psychology, in eschewing any concern with values he is in effect arguing for a stimulus–response approach to understanding legal phenomena.

In the second reading in Part II, Nonet vehemently rejects Black's theory, advocating a view of the sociology of law based on the heritage of jurisprudential ideas. In this respect he not only supports Selznick's view (1961) and that of the so-called Berkeley program but also aligns himself with the perspective of Cotterrell presented in Part I. He articulates four principles of the Berkeley program:

1. "The sociology of law must be jurisprudentially informed."
2. "The sociology of law must take legal ideas seriously."
3. "The sociology of law must have redeeming value for policy."
4. "The sociology of law must integrate jurisprudential and policy analysis."

What are the strength and weaknesses of each of these two theoretical perspectives? Are they as mutually exclusive as the authors contend?

The next three readings in Part II present different facets of functionalism as applied to legal systems. Parsons views law as a "generalized mechanism of social control that operates diffusely in virtually all sectors of society." The primary function of a legal system is "integrative." To perform this integrative function, a legal system, which comprises a set of rules, must solve problems pertaining to legitimation, interpretation, sanctions, and jurisdiction. Moreover, a legal system, according to Parsons, presupposes a "certain type of social equilibrium. Law flourishes particularly in a society in which the most fundamental questions of social values are not currently at issue or under agitation."

Pound, the founder of American "sociological jurisprudence," distinguishes three types of interests: individual, public, and social. He then undertakes an inventory of six categories of social interests— general security, security of social institutions, general morals, conservation of social resources, general progress, and individual human life. Pound claims that these interests "are recognized or are coming to be recognized in modern law." Although these interests can and do come into conflict with one another, he believes that there is a sufficient reservoir of value consensus to permit an orderly resolution of conflicting interests. "Looked at functionally, the law is an attempt to satisfy, to reconcile, to harmonize, to adjust these overlapping and often conflicting claims and demands . . . so as to give effect to the greatest total interests or to the interests that weigh most in our civilization, with the least sacrifice of the scheme of interests as a whole."

Cowan, a student of Pound, cogently argues for the need to supplement Pound's classification of individual, social, and public interests with a category of "group interests." By "group interests," Cowan refers to those stemming from the sociologist's "secondary group—associations, unions, societies, clubs, boards, councils, professions." He shows how group interests, rather than individual, public, or social interests, predominate in administrative law, labor law, and legislation. Inasmuch as "group interests" readily lead to social conflicts, Cowan's perspective serves as a bridge between a functionalist theory and a conflict theory of law.

Unlike a functionalist perspective on law and legal systems, "conflict theory" does not assume that there is a sufficient level of value consensus in a society to permit conflicting interests to be adjudicated harmoniously. Kelsen's penetrating exposition of the Marx–Engels theory of law shows that it is rooted in a theory of the state and of the class structure and rests on a proposition that law performs a function in the class struggle. As a component of the superstructure of society, law provides ideological justifications for the dominant ruling class vis-à-vis the subordinate working class. With the eventual abolition of capitalism and its replacement with socialism, progress towards a classless society will transform the state as well as law—both will tend to "wither away" since neither will be necessary as an instrument of class domination and exploitation.

Turk's conflict theory of law is not founded on the Marx–Engels theory of the state and class struggle. Rejecting the "moral functionalist" conception of law as a means of resolving conflicts, Turk advances the conception of law as power, that is, a set of resources whose control and mobilization can generate and exacerbate social conflicts. He identifies five distinct kinds of resource control: (1) war or police power, (2) economic power, (3) political power, (4) ideological power, and (5) diversionary power. With the aid of this concept of legal power, Turk develops twelve propositions concerning the conditions under which law promotes or facilitates conflict. Are these propositions empirically testable?

According to Turk, if these propositions were confirmed, they would "constitute the basis for a theory of law able to explain the conditions when and how conflict management may be accomplished by the control and mobilization of legal resources—i.e., a theory able to deal with conflict management as a problematic outcome, instead of a defining characteristic of law as a social and cultural phenomenon."

The socialization theory of Tapp and Levine represents a perspective on law and society that is on a different level of analysis from the other four theoretical perspectives. It is a social-psychological rather than a structural or sociological approach to legal phenomena. It is concerned with the process whereby legal and ethical values are acquired and how these, in turn, affect behavior. Drawing on the cognitive–developmental theories of Piaget and Kohlberg, Tapp and Levine discuss three types of legal reasoning: preconventional, conventional, and postconventional. Although the authors focus on the legal socialization of the citizenry, there is, of course, no reason to exclude the legal socialization, formal as well as informal, of lawyers, judges, legislators, administrative officials and other legal-system personnel. In fact, one plausible hypothesis is that the success with which the personnel of a legal system are legally socialized affects their fidelity to the law and their level of professional commitment to their roles. Likewise, the success with which the citizenry is legally socialized presumably affects its perception of the legitimacy of the legal system as well as its level of conformity to the law. Using Tapp and Levine's theory, how might one proceed to investigate to legal socialization of the personnel of a legal system as compared with rank-and-file citizens?

The sixth and last theoretical perspective, a systems theory of law and society, has thus far received less attention than any of the preceding five theories. The reading by Vanyo on the application of systems theory to environmental law provides an illustration of its potential usefulness. Underlying Vanyo's analysis are such basic concepts of systems theory as input and output vectors, state of system or subsystem variables, feedback processes, and so forth (Laszlo, Levine, and Milsum, 1974). There are, however, at least two impediments to the application of systems theory to law: (1) Systems theorists have not yet spelled out all the concepts and indicators needed for understanding the functioning of a total legal system of a society, and (2) there is a great dearth of systematic quantitative data on the functioning of the legal system in any society.

How would you compare the strengths and weaknesses of the six theoretical perspectives? Can you formulate a specific problem within the framework of each theoretical perspective? Can you formulate a testable proposition with the aid of each of the six theoretical perspectives?

References

Becker, T. L. (1964). *Political Behavioralism and Modern Jurisprudence.* Chicago: Rand McNally.

Kelsen, H. (1945). *General Theory of Law and State.* Trans. A. Wedberg. Cambridge, Mass.: Harvard University Press.

Laszlo, C. A., M. D. Levine and J. H. Milsum (1974). "A General Systems Framework for Social Systems." *Behavioral Science,* 19: 79-92.

Nagel, S. S. (1969). *The Legal Process from a Behavioral Perspective.* Homewood, Ill.: Dorsey.

4

The Boundaries of Legal Sociology
Donald Black

Contemporary sociology of law is characterized by a confusion of science and policy. Its analysis proceeds in the disembodied tongue of science, in the language of "system," "structure," "pattern," and "organization," or in the vocabulary of technique, of "needs," "functions," and "viability." Rarely does the language impart emotion, indignation, or even personal involvement on the part of the investigator. But while legal sociology is presented in this scientific language and scientific tone, normative considerations—the "ought" and the "just"—become subtly implicated.

Although legal sociologists typically criticize one another according to the usual scientific standards of methodological precision and theoretical validity, they frequently become preoccupied with the "policy implications" of their research. Occasionally, in assessing one another, they shed the mantle of science and become unabashedly political. Recently, for instance, a sociologist characterized the literature of legal sociology as bourgeois, liberal, pluralist, and meliorist.[1] He went on to argue that a more radical sociology is required, one that is "more critical in its premises and farther-reaching in its

Excerpt from "The Boundaries of Legal Sociology," *Yale Law Journal* 81 (May 1972), pp. 1086–1100, by permission of the author and publisher, The Yale Law Journal Company and Fred B. Rothman and Company.

proposals.[2] Whether liberal or radical, however, legal sociologists tend to share a style of discourse that deserves attention and comment.

It is my contention that a purely sociological approach to law should involve not an assessment of legal policy, but rather, a scientific analysis of legal life *as a system of behavior*. The ultimate contribution of this enterprise would be a general theory of law, a theory that would predict and explain every instance of legal behavior. While such a general theory may never be attained, efforts to achieve it should be central to the sociology of law. By contrast, the core problems of legal policymaking are problems of value. Such value considerations are as irrelevant to a sociology of law as they are to any other scientific theory of the empirical world. . . .

Legal Effectiveness

With one phrase, *legal effectiveness*, we capture the major thematic concern of contemporary sociology of law. The wide range of work that revolves around the legal-effectiveness theme displays a common strategy of problem formulation, namely a comparison of legal reality to a legal ideal of some kind. Typically a gap is shown between law-in-action and law-in-theory. Often the sociologist then goes on to suggest how the reality might be brought closer to the ideal. Law is regarded as ineffective and in need of reform owing to the disparity between the legal reality and the ideal.

Legal-effectiveness studies differ from one another, however, in the kinds of legal ideals against which their findings are measured. At one extreme are "impact studies" that compare reality to legal ideals with a very plain and specific operational meaning. Here the legal measuring rod is likely to be a statute whose purpose is rather clearly discernible or a judicial decision unambiguously declarative of a specific policy. The *Miranda* decision, for example, requiring the police to apprise suspects of their legal rights before conducting an in-custody interrogation, has a core meaning about which consensus is quite high.[3] Soon after *Miranda* was handed down by the Supreme Court, research was initiated to evaluate the degree of police compliance with the decision.[4] When the core meaning of a decision thus is clear, this type of research can be expected to show whether or not a decision has, in fact, been implemented. . . .

Finally, the sociologist may attempt to compare legal reality to an ideal grounded in neither statutory nor case law. Here the investigator assesses his empirical materials against standards of justice such as "the rule of law," "arbitrariness," "legality," or a concept of "due process" not explicitly anchored in the due process clause of the Constitution. Jerome Skolnick, for instance, asserts that the police employ the informer system in narcotics enforcement "irrespective of the constraints embodied in principles of due process."[5] But there is no indication of where Skolnick locates these principles. Presumably he realizes that no court in the United States has declared the practice illegal, and there is no reason to think such a decision is likely in the near future. In another study, Skolnick investigates plea-bargaining in the courtroom, concluding that the cooperation underlying this practice "deviates" from some unarticulated adversarial ideal. Similarly, Leon Mayhew, in arguing that the Massachusetts Commission Against Discrimination failed to define discrimination adequately and thereby ignored much illegal conduct, provides neither a legal argument nor an empirical referent for his interpretation of the Commission's proper mission.[6] In short, then, some studies in legal sociology seem to move beyond the law when they measure legal reality against an ideal.

At its most useful, legal-effectiveness research may be valuable to people in a position to reform the legal order. In this sense it consists of studies in *applied* sociology of law. This would appear to be particularly true of those investigations that relate empirical findings to legal ideals which are clearly expressed in the written law. Such research might provide legal reformers with a kind of leverage for change, though the mere evidence of a gap between law-in-action and law-in-theory would not in itself overwhelm all resistance to change. Who can imagine a study, after all, that would not discover such a gap? Little is more predictable about the law than that these gaps exist.

However, legal-effectiveness research sometimes moves beyond aplied sociology. When legal reality is compared to an ideal with no identifiable empirical referent, such as "the rule of law" or "due process," the investigator may inadvertently implant his personal ideals as the society's legal ideals. At this point social science ceases and advocacy begins. The value of legal-effectiveness research of this kind is bound to be precarious, for it involves, perhaps unwittingly, moral judgment at the very point where it promises scientific analysis. . . .

Law, Science and Values

Law can be seen as a thing like any other in the empirical world. It is crucial to be clear that from a sociological standpoint, law consists in observable acts, not in rules as the concept of rule or norm is employed in both the literature of jurisprudence and in every-day legal language. From a sociological point of view, law is not what lawyers regard as binding or obligatory precepts, but rather, for example, the observable dispositions of judges, policemen, prosecutors, or administrative officials. Law is like any other thing in the sense that it is as amenable to the scientific method as any other aspect of reality. No intellectual apparatus peculiar to the study of law is required. At the same time, a social science of law true to positivism, the conventional theory of science, cannot escape the limitations inherent in scientific thought itself. Perhaps a word should be said about these limitations.

Within the tradition of positivist philosophy, three basic principles of scientific knowledge can be noted. First, science can know only phenomena and never essences. The quest for the one correct concept of law or for anything else "distinctively legal" is therefore inherently unscientific.[7] The essence of law is a problem for jurisprudence, not science. Second, every scientific idea requires a concrete empirical referent of some kind. A science can only order experience, and has no way of gaining access to non-empirical domains of knowledge. Accordingly, insofar as such ideals as justice, the rule of law, and due process are without a grounding in experience, they have no place in the sociology of law. Third, value judgments cannot be discovered in the empirical world and for that reason are without cognitive meaning in science.[8]

It is for this last reason that science knows nothing and can know nothing about the effectiveness of law. Science is incapable of an evaluation of the reality it confronts. To measure the effectiveness of law or of anything else for that matter, we must import standards of value that are foreign to science. What is disturbing about the contemporary literature on legal effectiveness then is not that it evaluates law,[9] but rather, that its evaluations and proposals are presented as scientific findings. Far from denying this confusion, Philip Selznick has gone so far in the opposite direction as to claim that "nothing we know today precludes an effort to define 'ends proper to man's nature' and to discover objective standards of moral judgment.[10]

Legal sociologists involved in the study of effectiveness have thus come to advance a conception of scientific criticism of law. This is illogical; it is a contradiction in terms.

It is apparent by now that my critique of contemporary legal sociology is premised on the notion that sociology is a scientific enterprise and, as such, can be distinguished from moral philosophy, jurisprudence, or any other normatively oriented study—in other words, that the study of fact can be distinguished from the study of value. This is not to say that I am unaware of the criticisms that have been levied against a purely value-free social science. But while accepting these criticisms, I cannot understand the conclusion that the effort to develop an objective science of man should be abandoned.

It is important to understand precisely how values become involved in social science. One widely recognized intrusion of values occurs at the first stage of scientific inquiry: the choice of the problem for study. The values of the investigator may determine, for example, whether he selects a problem with great relevance for public policy or one of wholly academic interest. This intrusion of values was long ago noted by Max Weber, perhaps the most illustrious proponent of value-free sociology. Weber contended that the role of values in the choice of a problem is unavoidable and should be faced squarely, but he insisted that the problem, once selected, could and should be pursued "non-evaluatively."[11]

But I would go further than Weber and grant that these value orientations may bias the analysis of the problem as well as its selection. Though various methodological techniques have been developed to minimize the effects of these biases, good social science still requires a disciplined disengagement on the part of the investigator—so disciplined, in fact, that it may rarely be achieved. Various arguments can be made to the effect that bias is built into social science at its very foundations. For example, the claim has been made that every social science study necessarily implicates the investigator in the perspective of an actual hierarchical position, seeing social life from either the social top or the bottom, and is therefore inherently biased. For purposes of discussion I grant even this. Similarly it is arguable that all social science is, beyond science, a form of ideology, if only because it is by its nature an instance of social behavior subject to the scrutiny of the very discipline of which it is a part. Sociology, that is, can be analyzed sociologically. Sociology does not occur in a vacuum and is undoubtedly influenced by social forces. Accordingly, sociology may be viewed as ideology supporting either the defenders of the status quo or their opponents. . . .

In several senses, then, values enter into the activity of social science. While values may play a similar role in science of all kinds, it can at least be admitted that their role is especially visible and dramatic when man is studying himself. Values may be all the more prominent in the study of man's moral life, of which legal sociology is one branch. The major arguments against the possibility of a pure science of man, in short, seem to have some merit. But the crucial question is what all of this implies for the traditional distinction between fact and value. I say it implies nothing. In fact, much of the criticism of value-free sociology itself rests upon observable patterns of value impact upon social science and for that reason relies upon the fact-value distinction for its own validity.

We have seen that a social scientist may be affected by values in the choice of his problem and may be biased in his approach to it.

Critics of a value-free social science assert that these psychological effects, along with the ideological character of social science when viewed as the object of analysis itself, undermine the validity of social science. But this is to confuse the origins and uses of a scientific statement with its validity. *The fact that scientific statements are influenced by values does not make them value statements.* The psychological and social influence of values on scientific inquiry has no logical implications for the validity of a scientific proposition. Its validity is determined only by empirical verification. A value statement, by contrast, is not subject to such a test. How, for example, is the following statement to be empirically verified: "Democratic process is an ultimate good"? The fact that we can distinguish between scientific propositions and such value statements is all we need to assert the possibility of social science. In short, values may affect social science profoundly, but that is no reason to abandon the enterprise.[12]

Toward a Pure Sociology of Law

The proper concern of legal sociology should be the development of a general theory of law. A general theory involves several key elements that may not at first be obvious. To say that a theory of law is general means that it seeks to order law wherever it is found. It seeks to discover the principles and mechanisms that predict empirical patterns of law, whether these patterns occur in this day or the past, regardless of the substantive area of law involved and regardless of the society. By contrast, the contemporary study of law is ideographic, very concrete and historical. Legal scholars tend to rebel at the suggestion of a general theory of their subject matter. Nevertheless, unless we seek generality in our study of law, we abandon hope for a serious sociology of law.

If the sweep of legal sociology is to be this broad, a correspondingly broad concept of law is required. I like to define law simply as *governmental social control.* This is one possibility among many consistent with a positivist strategy. It is a concept easily employed in cross-societal analysis, encompassing any act by a political body that concerns the definition of social order or its defense. At the same time it excludes such forms of social control as popular morality and bureaucratic rules in private organizations. It is more inclusive than an American lawyer might deem proper, but more selective than anthropological concepts which treat law as synonymous with normative life and dispute settlement of every description, governmental or otherwise. If we are to have a manageable subject matter, our concept must construe law as one among a larger array of social control systems. And if we are to have a strategically detached approach, our concept must be value neutral. We need a theoretical structure applicable to the law of the Nazis as well as American law, to revolutionary law and colonial law as well as the cumbersome law of traditional China. What do these systems share, and how can we explain the differences among them?

Ultimately a theory is known and judged by its statements about the world. These statements both guide and follow empirical research. They propose uniformities in the relation between one part of reality and another. Thus a general theory of law is addressed to the relation between law and other aspects of social life, including, for instance, other forms of social control, social stratification, the division of labor, social integration, group size, and the structure and substance of social networks. At the moment we have only a small inventory of theoretical statements, or propositions, of this kind. The relevant literature is sparse, and many of our leads must come from the classic works of Maine,[13] Durkheim,[14] Weber,[15] Ehrlich,[16] Pound,[17] and the like. Marx, too, should not be forgotten, though he gave law only passing attention.[18] Apart from classical sociology and comparative jurisprudence, anthropological literature, notably the work of such scholars as Malinowski,[19] Hoebel,[20] Gluckman,[21] Bohannan,[22] and Nader,[23] has contributed more than sociology to a general theory of law. Contemporary sociologists tend to limit their attention to the American legal system, and even there, disproportionate emphasis is given the criminal justice system. Rarely do they compare American law to governmental social control in other societies; yet if legal sociology is not comparative, its conclusions will inevitably be time-bound and ethnocentric.

This is not to suggest that American criminal justice is unworthy of study. But one must address problems at a higher level of generality, thereby contributing to and benefiting from scholarship in other realms of law. If we investigate the police, for example, our fundamental interest as sociologists must be in what police work can teach us about law, generically understood, and we must bring to a study of the police whatever we know about other forms of legal life. From my standpoint, in other words, the major shortcoming of most sociological literature on the police is that it concerns the police alone, instead of treating police behavior as an instance of law. Often sociologists occupy themselves with the unique world of the policeman, his attitudes, hopes and fears, his relations with his fellow officers, his social isolation in the wider community—in brief, with the "human" dimensions of police work. Insofar as such studies rise above descriptive journalism or ethnography, then, they tend to focus upon the psychology of the policeman on his day-to-day round. Yet from a purely scoiological point of view it is not important to know that policemen are, after all, "human" or to know how their minds work. A pure sociology of law does not study humans in the usual sense. It studies law as a system of behavior. Taken in this sense, law feels nothing. It has no joy or sorrow or wonderment. Scientifically conceived as a social reality in its own right, law is no more human than a molecular structure. It has no nationality, no mind, and no ends proper to its nature. . . .

Police research should tell us something about the social control function of the police: What legal matters do they handle? How do they come to deal with those matters? What are the principles according to which they process their cases? Ideally a study would also tell us how police behavior resembles other known patterns of legal behavior and how it differs. We know, for example, that the police make arrests relatively infrequently when some other form of social control is available in the situation. Thus, they rarely make an arrest when one family member criminally offends another, a situation where other means of social pressure typically are at hand, whereas the same offense committed by one stranger against another is very apt to result in arrest.[24] This pattern of legal behavior is known to have analogues in a wide variety of legal settings, in civil as well as criminal cases, in the invocation of law as well as its application, in many countries and historical periods, and even in the evolution of law itself.[25] We may state the pattern as a theoretical proposition: Law tends to become implicated in social life to the degree that other forms of social control are weak or unavailable.[26] Hence, what we discover in the behavior of policemen turns out to be simply an instance of a much more general pattern in the conditions under which the law acts upon social life. We thereby add systematically to existing knowledge of this pattern, and, what is more, we can *explain* the behavior of the police, since it can be predicted and deduced from a more general proposition about law.[27] If the likelihood of legal control is greater where other forms of social control are absent, it follows that the police are more likely to arrest a stranger who, let us say, assaults a stranger than a son who assaults his father. To be able to explain something so mundane and microscopic as behavior in a police encounter with the same proposition that we use to explain the historical emergence of law itself is exciting and encouraging. It provides a glimpse of general theory in action. This kind of theoretical structure is built up and elaborated over time through a process of give-and-take between data and tentative propositions stated at a high level of abstraction. It is the classical pattern of scientific advance, and I cannot see why the sociology of law should be any less ambitious or any less rigorous.

Conclusion

We should be clear about the relation between sociological and legal scholarship. There is, properly speaking, no conflict of professional jurisdiction between the two. A legal problem is a problem of value and is forever beyond the reach of sociology. Jurisdictional conflict arises only when the sociologist makes policy recommendations in the name of science: In matters of legal policy, the lawyer must rely on his own wits.

But a more significant matter than jurisdictional clarity is the relation between pure and applied sociology of law. My view, hardly novel, is that the quality of applied science depends upon the quality of pure science. Just as major advances in mechanical and chemical engineering have been made possible by theoretical formulations in pure physics and chemistry, so legal engineering ultimately requires a general theory of how legal systems behave as natural phenomena. The case for a pure sociology of law does not rest solely on its social usefulness, but if utility is at issue, then in the long run the type of work I advocate is crucial. At present, applied sociology of law has little to apply. What more serious claim could be brought against it?

Notes

1. Currie, *Book Review*, 81 Yale L.J. 134 (1971), *reviewing* Law and the Behavioral Sciences (L. Friedman & S. Macaulay eds. 1969) *and* Society and the Legal Order, R. Schwartz & J. Skolnick eds. 1970). These two collections of the legal sociology literature not only collect representative materials but also attempt to explain the relevance of the materials, thereby providing excellent examples of the style of discourse now dominating the field.

2. *Id.* at 145. A striking feature of Currie's review is that he pays little attention to the scientific adequacy of the work he criticizes. Instead, he focuses more upon the reform implications of the existing work and condemns it on political rather than methodological or theoretical grounds. Thus, while he suggests that the work could greatly benefit from the perspectives of Marxian scholars, he fails to show that the Marxian approach to law has a superior explanatory power.

3. Miranda v. Arizona, 384 U.S. 436 (1966). Although there may be some disagreement as to the peripheral meanings of "custody" and "interrogation" (*see, e.g.*, Mathis v. United States, 391 U.S. 1 (1968); Orozco v. Texas, 394 U.S. 324 (1969)), there is little doubt that a suspect under arrest in a police station who is probingly questioned about his involvement in a crime is both in custody and under interrogation as these concepts are used by the Court. Moreover, no question remains as to the required *content* of an apprising of rights. 384 U.S. at 478-79. Yet, there may even be disagreement as to what constitutes an "adequate" and "effective" apprising of rights. *Id.* at 467.

Compare United States v. Fox, 403 F.2d 97 (2d Cir. 1968), *with* State v. Renfrew, 280 Minn. 276, 159 N.W.2d 111 (1968). For example, would a police procedure of giving the suspect a preprinted card listing his rights meet the requirement of an adequate and effective apprisal? Would that procedure meet the *Miranda* test if the suspect were illiterate?

4. *See, e.g.*, Project, *Interrogations in New Haven: The Impact of Miranda*, 76 Yale L.J. 1519 (1967).

5. J. Skolnick, Justice Without Trial 138 (1966).

6. L. Mayhew, Law and Equal Opportunity (1969), *reviewed*, Black, *Book Review*, 40 Soc. Inquiry 179 (1970). *See* Mayhew, *Teleology and Values in the Social System: Reply to Donald J. Black*, 40 Soc. Inquiry 182 (1970).

7. Philip Selznick, one of the most ambitious and influential students of legal effectiveness, considers the "cardinal weakness" of the sociological approach to law to be its "failure to offer a theory of the distinctively legal." Selznick, *The Sociology of Law*, 9 International Encyclopedia of the Social Sciences 51 (D. L. Sills ed. 1968).

8. *Id.* at 7–8. Some legal sociologists are willing to tolerate an obfuscation of factual and normative discourse. Selznick, for instance, while conceding that the separation of fact and value has some merit, nevertheless suggests that this distinction is meant for "unsophisticated minds." We must, he continues, unlearn this "easy and reassuring" formula from our "intellectual youth." Selznick finds a natural-law approach more appropriate for the mature thinker. Selznick, *Sociology and Natural Law*, 6 Natural L.F. 86 (1961).

9. As a rule I do not personally find the policy criticisms and proposals of legal sociologists to be particularly objectionable, the exception being those proposals that increase the power of the government to intervene in citizens' lives. Thus, for instance, I find the therapeutic approach to criminal offenders a frightening advance of an already too powerful criminal justice system. In fact, I align myself more broadly and precisely in the philosophical tradition of anarchism. For me, the validity of law is at all times contingent upon my own assessment of its moral validity, and thus I recognize no a priori legitimacy in the rule of law. For a brief introduction to this political ethic, see R. Wolff, In Defence of Anarchism (1970).

    I would add that the students of legal effectiveness I am discussing are, politically speaking, the elite of our society, however critical of the legal process they may seem. Indeed, the government often finances their research on its own effectiveness. It is my view that the confusion of fact and value operates as a form of mystification that helps to keep the established order intact. Nevertheless, I do not wish to use my status as a scientist to promote my political philosophy. *See* M. Weber, From Max Weber: Essays in Sociology 129–56 (H. H. Gerth & C. W. Mills transl. and eds. 1958).

10. Selznick, *supra* note 8 at 93–94.

11. *See* M. Weber, The Methodology of the Social Sciences 21–22 (E. A. Shils & H. A. Finch transls. 1949). For a direct attack on Weber's approach to these questions, see Gouldner, *Anti-Minotaur: The Myth of a Value-Free Sociology*, 9 Soc. Problems 199 (1962).

12. My critique of contemporary legal sociology arises from a very conventional conception of scientific method, a conception associated with the broader

tradition of positivist thought. I have not made and do not intend to make a philosophical defense of this tradition. I wish only to advocate a sociology of law true to basic positivist principles as they have come to be understood in the history of the philosophy of science.

13. *See, e.g.*, Ancient Law (1861), Village-Communities in the East and West (1871).

14. The Division of Labor in Society (G. Simpson transl. 1933); Professional Ethics and Civic Morals (C. Brookfield transl. 1957); *Two Laws of Penal Evolution* (M. Mileski transl. 1971) (available in my files).

15. Max Weber on Law in Economy and Society (M. Rheinstein ed., E. Shils & M. Rheinstein transl. 1954).

16. Fundamental Principles of the Sociology of Law (W. Moll transl. 1936).

17. *E.g.*, Social Control Through Law (1942); *The Limits of Effective Legal Action*, 27 Int'l J. Ethics 150 (1917); *A Survey of Social Interests*, 57 Harv. L. Rev. 1 (1943).

18. Marx did, however, inspire some interesting sociological work on law. *See, e.g.*, K. Renner, The Institutions of Private Law and Their Social Functions (O. Kahn-Freund ed., A. Schwartzchild transl. 1949); Pashukanis, *The General Theory of Law and Marxism*, in Soviet Legal Philosophy 111 (H. Babb transl. 1951).

19. The standard work is Crime and Custom in Savage Society (1926). This study is considered the first ethnography of law.

20. The Law of Primitive Man (1954); K. Llewellyn & E. Hoebel, The Cheyenne Way: Conflict and Case Law in Primitive Jurisprudence (1941).

21. *See, e.g.*, The Judicial Process Among the Barotse of Northern Rhodesia (1955). Gluckman provides a useful overview of legal anthropology in Politics, Law and Ritual in Tribal Society (1965).

22. Justice and Judgment Among the Tiv (1957); *The Differing Realms of the Law*, in The Ethnography of Law 33 (1965) (supplement to 67 Am. Anthropologist 33 (1965)).

23. E.g., *An Analysis of Zapotec Law Cases*, 3 Ethnology 404 (1964); *Choices in Legal Procedure: Shia Moslem and Mexican Zapotec*, 67 Am. Anthropologist 394 (1965).

24. Black, *The Social Organization of Arrest*, 23 Stan. L. Rev. 1087, 1107 (1971).

25. *Id.* at 1107–08 nn. 30–34.

26. *Id.* at 1108.

27. For a discussion of this type of explanation, see R. Braithwaite, Scientific Explanation: A Study of the Function of Theory, Probability and Law in Science (1953).

5

For Jurisprudential Sociology
Philippe Nonet

Ten years ago, in the first issue of this review [*Law and Society Review*], Carl A. Auerbach criticized some early statements of an emerging "Berkeley perspective" in the sociology of law (Auerbach, 1966).[1] Selznick, Skolnick, Carlin, and I were chided for proposing in various terms that a central concern of the sociology of law should be to study the social foundations of the ideal of legality (Selznick, 1961; 1968; Skolnick, 1965; Carlin and Nonet, 1968). . . .

"Pure Sociology"

Ten years (and countless hours of lecturing and discussion) later, the idea that sociology might properly seek to develop a normative theory of law remains unpopular. In fact, if we are to judge from its most recent manifestos, the opposition has hardened and escalated. In two recent essays (Black, 1972a; 1972b), Donald Black, who describes himself as "an uncompromising adherent of the positivist approach" (1972a: 709), reaffirms the doctrine that "value judgments cannot be discovered in the empirical world" (1972b: 1092). Hence, he argues, "value considerations are as irrelevant to a sociol-

Excerpt from "For Jurisprudential Sociology," *Law and Society Review* 10 (Summer 1976), pp. 525–545.

ogy of law as they are to any other scientific theory" (1972b: 1807), and "the quest for the . . . 'distinctively legal' is . . . inherently unscientific" (1972b: 1092). Black's point is not just to remind us of a problem of logic, or to warn us against a possible source of bias. Nor is it to urge a larger vision of the task of social science in the study of law. On the contrary, it is to define *limits* within which social inquiry must be confined, or lose its "purity."

According to Black, "a purely sociological approach to law should involve not an assessment of legal policy, but rather, a scientific analysis of legal life as a system of behavior" 1972b: 1087). When "sociologists move . . . beyond science and deal with questions of legal evaluation" (1972b: 1087), they "severely retard the development of their field. At best they offer an applied sociology of law— at worst, sheer ideology" (1972b: 1087). If research "relate[s] empirical findings to legal ideas which are clearly expressed in the written law" (1972b: 1089), then it constitutes applied sociology. But "when legal reality is compared to an ideal with no identifiable empirical referent, such as 'the rule of law' or 'due process,' the investigator may inadvertently implant his personal ideals as the society's legal ideals. At this point social science ceases and advocacy begins" (1972b: 1090). The investigator "leaves sociology and enters jurisprudence" (1972a: 712), which is inevitably "saturated with ideology and evaluation and interest" (1972a: 712).

At one point, Black concedes that "applied" sociology of law may be valuable to people interested in law reform (1972b: 1089). But eventually the concession is retracted, on the theory that "the quality of applied science depends upon the quality of pure science. . . . At present, applied sociology of law has little to apply. What more serious claim could be brought against it?" (1972b: 1100). Hence, the sociologist should return to his basic mission—the formulation of a "general theory of law," i.e., a theory that "seeks to discover the principles and mechanisms that predict empirical patterns of law, whether these patterns occur in this day or the past . . . regardless of the society" (1972b: 1096). . . .

As Black observes, "pure sociology" is deeply alien to the perspectives that have governed the growth of sociology. Even today, although the vast majority of social scientists sing and dance in ritual reaffirmation of its canons, in fact they all cheat constantly in their actual work. There, the focus (explicit or implicit) is on the clarification of values, the assessment of institutions, the evaluation of policy, the conditions that frustrate or facilitate aspirations. In that respect, the sociology of law does not differ from other fields in the discipline, e.g. stratification (read: distributive justice), or socialization (read: moral development). Obviously, sociology bears birthmarks of its origins in the normative study of politics, law, economics, culture. Furthermore, like it or not, the intellectual significance of sociological ideas remains largely derivative. In the absence of any autonomous (and persuasive) body of sociological theory, the conclusions of social inquiry continue to gain meaning and resonance primarily from what they contribute to political, legal, economic, and other branches of "normative" thought—in other words, to our understanding of the conditions and costs of the pursuit of various human aspirations, such as democracy, fairness, efficiency, intimacy.

Judging from past experience, that situation is not likely to change. If we were to teach only "pure sociology," we would have to graduate illiterates; and research so limited would only add to an already over-great indulgence in intellectual onanism. Having law, politics, economics to think about, we manage to retain some facts, some history, and some ideas to teach, thus saving our students from radical ignorance. Furthermore, law, politics, economics are not just subjects of theory; they are also key contexts of action within which social experience accumulates. . . .

Given its past accomplishments, "pure sociology" would seem a high-risk and very speculative intellectual investment. We should of course tolerate, and even encourage, the few who may try it. But it does not follow we should allow it to become a program for the rest of us. On the contrary, experience recommends what has been a cardinal tenet of the "Berkeley program" in legal sociology: just as other branches of sociology need to be informed by the normative thought on which they comment, so *sociology of law must be jurisprudentially informed* (Principle I). Even if a "pure sociology of law were to develop, we should still want to invest most of our resources in more tangibly fruitful ventures. The reason for that is the relatively low yield of purely theoretical work of any kind, in all sociology and all philosophy, in jurisprudence as well as in sociology of law. Hence another tenet of the Berkeley program (also, regrettably, the least observed): *sociology of law must have redeeming value for policy.* Never let any project stand on its theoretical merits alone (Principle II).

Prescribed Ignorance

Black does not deny the factual foundation of these principles. He deplores it, and urges instead that sociology sever its continuity with normative philosophy, and with its own history. Unfortunately, such a rupture entails serious and tangible intellectual costs, against which the speculative future of "pure" sociology cannot weigh heavily. The main cost is, of course, a severely impoverished education. In the event the point is not as obvious as I think it is, I shall let Black himself illustrate it. Our critic would have the sociology of law cut itself loose from its jurisprudential past. Thus he finds it regrettable that "normative" legal sociology "has become identified with debunkery and the unmasking of law." This orientation, he argues, "goes back to the legal realism movement. . . . Much legal sociology, then, is a new legal realism, appearing in the prudent garb of social science" (1972b: 1087, n. 4). A "pure" sociology of law would liberate itself from this unfortunate history. In this purified approach, we are told, law is seen

> as a thing like any other in the empirical world. It is crucial to be clear that from a sociological standpoint, law consists in observable acts, not in rules as the concept of rule is employed in both the literature of jurisprudence and in everyday legal language. From a sociological point of view, *law is not what lawyers regard as binding or obligatory precepts, but rather,* for example, *the observable dispositions of judges, policemen, prosecutors, or administrative officials* [1972b: 1091. Italics mine].

Now it should be apparent that this allegedly "sociological" approach to law has its own jurisprudential pedigree: it was last, and most forcefully, advocated by some legal realists.[2] It should also be clear that familiarity with its jurisprudential history would help inform the sociologists of the powerful objections to which this approach is vulnerable. Specifically, a jurisprudentially informed social scientist would be more likely to understand, along with H. L. A. Hart, that the sentence quoted above in italics is internally contradictory (in that the office of judge, policeman, etc. . . . is constituted by, and hence, cannot even be identified without reference to, rules), and seriously misleading as a guide for an empirical account of legal phenomena (in that it disregards the element of authority in legal phenomena) (Hart, 1961: especially 79–88; 132–144). Hence, he could hardly agree with Black's statement that the "sociological approach" so defined "does not conflict with the rule-oriented jurisprudence of H. L. A. Hart" (Black, 1972b: 1091 n. 15). Finally, he would be able to appreciate that, however "scientifically" inadequate, a focus on "the observable dispositions" of officials makes special sense if one's purpose is to expose the discrepancy between what officials do and what they ought to do. It presumes that very "debunking spirit" from which Black wants to rescue legal sociology.

If one agrees with Black (as I do) that debunking is too limited, too unpromising, and too easy a goal for sociological inquiry, perhaps the alternative is not to dismiss or ignore the role of values, rules, and other normative elements in legal phenomena, but rather to take them more seriously. This is part of the program H. L. A. Hart proposed for jurisprudence. It is also what Selznick proposed for legal sociology when, for similar reasons but in different words, he argued against the anti-formalist (read: rule-skeptical) mood that had pervaded the field and its immediate parents, i.e., legal realism and sociological jurisprudence (Selznick, 1968). . . .

Another basic tenet of the Berkeley program, which is: *the sociology of law must take legal ideas seriously.* (Principle III. Corollary: sociologists who want to study law should become legally literate.) Perhaps a difference between Auerbach and Selznick was that the former had greater confidence in the promise of legal realism, and the good sense of social science, than the latter could muster. In fact, legal realism was fraught with ambiguity in its posture towards legal ideas. On the one hand, it hoped to make legal thought more purposive, more policy-oriented, more aware of consequences, and hence, more informed by the problems of law inaction. On the other hand, its impatience towards legal formalism suggested a more radical critique of the inherent impotence of any legal thought. It was inevitable that such a perspective appeal to social scientists bent on demystification. Besides, it is all too comforting for the student of sociology to think he can study "pure" legal "behavior" (without bothering to learn about the complicated and obscure arguments that occupy lawyers), and still hope to capture all that "really" matters about the legal order. . . .

By now, it should be clear that Black's program for a "pure" sociology of law offers not just one, but two prescriptions for ignorance. Sociology should (1) ignore the problems, values, and doctrines of jurisprudence; (2) ignore the rules, principles, and policies that constitute law, as understood by all the pure sociologists.

Even the best intentioned and the strongest willed would find such vows of ignorance impossible to honor without breach. Black himself violates his religion in the very sermon he preaches. Thus he proposes that a definition of law as "governmental social control" (1972b: 1096) would satisfy the requirements of pure sociology. He finds that definition simple, as well as "consistent with a positivist strategy" (1972b: 1096). For example, it is obvious to Black that such a definition excludes from law "such forms of social control as . . . bureaucratic rules in private organizations" (1972b: 1096). Thus, it turns out, (a) rules are a "form of social control," and fall within the ambit of legal sociology if they are governmental; (b) the identification of the legal requires distinguishing between the "public" and the "private" sphere, a problem that has haunted jurisprudence and political theory, and which is the central preoccupation of the book [by Selznick] that Black rules out of sociology as an argument in jurisprudence (1972a).

Shortly thereafter, Black offers a "theoretical proposition" which, he thinks, exemplifies the kind of idea that pure sociology should aim to develop and test: "Law tends to become implicated in social life to the degree that other forms of social control are weak or unavailable" (1972b: 1099). It should be obvious that the conclusion that some form of social control is "weak or unavailable" presupposes the identification of some standard of need, or adequacy, or (might I venture) effectiveness, by which the control mechanism can be assessed. Thus, although pure sociology is barred from studying "legal effectiveness" (1972b: 1087) (because that involves unscientific evaluation), it appears it may, indeed must, evaluate the adequacy of non-legal forms of control. It is to Black's credit that his common sense is not always blinded by his positivist faith. One can hardly imagine a sensible study of social control that would not ask in one way or another: control to what end? by what means? with what results? at what cost? and other such evaluative questions. Black avoids the words, but does the job.

From this "theoretical proposition," Black argues, more specific generalizations can be "predicted and deduced" (1972b: 1099). He offers an example from a study he did of the conditions under which police resort to arrest: "The greater the relational distance between a complainant and a suspect, the greater the likelihood of arrest" (1971: 1107). Black explains that the police (i.e. law, governmental social control) will likely refrain from arresting a son who (allegedly) assaulted his father, because the family (i.e. another "means of social pressure") can probably handle "the situation"; by contrast, if one (e.g. a stranger) assaults a more distantly related other (e.g. another stranger), the probability of arrest is higher. This highly schematic story summarizes a complicated cost-benefit analysis of alternative means of control. It is unclear whether that analysis is made only by the police (whose conduct Black is just describing), or also by Black (who might then be arguing that the police's cost–benefit analysis usually comes to the same conclusion as his own). But whoever does the analysis, it involves assessing a problematic situation (a family quarrel) in which (a) several ends must be taken into account (punishing the offender? restraining the participants to prevent further offenses? upholding parental authority? facilitating a reconciliation? reducing risks and costs for law enforcement?), and (b) alternative policies (to arrest or not to arrest?) must be evaluated in the light of these normative criteria. This evaluation may be more or less routinized, more or less sensitive, more or less prompt, more or less accurate; and we may want to assess the conditions under which the quality of the policeman's analysis varies. We would then be evaluating the evaluation. Furthermore, the practical conclusions one might draw from the evaluation would depend in part upon how the many relevant ends would be ordered in a priority ranking. Thus, a legal order that gave high priority to upholding the authority of the criminal law, allowed police considerable resources, and had little regard for the family as an institution, would give its policemen decision criteria quite different from the criteria that would prevail if the family were highly valued, the criminal law were held in contempt, and the police were kept stingily understaffed.

Thus understood, Black's story makes new sense. Clearly, it no longer supports his "theoretical proposition," that is, the "purely sociological" "prediction" that police will "behave" (after having done all the thinking Black would like to ignore) in accordance with the stated pattern. The proposition is far too general, and has to be restated to incorporate the major conditions under which the predicted pattern can plausibly be expected. Note that at least some of these conditions would refer, implicitly or explicitly, to values, principles, and policies of the legal order, e.g. to how the legal order ranks the various ends its police must consider in deciding whether or not to arrest. Now it becomes apparent that Black's "theoretical proposition" is in fact the poorly disguised statement of a *principle of economy or restraint* by which some governments (or some officials of some governments, including the police Black studied) are sometimes guided. The "prediction" is a norm which directs government officials to save their resources for situations in which no other agency can take responsibility. The norm may itself reflect considerations of economy (avoid wasting scarce resources), or a more affirmative principle of deference to "private" institutions, or a general preference for minimal government. One must then wonder whether Black's enthusiasm for his "theoretical proposition" (he finds it "exciting and encouraging") (1972b: 1100) might not be a manifestation of his ideological preference for "the philosophical tradition of anarchism" (1972b: 1092, n. 23). For elsewhere in the paper he confesses that he finds "particularly objectionable" the policy proposals of legal sociologists that "increase the power of the government to intervene in citizens' lives" (1972b: 1092, n. 23).

Bias and Ideology

I could not resist making this last point, not because I find it important, but because *to Black* the ultimate sin of evaluative sociology is that the investigator is given opportunities, perhaps encouraged, to "inadvertently implant his personal ideals" (1972b: 1090) and drift from science to ideology. The arch enemy of "good science" is bias. That is why "good social science . . . requires a disciplined disengagement on the part of the investigator—so disciplined, in fact, that it may rarely be achieved" (1972b: 1093). Perhaps this principle of disengagement is the reason why Black urges upon us his program of willful ignorance. Of course, ignorance and impoverished education create their own risks of scientific error. In effect, we are asked to *prefer the risks of error by ignorance to the risks of error from bias.* . . .

Compared to bias, ignorance is far more damaging to the scientific enterprise. It diminishes the resources we have to analyze complex ideas, to make distinctions, to uncover hidden assumptions, briefly to correct faults in one's own as well as others' thinking. Furthermore, it reduces the chances that one will have many rather than few biases, and therefore none too strongly held, as each necessarily conflicts with some other. To prefer ignorance is to choose ideology as well as incompetence.

On close scrutiny, it turns out that ideology (in the sense just discussed) does not trouble Black too much. To assess police conduct *only* from the standpoint of its compliance with *Miranda* is to assume an ideological posture. But Black uses a study of this kind as an example of "applied" sociology (Black, 1972b: 1088), which he regards as scientifically legitimate. Two features seem to distinguish "applied" sociology from what Black regards as illegitimate evaluative sociology. First, the standard of evaluation has "a very plain and specific operational meaning (1972b: 1088). To the extent criteria of evaluation are complex and obscure, the assessment loses its scientific integrity. Second, the standard is drawn from a source other than the researcher's own preferences (although it may be congruent with them). Thus, if the standard is "a statute whose purpose is rather clearly discernible or a judicial decision unambiguously declarative of a specific policy" (1972b: 1088), the research is "applied" science. It should be obvious that these two criteria are likely to conflict with one another. A standard of evaluation borrowed from *one* statute or decision may be clear; but the relevant law is likely to comprise many statutes and decisions, and hence to be confused and ambiguous. To select one of these many criteria is to assume a partial and partisan standpoint. Similarly, one can have a "plain and specific operational" standard of judgment only if one agrees to defend a highly partisan viewpoint. The more complex, multiple, and hence obscure, are one's evaluation criteria, the wider the array of interests and values (other than one's own or any party's) they are likely to take into account.

Because Black's two ways of distinguishing applied from illegitimate evaluative sociology conflict with one another, I shall consider each separately. Let us begin with "clarity."

According to Black, clarity of meaning is what distinguishes narrow, specific policies (the kind of standards by which "applied" sociology evaluates legal behavior) from larger, more general ends (such as due-process, the Rule of Law, and other such standards which are the concern of jurisprudence, moral, and political philosophy, and by which illegitimate evaluative sociology assesses legal "reality"). To draw the line on that ground is to reduce scientific inquiry to the role of a bureaucratic investigation of compliance. As defined, "applied" legal sociology is perhaps less difficult than jurisprudential sociology. It is certainly not more scientific; on the contrary, it retreats from a major scientific responsibility of policy research, that is, the clarification of purpose. Whatever meaning a specific policy may have, it owes that meaning to some large purpose(s) or interest(s) it helps achieve in a particular context. Therefore, to evaluate the implementation of a policy is inevitably to further determine (clarify) what the pursuit of some larger ends requires (means) in the context under study. Research can, of course, determine whether the racial composition of classrooms meets the quantitative guidelines established by court decrees in school integration cases. But all judicial, bureaucratic, and "affirmative action" authorities to the contrary notwithstanding, that information alone would be meaningless, as full compliance with the guidelines is as compatible with increased racial conflict and poorer education, as it is with exactly opposite achievements. Good policy research would require that compliance with the guidelines be assessed in light of the ends of education and racial justice. This kind of assessment is precisely what we wish bureaucracies did more often, when we criticize them for transforming means (rules and routines of all kinds) into ends. Thus clarity, or rather the progressive clarification of values, is a *purpose, not a condition*, of policy research, as it is of jurisprudence and jurisprudential sociology. For this reason, a fourth tenet (Principle IV) of the Berkeley program is: *The sociology of law must integrate jurisprudential and policy analysis.*

Black's distinction between applied and jurisprudential sociology rejects that principle and amounts to yet another prescription for ignorance: it directs the sociologist to ignore the purpose of the policies he evaluates. Such a directive would sterilize policy-research. If the distinction also suggests that the purposes and logic of jurisprudential inquiry differ fundamentally from those of policy research, then it is doubly sterilizing. Jurisprudence lives and grows from what it learns from policy. For policy is the realm of action where abstract ideals are tested, redefined, and elaborated. Only by examining that experience can jurisprudence remain factually informed, and hope to clarify the dilemmas of moral and political choice.

Moral dilemmas, not moral causes, are the stuff of jurisprudence, as well as of moral and political theory. With this observation, let us turn to Black's second criterion for distinguishing philosophers from applied sociologists. The former, he thinks, *advocate* their "personal" preferences, whereas the latter *evaluate* in the light of standards set by others. . . . Black's objections to jurisprudential sociology are not that it advocates, but that it bases advocacy or evaluation upon the *personal* preferences of the analyst, rather than preferences imposed by some other source. Why the source of the standard should matter, if the intrusion of evaluation into the argument does not necessarily corrupt its logic, is the next obscurity we must consider.

Authority and Value

Obscure as it is, that question points to a central element in the creed of "pure sociology." Believers in that faith claim that science should not be used to give authority to values.

Clearly Black is not arguing that the "scientific validity" of evaluative research depends upon the source of the standard invoked. An "applied sociologist" might well personally believe in the policy by which he assesses legal behavior without thereby jeopardizing the legitimacy of his analysis. Conversely, an American jurisprudential sociologist who personally values and studies fidelity to "due process of law" is not exculpated by the fact that the Constitution of the United States gives authority to that standard.

What really matters to Black is that the applied sociologist usually makes *explicit* the authority for the standard he studies, whereas the jurisprudential sociologist is less apt to do so. Failing to disclose the source of one's standard makes one vulnerable to the charge of failing to separate clearly the normative from the factual elements in one's analysis, thus possibly misleading one's readers to believe that some normative statements are scientifically demonstrated truths. "What is disturbing about the contemporary literature on legal effectiveness then is not that it evaluates, but rather, that its evaluations and proposals are presented as scientific findings" (Black, 1972b: 1092-1093). To disown evaluative statements by indicating their authors are a legislature, or a judge, or for that matter anyone but a scientist, is a convenient way to avoid that risk.

There are good reasons why social scientists do not always clearly disclose the authority for their normative statements. For example, the sources may be too many, too diffuse, or simply too obvious. . . . When social scientists deal with a problem of value, they should be explicit about their own "personal" preference, or "bias." That rule, in turn, is just another way to satisfy the principle that scholars should not mislead their audiences about the scholarly merits of what they say or write *qua* scholars. With that principle, no one can reasonably disagree, even though reasonable men may differ about what specific conclusions they should draw from it. (The conclusions will vary in part with the assumptions one makes about one's audience's vulnerability to being misled. To establish an absolute requirement that normative statements be explicitly disowned is to assume all audiences suffer from excessive naiveté or debilitating deference to professorial authority.) . . .

To Black, the suggestion that science can assess, and knowledge can improve, the quality of moral judgments, is anathema. Thus he sees no justification for the view that law can benefit from "an accurate sociological analysis" (1972a: 713) of the world it governs. It is not clear why he objects to this view. Sometimes, it would seem, his quarrel is only with theses that by any reasonable judgment *overstate* what knowledge can do for moral choice. For example, he disagrees with "technocratic thought" (1972b: 1090) according to which "moral problems of *every sort* are translated into problems of knowledge and science, of know how" (1972b: 1090–1091. Italics mine.). But jurisprudential sociology is not committed to such overreaching. Sometimes, Black argues on moral or political grounds. If his anarchism entails a distaste for all kinds of authority, one can understand that he would object to the authority science is allegedly accorded, and to the alleged fact that "students of legal effectiveness . . . are . . . the élite of our society" (Black, 1972b: 1092 n. 23). But then one wonders why he should agree that moral philosophy has any competence, and legitimate authority, in the assessment of moral issues (Black, 1972b: 1092). If Black accepts that value statements be criticized on the basis of their "logical status in relation to a more general axiological principle" (Black, 1972b: 1095 n. 33), how can he object to criticism based upon the presence or absence of an empirically verified causal relation between (a) behavior that accords with a given value statement and (b) a class of outcomes defined by "general axiological principles"? Both kinds of criticism are based on the authority of reason. It is hard to see why it might be proper to reduce incoherence, but improper to reduce ignorance in moral discourse.

But most of the time, Black is not arguing that scientifically legitimate uses of science be restricted for moral reasons. Rather he is proposing that some uses of scientific inquiry, which might conceivably increase the quality of moral and political choice, be proscribed to preserve the "purity" of science. If there is any argument for the view that science should not be used to give or deny authority to values, it cannot be that the proposition follows any requirement of logic. Although Black does not offer it, there is an argument, and it is quite empirical. When scientific inquiry touches highly controversial and divisive moral issues, it creates a risk that the integrity and the authority of science as an institution will be threatened and undermined. Scientific debates may become politicized, the fervor of faith may displace dispassionate inquiry, and even the factual assertions of "scientists" may lose credibility. Undeniably, this risk exists, especially in the social sciences. . . . The risk is avoided, or at least reduced, if the scientific establishment commits itself to a principle of prudence: "Stay away from hot issues; leave politics to the politicians, morals to the moralists, law to the lawyers." Translated for publication in textbooks on the ethics and method of science, this counsel becomes the dogma of the separation of fact and value. The principle has considerable precedent in institutional experience. It is the foundation of bureaucracy: there, the separation of administration and policy protects the autonomy and integrity of bureaucratic expertise. In effect, "pure sociology" is an extension of bureaucratic principle to the management of the social scientific establishment. . . .

For Jurisprudential Sociology

Fortunately or unfortunately, the bureaucratic option is not truly open to the social sciences. There is no way to study human affairs and not to make statements about issues that matter deeply for the satisfaction of needs, the furthering of interests, the achievement of purposes, the fulfillment of aspirations, the development of capacities, in short, about values. The pure sociologist may try to remove all normative words from his language. But all he can do is to ban the words whose moral connotations he sees (fears? dislikes?), or define the connotations out of existence. Obviously he cannot help using the words whose normative meanings escape his attention. The effect is a social scientific Newspeak, which prohibits access to a vast and precious stock of cognitive resources. For the connotations that surround words such as law, government, control, democracy, equality, arrest, police, family, are the inchoate knowledge with which we think about the denoted phenomena. In attempting to rule normative meanings out of existence, "pure sociology" either deprives itself and its readers of that knowledge ("system of social stratification" is far purer than "inequality"), or requires denying the existence of that knowledge even as we use the words that evoke it (for either a word has been purified by definition, or the writer has overlooked the need for purification thus leaving the job to the reader). How else could we make sense of the following text: "By legal intelligence I mean the knowledge that a legal system has about law violations in its jurisdiction. . . . From a sociological standpoint, however, there is no 'proper' or even 'effective' system of legal intelligence. . . . [Let us therefore examine the l]imits of legal intelligence. Any legal system relying upon the active participation of ordinary citizens must absorb whatever naiveté and ignorance is found among the citizenry" (Black: 1973, 130-132). Either the language is English, and the reasoning incoherent, or the logic is proper, but we are forbidden to think of "intelligence," "naiveté," "ignorance," and "limits" as aspects of the quality and effectiveness of knowledge. Pure sociology cannot mean what it says.

Unfortunately, jurisprudence is no alternative to "pure" sociology. To prefer it would only be to choose another set of blinders. In fact, jurisprudence and pure sociology are deeply involved with one another: there is no better match for a sociology that denies the normative aspects of legal phenomena, than a legal philosophy blind to factual issues in the analysis of normative ideas. To Black, jurisprudence is as "logically" incapable of failing for lack of knowledge, as sociology is of failing for philosophical naiveté. What can disturb such a solid and comfortable relation of mutually respective ignorance?

Perhaps sociology can do so, it if returns to its historic intellectual task: that is, to enlarge the intellectual horizons of legal, political, economic, and other modes of normative thought; to broaden the concerns of these disciplines beyond the limits of their *specialized* institutional domains; to blur, not to draw, "boundaries," as between fact and value, law and politics, economy and society, policy and administration; to help all kinds of social thought recognize the relevance of facts, problems, interests, and values, of which they would not otherwise take account. Philosophy shared that intellectual responsibility until positivism sterilized it. Must sociology go through the same crisis? And if it must, where will that responsibility be assumed?

We need a jurisprudential sociology, a social science of law that speaks to the problems, and is informed by the ideas, of jurisprudence. Such a sociology recognizes the continuities of analytical, descriptive and evaluative theory. Analytical issues—e.g., the role of coercion in law; the relation of law to the state; the interplay of law and politics; the distinction between law and morality; the place of rules, principles, purpose, and knowledge in legal judgment; the tension between procedural and substantive justice—are taken as pointing to variable aspects of legal phenomena. The extent to which the law is coercive, vulnerable to politics, purposive, or open to social knowledge, is subject to variations that require empirical inquiry. At the same time, those jurisprudential-sociological variables condition the ends law can pursue, and the resources it can muster to serve those ends. To study such questions as: the kinds of sanctions and remedies that are available to legal institutions; the principles and structures of authority that characterize various legal processes; the way law receives and interprets political and moral values; the administrative resources legal agencies can deploy; the authority of purpose in legal reasoning—is also to assess the competences and limitations of different kinds of legal orders or legal institutions. Whatever knowledge is gained about these problems should contribute to formulating principles of institutional design, and guides for the diagnosis of institutional troubles. . . .

References

Auerbach, Carl A. (1966). "Legal Tasks for the Sociologist." 1 *Law & Society Review* 91.

Black, Donald J. (1971). "The Social Organization of Arrest." 23 *Stanford Law Review* 1087.

—— (1972a)."Book Review." 78 *American Journal of Sociology* 709, reviewing P. Selznick (1969).

—— (1972b). "The Boundaries of Legal Sociology." 81 *Yale Law Journal* 1086.

—— (1973). "The Mobilization of Law." 2 *Journal of Legal Studies* 125.

Carlin, Jerome and Phillipe Nonet (1968). "The Legal Profession." 9 *International Encyclopedia of the Social Sciences* 66. New York: Macmillan.

Hart, H. L. A. (1961). *The Concept of Law.* Oxford: Clarendon Press.

Holmes, Oliver Wendell (1897). "The Path of the Law." 10 *Harvard Law Review* 457.

Selznick, Philip (1961). "Sociology and Natural Law." 6 *Natural Law Forum* 84.

—— (1968). "The Sociology of Law." 9 *International Encyclopedia of the Social Sciences* 50. New York: Macmillan.

—— with the collaboration of Philippe Nonet and Howard M. Vollmer (1969). *Law, Society, and Industrial Justice.* New York: Russell Sage.

Skolnick, Jerome H. (1965). "The Sociology of Law in America: Overview and Trends." 12 *Social Problems* 4 (Supplement on "Law and Society").

Notes

1. The phrase "Berkeley perspective" or "Berkeley program" is mine. It is not meant to suggest all my colleagues at Berkeley agree with the propositions I have gathered under that convenient label. Such a consensus is too improbable at such a place.
2. The realists were fascinated by Holmes: "The prophecies of what the courts will do in fact, and nothing more pretentious, are what I mean by the law." (Oliver Wendell Holmes, 1897: 460-461).

FUNCTIONALIST THEORY

6

The Law
and
Social Control
Talcott Parsons

From a variety of points of view I think it can be said that law and sociology have an unusually wide area of overlapping interests. But for various reasons the exploration of these interests and the implications of the relationships have not been very adequately pursued. Perhaps the very extent to which sociology is such a young discipline plays a major part in bringing about this situation.

It may be useful to call attention, at the start, to two salient general considerations about the law as seen from a social scientist's point of view. In the first place, law is not a category descriptive of actual concrete behavior but rather concerns patterns, norms, and rules that are applied to the acts and to the roles of persons and to the collectivities of which they are members. Law is an aspect of social structure but one that lies on a particular level, which should be carefully specified. In a certain set of sociological terms I should call it an institutional phenomenon. It deals with normative patterns to which various kinds of sanctions are applied. This is a level that on general sociological grounds it is important to distinguish from that of the concrete structure of collectivities and roles in them.

Excerpt from "The Law and Social Control" in William M. Evan, ed., *Law and Sociology*. New York: The Free Press, 1962, pp. 56-72, by permission of the author and publisher.

The second salient characteristic of law is that it is nonspecific with respect to functional content at lower levels. Functional content, understood in the usual sociological senses, refers to such categories as economic, political, and a variety of others. There is law defining the Constitution and political processes within it. There is a law of business and of labor and the relations of business to labor. There is a law of the family, of personal relationships, and a variety of other subjects. Indeed *any* social relationship can be regulated by law, and I think every category of social relationship with which sociologists are concerned is found to be regulated by law in some society somewhere.

It seems justified to infer from these considerations that law should be treated as a generalized mechanism of social control that operates diffusely in virtually all sectors of the society.[1]

Law, of course, is not just a set of abstractly defined rules. It is a set of rules backed by certain types of sanctions, legitimized in certain ways, and applied in certain ways. It is a set of rules that stands in certain quite definite relationships to specific collectivities and the roles of individuals in them. Perhaps we can approach a little closer characterization of the place of law in a society by attempting to analyze some of these relationships, and by showing some of the conditions on which the effectiveness of a system of rules can be held to rest.

The Functions of Law and Some Structural Implications

Let us suggest that in the larger social perspective the primary function of a legal system is integrative. It serves to mitigate potential elements of conflict and to oil the machinery of social intercourse. It is, indeed, only by adherence to a system of rules that systems of social interaction can function without breaking down into overt or chronic covert conflict.

Normative consistency may be assumed to be one of the most important criteria of effectiveness of a system of law. By this I mean that the rules formulated in the system must ideally not subject the individuals under their jurisdiction to incompatible expectations or obligations—or, more realistically, not too often or too drastically. In the nature of the case, since they act in many different contexts and roles, individuals will be subject to many particularized rules. But the rules must somehow all build up to a single, relatively consistent system.

In this respect we may suggest that there are four major problems that must be solved before such a system of rules can operate determinately to regulate interaction. (Even though the questions are not explicitly put by the actors, an observer analyzing how the system operates must find some solution to each of them.)

The first problem concerns the basis of legitimation of the system of rules. The question is why, in the value or meaning sense, should I conform to the rules, should I fulfill the expectations of the others with whom I interact? What in other words is the *basis* of right? Is it simply that some authority says so without further justification? Is it some religious value, or is it that I and the others have some natural rights that it is wrong to violate? What is the basis of this *legitimation?*

The second problem concerns the *meaning* of the rule for me or some other particular actor in a particular situation in a particular role. In the nature of the case, rules must be formulated in general terms. The general statement may not cover all of the circumstances of the particular situation in which I am placed. Or there may be two or more rules, the implications of which for my action are currently contradictory. Which one applies and in what degree and in what way? What specifically are my obligations in this particular situation or my rights under the law? This is the problem of *interpretation.*

The third basic problem is that of the consequences, favorable or unfavorable, that should follow from conforming to the rules to a greater or lesser degree or from failing to conform. These consequences will vary according to the degrees of nonconformity and according to the circumstances in which, and reasons for which, deviation occurs. Under a system of law, however, the question of whether or not conformity occurs can never be a matter of indifference. This, of course, is the problem of *sanctions.* What sanctions apply and by whom are they applied?

Finally, the fourth problem concerns to whom and under what circumstances a given rule or complex of rules, with its interpretations and sanctions, applies. This is the problem of *jurisdiction,* which has two aspects: (1) What authority has jurisdiction over given persons, acts, and so on in defining and imposing the norms? (2) To which classes of acts, persons, roles, and collectivities does a given set of norms apply?

We may now attempt to say something about the conditions of institutionalizing answers to these questions in a large-scale, highly differentiated society. At the outset I want to suggest that a legal system must not itself be regarded in an analytical sense as a political phenomenon, although it must be closely related to political functions and processes. The two systems are most intimately related with respect to the problems of sanctions and of jurisdiction. Of these, the connection with respect to sanctions is in a sense the more fundamental.

We may speak of the existence of a continuum of sanctions, ranging from pure inducement to sheer and outright coercion. By inducement I mean the offer of advantages as a reward for actions that the inducer wishes his role-partner to perform. By coercion I mean the threat of negative sanctions for nonperformance of the desired course of action. Both inducement and coercion operate in all social relationships. The basis of the relation of law to political organization lies primarily in the fact that at certain points the question must inevitably arise as to the use of physical force or its threat as a means of coercion; that is, a means of assertion of the bindingness of the norm. If physical force is altogether excluded the ultimate coercive sanction is expulsion, as for example in the case of excommunication from the church. In many cases, however, expulsion will not be a sufficiently severe sanction to prevent undesirable action from taking place. And if it is not sufficient, resort must be had to force. Force is, at least in the preventive sense, the ultimate negative sanction.

Thus if rules are taken sufficiently seriously, inevitably the question will sometime be raised of resort to physical sanction in a preventive context. On the other hand, the use of force is perhaps the most serious potential source of disruption of order in social relationships. For this reason in all ordered societies there is at least a qualified monopoly of the more serious uses of physical force. This monopoly is one of the primary characteristics of the political organization, in its more highly developed forms leading up to the state. If, then, it becomes necessary in certain contingencies to use or threaten physical force as a sanction for the enforcement of legal norms, and if the legitimate use of physical force is monopolized in the agency of the state, then the legal system must have an adequate connection with the state in order to use its agencies as the administrators of physical sanctions.

The problem of jurisdiction is obviously closely linked with that of sanctions. One of the main reasons that the jurisdiction of political bodies is territorially defined is precisely the importance of the use of physical force in their functioning. Physical force can be applied only if the individual to whom it is directed can be reached in a physical location at a given time. It is therefore inherently linked to territoriality of jurisdiction. Hence a legal system that relies at certain points on the sanctions of physical force must also be linked to a territorial area of jurisdiction.

A further source of linkage between law and the state requires me to say a word about the imperative of consistency. On the level of the content of norms as such, this imperative exerts a strong pressure toward universalism (a trait that is inherent in systems of law generally). I spoke above of consistency from the point of view of not subjecting the same individual to contradictory rules. The obverse of this imperative is the recognition that, when a rule has been defined as a rule, it must be impartially applied to all persons or other social units that fall within the criteria that define the application of the rule. There are inherent limitations in systematizing legal systems, that is, in making them consistent, if this criterion of universalistic application cannot be followed.

In its practical implication this criterion of universalism, however, connects closely with territoriality, because it is only within territorial limits that enforcement of universalistically defined rules can effectively be carried out. It follows from these considerations that enforcement agencies in a legal system are generally organs of the state. They carry a special political character.

Enforcement agencies are, however, ordinarily not the central organs of the state. They are not primarily policy-forming organs but rather are organs that are put at the service of the many different interests that are covered by the rules of a legal system. The fact that even the enforcement agencies are not primarily political is vividly brought out by their relations to the courts. In most legal systems what they may do, and to a considerable degree how they may do it, is defined and supervised by the courts. Where enforcement agencies gain too strong a degree of independence of the courts, it may be said that the legal system itself has been subordinated to political considerations, a circumstance that does occur in a variety of cases.

The interpretive and legitimizing functions in law are even less directly political than are the sanctioning and the jurisdictional functions. First let us take the legitimation function, which concerns to an important degree the relation and the distinction between law and ethics.

We may say that, in the deeper sense, the lawyer as such tends to take legitimation for granted. It is not part of his professional function, whether as attorney or as judge, to decide whether the existence of a given rule is morally or politically justified. His function rather concerns its interpretation and application to particular cases. Even where, as under a federal system, there may be certain problems of the conflict of laws, it is the higher legal authority—for example, that of the Constitution—that is the lawyer's primary concern, not the moral legitimation of the Constitution itself. Nevertheless, the legal system must always rest on proper legitimation. This may take forms rather close to the legal process itself, such as the question of enactment by proper procedures by duly authorized bodies. For example, legislatures are responsible to electorates. But in back of proper procedures and due authorization of law-making bodies lies the deeper set of questions of ultimate legitimation.

In the last analysis this always leads in some form or other either to religious questions or to those that are functionally equivalent to religion. Law from this point of view constitutes a focal center of the relations between religion and politics as well as other aspects of a society.

Turning now to "interpretation," it must be noted that here again there are two basic foci of this function. One concerns the integrity of the system of rules itself; it is rule-focused. The other concerns the relation of rules to the individuals and groups and collectivities on whom they impinge. In a legal sense this latter function may be said to be client-focused. Taken together in these two aspects, the interpretive function may be said to be the central function of a legal system.

The first, the rule-focused aspect of the law, is primarily the locus of the judiciary function, particularly at the appellate levels. The second is the focus of the functions of the practicing legal profession. With respect to the judiciary certain sociological facts are saliently conspicuous. Wherever we can speak of a well-institutionalized legal system, the judiciary are expected to enjoy an important measure of independence from the central political authority. Of course, their integration with it must be so close that, for example, practically always judges are appointed by political authority. But usually (unless holding office for specified terms) they enjoy tenure, they are not removable except for cause, and it is considered most improper for political authority to put direct pressure on them in influencing their specific decisions. Furthermore, though not a constitutional requirement in the United States it is certainly general practice that judges, the more so the higher in the system, must be lawyers in a professional sense. This is not a function ordinarily open to the ordinary lay citizen.

Furthermore, the judicial function as part of the attorney's function is centered in a special type of social organization: the court. This is an organization that directly institutionalizes the process of arriving at decisions. This is done, of course, through the bringing of cases to the court for adjudication, in the course of which not only are the rights and obligations of individual petitioners settled but the rules themselves are given authoritative interpretations. We might perhaps say that authoritative interpretation in this sense is perhaps the most important of the judicial functions.

With respect to the legal profession in the sense of the practicing attorney, there is a conspicuous dual character. The attorney is, on the one hand, an officer of the court. As such he bears a certain public responsibility. But at the same time, he is a private adviser to his client, depending on the client for his remuneration and enjoying a privileged confidential relation to the client. This relation between lawyer and client parallels, to an interestingly high degree, that between physician and patient, its confidential character being one of the principal clues to this parallel. It is focused, however, on situations of actual or potential social conflict and the adjudication and smoothing over of these conflicts. It is not primarily person-oriented as the health-care functions are, but rather social relationship-oriented.

Performance of the interpretive function is facilitated, we have said, by such structural devices as "judicial independence" from political pressure, professionalization of the judicial role, and institutionalization of the decision-making process. These general kinds of structural facilities, however, are not sufficient to prevent the interpretive role from being the focus of certain inherent strains; and certain more specific mechanisms are required to check a tendency toward deviant reactions to the strains.

Law and Other Mechanisms of Social Control

Despite these general ways in which lawyers, as professionals, contribute to social control, it is important to note certain crucial differences between law and other control mechanisms. A useful point from which to approach the distinction, and from which to make clear its functional importance, is the set of remarks made above in connection with the functions of legitimation and interpretation.

From the combination of the interpretive function and that of legitimation, we may begin to understand some of the reasons for the emphasis in the law on procedural matters. As Max Weber put it, "the rationality of law is formal rather than substantive." Certainly one of the basic conceptions in our Anglo-Saxon legal systems is that of due process. Here, of course, it even goes to the point where the question of substantive justice may not be an issue, and injustice may have no legal remedy so long as correct formal procedure has been observed. It may be noted that if pressure becomes strong with reference to either the question of enforcement or the question of legitimation, it may operate against the integrity of the procedural traditions and rules. People who are sufficiently exercised about questions of substantive justice and injustice are often not strong respectors of complicated legal procedure. Similarly, if disobedience to law is sufficiently blatant and scandalous, there may be a demand for direct action that altogether by-passes the rules of procedure.

From this point of view, it may become evident that the prominence of and the integrity of a legal system as a mechanism of social control is partly a function of a certain type of social equilibrium. Law flourishes particularly in a society in which the most fundamental questions of social values are not currently at issue or under agitation. If there is sufficiently acute value conflict, law is likely to go by the board. Similarly it flourishes in a society in which the enforcement problem is not too seriously acute. This is particularly true where there are strong informal forces reinforcing conformity with at least the main lines of the legally institutionalized tradition. In many respects, modern England is a type case of this possibility.

Law, then, as a mechanism of control may be said to stand in a position midway between two other types of mechanisms:

(a) On the one hand, there are two classes of mechanisms that focus primarily on the motivation of the individual: those that operate through the media of mass communication—through the distribution and allocation of information and the concomitant emotional attitudes; and those that operate more privately and subtly in relation to the individual. Though there are many of these latter mechanisms, a particularly conspicuous one in our own society, administered by a sister professional group, is that of therapy. The line of distinction between questions that can be handled by legal procedure and those that involve therapy is a particularly important one.

(b) In another direction, the law must be distinguished from those mechanisms of social control that focus on the solution of fundamental problems of value orientation involving basic decisions for the system as a whole, rather than regulation of the relations of the parts to each other. Politics and religion both operate more in this area, and because of this difference it is particularly important to distinguish law from politics and religion.

Finally, it may perhaps be suggested that law has a special importance in a pluralistic liberal type of society. It has its strongest place in a society where there are many different kinds of interests that must be balanced against each other and that must in some way respect each other. As I have already noted, in the totalitarian type of society, which is in a great hurry to settle some fundamental general social conflict or policy, law tends to go by the board.

Both individually and collectively, law imposes restraints on precipitate and violent action. I might recall the words with which the recipients of law degrees are greeted by the President of Harvard University at every commencement. He says."You are now qualified to help administer those wise restraints which make men free."

Note

1. Of course it is better adapted to some problems of social control than to others. It is notorious that the more refined and settled sentiments of individuals cannot be controlled by legal prescription. Nevertheless, it is one of the most highly generalized mechanisms in the whole society. It is located primarily, as I said, on the institutional level. It is not isolated but is one of a family of mechanisms of control. At the end of this discussion I will sketch its relations to one or two others.

7

A Survey of
Social Interests
Roscoe Pound

There has been a notable shift throughout the world from thinking
of the task of the legal order as one of adjusting the exercise of free
wills to one of satisfying wants, of which free exercise of the will is
but one. Accordingly, we must start today from a theory of interests,
that is, of the claims or demands or desires which human beings,
either individually or in groups or associations or relations, seek to
satisfy, of which, therefore, the adjustment of relations and ordering
of conduct through the force of politically organized society must
take account. I have discussed the general theory of interests, the
classification of interests, and the details of individual interests in
other places.[1] It is enough to say here that the classification into
individual interests, public interests, and social interests was suggested
by Jhering.[2] As I should put it, individual interests are claims or demands or desires involved immediately in the individual life and
asserted in title of that life. Public interests are claims or demands or
desires involved in life in a politically organized society and asserted
in title of that organization. They are commonly treated as the
claims of a politically organized society thought of as a legal entity.
Social interests are claims or demands or desires involved in social life

in civilized society and asserted in title of that life. It is not uncommon to treat them as the claims of the whole social group as such.

But this does not mean that every claim or demand or desire which human beings assert must be put once for all for every purpose into one of these three categories. For some purposes and in some connections it is convenient to look at a given claim or demand or desire from one standpoint. For other purposes or in other connections it is convenient to look at the same claim or demand or the same type of claims or demands from one of the other standpoints. When it comes to weighing or valuing claims or demands with respect to other claims or demands, we must be careful to compare them on the same plane. If we put one as an individual interest and the other as a social interest we may decide the question in advance in our very way of putting it. . . .

In general, but not always, it is expedient to put claims or demands in their most generalized form, *i.e.*, as social interests, in order to compare them. But where the problems are relatively simple, it is sometimes possible to take account of all the factors sufficiently by comparing individual interests put directly as such. It must be borne in mind that often we have here different ways of looking at the same claims or same type of claims as they are asserted in different titles. Thus, individual interests of personality may be asserted in title of or subsumed under the social interest in the general security, or the social interest in the individual life, or sometimes from different standpoints or in different aspects, both of them. Again, individual interests in the domestic relations may be subsumed under the social interest in the security of social institutions of which domestic institutions are the oldest and by no means the least important. Again, the public interest in the integrity of the state personality may be thought of as the social interest in the security of social institutions of which political institutions are one form. When we have recognized and legally delimited and secured an interest, it is important to identify the generalized individual interest behind and giving significance and definition to the legal right. When we are considering what claims or demands to recognize and within what limits, and when we are seeking to adjust conflicting and overlapping claims and demands in some new aspect or new situation, it is important to subsume the individual interests under social interests and to weigh them as such. . . .

The body of the common law is made up of adjustments or compromises of conflicting individual interests in which we turn to some social interest, frequently under the name of public policy, to determine the limits of a reasonable adjustment.

In the common law we have been wont to speak of social interests under the name of "public policy." . . .³ For a time social interests were pushed into the background. It was said that public policy was "a very unruly horse, and when once you get astride it you never know where it will carry you."⁴ It was conceived that a court should be slow and cautious in taking public policy into account, and that if rules of law were to be limited in their application, or if exercise of individual powers of action was to be held down upon such grounds, the matter ought to be left to the legislature.

Questions of public policy came up in three forms: (1) in connection with the validity of contracts or similar transactions; (2) in connection with the validity of conditions in conveyances and testamentary gifts; (3) in connection with the validity of testamentary dispositions. Thus different social interests were weighed against a policy in favor of free contract ("right" of free contract) and a policy in favor of free disposition of property which was taken to be involved in the security of acquisitions and to be a corollary of individual interests of substance (rights of property). Accordingly, distrust of public policy grew out of a feeling that security of acquisitions and security of transactions were paramount policies. ". . . if there is one thing," said Sir George Jessel, "which more than another public policy requires it is that men of full age and competent understanding shall have the utmost liberty of contracting, and that their contracts . . . shall be enforced by Courts of justice."⁵

In truth, the nineteenth-century attitude toward public policy was itself only the expression of a public policy. It resulted from a weighing of the social interest in the general security against other social interests which men had sought to secure through an overwide magisterial discretion in the stage of equity and natural law.

Thus the conception of public policy was never clearly worked out, nor were the several policies recognized by the common law defined as were the individual interests to which the juristic thought of the last century gave substantially its whole attention. The books are full of schemes of natural rights. There are no adequate schemes of public policies. Often the weighing of social interests is disguised by reasoning about "causation," or by the drawing of what seem on their face arbitrary distinctions. But three general types of policies are clearly recognized as such in the law books of the last century. First and most numerous are policies with reference to the security of social institutions. As to political institutions, there is a recognized policy against acts promotive of crime or violation of law—in other words, a policy of upholding legal institutions—and a policy against acts prejudicially affecting the public service performed by public officers. As to domestic institutions, there is the well-known policy against acts affecting the security of the domestic relations, or in restraint of marriage. As to economic institutions, there are the policy against acts destructive of competition, the policy against acts affecting commercial freedom, and the policy against permanent or general restrictions on the free use and transfer of property. Secondly, there are policies with reference to maintaining the general morals. Thus there is a recognized policy against acts promotive of dishonesty. Also there is a recognized policy against acts offending the general morals. Thirdly, there are policies with reference to the individual social life: a policy against things tending to oppression, and a policy against general or extensive restrictions upon individual freedom of action. Some of the policies with respect to economic institutions suggest this same interest in the individual life.

In one way or another most of the social interests of which the law must take account today are at least suggested in the list of those recognized as policies in the common law. Yet one social interest which has governed the ideas of lawyers at all times and has played a controlling part in the thought of the immediate past is relatively little stressed as a policy. The social interest in the general security seems to have been thought of as something apart, as something involved in the very idea of law and entering into every legal relation as a necessary element. This appears clearly in nineteenth-century theories as to the end of law and in nineteenth-century juristic method. . . .

Perhaps enough has been said to show the practical importance of recognizing social interests as such, instead of thinking of policies, and of a more complete statement of them and a more adequate classification. Yet a satisfactory starting point for such a classification requires some consideration. A generation ago, as a matter of course, we should have relied upon logical deduction. We should have deduced the several social interests as presuppositions of generalized social existence. But schemes of necessary presuppositions of law or of legal institutions seem to be to be at bottom schemes of observed elements in actual legal systems, systematically arranged, reduced to their lowest terms, and deduced, as one might say, to order. I doubt the ability of the jurist to work out deductively the necessary jural presuppositions of society in the abstract.

At one time it seemed that a more attractive starting point might be found in social psychology. One need only turn to the list of so-called instincts in any of the older social psychologies in order to see an obvious relation between interests, as the jurist now uses that term, or what we had been wont to call natural rights or public policies, on the one hand, and these "instincts" or whatever they are now called, on the other hand. . . .

If we may not rely upon logical deduction nor upon a theory and classification of what were formerly called instincts, there remains a less pretentious method which may none the less be upon surer ground. If legal phenomena are social phenomena, observation and study of them as such may well bear fruit for social science in general as well as for jurisprudence. Why should not the lawyer make a survey of legal systems in order to ascertain just what claims or demands or desires have pressed or are now pressing for recognition and satisfaction and how far they have been or are now recognized and secured?

Social Interest in the General Security

In such a survey and inventory, first place must be given to the social interest in the general security—the claim or want or demand, asserted in title of social life in civilized society and through the social group, to be secure against those forms of action and courses of conduct which threaten its existence. Even if we accept Durkheim's view that it is what shocks the general conscience, not what threatens the general security, that is repressed, I suspect that the general conscience reflects experience or superstition as to the general safety. A common-law judge observed that there would be no safety for human life if it were to be considered as law that drunkenness could be shown to negate the intent element of crime where a drunk man kills while intoxicated though he would never do such a thing when sober. It should be noted how the exigencies of the general security outweighed the traditional theory of the criminal law.

This paramount social interest takes many forms. In its simplest form it is an interest in the general safety, long recognized in the legal order in the maxim that the safety of the people is the highest law. It was recognized in American constitutional law in the nineteenth century by putting the general safety along with the general health and general morals in the "police power" as a ground of reasonable restraint to which natural rights must give way. In another form, quite as obvious today but not so apparent in the past, before the nature and causes of disease were understood, it is an interest in the general health. In another form, recognized from the very beginnings of law, it is an interest in peace and public order. In an economically developed society it takes on two other closely related forms, namely, a social interest in the security of acquisitions and a social interest in the security of transactions. The two last came to be well understood in the nineteenth century, in which they were more or less identified with individual interests of substance and individual interests in freedom of contract. Yet a characteristic difference between the law of the eighteenth century and the law of the nineteenth century brings out their true nature. Eighteenth-century courts, taking a purely individualist view, regarded the statute of limitations as something to be held down as much as possible and to be evaded in every way. . . .

Modern courts came to see that there was something more here than the individual interests of plaintiff and defendant. They came to see that the basis of the statute was a social interest in the security of acquisitions, which demands that titles shall not be insecure by being open to attack indefinitely, and a social interest in the security of transactions which demands that the transactions of the past shall not be subject to inquiry indefinitely, so as to unsettle credit and disturb business and trade. . . .

Other examples of recognition of the security of transactions may be seen in the presumption as to transactions of a corporation through its acting officers, the stress which the courts put upon *stare decisis* in cases involving commercial law, and the doctrine allowing only the sovereign to challenge *ultra vires* conveyances of corporations. As to recognition of the social interest in the security of acquisitions, note the insistence of the courts upon *stare decisis* where rules of property are involved. In such cases it is an established proposition that it is better that the law be settled than that it be settled right.

Social Interest in the Security of Social Institutions

Second, we may put the social interest in the security of social institutions—the claim or want or demand involved in life in civilized society that its fundamental institutions be secure from those forms of action and courses of conduct which threaten their existence or impair their efficient functioning. Looking at them in chronological order, this interest appears in three forms.

The first is an interest in the security of domestic institutions, long recognized in the form of a policy against acts affecting the security of domestic relations or in restraint of marriage. Legislation intended to promote the family as a social institution has been common. There is a policy against actions by members of the family against each other. Today, although the law is becoming much relaxed, this social interest is still weighed heavily against the individual claims of married persons in most divorce legislation. It still weighs heavily against individual claims in the law as to illegitimate children. At times this has been carried so far that great and numerous disabilities have attached to such children lest recognition of their individual interests should weaken a fundamental social institution. . . .

A second form is an interest in the security of religious institutions. In the beginning this is closely connected with the general security. A chief point of origin of the criminal law, of that part of the law by which social interests as such are directly and immediately secured, is in religion. Sacrifice of the impious offender who has affronted the gods, and exclusion from society of the impious offender whose presence threatens to bring upon his fellows the wrath of the gods, are, in part at least, the originals of capital punishment and of outlawry. Religious organization was long a stronger and more active agency of social control than political organization. In the Anglo-Saxon laws the appeals or exhortations addressed to the people as Christians are at least as important as the threats addressed to them as subjects. One of the great English statutes of the thirteenth century recites that Parliament had met to make laws "for the common Profit of holy Church, and of the Realm."[6] It is only in relatively recent times that we have come to think of blasphemy as involving no more than a social interest in the general morals, of Sunday laws only in terms of a social interest in the general health, of heresy as less dangerous socially than radical views upon economics or politics, or of preaching or teaching of atheism as involved in a guaranteed liberty. Today what was formerly referred to this interest is usually referred to the social interest in the general morals. Questions as to the interest in the security of religious institutions have been debated in all lands.

In a third form the interest is one in the security of political institutions. This interest has weighed heavily in much twentieth-century legislation too familiar to require more than mention. When the public called for such legislation for the security of political institutions, absolute constitutional guarantees of free speech and natural rights of individual self-assertion, which in other times had moved courts to refuse to enjoin repeated and undoubted libels, lest liberty be infringed, were not suffered to stand in the way. If the individual interests involved had been conceived less absolutely and had been looked at in another light, as identified with a social interest in the general progress, they might have fared better.

Perhaps a fourth form of the interest in the security of social institutions should be added, namely, an interest in the security of economic institutions. Formerly, these were chiefly commercial. Today industrial institutions also must be taken into account. Judicial recognitions of a social interest in the security of commercial institutions are numerous. In a leading case in which it was determined that a bank note payable to bearer passed current the same as coin, Lord Mansfield grounded the judgment "upon the general course of business, and . . . the consequences to trade and commerce: which would be much incommoded by a contrary determination."[7] More than one decision in the last generation on labor law seems to go upon an interest in maintaining the industrial regime in the face of persistent pressure from the claims of organized workingmen. Some of the policies to be considered presently under the social interest in general progress might be referred to this head.

Social Interest in the General Morals

Third, we may put the social interest in the general morals, the claim or want or demand involved in social life in civilized society to be secured against acts or courses of conduct offensive to the moral sentiments of the general body of individuals therein for the time being. This interest is recognized in Roman law in the protection of *boni mores*. It is recognized in our law by policies against dishonesty, corruption, gambling, and things of immoral tendency; by treating continuing menaces to the general morals as nuisances; and by the common-law doctrine that acts contrary to good morals and subversive of general morals are misdemeanors. It is recognized in equity in the maxim that he who comes into equity must come with clean hands. Similar provisions are to be found in the private law and in the criminal law in other lands. Obstinately held ideas of morality may in time come in conflict with ideas arising from changed social and economic conditions or newer religious and philosophical views. In such cases we must reach a balance between the social interest in the general morals, and the social interest in general progress, taking form in a policy of free discussion. What was said above as to free speech and writing and the social interest in security of social institutions applies here also.

Social Interest in the Conservation of Social Resources

Fourth, there is the social interest in conservation of social resources, that is, the claim or want or demand involved in social life in civilized society that the goods of existence shall not be wasted; that where all human claims or wants or desires may not be satisfied, in view of infinite individual desires and limited natural means of satisfying them, the latter be made to go as far as possible; and, to that end, that acts or courses of conduct which tend needlessly to destroy or impair these goods shall be restrained. In its simplest form this is an interest in the use and conservation of natural resources, and is recognized in the doctrines as to *res communes*, which may be used but not owned, by the common law as to riparian rights and constitutional and statutory provisions where irrigation is practiced, by modern game laws, by the recent doctrines as to percolating water and surface water, and by laws as to waste of natural gas and oil. . . .

A closely related social interest is one in protection and training of dependents and defectives. It might from one point of view be called an interest in conservation of the human assets of society. In one form it was recognized long ago in the common-law system by the jurisdiction of the chancellor, representing the king as *parens patriae*, over infants, lunatics, and idiots. This jurisdiction has had a significant development in recent times in the juvenile court, and an extension to youthful offenders beyond the period of infancy is being urged. Again, there has been an extension of the idea of protection and training of dependents, on one hand to the reformation of mature delinquents, and on another hand to protection of the mature who are yet economically more or less dependent. This has gone a long way in recent times in social security or social insurance legislation and in small loan legislation. The latter has had a historical background in the interference of equity to prevent oppression of debtors and necessitous persons. Also after the first world war there was legislative recognition of a social interest in rehabilitation of the maimed. Much of the legislation referred to runs counter to the insistence upon abstract individual liberty in the juristic theory of the last century. It was formerly often pronounced arbitrary and so unconstitutional by courts whose dogmatic scheme could admit no social interest other than the general security. There has been a significant widening of the field of legally recognized and secured social interests. But for the most part the claims or demands here considered are better treated in connection with the social interest in the individual life.

Social Interest in General Progress

Fifth, there is the social interest in general progress, that is, the claim or want or demand involved in social life in civilized society, that the development of human powers and of human control over nature for the satisfaction of human wants go forward; the demand that social engineering be increasingly and continuously improved; as it were, the self-assertion of the social group toward higher and more complete development of human powers. This interest appears in three main forms, an interest in economic progress, and interest in political progress, and an interest in cultural progress. The social interest in economic progress has long been recognized in law and has been secured in many ways. In the common law it is expressed in four policies: the policy as to freedom of property from restrictions upon sale or use, the policy as to free trade and consequent policy against monopoly, the policy as to free industry, which has had to give much ground in recent legislation and judicial decision, and the policy as to encouragement of invention, which is behind patent legislation and there comes in conflict with the policy as to free trade. All of these policies have important consequences in everyday law. It may be thought that some of them should be classified rather as forms of a social interest in the security of economic institutions. As I read the cases, however, these demands have pressed upon courts and jurists from the standpoint of their relation to economic progress. If that relation fails, they are not likely to maintain themselves. Likewise the law has long recognized a social interest in political progress. In American bills of rights, and in written constitutions generally, a policy of free criticism of public men, public acts, and public officers, and a policy of free formation, free holding, and free expression of political opinion are guaranteed as identified with individual rights. Moreover, at common law, the privilege of fair comment upon public men and public affairs recognizes and secures the same interest. But the third form, the social interest in cultural progress, has not been recognized in the law so clearly. It may be said to involve four policies: a policy of free science, a policy of free letters, a policy of encouragement of arts and letters, and a policy of promotion of education and learning. The last two have been recognized to some extent in copyright laws and in American constitutional provisions for the promotion of higher learning. The first two have made their way more slowly because of conflict or supposed conflict with the security of religious and political institutions.

Closely connected with the interest in cultural progress is a social interest in aesthetic surroundings, which recently has been pressing for legal recognition. . . . In the United States, courts and legislatures were long engaged in a sharp struggle over billboard laws and laws against hideous forms of outdoor advertising. For a time also the interest pressed in another way in connection with town planning legislation. It is significant that the courts are now ready to admit a policy in favor of the aesthetic as reasonable and constitutionally permissible.

Social Interest in the Individual Life

Last, and in some ways most important of all, as we now are coming to think, there is the social interest in the individual life. One might call it the social interest in the individual moral and social life, or in the individual human life. It is the claim or want or demand involved in social life in civilized society that each individual be able to live a human life therein according to the standards of the society. It is the claim or want or demand that, if all individual wants may not be satisfied, they be satisfied at least so far as is reasonably possible and to the extent of a human minimum. Three forms of this social interest have been recognized in common law or in legislation: individual self-assertion, individual opportunity, and individual conditions of life. The first, the interest in free self-assertion, includes physical, mental, and economic activity. . . .

The most important phase of the social interest in individual self-assertion, from the standpoint of modern law, is what might be called the social interest in freedom of the individual will—the claim or interest, or policy recognizing it, that the individual will shall not be subjected arbitrarily to the will of others. This interest is recognized in an old common-law policy which is declared in the Fifth and Fourteenth Amendments. If one will is to be subjected to the will of another through the force of politically organized society, it is not to be done arbitrarily, but is to be done upon some rational basis, which the person coerced, if reasonable, could appreciate. It is to be done upon a reasoned weighing of the interests involved and a reasoned attempt to reconcile them or adjust them. This policy obviously expresses political and juristic experience of what modern psychology has discovered as to the ill effects of repression. . . .

I have called a second form the social interest in individual opportunity. It is the claim or want or demand involved in social life in civilized society that all individuals shall have fair or reasonable (perhaps, as we are coming to think, we must say equal) opportunities—political, physical, cultural, social, and economic. In American thinking we have insisted chiefly on equal political opportunities, since in the pioneer conditions in which our institutions were formative other opportunities, so far as men demanded them, were at hand everywhere. But a claim to fair physical opportunities is recognized in public provision of parks and playgrounds and in public provisions for recreation; the claim to fair cultural opportunities is recognized by laws as to compulsory education of children (although the social interests in general progress and in dependents are also recognized here) as well as by state provisions for universities and for adult education; the claim to fair social opportunities is recognized by civil rights laws; and the claim to fair economic opportunities is recognized, for example, in the legal right to "freedom of the market,"[8] and in the so-called "right to pursue a lawful calling,"[9] which is weighed with other social interests in regulating training for and admission to professions.

In a third form, an interest in individual conditions of life, the social interest in the individual life appears as a claim that each individual shall have assured to him the conditions of at least a minimum human life under the circumstances of life in the time and place. I have said minimum, which certainly was all that was recognized until relatively recent times. But perhaps we should now say reasonable or even equal. A claim for equal conditions of life is pressing and we can't put the matter as to what is recognized with assurance as we could have done a generation ago. Moreover, the scope of generally asserted demands with respect to the individual life is obviously growing. The Roman law recognized a policy of this sort, and it has long been recognized in American legislation. In weighing individual interests in view of the social interest in security of acquisitions and security of transactions, we must also take account of the social interest in the human life of each individual, and so must restrict the legal enforcement of demands to what is consistent with a human existence on the part of the person subjected thereto. . . .

When the law confers or exercises a power of control, we feel that the legal order should safeguard the human existence of the person controlled. Thus the old-time sea law, with its absolute power of the master over the sailor, the old-time ignominious punishments, that treated the human offender like a brute, that did not save his human dignity—all such things are disappearing as the circle of recognized interests widens and we come to take account of the social interest in the individual life and to weigh that interest with the social interest in the general security, on which the last century insisted so exclusively.

Conclusion

Such in outline are the social interests which are recognized or are coming to be recognized in modern law. Looked at functionally, the law is an attempt to satisfy, to reconcile, to harmonize, to adjust these overlapping and often conflicting claims and demands, either through securing them directly and immediately, or through securing certain individual interests, or through delimitations or compromises of individual interests, so as to give effect to the greatest total of interests or to the interests that weigh most in our civilization, with the least sacrifice of the scheme of interests as a whole.

Notes

1. Social Control Through Law (1942). 63–80; The Spirit of the Common Law (1921) 91–93; 197–203; Introduction to the Philosophy of Law (1922) 90–96; Interpretations of Legal History (1923) 158–64.
2. I Der Zweck im Recht (1877) 467–83, translated by Husick, Law as a Means to an End (1921) 348–59.
3. "Public Policy . . . is that principle of the law which holds that no subject can lawfully do that which has a tendency to be injurious to the public or against the public good. . . ." Lord Truro in *Egerton v. Lord Brownlow*, 4 H. L. Cas. I, 196, 10 Eng. Rep. 359, 437 (1853). "Whatever is injurious to the interests of the public is void, on the grounds of public policy." Tindal, C. J., in *Hornor v. Graves*, 7 Bing. 735, 743, 131 Eng. Rep. 284, 287 (1831). ". . . wherever any contract conflicts with the morals of the time and contravenes any established interest of society, it is void, as being against public policy." I Story, Contracts (1844) § 675.
4. Burrough, J., in *Richardson v. Mellish*, 2 Bing, 229, 252, 130 Eng. Rep. 294, 303 (C. P. 1824). See a full discussion in Fender v. St. John Mildmay, [1938] A. C. 1, and see *Mamlin v. Genoe*, 340 Pa. 320, 17 A. (2d) 407 (1941).
5. Printing & Numerical Registering Co. v. Sampson, L. R. 19 Eq. 462, 465 (1875).
6. Statute of Westminster I, 1275, 3 EDW. I, preamble.
7. *Miller v. Race*, 1 Burr. 452, 457, 97 Eng. Rep. 398, 401 (K. B. 1758).
8. *Jersey City Printing Co. v. Cassidy*, 63 N. J. Eq. 759, 766, 53 Atl. 230, 233 (1902). As to the economic theory behind this, see Hardy, *Market* (1937) 10 Encyc. Soc. Sciences 131.
9. *Butchers' Union Co. v. Crescent City Co.*, 111 U.S. 746, 762 (1884); Cummings v. Missouri, 4 Wall. 277, 321 (U.S. 1866); *In re Leach*, 134 Ind. 665, 34 N. E. 641 (1893); *Schnaier v. Navarre Hotel & Importation Co.*, 182 N.Y. 83, 87–89, 74 N.E. 561, 562 (1905); Wilkinson and Bregy, *Shoemakers' Children* (1942) 2 Bill of Rights Rev. 209.

8

Group Interests
Thomas A. Cowan

The time has come for legal scholars to study more intensively the nature of group interests. By "group interests" I mean interests urged, not in the name of individuals nor of society as a whole, but in the name of what sociologists call "secondary groups"—associations, unions, societies, clubs, boards, councils, professions. Even looser than these, but still having a group character, are taxpayers, consumers, "interested parties," and other amorphous collectivities.

Modern life is lived associatively. The new democracy is an aggregation of sub-groups, not primarily of individuals. Individual interests, to be preserved, must increasingly array themselves against group interests. To the nineteenth century clash of the interests of one individual against those of another, and the early twentieth century conflict between individual and social interests has been added a third variable, group interest.

It is quite evident that this third variable makes analysis of basic legal interests a complex matter. Not alone must the conception of group interests be distinguished from individual and social interests; the three must also be coordinated. Quite evidently the job is a more difficult one than that which faced jurisprudence in incorporating social interests into a body of law already heavily committed to the protection of the interests of the individual.

Individual interests are a primary concern of every matured system of law. We therefore start with a fairly good idea of what these indi-

Excerpt from "Group Interests," *Virginia Law Review* 44 (1958), pp. 331–345, by permission of the author and publisher.

vidual interests are. Social interests also have undergone almost a century of legal analysis. As Pound says,

> Social interests are claims or demands or desires involved in social life in civilized society and asserted in title of that life. It is not uncommon to treat them as the claims of the whole social group as such.

They are the demands civilization makes on the law. A society that recognizes only individual interests could presumably exist, but it is civilized only to the extent that it recognizes and enforces the claims of decent social living. Individual claims must always subscribe to the test of the competing claims of civilized society.

Group interests are neither wholly individual nor wholly social. To be sure, a system of law heavily weighted in favor of individual interests is apt to treat all groups which demand recognition as though they were individuals. This was the way the nineteenth century treated associations. Corporations were individuals; unincorporated associations were merely aggregates of individuals. On the other hand, to treat groups as merely social, that is, to see their demands only in the light of the interests of the whole society is possible only to a totalitarianism. Such "total governments" recognize only sub-groups of themselves.

It would be tempting to call a group interest a status and thus to put ourselves in the line of historical development of that valuable term. However, it will not do to call all group demands status demands. The reverse is perhaps true. Status demands are group demands. But the infinitely varied group demands of modern life can hardly be attributed to status except perhaps, as has already been suggested, in the sociologists' attenuated use of that term.

Historically, as Pound has shown, the common law has always had a strong preference for "status law." Maine's generalization was not true for the common law even at the time he formulated it almost a century ago. As for the present, it is necessary, as Pound has indicated, to say that the trend is the reverse, that is, from contract to status.

Groups make demands for themselves and resist the demands of individuals, other groups, and the whole of society. To this extent they are analogous to legal individuals which act in the same way. But the interests are not those of single individuals nor of a mere aggregate of individuals. Their claims are collective: the members of the union, association, whatnot, make the demands in a collective capacity. To this extent the interests are analogous to those of the whole society, in other words, to social interests.

A vast literature on the nature of human groups exists. It is not to our interest to examine that body of learning here. Whether the "group" is real, ideal, or nominal is a problem that need not detain us. For purposes of analysis, we can surely agree that the concept "group" is at least functional or operational. It does make a real legal difference whether we are dealing with claims of individuals, of groups, or of society as a whole. And if we can show, as I think we can, that contemporary law is struggling mightily to handle the conception of "group," and that in this struggle it is burdened with older notions of individual and social interests, then I think we shall have shown that the conception has demonstrated its own existence in a manner sufficiently forceful to warrant serious attention from students of the law.

There is one other important result that should follow from sustained attention to the matter of group interests. This is the fact that in American legal development group interests are often confused with social interests to the distinct disadvantage of the latter. In other words, lawmakers have often felt that in advancing protection to groups they are automatically taking care of the interests of society. This probably results from the fact that a group often appears to represent the public or social interest and frequently makes a specific claim to that effect when in fact it represents only its own selfish interests. We all understand and tend to correct the penchant of the individual for identifying the public good with his own good. The tendency of groups to identify the public interest with their own interest is much harder to counteract. Yet it stands to reason that to the extent that groups are in fact more powerful than individuals, their power to affect society as a whole is merely multiplied. There is no assurance whatever in any given case that this added power will be used for the benefit of society.

With these considerations in mind we are ready to turn to certain specific branches of the law to see how the analysis of group interests may be applied.

Administrative Law

If one were to call administrative law the law of groups or associations he would not miss the mark by much. To say this is not, of course, to say that administrative law is nothing more than the law of groups. It is merely to indicate the legal entities upon which administrative law chiefly operates. With this limitation in mind, it is fair to say that the incidence of administrative law falls mainly on groups or on individuals in their group or in their associative capacity.

Modern American administrative law began in the creation of the Interstate Commerce Commission, whose express purpose was to adjust the complex of conflicting interests arising in a vitally important sector of our expanding economy, the railroads. In the language of the jurisprudence of interests we may say that this immense system of conflicts forced recognition of the fact that the prevailing legal philosophy of the courts, that of preoccupation with individual interests (called "rights"), simply would not do. It was also felt that judicial recognition, in embryonic fashion, of social interests (called "police power") was equally inadequate. For the critical point was not the relationship of the railroads with those outside the "railroad complex." Ordinary law processes would suffice to adjust those conflicts. What was called for was an adjustment of conflict within and among the three dominant "railroad" groups: carriers, shippers, and "the public."

It was assumed, as it so often is in administrative law, that the public or social interest would be adequately taken care of by the administrative agency, despite the fact that it might easily be foreseen that constant preoccupation with the competing interests of such specialized groups as carriers and shippers might well force the administrative agency to push into the background such an amorphous and unrepresented matter as the public interest.

This threw onto the courts the burden of adjusting the older individual interests and those of the public. The courts took it for granted that the Commission could adequately adjust conflicting group demands. The judicial function then could be limited to an occasional interference in the interest of individual "rights" and to an increasing interference in the public or social interest.

Each of the great federal regulatory agencies involves in more or less acute form the conflict among the three types of interests. An extremely interesting case, *FCC v. Sanders Brothers Radio Station*,[1] illustrates the point. This case held that an existing radio station has no "right" to be protected against competition from a newcomer in the area, but has an "interest" sufficient to confer "standing" to contest the newcomer's application. The case has been severely criticized as an instance of overconceptionalism. In point of fact, fuller conceptualization would render the opinion fairly clear. The court read the statute as dealing primarily with the public interest. "Plainly it is not the purpose of the Act to protect a licensee against competition but to protect the public interest."[2] Therefore the existing licensee has no "right," *i.e.*, individual interest, to be protected from competition. But he has "standing" to sue, that is, his group interest is sufficient to entitle him to a place in the proceedings. The Court's reasoning is revealing. The Court intimated that, if the competitor has no standing, it may be that no one will be moved to act, and the public interest will go unrepresented. So the existing license-holder is given the task of protecting the public interest. A very doubtful guardian, one might say. Yet, once under way, the proceedings did in fact rest on a determination "in the public interest," made by the Commission.

How much of the confused law of "standing" would be straightened out by a careful analysis of its existing mixture of individual, group, and public or social interests I am not prepared to say. But that it could be of help in this important task I am sure. My impression is that in the huge pyramid which is administrative law, the broad base at the bottom allows almost anyone to take part. "Interested party" is almost literally anyone interested enough to get to the hearing in person or even by mail in the case of countless local boards, commissions, agencies, and others. Here at the bottom there may be no point whatever in sifting out the infinitely varied meanings of the qualifying term "interest." As one ascends the pyramid, however, differentiation occurs. Out of the primordial mass of interests, that of the citizenry, arises the notion of individual interest or right. Anyone hurt in person or property in ways traditionally recognized as justiciable may be heard. As we go further up we come upon the main business of the agency, the adjusting of group interests of taxpayers, utility consumers, carriers, passengers, shippers, union members, employer's associations, radio stations, power companies, and so on.

As the group interests clash with one another and with individual interests, it becomes obvious that something of the original mass is missing: the interests of the whole—social interests. By now we have reached the top layer of the pyramid, the courts. Here the issues, of standing and the rest, are mainly based on social interests.

The highest form of standing is the most conservative one: nineteenth century individual rights. These, however, are usually irrelevant since administrative agencies seldom deal with them except in group-interest contexts. Therefore, standing must next rest upon group interests. Here, by and large, the courts merely resolve contradictions which the agencies get themselves into or are too timid to resolve. Where both individual and group interests fail, there is nothing left but the social interest. It is usually assumed that the agency may represent this interest. If it does not, or even if it does, the court is the last guardian of this interest, which it may undertake to protect *sua sponte*. The court may even retroactively confer "standing" upon anyone who in fact brings it a record. In summary, the law of "standing" reflects in the main the difficulty of trying to fit group interests into judicial moulds devised for individual interests. It also shows the difficulty of adjusting social interests to this already overburdened system of unconscious conceptualism.

Certain administrative agencies, notably the Pure Food and Drug Administration, may subordinate both individual and group interests and concentrate on the social interest. When this happens, the agency may find itself engaged, to a more or less limited degree, in a policing operation.

Labor Law

Labor law is an area where everything from primitive regulation by self-help up to the most daring innovations on even comparatively modern legal conceptions takes place. Every tool in the legal kit, one might say, is brought into action in an endeavor to make the two most powerful groups in modern times give up war-ways for peace-ways. One hears of "cooling off periods," reminiscent of the medieval prohibitions against warfare on Fridays, Sundays, and holydays of obligation. On the other hand, injunction to cease and desist from refusing collectively to bargain is novel to the point of absurdity—a double negative designed to achieve a positive result.

Basically and essentially, labor law is a conglomerate of group interests imposed upon forms of law perfected in the nineteenth century for securing individual interests. The foremost analytical conception of nineteenth century individual interests is contract. The classic notion of contract is that of two adult males dealing at arm's length and agreeing on a matter of mutual advantage and disadvantage. Time-wise, contract law also is one-dimensional. The agreement comes into existence at a definite moment of time. Its terms are subject to the will of the parties before, during, and after agreement. It is the essence of private law. The public has but a minimal interest in it. Notions of public policy touch it only peripherally.

It is not surprising, therefore, that this perfect paradigm of individual interests theoretically should be regarded as too weak to carry the weight of group interests massively in opposition. What is surprising is that the device has proved to be so readily adaptable to the needs of the labor-management complex. The once-for-all notion of contract has given way to the continued status idea of a relation between labor and management. Though the old incidents of master-servant have disappeared to a large extent, there is still something of it left. Conceptually, though of course not in content, modern labor relations are more closely analogous to the older master-servant relation than to the nineteenth century contract of hire, where the two parties were looked upon as equal and as equally binding themselves by their individual will.

The overwhelming importance of group interests in this branch of the law leads to a slighting of the other two interests. Individual interests, unless they are of the most heavily protected sort, *e.g.*, bodily integrity, are apt to be sacrificed to the giant group interests. As for the public interest, this was and is apt to be lost sight of since the groups themselves are such a large part of the total population. Nevertheless the interest does directly come to the surface in disputes with a governmental employer. Somehow the outworn notion of sovereign governmental immunity is taken to be in point, when as a matter of fact the real inquiry concerns the public or social interest.

Preconditions to the agreement are also couched in nineteenth century phraseology of individual interests. The parties are commanded "to bargain collectively." The image evoked is that of horse-trading. Yet in point of fact the trading is not free but compulsory; the content of the bargaining is fixed by current notions of the employment relation, no important sector of which may be unilaterally omitted; and agreement can, in effect, be unilaterally compelled. The relation is a status relation and the interests are largely group. Individual "grievances" tend to be handled in group terms or not at all.

The adjustment of individual and social interests to the dominant group interests must be left mainly to the courts, or otherwise go unprotected. Many of the decisions, while they are couched in the language of statutory interpretation, appear frankly to recognize this necessity. Of course, this is not the sole concern of the courts. Intergovernmental conflicts and matters of group interest which the agencies have been unable to settle also require attention.

A frank recognition of the fact that individual interests have only a minor role to play in the labor-management complex might go a long way toward clearing up certain anomalies in this branch of the law. It would also make clear the fact that heavy emphasis upon group interests has left many important individual ones without even the protection previously afforded them by the nineteenth century jurisprudence of individual rights. . . .

Legislation

In theory as well as in fact, the legislative process is designed to test and then to consolidate into statutory law competing group interests. The legislature responds to pressures. Its ideal of justice is to have all proper pressures adequately represented. Needless to say, it assumes that only in this fashion can the social or public interest be protected.

Legislative protection of individual interests has always been a precarious matter. To begin with, the legislative process is poorly designed to distinguish between the selfish interests of individuals and the *social* interest in the fullness of individual life (individual rights). Delicately sensitive to pressures from individuals as well as from groups, the legislature has been forced more and more to seek devices to convert its apparent genuine preference for private legislation into a principled search for generalized public legislation.

The courts have aided in this process. In the nineteenth century, much judicial opposition to private legislation developed, and constitutional limitations were adapted or new ones invented to put restraints on the process. Legislation touching individual rights had to be "general," "prospective," "remedial," "procedural," "nonadjudicatory," and so on. Utilizing its newly acquired right to invalidate legislation and hinting darkly against "legislative abuses" in cases not going so far as directly to thwart the "popular will," courts virtually construed the legislatures out of the business of protecting individual rights. Statutes in derogation of individual rights were to be strictly construed.

Even the legislature's primary avowed role of guardian of the public interest was looked upon with disfavor by courts. Public policy in the main was restricted to its traditional exercise, and was restricted in its full operation by the legislature to the sphere of group interests. When the legislature attempted to adjust individual and social interests, the courts, until post New Deal times, were apt to invalidate the efforts.

Legislatures nowadays have won the battle to include in their adjustment of group interests, those of society and of the individual. But the fact that the courts do not interfere as vigorously with the legislative function does not mean that the legislature is doing the job adequately. Still organized in a way which at best is able to handle group interests, the legislature is poorly devised to safeguard social interests. And its attempts adequately to take account of individual interests are pitifully inadequate.

Conclusion

The foregoing are but a few illustrations of the vast influence which the modern "group movement" is having on the law. The effect is being felt in all other areas of the law as well. In criminal law administration, the older individualistic notions are being narrowly restricted to the actual trial, still pretty much a biparty affair, with the defendant representing individual interests and the prosecution, social interests. Beyond that the criminal administration complex takes over. Juvenile delinquency practice, probation, and parole virtually ignore the traditional processes of the criminal law. Indeed, post-sentencing procedure is largely out of the hands of prosecutor and judge. As the psychiatrist and social worker move into this area they are apt to take with them the concern for "group interests" which is so large a part of medical therapy.

Notes

1. 309 U.S. 470 (1940).
2. *Id.* at 475.

9

The Marx-Engels Theory of Law

Hans Kelsen

**Primacy of Economics over Politics in the Marxian
Theory of the Bourgeois (Capitalist) State**

The Marxian theory of law is inseparably connected with the
theory of state.[1] It is based on the assumption that the economic
production and the social relationships constituted by it (the *Produk-
tionsverhaeltnisse*) determine the coming into existence as well as the
disappearance of state and law. Neither phenomenon is an essential
element of human society; they exist only under definite economic
conditions, namely when the means of production are at the exclusive disposition of a minority of individuals who use or misuse this
privilege for the purpose of exploiting the overwhelming majority.
This implies the division of society into two groups of antagonistic
economic interests, two "classes," the class of the exploiting owners
of the means of production and the class of the exploited workers.

This is especially the situation of a society where the economic
system of capitalism prevails and society is split into the two classes
of the bourgeois (capitalists) and the proletariat. The state together
with its law is the coercive machinery for the maintenance of exploitation of one class by the other, an instrument of the class of ex-
ploiters which, through the state and its law, becomes the politically

Excerpt from *The Communist Theory of Law*, New York: Frederick A. Praeger,
Inc., 1955, pp. 1–38, reprinted by permission of Holt, Rinehart, and Winston.

dominant class. The state is the power established for the purpose of keeping the conflict between the dominant and the dominated class "within the bounds of 'order.'"[2] This "order" is the law, which—according to this view—although something different from the state, is in essential connection with the state. The state is "normally the state of the most powerful economically ruling class, which by its means becomes also the politically ruling class, and thus acquires new means of holding down and exploiting the oppressed class."[3] That means that the political power of the bourgeoisie is the effect of its economic power, that the bourgeoisie becomes the politically ruling class because it is the economically ruling class. This primacy of economics over politics is quite consistent with Marx' economic interpretation of history in general and of present society in particular. A society split into classes, says Engels, "needs the state, that means an organisation of the exploiting class for maintaining the external conditions of its production, especially for holding down by force the exploited class."[4] The dominance of one class over the other, which is the essence of the state, is identical with the exploitation of one class by the other, the dominant class being essentially the exploiting class.

Reality and Ideology

The interdependence which according to this economic or materialistic interpretation of society exists between the economic conditions on the one hand, and state and law on the other, is of decisive importance for the theory of state and in particular for the theory of law. It is usually assumed that Marx describes this interdependence in the well-known metaphor of a political and legal "superstructure" set up above the relationships of production constituting the economic structure of society. "Ideologies" form the superstructure, whereas the basis, the substructure, represents social reality. In his work *Zur Kritik der politischen Oekonomie* (Contribution to the Critique of Political Economy) he says:

> In the social production which men carry on they enter into definite relations that are indispensable and independent of their will; these relations of production correspond to a definite stage of development of their material powers of production. The sum total of these relations of production constitutes the economic structure of society—the real foundation, on which rise legal and political superstructures and to which correspond definite forms of social consciousness.[5]

The "superstructures" are "forms of social consciousness," which he later characterises as "ideological forms in which men become conscious" of social reality. It is usually assumed that Marx understands by "legal and political superstructures" law and state. Engels, *e.g.*, interprets the Marxian formula in the statement that "the economic structure of society forms the real basis, by which the total superstructure of legal and political institutions as well as religious, philosophical and other ideas [*Vorstellungsweisen*] of each historical period in the last analysis may be explained."[6] If this interpretation is correct and, hence, law has the nature of an ideology, the meaning of this term is of the utmost importance for a Marxian theory of law.

In his fragmentary work *Einleitung zu einer Kritik der politischen Oekonomie* (Introduction to the Critique of Political Economy) Marx says that in the study of social science it must be borne in mind that society is given "as in reality so in our mind."[7] Social ideology as a form of social consciousness is society as it is given in the human mind, in contradistinction to society as it is given in reality. In *Das Kommunistische Manifest* (Communist Manifesto) Marx and Engels refer to "the charges against communism made from a religious, a philosophical and, generally, from an ideological standpoint," thus meaning by ideology in the first place religion and philosophy. Then, they maintain that "man's ideas, views, and conceptions, in one word, man's consciousness changes with every change in the conditions of his material existence, in his social relations and his social life." Hence "ideology" means the content of man's consciousness, the ideas man forms in his mind of reality, especially of social reality.

But mostly Marx uses the term "ideology" not in this wider sense as identical with "idea," but in a narrower and decidedly deprecatory sense. By ideology he means a false consciousness, an incorrect—in contradistinction to a scientifically correct—idea of social reality. He says, in considering social transformations:

> the distinction should always be made between the material transformation . . . which can be described with the precision of natural science, and the legal, political, religious, aesthetic or philosophic—in short ideological forms in which men become conscious [of these transformations]. Just as our opinion of an individual is not based on what he fancies himself, so we cannot judge such a period of transformation by its own consciousness.[8]

The "ideological" consciousness is false because it is determined by the social situation of the man whose mind reflects the social reality, especially by the interests of the social group, or class, to which the man belongs. Marx has the rather naïve epistemological view according to which man's consciousness reflects—like a mirror—the real objects. In his main work, *Das Kapital*, Marx says, in opposition to Hegel's view that reality is a reflex of idea: "With me, on the contrary, the idea [*das Ideelle*] is nothing but the material transformed and translated in the mind of man [*das im Menschenkopf umgesetzte und uebersetzte Materielle*]."[9] And Engels writes in his pamphlet *Ludwig Feuerbach und der Ausgang der klassischen Philosophie:*[10] "We conceive of ideas . . . as pictures of real things"; and in his *Die Entwicklung des Sozialismus von der Utopie zur Wissenschaft:*[11] "thoughts are only more or less abstract images of the real things and events." An ideology is a form of consciousness that reflects social reality in a distorted way, it counterfeits something that, in reality, does not exist, it veils reality or something in it instead of unveiling it, it is a deception and even self-deception and, above all, it is an illusive consciousness. Hence there is always an antagonism or conflict between the reality and the ideological consciousness man has of this reality; and, since Marx speaks of conflicts or antagonisms as of "contradictions," there is always a contradiction between reality and ideology.

The epistemological doctrine which is at the basis of Marx' theory of ideology is formulated in these famous statements:

> The mode of production in material life determines the general character of the social, political and spiritual process of life. It is not the consciousness [*Bewusstsein*] of men that determines their existence [*Sein*] but, on the contrary, their social existence [*gesellschaftliches Sein*] determines their consciousness.[12]

Although the second sentence is supposed to express the same idea as the first, the two are not quite the same. In the first sentence only the "mode of production" is the determining factor, in the second, it is the entire "social existence." In the first sentence not only the "spiritual" but also the "social" and "political" process of life is the determined factor; in the second, it is only the "consciousness" which is identical with the spiritual process of life. By the "social" and "political" process of life law and state as social institutions may be understood; and this "social" and "political" process of life—as distinguished from the "spiritual" process of life in the first sentence—may very well be conceived of as part of the "social existence" of men referred to in the second sentence. Hence there is a strange ambiguity as to the meaning of the relationship between reality and ideology, which makes the foundation of Marx' theory of cognition highly problematical. This ambiguity plays a particular part in the theory of state and law when the question arises whether these social phenomena belong to the substructure, *i.e.*, the real basis, or to the ideological superstructure.

If Marx' sociological theory of knowledge is taken in its second version (the social existence of men determining their consciousness) the question arises whether a consciousness other than an ideological, *i.e.*, false, illusive consciousness is possible at all. Since man's consciousness is "ideological" in this sense because it is determined by man's social existence, the answer must be in the negative. Hence there can be no true, *i.e.*, objective theory of reality in general and of social reality in particular. It is evident that Marx cannot maintain his fundamental position, for the very statement that the social existence determines the consciousness of men must claim to be a true and that means an objective theory of the human consciousness, not determined by the social existence of the one who makes this statement. There can be no doubt that Marx presents his own social theory as a non-ideological, correct description of social reality, as a "science."

In an above-quoted statement Marx makes a clear distinction between a description of reality performed "with the precision of natural science," that is to say a "scientific" consciousness, and "ideological forms" in which man becomes conscious of social reality, that is to say, an ideological consciousness. As we shall see later, Marx explains the deficiency of an ideological consciousness by the deficiency of the social reality producing such an ideological consciousness. In the communist society of the future, which represents a perfect social reality, there will be no "ideological" consciousness; but there will be a consciousness, there will certainly be science; and if science, as a content of consciousness, is to be conceived of as ideology, not in the derogatory sense of the term but as something different from its object, *i.e.*, from reality reflected in the consciousness, the term "ideology" may be used not only in the sense of a false, illusive, but also in the sense of a scientifically correct, consciousness.

Marx was evidently aware of the fact that his doctrine of ideology endangers his own social theory. It is probably for the purpose of defending his theory against the objection to be a mere "ideology" in the derogatory sense of the term that in *Das Kommunistische Manifest*, he asserts that at a certain stage of the class struggle "the bourgeoisie itself supplies the proletariat with weapons for fighting the bourgeoisie," that "a portion of the bourgeoisie goes over to the proletariat and, in particular, a portion of the bourgeois ideologists, who have raised themselves to the level of comprehending theoretically the historical movement as a whole." Thus, these "bourgeois ideologists" cease to produce ideologies and develop a true science of the historical movement. But how is such a metamorphosis possible, how can they escape the fundamental law that their social existence, that is their belonging to the bourgeois class, determines their social consciousness? This is—seen from the point of view of Marx' social theory—a miracle.

State and Law as Reality

The typical and most characteristic ideology is religion. "Religion," says Marx, "is the general theory of this world"; and of religion he says that it is a "perverted consciousness of the world,"[13] the "opium of the people," an "illusion."[14] It is significant that Marx, when he denounces religion as an illusive ideology, defines it as a "theory." In a letter to Ruge he speaks of "religion and science" as of the "theoretical existence of man"[15] in contradistinction to his practical existence, that is, the "reality" of his true existence. In this sense only a theory, a function of cognition, a form of consciousness, not the object of theory or cognition, not reality—correctly or incorrectly—reflected in man's consciousness, could be characterised as ideological. Marx frequently speaks of ideology as a mere "expression" (*Ausdruck*) of reality and denounces as an ideological fallacy to take what is a mere "expression" of the reality for reality,[16] whereby he evidently presupposes that the expression is false, illusive. Hence, only a certain—namely a false—theory of the state or a certain—namely illusive—philosophy of law, not the state or the law, could be conceived of as an ideology. In accordance with his thesis that the social existence of man, that is, his social reality, determines man's social consciousness, Marx says that the state "produces religion as a perverted consciousness"[17] and opposes "the state together with the social reality connected with it" to the "legal consciousness, the most distinguished, most universal, to the rank of science elevated expression of which is the speculative philosophy of law,"[18] Here the state is presented as social reality upon which an illusive legal philosophy as an ideological superstructure is set up.

In his *Zur Kritik der politischen Oekonomie* he identifies the relationships of production, that is, the social reality in opposition to the social ideology, with legal relations. "At a certain stage of their development the material forces of production in society come in conflict with the existing relations of production—or what is but a legal expression for the same thing—with the property relations within which they had been at work before."[19] Property relations, that is, legal relations, are relations of production, that is, economic relations. "Property" or "legal" relations is only another name for relations of production, economic relations.[20] Marx, it is true, characterises here the law, just as he characterises ideology, as an "expression" of the relations of production, *i.e.*, an expression of the social reality. But the law is not—as an ideology by its very nature must be—a false, illusive expression, an expression which is in contradiction to the object that it expresses. The expression of economic reality which is the law, is in harmony with reality, corresponds to reality.

Marx rejects the view that sovereigns make law for the economic conditions. "Legislation, political as well as civil, could do no more than give expression to the will of the economic relations."[21] That economic relations have a "will" is a rather problematical metaphor. But the meaning of it is: that the law corresponds to the economic conditions which it "expresses," that the law is a correct, and hence not an ideological, expression of economic reality. "Law is only the official recognition of fact."[22] Marx says of the forms of division of labour: "Originally born of the conditions of material production, it was not till much later that they were established as law."[23] The law prescribing division of labour is in perfect harmony with division of labour in economic reality. That the law is an "expression" of economic conditions means that it is the product of economic reality, that it is its effect. But—according to Marx—the law is not only the effect of economic reality; the law has itself effects on this reality. In *Das Kapital* we read:

> By maturing the material conditions and the combination on a social scale of the process of production, it [the law] matures the contradictions and antagonisms of the capitalist form of production, and thereby provides, along with the elements for the formation of a new society, the force for exploding the old one.[24]

In his *Einleitung zu einer Kritik der politischen Oekonomie*[25] Marx writes:

> Laws may perpetuate an instrument of production, *e.g.*, land, in certain families. These laws assume an economic importance if large landed property is in harmony with the system of production prevailing in society, as is the case *e.g.*, in England.

In stressing the "harmony" of the law with the relationships of production, Marx goes as far as to characterise the positive law as "natural" law. He says of the English Factory Acts, they are "just as much the necessary product of modern industry as cotton yarns, self-actors, and electric telegraph."[26] "They develop gradually out of the circumstances as natural laws of the modern mode of production."[27] Marx expressly refers to "the effect of legislation on the maintenance of a system of distribution and its resultant influence on production." If the law is not "in harmony" with the conditions of production, it

ceases to be effective, as *e.g.*, in France, where in spite of the "legislative attempts to perpetuate the minute subdivision of land" achieved
by the revolution, "land ownership is concentrating again." In so far
as the law—or the fact Marx has in mind when he refers to "law"—is
an effect of economic reality and has itself effects on this reality,
that is to say, if the law is within the chain of cause and effect, it is
within reality, and hence belongs to the substructure of the ideological superstructure.

State and Law as Ideology

However, on the other hand Marx refers to the real state and the
existing law, and not to a theory of the state or a philosophy of law,
as to ideologies. In *Das Kommunistische Manifest* the charges against
communism made from an ideological standpoint are formulated as
follows: "Undoubtedly—it will be said—religious, moral, philosophical
and juridical ideas have been modified in the course of historical
development. But religion, morality, philosophy, political science,
and law constantly survived this change." Here morality and law are
placed as ideologies on the same plane with philosophy and science.
In *Die deutsche Ideologie*,[28] which is an important source for an
understanding of Marx' doctrine of ideology, Marx refers to "morality, religion, metaphysics, and other ideologies." Morality is an effective normative order regulating human behaviour; and if morality is
an ideology on the same level as religion and metaphysics, then law,
too, may be conceived of in this way. Marx says of the "laws" as well
as of "morality" that they are the "*ideelle* expression of the conditions of the existence" of the dominant class (conditioned by the
development of production) and by the "*ideelle*" expression he means
an ideological expression in opposition to the economic reality thus
expressed.

It is characteristic of "ideologists," says Marx, that "they take
their ideology for the creative force and the purpose of all social
relationships, although they are only their expression and symptom."[29] "The law," says Marx, "is only symptom, expression of
other relationships, on which the power of the state is based." The
real bases are the relationships of production.[30] It is especially the
legal institution of property which is the "legal expression" of "certain economic conditions, which are dependent on the development
of the forces of production"[31] for "the relationships of production
among the individuals must also express themselves as political and
legal relationships."[32] In his critique of Stirner, Marx reproaches this
philosopher of having taken "the ideological-speculative expression

of reality, separated from its empirical basis, for the very reality"; and as one of these ideological expressions of reality, mistaken as reality by Stirner, Marx points to the law.[33]

According to this view, the law—and not an illusive legal philosophy—is an ideological superstructure set up above the social reality, the relationships of production. Hence one is quite justified to interpret the "legal and political superstructures" referred to in *Zur Kritik der politischen Oekonomie* to mean the law and the state—as pointed out, Engels himself and consequently almost all interpreters of Marx do so—although Marx, a few lines later, identifies the law with the relationships of production, and, in other connections, characterises the state as a specific social reality producing ideology, and not as an ideology produced by a specific social reality.

If the law is part of the ideological superstructure as something different from and opposed to its substructure, the social reality constituted by economic relationships, then the law cannot be the effect of these relationships and, especially, cannot itself have effect on them. When Marx—in the above-quoted statements—admits an interaction between law and economics, he deals with law as with a social reality. If the law is a social reality in the same sense as economic production, then the scheme of super- and sub-structure is not applicable to the relationship between the two social phenomena. But it is just of the ideological superstructure that Engels maintains that it "influences" the substructure. In a letter to J. Bloch[34] he writes:

> The economic situation is the basis, but the various elements of the superstructure—political forms of the class struggle and its consequences, constitutions established by the victorious class after a successful battle, etc.—forms of law and then even the reflexes of all these actual struggles in the brains of the combatants: political, legal, philosophical theories, religious ideas and their further development into systems of dogma—also exercise their influence upon the course of the historical struggles.

That means that the ideological superstructure, especially the law as element of this superstructure, has effects on the substructure. Hence "ideology" is "reality" in the same sense as the economic relationships which Marx identifies with reality; and he must identify reality with economic relationships in order to oppose these relationships as 'reality' to that which he wants to disparage as 'ideology': above all, to religion. Since the identification of social reality with economic relationships is the essence of his economic interpretation of society, this interpretation breaks down as soon as 'ideologies' are recognised as 'realities'. A very characteristic application of this interpretation is Marx' statement:

> 'Society is not based upon law; this is a juridical fiction. On the contrary, the law must rest on society. It must be the expression of its common interests

and needs arising from the actual methods of material production against the caprice of the single individual'.[35]

The bourgeois doctrine, rejected by Marx, that society is based on law, means, if not intentionally misinterpreted, that the law—or more exactly formulated, certain acts by which law is created or applied—influences social life, without excluding that social life influences the formation of the law. Hence the rejected doctrine is not a juridical fiction. It is the description of social reality within which economic and legal elements are in a relationship of interaction or interdependence, a fact which Marx and Engels in the above-quoted statements admit.

The Future of the Law

As to the future of the law, there are only very few statements in the writings of Marx and Engels. They were probably of the opinion that what they said about the state applied also to the law, which they considered to be a coercive order issued by the state. It is obviously the law that Engels has in mind when he, in the above-quoted statement, refers to an "order" within the bounds of which the class conflict is kept by the state as an organisation of the ruling class. Neither Marx nor Engels had a clear idea of the relationships between state and law. That state and law are essentially connected with one another, they probably considered as self-evident; but they were more interested in the state aspect of society than in its law aspect. It may be assumed that according to the Marx–Engels doctrine of the state, the law as a coercive order and specific instrument of the state exists only in a society divided into two classes, a dominant exploiting and a dominated exploited class. In one of his most frequently quoted statements, Marx says that in the phase of transition from the proletarian revolution to the establishment of perfect communism, that is to say, during the period of the dictatorship of the proletariat, there will be still a law, but that this law, in spite of its progress as compared with the bourgeois law, will still be "infected with a bourgeois barrier (*mit einer buergerlichen Schranke behaftet*)."[36] By this not very fortunate metaphor he expresses the idea that the law of the socialist state will still have a certain bourgeois character, because there will still be a ruling class and a ruled class and hence a class antagonism; and that only "in the highest phase of communist society," that is, that phase where the socialisation of the means of production is completely achieved and all class antagonisms radically abolished, "can the narrow horizon of bourgeois law be completely overcome, and only then will society inscribe on its banner: from each according to his capacities and to each according to his needs." This may be interpreted to mean that in this phase of the development of communism there will be no law, because the law is by its very nature bourgeois law, and that means class law. It must, however, be admitted that the statement is ambiguous and that it may also be interpreted to mean that even in the perfect communist society there will be law, but not bourgeois law, meaning a coercive order guaranteeing the exploitation of one class by another, presented by an ideological doctrine to be the realisation of justice. Communist society will have law, but no "legal superstructure" because no ideological superstructure at all (provided that by legal superstructure not the real law but an illusive, apologetic doctrine of the law) is to be understood. There will be no reason to pretend that communist law is just, because communist law will really be just, legal reality will not be self-contradictory, its external form will be in complete harmony with its internal essence, its ideal destination, the idea of justice. Hence law may be conceived of as a normative order, and such a concept of the law will have no ideological character in the derogatory sense of the term. Since even the perfectly just reality of communist society will have a consciousness—there will be science, although no religion—the reflection of the real law in the consciousness of communist society, that is to say, the description of the law as a normative order . . . will not be in conflict with its immanent idea, for the law will really be identical with justice. . . .

Marx does not say that the law during the transition period of the dictatorship of the proletariat will be bourgeois law. He says only that the law of the socialist state will be infected with an evil of bourgeois society: inequality. He seems not to exclude the possibility of a law that is not infected with this evil, a law of true equality. But he adds to the words "a law of inequality" the words "as all law." Here, as mentioned before, the words, "all law" may, in conformity with the preceding words, mean bourgeois law as well as the law of the socialist state; the law of the communist society guaranteeing true equality is not included, because supposed to be justice. In this connection Marx says:

> These defects [the inequality of the law] are inevitable in the first phase of communist society, when, after long travail, it first emerges from capitalist society. The law can never be on a higher level than the economic structure of society and the evolution of civilisation conditioned by this structure.

This could be interpreted to mean: in the second phase of communist society, the economic structure of which will represent the highest possible degree of civilisation, the law, too, will reach the highest possible level. However, the words "as all law" may also mean what they say: all law whatsoever, so that there is no law even where the principle of true equality prevails.

It is important to note that the same ambiguity which characterises the view presented by Marx in his *Gotha Programme* concerning the future of the law in communist society is implied in the statements he makes in the same essay concerning the future of the state. Criticising the Programme's postulate of a "free state" he says:

> It is not at all the purpose of the workers . . . to make the state "free." In the German Reich the "state" is almost as "free" as in Russia. Freedom consists in transforming the state, which is not an organ superior to society, into an organ subordinated to society.[37]

Marx does not say that freedom consists in eliminating the state from society, but that it consists in organising the state in a way that it will become an instrument of society. As pointed out, he formulates the question of the future of the state as follows: "What are the changes which the state will undergo in the communist society?" He does not ask: Under what conditions will the state disappear? And he objects to the Gotha Programme that it does not deal with the revolutionary dictatorship of the proletariat, nor "with the future state of the communist society."[38] This statement may be interpreted to mean that there will be in the future communist society a state, although not a state which dominates society but a state dominated by society, a state which is an instrument of this society;[39] just as there will be—according to the above presented interpretation of Marx' statements about the future of the law—a just law in this society.

This interpretation of Marx' statements concerning the future of the law may be summarised as follows: There will be in communist society no law of inequality, hence no ideological, *i.e.*, illusive, legal theory, and no law pretending to be just; consequently there will be no law as an "ideology" in the derogatory sense of the term, but a real law of true equality, a law which will be the realisation of justice. If this law is conceived of as norm or normative order, it is an ideology in a non-derogatory sense—in the same sense as science will be an ideology of communist society. This view is confirmed by some statements he made in his *Einleitung zu einer Kritik der politischen Oekonomie*. There he says that "there can be no society where there is no property in some form," although it would be a mistake to assume that it must be private or individual property. Since property presupposes a legal order, the statement that there is no society without some form of property implies the view that where there is society there is law, expressed in the famous formula of Roman jurisprudence *ubi societas ibi jus.* He also says "that every form of production creates its own legal relations," from which follows that also in a communist society there must be law. As a matter of fact, he asserts in this connection:

All production is appropriation of nature by the individual and through a definite form of society. In that sense it is a tautology to say that property (appropriation) is a condition of production. But it becomes ridiculous when from that one jumps at once to a definite form of property, *e.g.*, private property (which implies, besides, as a prerequisite the existence of an opposite form, *viz.*, absence of property). History points rather to common property (*e.g.*, among the Hindus, Slavs, ancient Celts, etc.) as the primitive form, which still plays an important part at a much later period as communal property.[40]

If the nationalisation of the means of production achieved during the transition period of the dictatorship of the proletariat is to be maintained within the society of perfect communism, if here the means of production must remain at the exclusive disposition of the organs of the community and private property in these goods excluded, in order to maintain true equality, that is to say, if collective property of the community in the means of production has to be an institution of the future society, then there must be a law guaranteeing this status. However, it must be admitted that the other interpretation, according to which in the perfectly communist society of the future there will be no state and consequently no law, and that means that the social order will have no coercive, even no normative character, is not only not excluded but in conformity with the anarchistic tendency prevailing in the writings of Marx and especially of Engels.

Notes

1. Cf. my *Sozialismus und Staat*, 2. Aufl., Leipzig, 1923, and my *The Political Theory of Bolshevism*, University of California Press, Berkeley and Los Angeles, 1948.
2. Friedrich Engels, *Der Ursprung der Familie, des Privateigentums und des Staates*. Internationale Bibliothek, Stuttgart, 1920, p. 177 *et seq.*
3. Engels, *Der Ursprung der Familie etc.*, p. 180.
4. Engels, *Herrn Eugen Dührings Umwälzung der Wissenschaft (AntiDühring)*, Stuttgart, 1919, p. 302.
5. Karl Marx, *Zur Kritik der politischen Oekonomie*, herausgeg. v. Karl Kautsky, Stuttgart, 1919, p. lv.
6. Friedrich Engels, *Die Entwicklung des Sozialismus von der Utopie zur Wissenschaft*, 6 Aufl., Berlin, 1911. p. 33.
7. Marx, *Zur Kritik der politischen Oekonomie*, p. xliii.
8. *Loc. cit.*, p. lv-lvi.

9. Marx, *Das Kapital* (Volksausgabe, herausgeg. von Kautsky, 8. Aufl. 1928), I, p. xivii.

10. Friedrich Engels, *Ludwig Feuerbach und der Ausgang der klassischen Philosophie*, Marxistische Bibliothek, Bd. 3, p. 51.

11. Engels, *Die Entwicklung des Sozialismuss von der Utopie etc.*, p. 31.

12. *Zur Kritik der politischen Oekonomie*, p. lv.

13. Karl Marx, "Zur Kritik der Hegelschen Rechtsphilosophie." *Karl Marx— Friedrich Engels. Historisch-kritische Gesamtausgabe*, erste Abteilung, Bd. I-1, Frankfurt, 1927, p. 607.

14. *Loc. cit.*, Bd. I-1, p. 608.

15. *Loc. cit.*, Bd. I-1, pp. 573-574.

16. *Loc. cit.*, Bd. V, p. 453.

17. *Loc. cit.*, Bd. I-1, p. 607.

18. *Loc cit.*, Bd. I-1, pp. 613-614.

19. Marx, *Zur Kritik der politischen Oekonomie*, p. lv.

20. On the basis of this identification of legal relationships with economic relationships, some Marxian writers define the law as an aggregate of economic relationships in opposition to the bourgeois definition of the law as a system of norms. . . .

21. Karl Marx, *Misère de la Philosophie*. Gesamtausgabe, erste Abteilung, VI, p. 160.

22. *Loc. cit.*, p. 163.

23. *Loc. cit.*, p. 198.

24. Marx, *Das Kapital*, I, p. 443.

25. Marx, *Zur Kritik der politischen Oekonomie*, p. xxxii *et seq.*

26. *Das Kapital*, I, p. 422.

27. *Loc. cit.*, p. 231.

28. *Gesamtausgabe*, Bd. V, p. 16; cf. also pp. 21, 49.

29. *Loc. cit.*, p. 398.

30. *Loc. cit.*, p. 307; cf. also p. 321.

31. *Loc. cit.*, p. 335.

32. *Loc cit.*, p. 342.

33. *Loc. cit.*, pp. 261, 294.

34. Marx-Engels, *Correspondence 1846-1895*. A Selection. New York, 1935, p. 475.

35. *Karl Marx von den Koelner Geschworenen*, Berlin, 1895, p. 15.

36. This statement is made in a letter Marx wrote on May 5, 1875, to Bracke, concerning the draft of the Gotha Programme of the German Social-Democratic Party. The letter is published: *Neue Zeit*, IX-1, 1890-1891, p. 561 *et seq.*

37. *Loc. cit.*, p. 572.

38. *Loc. cit.*, p. 573.

39. The German text corresponding to the words "with the future state of the communist society" runs as follows: "*mit dem zukuenftigen Staatswesen der kommunistischen Gesellschaft.*" The term *Staatswesen* means by and large the same as *Staat*, that is, state. But it is significant that Marx does not use the more precise term *Staat*.

40. Marx, *Zur Kritik der politischen Oekonomie*, p. xix.; cf. also *supra*, p. 7.

10

Law as a Weapon in Social Conflict

Austin T. Turk

Despite persistent challenges by proponents of a wide range of alternative theoretical and ideological perspectives, the most prevalent conception of law explicit or implicit in recent research on law and society is that articulated most notably in the works of Fuller (1964, 1971) and Selznick (1961, 1968, 1969) and prominent in such influential sourcebooks as Aubert (1969), Nader (1969), and Schwartz and Skolnick (1970). Law is characterized as essentially a means for settling or precluding disputes by (a) articulating the requirements of an idea of justice (expressed as prerequisites for sustained interaction and the viable organization of social life), and (b) restraining those whose actions are incompatible with such requirements. Accordingly, the presumptive aims of socio-legal research are to determine how legal concepts, institutions, and processes function in preventing, minimizing, or resolving conflicts; how such legal mechanisms emerge or are created; how they relate to complementary non-legal mechanisms; and how they can be made more effective.

Not to deny either that law often does contribute to conflict management or that the quest for a just and secure social order is honorable and necessary, the objectives in this paper are (1) to note certain fundamental limitations of what may be termed the moral function-

Excerpt from "Law as a Weapon in Social Conflict," *Social Problems* 23 (February 1976), pp. 276-291, by permission of the author and publisher, The Society for the Study of Social Problems.

alist conception of law; (2) to marshal arguments for a conception of law free of those limitations—i.e., the conception of law as a form or dimension of social power (as empirically more a partisan weapon in than a transcendent resolver of social conflicts); and (3) to formulate a set of basic empirical propositions about law and social conflict to which the power conception of law directs socio-legal research.

Law as Conflict Management

To *define* law as a means of conflict management is to leave theory and research on law and society without an analytical framework independent of particular ethical and theoretical preferences and aversions. While it may facilitate critiques of totalitarian or bureau-pathic decisions and actions taken "in the name of law," such a definition appears at the same time to impede the development of an understanding of law in which evidence of its regulatory functions is integrated with evidence of its disruptive and exploitive uses and effects. Merely condemning the seamier side of law as perversions or departures from "the rule of law," and attributing them to human fallibility or wickedness, encourages neglect of the possible systemic linkages between the "good" and "bad" features of law as it is empiri-cally observed. Moreover, insofar as the moral functionalist concep-tion of law has directly or by default encouraged such neglect, it has left socio-legal research vulnerable to charges of bias favoring certain culture-specific ideas and institutions, and helped to provoke the radical counter-assertion that exploitation and disruption constitute the defining reality of law while regulation is only illusion and suppression. . . .

A related difficulty with the moral functionalist conception of law is that *legal* means of conflict management tend to be equated with *peaceful* ones; and there is a strong inclination to assume that con-sensual, non-coercive methods are the only really effective ways of preventing or managing conflicts. The difficulties with such assump-tions are exemplified in Barkun's (1968) volume appropriately en-titled *Law Without Sanctions*. . . .

At a more general theoretical level, the moral functionalist concep-tion of law impedes efforts to approach the scientific ideal of un-biased inquiry by encouraging investigators to define their research problems in terms of theoretical models derived from "natural law" and/or "functional-systems" assumptions. First, the bias introduced by natural law philosophy, even though secularized (cf. Selznick, 1961), leaves researchers unable to deal convincingly (i.e., in strictly naturalistic and empirically demonstrable propositions) with the observation or view that any idea of justice is founded ultimately upon faith, not upon empirical criteria. . . . Second, many crucial methodological and theoretical issues are not resolved but evaded to the extent that research begins with, instead of testing, the assumptions (a) that legal phenomena constitute a system, (b) that the system-referent is empirically obvious, or at least readily determined, and (c) that the system embodies the meritocratic or egalitarian prerequisities for social welfare. . . .

To summarize briefly, the major limitations of the moral functionalist conception of law for the purposes of socio-legal research are that it (1) introduces cultural bias into research by defining away the disruptive and exploitive aspects of law, (2) tends to equate legal with consensual methods or processes of conflict management, which are presumed to be more effective than coercive means, and (3) encourages research in which natural law and/or functional-systems assumptions are taken for granted. If research on law and society is to be even relatively unbiased by culturally, ethically, methodologically, and politically partisan assumptions, a more neutral and empirically-grounded conception of law is needed. The remainder of this paper is devoted to an attempt to develop such a conception.

Law as Power

It must be granted that people may use the language of norms and generally, more or less consciously, accept their constructions as binding in the absence of a centralized enforcement agency, or indeed of any reliable means of forcing conformity. However, as has already been observed, it is equally clear that they may come to believe that their interests are better served by violating the normative expectations of others. In this connection, the increasingly formal articulation of such expectations and the recognition or invention of the right to seek or attempt their enforcement . . . implies the increasing inability of people to get along with one another solely on the basis of tacit or consensual understandings. Furthermore, the persistence and growth of law as a cultural (symbolic, perceptual) and social (interactional, relational) reality is at least a kind of evidence that people have not yet found that they can do without such formalization, whether by a return to primitivism or by attaining some new consensual plateau. The effort to develop an adequate conception of law must, therefore, begin by recognizing the centrality of diversity and conflict in social life wherever law—provisionally understood as the process of formally articulating normative expectations— is discernible.

Given that law is intimately linked with social diversity and conflict, the most parsimonious explanation of the linkage seems to be that people find they cannot trust strangers. As the scale and complexity of social relatedness increase, so does the diversity of human experiences. The more diverse the experiences people have had, the more diverse their perceptions and evaluations of behavioral and relational alternatives may be. The greater the diversity of perceptions and evaluations, the greater may be the variability in what is perceived as justice in the specific terms of everyday life. (The implied distinction is between "norms in action" versus whatever similarities might be found in terms either of a general belief in justice as an abstract value, or of verbal responses to hypothetical questioning regarding the substantive meanings and relative importance of various normative statements or labels.) Aware that others' ideas of justice may vary from their own, people try—in accord with their own ideas and interests as they understand them—to maintain or gain control of, or to contest or evade, the processes by which normative expectations come to be formally articulated and enforced across, rather than only within, the boundaries of culturally homogeneous groups (whether the salient boundaries be those of families, clans, tribes, nations, or other groupings).

The empirical reality of law—apparently well understood in practice if not in theory—seems, then, to be that it is a set of resources for which people contend and with which they are better able to promote their own ideas and interests against others, given the necessity of working out and preserving accommodative relationships with strangers. To say that people seek to gain and use resources to secure their own ideas and interests is, of course, to say that they seek to have and exercise *power*. While the meaning of power is far from settled, a convenient starting point is to view power as the control of resources, and the exercise of power as their mobilization in an effort to increase the probability of acceptable resolutions of actual or potential conflicts. Although it helps to recognize that "law is power," a more specific conceptualization of what *kinds* of resource control are possible is necessary if we are to arrive at a useful understanding of what the general proposition means. I see five kinds of resource control, all represented in the cultural and social structural reality of law. These are (1) control of the means of direct physical violence, i.e., *war* or *police* power; (2) control of the production, allocation, and/or use of material resources, i.e., *economic* power; (3) control of decision-making processes, i.e., *political* power; (4) control of definitions of and access to knowledge, beliefs, values, i.e., *ideological* power; and (5) control of human attention and living-time, i.e., *diversionary* power.

1. Having the law on one's side in a conflict implies that one can rightfully use or call upon others (allies, champions, or the authorities claiming jurisdiction over the area, people, or matters involved) to use violence to support one's claims against others. Modern polities are characterized by the presence and availability of control agencies specializing in the accretion, organization, and use of the means of violence, and asserting the principle that violence is—excepting more and more narrowly defined emergency situations—a resource reserved for official use only. Decisions by authorities, including decisions regarding the respective claims of disputing parties, are accompanied by the implied threat of physical coercion should any of the affected parties refuse to act in accord with such decisions.

2. People's life chances are affected just as decisively by how much their economic power is enhanced or eroded by law. The invention and elaboration of property and tax laws, in particular, reflect and help implement decisions on (1) what kinds of activities, products, and people should be rewarded more and what kinds less, and (2) how great should be the range between maximum and minimum rewards. "Radicals" seek modifications of law so as to change the criteria for reward, and very often also to reduce the range of rewards; "liberals" seek modifications so as to insure at least a "decent" minimum in the range of rewards, and may accept—if they do not seek—some reduction in the range; "conservatives" resist modification, but may accept some "decent minimum." Though orderly (usually meaning limited and gradual) economic changes can be facilitated by law, economic decisions once articulated in and supported by law become postulates which further elaborations and even modifications of the law must satisfy. Radical economic changes, therefore, become increasingly difficult to effect by legal means because they require not legal reasoning to satisfy the postulates of a body of law, but rather a new set of postulates and thus a new body of law.

3. The formulae and procedures of legal decision-making are integral to the workings of politically organized societies. Organizational decisions are in significant ways influenced by and expressed through legal decisions. Most important, the law as culture and as social structure provides the rubric for articulating, interpreting, and implementing organizational norms and decisions. As a substantive and procedural model and as an ultimate support for institutional normative structures, the law contributes—as Selznick (1969) and many others have demonstrated—to private as well as public social ordering, and provides some of the weightiest criteria for assessing proposed changes and resolving internal as well as inter-organizational conflicts. While non-legal factors clearly affect political struggle

in general and organizational decision-making in particular, the law—as the most authoritative record of events and as the definitive model, criterion, and arbiter of rightness—is itself a political resource of major importance.

4. Legal concepts and thought-ways develop in the course of pragmatic efforts by men to comprehend problems of social interaction so as to manage them—including the problematics dominating the lives of other people. Though not in this regard different from other products of such efforts, law as culture has an especially strong impact upon the frames of reference people use to give meaning to their situations. Those definitions of the real, the true, and the worthy given legal expression or approval are thereby given the support of what is not only one of the most prestigious of cultural structures, but also that structure most directly supported by the apparatus of political control. The reality or value of alternative conceptions can be denied either by simply denying recognition in law, or else more forcefully by explicitly rejecting them in ways ranging from the most extreme forms of suppression to the most subtle forms of rejection in practice conjoined with verbal acceptance or toleration. Censorship by omission or commission is nonetheless censorship. Yet, the greatest importance of law as an ideological resource probably lies not in the facts of deliberate or inadvertent intervention on behalf of some perceptual alternatives versus others, but in the fact that legalism is the cultural bedrock of political order. The very concept of legality is designed to promote adherence to the ground rules of conventional politics . . . which amount to agreement among contending parties on the supreme value of their common membership in a polity which must be preserved.

5. Human attention and living-time are finite resources—a trite but profoundly consequential observation. Insofar as the rhetoric and the real workings of law occupy men's attention and time to the exclusion of other phenomena—perhaps of greater import for the probability and quality of life—the law exerts diversionary power. As entrepreneurs of the news, publishing, advertising, and entertainment industries have long known, at least the more reassuring, titillating, or lurid aspects of law can in the name of "human interest" and "information" be presented to capture and hold the public's attention. Nor have the obviously close links between diversionary and ideological power been neglected. Preoccupation with the law, especially in its more attractive and innocuous aspects, not only diverts attention from potentially more dangerous concerns (from the perspective of authorities, *de facto* oncluding loyal oppositions) but also reinforces the sense of law as an overwhelming, scarcely challengeable reality and criterion of reality.

The conception of law as a set of resources, as power, is method-ologically superior to the conception of law as conflict regulator in that the relationship between law and conflict is not assumed, but left open for investigation, and the distinction between legal and non-legal phenomena is grounded in empirical observations rather than normative assumptions. Instead of asking *how* law regulates conflict, the investigator   is encouraged to ask *whether* law regulates or generates conflict, or in what ways and in what degree the use of legal power does both. Instead of assuming that legal and non-legal actions and relations are somehow differentiated by criteria of moral legitimacy or functional necessity, the investigator asks whether and how the invocation of such criteria and the introduction of the dis-tinction itself exemplify the control and mobilization of ideological and diversionary resources. Freed from arbitrary ideological and theoretical constraints, the investigator directly confronts the empir-ical realities that legal power can be used in ways inconsistent as well as consistent with normative criteria of legality, that the empirical relevance of such criteria is decided by the actions rather than the claims of those who wield legal power, and that the law—since it is necessarily promulgated, interpreted, implemented, or enforced by people with spedific social and cultural involvements—can never really be neutral vis-à-vis social conflicts.

A particular advantage of the power conception of law is that it facilitates analysis of the *processes* (as distinct from particular struc-tures) by which normative expectations are given "cross-group" as well as "intra-group" significance—i.e., how they become formally binding upon people who themselves have neither generated such norms nor been socialized as children to accept them. At the most general analytical level, the processes are those—stigmatization and other forms of manipulation—any group uses to achieve some behavioral and relational coherence despite the varying idiosyncracies of its members. Nonetheless, as one's attention shifts from the most ephemeral and least differentiated forms of group life to more dur-able and complex social entities, the processes come more sharply into focus as the distinction between legal and nonlegal emerges and acquires increasing social and cultural reality. The power conception of law suggests analysis of these processes in the specific empirical terms of how people actually deal with one another, regardless of any conventional understandings or rationales about the existence and significance of particular legal phenomena. Thus, socio-legal research is cast not in terms of the assumed concreteness or meaning-fulness of the legal-nonlegal distinction, but in terms of the human actions creating the distinction, giving it empirical substance, and altering or erasing it.

Finally, the power conception of law gives socio-legal research a distinctive focus, related to but not confused with the general concerns of the social sciences with social order, conflict, and change. Instead of losing the legal-nonlegal distinction in the quest for knowledge useful in conflict management (as in Barkun's case), the distinction itself becomes in two ways the basis for defining research problems. First, the problematic status of the distinction implies the need for historical and anthropological studies to determine the specific conditions where it is introduced (and perhaps to suggest the conditions where it may be transcended) in social life. Second, as the core task of socio-legal research is taken to be that of developing a predictively useful understanding of the control and mobilization of legal resources, the availability of such resources is necessarily presupposed. That is, scientifically meaningful research questions about law and society become possible only when the concept of law is empirically grounded by the differentiation of legal from other cultural and social phenomena in one or more of the following ways: (1) verbal articulation of a set, in some degree a system, of explicit norms; (2) establishment of procedures for making, interpreting, implementing, and changing normative decisions; (3) occupational specialization in knowing the substantive law and in using the established procedures; (4) institution of explicit provisions for the enforcement of substantive and procedural norms, by actual or threatened deprivations; and (5) associated with any or all of the other ways, the display of symbolic trappings designed to emphasize the reality, rightness, and might of law.[1] Rather than some kind of essence, property, or function to be sought in an apparently unlimited variety of cultural and social configuration, "law" thus becomes an empirically specifiable set of objects of scientific attention.

In sum, in the power conception of law students of law and society are offered a methodologically tenable definition of the scope of their inquiry that includes it within the social scientific enterprise without reifying, mystifying, or obscuring the legal-nonlegal distinction. Given then the availability and amorality of legal power, the formulation and testing of propositions about the exercise of such power become central concerns for the scientific study of law as it is, as distinguished from doctrinal or applied research on behalf of law as someone believes it should or must be.[2] Because of the availability of so much work on law as a regulator and the relative paucity of work on law as a source and means of conflict, there is a particular need for propositions about ways in which law may generate or sharpen social conflicts. Accordingly, an effort has been made to develop several propositions indicating what seem to be the major ways law promotes or facilitates conflict. To the extent that these and related propositions are sustained and elaborated with greater precision in further research, they are expected to constitute the basis for a theory of law able to explain the conditions when and how conflict management may be accomplished by the control and mobilization of legal resources—i.e., a theory able to deal with conflict management as a problematic outcome instead of a defining characteristic of law as a social and cultural phenomenon.

Propositions: Law and Social Conflict

1. The availability of legal resources is in itself an impetus to social conflict, because conflicting or potentially conflicting parties cannot risk the possible costs of not having the law—or at least some law—on their side. When legal resources are not available or are negligible, parties are forced or able to rely upon nonlegal power to deal with the problematics of social interaction; law is irrelevant except perhaps in the loose sense of a generally recognized right of self-help for aggrieved parties able to assert. . . . As law becomes available, it becomes relevant as a contingency which must be met. It then becomes necessary to act so as to gain or increase control of legal resources, if only to neutralize them as weaponry an opponent might employ. The point is illustrated in the long effort by American southern whites to use the "white primary" and other ostensibly legal devices . . . supplemented by extralegal and illegal ones, to prevent blacks from using resources formally granted them by emancipation and subsequent legal enactments and decisions.

2. Given pressure to contend for control of legal resources, differential non-legal power can be expected to result at least initially in corresponding differences in legal power. The party with greater legal as well as non-legal power may then be able to increase its edge over weaker parties, even to the extreme of excluding the weaker altogether from access to the legal arena, cutting him off from even the opportunity to advance his claims and defend his interests "legally." For instance, since the formation of the inegalitarian South African nation in 1910, the weaker nonwhites have had their legal position steadily eroded, losing between 1936 and 1955 even voting rights guaranteed by the "entrenched clauses" of the South Africa Act (May, 1955: 47–78; see also Sachs, 1973: 143–145 and *passim*)— South Africa's constitution until it was superseded by the Republic of South Africa Constitution Act, 1961.

3. Legal power provides both the opportunity and the means to accomplish the effective denial of the reality of conflicts by making

it impossible or inordinately difficult for them to be articulated and managed—as amply demonstrated in the long and stubborn effort to deny legal recognition and support for the effective unionization of agricultural laborers (McWilliams, 1942; Tangri, 1967; Galarza, 1970).

However, the persistent recurrence of struggles against economic, racial, and other forms of domination and exploitation make it clear that issues which cannot be couched in the language of law, or will not be accepted as actionable or justiciable, eventually have to be fought out in non-legal arenae—where resolutions may be achieved, but often at greater cost and with less durability. It is, of course, true that the lack of appropriate legal mechanisms for managing some issues may result from unintended as well as intended actions. Nonetheless, even though the denial of access to law may be explicable in objective terms "objective" denial appears to be just as real in its consequences as "subjective."

4. Where power differences are rather less extreme, the availability of legal resources may encourage litigiousness—a word indicative of the fact that the presence of law encourages its use by parties hoping to improve their positions by methods relatively less dangerous or costly than non-legal power struggles, especially with formidable opponents. Parties confronting more powerful opponents may be encouraged to hope that by threatened or actual recourse to law they will be able to reduce, eliminate, or reverse initial power differences, or merely to extract some concession. For example, Nonet (1969: 81-83, 133-137) concluded that the New Deal turned law into an ally rather than an enemy of America trade unionism, so that the unions were encouraged to pursue a policy of self-help through legal advocacy instead of relying upon administrative procedures for handling workmen's compensation claims. On the other hand, stronger parties moving against weaker ones may find it advantageous to cloak their moves with legitimacy, especially to minimize the chance of third-party intervention on behalf of the underdog—as in the use of antitrust, conspiracy, right-to-work, and other laws to impede the development of effective labor unions (Blumrosen, 1962; Nonet, 1969: 81-83).

5. Apart from encouraging litigiousness, the availability of legal facilities decreases the pressure upon conflicting parties to resolve disputes in terms of the non-legal resources they can mobilize. Informal and private settlements, or at least accommodations to non-legal power differences (e.g., race relations "etiquette") seems less likely where the parties have the option or hope of legal recourse. Similarly, where an older legal system is giving way to a newer one, as in the Northern Rhodesian (Zambian) copperbelt, parties without recourse in the older system (e.g., young men protesting against

the power of their wife's kin to intervene in martial and familial affairs) may be encouraged to appeal "to norms irreconcilably opposed to those of the traditional tribal system" (Epstein, 1958: 222).

6. Articulation in law of social categories, boundaries, and roles—with their associated rights and obligations—can sharpen old conflicts and produce new ones. Heightened awareness of the problematics of social interaction and relatedness can decrease the chances of resolving or avoiding conflicts, because "bringing things out into the open" frequently hardens existing boundaries, cleavages, and inequities (whether objectively or perceptually "real") by making it less easy to ignore, tacitly live with, or quietly and informally erase or change them. Rather than a transformation of conflict into a form more amenable to a reasonable resolution, legalization of a conflict can amount to an escalation that makes genuine settlement more difficult. Recognition of such possibilities has often been used for resisting the use of law as an instrument of social change—e.g., the views of some southern moderates, as well as conservatives, in the 1950's regarding the probable impact of the U.S. Supreme Court's desegregation decisions (Tumin and Rotberg, 1957).

7. Legal procedural norms are often used to exclude or distort information essential to an adequate comprehension of empirical problems, and thus can impede or prevent conflict resolution. In particular, legal distinctions between admissible and inadmissible evidence tend to work against consideration of perceptual, or subjective factors—those perhaps not objectively important or recognizable by legal criteria but extremely important in terms of what is significant to some or all of the involved parties. European, especially Anglo-American, legal systems have frequently been critically contrasted with non-European systems (e.g., Epstein, 1958, 198–223; Gibbs, 1963; several of the selections in Nader, 1969) in which there are few if any restrictions upon what may be considered in determining the contextual significance of facts. These non-European systems emphasize the qualitative more than the formal aspects of what is seen as a continuing rather than an episodic relationship between the disputing parties. Similarly, though in a different vein, "bourgeois legalism" has been rejected by Marxists in favor of "socialist legality," where the emphasis is asserted to be (and in non-political cases normally is) upon the education of disputants and offenders to social awareness and responsibility (Berman, 1966: 277–384).

8. Legal formulae and processes tend to emphasize the limitation and cessation of overt conflict behavior, discouraging not only all-out battles of principle but even the recognition that at least some social conflicts are zero-sum, not variable-sum (e.g. czars vs. communists, white racists vs. black revolutionaries). To a considerable extent, law

is oriented to regulating the *symptoms* of conflict without getting at the more intractible problems of removing the *sources* of conflict. However tactical concern with symptoms may sometimes be dictated by a strategic concern to minimize political or other costs of dealing with those sources. Consider the frequently noted judicial preference, supported by and expressed in such operating principles as *stare decisis* and *certiorari*, for carefully delimited case-specific issues rather than open confrontations over the political and economic premises of "the given order." Nonetheless, insofar as the legalization of conflicts does no more than limit the means of conflict and/or obfuscate the real issues, as in zero-sum struggles, some or all of the conflicting parties may come to view legalization as simply another device for out-positioning an opponent or for gaining time to mobilize or regroup one's non-legal forces—an attitude characteristic of both revolutionaries and counter-revolutionary police agents.

9. The tactics required to accomplish a legal settlement can conflict with those required to accomplish a genuine settlement. Where communication between disputants may be essential for them to become aware of common interests with priority over those at issue, communication may be precluded by the risk of disclosing injurious facts, violating rules against collusion, or otherwise weakening or contaminating the case at hand. The terminology and style of public legal conflict—as in verbal exchanges in legislative and judicial proceedings—may emphasize instead of correcting the affective and cognitive biases associated with conflict. Obtaining formal, open concessions from opponents in the course of legal struggle can make it more difficult for them to back down or accept defeat, and can reduce the chances of building a fund of mutual trust with them as a way of making further conflicts more amenable to resolution. Such considerations appear to explain the reluctance of businessmen to conduct their transactions in strictly legalistic terms (Macaulay, 1963), as well as the opposition of many academics to the more explicit legalization of faculty–student relationships.

10. Legal decisions may prematurely signal the end of conflicts without actually resolving them. The processes of legal hearing, trial, and appeal often amount to rituals of dispute-settlement resulting in only illusory resolutions of conflicts, i.e., formal decisions that seem to settle disputes but do not do so on terms acceptable or even tolerable to the losers (and sometimes also the winners). Not only may dissatisfied parties be forced to seek redress by non-legal means in such present conflicts but the pretense of conflict resolution which they have experienced as the reality of law in action may make them far less willing to enter the legal arena in future conflicts. To the ex-

tent that law produces illusory instead of real conflict resolutions, it not only aggravates existing conflicts but also makes future conflicts more likely, and likely to be worse. Racial conflicts, for instance, have clearly not been resolved in South Africa by the legalization of a policy of racial separation—to be gradually accomplished during a "transitional" period of *dejure* white domination (Sachs, 1973), or in North America by the legalization of a policy of racial integration— to be gradually accomplished during a "transitional" period of over- coming *de facto* white domination "with all deliberate speed." . . .

11. Insofar as legal culture is incongruent with the social-behavioral realities of legal power as exercised by authorities, the law itself pro- motes cynicism, evasion, and defiance with respect to normative ex- pectations and decisions—even among its representatives and practitioners (on lawyers, see Blumberg, 1967; on police, see Galliher, 1971). The law provides authorities with the cloak of claimed impar- tiality, a difficult claim impossible to live up to always and entirely. Apart from predispositions arising from their social origins, legal offi- cials develop at least a partiality on behalf of their own organizational and career interests . . . and routines for categorizing and handling cases with as little effort and risk as possible. . . .

Moreover, whether or not authorities try to be unbiased, the intent of the law can never be identical with the effect of the law as experi- enced. Even the most "understandable" differences between inter- pretation and interpretation, interpretation and action, or action and action, may not be "understandable" to affected parties who believe themselves—probably correctly—to be disadvantaged by the outcome. Credit, tenancy, welfare, and other laws affecting economic oppor- tunities, privileges, and liabilities have often been shown to work sys- tematically against the poor (Caplovitz, 1963; Carlin, Howard, and Messinger, 1966; tenBroek, 1966).

The crucial point is that bias is not just a matter of intention or even objective behavior, much less a matter only of due process under formal rules. Bias is also—and for the tasks of conflict regula- tion most important—a matter of perception and inference. Law *believed* to be biased may be just as ineffective, or worse, as law that *is* biased.

12. Legal changes that precipitate or facilitate non-legal social and cultural changes inevitably—barring the improbable case of unanimity on the meaning and desirability of the changes—sharpen and produce conflicts. As new law supersedes old, older ideas and interests may be shunted aside or demoted to lower priority ratings—as will be those people whose identifications and commitments are defined in terms of those ideas and interests. Nowhere is the fact of law as a party with its own interests to safeguard and enhance, potentially in con-

flict with others, more inescapable to people than when legal power serves to override, subvert, or simply reject their values and ways. Regardless of the possible long-run impact of legally promoted changes, the short-run impact will certainly be some contribution to increasing and exacerbating conflicts—most especially conflicts between legal authorities and at least some of those over whom authority is claimed. The degree of conflict resulting from legal changes will, of course, vary with the type of innovation, the social characteristics of those affected, and other factors . . . from the relatively mild conflicts of conventional politics to the extreme conflicts resulting from legal intrusions into matters of sacred belief and practice—as in the Bolshevik attempt of the 1920's to impose sexual equality upon the largely Moslem peoples of Soviet Central Asia (Massell, 1968).

Conclusion

As many others have said in various ways, those engaged in socio-legal research must constantly question the assumptions so easily received from jurisprudence if the social science of law is to be more than a servant of established power, albeit a servant with critical intelligence. Socio-legal inquiry that assumes the goodness or badness of any set of cultural and social phenomena cannot be expected to produce valid and reliable knowledge of the full range of problematic relationships within that set and between that set and others. It had been argued in this paper that the most prevalent conception of law orienting contemporary socio-legal research—the "moral functionalist" conception of law as in essence a means of conflict regulation—is in this and other respects demonstrably inadequate for the purposes of scientific research, however useful it may be for other purposes. A far more adequate alternative, it has been further argued, is the power conception of law, which recognizes in law a set of resources whose control and mobilization can in many ways—as indicated in a series of propositional statements—lead toward instead of away from conflicts. While the specifics undoubtedly need extension, elaboration, and qualification, the formulation offered here will have served its purpose if it stimulates socio-legal theorists and researchers to be more alert to the often subtle realities of power and conflict. In any case, there should be no quarrel over the fact that law may indeed contribute to conflict management—not least by its role in creating, sustaining, denying, and changing the perceptions and understandings by which people live.

References

Aubert, Vilhelm (1969). (ed.) *Sociology of Law.* Baltimore: Penguin Books.

Barkun, Michael (1968). *Law Without Sanctions.* New Haven: Yale University Press.

Baxi, Upendra (1974). "Comment—Durkheim and legal evolution: some problems of disproof." *Law and Society Review* 8(Summer):645-651.

Berman, Harold J. (1966). *Justice in the U.S.S.R.: An Interpretation of Soviet Law.* Cambridge: Harvard University Press.

Blumberg, Abraham S. (1967). "The practice of law as a confidence game: organizational cooptation of a profession." *Law and Society Review* 1(June): 15-39.

Blumrosen, Alfred W. (1962). "Legal process and labor law: some observations on the relation between law and sociology." Pp. 185-225 in William M. Evan (ed.), *Law and Sociology.* New York: Free Press.

Caplovitz, David (1963). *The Poor Pay More.* New York: Free Press.

Carlin, Jerome E., Jan Howard, and Sheldon L. Messinger (1966). "Civil justice and the poor: issues for sociological research." *Law and Society Review* 1 (November): 9-89.

Epstein, A. L. (1958). *Politics in an Urban African Community.* Manchester: Manchester University Press.

Fuller, Lon L. (1964). *The Morality of Law.* New Haven: Yale University Press.

—— (1971). "Human interaction and the law." Pp. 171-217 in Robert P. Wolff (ed.), *The Rule of Law.* New York: Simon and Schuster.

Galarza, Ernesto (1970). *Spiders in the House and Workers in the Field.* South Bend, Ind.: University of Notre Dame Press.

Galliher, John F. (1971). "Explanations of police behavior: a critical review and analysis." *Sociological Quarterly* 12(Summer): 308-318.

Gibbs, James L., Jr. (1963). "The Kpelle Moot: a therapeutic model for the informal settlement of disputes." *Africa* 33: 1-11.

Hall, Jerome (1963). *Comparative Law and Social Theory.* Baton Rouge: Louisiana State University Press.

Macaulay, Stewart (1963). "Non-contractual relations in business: a preliminary study." American Sociological Review 28(February): 55-67.

Massell, Gregory J. (1968). "Law as an instrument of revolutionary change in a traditional milieu: the case of Soviet Central Asia." *Law and Society Review* 2(February): 179-228.

May, Henry J. (1955). *The South African Constitution.* Third Edition. Cape Town: Juta.

McWilliams, Carey (1942). *Ill Fares the Land: Migrants and Migratory Labor in the United States.* Boston: Little, Brown.

Nader, Laura (ed.) (1969). *Law in Culture and Society.* Chicago: Aldine.

Nonet, Philippe (1969). *Administrative Justice: Advocacy and Change in a Government Agency.* New York: Russell Sage Foundation.

Sachs, Albie (1973). *Justice in South Africa.* Berkeley: University of California Press.

Schermerhorn, Richard A. (1961). *Society and Power.* New York: Random House.

Schwartz, Richard D. (1974). "Legal evolution and the Durkheim hypothesis: a reply to Professor Baxi." *Law and Society Review* 8(Summer): 653–668.

Schwartz, Richard D. and James C. Miller (1964). "Legal evolution and societal complexity." *American Journal of Sociology* 70 (September): 159–169.

Schwartz, Richard D, and Jerome H. Skolnick (eds.) (1970). *Society and the Legal Order.* New York: Basic Books.

Selznick, Philip (1961). "Sociology and natural law." *Natural Law Forum* 6: 84–108.

—— (1968). "The sociology of law." Pp. 50–59 in David L. Sills (ed.), *International Encyclopedia of the Social Sciences,* vol. 9. New York: Macmillan, Free Press.

—— (1969). *Law, Society, and Industrial Justice.* New York: Russell Sage Foundation.

Tangri, Beverly S. (1967). *Federal Legislation as an Expression of United States Public Policy Toward Agricultural Labor, 1914–1954.* Unpublished Ph.D. dissertation, University of California.

tenBroek, Jacobus (ed.) (1966). *The Law of the Poor.* San Francisco: Chandler.

Tumin, Melvin M. and Robert Rotberg (1957). "Leaders, the led, and the law: a case study in social change." *Public Opinion Quarterly* 21(Fall): 355–370.

Turk, Austin T. (1969). *Criminality and Legal Order.* Chicago: Rand McNally.

—— (1972). *Legal Sanctioning and Social Control.* Washington D.C.: Supt. of Docs., U.S. Government Printing Office, DHEW Pub. No. (HSM) 72–9130.

Wirt, Frederick M. (1970). *Politics of Southern Equality: Law and Social Change in a Mississippi County.* Chicago: Aldine.

Wolff, Robert P. (ed.) (1971). *The Rule of Law.* New York: Simon and Schuster.

Notes

1. The extent to which sequential or functional relationships may be found among these indicants of the five kinds or dimensions of legal power is an empirical question. Though not directly pertinent, the mediation-courts-punishment-police-counsel cumulative scale order that seems to be emerging from the work of Schwartz and others (Schwartz and Miller, 1964; Wimberley, 1973; Baxi, 1974; Schwartz, 1974) suggests that some such relationships may well exist.

2. While the distinction is essentially that proposed by Jerome Hall (1963: 42) between "normative" or "humanistic legal sociology" (which he approves) and "scientific legal sociology" or "legal science" (which he disapproves), there is no compelling reason to oppose these two kinds of inquiry to each other. The point is merely that for those whose primary aim is to develop scientific knowledge of law as a social and cultural phenomenon an appropriately objective conception of law is essential. For those with other primary objectives, the moral functionalist or some other "committed" conception may well be more useful.

11

Legal Socialization

June Louin Tapp and Felice J. Levine

How do individuals reason relative to their legal worlds? What are their conceptions of rules and roles? What capacities do they demonstrate for considering notions of law, justice, obligation, and rights? Such questions are basic to understanding people's relationships to law.

This article presents a social-psychological, developmental model designed to describe and analyze the legal reasoning of the individual. In the not too distant past, such an exercise might have been regarded as purely speculative. But it is no longer necessary to infer the characteristics of individual legal development, the dynamics of legality, and the bases for an ethical utilization or mobilization of law from casual conversation or conceptual debate. Social scientific studies have begun to provide the requisite data for informed analysis.

Our theory of legal socialization and development posits three distinct levels of legal reasoning: preconventional, conventional, and postconventional. Legal reasoning is essentially a cognitive process that defines a person's basic problem-solving strategies and conceptual framework relative to law and legal systems. There is substantial empirical evidence that stable, consistent reasoning patterns underlie individuals' perspectives toward law. We aim to specify and trace the

Excerpt from "Legal Socialization: Strategies for an Ethical Legality," *Stanford Law Review* 27 (1974), pp. 1–72. Copyright © 1974–75 by the Board of Trustees of the Leland Stanford Junior University. Reprinted by permission.

development of these structuring patterns and indicate how they guide human legal decisionmaking. . . .

Most citizens acquire their notions of rules, laws, and obedience, and develop strategies for utilizing the law through, an interaction between natural cognitive structures and a host of "legal" environments such as the home, school, friendship circle, or court. Since these variables generally influence all social development, it is important to separate legal from political and moral socialization. While there is clearly some overlap, there are differences in emphasis among the three areas in terms of socializing contexts (jury versus political caucus), indicators of authority (judge versus mayor), and ethical concerns (justice versus party loyalty). The term "legal socialization" refers to the development of values, attitudes, and behaviors toward law. It focuses on the individual's standards for making sociolegal judgments and for resolving conflicts, pressing claims, and settling disputes. Emphasizing both "positive" and "negative" aspects of learning about the institution of law specifically and all authoritative rule-systems generally, legal socialization evidences the influence of social variables that can facilitate or retard the development of legal reasoning capacities.

Optimally, legal socialization works to clarify and elaborate reciprocal role orientations and rights expectations in relation to law, not to institutionalize blind obedience or preach the goodness of specific rules. The goal is to stimulate the efficient, accommodative, and principled legal development of both the individual and systems of law. The essence of this goal is captured in Philip Selznick's observation that, "[i]n its richest connotation, legality evokes the Greek view of a social order founded in reason, whose constitutive principle is justice."[1] Thus, the problem for legal socializers is to ensure that they encourage expression and independence, rather than repression and dependence, so that ultimately the individual can develop comprehensive reasoning principles, well suited to analyzing complex problems and integrating diverse inputs.

The Law as Socializing Agent

The growth of the law as a socializing instrument. The burgeoning trend of legal activity in contemporary societies, evidenced by a greater use of legal resources and solutions, underscores the increased impact of law. It also indicates the necessity for reinterpretation of the law's educative or socializing function. This pattern is apparent not only in developed nations in the East and West, but in "Third World" settings as well. The respective legal and psychological works of Berman[2] and Bronfenbrenner,[3] for example, on the United States and the Soviet Union, describe the allocation of "social" education functions to other than customary socializing agents. While traditionally the home and the school have been identified as the predominant socializers of ethical values and of a sense of competence, increasingly the law has become a primary educative institution. . . .

Congruence with psychological potential. Since the development of mature, ethical legal judgments is affected substantially by the nature of "legal" environments, we must consider whether the law has a socializing framework that is both philosophically and psychologically compatible. Laws that are incompatible with psychological capacities or ethical values create confusion regarding the meanings of compliance and deviance, rights and responsibilities, obligation and loyalty. Harold Berman put the issue succinctly: "The official law of the state, with its authoritative technical language and its professional practitioners, cannot do violence to the unofficial law-consciousness of the people without creating serious tensions in society."[4] Ultimately, the law's role and efficacy will be measured by its success in moving humankind to attitudes and acts of justice. If legal rules are incongruent with the "law-consciousness" of the people, modes of deviance, dissent, and distrust will prevail,[5] and the probability of stimulating a higher-order sense of legality in both individuals and institutions will be substantially reduced. . . .

Levels of Legal Development

Our legal levels theory reflects a confluence of cognitive-developmental psychology and jurisprudence. . . .

The cognitive-structural-stage theories of moral development and thought introduced by Jean Piaget[6] and advanced by Lawrence Kohlberg[7] have substantially influenced our levels model of legal reasoning and ethical legality. Piaget hypothesizes the centrality of intellectual development in the acquisition of moral values as well as in the acquisition of linguistic or mathematical ideas. In exploring the domain of children's morality, Piaget stresses the interaction of "natural" and "social" influences on emergent concepts of rules and justice. Guided by a stage and structure approach to human reasoning, Piaget roots his morality theory in assumptions about the human organism's capacity to develop, formalize, and utilize rational alternatives systematically. While noting a premoral stage wherein the individual is incapable of causal thought, he primarily emphasizes two progressive levels of morality—heteronomous and autonomous. At the heteronomous stage the individual sees authorities as warranting unilateral respect and their rules as obligatory, sacred, and immutable. The structuring of thought in oriented to "obligations . . . determined by the law or the order itself, independent of intentions and relationships."[8] At the autonomous stage, obligations are defined in terms of mutual respect, reciprocity, and responsibility, and "an essential product . . . is the sense of justice . . . [wherein] justice prevails over obedience itself."[9]

Postulating six stages (three levels) of moral development, Kohlberg has tested cognitive developmental theory both longitudinally and cross-culturally.[10] His moral development typology is adaptable to the study of many different aspects of moral judgment. Since our legal levels model is in part a variation and application of Kohlberg's levels to legal reasoning, we do not elaborate upon his stage typology here. We note, however, that the Kohlberg model has furnished a valuable perspective for analyzing a number of areas of social development. For example, in addition to our explorations in the realm of law, other investigators have employed his framework for studying political ideological thought.

The major thrust of Kohlberg's research to date aims at verification of an invariant sequence of moral stages. Basic to his structural-developmental approach are the propositions (a) that there are distinctive, organized structures of thinking which are generally stable across situations, (b) that these modes of thought develop in an invariant stage sequence, each stage reflecting a more accommodative mode of differentiation and integration, and (c) that the process of development is self-regulated but is also affected by interaction with environmental conditions. . . .

Our theory of legal levels builds also upon jurisprudential frameworks. Foremost among those who have enhanced our perspective on legal socialization and development are Lon L. Fuller,[11] a proponent of legal naturalism, and John Rawls,[12] a moral philosopher. Both appreciate the interdependence of the moral, legal, and psychological. Their analytic constructs take account of the interactive components of individual and institutional legal development and acknowledge the logical and psychological conditions for developing an ethical legality. Their emphasis on legal developments as an interactive, purposive process and their attention to the potential of individuals and social institutions correspond closely to our own assumptions. Further, their philosophical orientation lends credence to our conclusion that the law can be a major mechanism for gaining a sense of self and for integrating the ideal and real demands for justice and for maintenance of social order.

While many of Fuller's ideas have shaped our general theory,[13] his discussion of dual moralities is especially germane to our legal levels model. For Fuller the law is ultimately inspired by a morality of aspiration subsuming a morality of duty. The morality of aspiration is the life "of excellence, of the fullest realization of human powers."[14] The morality of duty specifies the basic rules requisite for social order. While a person, as either a citizen or an official, may not attain his full capacity, there is no condemnation for failing "to embrace [such] opportunities. [However, there is condemnation] for failing to respect the basic requirements of social living."[15]

In essence, Fuller's discussion of the relationship between the morality of aspiration and the morality of duty implies a developmental progression, most clearly evident in his "invisible pointer that marks the dividing line where the pressure of duty leaves off and the challenge of excellence begins."[16] In moving from duty to aspiration, Fuller's analysis resembles Piaget's shift from an amoral to a juridical position. Illustratively, such a shift is reflected in the understanding that a "mere respect for constituted authority must not be confused with fidelity to law."[17] Philosophically and psychologically, there is an advance from a dependent, hedonistic, and uncritical state to an independent, altruistic, and rational manner. As with Piaget, there is a basic commitment to seeing humans as increasingly interactive and intellective, capable of rationality and, therefore, of an ethical legality.

The jurisprudential construct of John Rawls has also helped to clarify our ideas about justice, law, and obedience, as well as corroborate our model of legal levels. To Rawls, "moral feelings are a normal feature of human life,"[18] and a sense of justice is a psychological and logical developmental phenomenon. Adopting primarily a cognitive psychological orientation, he postulates that a "sense of justice may be viewed as the result of a certain natural development."[19] For Rawls, the acquisition of a sense of justice "takes place in stages connected with the growth of knowledge and understanding."[20] In addition, this intellectual development is enhanced through the social interaction and communication found in a well-ordered society.

Drawing heavily upon Piaget's model, Rawls details three progressive stages of justice based on authority, association, and principle. The experiences of trust and love, cooperation and friendship, roletaking and empathy, facilitate the development of a principled position. Rawls recognizes that the ethic of justice, although part of the individual's "natural" capacity, requires the "social" nourishment of love and trust, participation and mutuality, shared activity and reciprocity.

In addition to describing the developmental process for acquiring a sense of justice, Rawls identifies this sense of justice as a prerequisite for development of a universal ethic. [His] approach is pluralistic and individualistic, thus permitting analysis of both the individual and the institutional potential for an ethical utilization of law. In his schema he adroitly synthesizes the moral and legal with the political and psychological while clarifying the choice for justice as rational, possible, and necessary.

A Theory of Legal Development

Cross-cultural congruence in development. Basic to our theory of legal development and legal reasoning is the proposition that across cultures certain detectable regularities in modes of legal thought identify individuals' interactions with systems of law. Our emphasis on a legal levels typology stems from the assumption that the stages of individual development are characterized by distinctive ways of thinking about legal values and relating to legal systems. Focusing on cognitive structure is not inconsistent with recognizing the impact of affective states. . . .

We are interested in the basic structure of reasoning (*i.e.*, how legal issues are defined and judgments are made), and we expect to find the same stages of development in all cultures. Although a specific legal attitude or action may vary by culture, group, or even person, an individual's level of legal reasoning can generally explain variations in the content of expressions or orientations toward law. Thus, our focus on forms of thought offers a universal framework for organizing and structuring legal cognitions that simultaneously incorporates both individual and cultural diversity. An important corollary of such a model is that socialization strategies, whether moral, legal or political, share common features regardless of their specific content or context. Later we consider the implications for legal socialization of conceptualizing legal development as part of the general process of social development and value education.

Primacy of age over culture. Like moral development, legal development "does not represent an increasing knowledge of cultural values; rather, it represents the transformations that occur in the . . . form of thought and action."[21] Cross-cultural and longitudinal age trend data support Piaget's and Kohlberg's postulations of moral judgment stages. Age trends discernible from Hess and Tapp's cross-cultural work on socialization into compliance systems and from Minturn and Tapp's cross-national research on the justice of aggressive confrontations also suggest the potency of age over culture in determining the development of concepts related to authority and rules, aggression and justice.[22] Subsequent studies further support the hypothesis of universality of age-related sequencing in the growth of ideas concerning law and justice.[23] The effects of culture are thus primarily related to variations in the rate of development, rather than to determinations of the form or qualities of the progression itself—whether moral or legal.

Legal levels theory. A levels typology yields classifiable, interdisciplinary (psycholegal) conceptualizations that are observable cross-culturally. Cross-cultural study permits investigation of individual differences in development and simultaneously considers universal socialization strategies. While any typology is subject to the problem of ideal types, our legal levels theory provides a set of working hypotheses useful in attempting to clarify and describe the legal worlds of individuals and institutions.

a. Progression of legal reasoning. Legal reasoning is a conceptual framework for interpreting, defining, and making decisions about roles and rules, rights and responsibilities. The various levels of reasoning can best be depicted as successive restructurings of ways to analyze problems and accommodate human interactions. For example, a person's thought structure determines how he/she reasons about accepting or rejecting a substantive law and attempting to reform or maintain it.

The configuration of legal reasoning stages is best characterized by three major progressions: the preconventional (I), a sanction-oriented, deference stance; the conventional (II), a law-and-order, conformity posture; and the postconventional (III), a law-creating, principled perspective. Of these the second, or conventional system-maintenance level, is modal in most societies. This finding is supported by the research of social psychologists wherein a substantial majority of the subjects conform to a group or authority norm. Nevertheless, there is considerable evidence that individuals generally have the ability to reach the highest level of legal reasoning.

Observable, representative numbers of people develop their legal competencies to exercise an ethical utilization of law. The presence of exemplary figures across cultures and the empirical psychological data in colleagues' and our work emphasize the capacity for an ethical legality. Thus, a compelling task in so-called developing and developed countries is to construct socializing conditions that increase the number of ethical and critical persons who can act on a principled basis in developing and evaluating rule norms.

b. Modes of legal reasoning. The meaning of "higher" or "highest" levels of development often troubles the cognitive oriented psychologist in the creation of paradigms or the interpretation of results. We are persuaded by the Piagetian notion that higher implies better at problem solving, integrating differences, and incorporating logical and psychological concepts. The view that the sequence of stages represents a progressive development has also guided Rawls: At the last stage "all the subordinate ideals are finally understood and organized into a coherent system by suitably general principles. The virtues of the other moralities receive their explanation within . . . the more comprehensive conception [which is] continuous with these principles but extending beyond what they enjoin."[24]

Preconventional reasoning. With this orientation in mind, we conceive a unified system of levels of legal development, each characterized by a certain style of legal reasoning. Individuals at level I—the preconventional level—exhibit a mode of legal reasoning based on fear of punishment from authority, apprehension about physical harm, or deference to power. Preconventional views of law and legal obligation are guided by a focus on external consequences and authority. An instrumental hedonism tempers legal valuations. When a sense of rights is invoked, it is expressed in personal and material, not in reciprocal or sociocentric, terms. For a preconventional person, notions of retaliatory justice and literal exchange pervade one's orientation. Conceptualizing the generality of law is absent in reasoning legal actions and attitudes.

Conventional reasoning. At level II, the law maintenance level, people are concerned with role expectations and their fulfillment. Commitment to the community is tied to performing as a good girl (woman) or good boy (man). At this law-and-order, conventional level, obedience and likewise disobedience stem from perceived requirements of personal and social conformity. Practically, justice is synonymous with majority vote; individual rights are obscured in the domination of group norms; and equality implies no more than the impartial application and interpretation of rules. At level II, rights can easily be confused with privileges conferred by virtue of one's social role. At the core of this reasoning is the assumption that certain role expectations and social norms must be maintained for orderly and beneficial individual and group living.

Postconventional reasoning. Postconventional level III represents the law-creating, legislative perspective. Principled, thinking individuals are developmentally advanced because they see the need for social systems and yet can differentiate between the values of a given social order and universal ethics. From a postconventional frame of reference, legal directives are not derived from the dictates of a unilateral authority. They are human constructs reflecting the active, consensual participation of equals moving toward shared expectations. At this level of legal thought, people have the competence to entertain principles of social contract, mutuality, and "universal" rights as baselines for guiding attitudes and actions. Postconventional legal reasoners distinguish principles of justice from concrete laws and societal conventions so that they can evaluate the system itself in terms of criteria for an ethical legality. While valuing social systems and stable role expectations, individuals at level III appreciate the need to make independent ethical choices.

The development of principled or postconventional reasoning is congruent with "perfecting" legal, political, and moral systems. Ultimately, principled judgment is tested in real life stances on such current individual and social issues as the provision of legal services for the poor, protection of human subjects in biomedical or social research, and affirmative action on behalf of the rights-deprived. In determining whether to attempt actively to resolve ethical conflicts with law or merely to conform, postconventional valuation is guided by an appreciation of the rights and conditions of others and by a priori, general agreements that are compatible with one another. . . .

Conclusion

From a socialization perspective, the capacity of the individual to achieve an ethical legality is affected by opportunities for equal access to and participation in the administration of justice. Essentially the goal of legal socialization is to stimulate a reciprocal rights-consciousness and legal competence. Therefore, a comprehensive program of legal education must impart knowledge, enhance a sense of mutual rights and remedies, stimulate reasoning skills for contemplating and utilizing diverse alternatives, and cultivate in the individual a self-concept as a creator as well as consumer of law.

The generally low level of legality apparent in both developing and developed countries tends to indicate that more than increasing legal resources and knowledge about rights is required to stimulate a postconventional utilization of law. To raise the level of legal competence and more generally increase self-esteem and confidence, comprehensive "legal literacy" efforts need to commence.[25] Such efforts should be part of a broad, societal commitment to socialize and resocialize individuals to become more interactive, self-reliant participants in multiple systems of law. Only then can we achieve the essence of ethical legality.

In sum, if the legal system and the general population are both to attain an ethical level of legal development, we must recognize the dynamic relationships between the individual and the system and socialize both simultaneously. Fostering community legal systems and innovations in legal education and legal services programs consistent with modifications suggested by legal socialization theory and data would constitute a significant beginning in this regard. . . .

Notes

1. P. Selznick, *Law, Society, and Industrial Justice* 18 (1969).
2. H. Berman, Justice in the U.S.S.R. (rev. ed. 1963); Berman, *The Educational Role of the Soviet Court*, 21 Int'l Comp. L.Q. 81 (1972). . . .
3. U. Bronfenbrenner, Two Worlds of Childhood: U.S. and U.S.S.R. (1970); Bronfenbrenner, *Soviet Methods of Character Education: Some Implications for Research*, 57 Relig. Educ. Research Supp. 345 (1962).
4. H. Berman, *supra* note 2, at 279. In articulating his conception of "law-consciousness," Berman noted the substantial influence of the early 20th-century Polish-Russian jurist Leon Petrazhitsky who "distinguished between the 'official' law of the state and the 'unofficial' or 'intuitive' law that exists in the consciousness of people." Berman, *The Use of Law to Guide People to Virtue: A Comparison of Soviet and American Perspectives, supra* note 2. *See also* H. Berman, *supra* note 12, at 420–23; J. Shklar, *Legalism* (1964), at 58–60.

   Legislation on victimless crimes (homosexual relations between consenting adults, drunkenness, and use of marijuana) poignantly exemplifies the problem of a lack of congruence between the "official" law and the "law-consciousness" of the people. That these are as much the insights of behavioral scientists as legal deterrence theorists is evidenced, for example, in E. Schur, Crimes Without Victims (1965); F. Zimring & G. Hawkins, Deterrence (1973); Andenaes, *Deterrence and Specific Offenses*, 38 U. Chi. L. Rev. 537 (1971); Andenaes, *The General Preventive Effects of Punishment*, 114 U. Pa. L. Rev. 949 (1966); Berkowitz & Walker, *Law and Moral Judgments*, 30 Sociometry 410 (1967); Zimring & Hawkins, *Legal Threat as an Instrument of Social Change*, 27 J. Soc. Issues, No. 2, at 33 (1971); Zimring & Hawkins, *Deterrence and Marginal Groups*, 5 J. Crime & Delinq. 100 (1968).
5. This is not to say that the "law-consciousness" of individuals at any point in time and development defines what is an ethical legality and that legal authorities—upon ferreting out expectations, values, and norms—must simply institute a compatible system. The view that the institution of law ought to be merely a summation, reflection, or consensus of legalities obscures the human potential for legal development, the effect of social variables, and the socializing role of law for individual as well as system maintenance and change. We do, however, view incompatibilities between the law and individual law-consciousness as having an impact on the development of an ethical legality in both the individual and institution. . . . For a review of jurisprudential considerations, *see* J. Cohen, R. Robson & A. Bates, Parental Author-

ity: The Community and the Law 3-22 (1958). Cohen, Robson and Bates' study is one of the first attempts to measure community sentiments—the "moral" sense of the community—toward law.

6. For his major works regarding a levels approach to human reasoning, a particular debt is due the seminal contributions of Jean Piaget. *See, e.g.,* J. Piaget, The Child's Conception of the World (1929); J. Piaget, Judgment and Reasoning in the Child (1928); . . . J. Piaget, Science of Education and the Psychology of the Child (1970); J. Piaget, Six Psychological Studies (D. Elkind ed. 1967); J. Piaget, Structuralism (1970); J. Piaget & B. Inhelder, The Psychology of the Child (1969). Excellent reviews of Piaget's work appear in R. Brown, Social Psychology 403-07 (1965); J. Flavell, The Developmental Psychology of Jean Piaget (1963).

7. . . . Exemplary works include L. Kohlberg, The Development of Modes of Moral Thinking and Choice in the Years Ten to Sixteen, 1958 (unpublished doctoral dissertation, University of Chicago); Kohlberg, *From Is to Ought,* in Cognitive Development and Epistemology 151 (T. Mischel ed. 1971); Kohlberg, *The Child as a Moral Philosopher,* Psychol. Today, Sept. 1968, at 24; Kohlberg, *Development of Moral Character and Moral Ideology,* in I Review of Child Development Research 383 (M. Hoffman & L. Hoffman eds. 1964); Kohlberg, *The Development of Children's Orientations Toward a Moral Order: I. Sequence in the Development of Moral Thought,* 6 Vita Humana 11 (1963). *See* Kohlberg & Kramer, *Continuities and Discontinuities in Childhood and Adult Moral Development,* 12 Human Develop. 93 (1969) . . . Rest, Turiel & Kohlberg, *Level of Moral Development as a Determinant of Preference and Comprehension of Moral Judgment Made by Others,* 37 J. Personal. 225 (1969).

8. J. Piaget & B. Inhelder, *supra* note 6, at 125.

9. *Id.* at 127.

10. . . . Kohlberg, *From Is to Ought, supra* note 7; Kohlberg, *The Child as a Moral Philosopher, supra* note 7, *see* Kohlberg, *Stages of Moral Development as a Basis for Moral Education,* in Moral Education: Interdisciplinary Approaches 23 (G. Beck, B. Crittenden & E. Sullivan eds. (1971); Kohlberg & Gilligan, *The Adolescent As A Philosopher: The Discovery of the Self in a Postconventional World,* 100 Daedalus 1051 (1971). A full report of the work of Kohlberg and his associates is forthcoming in Moralization: The Cognitive Developmental Approach (L. Kohlberg & E. Turiel eds., forthcoming 1975). For an illustrative cross-cultural report, *see* Turiel, Kohlberg & Edwards, *Cross-cultural Studies of Moral Development.* . . .

11. The extensive writings of Fuller have provided enrichment for our psycholegal perspective. *See* L. Fuller, Anatomy of the Law (1968); L. Fuller, The Morality of Law (rev. ed. 1969); L. Fuller, The Justification of Legal Decisions, Aug.-Sept. 1971, at i (paper presented at the World Congress for Legal and Social Philosophy); Fuller, *Human Interaction and the Law,* 14 Am. J. Juris. I (1969). . . .

12. . . . *See, e.g.,* Rawls, *The Justification of Civil Disobedience,* in Civil Disobedience: Theory and Practice 240 (H. Bedau ed. 1969); Rawls, *Distributive Justice,* in Philosophy, Politics and Society 58 (P. Laslett & W. Runciman

eds. 1967); Rawls, *Justice As Fairness*, 67 Phil. Rev. 164 (1958); Rawls, *The Sense of Justice*, 72 Phil. Rev. 281 (1963); Rawls, *Two Concepts of Rules*, 64 Phil. Rev. 3 (1955).

13. *E.g.*, communication, interaction, shared activity, purposive striving, internal morality of law, and ethics of the role. *See* references to Fuller's work cited in note 11 *supra* for an overview of his framework. . . .

14. L. Fuller, The Morality of Law, *supra* note 11, at 5.

15. *Id.* at 6.

16. *Id.* at 9-10.

17. *Id.* at 41.

18. J. Rawls, *A Theory of Justice*, 1971, at 487.

19. Rawls, *The Sense of Justice*, *supra* note 12, at 281-82.

20. J. Rawls, *supra* note 18 at 495.

21. Turiel. *Stage Transition in Moral Development* in *Second Handbook of Research on Teaching*, at 735 (R. Travers ed. 1973). We emphasize that legal development does not result in homogeneous attitudes and actions. Higher stage reasoning is coincident with an increased tolerance of diversity and an ability to accommodate and integrate various perspectives.

22. The data included the perceptions of some 5,000 children in six countries and seven cultures. R. Hess & J. Tapp, Authority, Rules, and Aggression: A Cross-National Study of Socialization into Compliance Systems (Part I), Mar. 1969 (report submitted to U.S. Office of Education, Project 2947); L. Minturn & J. Tapp, Authority, Rules, and Aggression: A Cross-National Study of Children's Judgments of the Justice of Aggressive Confrontations (Part II), Oct. 1970 (report submitted to U.S. Office of Education, Project 2947).

23. *See, e.g.*, Levine and Tapp, *How the Public Relates to Law: Juveniles as a Case in Point*, in J. Tapp and F. Levine, *Legal Socialization: Issues for Psychology and Law* (forthcoming, 1975). Gallatin & Adelson, *Individual Rights and the Public-Good: A Cross-National Study of Adolescence*, 2 Comp. Pol. Studies 226 (1970); Gallatin & Adelson, *Legal Guarantees of Individual Freedom: A Cross-National Study of the Development of Political Thought*, 27 J. Soc. Issues, No. 2, at 93 (1971). For further illumination of developmental and cross-cultural patterns, *see, e.g.*, F. Greenstein, Do American Children Learn to Respect Authority: A Comparative Analysis, 1971 (paper presented at the Centennial lecture at the University of Arkansas); A. Sarat, Compliance and the Law, 1973 (unpublished doctoral dissertation, University of Wisconsin); Gorsuch, *Stages of Ethical Reasoning and Moral Norms of Carib Youth*, 4 J. Cross-Cultural Psychol. 283 (1973); Greenberg, *Children and Government: A Comparison Across Racial Lines*, 14 Midwest J. Pol. Sci. 249 (1970).

24. J. Rawls, *A Theory of Justice*, (1971), at 478-79.

25. Levine and Preston, *Community resource orientation among low-income groups*, 1970 *Wisc. L.R.* 80 at 112-13, concluded their empirical analysis of the utilization of legal services by low income groups with a call for broad, comprehensive legal literacy programs. To accomplish this goal, the law school—and the legal profession—will need to accept an active role. As Cahn

& Cahn have indicated, "If there is any area in which the law school pre-eminently can make a unique contribution to the restructuring of the legal system, it will be in using its accrediting and training role, to expand the manpower of the legal profession and to disseminate legal knowledge to the population at large. The law school in the future will have to begin working with colleges and high schools—and even grammar schools. . . . [It] will have to take responsibility for imparting to the populace at large not merely rote legal knowledge, but a sensitivity to those fundamental values of due process, fair play, free speech, privacy and official accountability." Cahn and Cahn, *Power to the People or the Professions?—The Public Interest in Public Interest Law, 79 Yale L.J.* 1005 (1970) at 1030–31.

12

Dynamics of the Legal Process
James P. Vanyo

There has developed over the last 20 to 30 years a body of knowledge referred to as operations research and systems analysis. Systems analysis in particular provides a tool for quantitatively analyzing and predicting the behavior of dynamic systems. It can be applied equally well to a technical system such as a space vehicle or the human body or to an operational system such as a corporation or the legal process.

As an example, consider the torts of nuisance and trespass as applied to environmental matters. The tort of nuisance has an extended history. In an early case (1705) a defendant was found liable when his sewage percolated into the cellar of an adjoining house.[1] In 1899 pollution of a stream which inconvenienced downstream property owners was held to be a nuisance.[2] Both of these were private nuisances—a term applied to an unreasonable interference with the interest of an individual in the use or enjoyment of land. When pollution killed fish, there was an interference with a public interest; it became a public nuisance; and it was prosecutable by the state. Note that a private party may act on a public nuisance only if he suffers special damage different from the damage suffered by the public in general. Also a nuisance requires a substantial interference; an occasional unpleasant odor, for example, is not sufficient.

However, a trespass may consist of a mere technical invasion and

Reprinted from "Dynamics of the Legal Process and Environmental Law," *California Trial Lawyers Journal* 10 (Fall 1971), pp. 44–50, by permission of the author and publisher, California Trial Lawyers Association.

further is occasionally the basis for punitive damages in addition to the actual damages incurred. The majority of decisions hold that a trespass has to be by a tactilely perceivable object—a rock, a person, a stream of water, etc. Recently, Oregon and California have recognized trespass by fumes, dust, and noise.[3,4]

In a 1970 review article[5], Evans and Kratter presented arguments for the existence of "A New Tort: Mass Trespass by Air Pollution," in which they would permit use of a class action. Use of the trespass concept would avoid the need to show special damages and would permit the granting of punitive damages as a deterrent. A legislative approach[6] was presented by Senator Moscone of the California Senate, who authored a bill to expand the definition of nuisance to include anything potentially injurious to health, or which constitutes air, water, or noise pollution. It would permit a private person to maintain an action for a public nuisance in certain instances and would permit the person to collect costs and attorney's fees if successful. All three of the above approaches are probably indicative of a coming trend.

This discussion of nuisance and trespass illustrates the type of legal thinking and development that makes up much of the legal process. General rules of law are formulated from a series of court decisions based on isolated-fact situations. A continuing series of legislative enactments parallel the court decisions. They are complemented by changes in governmental structure.

As the social scene changes further, continued application of the rules and laws may yield results that will again appear unattractive. In response to this stimulus, other law review articles will be written; judges will again experiment with departures from precedent; and legislators will again author new bills. This dynamic continuum—too fast for some, too slow for others—is discussed further as part of a systems approach.

Systems analysis, sometimes referred to in special cases as "servo theory" or "control theory," deals with the understanding and control of dynamic processes involving "feedback." Feedback is that characteristic of a system whereby the result (output) affects the cause (input). Such a system must be carefully balanced to avoid erratic system response.

In a dynamic system, too much feedback (overcontrol) results in oscillations of increasing amplitude, which reach a steady state only if sufficient damping is present to absorb the excess energy. If too much damping exists the system fails to respond to any stimuli. The optimum dynamic system is one in which feedback and damping are balanced so that the system responds as quickly as possible without going into destructive oscillations.

The techniques of systems theory are very well established and have become very generalized.[7] In applying the theory to the legal process, the difficulty is in collecting the necessary data and formulating the problem—not in solving the problem once it is stated.

The block diagram of a simplified model of the legal process is shown in Figure 1. In Figure 1, responses (e.g., motion or energy for a technical system—information or social action for a nontechnical system) flow in the direction of the arrows. The rectangles denote the condition or state of different portions of the systems. The circles with the + symbols denote that the output of two or more portions of the system are added together to produce the total input to a subsequent portion of the system. The essential characteristic showing that feedback exists is the closed loop structure of the block diagram. A system in which all responses flow in one direction is not a closed loop and does not have feedback.

In order to solve dynamic systems problems a technique called simulation[8] is used often. It is probably the most useful and most general of all the operations research and systems analysis concepts. As used today, simulation is a technique for reproducing situations that occur in the real world. Changes are made inside the computer resulting in variations in the computed result. These results are used to infer that similar results would occur in the real world if the same variations were made. The utility of the results depends of course on the accuracy of the data. Almost any kind of a problem, technical or

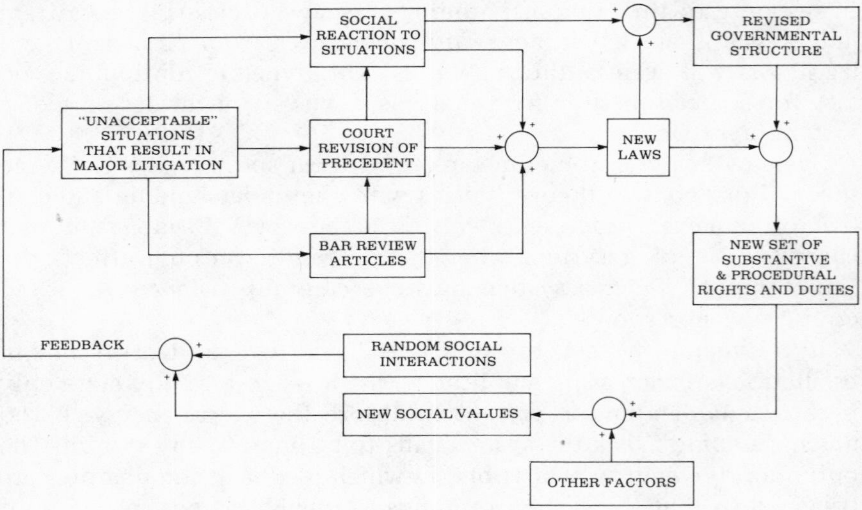

FIGURE 1. Simplified Block Diagram of the Dynamics of the Legal Process

nontechnical, can be solved. The essential ingredients are a large computer and imagination.

An an example, one may wish to assess the impact of changing a specific legal procedure relative to the practice of law. Consider the following problem and some of the possible solutions:

"One of the greatest constraints on the use of the legal process in environmental matters has been the inability of attorneys to earn a living while specializing in the practice of environmental law. A number of law firms, acting in the public interest, are currently supporting young attorneys who practice solely in environmental areas. However this has an obvious limitation: Members of the firm doing the more mundane but profitable work to support the environmental attorneys will eventually become unhappy and seek to stop the arrangement. The use of trusts is a possible solution, as are class actions. Both of these have procedural disadvantages and also place the attorney in a situation bordering on advertising. Groups such as the Sierra Club offer a solution but with the difficulty of proving a standing to sue. An additional solution is to award court costs and reasonable attorney fees to a litigant who successfully prosecutes an environmental suit and thereby protects the public interest. Taxpayers' suits usually award costs and attorney's fees, as do a number of other actions."

In this example, one may desire to assess the impact of awarding costs and attorney's fees in environmental actions relative to the overall public benefit. The results, if favorable, could be used as support for the proposed change. If not favorable, the results could be used to seek a more desirable change.

One real utility in all of the techniques of operations research and systems analysis lies in the ability of rationally quantifying and then mathematically manipulating quantities that to many persons would appear to be "nonmeasurable." Measurements may be based on physical laws or they may be based on an arbitrary but definable scale. A valid arbitrary scale could be, say, zero for "least" up to 100 for "most" of a definable quantity. Most physical dimensions in science originated as arbitrary but definable scales. Only after a phenomenon was well understood were the arbitrary scales related to general physical laws.

Measurable may also be categorized as exact or approximate. An assumption of exact values and exact laws leads to a deterministic world. The real world is probabilistic and includes the fact that even physical laws do not always hold and that all data and measurements are inexact. A sophisticated analysis treats a problem in a probabilistic way and yields an expected answer plus some measure of its accuracy. One can make an estimate of any physical, emotional, or intellectual concept with at least some estimable degree of accuracy and therefore obtain a mathematical solution in a probabilistic sense.

The entire spectrum of legal-technical-environmental problems is susceptible to these techniques. For example one may assess:

1. changing the structure of administrative agencies
2. the effect of imposing on corporate directors an obligation to evaluate the impact of their operations on the environment
3. the effect of automatically assigning a specific revenue source to a specific use
4. variations in court procedure
5. the effect in general of revisions in laws

The use of impact reports and cost–benefit analyses, as used in environmental matters, are precursors to the analyses described here. Initially the validity of the results will be limited. Eventually such tools will enable attorneys and legislators to assess the impact of their proposals with a useful degree of accuracy.

Notes

1. Tenant v. Goldwin, 1 Salk. 360 (1705).
2. *Smith v. City of Sedalia*, 152 Mo. 283, 53 S.W. 907 (1899).
3. Roberts v. Permanente Corporation, 188 Ca. App. 2nd 526, 10 Cal. Rptr. 519 (1961).
4. Davis v. Georgia-Pacific Corp., 445 P. 2nd 481 (1968).
5. Evans Marjorie W. and L. M. Kratter, "A New Tort: Mass Trespass by Air Pollution," *California Trial Lawyers Journal*, vol. IX, no. 4, Fall 1970.
6. Moscone, George R. (Senator), California Senate Bill 490 (1971).
7. Forrester, Jay W., *Principles of Systems*, Wright-Allen Press Inc., Cambridge, Mass., 2nd edition (1968).
8. Morgenthaler, G. W. "The Theory and Application of Simulation in Operations Research", in *Progress in Operations Research*, vol. 1, R. L. Ackoff (ed.), pages 363–419, Wiley and Sons (1961).

PART III

Social-Structural Theory of Law: Normative Analysis

Of the six theoretical perspectives on law and society reviewed in Part II, which, if any, can be used to illuminate the functioning of a legal system? Although systems theory can potentially provide a theoretical framework for the sociology of law that would integrate some fruitful ideas from alternative theories and guide future research, it is still in embryonic form (Evan, 1978). As an interim solution to the problem of providing a frame of reference for this field, I shall combine some insights of systems theory—as articulated in the reading by Vanyo and in the works of others (Laszlo, Levine, and Milsum, 1974; Buckley, 1967, 1968)—with Parsons's four structural components of social systems: values, norms, roles and collectivities (Parsons, 1961: 41–44; Evan, 1975: 387–388). I shall refer to this theoretical amalgam in the remainder of this book as a "social-structural theory of law."

Any subsystem or institution of a societal system, whether it be a legal system, a family system, an economic system, a religious system, etc., can be decomposed into four structural elements: values, norms, roles, and organizations. The first two elements relate to a cultural or normative level of analysis and the latter two to a social-structural level of analysis. Interactions between two or more subsystems of a society are mediated by cultural as well as by social-structural elements. As Parsons pointed out in the selection in

Part I, law is a generalized mechanism for regulating behavior in the several subsystems of a society. At the normative level of analysis, law entails a "double institutionalization" of the values and norms embedded in other subsystems of a society. In performing this reinforcement function, law develops "cultural linkages" with other subsystems, thus contributing to the degree of normative integration that exists in a society. As disputes are adjudicated and new legal norms enacted, a value from one or more of the nonlegal subsystems is tapped and provides an implicit or explicit justification for legal decision-making.

From a sociological perspective, values are conceptions of that which is desirable. They are conceptions of ideals, which can only be approximated, never attained. These conceptions—e.g., value of property, value of individual liberty, value of privacy, value of equality—are part of the cultural underpinnings of the various subsystems of a society. In other words, values are institutionally linked concepts. In each of the social institutions or subsystems of a society—be it the family, religion, the economy, the educational system, the legal system, or something else—there are dominant values guiding the respective norms, roles, and organizational components of each of these structures. Thus, for example, love and nurturance are values underlying the family; the production and distribution of wealth dominate the economy; and justice is the heart of the legal system. Each of the values may represent complex concepts of what is deemed desirable; associated with each of them are diverse norms, both legal and nonlegal. Unlike a value, a norm carries with it a sanction, negative for violating it, and positive for conforming to it. (With these distinctions in mind, analyze the legal documents in Appendix I.)

At the social-structural level of analysis, interactions between the legal system and other subsystems of society are mediated by the occupants of roles as individuals and by the members of organizations within and without the legal system. We shall consider the role and organizational elements of a social-structural theory of law in Parts IV and V, respectively. The aggregate nature of the interactions of the legal system with the other subsystems of a society, that is, what we include under the rubric of the interinstitutional level of analysis, will be taken up in Part VI.

In systems-theoretic terms, the values and norms of a legal system may be viewed as goal parameters in comparison with which the performance of a legal system may be objectively assessed. The inability of a legal system to develop "feedback loops" and "closed-loop systems" to monitor and assess the efficacy of its outputs makes it vulnerable to various types of failures. Instead of generating "negative feedback," i.e., self-corrective measures, when legal personnel or rank-and-file citizens fail to comply with the law, the system is subjected to "positive feedback" of a detrimental sort (Laszlo, Levine, and Milsum, 1974). In Part VII we shall examine the problems of legal system failure in relation to efforts at planned social change.

What are some implications of our social-structural perspective on law? In the first place, the legal system is not viewed as only an immanently developing set of legal rules, principles, or doctrines insulated from other subsystems of society, a view commonly held by some legal scholars and legal practitioners. Second, the personnel of the legal system, whether judges, lawyers, prosecutors, or administrative agency officials, activate legal rules, principles or doctrines in the course of performing their roles within the legal system. Third, formally organized collectivities, be they courts, legislatures, law enforcement organizations, or administrative agencies, perform the various functions of a legal system. Fourth, in performing these functions, the formally organized collectivities constituting a legal system interact with individuals and organizations representing interests embedded in the nonlegal subsystems of society. In other words, each of the institutions or subsystems of a society—legal and nonlegal—has the same structural elements: values, norms, roles, and organizations. Interinstitutional interactions involve an effort at coupling these structural elements across institutional boundaries. An important challenge to the sociologist of law is to discover the diverse couplings or linkages—cultural and social-structural—between the legal system and the nonlegal systems in terms of the four constituent structural elements. Another challenge is to ascertain the impact of these linkages on the behavior of legal personnel and on the behavior of the citizenry, on the one hand, and to measure the impact of "double institutionalization" on societal goals, on the other.

In the first reading in Part III, Jane and William Pease present a vivid historical account of the passage and administration of the Fugitive Slave Law of 1850. The reluctance of the Northerners to comply with the constitutional provision for the return of fugitive slaves led to Southern demands for strict enforcement. To implement the constitutional protection of property rights in slavery, Congress passed a law in 1793 to ensure extradition of fugitives from slavery. Opposition to the 1793 statute grew with the emergence and growth of the antislavery movement, leading eventually to a new statute, the Fugitive Slave Law of 1850. The clash in values between the property rights in slaves and the human rights of slaves evoked further opposition in the North, where the law, lacking in perceived legitimacy, was widely flouted.

That the dominant values of the several subsystems constituting a society can and do conflict with one another is illustrated in the selection by Evan on the law of evidence. The value of justice under-girding law has stimulated the development of various testimonial privileges; the value of truth, which is the foundation of the sub-system of science and technology, is also reflected in some of the admissibility rules of evidence. Whereas some of the admissibility rules are concerned with promoting the search for truth, testimonial privileges such as those against self-incrimination, interspousal privileges, attorney–client privileges, and so forth, are oriented to ensuring that justice is done even if it be at the expense of truth. In *Rochin v. California*, the value conflict between truth and justice is clearly articulated.

Regardless of the values underlying one or more legal norms, several generic questions can be asked. To what extent is the target population of a given legal norm aware of the existence of the norm (Podgórecki *et al.*, 1973)? And to what extent do they support or legitimate that norm? In Sarat's selection the relationship between knowledge and value consensus is tellingly posed. Why do you sup-pose these two dimensions of legal norms are not positively corre-lated? Why does dissatisfaction with the legal system increase as knowledge about it increases? Why is willingness to comply unrelated to knowledge? What are the implications of these findings for a theory of legal socialization?

Two other dimensions of legal norms, apart from knowledge and value consensus, relate to punishment: the degree of certainty and the severity of punishment. In the reading by Antunes and Hunt, the authors, after systematically reviewing the literature on deterrence, investigate the relative impact of certainty and severity on the deter-rence of crime in forty-nine states. They conclude that a multiplica-tive model in which certainty and severity are combined is a good predictor of crime rates. In addition, they discovered that "the impact of severity is filtered through the certainty value," that is, that severity makes a difference only under conditions of certainty of punishment. Why do you suppose that certainty of punishment is more effective in deterring crime than is severity?

Yet another dimension of legal norms is the degree of compliance or conformity. In an arresting analysis of the legal system of Com-munist Czechoslovakia, Otto Ulč, a former judge, explains the preva-lence of pilferage of state property. He appears to be suggesting that in the absence of value consensus or of perceived legitimacy of the legal order, there is widespread noncompliance with the law. But lest the reader conclude that the problem of compliance is associated exclusively with the citizenry, the reading by Ahart forcefully reminds us that legal personnel charged with enforcing a law may themselves be guilty of violating a law, whether by acts of omission or commission. How would you apply Tapp and Levine's theory of legal socialization to Ahart's findings?

References

Buckley, W. (1967). *Sociology and Modern Systems Theory.* Englewood Cliffs, N.J.: Prentice-Hall.

Buckley, W., ed. (1968). *Modern Systems Research for the Behavioral Scientist.* Chicago: Aldine.

Evan, W. M. (1975). "The International Sociological Association and the Internationalization of Sociology." *International Social Science Journal,* XXVII: 385-393.

Evan, W. M. (1978). "Systems Theory and the Sociology of Law." Presented at the Ninth World Congress of Sociology in Uppsala, Sweden, August 1978 (to appear in my forthcoming book *Law and Social Structure*).

Laszlo, C. A., M. D. Levine and J. H. Milsum (1974). "A General Systems Framework for Social Systems." *Behavioral Science,* 19: 79-92.

Parsons, T. (1961). "An Outline of the Social System." Pp. 30-79, in T. Parsons, E. Shils, K. D. Naegel, and J. R. Pitts, eds., *Theories of Society.* Vol. 1. New York: Free Press of Glencoe.

Podgórecki, A., *et al.* (1973). *Knowledge and Opinion About Law.* London: Martin Robertson and Co.

13

The Fugitive Slave Law

Jane H. Pease and William H. Pease

Seldom since the United States became a nation has any law generated as much moral opposition as did the Fugitive Slave Law of 1850. Never have property rights and civil liberties clashed more starkly than when men and women in the free states were called on to return fugitive slaves to bondage. Nonetheless, the tensions they faced had long been building and had their roots in the very framing of the Constitution in 1787. By then several Northern states had already ended slavery within their own borders; yet the constitutional convention in its efforts to achieve a more strongly unified nation acted to insure the interests of slave holders. In doing so, the convention adopted a compromise which provided that each slave be counted as three fifths of a person for purposes of both taxation and congressional representation, and which forestalled ending the African slave trade for at least twenty years. Finally its members expressly wrote into the Constitution the provision that "No Person held to Service or Labour in one State, under the Laws thereof, escaping into another, shall, in Consequence of any Law or Regulation therein, be discharged from such Service or Labour, but shall be delivered up on Claim of the Party to whom such Service or Labour, may be due" (Art. IV, Sec. II, Par. 3.). Both Northerners and South-

Excerpt from *The Fugitive Slave Law and Anthony Burns: A Problem in Law Enforcement.* Philadelphia: J. B. Lippincott Company, 1975, pp. 3-23, by permission of authors and publisher.

erners believed that these were necessary provisions to balance sectional interests and soothe sectional fears.

In 1808, Congress ended the international slave trade and that issue was, thereafter, little debated. Never until post-Civil War Reconstruction was federal action taken to amend the three fifths ratio. But the third provision twice required national legislation and ultimately created far more sectional rancor than it allayed. That this would be the case was not initially clear. In 1793, Congress first provided for enforcing the return of fugitives from labor in an act designed primarily to insure extradition of fugitives from justice. The law required that federal, state, and local officials in any state to which a fugitive had escaped from another were responsible for his return once the owner or his agent had apprehended the runaway. That Congress anticipated some Northern opposition to the law was evident in the provision that any one who helped a slave escape or hid him from his master was subject to a $500 fine. Despite that provision, the law at first provoked little overt opposition and was regarded simply as a means to implement a binding constitutional obligation.

Limiting the 1793 Law

Before long, however, the finality implicit in that constitutional compromise began to crumble. Northerners, many of whom were troubled by slavery though they did not support black equality with whites, hesitated to return slaves escaping into their states. While they might tolerate slavery as an institution elsewhere and recognize rights to property in slaves, they would not themselves act to deprive individual human beings of liberty. So, even before a broadly based antislavery movement had emerged, there was resistance to the law's enforcement. In Pennsylvania, which had long sustained a society for promoting the abolition of slavery and had early acted to end slavery within its own borders, the legislature passed laws in 1820 and 1826 to define and limit the state's role in enforcing the 1793 federal statute. Though these laws regularized the procedures by which claimants might recover their property, they also stipulated somewhat more adequate protection for alleged fugitives. They provided, for instance, that their cases would be heard by judges rather than by mere aldermen or justices of the peace and that certain standards of evidence would be maintained. They also levied severe penalties against the illegal seizure (kidnapping) of free blacks.

More persistent and overt opposition to the 1793 statute emerged with the antislavery movement's growth after 1830. . . . Although fugitives were most often aided by blacks, white abolitionists also helped, giving legal and financial aid as well as shelter and sustenance. More formally, vigilance committees were organized to coordinate these efforts in cities to which runaways most frequently came. In addition, in individual cases, local Negroes used mob action to rescue fugitives from law officers, as they did in Detroit and Buffalo; and in Boston a group of angry black women spirited a refugee out of a court room in the very presence of the presiding judge. By 1840 it was clear that abolitionists were willing to use both legal and illegal means to protect the new-found liberty of human beings who had, in their flight north, rebelled against being mere chattel.

Necessarily these activities provoked serious clashes between the Southern determination to protect slave property and the increasing Northern proclivity to pit the human rights of the slave against the property rights of the master. Frequently the issue focussed on the responsibility of Northern state officials to facilitate enforcement of the 1793 law and on Southern moves to circumvent obstacles which increasingly blocked the return of runaways. In 1839 the governor of Virginia, impatient with the failure of the 1793 law to return slaves escaping from his state on Northern vessels, called upon New York governor William Seward to extradite three sailors "charged with having feloniously stolen a negro slave"[1] in Virginia. Arguing that, because slavery did not exist in New York, the state could recognize no such crime. Seward refused to extradite the sailors. Three years later, the federal Supreme Court moved to define more precisely the state's responsibility in fugitive slave law cases. Edward Prigg, a Maryland resident, had seized his fugitive slave and her children and removed them from Pennsylvania in clear violation of the legal processes required by that state's 1826 law. After a state court had tried and convicted Prigg, both Maryland, concerned with her citizens' property rights, and Pennsylvania, eager to protect her residents' civil liberties, backed Prigg's appeal to the Supreme Court. That tribunal deliberated two central points: first, whether the power to legislate under the fugitive slave provision of the Constitution resided with the nation or with the states; and second, whether federal law could oblige state officials to execute the federal fugitive slave law.

The decision, written by Justice Joseph Story, ruled that there was no constitutional requirement that state authorities must in any way assist in returning fugitive slaves, although state magistrates might, if they chose, "exercise that authority, unless prohibited by state legislation."[2] But except for that point, congressional legislation on the subject took precedence over all state legislation. The nimbleness of the Court's finding elicited mixed responses from both pro- and anti-slavery people—each side finding some merit and some fault with it.

Nonetheless the decision marked a fundamental shift in Southern views of federal and state power. Many Southerners heretofore associated with a strict states' rights position, which prohibited federal interference with their peculiar institution, now pressed for an extension of federal power to protect their property rights. By contrast, antislavery Northerners demanded a strict observance of the states' power to guarantee to all their residents, including fugitives, the rights of habeas corpus and trial by jury.

As a result of the Prigg decision, personal liberty laws similar to those of Pennsylvania proliferated in the Northeast. Even before 1842, both New York and Vermont had guaranteed fugitives the rights to jury trial and counsel. Thereafter, Massachusetts, responding specifically to the arrest of the fugitive George Latimer in Boston, prohibited the use of state jails for detaining fugitives as well as any participation by state officials in enforcing the fugitive slave law. Subsequently Pennsylvania, Rhode Island, and Vermont also forbade state officials, as one observer put it, to "act the part of bull-dog for the South, to seize and hold their runaway slaves,"[3] or otherwise to assist in enforcing the law.

The Compromise of 1850

Over the years therefore Northern unwillingness to implement the constitutional provision for the return of fugitives from labor trenched on Southern demands for its strict enforcement and led to a fundamental constitutional issue. To the South, this guarantee of its property rights was part of a compromise which had led it to accept the Constitution in the first place. Antislavery Northerners, unwilling to be bound by a compromise they considered an infringement of human rights, argued a superior moral commitment or "higher law" which absolved them from complying with the obligations imposed by the Constitution. This disagreement over the binding nature of a fundamental national compromise festered in the congressional debates which followed the Mexican War. Confronted with newly acquired territory, where slavery's status required definition, Congress argued not only the federal government's power to establish or ban slavery but its responsibility to insure the return of fugitives.

In January 1850 Senator Henry Clay of Kentucky, venerated for his past role in mediating national crises, proposed one more national compromise whereby the United States might balance opposing sectional issues. In the process Southerners were asked to surrender a parity of free and slave states, which the admission of California as a free state involved, in return for equal access for slave owners to the rest of the Mexican cession and a new and binding fugitive slave law. In turn antislavery Yankees were to be pacified with abolition of the slave trade in the District of Columbia. . . .

The puzzle facing Congress, therefore, was how to protect Southern slave interests and, simultaneously, satisfy Northern civil liberties demands. Was it possible to satisfy both claims and avoid the clash between property rights and human freedom? Some, at least, saw a way out by a system of financial compensation. Maryland Senator Thomas Pratt, reflecting his state's practical interest in a solution of the problem, proposed that the federal government pay the claimant the value of any runaway slave who was located by his owner in another state but for some reason was not then returned. . . . The constitutional compromise, the law of 1793, and the Prigg decision, Pratt insisted, all asserted the federal government's responsibility to insure the return of fugitives from labor. It followed logically from that premise that if government could not fulfill its obligations it should make good its failure by compensating the owner for his loss.

Pratt's proposal, offered late in August 1850, attracted some support but failed to satisfy objections made to it from both North and South. Senator Dayton of New Jersey opposed it because he feared it would drain the federal treasury. The rationale behind Pratt's proposal could be extended to hold the federal government responsible, at unimaginable cost to the taxpayers, for all damages incurred when any federal law was broken. . . . And that, even were the compensation limited to the fugitive slave obligation, would lead to fraud, for who would genuinely try to recover property when he could so easily claim compensation. . . . Thus North and deep South rejected this border state proposal. . . .

What options, then, were open to the South in her efforts to protect slave property? Compensation held at least the potential for subsequent federal intervention to effect emancipation. Reliance on Northern prejudice to produce state legislation excluding all Negro migrants simply did not work in the Northeast. And Southern defense of states' rights perversely fed the arguments of antislavery spokesmen, who used them to reject any extension of federal power protecting slave interests. Caught in this quandry, Virginia's Senator Mason asserted that the right to hold property in slaves was absolute and precedent to all other rights. Strange doctrine from the home state of Thomas Jefferson! Equally ironically, the doctrine of absolute right could be turned around by antislavery men who claimed that Christian teaching and moral law established a "higher law" which forbade their returning refugees from slavery. And if the higher law overshadowed constitutional obligation in the North, Southerners threatened to meet its challenge in ways equally unconstitutional. Once again it was Mason who warned that if a new fugitive law did not provide slaveowners adequate protection he would recommend that his fellow Southerners "provide by law for reprisals upon the property of the citizens of any offending State," concluding, "I know of no other mode of redress against those who acknowledge no obligation either of honor or of law."[4] . . . And at the extreme fringe of constitutional challenge R. Barnwell Rhett of South Carolina posed the ultimate solution of disunion. He urged Congress to repeal federal fugitive slave legislation and thus test the Northern states' will to meet their constitutional commitments. If they failed to act on their own, Rhett concluded, the disunion that would inevitably follow would be of their own making. Nothing would have pleased the most fanatic abolitionists more, for they too sought disunion and destruction of a constitution which protected slavery.

The New Fugitive Slave Law

Neither Southern nor Northern moderates, however, sought to strain the Constitution further but rather to preserve union. So in mid-September 1850, after eight months of almost continuous debate on all measures embodied in Clay's compromise, the Congress passed a fugitive slave bill which President Fillmore then signed. In substance it involved an extended roster of federal officials responsible for enforcing the return of fugitives, provided a simplified procedure for claimants, pressed private citizens—though not state officials—into its service, and in no way met Northern demands for judicial protection for alleged slaves. Specifically it empowered commissioners of federal circuit courts and persons specially appointed by the federal superior courts in the territories, as well as those courts themselves, to issue certificates entitling claimants of fugitive slaves to take their property back to the state or territory from which the slaves had fled, provided only that satisfactory proof was presented to such commissioner or other official that the prisoners were the fugitives as alleged and did owe service. The law charged federal marshals and their deputies to execute all warrants for the arrest of alleged fugitives issued by the commissioners and the courts and to be financially accountable should the fugitives escape. In pursuance of their duties, the marshals were authorized "to summon and call to their aid the bystanders, or *posse comitatus.*" But, should the claimant so prefer, he might seize a fugitive on his own responsibility without a warrant. Once the fugitive was seized, the law continued, an affidavit certified by any court in the state or territory from which the alleged slave had escaped was all that was required to establish the slave's identity and the fact that he owed service from which he had fled. If the fugitive met the affidavit's description, the commissioner or court was required to issue a certificate for his rendition. At no time during this process was the alleged fugitive allowed to testify in his own behalf. And of course there was no provision for habeas corpus, jury trial, counsel, or the like.

The law also extended special aid against the dangers of illegal intervention to forestall the slave's return. Should the claimant or his attorneys file an affidavit after the certificate for return had been issued that a rescue attempt was anticipated, the marshal or other federal official holding the slave was "to remove him to the State whence he fled" at federal expense. Finally, those who obstructed the law were subject to a $1,000 fine and six months imprisonment and liable for an additional $1,000 damages should the owner bring civil suit. The federal government bore the expense of the usual fees for the marshal, deputies, and clerks unless the claimant failed to make good his claim. The commissioner was paid a $10 fee for his services if he found for the claimant, but only a $5 fee if he found against him.

By these terms slaveholders seemed to have gained strong new protection for their property. The financial arrangements, the terms of punishment, the nature of evidence required to establish legal grounds for the return of a fugitive, and the obligation imposed upon all citizens to assist in the capture and rendition of fugitives added force which the 1793 law had lacked. But even so, was it enforceable? Its very passage had been achieved only by the planned absenteeism of a large group of free state senators whose compromise consisted in not voting against the measure. North and South alike admitted that the law offended the mores and morals of many Northern communities. And even if the law could be enforced, would it curtail the property loss which border states experienced? Where slavery was least profitable as a labor system and least viable as an economic institution, would most owners undertake the expense of tracking down their runaways and employing agents and counsel to reclaim balky and unreliable servants?

Still and all, the Fugitive Slave Law of 1850 was of major importance to the South in its symbolic guarantees of property in slaves backed by the weight of the federal government. Its enactment alone confirmed the South's interpretation of the Constitution and the lasting nature of its sectional compromises. But if this symbol was to retain its meaning, then on those occasions when it was applied, it must be applied successfully. The federal government must demonstrate its resolution and firmness, and the North must comply if Henry Clay's compromise was to last. The line was drawn; the test was yet to come. . . .

Testing the Law

. . . No sooner had the bill become law than petitions reached Congress seeking its repeal. . . . They echoed familiar themes, that the law itself was both unfair and immoral, and roused Southern fears that a petition campaign similar to that of 1836 designed to rally Northern opposition to slavery was under way. . . .

But times had changed and the petition issue quickly fell behind antislavery events. The language of abolitionist attacks on the new law was no longer supplicatory but bristlingly defiant. Even before congressional debate on the bill had ended, groups in Massachusetts and New York had publicly urged disobedience and advised fugitives to arm themselves for self-defense. When the bill became law anguished abolitionists became still more militant. . . .

Blacks as well as whites openly challenged the new law. . . . In mass meetings throughout the North they closed ranks, emphasizing less the abstract morality of a higher law than the imperatives of simple survival. "Shall we resist Oppression? Shall we defend our Liberties? . . .

While these protests were broached, the South, the beneficiary of the new law, stood willing, for a time, to let the matter rest. . . . Yet only to a point. They tolerated Northern defiance so long as it remained verbal. But when professions of higher law and moral obligation were converted into overt acts to evade the law, tolerance quickly diminished.

Boston, in the Southern mind the focus of antislavery activity, gave the law its first major test. Even before February 15, 1851, when the Shadrach case broke, the city had seen the law thwarted. William and Ellen Craft, whose escape from Georgia with Ellen impersonating William's white master had been widely publicized, were in town when the fugitive bill became law. With their arrest under it already in preparation, abolitionists hastily sent them off to England. Thus it seemed imperative to federal officials that the first full-fledged application of the law in Boston be successful.

In mid-February, then, John Caphart of Norfolk, Virginia, obtained from Commissioner George T. Curtis an arrest warrant for Frederick Wilkins, popularly known as Shadrach. Still smarting from the Craft affair, deputy federal marshal Patrick Riley carefully staked out the Cornhill Coffee House were Wilkins was a waiter. Then on Saturday morning, February 15, he and his men arrested the black man. Word of the arrest spread quickly, and within hours five well-known Boston Lawyers volunteered as counsel for the defendant. To give them time to develop their case, Curtis granted a delay in the hearings until the following Tuesday.

Up to that point all had gone according to script, despite the fact that Marshal Riley had no place to keep his prisoner other than the courthouse, where the federal government rented courtroom space. Denied by Massachusetts law the use of any state jails for holding a fugitive slave, Riley was made doubly insecure by the mayor's refusal of special police protection at the courthouse and the commander of the Boston naval yard's refusal to use his facilities for Shadrach's safe-keeping. His legitimate fears for his prisoner's incarceration were, however, short-circuited in a most unexpected manner. After Curtis had granted the delay, the courtroom gradually emptied. The lawyers and commissioner had already left when suddenly a door burst open and a crowd of blacks, pushing Riley and his men aside, swarmed into the room, encompassed Wilkins, and swept him out the opposite door. When next heard from, Wilkins was safe in Montreal.

Marshal Riley's careful preparations and official Washington's sharp response to Wilkin's escape strongly suggest that his arrest was intended to demonstrate a firm federal intention to enforce the law regardless of Northern opposition. The executive branch had made its concern clear. Only a month after he signed the bill into law, President Fillmore had pledged himself to enforce it faithfully as part of his constitutional duty. Two months later, in his first annual message, he called on all Americans to obey the law as the only way to insure that American government remained one of laws, not of men. If the law offended, it must be repealed legally, not defied. . . .

The rescue, however, cast doubt on this resolution. Within three days Congress had considered the matter and called for the relevant executive documents. The president, in turn, used this opportunity to elaborate his views. By February 18, he had already ordered all federal civil and military officers to aid in Wilkins's recapture and simultaneously had directed the government to prosecute those who had aided and abetted the escape. Then, in his message to Congress which accompanied these documents, Fillmore went on to condemn Massachusetts's personal liberty laws and especially its denial of state jail facilities in fugitive cases. Because of that state's uncooperativeness, he sought congressional action to empower him to call the state militia into federal service without the time-consuming proclamation process which existing law required. . . .

Congressional assessment of the Shadrach case varied. Kentucky

Whig Henry Clay saw in it an invitation to a strong law-and-order stand. Though he also noted that it involved a black threat to white dominance, the thrust of his argument lay elsewhere. "If to-day the law upon the subject of fugitive slaves is obstructed by violence and force, and its execution prevented, what other law on our statute-book may not to-morrow be obstructed by equal violence and its execution prevented? What department of the Government," Clay continued fervently, "what Government itself, will not be opposed by violence and by force, and thus its very existence be threatened?"[5] Across the aisle, Iowa Senator Augustus Caesar Dodge had already seconded his more famous colleague's sentiments. "I am . . . in favor of steps being taken such as will at the threshold stop all resistance to the law."[6]

Antislavery senator John Hale of New Hampshire, on the other hand, thought the president had blown the Shadrach affair out of all proportion. It was, he said, nothing more than a "momentary impulse to successful resistance to law," common to all civilizations at all times. The reaction of the government, he warned, was excessive. "If upon every such occasion such a parade as this is made, it will bring the Government into contempt. . . . Instead of strengthening, you weaken; instead of giving respect, you take it away."[7]

Southern senators denied Hale's analysis. Many say in the rescue evidence of a larger conspiracy, "the acting out of a great and widely-spread scheme throughout no small portion of New England,"[8] as North Carolina Senator George Badger said. Senator Hopkins Turney of Tennessee claimed that closely knit groups or "clubs" of anti-slavery Northerners stayed constantly on the alert to frustrate the law. And Stephen Douglas of Illinois, prime promoter of the 1850 compromise, agreed with these conclusions. For others the rescue bespoke less a conspiracy against the law than its basic inutility. Senator Butler, a strong supporter of the Mason bill, now agreed with Jefferson Davis that the law was futile (Document I-C-2). Only military force, Butler thought, could enforce it. The crux was, as Davis had said, that "there was not a sentiment in the northern States to enforce the law, and without that public sentiment, without that consent . . . the law was useless."[9] . . .

These critiques did not, however, shake Fillmore's determination to enforce the law and vindicate the 1850 compromise. He assigned Daniel Webster, the strongest member of his cabinet, to coordinate the prosecution of the Shadrach case. Richard Henry Dana, counsel for several of the defendants, learned from the federal district attorney that it was Webster who called the moves in the various trials and who would not drop the matter even after the jury refused to convict in several cases.

Webster's course could have been predicted from his public statements. In May 1851, for instance, he told an Albany, New York, audience that the fugitive slave law was "fair, reasonable, equitable, and just" and gave "the Southern States what they were entitled to, and what it was intended originally they should receive."[10] But he also went beyond support for the 1850 compromise to excoriate those who had already chosen to set the law at naught. Verbal opposition fell within the boundaries of free speech, but action on such opposition was, he asserted, nothing short of treason. Thus Webster's and Fillmore's determination to punish the Shadrach rescuers was not only a question of enforcing one unpopular law but of punishing traitors who threatened the national existence. . . .

In another case shortly after Webster's speech, the federal government was more successful. Thomas Sims, recently from Georgia, was seized, and in the absence of effective black or white antislavery support, was returned to slavery.

President Fillmore was delighted. "I congratulate you and the country," he wrote to Webster, "upon a triumph of law in Boston. She has done nobly. She has wiped out the stain of the former rescue [of Wilkins] and freed herself from the reproach of nullification.[11]

Forcible Resistance

In some other fugitive cases, however, the administration was less successful. Early in September 1851, Maryland slaveholder Edward Gorsuch, accompanied by a federal marshal, arrived in the southeastern Pennsylvania village of Christiana to reclaim four escaped slaves. Warned in advance of his approach, the fugitives hid in the house of William Parker, where other local blacks rallied to their protection. Not to be deterred, Gorsuch and his associates persisted until a gun battle occurred in which Gorsuch was killed and his son gravely wounded. When it was all over the four fugitives had disappeared, and Parker fled to Canada.

Once again the federal government acted to punish where it had not prevented. Some fifty marines were dispatched to Christiana where they turned the local hotel into a jail and courthouse from which the affair was investigated. Several weeks later, acting on Webster's conception of the offence, the government obtained indictments against some forty participants, not for violation of the Fugitive Slave Law but on charges of treason. Only one of them, Castner Hanway, a local white Quaker, was tried, and he was acquitted. Failing to win the first case, the federal district attorney George W. Ashmead dropped the treason charges against the others and sought no further indictments on lesser grounds. Thus once again the Fugitive Slave Law had been successfully challenged.

After the Christiana affair but before the trials, yet another successful defiance of the law occurred at Syracuse in upstate New York. There on October 1 Jerry McHenry was arrested as a fugitive. Both the timing and the locale suggested to many that Webster was seeking another dramatic demonstration that the government could and would enforce the law. Syracuse lay not only in the heart of politically oriented antislavery country but was also a major transfer point on the Underground Railroad, efficiently overseen by two clergymen, white Samuel J. May and black Jarmain Loguen. Taking a fugitive there would strike at a major flight route to Canada. But McHenry had been in Syracuse for some time and was well known to its inhabitants. Why then did federal officials select him and choose October 1 for the arrest, just when the local agricultural fair and a Liberty party regional convention brought mobs of people to town, many of them abolitionists? The evidence suggests either careless ineptitude or a careful choice to draw attention to the case.

Immediately after McHenry's arrest, a battery of lawyers offered counsel and were present at the preliminary hearing which began that same afternoon. When the proceedings recessed at about two-thirty, a group of blacks made their way into the court room, snatched up McHenry, and rushed him out, much as Boston blacks had done in the Shadrach rescue. They failed, however, to meld into the crowds, and police pursued them down the streets, around corners, and over a bridge. Finally the chase ended with the fugitive again in the hands of the police, who returned him to the Justice House. There he was placed under close guard. At five o'clock the hearings resumed, and at seven o'clock recessed until the following morning. Meanwhile, however, Unitarian minister May and Liberty party leader Gerrit Smith had planned a second rescue. At nine o'clock that evening the milling crowd, which had been throwing stones at the Justice House, invaded it, drove back the guards, freed McHenry and carried him victoriously on their shoulders to Bratnell's Hotel. There he was hurried away in a carriage, hidden for several days, and finally delivered across the lake to Canada.

In hindsight sober citizens speculated on the melodrama of McHenry's arrest and escape. The Syracuse *Journal* was sure that with care and efficiency the unpopular Fugitive Slave Law could be enforced in the city. Positing that "there would have been no disturbance, and [that] any attempt at a rescue would have been frustrated" had the government been able to "inspire the public with respect" or "been capable of managing a matter of this importance with judgment and wisdom,"[12] the newspaper blamed federal authorities for botching the whole affair. Testimony to their failure was the sole injury of the day, the broken arm of a marshal who, in fleeing the mob, had jumped from a window.

Once again federal resolution stiffened after the event—this time in a series of trials which lasted for nearly two years. Once again the district attorney laid treason charges against the leaders, including May and Smith, who were arraigned in nearby Auburn, home town of William Seward. There the senator went bond for their bail, entertained them, and agreed to act as defense counsel should his services be necessary. But in mid-November, when the government sought indictments from a grand jury on the treason charges, it was rebuffed. Not won over by the logic of Webster's treason theory, the grand jurors returned indictments merely for participating in riot and obstructing the return of a fugitive. . . . In his annual message of December 1851 President Fillmore emphasized again a determination to enforce the law. Like Webster he saw in opposition to it more than simple lawbreaking. Those who disobeyed it attacked the Constitution and thereby betrayed "their wish to see that Constitution overturned." If his administration was to prevent potential traitors from "rend[ing] asunder this Union,"[13] it had to take action. Yet what could it do? Not only had it failed to prevent three spectacular rescues; it had had little success in punishing the transgressors. In both the Shadrach and Christiana cases no one was found guilty on federal charges; and in the Jerry prosecutions only one defendant, Enoch Reed, a black man, was convicted, and that not under the controversial 1850 law but under the old 1793 statute. Of the other Jerry defendants who reached trial, two were set free by hung juries and one was acquitted; the cases against all the rest were finally abandoned.

While the government pressed its enforcement program with minimal success, abolitionists continued to attack the new law. . . . The new mood was nowhere better defined, however, than in an 1851 resolution of the American Anti-Slavery Society. "As for the Fugitive Slave Law, we execrate it, we spit upon it, we trample it under our feet."[14]

The Politics of Repeal

The conflict over early attempts to enforce the Fugitive Slave Law also marked election-year politics in 1852. In the Congress, while they recognized its practical futility, antislavery legislators repeatedly raised the question of repeal, though they frequently had to stretch a point to relate their remarks to the topic directly under debate. The only major speech for repeal, however, came from Massachusetts's new senator, Charles Sumner. . . .

On July 27 Sumner had created an opening for his attack on the fugitive law. No one could limit his speaking directly to the business of the Senate; he launched a three-and-three-quarter-hour carefully structured and well-memorized oration. Slavery, he argued, was exclusively a matter for state responsibility. The return of fugitives, therefore, could not constitutionally be undertaken by the federal government. To the contrary, each state must decide how to meet its obligation and could approach the problem from the assumptions of a free rather than a slave state. The only clear-cut restraint on state action was the constitutional requirement that it not legislate freedom for fugitives bound to service in other states. . . . The debate which followed showed clearly that Sumner's intent was less letting each state take responsibility for returning fugitives than rendering the constitutional provision for such return inoperative.

Although Sumner's amendment won only four votes, its overwhelming defeat reflected less the convictions of Northern senators than the imperatives of election-year politics. With few exceptions, senators could not appear loyal to their party's platform and also support the Massachusetts senator. On the other hand, for Free Soilers like John P. Hale, the party's presidential candidate, it was easy because his party's platform read "that the Fugitive Slave Act of 1850 is repugnant to the Constitution, to the principles of the common law, to the spirit of Christianity, and to the sentiments of the civilized world."[15] Sumner was only proposing to realize their common party's goal.

But for antislavery Whigs the choice was not so easy. Members of a national party, they were caught in the constraints of practical politics. Though they were not enchanted by the Whig presidential candidate, Winfield Scott, they hoped he could be elected and that when he was elected, they could control him. Their party's platform, however, reflected Fillmore's loyalty to the 1850 Compromise and his determination to enforce the Fugitive Slave Law. Explicitly rejecting repeal, its only sop to the law's opponents was an oblique reference to alteration at some indeterminate future date.

For Democrats there was even less latitude. Their platform fully supported the fugitive law as a permanent and constitutionally binding obligation. Although their presidential candidate, New Hampshire's Franklin Pierce, had once indiscreetly confessed his dislike for the law, his public record belied the slightest antislavery tinge. From 1836, when as a young congressman he had supported the gag resolution against receiving antislavery petitions, he set the course he there-after followed, supporting the Southern wing of his party. In 1850 he had forced the Democratic gubernatorial candidate in New Hampshire to resign after the latter had repudiated the Fugitive Slave Law. Later Pierce persuaded both his state party convention and a state constitutional convention to endorse the 1850 Compromise and particularly the fugitive law. . . .

Despite lingering doubts among some Southerners that he might not be wholly sound on the fugitive slave question—and his preelection correspondence indicates that that was one of three major issues raised against him during the campaign—his past record met the challenge. When the votes were counted Pierce had 200,000 majority over Scott, while the total Free Soil vote amounted to less than 157,000. Pierce saw in the election tally a talisman of sectional harmony and a mandate for vigorous enforcement of the fugitive law. To Horace Greeley, antislavery editor of the New York *Tribune*, the election meant roughly the same thing. "There is no probability," he wrote, "that . . . the Fugitive Slave Law . . . will be altered by Congress during the present generation."[16] The desire for harmony seemed to have triumphed over the higher law.

Notes

1. William Henry Seward, "Annual Message to the Legislature," January 7, 1840, in George Ellis Baker, ed., *Works of William H. Seward* (New York: Redfield, 1853-54), 2: 221.
2. *16 Peters, Justice Story's Opinion*, 608, quoted in Marion Gleason McDougall, *Fugitive Slaves* (1891; New York: Bergman Publishers, 1967), 109.
3. George L. Clarke to Frederick Douglass, February 18, 1848, in *North Star*, March 3, 1948.
4. U.S. Congress, Senate, *Congressional Globe*, 31st Cong., 1st sess., January 28, 1850, 236.
5. U.S., Congress, Senate, *Congressional Globe*, 31st Cong., 1st sess., August 19, 1850, Appendix, 1585.
6. *Ibid.*, 31st Cong., 2nd sess., February 22, 1851, Appendix, 310.
7. *Ibid.*, 31st Cong., 2nd sess., February 21, 1851, Appendix, 296.
8. *Ibid.*, 31st Cong., 2nd sess., February 21, 1851, Appendix, 301.
9. *Ibid.*, 31st Cong., 2nd sess., February 18, 1851, 598.
10. Daniel Webster, *Works* (7th edition. Boston: Little, Brown and Co., 1853), 2: 575.
11. Millard Fillmore to Daniel Webster, April 16, 1851, quoted in Stanley W. Campbell, *The Slave Catchers: Enforcement of the Fugitive Slave Law, 1850-1860* (Chapel Hill: University of North Carolina Press, 1970), 99-100.

12. Syracuse *Journal*, n.d., reprinted in *Frederick Douglass' Paper*, October 9, 1851.

13. James D. Richardson, comp., *A Compilation of the Messages and Papers of the Presidents* . . . (New York: Bureau of National Literature, 1897–1917), 6: 2674.

14. *National Anti-Slavery Standard*, May 15, 1851.

15. Kirk H. Porter and Donald Bruce Johnson, *National Party Platforms, 1840–1956* (Urbana: University of Illinois Press, 1956), 18.

16. Quoted in Stanley W. Campbell, *The Slave Catchers: Enforcement of the Fugitive Slave Law, 1850–1860* (Chapel Hill: University of North Carolina Press, 1970), 179.

14

Value Conflicts
in the Law
of Evidence
William M. Evan

The case of *Rochin v. California* (342 U.S. 165, 1951) introduces our problem of science, value, and law. Three deputy sheriffs illegally entered Rochin's house and forced their way into his bedroom, where they found two capsules on a stand beside the bed. When the officers asked whose they were, Rochin seized the capsules and put them in his mouth. The officers then assaulted him in an effort to extract the capsules. Failing in this, they handcuffed him and took him to a hospital where, at their direction, a doctor forced an emetic solution through a tube into Rochin's stomach. This "stomach pumping" brought up the capsules, which contained morphine. The capsules were used as the chief evidence for Rochin's conviction. The decision was upheld in the appellate court but reversed by the Supreme Court of the United States on the ground that it violated the Due Process Clause of the Fourteenth Amendment.

In this case the California narcotics law, designed presumably to protect the health and morals of the public, was subordinated to the Due Process Clause, which safeguards the citizen against the abusive and arbitrary exercise of authority by the state. The conviction was reversed not because of any doubt about the validity of the evi-

Reprinted from *American Behavioral Scientists* 4 (November 1960), pp. 23-26, by permission of the publisher, Sage Publications, Inc.

dence of violation of the narcotics law, but because of the methods by which it was obtained. Justice Felix Frankfurter, in giving the majority opinion, analogized the case to a conviction based on a coerced confession: "This course of proceeding by agents of government to obtain evidence is bound to offend even hardened sensibilities. They are methods too close to the rack and the screw to permit of constitutional differentiation." One concurring justice argued that the evidence was secured in violation of the Fifth Amendment. Another concurring justice contended that the conviction violated the Fourth Amendment, which proscribes "unreasonable search or seizure."

In Pursuit of Justice

In the case of *Rochin v. California*, as in all cases, the avowed objective of the court is a just decision. "Justice" is the desired end of the judicial process and one of the institutionalized means to achieve this end is the law of evidence. The concept of justice, like that of law, however, continues to be the subject of controversy in jurisprudence. Exponents of natural law conceive of justice and law as transcendental values rooted in divine will, whereas adherents of legal positivism contend that they are an expression of the will of a sovereign state.

From a sociological rather than a jurisprudential point of view, law is a body of norms with institutionalized methods of enforcement and justice is a set of cultural values justifying them. Thus, justice might be called a complex of political, religious, economic, familial, and other institutionalized values—of the culture of one or more societies—which serves as the foundation of law. Or as Rene Savatier puts it, law is "the incarnation of justice and all the moral values which go with it."[1] And the courts administering justice adjudicate disputes in terms of some working conception, however accurate or inaccurate, of the values comprising justice. The empirical basis of the court's conception of the community's "sense of justice" has only recently been systematically investigated.[2]

The law of evidence, from a sociological point of view, is a body of rules governing judicial investigations into questions of *fact*, designed to regularize the behavior of actors in a significant type of social situation. As one of its functions, it purportedly assists in "the discovery of truth in trials." As an instrumental value designed to achieve the goal of justice, however, the law of evidence may come into conflict with some component values of justice. Analysis of this recurrent legal situation provides an opportunity to identify, among other things, the values, conflict of values, and hierarchy of values embodied in law and reflected in judicial decisions.

The system of rules comprising the law of evidence is a product of centuries of development toward rationalization. Legal scholars have termed this body of law a "child of the jury trial system." With the rise of the English jury system in the thirteenth century, such "irrational" methods as trial by oath, by ordeal, by battle, and by other rituals were gradually eliminated. Inquisitorial procedures by church and state were replaced by an adversary court system. The reliance on a group of one's peers to determine the facts of a case democratized the administration of justice and provided protection against arbitrary acts by government or ecclesiastical authorities. As the law of evidence slowly evolved along with common law, it underwent a process of rationalization and secularization. As Max Weber pointed out, the previous "formally irrational" trial systems, with their dependence upon magic and divine interposition, were superseded by "formally rational" procedures more in harmony with the ethos of modern science. These rational, secular, and democratic changes in the legal system—changes associated with the emergence of the liberal state—were functional requirements for the rise of capitalism.[3]

The Role of Science

In the modern era the value of truth is identified preeminently with the ethos of science. And in keeping with the historical trend toward rationalization in the law of evidence, the legal profession is making relatively increasing use of social science methodology in determining questions of fact. Survey data, for example, have been given judicial consideration in a number of cases, though they are still not consistently admitted as evidence. In some cases survey data have been excluded on the ground that they violated the hearsay rule, since the interviewees were not available in court for cross-examination. Content analysis has been used in several instances; and recently, psycholinguistic techniques have been employed in a criminal case to ascertain whether a confession was coerced.

Notwithstanding the long-term rationalization process in the law of evidence, a court trial has hardly been transformed into a scientific investigation. Conflicts of cultural values intrude forcibly. Whereas the search for truth in the form of verifiable and abstract knowledge is, ideally, the controlling factor in the conduct of a scientific inquiry, values other than the pursuit of truth—as illustrated in the case of *Rochin v. California*—dominate a trial.

Technical specialists do not disinterestedly investigate all available data bearing on a case and report their findings to a judge, who in turn arrives at a decision by finding the best "fit" between the data and an unambiguous law. Instead, in accordance with the adversary court system counsel for each party presents partisanly selected data, subject to admissibility rules of evidence, often to a jury of laymen who arrive at a verdict. A striking paradox may be briefly noted: the existing adversary court system presupposes a "perspectivistic" approach to truth, as opposed to the non-perspectivistic or objective approach which underlies the methodology of scientific inquiry as well as the inquisitorial court system current in the Middle Ages and in modern totalitarian states.

Unlike the canons of scientific inquiry, the law of evidence includes an elaborate body of rules of admissibility, some of which have the general effect of promoting the search for truth, and others of obstructing it. In the former category are rules of hearsay, original writings, authentication of documents, testimonial qualifications, and impeachment of witnesses. These attempt to ensure that answers of more probative values are given to controverted questions of fact. They are also designed to exclude evidence to which lay jurors might attach too much weight.

The Case of Testimonial Privilege

Testimonial privileges, on the other hand, are rules that tend to obstruct the search for truth. They include, on the one hand, privileged *acts* such as self-incrimination; and, on the other hand, *privileged communications* such as those between attorney and client, physician and patient, husband and wife, and priest and penitent.

The rationale for the testimonial privilege is phrased in terms of "social policy," *viz.*, that values such as marital harmony and stability take precedence over the ascertainment of truth. "The basic reason the law has refused to pit wife against husband or husband against wife in a trial where life or liberty is at stake," says Justice Black, "was the belief that such a policy is necessary to foster family peace, not only for the benefit of husband, wife, and children, but for the benefit of the public as well." (*Hawkins v. U.S.*, 79 S. Ct. 136, 138, 1958.)

Similarly, it is argued that the religious values of the priest–penitent privilege and the delicacy of health considerations in the doctor-patient privilege must be protected in a court trial, even if it be at the expense of rationality in the fact-finding procedure. Thus the rules of testimonial privilege, as distinct from most exclusionary rules of evidence, point to a conflict between means and ends in the law of evidence: the ascertainment of truth of litigated propositions vs. the preservation of values embedded in various institutions and also comprising elements of the concept of justice. So "truth is barred."

Testimonial privileges may be waived, since they are options conceded to classes of persons to decline giving certain testimony. How often are these privileges in fact claimed? When they are claimed, how crucial does the excluded testimony *appear* to be to the structure of the evidence presented and to the judicial decision? To what extent are present rules of privileged communications held essential or desirable by the various professions and client-publics? Is the public at large in favor of an extension or a restriction of testimonial privileges pertaining to professions?

One condition necessary for the establishment of privilege is that "the *relation* must be one which in the opinion of the community ought to be sedulously fostered."[4] With respect to the husband–wife privilege, Justice Steward in *Hawkins v. U.S.* raises a relevant empirical question: "Before assuming that a change in the present rule would work such a wholesale disruption of domestic felicity as the court's opinion implies, it would be helpful to know the experiences in those jurisdictions where the rule has been abandoned or modified."

A similar question may be asked with respect to the priest–penitent and physician–patient rules of privilege. Is the professional–client relationship at all impaired in those States which do not have these privileges? Since the confidentiality of the professional–client relationship is prescribed in the codes of ethics of all professions and is a culturally approved relationship, it is doubtful whether the relationship would be jeopardized in the absence of rules of privileged communications. In jurisdictions in which statutory provisions for these privileges or such common-law rules do not exist, are those privileges informally recognized or judicially noticed? If they are judicially noticed, is it because the courts take cognizance of the "customs" of the professions?

Apart from the explicit values which the rules of privileged communication seek to protect, it is not fortuitous that the only occupations covered are such long-established professions as law, clergy, and medicine. This may be partly a reflection of the prestige of these occupations and their organizational power to protect their vested interests. By contrast, such new professions as journalism, accounting, and social work—except in a few jurisdictions—are not covered by these privileges.

In this respect, the old profession of teaching is an anomaly. Why are teacher-student communications, particularly at the college level, not privileged? If the legal status of teaching and the new professions is explained by differential organizational power, rather than by other factors, a question arises: As these professions develop strong organizations, will they demand statutory extensions of the rules of privileged communication?

Moreover, given a general trend toward professionalization of various occupations and a further extension of occupational licensing laws, may we expect an increase in the number of occupations covered by testimonial privileges? If testimonial privileges *are* extended to an increasing number of occupations, the secular trend toward a rationalization in the law of evidence will be impeded, leading to more value conflicts between the instrumental and the terminal values of the judicial process.

If the trend toward rationalization does continue, however, testimonial privileges may be reduced or eventually eliminated. In the opinion of one legal scholar, Charles McCormick, "The manifest destiny of evidence law is a progressive lowering of the barriers to truth. . . . One may hazard a guess . . . that in a secular sense privileges are on the way out."[5] If this prediction proves accurate, value conflicts may be minimized or resolved. Two dysfunctional consequences of the testimonial privileges would also be reduced or eliminated. We would be better able to predict the results of the litigation process, which is now difficult in part because of uncertainty as to what evidence will be withheld due to testimonial privileges. The social control function of law would be strengthened in that fewer guilty persons would be able to evade punishment with the aid of the law of evidence.

However, if value conflicts are resolved in favor of more rational trial procedures, we may pay a high social cost. Some of the rules of evidence may interfere with a rational investigation of questions of fact, but they also protect the rights of the citizen against the state's monopoly of coercive power and protect values of society that presumably are widely cherished.

Thus we are faced with a dilemma. If, on the one hand, the value conflicts are resolved in favor of increasing *rational* trial procedures, some of the rights of the citizen against the state and some societal values may be threatened. On the other hand, if the value conflicts are resolved in favor of *traditional* trial procedures, to preserve some values of major institutions of our society, the rational pursuit of truth is not only obstructed but judicial predictability is lowered and social control is impaired.

Value conflicts are endemic to complex societies. The type and frequency of value conflicts will vary from one society to another. The legal system provides many problems of value conflicts, as we have seen. An analysis of rules of evidence, or even more particularly testimonial privileges pertaining to occupations, would throw light on the interrelations between selected occupations and the legal system, and it would contribute to an understanding of the rise and decline of legal norms.

Notes

1. In "Law and Progress of Techniques," *Intl. Social Science Bulletin*, IV (1952), p. 310.
2. See Julius Cohen, Reginald A. H. Robson, and Alan Bates, "Ascertaining the Moral Sense of the Community," *Journal of Legal Education*, VIII (1955), pp. 137-49; and their monograph, *Parental Authority*, Rutgers U. Press, 1958.
3. *Law in Economy and Society*, Cambridge: Harvard U. Press, 1954, pp. xlviii-lxiii, 61-64, 73, 227-28.
4. John H. Wigmore, *A Treatise on the Anglo-American System of Evidence in Trials at Common Law.* Boston: Little, Brown and Co., 1940, Vol. 1, p. 531.
5. *Handbook of the Law of Evidence*, St. Paul: West Publishing Co., 1954, pp. 165-66.

15

Support for the Legal System
Austin Sarat

The legal system—the institutions, processes, and officials responsible for making, administering, and enforcing the law—considered as a whole makes important functional contributions to our society and polity (Friedman, 1969). Those who make, administer, and enforce the law play active and important roles in regulating social relationships, resolving conflicts, and allocating goods, services, power, prestige, and other scarce resources (Aubert, 1974). Among the factors influencing the behavior of these performing these functions, students of the legal system have increasingly come to recognize the importance of public opinion. This recognition has accompanied the realization that the capacity of the courts, police, and other legal institutions to perform their functions is to a large extent dependent on the level of public support for them . . . and it is reflected in the growing number of studies which have employed the concept of support in their analyses of the legal system (Rodgers and Lewis, 1974; Murphy and Tanenhaus, 1968, 1974; Skogan, 1971; Boynton et al., 1968; Richardson et al., 1972; Walker, 1972; Engstrom and Giles, 1972).

The concept of support is itself relatively new in the social sciences, yet it has already evoked considerable interest and stimulated

Excerpt from "Support for the Legal System: An Analysis of Knowledge, Attitudes, and Behavior," *American Politics Quarterly* 3 (January 1975), pp. 3–24, by permission of the author and publisher, Sage Publications, Inc.

a substantial body of research. This concept was first introduced into our lexicon about a decade ago by Easton (1965). Although Easton was primarily concerned with explaining the way in which support contributed to the persistence of the political system, his analysis seems no less relevant for the study of legal institutions and behavior. In his writing (1973: 38-39), Easton defined support as "any kind of favorable orientation that prepares a person to act on behalf of or in opposition to a political object," and he identified two varieties of support which he called "specific" and "diffuse." . . .

From his original general and theoretical formulation have followed numerous attempts to refine and analyze the theory of political support. Those who have studied the state of public support for various political and legal institutions have begun to identify and investigate some of the most important issues and hypotheses in Easton's original theoretical statement.

Among the most important of these issues is the extent to which public support for political and legal institutions is or is not compatible with the ideal of an "informed citizenry." While classical democratic theorists regard widespread public interest in and knowledge about politics as an important cornerstone of democratic institutions (Bachrach, 1967), many contemporary social scientists argue that democratic institutions function best when the public is neither too informed about nor interested in their operations (Lipset, 1963; Dahl, 1961; Key, 1961; Budge, 1970). In fact, as Edelman (1971) suggests, the continued viability of the myths and symbols which legitimize governmental institutions may be dependent upon the vagueness and ambiguity which characterizes the way most people perceive and think about politics and government.

Others who have studied specific political and legal institutions have found this same inverse relationship between knowledge and support which theorists like Edelman predict. For example, those who have studied support for the U.S. Supreme Court report that diffuse support for the court is generally relatively high; at the same time, however, they report that knowledge about the way the court operates and its specific decisions is quite low. Those who know more about either the institution or its decisions seem to be uniformly less supportive, e.g., less likely to approve specific decisions and less likely to believe in the legitimacy of the court, than those whose evaluations of the court are ill-informed. . . . The incompatibility of knowledge and support has also been noted in studies of public attitudes toward the police (Bayley and Mendelsohn, 1969; McIntyre, 1967; Coopersmith, 1971), toward lower courts (Skogan, 1971) and toward various legal institutions and practices in several European countries (Podgorecki et al., 1973). The inverse relationship of knowledge and support may occur because as people come to know more about political and legal institutions they may come to realize the extent to which such institutions, and the people who run them, fall short of their expressed ideals and functions. Increased knowledge highlights the gap between the way people expect governmental institutions to operate and the way they in fact function. This may be especially true when, in the case of institutions like the courts, the way people think they function is dramatically out of line with their operating reality. . . .

Another important issue in the theory of political support involves the relationship of what Easton has called "covert" and "overt" expressions of support (1965). According to Easton's formulation, support for government and its institutions can be manifest both in what people think and in how they behave. However, the relationship between these two ways of expressing support is, for Easton, not self-evident. It is an issue to be examined and investigated.

Most of those who have studied support either for the political system as a whole or for any of its component parts have not investigated the linkage between the way people feel about these objects and the way they behave. Students of support have tended to focus exclusively on the covert, attitudinal dimension of support. There have been, however, several recent studies which have tried to explicitly investigate the linkage of supportive attitudes and behavior. Dennis, for example, in his study of support for the institution of elections examined the relationship of support for the electoral system and participation in elections. He found that one component of support, what he calls "voting duty," was significantly related to this kind of behavior, while two other components, "approval of electoral processes and efficacy of elections," were not (Dennis, 1970). This finding is important in illustrating how support for a political object may influence behavior with respect to that object. Additionally, it indicates that by disaggregating support, by examining various dimensions of a generally supportive attitude, we may get a clearer picture of the way in which that attitude influences political behavior.

Like Dennis, Muller has investigated the effects of supportive attitudes on political behavior. Focusing on support for national governmental institutions, Muller reports (1970: 408) what he calls a "moderately strong relationship" between the attitudes of the students he surveyed and their "intention to avoid disruptive behavior." Others, however, have found that the linkage of attitudinal support and specific behavior is quite weak. For example, Rodgers and Lewis report that there is virtually no relationship between support and obedience to law. They suggest that whether an individual obeys the law and/or avoids engaging in "unconventional" political behavior may be dependent on factors far more specific and concrete than general beliefs in the legitimacy of the regime or diffuse support for political authorities (Rodgers and Lewis, 1974). The varying relationships which Dennis, Muller, and Rodgers report between covert and overt support are a function, to some extent, of differences in the objects they studied and of the different ways in which they operationalized the concepts of covert and overt support. Nevertheless, their work highlights the importance of investigating the relationship of attitudes and behavior in the theory of political support.

This paper is concerned with the problem of support as it applies to the legal system. . . . I will examine the degree to which support for the legal system is associated with knowledge of it and the degree to which that support is reflected in behavior.

Support for the Legal System

. . . Easton himself has recognized the difficulties inherent in trying to operationalize the concept of support and has recently suggested that instead of trying to measure support in an additive way, namely by defining all the components of an object and asking questions about each component on the assumption that attitudes toward the object as a whole will be equal to the sum of attitudes toward the components, those interested in studying support might try to measure it in a "holistic" manner. Specifically, he suggests that we treat objects or systems as wholes and try to measure attitudes toward the object or system under study in a general way (Easton, 1973). The measurement of support for the legal system employed in this research follows the second strategy. Support was measured by nine Likert-type attitudinal statements. These items did not deal with courts, police, lawyers, or other specific elements of the legal system; rather they all were designed to tap support for law and the operation of the legal system as a whole. They were included in a larger survey administered to a random household probability sample of the adult (over eighteen years old) population of Madison, Wisconsin in January 1973. People (220) were interviewed in person by employees of the Wisconsin Survey Research Lab.

The data arrayed in Table 1 indicate that support for law and the legal system varies considerably. When asked to consider the way the legal system is currently operating, large numbers of the people interviewed registered disapproval. For example, while almost everyone (92%) agrees that law should reflect the wishes of the majority

TABLE 1. Support Items (in percentages)

	STRONGLY AGREE 1	2	3	AGREE/DISAGREE 4	5	6	STRONGLY DISAGREE 7	DON'T KNOW
(1) I must always obey the law	41.4	22.7	6.4	11.4	5.9	4.1	8.2	5
(2) The individual who refuses to obey the law is a menace to society.	41.8	17.7	9.5	18.6	4.5	3.2	4.5	0
(3) Disobedience of the law can never be tolerated.	19.1	10.0	11.4	20.5	10.0	10.5	17.7	.9
(4) A person should obey the law even if it goes against what he thinks is right.	27.4	20.9	15.9	15.9	5.9	5.9	7.7	.5
(5) Personal circumstances should never be considered an excuse for lawbreaking.	19.5	11.8	10.0	12.3	15.0	13.2	16.4	1.9
(6) It would be difficult to break the law and keep my self-respect.	39.5	19.5	6.8	12.7	4.5	7.3	8.2	1.4
(7) We would be better off with fewer laws.	12.1	15.5	21.5	14.1	5.0	17.7	12.7	1.4
(8) Something must be done to improve the way the legal system operates and the laws it produces.	12.3	22.3	24.5	22.3	6.3	7.7	3.2	1.4
(9) The law in this country generally reflects the wishes of the majority.	9.1	9.1	9.5	22.3	18.6	17.3	12.7	1.4

171

of the peoples, only 27% believe that the law generally meets this standard.[1] For most others, the law does not live up to an important democratic norm. Furthermore, almost one-half of those interviewed state that the law tries to do too much, that too many things are regulated by law, and that "We would be better off with fewer laws." Finally, 59% of the Madison sample believe that change is needed, that "something must be done to improve the way the legal system operates and the laws which it produces."

The dissatisfaction which seems to emerge from these responses exists, however, alongside an equally prevalent belief in the obliga- tory character of legal action. Most of those interviewed (64%) agree that "A person should obey the law even if it goes against what he thinks is right." Furthermore, two items dealing with attitudes toward lawbreakers elicit uniform and impressive support for the legal system. Almost seven out of every ten of the people interviewed believe that disobedience to the law is harmful to the society, and over two-thirds of those in the sample say that they would lose respect for themselves if they disobeyed the law. The feeling of obligation reflected in these items exists, as we have seen, alongside considerable questioning of the current state of the legal system. This paradox may reflect a type of resignation in public affairs, a sense that while an individual may not like the way things are going he must nevertheless acquiesce, a response associated with the emphasis on an "obedient" conception of citizenship which most people learn as children. . . . Alternatively it may reflect a willingness to go along while attempts at reform are made, a sense that current problems do not undercut the basic legitimacy of the legal system. In either case, it is a paradox which illustrates Easton's (1965: 269–277) contention that current popular dissatisfactions do not automatically threaten the legitimacy and popular support of particular governmental institutions or of the political system as a whole.

The items arrayed in Table 1 display, as we have seen, a varied pattern of responses. These items were designed to tap two separate dimensions of support for the legal system, specifically, having to do with the way respondents viewed their general legal obligations (items 1–6) and the way they evaluated the current operation of the legal system (items 7–9), dimensions roughly parallel to Easton's categorization of diffuse and specific support. In order to test the extent to which this hypothesized division was, in fact, reflected in responses to the nine support items, the items were analyzed in a common-item pool using factor analysis. If this division is empirically valid, there should be a clear factorial division between items 1–6 in Table 1 and items 7–9. In fact, a Kaiser Varimax rotated solution applied to these nine items demonstrates empirical support for the

TABLE 2. Factor Analysis of Support Items

ITEM	FACTOR I	FACTOR II
(1)	.661	-.363
(2)	.634	-.202
(3)	.751	-.045
(4)	.711	-.073
(5)	.612	-.002
(6)	.746	-.168
(7)	-.306	.528
(8)	-.267	.695
(9)	-.319	.555
Percentage of total variance (cumulative)	37.1	51.5
Percentage of explained variance (cumulative)	72.8	100.0

NOTE: Missing values were handled by recoding to the mean for each item.

hypothesized division of the support items; that is, as Table 2 indicates, items designed to measure each component of support tend to load highly on separate factors, and these factors combined explain 51% of the total variance.[2] This analysis offers some assurance that the items measure distinct components of support, components which conform to the theoretical distinctions generally recognized in the literature on support. Thus, the nine items were grouped into two scales: the first, based on items 1–6, tapping general "willingness to comply" with the law, and the second, composed of items 7–9, tapping "satisfaction" or dissatisfaction with the legal system as it currently operates.

Using the two dimensions of support which emerge from the rotation procedure, I factor scored respondents in my sample.[3] In the analysis that follows, these scores are used first to examine the relationships which exist between knowledge of the legal system and the dimensions of satisfaction and willingness to comply, and second, to assess the relationship of both dimensions of covert support and supportive behavior.

Knowledge and Support

As suggested above, one of the analytic issues which previous studies of support have highlighted is the relationship between what people know about and how they feel toward various political and legal institutions. Such studies demonstrate that support for many of these institutions varies inversely with knowledge of them. In order to test the extent to which this same type of relationship occurs in considering support for the legal system, each of the respondents was presented with ten items describing various legal rules, processes, and functions, and asked to indicate whether the items accurately portrayed the particular rule, process, or function in question.

As Table 3 indicates, the respondents, taken as a whole, displayed a relatively high level of knowledge about almost all of the rules, processes, and functions which were described in the ten items. For example, almost everyone knew that a policeman must inform a suspect of his rights before questioning him; additionally, over 80% of those interviewed were aware of the prohibition in our legal system of ex post facto lawmaking, correctly perceived that the judge in a criminal trial does not have prosecutorial functions, and that such trials are usually public. The highest levels of knowledge were displayed about these various elements of the criminal justice system, elements widely publicized in the mass media. It is this mass media dissemination of information which may account for the relatively high level of knowledge which the respondents displayed. The dissemination of information about the legal system is not, however, uniform. For instance, over 40% of those interviewed did not know that the attorney general of Wisconsin does not have to give his permission before a police search can be conducted; an equally high percentage did not seem to know about the guarantee against self-incrimination. Finally, knowledge about the civil side of the law and its operations was, on the whole, lower than even the least well-known of the criminal aspects. This may reflect the fact that civil processes are generally less well publicized and are the subject of much less attention in the mass media. In any case, the fact that my respondents knew less about civil than criminal processes is in line with the findings of others (*Michigan Law Review*, 1973; Williams and Hall, 1972) and, more importantly, it suggests a potential problem in our legal system. Legal knowledge is a fundamental requisite for citizens in a competitive economic and political system. Only people who know what their rights are and how the legal system works can defend themselves against intrusions on their freedom and use that system to achieve their goals or ameliorate undesired conditions. . . . The people in this admittedly limited sample seem better prepared to defend themselves, to know their rights vis-à-vis the police or other law enforcement agencies, than to use the legal system as a resource in their lives.

Since the primary purpose of this study was to assess the impact of knowledge on support for the legal system, each respondent was given a knowledge score based on the number of items which they

T A B L E 3 . Knowledge of the Legal System

	ANSWER GIVEN BY RESPONDENTS (IN PERCENTAGES)		
	True	*False*	*Don't Know*
(1) The attorney general of Wisconsin has to give his permission before a policeman can search someone's home.	22.2	59.1[a]	17.7
(2) If an innocent man is arrested it is up to him to prove that he is not guilty.	24.1	73.2[a]	2.7
(3) Criminal trials in the United States are usually secret.	6.8	86.4[a]	6.8
(4) A man who has committed a crime can be made to answer questions about the crime in court.	42.3	47.7[a]	10.0
(5) It is the job of a judge to prove that a man accused of a crime is guilty.	11.8	85.5[a]	2.7
(6) Before a policeman questions a person accused of crime, he must inform the suspect of his right to remain silent.	96.4[a]	2.3	1.4
(7) If you owe money to a store and have refused to pay your debt, the owner of the store can get a court order attaching part of your salary or wages until you have made arrangements to pay.	62.7[a]	19.1	18.2
(8) In order to drive a car in this state, you must have liability and collision insurance.	38.2	53.2[a]	8.6
(9) A citizen may be arrested and punished for violating a law which did not exist when he committed the act prohibited by law.	5.0	86.8[a]	8.2
(10) If you wanted to and could afford it you could take any court case all the way up to the Supreme Court of the United States.	53.2	34.1[a]	12.7

[a]Indicates the correct answer.

correctly identified as being either accurate or inaccurate. The relationship of these scores and the two dimensions of support is presented in Table 4.

Table 4 shows that the relationship of knowledge and these dimensions is not uniform. With respect to the first, willingness to comply,

TABLE 4. Bivariate and Partial Correlations (Pearson's r)
Between Knowledge and Support for the Legal System[a]

	BIVARIATE	PARTIAL
Willingness to Comply	.11	.08
Satisfaction	-.36[b]	-.30[b]

[a]Controlling for education.
[b]Significant at .01 level.

there is a slight, but insignificant relationship between what people
know about law and the legal system and their general feelings about
whether law should or should not be obeyed. The norm of law abid-
ingness appears so strong, as previous studies of both adults and
children have shown (Boynton et al., 1968; Rodgers and Taylor,
1970; Hess and Torney, 1967), that it is adhered to no matter what
people know about the way the legal system operates or the laws
and rules which govern their lives.

The picture changes dramatically when the second dimension of
support is considered. The inverse relationship which others have
reported between knowledge and support emerges most clearly when
we examine the way in which the respondents evaluate the current
state of the legal system. More than one-half (52%) of those high in
their knowledge of the law and the legal system are low in their
level of satisfaction. On the other hand, almost two-thirds (63%) of
those who had little knowledge are high in their level of satisfaction.

Table 4 also demonstrates that the varying relationship of knowledge and the two dimensions of support is not significantly altered
when we control for the effect of education. The more a person
knows about the legal system, the more dissatisfied he is likely to be
no matter how well or how poorly he is educated. Those who know
more about the legal system appear to be acutely aware of its problems and failings. Yet at the same time, they appear willing to
acknowledge a general obligation to comply with its decisions, an
acknowledgement which may well contribute to the maintenance of
the very system with which they are dissatisfied.

Covert Support and Supportive Behavior

Easton (1965: 158), in describing the role which the "support
input" plays in the political system, suggests that support enables
political authorities "to make decisions, to get them accepted as
binding and to put them into effect." According to this line of

reasoning, support for the political system should be associated with compliance (behavioral conformity) with its authoritative decisions. Support, suggests Easton, is only meaningful to the extent that people express it in their overt behavior. As indicators of this kind of behavioral support he suggests (1965: 165) that we look at

> the regularity with which citizens or subjects perform their obligations; manifestations of open hostility such as breaches of the law . . . and expressions of preferences for other systems through emigration or separatist activities. Hence the ratio of deviance to conformity as measured by violations of laws, the prevalence of violence, the size of dissident movements, or the amount of money spent for security would provide individual indices of support.

Those who express supportive sentiments toward a particular institution or system should behave in a way which contributes to the effectiveness of that institution or system. No matter how that behavior is operationalized, if support is a meaningful concept in political analysis then we should expect to find that differences in covert support are reflected in differences in behavioral or overt support.

As indicated earlier, this hypothesis has been the subject of some attention in other research; however, few have tried to test it by employing measures of the way people actually behave. Ideally one would like to be able to observe directly and note the way people behave with respect to the legal or political system. Such a strategy is, however, usually too costly and too difficult to carry out. As a result, the generally preferred way to measure behavior is to examine some close approximation; although it is not without problems, the best approximation of directly observing behavior is allowing people to report on their own behavior.

Two especially vexing problems plague reported behavior measures. The first is, of course, the problem of recall. People may or may not accurately recall the way they behaved in the past and/or they may remember their behavior in a highly selective fashion. . . . The added problem in this case is that the behavior in question is by definition "deviant." Violations of the law, whether or not they result in the imposition of external sanctions, are generally condemned by most people. As a result, an individual who violates the law may be reluctant to admit having done so, reluctant because of his fear of the disapproval of others, or reluctant because of his own negative evaluation of lawbreaking. In either case, this reluctance is likely to bias reported behavior measures in such a way as to underestimate the incidence of illegality. Although it is theoretically possible to compare reports of behavior with statistics on crime and thus get some idea of the degree of distortion in the reported behavior measure, this type of external validation is not possible where, as in this study, the researcher was not concerned with violations of the law committed within a specified period of time. However, where such a procedure has been employed, reported behavior measures have stacked up rather well. . . . People appear willing, in a setting of relative anonymity, to discuss the incidences and occasions on which they have violated the law. Although there is no guarantee that the same willingness was at work in this study, it adds some credence to the data presented below.

Each person interviewed was presented five types of behavior and asked to indicate if he had ever engaged in each and, if so, how frequently. The behaviors which were the subject of inquiry all involved violations of the law, and they ranged in seriousness from littering to battery. I recognize that obedience to even the most trivial of laws is the product of a variety of factors beyond feelings of support for or alienation from the legal system. This paper, however, is not concerned with why people do or do not obey the law as such; rather it is concerned specifically with the relationship of support for the legal system and behavioral obedience. Furthermore, while the kinds of behaviors which were measured may not seem as dramatic or important as participating in protest demonstrations or violent "anti-system" behavior, to overlook their impact would be, I believe, a mistake. As Gerstein (1970) suggests, only where people obey the everyday, ordinary, and unspectacular rules of the legal system can it efficiently perform its social control, dispute settlement, and resource allocation functions.

As Table 5 indicates, the range of variation in supportive behaviors is great. Over 70% of those interviewed admit having littered and over one-half recall incidents of driving under the influence of alcohol. On the other hand, almost three-quarters of the respondents denied ever having committed battery and an even greater percentage say that they have never smoked marijuana. As a general rule, more people report incidents of disobedience the less "serious" the law; this in itself may indicate only that they were more reluctant to admit to violating laws where there are potentially severe sanctions involved or it may itself be considered an important aspect of behavioral support for the legal system.

Using frequency of noncompliance with these laws as my dependent variable, I calculated bivariate correlations for each dimension of support. As Table 6 indicates, the relationship of support for the legal system and the reported frequency of noncompliance varies with the dimension studied. Insofar as the level of satisfaction is concerned, there is almost no relationship. Whether people feel satisfied with the current operation of the legal system has little or no relationship to whether or not they behave in compliance with its

TABLE 5. Reported Behavior Items (in percentages)

Question

I'd like to ask you about some things that most people have done at one time or another; we are trying to find out which of these things has been done by the largest number of people. Please indicate whether you have done each of the following things very frequently, frequently, sometimes, seldom, or never.

	VERY FREQUENTLY	FREQUENTLY	SOMETIMES	SELDOM	NEVER
(1) I have made enough noise to disturb the neighbors.	.5	1.4	19.5	36.8	41.8
(2) I have littered in violation of the law.	.5	1.8	21.0	48.2	27.7
(3) I have driven an automobile while intoxicated.	.9	3.2	23.6	26.4	45.9
(4) I have smoked marijuana.	.0	3.2	5.0	10.0	81.8
(5) I have hit someone in the midst of an argument.	.5	.5	5.0	20.9	73.2

T A B L E 6 .   Bivariate Correlations Between Support for the Legal System and Two Measures of Compliance to Law

	REPORTED BEHAVIOR	HYPOTHETICAL SITUATIONS
Willingness to Comply	-.33[a],[c]	.20[b]
Satisfaction	.02	-.01

[a]Significant at .01 level.
[b]Significant at .05 level.
[c]This relationship is negative because higher scores on the reported behavior measure indicate more frequent noncompliance.

outputs. However, the first dimension of support, which was labeled "willingness to comply," is significantly and strongly related to that behavior. Those who believe that people are obligated to obey the law are less likely than others to behave in a noncompliant manner.

In order to test the possibility that the reported-behavior measure might be so closely related to the willingness-to-comply dimension of support as to produce an artificially high relationship, an alternative, and less direct measure of overt support for the legal system was also utilized. . . . Each respondent was presented with five questions which asked the respondents whether the law should be obeyed in hypothetical situations involving other people. These situations involved a local court decision on free speech, a state anti-discrimination statute, a Supreme Court ruling on the rights of criminal defendants, the Selective Service law, and a state anti-pollution statute.[4]

Table 6 also shows that when respondents' scores on these hypothetical situations are aggregated into a single indicator and correlated with the two dimensions of support, the same pattern noted above recurs. Although the relationships are somewhat weaker, the willingness to comply is significantly associated with this second measure of overt support for the legal system and the level of satisfaction is not.

Summary and Conclusions

In this paper support for the legal system was measured in terms of two specific dimensions, which I called willingness to comply and satisfaction. It was found that while satisfaction seems relatively low, the willingness to comply is, nevertheless, quite high. This is something of a paradox, but not an unexpected one. As Easton noted in his original formulation, while people may be dissatisfied with the way an institution or object is operating they may continue to accord it support, in this case expressed in the form of a continuing acknowledgment of an obligation to comply. However, he cautions that such dissatisfaction may, if it persists over time, erode support in all its forms (1965). The findings of this paper suggest that the legal system may be faced with this problem, although without longitudinal data we can not know how serious it is or is likely to become.

Having measured support, three questions were posed: first, to what extent is support for the legal system associated with "informed public opinion;" second, to what extent are supportive attitudes associated with behavior which contributes to the effectiveness of the legal system, and third, do these relationships differ when we consider different dimensions of support?

In answer to the first question, the data indicate that support declines as knowledge increases, that knowledge of and support for the legal system are inversely related but that this is true only when we examine satisfaction with the legal system. This finding seems to add support to the body of literature which indicates a basic incompatibility between public knowledge of and support for political institutions.

In terms of democratic theory this research seems to bolster the position of those who believe that the stability of democratic institutions rests on public ignorance and apathy. In terms of the legal system itself, to the extent that its performance and persistence ultimately depend on the input of support, then the legal system may be best served by the fact that for many people it is a somewhat mysterious and incomprehensible object. So long as people have an idealized and unrealistic conception of the way the legal system operates, a conception conveyed by the mass media and other popular sources, support for it is likely to remain at least relatively widespread; where this conception is tempered by information, as it is for many people in my sample, support, at least as reflected in feelings of satisfaction, is likely to erode. The gap between beliefs about the way the legal system operates and the way it in fact operates leaves considerable room for disillusionment when people come to perceive the extent of this gap (Patterson et al., 1969). The fact that the gap between beliefs and reality is considerably less with respect to explicitly political institutions may explain the fact that increased knowledge of the way they do operate does not erode support in quite the same way as it does for legal or judicial institutions or processes (Boynton et al., 1968).

The relationship of supportive sentiments and behavior is as important as, if not more important than, the relationship of knowledge and support. If support for an institution or a system were not related to the way people behave with regard to that institution or system, then the growing emphasis on the study of political support would seem to be somewhat misdirected. This is not, however, the case in this research. Using a measure of reported behavior, specifically, instances of noncompliance with the law and an indicator based on hypothetical situations. I found that those who were more supportive of the legal system were more likely to behave in a compliant manner and to favor such behavior in others than those who were less supportive.

The relationships between knowledge and support and between covert and overt support are in each case significantly affected by disaggregating the concept of support. As we saw earlier, with respect to knowledge its influence is limited to feelings of satisfaction with the present legal system; on the other hand, when we turn to the relationship of covert and overt support it is the dimension of the willingness to comply which takes on greater importance. These findings indicate the need to describe the measure support in complex terms, to use multidimensional operationalizations, and to treat the dimensions of support as separate and important in their own right.

References

Armour, D. J. and A. S. Couch (1972). *Data-Text Primer*. New York: Free Press.

Aubert, V. (1974). "The functions of law." (unpublished manuscript)

Bachrach, P. (1967). *The Theory of Democratic Elitism*. Boston: Little, Brown.

Bayley, D. and H. Mendelsohn (1969). *Minorities and the Police*. New York: Free Press.

Boynton, G. R. et al. (1968). "The structure of public support for legislative institutions." *Midwest J. of Pol. Sci.* 12: 163-180.

Budge, I. (1970). *Agreement and the Stability of Democracy*. Chicago: Markham.

Coopersmith, S. (1971). *Student Attitudes Toward Authority, Law and Police*. Davis, Calif.: Institute for Governmental Affairs.

Dahl, R. (1961). *Who Governs?* New Haven: Yale University Press.

Dennis, J. (1970). "Support for the institution of elections by the mass public." *Amer. Pol. Sci. Rev.* 64: 819-835.

Easton, D. (1973). "Theoretical approaches to political support." Unpublished Manuscript.

—— (1965). *A System Analysis of Political Life*. New York: Wiley.

Edelman, M. (1971). *Politics as Symbolic Action*. Chicago: Markham.

Engstrom, R. and M. Giles (1972). "Expectations and images: a note on diffuse support for legal institutions." *Law and Society Rev.* 6: 631-636.

Friedman, L. (1969). "Legal culture and social development." *Law and Society Rev.* 4: 29-44.

Gerstein, R. (1970). "The practice of fidelity to law." *Law and Society Rev.* 4: 479-493.

Harmon, H. (1967). *Modern Factor Analysis*. Chicago: University of Chicago Press.

Hess, R. and J. Torney (1967). *The Development of Political Attitudes in Children*. Garden City, N.Y.: Anchor.

Key, V. O. (1961). *Public Opinion and American Democracy*. New York: Knopf.

Lipset, S. M. (1963). *Political Man*. Garden City. N.Y.: Anchor.

McIntyre, J. (1967). "Public attitudes toward crime and law enforcement." *Annals of the Amer. Assn. of Pol. and Social Sci.* 347: 34–46.

Michigan Law Review (1973). "Legal knowledge of Michigan citizens." *Michigan Law Rev.* 71: 1463–1486.

Muller, E. (1970). "Correlates and consequences of beliefs in the legitimacy of regime structures." *Midwest J. of Pol. Sci.* 14: 392–412.

Murphy, W. and J. Tanenhaus (1974). "Explaining diffuse support for the United States Supreme Court." *Notre Dame Lawyer* 49: 1037–1044.

—— (1968). "Public opinion and the United States Supreme Court." *Law and Society Rev.* 2: 357–384.

Patterson, S. et al. (1969). "Perceptions and expectations of the legislature and support for it." *Amer. J. of Sociology* 75: 62–76.

Podgorecki, R. et al. (1972). *Knowledge and Opinion About Law*. London: Robertson.

Richardson, R. et al. (1972). *Perspectives on the Legal Justice System*. Chapel Hill, N.C.: Institute for Research in Social Science.

Rodgers, H. and E. Lewis (1974). "Political Support and Compliance Attitudes." *American Politics O.* 2: 61–77.

Rodgers, H. and G. Taylor (1970). "Preadult orientations toward legal compliance." *Social Sci. O.* 51: 539–551.

Skogan, W. (1971). "Judicial myth and judicial reality." *Washington University Law O.* 1971: 309–334.

Walker, D. (1972). "Contact and support: an empirical assessment of public attitudes toward the police and courts." *North Carolina Law Rev.* 51: 43–78.

Williams, M. and J. Hall (1972). "Knowledge of the law in Texas." *Law and Society Rev.* 7: 99–118.

Notes

1. This question is not included in Table 1. It read "The legal system in this country *should* generally reflect the wishes of the majority of the people."
2. A three-factor solution explained less than 3% more of the factor variance. Conventionally, factors with a factor "root" of less than 1 or which add no more than 5% to the total explained variance are not considered to be significant or to merit interpretation (Harmon, 1967).
3. Factor scores were computed for each respondent on each dimension. Scores are based on standard deviations from the mean for each factor (Armour and Couch, 1972; Harmon, 1967).
4. The hypothetical situations included the following:

   1. A local school board refuses to allow an avowed communist to speak in a local high school because it believes communism to be dangerous and

un-American. The school board makes this decision even though a court has ruled that the communist has a constitutional right to speak and has ordered the scholl board to let him do so.

2. A local businessman needs a foreman, but refuses to hire a black man even though he has the experience and qualifications needed for the job. He refuses to hire the man in spite of a state law forbidding such discrimination.

3. A policeman refuses to allow an ex-convict, who had committed several robberies in the past, to see a lawyer and questions him until the person admits he committed another crime. The policeman does this in spite of a Supreme Court ruling that all persons accused of crime must be provided with a lawyer before questioning.

4. A draft-eligible young man, who disagreed with the war in Vietnam and left the country to avoid being drafted, wants to come back to this country. Should the law which makes draft evasion a crime be enforced or would it be better not to enforce it in this case and let him back into this country without punishing him?

5. An industry continues to pollute the Wisconsin River even though the state legislature has passed a law requiring all industries to stop such pollution. The owner of the industry claims that the cost of complying with the law would force him out of business.

In each situation, the people interviewed were asked whether the law should be enforced. Aggregate scores were derived by assigning 1 for each positive response and 0 for each negative response and summing the item scores.

16

The Impact of Certainty and Severity of Punishment
George Antunes and A. Lee Hunt

It is generally agreed that a legitimate reason for the existence of governments is to procure for the citizenry the safety and security of their persons and possessions. Unfortunately, governments are never fully successful in this regard, with the result that they have as a major problem the task of reducing dangerous crime. Many public officials in the United States have advocated the use of more severe penal sanctions as a means of deterring crime. Unfortunately, very little research has been conducted to ascertain the deterrent effect of criminal sanctions, or to determine the possible impact of longer prison sentences on levels of serious crime. The preponderance of arguments both for and against punitive sanctions are founded on ethical grounds or "common sense," and generally have been advanced without scientific support. Indeed, implicit in our criminal justice policies are the hypotheses that the certainty and severity of punishment will deter crime.[1] However, scholars have undertaken

Excerpt from "The Impact of Certainty and Severity of Punishment on Levels of Crime in American States: An Extended Analysis," *Journal of Criminal Law and Criminology* 64 (1973), pp. 486–493. Reprinted by special permission of The Journal of Criminal Law and Criminology. Copyright © 1974 by Northwestern School of Law, vol. 64, no. 4.

relatively little systematic research to discover the extent to which these hypotheses enjoy empirical support.

The relevant research can be covered briefly. First, however, it will be helpful to distinguish two types of deterrence: *special* (the specific deterrence of a given individual), and *general* (the overall reduction in crime due to the inhibitory effect of sanctions on an aggregate of persons). As Packer notes:

> These two are quite different although they are often confused in discussion of problems of punishment. For example, it is sometimes said that a high rate of repeat offenses, or recidivism as it is technically known, among persons who have already been once subjected to criminal punishment shows that deterrence does not work. The fact of recidivism may throw some doubt on the efficacy of *special* deterrence, but a moment's reflection will show that it says nothing about the effect of *general* deterrence.[2]

It is general deterrence which we wish to examine in this paper. Thus, we may safely disregard the rather extensive literature indicating that both incarceration and "treatment" intended to reform are often markedly unsuccessful in attaining that goal.

We may also disregard the studies focusing on the deterrent effect of capital punishment. We do so because capital punishment, although quite severe, is remarkably uncertain. Murder is the only crime for which execution has been employed enough to be statistically meaningful. However, whatever the findings of research on the deterrent effect of capital punishment may be, they cannot be generalized to crimes other than murder. Further, it should be noted that there are some problems in generalizing the deterrent effect of capital punishments even to the set of all murders. The vast bulk of persons convicted of homicide are incarcerated, not executed. In fact, the death penalty rarely has been imposed in recent years. Even those sentenced to death are able to delay execution through lengthy, and often successful, appeals.

We now turn our attention to other empirical studies of the deterrent impact of sanctions. One major thrust in the empirical literature involving the study of murder is an initial work by Gibbs.[3] He constructed aggregate measures of certainty of punishment based on the number of state prison admissions for homicide in 1960, divided by the mean number of homicides known to police for 1959 and 1960. Severity of punishment was measured as the median number of months served by all persons in prison on December 31, 1960. Although some may take exception to the respective measures of these variables, we find the operations adequate. Utilizing data from the Federal Bureau of Investigation's *Uniform Crime Reports* and the *National Prisoner Statistics*, Gibbs computed certainty and severity values for each of the forty-eight states *circa* 1960. Dichotomizing this data, Gibbs used Chi-square tests and phi correlations to assess the impact of certainty and severity of punishment on rates of homicide known to the police in 1960.

Gibbs reported an inverse relationship between the homicide rate and both independent variables, and concluded that his findings, contrary to common assertion, demonstrated evidence of a relationship between the crime rate and legal reactions to crime.

Following Gibbs, and utilizing the same data, Gray and Martin[4] reported a series of regression models which also demonstrated moderate, inverse associations between the variables. Specifically, the homicide rate correlated -.37 with severity, and -.28 with certainty. The multiple correlation indicating the combined effects of both certainty and severity on homicide was .47, thus accounting for 22 percent of the variance. Gray and Martin also computed several regression analyses in which the data were subjected to a natural logarithm transformation. This produced no change in the correlation between certainty and homicide, but the correlation of the latter with severity increased to -.51. The multiple correlation of the transformed data increased to .61, accounting for 38 percent of the variance. Gray and Martin concluded that the independent variables have a demonstrable, and equally weighted, impact on the homicide rate.

Attempting to clarify methodological issues raised in these studies, Bean and Cushing[5] performed a second re-analysis of Gibbs' data. They found that the data did not violate assumptions of normality, and therefore did not need to be transformed in order to meet the assumptions for using multiple regression. They also tested the data for departures from linearity. When no significant departures were found, they concluded that the logarithmic transformation models presented by Gray and Martin did not result in a significant increase in prediction and, thus, the models must be ruled out on the grounds of parsimony.

Bean and Cushing extend the Gray and Martin model by incorporating an etiological variable. Examining the residuals of the multiple regression of certainty and severity on homicide rate, they found that "most of the large positive residuals occurred for southern states and most of the large negative residuals for non-southern states."[6] To investigate the hypothesis that the effects of certainty and severity are contingent upon region, a revised regression model incorporating "region" as a variable was tested. This resulted in the squared multiple correlation increasing from .22 to .69. Indeed, the squared correlation between region and homicide rate was a startling .62.

The concept "region" is a surrogate for various unmeasured variables. To demonstrate the theoretical importance of "region," Bean and Cushing replace this variable with a measure of "percent black population."[7] Utilizing this variable and measures of certainty and severity as the independent variables, they observe a squared multiple correlation of .76. Examining the slopes of the certainty and severity variables in this regression, they conclude that when percent black population is controlled as an etiological variable, "the variable measuring legal reactions to crime retained its association with criminal homicide rate in a direction consistent with the deterrence hypothesis."[8]

These studies of homicide converge on the finding that certainty and severity of punishment exhibit a moderate deterrent impact. One might ask, however, whether this is typical of the relationship between these two independent variables and other types of crimes. A separate set of deterrence studies examines this question, primarily by utilizing the seven FBI Index crime categories.

Tittle[9] analyzed data on the FBI Index crimes, including homicide. Although his operational measures of certainty and severity differed slightly from those employed in previous studies, this work seems generally comparable. All the variables were grouped into rank categories and the ordinal statistic Tau c was employed to assess the impact of certainty and severity on crime rates for each of the seven crime categories. This analysis produced a moderate to weak inverse association between certainty and crime rates for each of the seven crimes. These ranged from a high of -.57 for sex offenses to a low of -.08 for auto theft. The correlation between murder and certainty was -.17. However, when the severity variable was examined a *negative* association, -45, was found *only* between severity and homicide. The relationship between severity and each of the six other crime categories was *positive*, ranging from a high of .26 for sex offenses to a low of .04 for auto theft. These findings are contrary to the commonly proposed deterrence hypothesis.

Waldo and Chiricos also incorporated the seven FBI Index crimes in an examination of the impact of certainty on crime rates across three time points: 1950, 1960 and 1963.[10] Two time points were utilized in testing the impact of severity: 1960 and 1964. This analysis further sought to assess the impact of changes in levels of certainty, and severity on two dependent variables: crime rates and changes in crime rates. All the data were dichotomized, and phi correlations were computed as measures of impact. With respect to certainty, the results for all three time periods generally supported the findings of Tittle and others. All the correlations were negative and low to moderate in magnitude, with the exception of homicide in 1950, which was +.02.

No pattern emerged from the analysis of changes in levels of certainty and severity on changes in crime rates. Waldo and Chiricos conclude that evidence in support of a deterrent impact for levels of certainty or severity on crime rates is not sufficiently demonstrated in their analysis to justify acceptance of the deterrence hypothesis.[11]

Summary of Conclusions from Empirical · Research on Deterrence

First, it is evident that certainty of punishment has a mild deterrent impact on crime rates. This is demonstrated in all the studies reviewed, in spite of varying measurement operations, time points and methods of analysis. At least in this respect, the theory of deterrence receives some support.

Secondly, severity of punishment exhibits a moderate deterrent impact on homicide rates, but is unrelated to crime rates for other types of crimes. If this is the case, what attributes distinguish homicide from the other six crime categories which would account for the differential deterrent impact of severity? Several aspects of homicide can be considered in this regard. From studies of the etiology of crime we know that murder, in contrast to other types of crime, occurs in or near the home. The murderer is usually a member of the family or someone well known to the victim. Finally, in contrast to many other crimes, murder is usually done without reflection in a moment of high passion. From this, the following points can be drawn:

1. All other things being equal, the deterrent impact of certainty and severity should be greater for a rational, economic crime like burglary, than for a spontaneous emotional crime like murder.
2. Since there is frequently a connection between murderer and victim, most murders are "solved." This means that the certainty rate for murders as a category of crime should be much higher than the certainty rate for other types of crime. This is borne out by the data reviewed above.

With respect to the existing research findings, these two points imply the following:

1. Certainty, acting alone, has a deterrent impact on crime rates.
2. Given the impact of severity on murder, severity should have an even greater impact on other crimes. Since it does not, it is plausible to hypothesize that *severity only has a deterrent impact when the certainty level is high enough to make severity*

salient. Any deterrent impact from severity depends on the level of certainty.

Severity can be most effectively integrated into a deterrence theory by formulation of a model in which the effects of severity operate interactively with the effects of certainty. The basic hypothesis would be that deterrence, as measured by crime rate, is some function of the product of certainty and severity. A more complicated model allows a separate causal link between deterrence and certainty, as well as that between the product of certainty and severity. (These models are described in greater detail, as models 3 and 2 respectively, in Figure 1.)

Research Design

The dependent variable in the analysis performed in this paper is "crime rate." This is a *per capita* measurement of the number of crimes per 100,000 inhabitants in each of 49 states. Seven categories of crime are examined as dependent variables: homicide, sex crimes, robbery, assault, burglary, larceny and auto theft.

Certainty of imprisonment and severity of sentence are determined for each of these crime categories and are treated as independent variables. The "certainty" variable is calculated by dividing the number of persons admitted to prison for a given crime in year "x" by the number of the type of crime known to police in year "x-1." The measure of "severity of sentence" is the median length of sentence served by all those in prison for a given crime on any specified reporting date.

The number of crimes known to police in 1959 and 1960 and the crime rates for 1960 were collected from the FBI's *Uniform Crime Reports*, 1960. Information about admission to state prisons and median sentence length were obtained from the Federal Bureau of Prisons' *Characteristics of State Prisoners*. Thus, in this analysis, "certainty" will be indicated by the number of persons admitted to state prisons in 1960 divided by the number of crimes known to the state

FIGURE 1.   Alternative Regression Models

$$(1)\ y = a + b_1 C + b_1 S + e$$
$$(2)\ y = a + b_1 C + b_2 CS + e$$
$$(3)\ y = a + b_1 CS + e$$
$$(4)\ y = a + b_1 C + e$$
$$(5)\ y = a + b_1 S + e$$

police in 1959. "Severity" is the median sentence served by persons incarcerated on December 31, 1960.

One aim of this study is to extend the analyses of Tittle and of Chiricos and Waldo through the application of interval level statistics to similar data. We thereby avoid the limitations imposed by collapsing data into ordinal or nominal categories, and instead, may retain information about relationships which is frequently lost by the use of the less powerful nonparametric techniques.

Accordingly, we employ the following techniques in our analysis: First, we replicate Tittle's work by computing the bivariate relationships between certainty and crime rate for each of the seven index crime categories. Then, we make the additional comparison of crime rates and severity. The combined predictive effects of certainty and severity considered simultaneously are then explored through a series of linear multiple regressions.

To examine the hypothesis that severity has a deterrent impact on crime rates only under conditions of high certainty, we compute for each type of index crime a regression model of the following form:

$$y = a + b_1 CS + e$$
where: y is a crime rate
a is a constant
b_1 is a least squares regression coefficient
C is certainty of imprisonment
S is severity of sentence
e is the residual error

In this equation, note that severity, whatever its value, will have a predictive impact only when certainty is greater than zero. As certainty approaches one, severity approaches its maximum impact value. The second hypothesis—that certainty has an independent deterrent effect in addition to the effect of its interaction with severity—is explored through a regression equation of the form:

$$y = a + b_1 C + b_2 CS + e$$
where: y is a crime rate
a is a constant
b_1 and b_2 are least squares regression coefficients
C is certainty of imprisonment
S is severity of sentence
e is the residual error

A listing of the five alternative regression models to be examined is provided in Figure 1. We turn now to an analysis of our data in order to ascertain the empirical viability of the alternative models.

TABLE 1. Bivariate Regressions of Crime Rates in States (1960) on Certainty and Severity for Seven Categories of Crime

CRIME CATEGORY	CERTAINTY			SEVERITY		
	Slope	r	r²	Slope	r	r²
Murder..............	-4.3	-.19	.04	-.07	-.39	.15
Rape................	-8.1	-.56	.31	.13	.30	.09
Robbery............	-75.0	-.32	.10	.48	.10	.01
Assault.............	-118.2	-.27	.07	2.10	.18	.03
Burglary...........	-3639.8	-.40	.13	5.10	.09	.01
Larceny............	-1441.7	-.36	.13	1.36	-.06	.00
Auto-theft..........	-1807.3	-.30	.09	.49	.03	.00

Analysis of the Data

The first step in the analysis consists of a series of bivariate regressions between certainty and severity (as independent variables), and crime rates (as the dependent variables) for the seven index crimes. Table 1 presents the product–moment correlations and the regression slopes from these equations.

Turning to these results, we observe that the correlations on "murder" agree with other findings reported, *i.e.*, certainty and severity demonstrate a slight negative relationship with homicide rates. Furthermore, for all seven categories of index crimes, these results generally agree with those reported by Tittle and also by Waldo and Chiricos. Certainty exhibits a slight to moderate negative relationship with each of the seven types of crime rate, while severity demonstrates a weak positive relationship (with the exception of homicide). In our analysis, we found, unlike Tittle, a negative relationship between the crime rate for larceny and severity. However, the magnitude of the correlation is so slight (-.06) that no inference about the sign is allowable.

On the basis of the findings presented in Table 1 we, too, would be led to reject the hypothesis that both certainty and severity have a deterrent effect on crime. The evidence mustered at this point would suggest a policy direction which aims at increasing the certainty of punishment. The commonly held opinion that severe sentencing will lead to a reduction in crime rates simply finds no empirical support in these data.

Noting the anomalous results with regard to the relationship between homicide rate and severity, we were led to our original hypothesis that severity would have a deterrent impact on crime rates only under conditions of high certainty. Accordingly, we outlined two possible configurations of this interactive relationship in the regression models presented in Figure 1. These models represent an exploratory attempt to create a viable, parsimonious theory of deterrence in which predictive capabilities are enhanced without the necessity of including additional variables.

The usefulness of these regression models with respect to each of the seven crime categories may be ascertained by examination of Table 2, which offers a summary of the explanatory capabilities (as expressed by R^2) for each of these models for each type of crime.

In the summary presented in Table 2, models 4 and 5 represent, respectively, the simple linear effects of certainty of punishment and severity of sentence actually served acting alone on actual crime rates. In these models we make observations which are consistent with our

TABLE 2. Summary of Predictive Models (R^2)

REGRESSION MODEL	1 (C + S)	2 (C + CS)	3 (CS)	4 (C)	5 (S)
Dependent Variable:					
Homicide	.21*	.19	.19*	.04*	.15*
Rape	.31	.31*	.20*	.31*	.09
Robbery	.11*	.16*	.07*	.10*	.01
Assault	.08	.15	.13*	.07*	.03
Burglary	.16	.16	.12*	.13*	.01
Larceny	.14*	.18*	.18*	.13*	.00
Auto-theft	.10	.09	.06*	.09*	.00
Average R^2	.16	.18	.14	.12	.04

*Slope(s) of the regression equation negative.

initial bivariate observations, that is, severity, acting alone, accounts for very little of the explained variation in crime rates, regardless of type of crime. Furthermore, the regression coefficients for model 5 are almost all positive in sign (the exceptions being homicide and larceny), indicating that higher levels of severity are associated with *higher* levels of crime. The positive nature of this association is worthy of only passing notice, since the strength of association is generally slight. With the single exception of homicide rate, the severity variable consistently accounts for less than ten percent explained variation, and, in four types of crime, predicts less than one percent. Of the five alternative regression models, the severity model (number 5) is the weakest predictive scheme.

Considering the effects of the certainty variable acting independently, the average variance explained increases to 12 percent. For all seven categories, the slope of the regression equation is negative. Thus, these correlations are interpretable as demonstrating a consistent deterrent effect on levels of crime.

In the simple multiplicative model 3, the average amount of explained variance is fourteen percent. More importantly, every regression slope in this model is negative in direction, supporting a deterrence interpretation.

Model 1 considers the linear, additive effects of certainty and severity. For homicide, burglary and auto theft this model is one of the strongest predictors, with an average R-square of .16. However, only three of the seven equations have the requisite negative regression slopes. Thus, the increased predictive power is of little use because the model cannot provide interpretations to consistently support the deterrence hypothesis.

In model 2, the effects of severity are not only examined in an interactive context with certainty (as in model 3), but allowance is made for an additional, separate link between certainty and crime rates. This model articulates the more elaborate hypothesis about the conditions under which severity may combine with certainty to influence crime rates. However, from the data analysis, we see that model 2 is not markedly better in predictive power than either the simple additive or simple multiplicative models (models 1 and 3 respectively). Moreover, the regression slopes in model 2 are negative for only three of the seven dependent variables. Thus, model 2, although viable in terms of predictive power, generally does not conform to the requirements of a deterrence model.

Summary and Conclusion

In this paper we have attempted to distinguish the independent and interactive effects of certainty of punishment and severity of sentence on the level of crime rates in the American states. We have applied several regression models in a test of the effects of these variables in the general deterrence of crime.

From this analysis we find no support for severity of sentence acting alone as a deterrent to crime. However, we find a consistent, moderate effect for certainty of punishment acting to reduce crime rates. Attempts to improve predictive capability through a theoretically formulated model, in which severity exerts an impact on crime rates only under conditions of high certainty, are partially successful. The more complicated version of this model, which hypothesizes both an effect from certainty and severity combined, and a separate effect from certainty acting alone, is the best predictor of crime rates. Nevertheless, it is theoretically uninterpretable. The simpler model, in which certainty and severity combine to jointly influence crime rates, demonstrates good prediction relative to the alternative arrangements of the independent variables. It is theoretically interpretable. In our judgment, this model plausibly demonstrates that certainty and severity do have a moderate deterrent effect upon rates of crime. However, it should be kept in mind that certainty, considered by itself, has a moderate deterrent effect for all crimes, while severity acting alone is not associated with lower rates of crime. When certainty and severity are combined, as is the case of our model, then the impact of severity is filtered through the certainty value. This means that increasing severity in a condition of low certainty will have little effect on crime rates.

As Zimring and Hawkins have noted, sentences in the United States are currently quite severe in comparison to those imposed in Western Europe.[12] It is quite likely that spending additional funds to keep convicts in prison for longer periods of time will not result in any meaningful increase in general deterrence. Monies spent in this fashion will simply be wasted. Indeed, increasing the severity of sentences may have the unintended consequence of reducing the level of special deterrence through increased recidivism. There are a number of reasons why more severe sentences might cause higher rates of recidivism. Among them are the increased social stigmatization associated with longer sentences, the inability of those sanctioned and released to live normally in society after prolonged incarceration and a heightened sense of alienation and injustice caused by lengthy incarceration under a condition of low certainty of imprisonment. In our opinion, the appropriate criminal justice policy is one which attempts to reduce crime by increasing the probability of apprehension and prosecution. This would have the advantage of not only increasing the level of general deterrence, but might also result in an increased sense of the fairness of punishment and lower rates of recidivism.

Notes

1. For example, over twenty years ago Edwin Sutherland observed the following:

   The conventional policy has been to punish those who are convicted of crimes, on the hypothesis that this both reforms those who are punished and deters others from crimes in the future. Also, according to this hypothesis, crime rates can be reduced by increasing the severity, certainty, and speed of punishment. E. Sutherland, Principles of Criminology 613 (4th ed. 1947).

2. H. Packer, The Limits of the Criminal Sanction 39 (1968).

3. Gibbs, *Crime, Punishment, and Deterrence*, 48 Soc. Sci. Q. 515 (1968).

4. Gray & Martin, *Punishment and Deterrence: Another Analysis of Gibbs' Data*, 50 Soc. Sci. Q. 389 (1969).

5. Bean & Cushing, *Criminal Homicide, Punishment, and Deterrence: Methodological and Substantive Reconsiderations*, 52 Soc. Sci. Q. 277 (1971).

6. *Id.* at 283.

7. Bean & Cushing, *supra* note 5, at 287.

8. Bean & Cushing, *supra* note 16, at 289.

9. Tittle, *Crime Rates and Legal Sanction*, 16 Social Problems 409 (1969).

10. Chiricos & Waldo, *Punishment and Crime: An Examination of Some Empirical Evidence*, 18 Social Problems 200 (1970).

11. Chiricos & Waldo, *supra* note 10, at 211–213. This contention is refuted by Bean and Cushing, *supra* note, at 279.

12. E. Zimring & G. Hawkins, *Deterrence: The Legal Threat in Crime Control* (1973), at 56.

17

"He Who Does Not Steal from the State ...
Otto Ulč

. . . steals from his family." In pre-Communist days, this witticism would hardly have been understood. Since then, however, it has acquired the power of proverbial wisdom, indicating a major ailment of Czechoslovak society and a persistent headache of the leadership. The pilferage of socialist property is the most popular crime in the country. Never before has so much been stolen by so many, the Party bewails. The statistics on national economic losses as a result of pilferage vary, according to time, to the willingness of the leadership to reveal honest figures, and to the nature of the audience. At our closed judicial meetings, we were told that "privatization" of public wealth retarded planned economic development by roughly twenty per cent. I cannot quite visualize just what that involved, but I certainly do know that the section on pilferage in the Criminal Code represented the bulkiest segment of Czechoslovak adjudication and grew steadily despite all efforts to prevent, punish, and educate.

Pilferage of Socialist Property

Traditionally, the Czechs were not a nation of thieves. Whatever their flaws, an endemic dishonesty was not among them. But values

Excerpt from *The Judge in a Communist State: The View from Within.* Athens, Ohio: Ohio University Press, 1972, pp. 166–174, by permission of the author and publisher.

changed with the times. The corrosion of public respect for some one else's possessions was largely the Party's own doing. First the System taught that the sanctity of private property was a bourgeois device, a devious trick to keep the toiling masses under the yoke of economic oppression. Accordingly, the state expropriated fortunes, and the have-nots applauded. Somewhere along the way, however, the swollen ranks of the have-nots lost any feelings of respect for any property, whoever might be the owner. As it turned out, the only landlord left in the national edifice was the Party.

The expropriators' appetites exceeded their digestive capacity. It would have been impressive and very revolutionary if the sky had been the limit for nationalization. But at some stage the voracious state should have realized that it had become the owner of more wealth than it could possibly protect. No matter how numerous the army of full-time guardians, they would never be equal to the task of controlling, checking, and re-checking the rest of the population with access to socialist factories, socialist fields, and socialist services. The volume and unpredictability of the public inventory had become an open temptation, and man was easily tempted.

If my toilet plumbing leaked several sources were open to me: I could place an order for the repair with the appropriate municipal enterprise. With luck, in about a year the defect would be remedied. But, if, having become accustomed to the convenience of a flushing toilet, I had no wish to wait four seasons, I might take the risk of committing the crime of "complicity in parasitism" and hire a craftsman who operated without a license, for profit. But in all probability, because of the expense of such a plumber, I would decide to repair the toilet myself. For this I would need materials, and the state retail stores carried none. So I would choose to steal ("de-nationalize") the material from the factory where I worked. If I could not get hold of the necessary pipes, a friend would. In return, I would agree to provide him with valuables he needed that I had access to. Whether I was a waiter, a store manager or a diamond cutter, I would feel, justly or not, underpaid and so seek a way to supplement my income through illegal, though in my opinion not unjustified, means. My frustration with the political status quo and my inability to change it could be mitigated by a furtive project of petty theft, which in my own eyes would be both daring—I would be a *practicing* anti-Communist!— and highly utilitarian. To blow up President Novotný along with the entire Hradčany Castle would make little sense to someone simply in need of a sack of garlic. All the valiant efforts of the Party to exhort the masses to protect *posvátné* ("sacred") socialist property were no match for the attitudes of the alienated men who easily became stealing men.

The public condoned incidents of "de-nationalization," provided the appetite of the pilferer was not boundless, and/or the crime harmed no one but the state. Pilferage often advanced to the level of art, as exemplified by the case of Prague chimneysweeps. Some members of this sooty craft worked out a bizarre, Chaplinesque, and very successful scheme to raise their living standards. First, they made a deal with a group of employees at the Prague slaughter house. Then, they signed a *socialistický závazek* ("socialist endeavor pledge") to clean the chimneys in the classless fatherland, day and night—especially during the night and in particular at the premises of the slaughter house. While their accomplices produced salami inside the building, the shockworkers on the roof fished for the products, in keeping with their calling, down the chimneys. Ludicrous as it may sound, this project lasted for a long time and proved very profitable. The average reaction to this enterprise was one of amusement rather than indignation or desire for revenge.

The ingenuity of these plotters was by no means atypical. Many showed remarkable imagination in securing more than their assigned shares of the socialist pie. As a rule, however, being a successful pilferer did not require a mastermind. The average offender could operate undetected because of the seemingly irremediable deficiency in the control system. The State's eagerness to supervise each and every aspect of economic life was submerged in a deluge of conflicting regulations, and often the only outcome was confusion. Take, for example, the case of an aging though not maturing lady, the head accountant in charge of paychecks at the Plzeň papermill. She happened to be very much enamoured of K., the Prague Opera star who even at the time of this writing infatuates his female audiences. The lady's organizational talent was accompanied by an extraordinary generosity. She bought her hero sets of silk pajamas and paid outrageous sums for taxi trips from Prague half across Bohemia, to Karlsbad and, of course, also to Plzeň. The prosecutor later submitted scores of enraptured letters written by the defendant to K., and the court file was rather interesting to read. The justices, drowning in these lyrical incantations, could not avoid noticing several points which seemed to have escaped everyone else. How had it been possible, in an environment in which spying had become second nature, for a person to lead a life of such ostentatious affluence, far in excess of her legitimate means, and still remain undetected? More importantly, how had the defendant managed for years to add scores of non-existent employees to the payroll and pocket the salaries for her own use? The total sum embezzled amounted to the monetary value of ten years' work by the average salaried employee. The defendant was sentenced to a term of ten years. Nothing at all happened to the officials supposedly responsible for the overall control and supervision at the papermill.

This example of improper auditing was by no means exceptional. In Plzeň we had a department store, *Obchodní Domy*, where a floor manager was indicted on the suspicion of having pilfered state property. A lengthy trial ended in his acquittal. Despite the loads of paper work with which the employees had to wrestle, it was impossible either to get any picture of the store's business transactions, or to figure out upon which floor the losses, if any, had occurred. The prosecutor was so furious that he contemplated indicting the senior executive for gross negligence in the administration of entrusted state funds. Before such an action could be initiated, however, the Provincial Party Secretariat conceived of a better idea. The Secretary thought of a way to promote this incompetent bungler to a more responsible and more demanding position with the Ministry of Domestic Trade in Prague.

The Penal Code

The manifold endeavors of the populace to disencumber the state of its many possessions came under the heading of the notorious Section 245 of the 1950 Penal Code:

1. Whoever pilfers property which is in national or cooperative ownership by
    a. appropriating an article of such property by taking possession of it,
    b. appropriating an article of such property which was entrusted to him, or
    c. enriching himself to the detriment of such property, shall be punished by imprisonment for a term of up to five years.
2. Equally shall be punished he who intentionally damages national or cooperative property, especially by destroying, damaging or rendering useless the articles of such property.
3. An offender shall be punished by imprisonment for a term of five to ten years,
    a. if he commits such act described in paragraph 1 for gain,
    b. if by such act described in paragraph 1 or 2 causes considerable damage, or
    c. if other especially serious consequence is present.
4. The offender shall be punished by imprisonment for a term of ten to twenty years if by the act described in paragraph 1 or 2 he by misusing his position as public official, causes considerable damage.

The weakest spot of the provision was Section 1, lit. c, calling for the punishment of a person "who enriches himself to the detriment of such property." Around this vague formula revolved a maze of sophistry and juridicial pseudoargumentation. For example, consider this charge: A number of state restaurant managers worked out a profitable deal with the meat suppliers from the municipal slaughter house. They upgraded inferior merchandise—including some meat condemned by the veterinarian as a health hazard—to top quality meat. This was then served to customers. Common sense would presumably have concluded that the only losers were the customers. Only their stomachs suffered, and only their pockets had been cheated. The courts knew otherwise. The fraud was interpreted as pilferage of socialist property. By the same token, if I bought a lollipop in a state retail store for double the proper price, the excess which I paid would be considered "pilferage of socialist property." The state suffered the damage, not I. Therefore, I would be left with no legal claim to recover the loss.

This quaint reasoning could be traced back to the concept of management of entrusted socialist property. This concept held the manager liable—criminally and/or materially—for all losses but did not entitle him to keep any surpluses. Surplus, irrespective of the way it had been acquired, belonged to the state. This strange logic was hardly likely to promote honesty among the sales personnel. Let us suppose I was the manager of a candy store with two sales girls helping me to sweeten the life of the toiling masses. I suspected one of the girls of stealing. Probably both were doing so—and needed to, in view of their low wages. Yet, according to the terms of the "contract of material responsibility," I as manager would be solely liable for the losses. Something had to be done to compensate for the money that vanished from the cash register, and for the merchandise which disappeared from the shelves. The customers also stole, and so did I, because I, too, felt underpaid. In order that I might not be on the losing side on Tuesday, Monday would be the right time to cheat the lollipop buyer. The surplus would be stowed away in an emergency fund for the lean days ahead.

Pilferers came in all sizes. The mastermind behind the largest affair in all the years of the Plzeň people's democratic existence was a man of the poetic surname Konvalinka—"Lily of the Valley" in English. Mr. Konvalinka was employed by the state monopoly Benzina as a supervisor and repairman of the metering system for all the filling stations in Western Bohemia. The job turned into a bonanza. The supervisor conspired with a vast number of station attendants to adjust the gas pumps to indicate more fuel than actually had been received by the customers. The difference was then sold and the profit split between the dealer and Konvalinka. No one but the customer suffered under Konvalinka's scheme, but again, when the affair came into the open, the culprits were tried and sentenced to stiff terms for having pilfered socialist property, and all compensation was paid to the state.

The algebra of the cited Section might read as follows: wrongdoer A. who defrauds citizen B. is punished because of damaging the State C. The State emerges from the trial as the only beneficiary, with sole title to compensation for damages.

I would like to give one more example in this connection—an absurd story involving phonograph records. The totalitarian state applies political criteria to nearly everything. Thus, in the case of phonograph records, prices started from a low of five crowns for speeches of the leaders, anthems and revolutionary songs, to a ceiling price of over thirty crowns for a jazz disk. One Sunday, during a fair, a truck arrived in town bearing the name of an unknown national enterprise. This in itself provoked no suspicion, because if anything abounded in Czechoslovakia, it was obscurely titled socialist undertakings. The employees of the mysterious outfit drew a large crowd by broadcasting the feeble-minded hit of the season, *A hloupý Honza se jen smál* ("Silly Johnny did not stop laughing"). The high price of thirty crowns did not deter the customers, who soon bought out the supply. The truck left for an unknown destination. A rather annoying discovery awaited the buyer, at home. When they played the record, they discovered that only the label was genuine—they had bought a rendering of the national anthem of the Union of Soviet Socialist Republics, available in unlimited supply in local stores for a paltry five crowns. The vanished entrepreneurs had made a handsome profit of twenty-five crowns per record. The enraged customers reported the nefarious trick to the police, who prepared "a case against the unknown culprit." When the story came to our attention at the court, we were anxious to meet the practitioners of such mercurial ingenuity. Our wish remained unfulfilled; the offenders were never apprehended. Yet another case against "pilferers of socialist property" had to be closed.

Even when the state succeeded in apprehending a culprit, arrest and punishment were one thing; the recovery of—or compensation for—the stolen property was another. The punitive hand of the System was busy while the economic hand was reaching into an empty pocket. The prosecutors and the criminal law judges, piling up their achievements in socialist competition and production quotas, cared about the penalty but hardly at all about the indemnity. The recovery of losses was left to our civil law bench. . . . Thousands of managers were convicted and sentenced without the state ever collecting one cent from them. What could be done about an ex-housewife who, after having brought a grocery store to bankruptcy and served her term in jail, returned to the household? There were no means of recovering losses from a propertyless and unemployed wife and mother.

Let us now assume it is winter, with ice everywhere and slippery roads. You are driving your own car and cause a collision. If the other car involved in the accident is privately owned, the incident is reported to the state insurance company, which will settle the bill. If, however, you happened to ram a socialist automobile, you become subject to criminal prosecution according to Section 246 of the Penal Code. This provision reads: "Whoever causes through negligence a not insignificant amount of damage to national or cooperative property, shall be punished by imprisonment for a term up to one year." The 1955 volume of the "Collection of Decisions of Czechoslovak Courts," for example, listed under Number 20 a verdict of the District Court in Kraslice. Two drivers—one employed by the Party District Secretariat, the other by the District People's Committee— were tried and sentenced under Section 246 on the grounds that they "should have known that both cars were a part of national property." Apparently the drivers, fortified by this knowledge, would have found the roads less slippery.

This provision linking negligent damage to property with criminal liability constitutes a dangerous departure from the rudimentary concept of justice. I do not believe that this deterrent formula saved much socialist property. It certainly did not save those who, with no intent to harm the cause of socialism, found themselves regarded and treated as criminals.

Speculation, any thought of profit—or, at times, any thought at all—as parasitism, depending greatly on the socio-political classification of the person in question.

Theft of Private Property

Compared with misdeeds against socialist ownership, those against private property were treated far less severely. While the pilferers from the state were frequently punished by a term of ten years, the maximum sentence for larceny of private possessions was two years. If private property was less protected, it was also less threatened.

Despite the severity of the sanctions, the offender generally preferred to leave unmolested his equally non-affluent fellow citizen, and steal from the distended coffers of the state. By and large, pickpockets became relics of a nostalgic past. It is true that some stubborn adherents still practiced this obsolete trade, but the politically up-to-date courts did not take them too seriously. In the days of hectic campaigns against pilferers and assorted wreckers of socialist construction, it was inappropriate to be too concerned with an old-fashioned thief. Once I witnessed the trial of a gentle grandfather. It was his golden anniversary—the fiftieth time in his long career he was facing the bench for petty theft. The defendant seemed so hopelessly behind the times that the court did not even bother with any token political verbiage about class struggle, world peace, etc.; the quaintly relaxed atmosphere of the proceedings was undisturbed.

The new 1961 Criminal Code remedied some of the inadequacies of the old law. However, low respect for the "sacred socialist owner-ship" continues to be one of the major concerns of the government. The Czechoslovak press has begun to admit the widespread popular-ity of pilfering, and there is even talk of a revival of larceny and other threats to personal property.

18

Evaluating Contract Compliance
Gregory J. Ahart

The Federal contract compliance program is mandated by Executive Order 11246, signed in 1965, which forbids discrimination in employment by Government contractors and subcontractors on the basis of race, color, religion, or national origin. The order was amended in 1967 to forbid discrimination in employment on the basis of sex as well. It requires Government contractors to take affirmative action to insure that job applicants and employees are not discriminated against on the basis of race, color, religion, national origin, or sex.

Contractors subject to the requirements of the program must ensure that equal employment opportunity principles are followed at all company facilities, including those facilities not engaged in work on a Federal contract. For example, if a Government agency enters into a contract with a contractor in Washington, D.C., and that contractor has other facilities scattered throughout the United States, each of the contractor's facilities is required to comply with the provisions of the Federal contract compliance program.

Each nonconstruction contractor that has 50 or more employees and a Government contract of $50,000 or more is also required to

Excerpt from "Evaluating Contract Compliance: Federal Contracts in Nonconstruction Industries," *Civil Rights Digest* 7 (Fall 1974), pp. 35–45, reprinted by permission of the author.

prepare a written affirmative action plan (AAP) applicable to each of its facilities.

To meet the standards for acceptability set forth in regulations issued by the Secretary of Labor, the AAP must include specific types of data. These include: (1) goals for improving the employment of minorities and females in those cases where the contractor is found to be deficient (i.e., where the contractor is presently employing fewer minorities and/or females than would reasonably be expected considering their availability within an area where the contractor can be expected to recruit); and (2) timetables for achieving those goals. Following this plan, the contractor should be able to increase materially the utilization of minorities and women at all levels and in all segments of its work force where deficiencies exist.

Various sanctions are authorized if a Government contractor fails to prepare an acceptable AAP or to exercise good faith in implementing it. These include contract suspension, contract cancellation, debarment from future Government contract, and referral to the Department of Justice for court action under Title VII of the Civil Rights Act of 1964.

Responsibility for administration of the Executive order is assigned to the Secretary of Labor. The Secretary has redelegated some of his authority (including the authority to designate agencies to act as compliance agencies) to the Director of the Office of Federal Contract Compliance (OFCC) within the Department's Employment Standards Administration. . . .

The Compliance Agencies

The primary responsibility for enforcing the Executive order and related guidelines rests with the Federal agencies designated as compliance agencies, which at the time General Accounting Office (GAO) began its review numbered 13 for nonconstruction contractors. These were:

Agency for International Development (AID)
Atomic Energy Commission (AEC)
Department of Agriculture
Department of Commerce
Department of Defense (DOD)
Department of Health, Education, and Welfare (HEW)
Department of the Interior
Department of Treasury
Department of Transportation
General Services Administration (GSA)

National Aeronautics and Space Administration (NASA)
United States Postal Service (USPS)
Veterans Administration (VA)

OFCC assigns to each of the compliance agencies the responsibility for contractors in specified industries. This assignment is made primarily on the basis of standard industrial classification codes, irrespective of which Government agency has entered into the contract. For example, GSA is responsible for the utilities and communications industries. Treasury is responsible for banking institutions, and HEW is assigned universities and hospitals. . . .

The compliance agencies are responsible for performing compliance reviews of Government contractors within the industries assigned to them. Compliance reviews (including pre-award reviews, initial compliance reviews, followup reviews, and complaint investigations) consist of investigation by a compliance officer who conducts an in-depth and comprehensive analysis of each aspect of the contractor's employment policies, systems, and practices to determine adherence to the nondiscrimination and affirmative action requirements. Where the review discloses that the contractor has not prepared a required AAP, has deviated substantially from his approved AAP, or has a program which is unacceptable, a "show cause notice" is required to be issued.

The show cause notice affords the contractor a period of 30 days to show cause why enforcement procedures should not be instituted. If the contractor fails to show good cause for his failure to comply with the program or fails to remedy that failure, debarment or other appropriate sanction actions are required to be initiated, and the contractor must be given the opportunity of having a formal hearing before sanction actions are imposed.

Scope of Review

. . . The GAO review, which is still under way, is directed toward an evaluation of:

- Compliance agencies' efforts in implementing OFCC guidelines for conducting compliance reviews and complaint investigations,
- Application of enforcement measures available to the compliance agencies,
- OFCC's guidance to the Federal agencies assigned compliance review responsibility for nonconstruction contractors, and
- The coordination of compliance review and complaint investigation activities between OFCC and the Equal Employment Opportunity Commission. . . .

The Implementation

Results to date show that compliance agencies are not adequately implementing the guidelines prescribed by the Secretary of Labor and OFCC for carrying out the contract compliance program. More specifically:

1. Only one of the 13 compliance agencies has identified all contractors for which it is responsible.
2. Some compliance agencies do not always perform the required pre-award reviews.
3. Most compliance agencies make periodic compliance reviews at only a small percentage of the total number of estimated contractor facilities for which they are responsible.
4. DOD and GSA are approving contractors' AAPs although these AAPs do not meet OFCC's guidelines.
5. Sanction actions prescribed by the Executive order for non-compliance are seldom imposed.

OFCC guidelines provide that each compliance agency is responsible for assuring that all the contractors in its assigned area of responsibility comply with the Executive order and implementing guidelines. However, OFCC has not developed a centralized system to identify all contractor facilities for which each compliance agency is responsible.

Officials of GSA and DOD . . . stated that they did not have complete information showing all contractor facilities in their regions for which they were responsible. Headquarters officials at 12 of the 13 nonconstruction compliance agencies also advised GAO that they too did not have complete information showing the identity of all contractor facilities under their responsibility. Only at NASA did officials state that they had complete information on all contractor facilities for which NASA was responsible. They also stated, however, that NASA—unlike the other compliance agencies—is only responsible for contractors having NASA contracts and which are located on or near NASA installations.

If a compliance agency is unaware that a particular business firm is a Government contractor, it will obviously not review the contractor to determine if it is in compliance. Without knowledge of the identity of all contractor facilities for which it is responsible, the compliance agency can not systematically select for review those contractor facilities which offer the most potential for improving equal employment opportunity.

More accurate identification of contractor facilities under each compliance agency's responsibility is not necessarily difficult. . . .

Pre-award Reviews

Department of Labor (DOL) regulations require that before an agency awards a contract of $1 million or more, the awarding agency must first assure itself that a compliance review of the contractor has been performed within the preceding 12 months and that the contractor was in compliance with all provisions of the contract compliance program. When the contracting agency is not the responsible compliance agency for a particular contractor, the contracting agency is required by DOL regulations to request pre-award clearance from the responsible compliance agency. If the latter has not performed a compliance review of the contractor within the preceding 12 months, pre-award clearance may not be granted until a pre-award review takes place and the contractor is found in compliance.

In some instances compliance agencies are granting pre-award clearances without having performed the required compliance reviews. In others, contracting officers are apparently awarding contracts in excess of $1 million without requesting a pre-award clearance from the responsible compliance agency. . . .

GAO reviewed six requests by DOD for pre-award clearance received by the Department of the Interior during calendar year 1973. The Department of the Interior issued pre-award clearances to DOD in all six instances. The review showed, however, that in four of the six instances COL requirements for pre-award reviews were not followed. In these four instances, the contractors had not been reviewed during the preceding 12 months, nor had pre-award reviews been performed.

A Department of the Interior compliance official stated that when a request for pre-award clearance is received, a pre-award review is not performed even if the prospective contractor had not been reviewed during the preceding 12 months. Pre-award clearances are withheld only if there are outstanding show cause notices against prospective contractors.

DOL regulations require that compliance agencies must respond to requests for pre-award clearances within 30 days. But the Department of the Interior compliance official stated that as a practical matter, it is not possible to perform an in-depth pre-award compliance review and persuade contractors to resolve deficiencies within the 30-day period. . . .

The Number of Reviews

The GAO review showed that with one exception—NASA—the compliance agencies are performing compliance reviews at a relatively small percentage of the estimated total number of contractor facilities for which they are responsible. . . . In April and September 1973 OFCC reviewed NASA's enforcement of the Executive order and implementing guidelines and found that (1) NASA was not consistently following OFCC's standards and requirements, and (2) NASA was apparently reluctant to issue show cause notices or take sanction actions.

Table 1 shows for each compliance agency the number of compliance reviews performed during fiscal years 1973 and 1974 . . . expressed as a percentage of the total number of contractor facilities for which those agencies estimate they are responsible. Eight of the 13 nonconstruction compliance agencies reviewed less than 15 percent of their contractor facilities in fiscal 1973. Four agencies reviewed 17 to 28 percent. . . .

Affirmative Action Plans

Compliance reviews are often directed towards an evaluation of, and approval or rejection of, contractors' AAPs. In this regard, OFCC has specified certain requirements which must be included in AAPs.

To determine the consistency of application of OFCC regulations and the adequacy of approved AAPs, a random sample of 120 AAPs approved during the first 9 months of fiscal year 1974 was selected for review. The sample consisted of 20 approved by DOD and 20 approved by GSA in each of the three regions reviewed. The investigators analyzed each of the AAPs to determine if they meet the requirements for acceptable AAPs as established by OFCC.

Based on the analyses. 42 (or 70 percent) of the 60 GSA-approved AAPs, and 12 (or 20 percent) of the 60 DOD-approved AAPs did not meet OFCC's guidelines and should not have been approved. In most instances, GSA and DOD regional officials agreed with this conclusion.

One deficiency frequently noted was that the AAPs did not contain a sufficient breakdown of job categories. The job category of "salesworkers" might include highly paid salesmen selling expensive merchandise on a commission basis as well as over-the-counter salesclerks earning the minimum wage. If a contractor were to discriminate against females and limit them to salesclerk positions, and if the data on these two types of jobs were combined in the AAP, it would

T A B L E 1. Small Percentage of Government Contractor Facilities Reviewed

COMPLIANCE AGENCY	ESTIMATED NUMBER OF CONTRACTOR FACILITIES ELIGIBLE FOR REVIEW (AS OF MARCH 1974)[1]	REVIEWS PERFORMED EXPRESSED AS A PERCENTAGE OF EST. NUMBER	
		FY 1973	FY 1974 (TO 3/31/74)
AEC	4,140	14%	12%
Agriculture	21,200	4	2
AID	1,200	12	4
Commerce	780	28	20
DOD	36,000	17	11
GSA	23,000	13	10
HEW	3,420	13	7
Interior	4,000	19	10
NASA	260	100	79
Postal Service	19,000	21	3
Transportation	380	8	7
Treasury	6,000	8	6
VA	12,480	1	1
Total	131,860	13	7

[1] With one exception neither OFCC nor the compliance agencies have data showing: 1) the identity of all of the Government contractors for which they have compliance review responsibility or 2) the total number of employees of Government contractors in their assigned industries.

not be possible by reviewing the AAP to discern a possible pattern of discrimination against females for further investigation. Other deficiencies noted included inadequate work force utilization analyses and the lack of goals and timetables as required by OFCC regulations.

In one regional office, GSA representatives were unable to provide GAO with copies of several AAPs that their records showed as having been approved. The GSA representatives stated that errors had been made in reporting these AAPs as approved; in fact, GSA had not reviewed nor approved the AAP in question. The proportion of deficient AAPs ranged from a low of 15 percent in the DOD Chicago region to a high of 80 percent in the GSA Washington region.

GAO investigators concluded that OFCC has not adequately monitored the implementation of the Executive order by the compliance agencies. If OFCC had been adequately monitoring and supervising the compliance agencies, it is likely that the failure of GSA and DOD to meet OFCC's standards with respect to reviewing and approving AAPs would have been detected by OFCC and could have been brought to the attention of appropriate GSA and DOD officials for corrective action.

In reviewing the 20 AAPs approved by the San Francisco DOD regional office and 15 AAPs approved by the San Francisco GSA regional office, investigators compared the employment of females by job category during the current year and the prior year (see Table II). Five of the GSA-approved AAPs could not be used in the comparison because GSA files did not contain sufficient information.

Table 2 shows a net increase in employment of 2,808 by the 35 contractors. Females accounted for 1,260 or 45 percent of this increase. However, there was a net decline of two females holding upper echelon jobs (officials, managers, and professionals), and most of the increase in female employment occurred in the office and clerical, craftsman, operative, laborer, and service worker categories.

Investigators found that GSA was performing compliance reviews at contractor facilities which had a relatively small number of employees. For example, in the San Francisco region the average number of persons employed by the 20 GSA-approved contractors whose AAPs were selected for review was 122 persons. In contrast, the average number of persons employed by the 20 DOD-approved contractors was 909 persons. Similar variations were noted in the Chicago and Philadelphia regions.

Selecting Contractors for Review

The difference in the industries assigned to GSA and DOD may partly contribute to the differences in the sizes of the contractor

TABLE 2. Review of 35 AAPs Approved by DOD and GSA in San Francisco Region

JOB CATEGORY	FEMALES AS PERCENTAGE OF WORKFORCE		INCREASE (DECREASE) IN FEMALE EMPLOYEES	
	Prior year	Current year	Number	Percent of total increase
Officials, managers & professionals	5.7%	5.4%	(2)	—
Technicians	12.6	14.3	132	10%
Salesworkers	8.0	10.8	8	1
Office & clerical craftsmen, operatives laborers, service workers	38.4	41.7	1,122	89
Totals	27.3	29.8	1,260	100%
	Prior year	Current year	Increase	Percent Increase
Total number of employees	16,981	19,789	2,808*	17%
Total number of female employees	4,638	5,898	1,260*	27%

*Females accounted for 45% of the net increase in jobs.

facilities being reviewed by GSA and DOD. However, a major cause of the difference is that policies on selecting contractors for review differ.

DOD policy states that contractor facilities are to be considered for review in descending order of the number of their employees. Based on this policy and the capability of the DOD compliance staff, contractor facilities with less than 200 employees generally will not be selected for review.

The GSA Chicago and Washington regions expect each compliance officer to complete six compliance reviews per month, while the GSA San Francisco region expects its compliance officers to complete four reviews per month. Consequently, in two of the three regions reviewed, GSA compliance officers indicated that they often selected small contractors which require less time to review, so that they could complete the designated number of reviews per month.

Small contractors should not be excluded from the review process. But the Federal contract compliance program should generally emphasize reviewing contractors with the greatest underutilization of women and minorities and with the most hiring and promotion opportunities, rather than selecting contractors on the basis of achieving a standard or recommended number of reviews per month.

In this regard, OFCC has developed a system to be used by the compliance agencies to identify those contractor facilities where compliance with the Executive order is below that which could be expected by the presence of minorities and women in the area work force. OFCC guidelines state that compliance agencies are to use this method as a primary criterion to select contractors for review. GAO's review showed, however, that the nonconstruction compliance agencies were not fully implementing the OFCC system for selecting contractor facilities for review, but rather were relying on internally developed selection criteria which varied among agencies.

Table 3 shows that the compliance agencies issued relatively few "show cause" notices—in less than 2 percent of the reviews conducted—and imposed even fewer sanction actions.

The data in Table 3 could be interpreted in either of two ways: (1) most contractors are complying with the requirements of the Executive order and there is little need for show cause notices or sanction actions; or (2) the compliance agencies are reluctant to issue show cause notices and to take sanction actions against contractors who are not in compliance.

Indications are that the latter is true. DOD and GSA representatives stated that they attempted to persuade contractors to comply with the Executive order and implement guidelines through conciliation efforts rather than by invoking formal sanction actions.

Officials of the Department of Commerce and the Department of

TABLE 3. Show Cause Notices and Sanctions Imposed for Fiscal Years 1972, 1973, and 1974 (to 3/31/74)

COMPLIANCE AGENCY	REVIEWS CONDUCTED	SHOW CAUSE NOTICES ISSUED		SANCTIONS IMPOSED[1]
		Number	Percentage of reviews conducted	
AEC	1,596	41	2.6%	0
Agriculture	1,820	19	1.0	0
AID	287	13	4.6	0
Commerce	604	1	.2	0
DOD	15,855	127	.8	0
GSA	7,071	276	3.9	1[2]
HEW	974	4	.4	0
Interior	1,012	34	3.4	0
NASA	714	1	.1	0
Postal Service	9,684	0	.0	13[3]
Transportation	109	10	9.1	0
Treasury	1,112	0	.0	0
VA	593	10	1.7	0
Totals	41,431	536	1.3%	14

[1] Does not include proposed sanction actions or pre-award clearances withheld.
[2] One company was debarred after the firm declined to request a hearing.
[3] Thirteen trucking companies were referred to the Department of Justice for appropriate legal action and a consent decree has been entered into with the companies under which the companies have agreed to stop their discriminatory practices.

215

the Treasury said that they follow the practice of issuing informal pre-show cause notices, or warning letters in lieu of show cause notices, to contractors that have not been fully responsive to OFCC requirements. These notices, however, do not automatically require further sanction actions if the contractor fails to show good cause why sanction actions should not be imposed.

For the fiscal years 1973 and 1974 . . . these two agencies performed about 1,200 compliance reviews, issued no show cause notices, and had not initiated any sanction actions. A Department of Transportation official told GAO that the issuance of a show cause notice only points to the failure of the compliance agency's conciliation function.

Moreover, the Director of AID's compliance program said that her agency had not found it necessary to proceed to the hearing stage of the sanction process but that if it had been necessary, she would have had to have OFCC's assistance because she was not familiar with all of the requirements for initiating a hearing.

Clarifying OFCC Guidance

The Secretary of Labor and OFCC have established and published certain guidelines to assist the compliance agencies in carrying out their compliance review and enforcement responsibilities under the Executive order. Despite this, however, the GAO review showed— and the compliance agencies generally agreed—that clarification of certain guidelines and additional guidance was needed in several areas to enable the compliance agencies to carry out their assigned responsibilities more effectively. Two of the most important areas in which additional DOL guidance was needed concern 1) employees who are victims of "affected class" discrimination and related remedies and 2) employee testing and selection procedures.

One of the guidelines issued by DOL is known as Revised Order No. 4 which, in part, requires that before a contractor is found in compliance, the contractor must first agree to provide relief to "affected class" employees who have been subjected to discrimination in the past and who continue to suffer its effects.

Neither Revised Order No. 4 nor other DOL guidelines establish specific criteria for identifying or remedying affected class problems. Revised Order No. 4 merely states that relief for members of an affected class must be afforded in order for a contractor to be found in compliance. According to an OFCC official, remedies can include 1) revised transfer and promotion systems and 2) financial restitution, or "back pay."

Officials of three compliance agencies (VA, USPS, and the Department of Transportation) said that their compliance officers did not determine in their reviews whether affected class situations existed, or whether back pay relief was called for, because DOL had not provided sufficient instructions or guidelines to enable such determinations to be made. . . .

Testing and Other Selection Procedures

In addition to setting forth guidelines explaining the affirmative action requirements of the Executive order, DOL has issued a series of special guidelines on the implementation of the order's nondiscrimination clause. One of these special guidelines concerns employee testing and other selection procedures.

The testing and selection procedures apply to those employment selection criteria which have an adverse affect on the opportunities of minorities or women in terms of hiring, transfer, promotion, training, or retention. If a test or other selection method used by the contractor tends to reject a disproportionate number of minority members or women, then the contractor must show that the test has been validated; that is, that any existing differential rejection rates, based on the test, are relevant to performance on the jobs in question.

Whenever agency compliance officers have questions about the adequacy of a testing validation study submitted by a contractor, OFCC guidelines provide that compliance agencies should refer the study to OFCC. As of July 1974, only one OFCC staff member was assigned to review testing validation studies, resulting in a 6 to 8-month backlog of about 32 validation studies to be analyzed. . . .

Despite its responsibility, OFCC has done very little to implement a program or system for monitoring the compliance agencies responsible for nonconstruction contractors to ensure that the program is administered in a uniform and effective manner.

At the three OFCC regional offices which GAO visited—Chicago, Philadelphia, and San Francisco—the staff devoted almost all its efforts to monitoring compliance agencies' enforcement of the Executive order as it applied to construction contractors and virtually no effort to monitor enforcement for nonconstruction contractors. . . .

Joint Responsibility

Contractors for which OFCC has responsibility under Executive Order 11246 also fall within EEOC's responsibilities under Title VII of the Civil Rights Act of 1964.

The two agencies signed a memorandum of understanding on May 20, 1970, designed to reduce duplication, exchange information, and establish procedures for processing cases against Government contractors subject to the provisions of the Executive order. GAO's review showed, however, and representatives of most of the compliance agencies agreed that the provisions of the memorandum were not being fully followed.

The memorandum provides, in part, that OFCC would check with EEOC prior to conducting compliance reviews to determine if outstanding discrimination complaints had been filed with EEOC. Representatives of five compliance agencies (DOD, USPS, Departments of the Interior, Treasury, and Transportation) informed GAO that their compliance officers, acting on behalf of OFCC in making compliance reviews, were not routinely checking with EEOC before conducting compliance reviews. As a result, these compliance agencies were approving contractor's AAPs without considering whether complaints had been registered with EEOC.

GAO investigators reviewed complaint listings at EEOC to determine whether there were outstanding complaints against the individual contractors whose AAPs were reviewed. Eighteen of the 60 DOD contractor facilities and 14 of the 60 GSA contractor facilities had outstanding complaints filed against them with EEOC at the time the compliance reviews were performed. It appeared that the complaints on 14 of the 18 DOD contractor facilities and 13 of the 14 GSA contractor facilities were not considered at the time the compliance reviews were conducted.

As early as March 1972, AID requested guidance from OFCC concerning the approval of AAPs when there were outstanding complaints on file with EEOC against the contractors. As of July 1974, however, OFCC had not yet issued any written guidance to AID on this subject.

In another instance, DOD had made at least two compliance reviews of a contractor and each time found the contractor to be in compliance with the Executive order. The two were completed during October 1973 and May 1974. As early as October 1970, however, EEOC had determined that a number of employment practices of the same contractor discriminated against female employees. For example, according to EEOC, the company paid males more than females for performing equal work.

As a result of its findings, EEOC is presently in the process of bringing suit charging the contractor with violation of Title VII of the Civil Rights Act of 1964.

EEOC's chief compliance officer said that the memorandum of understanding has been inoperative for several years. He asserted that

EEOC no longer needs OFCC's enforcement power since EEOC now has litigation authority which is more effective than OFCC's enforcement powers.

He also stated that EEOC no longer sends OFCC any information on its activities, but EEOC still receives and incorporates charges from the compliance agencies in its employment discrimination settlements. OFCC and EEOC are in process of redefining and clarifying this memorandum.

It should be pointed out that OFCC recognizes the need for improvement in various aspects of its compliance program. In a memorandum for fiscal year 1976, OFCC sets forth certain planned improvements in the contract compliance program. These include:

- Plans to establish an audit review system to review the compliance agencies and prepare annual formal evaluations of each agency;
- New or revised regulations on affected class, back pay relief, sex discrimination, testing and selection, and religious discrimination, for fiscal year 1975;
- Response to requests by compliance agencies for specific guidance, interpretation, and clarification, from OFCC within 10 days of receipt;
- Guidelines for performing compliance reviews and issuing show cause notices; and
- A memorandum of understanding with the Department of Justice and EEOC which would include coordination of target selections, data exchange, and enforcement procedures.

APPENDIX I:

LEGAL DOCUMENTS

Values and Legal Norms

A. *Eisenstadt* v. *Baird* 405 U.S. 438 (1972)
B. Filial Piety, Patricide and Equality Under the Law (The Fukuoka Patricide Decision)
C. The Universal Declaration of Human Rights, 1948
D. Convention on the Prevention and Punishment of the Crime of Genocide, 1948
E. Treaty on the Non-Proliferation of Nuclear Weapons, 1968

Introduction

Although a legal norm has an underlying value that constitutes its justification, the linkage is not always explicit. In each of the five documents in this Appendix, the relation between the norm and the value in which it is grounded is visible and significant.

A Massachusetts law prohibiting the distribution of contraceptives to unmarried persons but allowing married persons to obtain them, provided they are dispensed by physicians and pharmacists, had as one of its purposes to "discourage premarital sex." In *Eisenstadt* v. *Baird*, the U.S. Supreme Court found that this law violated the Equal Protection Clause of the Fourteenth Amendment by providing "dissimilar treatment for married and unmarried persons who are similarly situated."

In the Fukuoka patricide decision, the contending values are filial piety and the principle of equality under the law. A trial court in Japan found the defendant guilty of murdering his father, a "lineal ascendant," an act which according to a section of the Criminal Code warrants a more severe penalty than if the victim were not a lineal ascendant. The trial court, however, refrained from applying the relevant section of the Code on the grounds that it violated the principle of equality under the law guaranteed under the 1947 Constitution. The Japanese Supreme Court held for the appellant, the prosecution, claiming that the trial court had misapplied the constitutional principle of equality under the law and that this principle did not vitiate "filial piety" and the values involved in parent–child relations and other family relations. Moreover, the values underlying relations among family members, the court claimed, involve "a universal moral principle recognized by all mankind without regard to past or present or East and West."

The next three documents—the Universal Declaration of Human Rights, the Genocide Convention, and the Nuclear Non-Proliferation Treaty—affirm values in the name of mankind and the international community of nations. The values articulated in the thirty articles of the Universal Declaration of Human Rights are grounded in the general principle of "inherent dignity and of the equal and inalienable rights of all members of the human family." Similarly, the Genocide Convention asserts the right to life of every national, ethnic, racial and religious group. And the Treaty on Non-Proliferation of Nuclear Weapons seeks to protect mankind from the danger of a nuclear war. All three legal documents represent groping efforts to contribute to the body of international law so as to affirm the universal values of life, dignity, and equality of all human beings and of all groups of human beings.

To what extent do the six theoretical perspectives surveyed in Part II and the social-structural theory of law sketched in Part III throw light on the documents in Appendix I? Where do the courts look to find the values or goals underlying statutes or rules of law? To their own theories? To the legislative body? And where does the legislature look? Compare the United States Supreme Court's efforts at justifying their opinions, in terms of values, with those of the Japanese Supreme Court. How does the task of ascertaining values differ in the international forum?

Values and Legal Norms

A—*Eisenstadt v. Baird*
405 U.S. 438 (1972)

Mr. Justice BRENNAN delivered the opinion of the Court.

Appellee William Baird was convicted at a bench trial in the Massachusetts Superior Court under Massachusetts General Laws c. 272, §21, first, for exhibiting contraceptive articles in the course of delivering a lecture on contraception to a group of students at Boston University and, second, for giving a young woman a package of Emko vaginal foam at the close of his address. The Massachusetts Supreme Judicial Court unanimously set aside the conviction for exhibiting contraceptives on the ground that it violated Baird's First Amendment rights, but by a four-to-three vote sustained the conviction for giving away the foam. . . . Baird subsequently filed a petition for a Federal writ of habeas corpus, which the District Court dismissed. . . . On appeal, however, the Court of Appeals for the First Circuit vacated the dismissal and remanded the action with directions to grant the writ discharging Baird. . . . This appeal by the Sheriff of Suffolk County, Massachusetts, followed, and we noted probable jurisdiction. . . .

Massachusetts General Laws c. 272, §21, under which Baird was convicted, provides a maximum five-year term of imprisonment for "whoever . . . gives away . . . any drug, medicine, instrument or article whatever for the prevention of conception," except as authorized in §21A. Under §21A, "[a] registered physician may administer to or prescribe for any married person drugs or articles intended for the prevention of pregnancy or conception. [And a] registered pharmacist actually engaged in the business of pharmacy may furnish such drugs or articles to any married person presenting a prescription from a registered physician." As interpreted by the State Supreme Judicial Court, these provisions make it a felony for anyone, other than a registered physician or pharmacist acting in accordance with the terms of §21A, to dispense any article with the intention that it be used for the prevention of conception. The statutory scheme distinguishes among three distinct classes of distributees—*first*, married persons may obtain contraceptives to prevent pregnancy, but only from doctors or druggists on prescription; *second*, single persons may not obtain contraceptives from anyone to prevent pregnancy; and, *third*, married or single persons may obtain contraceptives from anyone to prevent not pregnancy, but the spread of disease. This construction of State law is, of course, binding on us. . . .

The legislative purposes that the statute is meant to serve are not altogether clear. In *Commonwealth* v. *Baird*, the Supreme Judicial Court noted only the State's interest in protecting the health of its citizens: "[T]he prohibition in §21," the court declared, "is directly related to" the State's goal of "preventing the distribution of articles designed to prevent conception which may have undesirable, if not dangerous, physical consequences." . . . In a subsequent decision, *Sturgis* v. *Attorney General*, . . . the court, however, found "a second and more compelling ground for upholding the statute"—namely, to protect morals through "regulating the private sexual lives of single persons." The Court of Appeals, for reasons that will appear, did not consider the promotion of health or the protection of morals through the deterrence of fornication to be the legislative aim. Instead, the court concluded that the statutory goal was to limit contraception in and of itself—a purpose that the court held conflicted "with fundamental human rights" under *Griswold* v. *Connecticut*, 381 U.S. 479 (1965), where this Court struck down Connecticut's prohibition against the use of contraceptives as an unconstitutional infringement of the right of marital privacy. . . .

We agree that the goals of deterring premarital sex and regulating the distribution of potentially harmful articles cannot reasonably be regarded as legislative aims of §§21 and 21A. And we hold that the statute, viewed as a prohibition on contraception *per se*, violates the rights of single persons under the Equal Protection Clause of the Fourteenth Amendment. . . .

II

The basic principles governing application of the Equal Protection Clause of the Fourteenth Amendment are familiar. . . . The question for our determination in this case is whether there is some ground of difference that rationally explains the different treatment accorded married and unmarried persons under Massachusetts General Laws c. 272, §§21 and 21A. For the reasons that follow, we conclude that no such ground exists.

First. Section 21 stems from Stat. 1879, c. 159, §1, which prohibited, without exception, distribution of articles intended to be used as contraceptives. In [1917], the Massachusetts Supreme Judicial Court explained that the law's "plain purpose is to protect purity, to preserve chastity, to encourage continence and self restraint, to defend the sanctity of the home, and thus to engender in the State and nation a virile and virtuous race of men and women." Although the State clearly abandoned that purpose with the enactment of §21A at least insofar as the illicit sexual activities of married persons are concerned, . . . the court reiterated in *Sturgis* v. *Attorney General, supra*, that the object of the legislation is to discourage premarital sexual intercourse. Conceding that the State could, consistently with the Equal Protection Clause, regard the problems of extramarital and premarital sexual relations as "[e]vils . . . of different dimensions and proportions, requiring different remedies," . . . we cannot agree that the deterrence of premarital sex may reasonably be regarded as the purpose of the Massachusetts law.

It would be plainly unreasonable to assume that Massachusetts has prescribed pregnancy and the birth of an unwanted child as punishment for fornication, which is a misdemeanor under Massachusetts General Laws c. 272, §18. Aside from the scheme of values that assumption would attribute to the State, it is abundantly clear that the effect of the ban on distribution of contraceptives to unmarried persons has at best a marginal relation to the proffered objective. . . . Like Connecticut's laws, §§21 and 21A do not at all regulate the distribution of contraceptives when they are to be used to prevent not pregnancy, but the spread of disease. . . . Nor, in making contraceptives available to married persons without regard to their intended use, does Massachusetts attempt to deter married persons from engaging in illicit sexual relations with unmarried persons. Even on the assumption that the fear of pregnancy operates as a deterrent to fornication, the Massachusetts statute is thus so riddled with exceptions that deterrence of pre-marital sex cannot reasonably be regarded as its aim.

Moreover, §§21 and 21A on their face have a dubious relation to the State's criminal prohibition on fornication. As the Court of Appeals explained, "Fornication is a misdemeanor [in Massachusetts], entailing a thirty dollar fine, or three months in jail. . . . Violation of the present statute is a felony, punishable by five years in prison. We find it hard to believe that the legislature adopted a statute carrying a five year penalty for its possible, obviously by no means fully effective, deterrence of the commission of a ninety-day misdemeanor." . . . Even conceding the legislature a full measure of discretion in fashioning remedies for fornication, and recognizing that the State may seek to deter prohibited conduct by punishing more severely those who facilitate than those who actually engage in its commission, we, like the Court of Appeals, cannot believe that in this instance Massachusetts has chosen to expose the aider and abetter who simply *gives away* a contraceptive to *20* times the *90-day* sentence of the offender himself. The very terms of the State's criminal statutes, coupled with the *de minimis* effect of §§21 and 21A in deterring fornication, thus compel the conclusion that such deterrence cannot reasonably be taken as the purpose of the ban on distribution of contraceptives to unmarried persons.

Second. Section 21A was added to the Massachusetts General Laws by Stat. 1966, c. 265, §1. The Supreme Judicial Court in *Commonwealth* v. *Baird, supra*, held that the purpose of the amendment was to serve the health needs of the community by regulating the distribution of potentially harmful articles. It is plain that Massachusetts had no such purpose in mind before the enactment of §21A. As the Court of Appeals remarked, "Consistent with the fact that the statute was contained in a chapter dealing with 'Crimes Against Chastity, Morality, Decency and Good Order,' it was cast only in terms of morals. A physician was forbidden to prescribe contraceptives even when needed for the protection of health. . . ." Nor did the Court of Appeals "believe that the legislature [in enacting §21A] suddenly reversed its field and developed an interest in health. Rather, it merely made what it thought to be the precise accommodation necessary to escape the *Griswold* ruling." . . .

Again, we must agree with the Court of Appeals. If health were the rationale of §21A, the statute would be both discriminatory and overbroad. Dissenting in *Commonwealth* v. *Baird*, . . . Justices Whittemore and Cutter stated that they saw "in §21 and §21A, read together, no public health purpose. If there is need to have a physician prescribe (and a pharmacist dispense) contraceptives, that need is as great for unmarried persons as for married persons." The Court of Appeals added: "If the prohibition [on distribution to unmarried persons] is to be taken to mean that the same physician who can prescribe for married patients does not have sufficient skill to protect the health of patients who lack a marriage certificate, or who may be currently divorced, it is illogical to the point of irrationality." . . . Furthermore, we must join the Court of Appeals in noting that not all contraceptives are potentially dangerous. As a result, if the Massachusetts statute were a health measure, it would not only invidiously discriminate against the unmarried, but also be overbroad with respect to the married. . . .

Third. If the Massachusetts statute cannot be upheld as a deterrent to fornication or as a health measure, may it, nevertheless, be sustained simply as a prohibition on contraception? The Court of Appeals analysis "led inevitably to the conclusion that, so far as morals are concerned, it is contraceptives per se that are considered immoral—to the extent that *Griswold* will permit such a declaration." . . . The Court of Appeals went on to hold . . . :

> To say that contraceptives are immoral as such, and are to be forbidden to unmarried persons who will nevertheless persist in having intercourse, means that such persons must risk for themselves an unwanted pregnancy, for the child, illegitimacy, and for society, a possible obligation of support. Such a view of morality is not only the very mirror image of sensible legislation; we consider that it conflicts with fundamental human rights. In the absence of demonstrated harm, we hold it is beyond the competency of the state.

We need not and do not, however, decide that important question in this case because, whatever the rights of the individual to access to contraceptives may be, the rights must be the same for the unmarried and the married alike.

If under *Griswold* the distribution of contraceptives to married persons cannot be prohibited, a ban on distribution to unmarried persons would be equally impermissible. It is true that in *Griswold* the right of privacy in question inhered in the marital relationship. Yet the marital couple is not an independent entity with a mind and heart of its own, but an association of two individuals each with a separate intellectual and emotional make-up. If the right of privacy means anything, it is the right of the *individual*, married or single, to be free from unwarranted government intrusion into matters so fundamentally affecting a person as the decision whether to bear or beget a child. . . .

On the other hand, if *Griswold* is no bar to a prohibition on the distribution of contraceptives, the State could not, consistently with the Equal Protection Clause, outlaw distribution to unmarried but not to married persons. In each case the evil, as perceived by the State, would be identical, and the underinclusion would be invidious. . . . We hold that by providing dissimilar treatment for married and unmarried persons who are similarly situated, Massachusetts General Laws c. 272, §§21 and 21A, violate the Equal Protection Clause. The judgment of the Court of Appeals is affirmed. . . .

B—Filial Piety, Patricide and Equality Under the Law, 1950 (The Fukuoka Patricide Decision), Hanreisbu, IV, No. 10, 2037 (Criminal)*

References

Criminal Code. Article 205. 1. A person who inflicts a bodily injury upon another and thereby causes his death shall be punished with imprisonment at forced labor for a fixed term of not less than two years.

2. When committed against a lineal ascendant of the offender or of his or her spouse, imprisonment at forced labor for life or for not less than three years shall be imposed.

Constitution of Japan. Article 14. All of the people are equal under the law

*Excerpt from John M. Maki, *Court and Constitution in Japan*, Seattle: University of Washington Press, 1964, pp. 130-138, by permission of the publisher.

and there shall be no discrimination in political, economic or social relations because of race, creed, sex, social status or family origin.

Peers and peerage shall not be recognized.

No privilege shall accompany any award of honor, decoration or any distinction, nor shall any such award be valid beyond the lifetime of the individual who now holds or hereafter may receive it.

Formal Judgment

The original judgment shall be quashed. The case shall be returned to the Fukuoka District Court.

Reasons. Regarding the reasons for appeal by the prosecution: The appeal by the prosecution states that the original decision recognized that the accused inflicted on his lineal ascendant an injury resulting in death, yet failed to apply paragraph 2 of Article 205 of the Criminal Code and disposed of the case under paragraph 1 of the same article on the ground that paragraph 2 violates the spirit of Article 14 of the Constitution. The argument for appeal contends that this decision is contrary to law and should be quashed, because it is based on a misunderstanding of the intent of the constitutional provision and because the penal provision that should have been applied was not applied.

The original judgment states in its "Reasons":

The provision of Article 205, paragraph 2, of the Criminal Code, viewed in the light of its origin, fondly preserved under the name of a so-called beautiful custom a matter which derived from the idea of severe punishment for patricide, which was regarded as the equivalent of the murder of one's lord because it was considered to be treachery against a parent who, in respect to the child, was viewed as the family head or as a protector or as a figure of authority. Thus, in the final analysis, this provision, derived as it is from quite feudalistic, antidemocratic, and antilibertarian ideas, runs counter to the grand spirit of the Constitution, which stresses the legal equality of all human beings.

In stating this, the original judgment holds that the said provision is contrary to the egalitarian democratic spirit of Article 14 of the Constitution and is thus unconstitutional.

Article 14 of the Constitution enunciates the principle of equality under the law for the people and provides that there be no discrimination in political, economic, or social relations because of race, creed, sex, social status, or family origin; this states the equality for all men of the value of human personality. Therefore, it is none other than an expression of the great principle that there be neither special rights nor the infliction of especially disadvantageous treatment on the grounds of differences in race, religion, sex, occupation, social status, and so forth. That slavery and special rights of peers are no longer recognized and that under the new Civil Code the incompetency of the wife and the special privileged position of the head of the house are abolished are also due to this principle. But this does not mean that the law is prevented from laying down appropriate, concrete provisions as required by morality, justice, or the specific purposes to be served by the law—taking into consideration within the scope of the principle of equality of the people such circumstances as age, natural qualities, occupation, or special relations with others. The reason for the more severe punishment of murder or injury resulting in death when committed against lineal ascendants as stipulated in the Criminal Code compared with ordinary cases of the same crimes is that the Code attributes special importance to the moral duties of the child toward his parents; the provision is merely a concrete legal provision, based on the requirements of morality.

The original decision points out that such an attribution of importance to the child's moral duties to his parents arose from feudalistic, antidemocratic ideas and that it is allowed to exist only in a familistic society based on ideas such as "the unity of loyalty and filial piety" and "ancestor worship"; but morality, controlling such relations as those between husband and wife, parent and child, or brother and sister is the great fountainhead of human ethics, a universal moral principle recognized by all mankind without regard to past or present or East and West. In other words, it must be said that this principle belongs to what in theory is called natural law. Therefore, with the exception of England and the United States, which are common law countries, we can find many examples of legislation providing more severe punishment for crimes against lineal ascendants than in ordinary cases. Whereas the original decision found that a morality that attaches special importance to the moral duties of children toward parents is feudalistic and antidemocratic, we find that this is a confusion of the natural relations between parents and children with the artificial social family system centering around the head of the house, which is negated under the new Constitution. In short, it [the original decision] indiscriminately rejects existing beautiful customs for the reason that they are feudalistic and antidemocratic and that it makes the same mistake as the present trend of the world, which falls into the evil of "throwing out the baby with the bath water."

Furthermore, by our interpretation of Article 14, paragraph 1, of the Constitution, the relations between parents and children do not fit under any of the categories, such as social status, and so forth, which are mentioned therein as reasons for discriminatory treatment. Also, the provision of the said article and paragraph that states that all of the people must in principle be treated equally in their political, economic, and social relations considers their position in regard to basic rights and duties from their place as subjects of those rights. It does not prohibit treatment of the people that varies according to their respective differences as objects in the several legal relationships applying to them. The original decision states that applying a more severe penalty when the victim is a direct lineal ascendant is tantamount to establishing, in regard to both the protection of human life and to punishment, a distinction among the people between those who are "special" and those who are "ordinary" and that, therefore, giving special protection to lineal ascendants as compared with ordinary people results in an inequality under law. However, it is reasonable to interpret the main object of the legislation as not being focused on the protection of the lineal ascendant who is the victim, but rather on a special consideration of the antimoral character of the descendant who is the assailant, the occasional greater protection thus given to lineal ascendants being merely a reflection of this.

Furthermore, the original decision holds that affection among relatives, as we know it, does not originate in legal provisions and that although family relations can be considered in weighing penalties, this is no reasonable basis to provide for inequality [of punishment] therein by means of law. However, we find that if it is feudalistic and antidemocratic, as the original judgment states, to emphasize the morality of children and parents and if, consequently, a law based on this emphasis is unconstitutional, then it is also unconstitutional to take these circumstances into consideration in weighing penalties when rendering judgment. Or, stated conversely, if one can take these circumstances into consideration constitutionally, then it is also possible constitutionally to go a step further and to objectify them in the form of law.

The original judgment points out that when the victim is a lineal descendant or spouse, paragraph 1 of Article 205 of the Code applies, and it criticizes the imbalance and the resulting inequality between this situation and a case in which the victim is a lineal ascendant. But the definition of the range of relatives who are victims in this kind of crime is a matter of legislative policy. The legislation of various countries is not always in agreement on this point. Therefore, when the original judgment points this [inequality] out in finding the said article and paragraph unconstitutional, it is confusing constitutional issues and legislative issues, just as is stated in point 6 of the Statement of Reasons for Appeal.

Such being the case, the provisions of Article 205, paragraph 2, of the Criminal Code have definitely remained valid from the time the new Constitution came into effect to today; therefore, the original judgment, which rejected the application of this paragraph in spite of the factual finding that the defendant killed his lineal ascendant and disposed of this case under paragraph 1 of Article 205, which deals with injury causing death in ordinary cases, is illegal because it misinterpreted Article 14, paragraph 1, of the Constitution and failed to apply the penal provisions that should have been applied. Thus, the appeal is well founded. . . .

The minority opinion of Justice Mano Tsuyoshi follows:

The original decision found that the provision of Article 205 of the Criminal Code relating to injury causing death of a lineal ascendant is unconstitutional and null and void. Against this judgment the prosecution lodged an appeal, contending that the said article is in accord with the Constitution. As I believe, in conclusion, that the decision of unconstitutionality in the original judgment should be accepted, I find that the appeal of the prosecution in this case should be dismissed. The outline of my reasons is as follows:

The Constitution declares in Article 14 that "all of the people are equal under the law." Over the front entrance of the building of the Supreme Court of the United States of America four words are engraved in marble: "Equal justice under law." What do they mean? Needless to say, they extol the great principle of "equality under the law, ' based on democracy. This principle is also solemnly declared in Article 2 of the Universal Declaration of Human Rights of the United Nations. The basis of democracy lies in the equality of individuals founded on human dignity, in other words, on equality of all personalities. And the basis of the equality of individuals lies in the spirit of independence and self-respect that guides unrestrained and free individuals to act—not from external coercion, but with a spontaneity arising from the profound inner self and, inseparably related to this, with a spirit of self-responsibility. To respect one's own independence and responsibility is at the same time to respect the independence and responsibility of others and to respect humanity. This respect, whether of one's own personality or of someone else's, is not simply a means but always an end. Thus, one necessarily becomes conscious of the equality of all personalities. After all, democracy has as its basis the equality among individuals of fundamental human rights. This principle of equality under law is generally recognized as the outcome of a long history, and is clearly proclaimed in Article 14 of the new Constitution.

To make a distinction with respect to Article 205 of the Criminal Code between injury causing death of lineal ascendants and injury causing death of other persons and to impose an especially severe penalty in the former case is obviously inequality of treatment, a violation of the above-mentioned great principle of equality under law, and in contravention of Article 14 of the Constitution. . . .

The majority opinion repeatedly emphasizes morality between parents and children and this may easily appeal to those among the masses who do not understand democracy. But what would remain if we subtract from the morality of children toward parents (direct ascendants) the proper democratic morality based on the dignity of man and the respect of personality? There would be only (1) the voluntary obedience and services of children to parents based on natural affection and (2) the duty of obedience and service as return for the *on*[1] which they receive from their parents. These should be left essentially to the free will of the individual, and it is not proper to make them into a relationship of rights and duties under law or to give them other kinds of legal protection. Rather, they belong to a domain in which moral values are to be purified and enhanced under an increasing feeling of freedom in the absence of legal coercion. In a rational, democratic state, as opposed to a primitive society in which moral issues are not distinguished from but are intermingled with legal issues, it is necessary to distinguish rationally between what is properly a moral issue and what is properly a legal issue. Thus, it is necessary to enact laws consistent with morality after making a critical examination of the peculiar functional differences between law and morality. Through all ages the morality of children toward parents was commonly called filial piety and centered around the duty of absolute obedience and service in gratitude and in repayment for the *on* received from the parents. This *on* was said to be "deeper than the sea and higher than the mountains." The argument that the core of such filial piety is repayment for *on* rests on the same basic principle as the feudal relationship of vassalage, the core of which is a return through service by feudal warriors for a fief, stipend, or allowance bestowed by the lord. This filial piety is a relationship between parents, who hold a superior status, and children, who hold an inferior status in the social organization; in other words, it is a relationship between persons unequal in status and not a relationship between equal individuals. Thus what was called filial piety in the past was the basis of the family system, the foundation of a system of patriarchy that was a kind of relationship of authoritarian control and at the same time had a strong feudalistic coloration. This is indeed an undeniable historical fact. The new filial piety should be a truly voluntary, free, uncoerced, and sound morality based on the principle of equality of personality. As seen above, there has been for a long time a difference in social status between parent and child as superior and inferior. And the provisions of severe punishment for patricide or injury causing death of lineal ascendants, which were established as norms of filial piety arising from this difference of status, are in violation of the examples stipulated in Article 14 of the Constitution.

The majority opinion states that the reason for the provisions for more severe penalty for injury causing death of a lineal ascendant in the Criminal Code is that the code attaches importance to the moral duty of the child toward its parents and that

> morality, controlling such relations as those between husband and wife, parent and child, or brother and sister is the great fountainhead of human ethics, a universal moral principle recognized by all mankind without regard to past or present or East and West. in other words, it must be said that this principle belongs to what in theory is called natural law.

But if under the name of morality provisions for inequality can be made at random, like bamboo sprouts coming up after a rain, by saying "this is morality between parent and child, that is morality between husband and wife, this is morality between brother and sister, that is morality among relatives, this is morality between teacher and pupil, that is morality among neighbors, and this is such-and-such morality," what will become of the principle of "equality under the law," which is emphatically proclaimed by the new Constitution? I shudder at the thought. The provisions of the Criminal Code governing the murder of lineal ascendants and those governing the crime of inflicting injury on them resulting in death are said to be almost valueless in practice and even harmful at times. This may be proved by statistics. There is no necessary, rational justification for violating the great principle of equality. Therefore, I cannot agree at all with the majority opinion which, even though these provisions clearly involve inequality as pointed out above, vaguely states in the name of morality that they are not in violation of the principle of equality. . . .

Note

1. *On* may be roughly translated as meaning "the benefits for which one is indebted to a superior." For a detailed discussion of *on* see Ruth Benedict, *The Chrysanthemum and the Sword* (Boston: Houghton Mifflin, 1946), pp. 99 ff. (Translator's note.)

C—The Universal Declaration of Human Rights, 1948,
United Nations, General Assembly Official Records,
Resolutions, 3 (pt. 1)
(A/810), at 71–78

Preamble

Whereas recognition of the inherent dignity and of the equal and inalienable rights of all members of the human family is the foundation of freedom, justice and peace in the world,

Whereas disregard and contempt for human rights have resulted in barbarous acts which have outraged the conscience of mankind, and the advent of a world in which human beings shall enjoy freedom of speech and belief and freedom from fear and want has been proclaimed as the highest aspiration of the common people,

Whereas it is essential, if man is not to be compelled to have recourse, as a last resort, to rebellion against tyranny and oppression, that human rights should be protected by the rule of law,

Whereas it is essential to promote the development of friendly relations between nations,

Whereas the peoples of the United Nations have in the Charter reaffirmed their faith in fundamental human rights, in the dignity and worth of the human person and in the equal rights of men and women and have determined to promote social progress and better standards of life in larger freedom.

Whereas Member States have pledged themselves to achieve, in co-operation with the United Nations, the promotion of universal respect for and observance of human rights and fundamental freedoms,

Whereas a common understanding of these rights and freedoms is of the greatest importance for the full realization of this pledge,

Now, therefore,

The General Assembly Proclaims

This Universal Declaration of Human Rights as a common standard of achievement for all peoples and all nations, to the end that every individual and every organ of society, keeping this Declaration constantly in mind, shall strive by teaching and education to promote respect for these rights and freedoms and by progressive measures, national and international, to secure their universal and effective recognition and observance, both among the peoples of Member States themselves and among the peoples of territories under their jurisdiction.

Article 1

All human beings are born free and equal in dignity and rights. They are endowed with reason and conscience and should act towards one another in a spirit of brotherhood.

Article 2

Everyone is entitled to all rights and freedoms set forth in this Declaration, without distinction of any kind, such as race, colour, sex, language, religion, political or other opinion, national or social origin, property, birth or other status.

Furthermore, no distinction shall be made on the basis of the political, jurisdictional or international status of the country or territory to which a person belongs, whether it be independent, trust non-self-governing or under any other limitation of sovereignty.

Article 3

Everyone has the right to life, liberty and security of person.

Article 4

No one shall be held in slavery or servitude; slavery and the slave trade shall be prohibited in all their forms.

Article 5
No one shall be subjected to torture or to cruel, inhuman or degrading treatment or punishment.

Article 6
Everyone has the right to recognition everywhere as a person before the law.

Article 7
All are equal before the law and are entitled without any discrimination to equal protection of the law. All are entitled to equal protection against any discrimination in violation of this Declaration and against any incitement to such discrimination.

Article 8
Everyone has the right to an effective remedy by the competent national tribunals for acts violating the fundamental rights granted him by the constitution or by law.

Article 9
No one shall be subjected to arbitrary arrest, detention or exile.

Article 10
Everyone is entitled in full equality to a fair and public hearing by an independent and impartial tribunal, in the determination of his rights and obligations and of any criminal charge against him.

Article 11
(1) Everyone charged with a penal offence has the right to be presumed innocent until proved guilty according to law in a public trial at which he has had all the guarantees necessary for his defence.
(2) No one shall be held guilty of any penal offence on account of any act or omission which did not constitute a penal office, under national or international law, at the time when it was committed. Nor shall a heavier penalty be imposed than the one that was applicable at the time the penal offence was committed.

Article 12
No one shall be subjected to arbitrary interference with his privacy, family, home or correspondence, nor to attacks upon his honour and reputation. Everyone has the right to the protection of the law against such interference or attacks.

Article 13
(1) Everyone has the right to freedom of movement and residence within the borders of each state.
(2) Everyone has the right to leave any country, including his own, and to return to his country.

Article 14
(1) Everyone has the right to seek and to enjoy in other countries asylum from persecution.

(2) This right may not be invoked in the case of prosecutions genuinely arising from non-political crimes or from acts contrary to the purposes and principles of the United Nations.

Article 15

(1) Everyone has the right to a nationality.

(2) No one shall be arbitrarily deprived of his nationality nor denied the right to change his nationality.

Article 16

(1) Men and women of full age, without any limitation due to race, nationality or religion, have the right to marry and to found a family. They are entitled to equal rights as to marriage, during marriage and at its dissolution.

(2) Marriage shall be entered into only with the free and full consent of the intending spouses.

(3) The family is the natural and fundamental group unit of society and is entitled to protection by society and the State.

Article 17

(1) Everyone has the right to own property alone as well in association with others.

(2) No one shall be arbitrarily deprived of his property.

Article 18

Everyone has the right to freedom of thought, conscience and religion; this right includes freedom to change his religion or belief, and freedom, either alone or in community with others and in public or private, to manifest his religion or belief in teaching, practice, worship and observance.

Article 19

Everyone has the right to freedom of opinion and expression; this right includes freedom to hold opinions without interference and to seek, receive and impart information and ideas through any media and regardless of frontiers.

Article 20

(1) Everyone has the right to freedom of peaceful assembly and association.

(2) No one may be compelled to belong to an association.

Article 21

(1) Everyone has the right to take part in the government of his country, directly or through freely chosen representatives.

(2) Everyone has the right of equal access to public service in his country.

(3) The will of the people shall be the basis of the authority of government; this will shall be expressed in periodic and genuine elections which shall be by universal and equal suffrage and shall be held by secret vote or by equivalent free voting procedures.

Article 22

Everyone, as a member of society, has the right to social security and is entitled to realization, through national effort and international co-operation and in accordance with the organization and resources of each State, of the economic, social and cultural rights indispensable for his dignity and the free development of his personality.

Article 23

(1) Everyone has the right to work, to free choice of employment, to just and favourable conditions of work and to protection against unemployment.

(2) Everyone, without any discrimination, has the right to equal pay for equal work.

(3) Everyone who works has the right to just and favourable remuneration ensuring for himself and his family an existence worthy of human dignity, and supplemented, if necessary, by other means of social protection.

(4) Everyone has the right to form and to join trade unions for the protection of his interests.

Article 24

Everyone has the right to rest and leisure, including reasonable limitation of working hours and periodic holidays with pay.

Article 25

(1) Everyone has the right to a standard of living adequate for the health and well-being of himself and of his family, including food, clothing, housing and medical care and necessary social services, and the right to security in the event of unemployment, sickness, disability, widowhood, old age or other lack of livelihood in circumstances beyond his control.

(2) Motherhood and childhood are entitled to special care and assistance. All children, whether born in or out of wedlock, shall enjoy the same social protection.

Article 26

(1) Everyone has the right to education. Education shall be free, at least in the elementary and fundamental stages. Elementary education shall be compulsory. Technical and professional education shall be made generally available and higher education shall be equally accessible to all on the basis of merit.

(2) Education shall be directed to the full development of the human personality and to the strengthening of respect for human rights and fundamental freedoms. It shall promote understanding, tolerance and friendship among all nations, racial or religious groups, and shall further the activities of the United Nations for the maintenance of peace.

(3) Parents have a prior right to choose the kind of education that shall be given to their children.

Article 27

(1) Everyone has the right freely to participate in the cultural life of the community, to enjoy the arts and to share in scientific advancement and its benefits.

(2) Everyone has the right to the protection of the moral and material interests resulting from any scientific, literary or artistic production of which he is the author.

Article 28

Everyone is entitled to a social and international order in which the rights and freedoms set forth in this Declaration can be fully realized.

Article 29

(1) Everyone has duties to the community in which alone the free and full development of his personality is possible.

(2) In the exercise of his rights and freedoms, everyone shall be subject only to such limitations as are determined by law solely for the purposes of securing due recognition and respect for the rights and freedoms of others and of meeting the just requirements of morality, public order and the general welfare in a democratic society.

(3) These rights and freedoms may in no case be exercised contrary to the purposes and principles of the United Nations.

Article 30

Nothing in this Declaration may be interpreted as implying for any State, group or person any right to engage in any activity or to perform any act aimed at the destruction of any of the rights and freedoms set forth herein.

D—Convention on the Prevention and Punishment of the Crime of Genocide, 1948, United Nations Treaty Series, Volume 79, at 279

The Contracting Parties,

Having considered the declaration made by the General Assembly of the United Nations in its resolution 96 (1) dated 11 December 1946 that genocide is a crime under international law, contrary to the spirit and aims of the United Nations and condemned by the civilized world;

Recognizing that at all periods of history genocide has inflicted great losses on humanity; and

Being convinced that, in order to liberate mankind from such an odious scourge, international co-operation is required,

Hereby agree as hereinafter provided:

Article I

The Contracting Parties confirm that genocide, whether committed in time of peace or in time of war, is a crime under international law which they undertake to prevent and to punish.

Article II

In the present Convention, genocide means any of the following acts committed with intent to destroy, in whole or in part, a national, ethnical, racial or religious group, as such:

a. Killing members of the group;
b. Causing serious bodily or mental harm to members of the group;
c. Deliberately inflicting on the group conditions of life calculated to bring about its physical destruction in whole or in part;
d. Imposing measures intended to prevent births within the group;
e. Forcibly transferring children of the group to another group.

Article III

The following acts shall be punishable:

a. Genocide;
b. Conspiracy to commit genocide;
c. Direct and public incitement to commit genocide;
d. Attempt to commit genocide;
e. Complicity in genocide.

Article IV

Persons committing genocide or any of the other acts enumerated in article III shall be punished, whether they are constitutionally responsible rulers, public officials or private individuals.

Article V

The Contracting Parties undertake to enact, in accordance with their respective Constitutions, the necessary legislation to give effect to the provisions of the present Convention and, in particular, to provide effective penalties for persons guilty of genocide or of any of the other acts enumerated in article III.

Article VI

Persons charged with genocide or any of the other acts enumerated in article III shall be tried by a competent tribunal of the State in the territory of which the act was committed, or by such international penal tribunal as may have jurisdiction with respect to those Contracting Parties which shall have accepted its jurisdiction.

Article VII

Genocide and the other acts enumerated in article III shall not be considered as political crimes for the purpose of extradition.

The Contracting Parties pledge themselves in such cases to grant extradition in accordance with their laws and treaties in force.

Article VIII

Any Contracting Party may call upon the competent organs of the United Nations to take such action under the Charter of the United Nations as they consider appropriate for the prevention and suppression of acts of genocide or any of the other acts enumerated in article III.

Article IX

Disputes between the Contracting Parties relating to the interpretation, application or fulfilment of the present Convention, including those relating to the responsibility of a State for genocide or for any of the other acts enumerated in article III, shall be submitted to the International Court of Justice at the request of any of the parties to the dispute. . . .

E—Treaty on the Non-Proliferation of Nuclear Weapons, 1968
United Nations Treaty Series, Volume 729, at 161.*

The States concluding this Treaty, hereinafter referred to as the "Parties to the Treaty",

Considering the devastation that would be visited upon all mankind by a nuclear war and the consequent need to make every effort to avert the danger of such a war and to take measures to safeguard the security of peoples,

Believing that the proliferation of nuclear weapons would seriously enhance the danger of nuclear war,

In conformity with resolutions of the United Nations General Assembly calling for the conclusion of an agreement on the prevention of wider dissemination of nuclear weapons,

Undertaking to co-operate in facilitating the application of International Atomic Energy Agency safeguards on peaceful nuclear activities,

Expressing their support for research, development and other efforts to further the application, within the framework of the International Atomic Energy Agency safeguards system, of the principle of safeguarding effectively the flow of source and special fissionable materials by use of instruments and other techniques at certain strategic points,

Affirming the principle that the benefits of peaceful applications of nuclear technology, including any technological by-products which may be derived by nuclear-weapon States from the development of nuclear explosive devices, should be available for peaceful purposes to all Parties to the Treaty, whether nuclear-weapon or non-nuclear-weapon States.

Convinced that, in furtherance of this principle, all Parties to the Treaty are entitled to participate in the fullest possible exchange of scientific information for, and to contribute alone or in co-operation with other States to, the further development of the applications of atomic energy for peaceful purposes

Declaring their intention to achieve at the earliest possible date the cessation of the nuclear arms race and to undertake effective measures in the direction of nuclear disarmament.

Urging the co-operation of all States in the attainment of this objective,

Recalling the determination expressed by the Parties to the 1963 Treaty banning nuclear weapon tests in the atmosphere, in outer space and under water in its Preamble to seek to achieve the discontinuance of all test explosions of nuclear weapons for all time and to continue negotiations to this end, . . .

*Signed at London, Moscow, and Washington on 1 July 1968.

Have Agreed as Follows:

Article I

Each nuclear-weapon State Party to the Treaty undertakes not to transfer to any recipient whatsoever nuclear weapons or other nuclear explosive devices or control over such weapons or explosive devices directly, or indirectly; and not in any way to assist, encourage, or induce any non-nuclear weapon State to manufacture or otherwise acquire nuclear weapons or other nuclear explosive devices, or control over such weapons or explosive devices.

Article II

Each non-nuclear-weapon State Party to the Treaty undertakes not to receive the transfer from any transferor whatsoever of nuclear weapons or other nuclear explosive devices or of control over such weapons or explosive devices directly, or indirectly; not to manufacture or otherwise acquire nuclear weapons or other nuclear explosive devices; and not to seek or receive any assistance in the manufacture of nuclear weapons or other nuclear explosive devices.

Article III

1. Each non-nuclear-weapon State Party to the Treaty undertakes to accept safeguards, as set forth in an agreement to be negotiated and concluded with the International Atomic Energy Agency in accordance with the Statute of the International Atomic Energy Agency and the Agency's safeguards system, for the exclusive purpose of verification of the fulfilment of its obligations assumed under this Treaty with a view to preventing diversion of nuclear energy from peaceful uses to nuclear weapons or other nuclear explosive devices. Procedures for the safeguards required by this article shall be followed with respect to source or special fissionable material whether it is being produced, processed or used in any principal nuclear facility or is outside any such facility. The safeguards required by this article shall be applied on all source or special fissionable material in all peaceful nuclear activities within the territory of such State, under its jurisdiction, or carried out under its control anywhere.

2. Each State Party to the Treaty undertakes not to provide: (*a*) source or special fissionable material, or (*b*) equipment or material especially designed or prepared for the processing, use or production of special fissionable material, to any non-nuclear-weapon State for peaceful purposes, unless the source of special fissionable material shall be subject to the safeguards required by this article.

3. The safeguards required by this article shall be implemented in a manner designed to comply with article IV of this Treaty, and to avoid hampering the economic or technological development of the Parties or international cooperation in the field of peaceful nuclear activities, including the international exchange of nuclear material and equipment for the processing, use or production of nuclear material for peaceful purposes in accordance with the provisions of this article and the principle of safeguarding set forth in the Preamble of the Treaty.

4. Non-nuclear-weapon States Party to the Treaty shall conclude agreements with the International Atomic Energy Agency to meet the requirements of this article either individually or together with other States in accordance with the

Statute of the International Atomic Energy Agency. Negotiation of such agreements shall commence within 180 days from the original entry into force of this Treaty. For States depositing their instruments of ratification or accession after the 180-day period, negotiations of such agreements shall commence not later than the day of such deposit. Such agreements shall enter into force not later than eighteen months after the date of initiation of negotiations.

Article IV

1. Nothing in this Treaty shall be interpreted as affecting the inalienable right of all the parties to the Treaty to develop research, production and use of nuclear energy for peaceful purposes without discrimination and in conformity with articles I and II of this Treaty.

2. All the Parties to the Treaty undertake to facilitate, and have the right to participate in, the fullest possible exchange of equipment, materials and scientific and technological information for the peaceful uses of nuclear energy. Parties to the Treaty in a position to do so shall also co-operate in contributing alone or together with other States or international organizations to the further development of the applications of nuclear energy for peaceful purposes, especially in the territories of non-nuclear-weapon States Party to the Treaty, with due consideration for the needs of the developing areas of the world.

Article V

Each Party to the Treaty undertakes to take appropriate measures to ensure that, in accordance with this Treaty, under appropriate international observation and through appropriate international procedures, potential benefits from any peaceful applications of nuclear explosions will be made available to non-nuclear-weapon States Party to the Treaty on a non-discriminatory basis and that the charge to such Parties for the explosive devices used will be as low as possible and exclude any charge for research and development. Non-nuclear-weapon States Party to the Treaty shall be able to obtain such benefits, pursuant to a special international agreement or agreements, through an appropriate international body with adequate representation of non-nuclear-weapon States. Negotiations on this subject shall commence as soon as possible after the Treaty enters into force. Non-nuclear-weapon States Party to the Treaty so desiring may also obtain such benefits pursuant to bilateral agreements.

Article VI

Each of the Parties to the Treaty undertakes to pursue negotiations in good faith on effective measures relating to cessation of the nuclear arms race at an early date and to nuclear disarmament, and on a treaty on general and complete disarmament under strict and effective international control.

Article VII

Nothing in this Treaty affects the right of any group of states to conclude regional treaties in order to assure the total absence of nuclear weapons in their respective territories. . . .

Article X

1. Each Party shall in exercising its national sovereignty have the right to withdraw from the Treaty if it decides that extraordinary events, related to the subject-matter of this Treaty, have jeopardized the supreme interests of its country. It shall give notice of such withdrawal to all other Parties to the Treaty and to the United Nations Security Council three months in advance. Such notice shall include a statement of the extraordinary events it regards as having jeopardized its supreme interests.

2. Twenty-five years after the entry into force of the Treaty, a conference shall be convened to decide whether the Treaty shall continue in force indefinitely, or shall be extended for an additional fixed period or periods. This decision shall be taken by a majority of the Parties to the Treaty.

PART IV

Social-Structural Theory of Law: Role Analysis

The second component of our social-structural theory of law deals with the analysis of roles of legal personnel. In complex societies, in contrast with relatively simple, preliterate societies, legal systems tend to become increasingly differentiated not only with respect to the number and types of legal rules but also with respect to the number of legal roles. Whatever roles are institutionalized in a legal system, the task of the sociologist is to develop or apply a theory with which to analyze the behavior of legal personnel. We shall use role theory to perform this task.

The concept of role has a long history in anthropology, sociology, and psychology. In his classic formulation, Linton (1936) distinguished "role" from "status," the latter referring to a position in a social system and the former to the behavioral aspect associated with a given status.

In a legal system, as in any subsystem of a society, there are several institutionalized statuses and their accompanying roles. Among the principal legal roles in a complex society are the judge, the lawyer, the legislator, the government administrator, the prosecuter, and the police officer. Each of these and other legal roles may be analyzed from at least three perspectives: (1) role expectations, (2) role orientations, and (3) role behavior.

The role expectations of legal personnel may be based on legal rules, administrative regulations, "codes of ethics," etc. Because there is often an absence of consensus on role expectations (Gross, Mason, and McEachern, 1958), role occupants exercise a measure of discretion in discharging their role obligations. How much discretion and what type of discretion is exercised by a role occupant in a legal system is partly a function of his/her orientations or attitudes toward role expectations.

The role orientations of a lawyer, judge, prosecutor, or occupant of any other legal role are partly a function of the socialization process, which includes a formal as well as an informal phase. The formal phase may consist of a period of formal training, such as occurs in a law school; the informal phase occurs during an individual's role incumbency as he/she interacts with various "role-partners" who constitute an incumbent's "role-set" (Merton, 1957: 368–380). As Merton has noted, each role occupant does not necessarily interact with only one other person in a complementary role relationship— as in the case of an employer–employee relationship or a teacher– student relationship—but with a number of other role-partners who impinge on his/her particular role.

Role behavior, as distinct from role orientations and role expectations, involves overt actions—principally decision-making in the case of legal roles—that may take a multitude of forms. In the case of legal roles, role behavior is a function in part of role expectations and role orientations. Additional factors affecting the behavior of role incumbents are the expectations and demands of role-set members which may give rise to what have been referred to as "role-set conflicts." No matter how role-set conflicts are resolved, they will invariably affect the behavior of role incumbents (Evan and Levin, 1966).

Other factors that may influence a role incumbent's behavior are his or her concurrent statuses, collectively designed as "status-sets," and past or possible future changes in status, which have been referred to as "status-sequences" (Merton, 1957: 380–384). Both status-sets and status-sequences may be sources of conflict which, upon resolution, will influence the behavior of a role incumbent.

The concepts and propositions outlined above are illustrated in the readings in Part IV and in the legal documents in Appendix II. In the first selection, by Judge Lois Forer, she graphically describes not only her role-set in a trial court but also her role behavior during an average day in the course of which she is expected to dispose of about twenty cases.

In a pioneering study, Carlin establishes that the ethical orientations and behavior of lawyers are a function of the size of their law firms, which also determines the nature of their clientele and the type of courts and agencies with which they have contact. How would you use the concept of "role-set" to help explain differences in the ethical attitudes and behavior of lawyers? Given Carlin's findings, what changes, if any, do you think the American Bar Association should make in its code of ethics (Morgan, 1977)?

In the reading on legislators, Eulau conceptualizes three role orientations—the representative, the politico, and the trustee—and reports some research findings on the differential distribution of these orientations among state legislators. Were you surprised by the high frequency of a "trustee" orientation among the legislators in Eulau's study? What are the relative merits of the three role orientations of legislators from the vantage point of safeguarding the democratic process?

Nagel's analysis of the role behavior of commissioners of federal administrative agencies involves an analysis of status-set attributes, particularly that of political party affiliation. He found that commissioners who were Democrats tended to decide cases more frequently in a "liberal" direction—i.e., pro-labor, pro-consumer, and pro-small businessman—than Republican commissioners. This finding and others lead Nagel to conclude that the policy of appointing commissioners of federal administrative agencies with due recognition of their political party affiliation should be retained. A counter-argument might be made in favor of appointing nonpartisan commissioners who are acknowledged experts in a particular body of knowledge pertinent to the operations of a given agency. Compare the pros and cons of this view with Nagel's policy recommendation.

References

Evan, W. M. and E. G. Levin (1966). "Status-Set and Role-Set Conflicts of the Stockbroker." *Social Forces*, 45:73–83.

Gross, N., W. S. Mason and A. W. McEachern (1958). *Explorations in Role Analysis: Studies of the School Superintendency Role.* New York: Wiley.

Linton, R. (1936). *The Study of Man.* New York: Appleton-Century.

Merton, R. K. (1957). *Social Theory and Social Structure.* Revised enlarged edition. Glencoe, Ill.: Free Press.

Morgan, T. D. (1977). "The Evolving Concept of Professional Responsibility." *Harvard Law Review*, 90: 702–743.

19

One Day in the Life of a Trial Judge

Lois G. Forer

For most Americans, the courts are the agency to which they must turn for redress. And, of course, it is in courts that the hundreds of thousands of adults accused of crime, mental illness, alcoholism and drug addiction, and the children accused of everything from murder to receiving inadequate parental care, are tried. More than 19,500 of the 20,000 courts in America are trial courts. It is here that most people get whatever justice they will receive from the judicial system.

The Trial Court

Only the lawyers and judges who are in these trial courts on a daily basis really know what happens there. Neither the leaders of the bar nor the legal scholars spend much, if any, time in these tribunals. Most treatises on law discuss legal principles, landmark cases and changing doctrines. They analyze the difficult issues presented to the appellate courts and focus primarily on their opinions.

There is one United States Supreme Court. There are ten appellate

Excerpt from *The Death of the Law*, New York: David McKay Company, Inc. 1972, pp. 79-98. Reprinted by permission of Curtis Brown, Ltd. and the author.

federal courts. Each state has a supreme court and one or two inter-
mediary appellate courts. All of these courts pass upon only a very
small fraction of the cases that are brought before the trial courts.
The role of the trial courts in providing or failing to provide fair and
just treatment for millions of Americans is a significant factor in
creating a nation of scofflaws.

Our knowledge of what happens in these trial courts is fragmentary. We do not even know how many cases—criminal and civil—are
brought to court or how many are actually tried.

Statistics with respect to the number of cases litigated are incomplete. Many cases are dropped or settled before trial. Many criminal
prosecutions are withdrawn. No one knows why. No one knows
whether justice was served by these abortive legal actions. The only
certain fact is that the number of cases is enormous and increasing
every year. The federal court system does maintain fairly complete
records. In 1950, 44,454 civil cases and 36,393 criminal cases were
commenced in the federal courts. In 1971, 93,396 civil cases and
41,290 criminal cases were filed in the same federal courts. Corresponding increases in numbers of cases seem to have occurred in state
and local courts. The exact numbers are difficult to ascertain. One
can, however, estimate from a limited set of statistics. In Philadelphia, which has a population of not quite 2 million, some 25,000
civil cases and 16,000 criminal prosecutions, excluding juvenile and
domestic relations cases, were instituted in 1971. The national
population in 1971 was in excess of 200 million. Extrapolating these
figures, one concludes that probably at least 2.5 million civil cases
and more than 1.6 million criminal prosecutions were instituted in
the United States in 1971.

Few of these cases were noted by the scholars. They devoted the
greater part of their attention to the four hundred cases decided on
the merits each year by the United States Supreme Court. A single
trial judge may decide four hundred cases in less than two months.

The emphasis upon appellate court decisions, and especially the
opinions of the United States Supreme Court, obscures our very real
ignorance of the operations of the law in more than 99 percent of
the cases, those in which no appeal is taken. The number of major
cases actually tried before judge and jury is relatively small. The vast
majority of lawsuits are disposed of in brief hearings, unnoticed by
the public, forgotten by all but the victim and the accused or the
plaintiff and the defendant. . . . Despite the overwhelming quantity
of studies of the judicial process, the courts and the administration
of justice in the United States, very little is known or written about
the normal, uncelebrated processing of cases.

On a typical day in criminal motions court, fifteen to twenty cases are listed, of which two or three are "add ons" (matters that have come up at the last minute or that don't fit in any recognized category). In addition, there are applications for bail and reduction of bail. On the average, a judge in such a court must make decisions in twenty cases each day.

Even though the hearings are brief and hasty, a large corps of supporting personnel is needed to man any courtroom. There is at least one court officer to swear in the witnesses and take charge of opening court, maintaining order and calling the cases. There are also a clerk who brings in the files, keeps the records, enters the orders and returns the papers at the end of the day; a sheriff to bring in the handcuffed prisoners, remove the manacles while they testify, reshackle them and return them to the cell block; usually another sheriff or policeman armed with gun, nightstick and blackjack for security purposes (a courtroom is not a safe place). There are also: a court stenographer who must record every word of testimony; the prosecutor, the defender, and the policemen and detectives who will testify. Occasionally there are witnesses for the defense—poor, frightened people who sit waiting for they know not what. A few privately retained attorneys rush in and out to see when their cases will be reached. And there is the judge seated on a dais in a black robe. The judge has awesome powers over individuals but is subjected to many limitations. The judge is deferentially addressed as "Your Honor," but he can no more control the matters that are brought into court than the worker on an assembly line at General Motors can control the pieces of machinery that are borne along the conveyor belt in front of him. Fragments of human lives pass before the bench in unending procession.

The factory worker can only tighten or loosen a screw. He cannot change the shape or design of the product; he cannot see it whole. The trial judge, too, has a very limited function. He can only tighten or loosen the screws of the system very slightly. He can raise or lower bail; imprison or free the accused; suppress or admit a confession; permit or deny the defense information with respect to the alleged crime. There is little, if anything, a judge can do for the people he sees briefly each day.

For these cases, any old room will do. In many cities and counties the courthouse is an old, dilapidated building, too small and too antiquated to cover the needs of the community. The courtroom is often dirty, ill ventilated and depressing. It bears little resemblance to the spacious marble halls in which appeals are argued. An appellate court is composed of several members, usually seven or nine. Such a court hears argument by counsel and reads briefs in which the points of law have been carefully researched and analyzed. The court adjourns and deliberates, perhaps for weeks or months, and then ultimately files a written opinion which has been prepared by law clerks (often the most capable young law graduates), reviewed by the judges, revised, and finally issued after searching deliberation. The trial judge must rule on most matters from the bench, when a motion is made. Judge John Parker of the Court of Appeals for the Fourth Circuit is reported to have told this story. He, an appellate judge, said to a trial judge: "It has always been a matter of wonder to me how a trial judge who must decide so many questions on the spur of the moment makes so few mistakes." The trial judge replied, "I always marvel that appellate judges, who have so much time to consider, make so many damn mistakes."

Criminal Motions Court

A trial judge is under constant pressure to decide at once. For example, the sheriff and a guard from Kentucky are in the court room, ready to take a fugitive back from Pennsylvania to Kentucky. The judge cannot tell them to return in a few days after he thinks about the question and researches the law.

At nine thirty the court personnel begin to assemble. The crier opens court. "All rise. Oyez, oyez, all persons having business before the Court of Common Pleas Criminal Division come forth and they shall be heard. God save this honorable court. Be seated and stop all conversation. Good morning, Your Honor." The crier calls out the names of the defendants. Most of them are represented by the public defender. He checks his files. One or two names are not on his list. A quick phone call is made to his office to send up the missing files.

On one particular day when I was sitting in criminal motions court, three cases had private counsel. One had been retained by the defendant. The other two had been appointed by the court to represent indigents accused of homicide. Where are these lawyers?

As is customary, the court officer phones each of them and reminds his secretary that he has a case listed and he must appear. Several of the defendants are not present. The prison is called to locate the missing parties. The judge, if he wishes to get through his list, must find the lawyers and litigants and order them to come to court.

Frequently the prosecutor cannot find his files. When he does, he discovers that a necessary witness has not been subpoenaed. The case must be continued to another day. The other witnesses, who are present and have missed a day's work, are sent home. The defendant is returned to jail to await another listing. Often cases are listed five and six times before they can be heard. One day in motion court is like any other—filled with murder, rape, robbery, larceny, drug addiction, poverty and despair.

On this day there were three extraditions. Amos R. was wanted in South Carolina. Seven years ago he had escaped from jail and fled north. Since then he has been living in Philadelphia. He has married here and has two children. His wife and children are in the courtroom. He is employed. He has not been in trouble since leaving South Carolina. Ten years ago Amos was convicted of stealing a car and sentenced to nine to twenty years in prison. He had no prior record. In Pennsylvania, he would probably have been placed on probation or at most received a maximum sentence of two years.

Now he testifies that he didn't steal the car, he only borrowed it. Moreover, he didn't have a lawyer. When he pleaded guilty he was told he would get six months. It is probably true. Also, he was undoubtedly indicted by a grand jury from which Negroes were systematically excluded. All of these allegations would be grounds for release in a postconviction hearing for they are serious violations of Constitutional rights. But they are irrelevant in extradition hearings. The only issues that the judge may consider before ordering this man to leave his family and shipping him off to serve eighteen more years in prison are whether he is in fact the Amos R. named in the warrant and whether the papers are in order. There is little judicial discretion. One is often impelled by the system to be an instrument of injustice.

This is the dilemma of a judge and of many officials in the legal system. Following the rule of law may result in hardship and essential unfairness. Ignoring the law is a violation of one's oath of office, an illegal act, and a destruction of the system. Some choose to ignore the law in the interests of "justice." Others mechanically follow precedent. Neither course is satisfactory. The judge who frees a defendant knows that in most instances the state cannot appeal. Unless there is an election in the offing and the prosecutor chooses to use this case as a political issue, there will be no repercussions. But it is his duty, as it is that of the accused, to obey the law. If the judge is not restrained by the law, who will be? On the other hand, it is unrealistic to say, "Let the defendant appeal." In the long period between the trial judge's ruling and that of the higher court, if it hears the appeal, a human being will be in jail. One does not easily deprive a person of his liberty without very compelling reasons. Almost every day, the guardians of the law are torn between these conflicting pulls.

After hearing the life story of Amos R., as reported by the prosecutor, the young defender said, "Mr. R. wishes to waive a hearing."

I looked at the lawyer. "Mr. R., do you know that you have a right to a hearing?"

"Yes."

"Have you consulted with your attorney about waiving a hearing?"

"My attorney?" R. looks bewildered.

"Your lawyer, the defender," I pointed to the young man.

"Oh, him," R. replies, "Yes, I talked to him."

"How long?"

"Bout two minutes."

"Your Honor," says the defender, "I have spoken to the sheriff. There is no question that this is the Amos R. wanted. The papers are in order."

I search through the official-looking sheaf of documents with gold seals and red seals and the signatures of two governors, hoping to find a defect, a critical omission. At last I discover that Amos R. was arrested in New Jersey on a Friday night. He was not taken to Pennsylvania until the following Monday. It is eighty-nine days that he has been in jail in Pennsylvania. The extradition hearing must by statute be held within ninety days of arrest. By adding on the three days he was in custody in New Jersey, I conclude that the ninety-day time limit has not been met. Amos R. is once again a free man. This happy ending is unusual. Bureaucratic inefficiencies seldom redound to the benefit of the individual.

The next four matters are bail applications. All the defendants fit the stereotype. They are black males under the age of thirty. Only one is in the courtroom. The others are in the detention center. It is too much trouble and too expensive to transport them to court for a bail hearing. I must decide whether to set free or keep locked up a man whom I cannot see or talk to. If I do not release him, he may be in jail for as long as a year awaiting trial. The law presumes that he is innocent. I look at the applications. This is not the first arrest for any of them. There are records going back to age nine, when Daryll was first incarcerated for truancy.

"The defendant's juvenile record may not be used against him in adult court," I remind the prosecuting attorney.

"I know, Your Honor," he replies apologetically, "but the computer prints out all the arrests."

"How many convictions?"

The computer does not give the answer to that question. So knowing only the number of arrests and not the number of acquittals almost creates a presumption of guilt rather than of innocence.

One man is accused of rape. The record shows that his prior offenses were larceny of an automobile and, as a child, running away from home. The police report indicates that when the police arrived the defendant was in the complainant's apartment with his clothes off. He left so quickly that he abandoned his shoes and socks. The complainant admitted knowing him and gave his name and address to the police. No weapon was involved.

My usual rule of thumb is a simple one: "If he had time to take off his shoes, it isn't rape."

Before releasing an alleged rapist from jail, possibly to prey on other victims, I want to see him. Although Lombroso's theory that one can tell a criminal by his physical appearance is out of fashion, I still want to see and speak to the accused, but he is not in the courtroom. Perhaps his lawyer, the defender, can give some helpful information. However, the defender has never seen the accused. Someone else interviewed him on a routine prison visit. No one knows whether he has a family, a job, a home.

"Please have this defendant brought to court tomorrow and get me some information on him," I tell the defender.

He replies, "I'm sorry, Your Honor. I'll be working in a different courtroom tomorrow. There is no way I can find out about this man."

"We're dealing with human beings, not pieces of paper," I expostulate. "You are his lawyer. You should know him."

The young defender sadly shakes his head. "Your Honor, I work for a bureaucracy."

So do I, I remind myself, as I look at the clock and see that it is past 11:00 and there are fourteen more matters to be heard today.

I refuse bail for a fourteen-year-old accused of slaying another child in a gang rumble. Will he be safer in jail than on the street, where the rival gang is lying in wait for him? I do not know. The boy is small and slender. The warden will put him in the wing with the feminine homosexuals to save him from assault. I mark on the commitment sheet that the boy is to attend school while in prison awaiting trial. But if the warden does not honor my order, I will not know it. . . .

As the silent, defeated prisoners are brought before me I think of Emma Lazarus' hopeful words: "Bring me . . . the wretched refuse of your teeming shores." These people—almost all native-born Americans (Puerto Ricans are Americans, too)—are our wretched refuse. But they have no promised land across the seas. They have only the cell block at the detention center from which they are brought to me, or the cell block at another prison to which they will ultimately be sent.

Most of them are young—under thirty. I also see children who are charged with homicide. They are denied even the nominal protections of the juvenile court and are "processed" as adults. The fourteen-year-old accused of slaying another child in a gang rumble; the sixteen-year-old dope addict, surprised while burglarizing a house, who panicked and shot the unwary owner; the girl lookout for the gang, who is accused of conspiracy and murder. Many of these children are themselves parents. Can they be turned back to the streets? I refuse bail for an illiterate fifteen-year-old accused of murder and note on the bill of indictment that he be required to attend school while in detention. I ask the court-appointed lawyer to check with the warden and see that the boy is sent to class. But is there a class in remedial reading at the detention center? Who will pay for it? Not the overburdened public schools or the understaffed prisons. It is not a project likely to find a foundation grant. What startling research can be developed from teaching a fifteen-year-old illiterate slayer to read?

A perplexed lawyer petitions for a second psychiatric examination for his client. The court psychiatrist has found him competent to stand trial but the lawyer tells me his client cannot discuss the case with him. Randolph, who is accused of assault with intent to kill, attacked a stranger in a bar and strangled the man, almost killing him. Fortunately, bystanders dragged Randolph away. I ask to speak with Randolph. A big, neatly dressed Negro steps up to the bar of the court. He speaks softly, "Judge," he says, "I'm afraid. I need help."

Randolph is out on bail. This is his first offense. He has a good work record. He is married, has two children, and lives with his family. It is Friday morning. I fear what may happen over the weekend. The court psychiatric unit is called.

"We've got people backed up for a month," the doctor tells me. "Even if I took Randolph out of turn I couldn't see him until next week." When he does see Randolph it will be a forty-five-minute examination. A voluntary hospital commitment seems to be the only safeguard. But at least he will be watched for ten days. Gratefully, Randolph promises to go at once to the mental health clinic. What will happen to him after the ten-day period?

There is no time to wonder. The next case is waiting. The parade of accused muggers, robbers and thieves continues. . . .

At 4:45 P.M., I ask hopefully, "Have we finished the list?" But no, there is an application for a continuance on an extradition warrant. The papers from the demanding state have not arrived. It is a routine, daily occurrence.

I look around the courtroom. By this hour only the court personnel and a few policemen and detectives are present. "Where is the defendant?" I inquire. The prosecutor does not know. He is not responsible for producing him. The defender does not have him on his list. "Is he in custody?" I ask. We all search the records and discover that he was arrested more than five months ago. There is no notation that bail has ever been set. No private counsel has entered an appearance. A deputy sheriff checks and reports that he has not been brought up from the prison. The computerized records show that this man has never had a hearing. Hardened as we are, the prosecutor, the defender and I are horrified that someone should be sitting in jail all this time without ever having had an opportunity to say a word. Is he, in fact, the person wanted for an offense allegedly committed years ago and hundreds of miles away? Was he ever there? Is he a stable member of society? Has he a family, a job, a home? Is he a drug addict? No one knows. The papers do not indicate. No one in the courtroom has ever seen him. Each of us makes a note to check on this forgotten prisoner whom the computer may or may not print out for appearance on some other day in some other courtroom.

Criminal Trial Court

The scene in criminal trial court is similar. Most of the cases are "waivers" and guilty pleas. The accused may waive his Constitutional right to be tried by a jury of his peers and be tried by a judge alone. Fewer than 5 percent of all cases are tried by jury. In most cases, the accused not only waives his right to a jury trial but also to any trial and pleads guilty. Before accepting a waiver or a plea, the accused is asked the routine questions.

Day after day defense counsel recites the following formula to poor, semiliterate defendants, some of whom are old and infirm, others young and ignorant. Read this quickly:

Do you know that you are accused of [the statutory crimes are read to him from the indictment]?

Do you know that you have a right to a trial by jury in which the state must prove by evidence beyond a reasonable doubt that you committed the offenses and that if one juror disagrees you will not be found guilty?

Do you know that by pleading guilty you are giving up your right to appeal the decision of this court except for an appeal based on the jurisdiction of the court, the legality of the sentence and the voluntariness of your plea of guilty? [The accused is not told that by the asking and answering of these questions in open court he has for all practical purposes also given up this ground for appeal.]

Do you know that the judge is not bound by the recommendation of the District Attorney as to sentence but can sentence you up to ——— years and impose a fine of _____ dollars? [The aggregate penalty is read to him. Judges may and often do give a heavier penalty than was recommended. They rarely give a lighter sentence.]

Can you read and write the English language?

Have you ever been in a mental hospital or under the care of a psychiatrist for a mental illness?

Are you now under the influence of alcohol, drugs, or undergoing withdrawal symptoms [from being off the use of drugs]?

Have you been threatened, coerced or promised anything for entering the plea of guilty other than the recommendation of sentence by the District Attorney?

Are you satisfied with my representation?

All this is asked quickly, routinely, as the prisoner stands before the bar of the court. He answers "Yes" to each question.

If it were read aloud to you in the frightening atmosphere of a courtroom by a lawyer whom you had not retained, whom you had seen for the first time that day, would you be able to reply "Yes" knowingly and intelligently?

The final question is: "Are you pleading guilty because you are guilty?" The defendant looks at the defender, uncertainly.

"Have you consulted with your lawyer?" I inquire.

"Right now. 'Bout five minutes."

"We'll pass this case until afternoon. At the lunch recess, will you please confer with your client," I direct the defender.

I am not being fair to the young lawyer. He is entitled to eat lunch. He seldom has a chance to do so because he must call for missing files, check to see what has happened to the clients he has never seen and who have not appeared. Now I am ordering him to confer with this man. It is an exercise in futility, like so much that we do.

In the afternoon, the accused, having talked with the lawyer for another ten minutes, again waives his right to a trial. He has been in jail more than eight months. The eight months in jail are applied to his sentence. He will be out by the end of the year—sooner than if he demanded a trial and was acquitted.

The plea has been negotiated by the assistant defender and the assistant prosecutor. The defendant says he was not promised anything other than a recommendation of sentence in return for the guilty plea. But the judge does not know what else the defendant has been told, whether his family and friends are willing to come and testify for him, whether his counsel has investigated the facts of the case to see whether indeed he does have a defense. The magic formula has been pronounced. The judge does not know what the facts are. Did the man really commit the offense? Even if there were a full-scale trial, truth might not emerge. Many of the witnesses have long since disappeared. How reliable will their memories be? The policeman will say he did not strike the accused. The accused will say that he did. Friends and relatives will say that the accused was with them at the time of the alleged crime. The victim, if he appears, will swear that this is the person whom he saw once briefly on a dark night eight months ago.

The lawyers are in almost equal ignorance. The prosecutor has the police report. The defender has only the vague and confused story of the accused. The judge is under pressure to "dispose" of the case. There is a score card for each judge kept by the computer. The judges have batting averages. Woe betide those who fail to keep pace in getting rid of cases. A long trial to determine guilt or innocence will put the judge at the bottom of the list. The prosecutors and public defenders also have their score cards of cases disposed of. Private defense counsel—whether paid by the accused or appointed by the court and paid by the public—has his own type of score card. For the fee paid, he can give only so many hours to the preparation and trial of this case. He must pay his rent, secretary and overhead. All of the persons involved in the justice system are bound by the iron laws of economics. What can the defendant afford for bail, counsel fees, witness fees, investigative expenses? All of these questions will inexorably determine the case that is presented to the court. . . .

Motions in Civil Court

Motions in civil court are disposed of even more quickly and casually. The defendant files a motion for judgment on the pleadings. If it is granted, the plaintiff has lost his cause of action. He is out of court and can never get a trial on the issue involved.

A motion to take off a judgment is filed and opposed. There was never a trial. The plaintiff had simply signed a note when he bought his appliances on time. The TV didn't work and so he stopped paying. Now there is a judgment against him for the balance of the payments plus interest and costs of the proceeding. It amounts to more than the retail price of the TV set. The federal courts have ruled that judgment notes are, in certain circumstances, unconstitutional. By artful pleadings the plaintiff's counsel must try to bring his client within the scope of those decisions and also meet the onerous conditions for taking off a judgment. The seller asserts that the pleading fails to meet the rules.

A couple who bought a house ten years ago now want to move but they find that there is a lien against their property and they cannot sell the house. A motion to quiet title is filed. Have the necessary elements been pleaded?

A woman badly injured in a collision between a train and a bus brought suit against both companies. Her lawyer wants the accident reports of the company investigators. They will not turn them over to him, so he files a motion. Both companies resist. Without the reports the women cannot prove negligence.

In all these matters and hundreds of others the disposition of the motion will decide whether the parties can legally or feasibly pursue their claims. Oral arguments are brief—perhaps ten or fifteen minutes. The judge, with the help of a law clerk—who is usually young, inexperienced and often unaware of the critical significance of the decision—disposes of twenty or thirty motions a day. Many of them raise questions, like the confession of judgment note, which will ultimately be decided by an appellate court in another case years later. When there is a concurrence of public outrage, a flagrantly unfair case, and a judge willing to overturn decades or centuries of precedent, the harshness of the common-law rule that governs the disposition of such cases will be set aside. Meanwhile, there are countless people whose rights and economic existence are determined by whether a document filed in court fits within the Procrustean bed of the law.

At the end of a long day in court, even the crier remarks despairingly, "There must be a better way." But we go on day after day in the same old unsatisfactory way.

Doing Justice

At the end of a day in which as a judge I have taken actions affecting for good or ill the lives of perhaps fifteen or twenty litigants and their families, I am drained. . . .

Was Cottle really guilty? I will never know. Fred made bail. Will he attack someone tonight or tomorrow? One reads the morning paper with apprehension. It is safer for the judge to keep them all locked up. There will be an outcry over the one prisoner released who commits a subsequent offense. Who will know or care about the scores of possibly innocent prisoners held in jail? . . .

Before the reader can consider possible alternatives or remedies, he must see, hear and smell the squalor and despair of the nation's trial courts. He must understand the haste, the "speed up" in which disposing of cases is more important than doing justice.

The trial judges, who know intimately what is so wrong and so unjust, have rarely spoken out. Many of them cannot afford to resign from a position which they find brutalizing and degrading. A few judges have done so. Their resignations and condemnations have passed almost unnoticed—one cog in the machine replaced by another. The majority of us know that and we are simply too tired to speak out.

We know that the critic is asked accusingly: "If things are so bad, what remedy do you propose?" The honest answer—that the problems are enormous, complex and interrelated, that it is not possible for one person in his spare time to devise a new approach that will meet so many diverse and competing interests, that much more information, skill and expertise are required—seldom satisfies. With unconscious Panglossian chauvinism, most members of the legal profession continue to proclaim that ours is the best of all legal systems. Those of us who daily see the law in action know that, whether or not it is the best of all existing systems, it certainly cannot be the best of all possible systems. On the whole we limit our discussions and proposals to small specifics because we can suggest feasible, immediate remedies only for such matters and we are obsessed with the need to get through the day, doing as little harm and as much kindness as the system permits.

20

Lawyers' Ethics
Jerome E. Carlin

Lawyers are informed of their ethical obligations through several official or quasi-official sources: the canons of ethics of the various bar associations; the published opinions of committees on professional ethics; court rules for the regulation of lawyers' conduct; court decisions in disciplinary and other cases involving lawyers; legislative provisions "that the conviction of certain specified offenses shall necessitate the lawyer's disbarment;"[1] and finally, the definition and interpretation of standards contained in the various texts, treatises, and casebooks on legal ethics.[2] Lawyers are also guided by unwritten norms, customs, and practices that have evolved out of the needs and problems of the legal profession.

The standards gleaned from these sources speak to three main areas of ethical responsibility: obligations to *clients*, to *colleagues*, and to the *administration of justice*. Official standards respecting clients include rules relating to the conversion of clients' funds, commingling, overcharging, conflicts of interest, abuse of confidential information, misinforming, and client neglect. Norms for dealing with colleagues prohibit solicitation of cases, breaking an agreement with a colleague, bypassing him and dealing directly with his client, or deceiving him. Finally, rules affecting the administration of justice prohibit payoffs (bribes and gifts to obtain preferential treatment) and fraud (false representation, concealment of evidence, pressing

Excerpt from Chapters 3 and 4 of *Lawyers' Ethics: A Survey of the New York City Bar*. New York: Russell Sage Foundation, 1966, pp. 41–81, by permission of the author and publisher, Basic Books, Inc.

unfounded claims), principally in the courts and administrative agencies.

Selection of Items for the Ethics Measure

. . . We decided to measure lawyers' ethical behavior on the basis of their own reports of how they had acted in certain situations where norms might be violated. The initial task, therefore, was to devise questionnaire items setting forth a variety of ethical conflicts. A large number of such items were assembled from information obtained in informal interviews with selected lawyers and from texts and other materials on legal ethics, including the published opinions of committees on professional ethics.

To narrow down the number of ethics items, a preliminary study was conducted. The main purpose of this study was to select items that met the following criterion: the item should represent the kind of conflict situation in which lawyers judged as unethical by their colleagues would actually report taking the unethical action. In other words, we wanted items such that a lawyer rated ethical or unethical by his colleagues would also be rated ethical or unethical by us. . . .

Differential Acceptance of Ethical Norms

In the preliminary study we asked lawyer-respondents whether they approved or disapproved of what Lawyer A had done under the circumstances set forth in the hypothetical situation. On the basis of answers to this question we developed a measure of the *acceptance* of ethical standards.

As might be expected, the official standards of the bar are differentially accepted. This differential acceptance was consistently evident in the preliminary study: the same results appeared whether acceptance was measured by lawyer-respondents' disapproval of unethical action, by the saliency of norms to lawyer-informants, or by lawyer-respondents' estimates of the prevalence of particular unethical practices.

Degree of acceptance of norms is associated with the type of ethical obligation involved. Norms dealing with lawyer–client relations are most likely to be accepted. Justice norms that prohibit bribing officials and colleague norms concerning specific types of unfairness find somewhat less acceptance. Justice norms involving manufacture of evidence and various omissions in dealings with courts, agencies, or other parties to a controversy are much less frequently accepted, while colleague norms concerning solicitation of legal business are deemed least important of all. . . .

Acceptance and the Status Structure of the Bar

Not only are ethical standards differentially accepted by lawyers, there appears to be a distinct pattern of acceptance that reflects the status structure of the bar. In considering whether there is such a pattern, it is useful to bear in mind three possible models that might be encountered in the absence of complete consensus on norms:

1. Random Disagreement: where knowing the lawyer's social status in the bar would not allow us to predict which norms he accepts. Thus, for any given norm or set of norms lawyers in each stratum would have an equal probability of accepting or rejecting the standard; there would be no *patterned* acceptance or rejection of standards by social strata.

2. Plural Standards: where members of various strata uphold different or opposing norms. Acceptance of standards would be patterned, but members of each stratum would hold to their own unique norms. If this were the case, we would be in the position of measuring one group's behavior in terms of another's standards.

3. Norm Hierarchy: where everyone upholds certain basic norms, but a subgroup accepts additional, more demanding norms.

Which model best describes the situation in the New York City bar? The pattern of acceptance of ethical norms is revealed in Table 1. Here it is shown that on eight of the items a large majority of lawyers in each stratum (as defined by size of firm) disapprove of the unethical action; the standards involved in these items will be known as *bar norms*, that is, they are norms generally accepted in the bar as a whole. On four items, less than half of the lawyers in each stratum disapprove of the unethical action; these are classified as *paper norms*, that is, norms not generally accepted in any stratum of the bar. Finally, the ethical standards embodied in three items are accepted by most large-firm lawyers, but by a much smaller proportion of small-firm lawyers; these are defined as *elite norms*.

In the New York City bar, then, the patterning of norms appears to correspond most closely to the third model, the normatively hierarchical system. A large majority of lawyers at all status levels accept certain basic standards (the bar norms) and reject others (the paper norms), and a subgroup, the upper-status lawyers, accept cer-

TABLE 1. Acceptance of Ethical Norms by Size of Firm

ETHICS ITEM[a]	PER CENT OF LAWYERS DISAPPROVING THE UNETHICAL ACTION				
	Large firm	Medium	Small	Individual practice	Percentage difference
Bar Norms					
Client Kickback:					
money	98	93	95	90	+ 8
Stock Purchase	97	89	84	90	+ 7
Police Payoff	87	83	82	83	+ 4
Package Deal	82	83	80	77	+ 5
Assault Charge	75	73	73	72	+ 3
Divorce	68	70	79	72	- 4
Syndicate Sale	72	65	60	60	+12
Client Payoff: "don't tell me"	72	70	50	59	+13
Elite Norms					
Commission: accept without informing client	94	75	52	51	+43
Client Payoff: "risky but your business"	62	46	42	39	+23
Referral Fee	55	29	16	16	+39
Paper Norms					
Client Kickback: gift, free advice	45	44	46	39	+ 6
Conflict of Interest	35	35	30	36	- 1
Commission: take into consideration	20	10	8	7	+13
Christmas Cards	13	7	8	6	+ 7
Oral Contract[b]	58	52	45	45	+13
	(60)	(204)	(161)	(376)	

[a]See Table 27 for synopsis of ethics items. This list contains 16 instead of 13 items because three check-list items (items in which respondents were presented with two unethical as well as various ethical actions) were split into two separate items. The two unethical alternatives in each of the three check-list items (numbers 91, 95, and 99) were defined as distinct items for purpose of this analysis.

[b]Since the oral contract item does not fit into the bar, elite, or paper norm category, it was excluded from this classification.

tain additional (elite) norms that are matters of indifference to lower-status lawyers. The lower-status lawyers do not appear to have their own professional norms which elite lawyers do not accept. . . .

Important substantive differences distinguish bar norms from elite and paper standards. Bar norms proscribe such generally disapproved behavior as bribery, fraud, cheating, and stealing. They are, therefore, closest to, and may be indistinguishable from, community-wide standards of morality. Most of the operative norms of the legal profession simply require lawyers to conform to ordinary standards of honesty and fair dealing. That these norms are officially reiterated undoubtedly arises from the fact that lawyers are under special pressure to violate general moral standards, and encounter more opportunities to do so.

Elite and paper norms, on the other hand, proscribe behavior not necessarily immoral or unethical in the wider community.[3] Indeed such behavior may be perfectly proper within the business community. Examples are norms that prohibit lawyers from advertising their services and from accepting (or giving) commissions for sending (or receiving) business. Other paper and elite norms involve fairly technical considerations, such as conflicts of interest among clients and adjustment of colleague relations. The paper and elite norms are thus peculiarly incident to the lawyer's role as a professional and his membership in a professional community. Moreover, his claim to being engaged in a "higher" calling, of being more than a business-man, is based largely on these distinctively professional norms.

If we now consider the pattern of acceptance within the different status groups in the bar, we find that two out of three high-status (large-firm) lawyers accept more than the bar norms, while low-status lawyers (in small firms and individual practice) for the most part accept only the bar norms (Table 2).

TABLE 2. Acceptance of Various Types of Norms by Size of Firm

ACCEPTANCE SCALE	PER CENT OF LAWYERS			*Individual practice*
	Large firm	*Medium*	*Small*	
Bar plus	65	51	35	32
Bar only	12	22	35	36
None	5	18	22	26
Nonscale	15	9	8	6
Total	100	100	100	100
	(60)	(198)	(158)	(362)

The Ethical Behavior Index:
Violators and High Conformers

The preceding sections have discussed *acceptance* of ethical norms. We now turn to a closer examination of *adherence* to ethical norms. Adherence, as was indicated earlier, is measured by lawyers' reported behavior in particular ethical conflict situations. . . .

An Ethical Behavior Index was constructed using all 13 of the ethics items included in the survey questionnaire. In analyzing the responses to these items by the 801 lawyers in the final survey, it was found that the items were all positively correlated with one another; those who gave the ethical response to one item (would take or had taken the ethical action) were likely to give the ethical response to each of the other items. The respondent's score on the Ethical Behavior Index was calculated by giving a point for each response indicating conformity with the official standard. Respondents' scores on this Index could range from 0 to 13. These scores were then grouped into three categories: respondents who reported they had taken (or would take) the ethical action on 10 to 13 items were classified as "high"; those reporting the ethical action on 7 to 9 items were rated "middle"; and those reporting the ethical action on fewer than seven were rated "low." Those scoring high are designated as "high conformers"; those scoring low as "violators." . . .

We have seen that the status structure of the bar is related to a particular patterning of *acceptance* of ethical standards. If we now cross-tabulate size of firm with the Ethical Behavior Index ratings, we find that there is also a strong correlation between a lawyer's status in the bar and *adherence* to ethical norms (Table 3). The majority of lawyers in the large firms are high conformers. As firm

TABLE 3. Ethical Behavior Index Ratings by Size of Firm

ETHICAL BEHAVIOR INDEX RATING	PER CENT OF LAWYERS			
	Large firm	Medium	Small	Individual practice
High (conformers)	57	39	22	20
Middle	38	38	50	47
Low (violators)	5	20	26	30
No answer	0	3	2	3
Total	100 (60)	100 (204)	100 (161)	100 (376)

size decreases, the proportion of high conformers decreases from 57 per cent of large-firm lawyers to 20 per cent of individual practitioners. Correspondingly, as size of firm increases, the proportion of violators decreases, from 30 percent of individual practitioners to only 5 per cent of large-firm lawyers. . . .

A major finding [in this section] is that status in the bar as measured by size of firm is strongly associated with ethical behavior. Large-firm lawyers tend to score much higher on the Index of Ethical Behavior than lawyers in small firms and individual practice. It was previously shown that size of firm largely determines the nature of a lawyer's clientele and the level of the court or agency with which he comes into contact. Small-firm lawyers have a low-status clientele, large-firm lawyers a high-status clientele. Similarly, small-firm lawyers come into contact mainly with lower-level courts and agencies, large-firm lawyers deal mainly with upper-level courts and agencies. . . .

Client Relations

The lawyers's clientele has considerable influence on his ethical conduct. Our principal finding is: the lower the status of the clientele, the higher the rate of violation by members of the bar (Table 4).

Lawyers with low-status clients serve a disproportionate number of individual proprietors and small, closely held corporations in retail, personal service, and light manufacturing industries, and middle- to low-income individuals of minority ethnic background. Lawyers with this type of clientele are subject to far more temptations, opportunities, and client pressures to violate ethical norms than are lawyers with high-status clients who serve primarily large, wealthy corporations, and well-to-do individual clients from old American families. Moreover, because of the nature of their practice, lawyers with low-status clients are less able to resist these temptations, opportunities, and pressures.

T A B L E 4.   Violation by Client Status

CLIENT STATUS	PER CENT VIOLATORS
Low	42 (188)
Low-middle	29 (137)
High-middle	20 (253)
High	15 (194)

Temptation

The lower the status of the lawyer's clientele, the more precarious and insecure his practice. Lawyers with low-status clients tend to have an unstable clientele; that is, they have a higher rate of turnover in business and individual clients (Table 5). The small businessman is more likely than a large corporation to shop around and switch attorneys: he may be on the lookout for a less expensive, sharper, and more compatible lawyer. This type of client is also more likely to divide his legal business among several lawyers, and to have only occasional need for legal service. Lower- to middle-income individuals are less likely to use lawyers, and when they do, they are likely to bring matters of a nonrepeating character. Lawyers with low-status clients also report more competition from other lawyers in obtaining clients, and that they have been hurt by such competition. This reflects the weak and intermittent demand for legal services from lower-status clients, the relatively large number of lawyers whose practice is restricted to such clients, and the many nonlawyers who are willing and able to perform similar services often at a lower price.

Insecurity of practice leads to violation of basic bar norms, whether this insecurity is measured by instability of clientele or competition from other lawyers. Indeed, it is the combination of instability and competition that produces the highest rate of violation. Moreover, the effect of insecurity on violation is especially marked among lawyers who have a low-status clientele.

On common sense ground, one would expect the lawyer who must rely on a precarious, low-status clientele to be more tempted than

TABLE 5. Insecurity of Practice by Client Status

	LOW-STATUS CLIENTS[a]	HIGH-STATUS CLIENTS
Percent of lawyers who report:		
Unstable clientele[b]	59	28
High competition from other lawyers[c]	43	24
	(332)	(460)

[a]"Low" includes both low and low-middle; "high" includes both high and high-middle.
[b]Includes both unstable and moderately unstable. Stability of Clientele Index defined in terms of degree of turnover in both individual and business clients.
[c]That is, lawyers who report a great deal of competition among lawyers in obtaining clients and that they have been hurt by this competition.

other lawyers to violate. He has less to lose and perhaps something to gain. Some client-related items in the Ethical Behavior Index contain norms forbidding the lawyer to realize financial gains that might be perfectly proper in the business community: for example, accepting a title company commission without the client's consent. Colleague-related canons that enjoin client solicitation and advertising hamper the lawyer who is dependent on a transient clientele and is in a highly competitive market. Furthermore, in such a market, concessions to client demands to violate ethical standards may be viewed as one way of getting and retaining clients. . . .

Opportunity to Exploit Clients

To the extent that lawyers have access to secret or confidential information about their clients' business affairs, they are likely to encounter opportunities to realize some financial gain to the detriment of their clients. Low-status clients are much more likely to provide such opportunities than high-status clients: 70 per cent of lawyers with low-status clients encounter frequent opportunities for exploiting clients, compared to 43 per cent of lawyers with high-status clients. Opportunity to exploit clients is a major source of norm violation. As one respondent noted, "An unscrupulous lawyer can burn his client alive." . . . Client expendability is most likely to result in violation when the lawyer has frequent opportunities to exploit his clients (Table 6). Susceptibility to temptation must be

T A B L E 6 . Violation by Opportunity to Exploit Clients and Client Expendability

| | PER CENT VIOLATORS | | |
| | *Opportunity to exploit clients*[a] | | |
CLIENT EXPENDABILITY[b]	HIGH	MODERATE	LOW
High	61 (41)	32 (28)	22 (45)
Moderate	37 (73)	29 (76)	21 (95)
Low	16 (49)	21 (72)	17 (69)

[a]Defined by the number of client-related ethical conflict situations occurring in a lawyer's practice: 4 to 6 items classified as "high," 2 to 3 as "moderate," and one or none as "low" opportunity to exploit.
[b]Lawyers with an unstable or moderately unstable clientele whose largest client accounts for less than 13 per cent of their income are defined as "high" on client expendability. Those with a stable clientele whose largest client accounts for 13 per cent or more of their income are defined as "low." All others are "moderate."

accompanied by opportunity, and opportunity by temptation, before either becomes a significant source of violation. . . .

Client Pressure

In the preceding discussion, the low-status client was seen as victim. But the client himself can put pressure on the lawyer to violate ethical norms. Examples are pressures from clients to bribe or use improper influence with public officials, to press unfounded or fraudulent claims, or to break a promise to another lawyer.

Lawyers with low-status clients report more frequent client pressure than lawyers with high-status clients: 30 per cent of the former said that their clients had put pressure on them, either sometimes or often, compared to 16 per cent of the latter. This may reflect the marginal economic position of the low-status client, who, like his counterpart in the bar, is more willing to engage in certain illegitimate practices.

That client pressure leads to violation is shown in Table 7. There are, however, substantial differences in lawyers' capacities to resist, depending upon the nature of their practice. Lawyers who have an unstable clientele, and who derive a major portion of their income from their largest client, are the most sensitive to client pressure. . . .

Client Relations and Conformity to Higher Level Norms

The preceding discussion has inquired into the influences of clientele and practice on rates of violation of generally accepted norms of conduct. We shall now consider briefly the effect of the lawyer's clientele on conformity to higher-level, more demanding norms.

TABLE 7.   Violation by Client Pressure

HOW OFTEN HAVE CLIENTS EXERTED PRESSURE ON YOU TO ENGAGE IN PRACTICES CONTRARY TO YOUR STANDARDS?	PER CENT VIOLATORS
Very often	48 (23)
Sometimes	35 (140)
Rarely or never	22 (594)

TABLE 8. High Conformity by Client Status

CLIENT STATUS	PER CENT HIGH CONFORMERS[a]
High	44 (195)
High-middle	34 (254)
Low-middle	18 (137)
Low	14 (189)

[a]Defined as reporting the ethical action in 10 or more of the 13 ethics items.

Once again the status of the clientele seems to be of paramount importance. The higher the status of his clientele the more likely the lawyer is to conform to distinctively professional norms (Table 8).

Lawyers with high-status clients, as we have seen, are less likely to be exposed to client-related pressures to violate. It is plausible to assume that the higher rates of conformity among lawyers with high-status clients are the result of their greater insulation from such pressures. . . .

We have found that by taking client-related pressures into account we can partly interpret the relation between having low-status clients and violating basic bar norms. These same conditions, however, do not explicate the relation between having high-status clients and conformity to higher level norms. . . .

Notes

1. Drinker, Henry S., *Legal Ethics.* Columbia University Press, New York, 1954, pp. 41-42.
2. For a comprehensive collection of opinions, see *Opinions of the Committees on Professional Ethics of the Association of the Bar of the City of New York and the New York County Lawyers' Association*, ColumbiaUniversity Press, New York, 1956. Cheatham, Elliott E., *Cases and Materials on the Legal Profession*, 2d ed., The Foundation Press, Brooklyn, 1955; Prisig, Maynard E., *Cases and Materials on the Standards of the Legal Profession*, West Publishing Co., St. Paul, Minn., 1957; MacKinnon, F. B., "Study of the Ethical Problems of Lawyers in Private Practice," Harvard Law School Project, unpublished manuscript, 1955; and the *Report of the Special Committee of the American Bar Foundation on Canons of Ethics*, American Bar Foundation, Chicago, 1958.
3. Durkheim has noted with reference to these more specifically professional norms: "There are no moral rules whose infringement, in general at least, is looked upon with so much indulgence by public opinion. [Their] transgressions . . . come in merely for rather vague censure outside the strictly professional field. They count as venial." Durkheim, Emile, *Professional Ethics and Civil Morals*, The Free Press, Glencoe, Ill., 1958, p. 6.

21

The Legislator
as Representative
Heinz Eulau

The problem of representation is central to all discussions of the functions of legislatures or the behavior of legislators. For it is through the process of representation, presumably, that legislatures are empowered to act for the whole body politic and legitimized. And because, by virtue of representation, they participate in legislation, the represented accept legislative decisions as authoritative. It would seem, therefore, that legislation and representation are closely related. . . .

Our purpose here, however, is less ambitious than a full-scale investigation of such relationships. It is to eliminate those particular ambiguities in the concept of representation which concern the actions or behavior of representatives, by use of the concept of "role," and to demonstrate the utility of this approach for further research relevant to the theory of representation.

. . . A convenient and useful starting point in theoretical clarification is Edmund Burke's theory of representation. For, in following his classic argument, later theorists have literally accepted Burke's formulation and ignored its contextual basis and polemical bias. Burke ingeniously combined two notions which, for analytical

Excerpt from John C. Wahlke, Heinz Eulau, William Buchanan, and LeRoy C. Ferguson, *The Legislative System: Explorations in Legislative Behavior.* New York: John Wiley and Sons, Inc., 1962, pp. 267-286. Reprinted by permission of the author and publisher.

purposes, should be kept distinct. In effect, he combined a conception of the focus of representation with a conception of the style of representation. "Parliament," Burke said in a famous passage,

> . . . is not a *congress* of ambassadors from different and hostile interests; which interests each must maintain, as an agent and advocate, against other agents and advocates; but Parliament is a *deliberative* assembly of *one* nation, with *one* interest, that of the whole; where, not local purposes, not local prejudices ought to guide but the general good, resulting from the general reason of the whole.[1]

The sentence indicates that Burke postulated two possible foci of representation: local, necessarily hostile interests, on the one hand; and a national interest, on the other hand. He rejected the former as an improper and advocated the latter as the proper focus of the representative's role. But in doing so, he also linked these foci of representation with particular representational styles. If the legislature is concerned with only one interest, that of the whole, and not with compromise among diverse interests, it follows that the representative cannot and must not be bound by instructions, from whatever source, but must be guided by what Burke called "his unbiased opinion, his mature judgment, his enlightened conscience." Moreover, Burke buttressed his argument by emphasizing the deliberative function of the legislature, presumably in contrast to its representational function. Yet if one rejects his notion of the legislature as only a deliberative body whose representational focus is the whole rather than its constituent parts, the logic of Burke's formulation is no longer necessary or relevant.

Today, many "publics" constitute significant foci of orientation for the representative as he approaches his legislative task. Under the conditions of a plural political and social order, these foci of representation may be other than geographical interests, be they electoral districts or the larger commonwealth. The modern representative faces similar choices concerning the style of his representational role not only vis-à-vis his constituency or state and nation, but vis-à-vis other clienteles, notably political parties, pressure groups, and administrative agencies. From an analytical point of view—though not, of course, from an empirical standpoint—the style of the representative's role is neutral as far as these different foci of representation are concerned. Regardless of his focus of representation—a geographical unit, a party, a pressure group, or an administrative organization—he is not committed to take either the role of free agent, following his own convictions, or the role of delegate, bound by instructions. In other words, Burke's linkage of a particular areal focus of representation with a particular representational style constitutes only a special case in a generic series of empirically possible relationships between different foci of representation and appropriate styles of representation. . . .

Perceptions of the Representational Role

Representational-role orientations were derived from responses to the following two questions:

How would you describe the job of being a legislator—what are the most important things you should do here?

Are there any important differences between what you think this job is and the way your constituents see it?

Responses to these questions yielded three major representational-role orientations: trustee, delegate, and politico. In the following we shall describe these orientational types as they were defined by legislators themselves.

Trustee. The role orientation of trustee finds expression in two major conceptions of how decisions ought to be made. These conceptions may occur severally and jointly. There is, first, a moralistic interpretation. The trustee sees himself as a free agent in that, as a premise of his decision making behavior, he claims to follow what he considers right or just, his convictions and principles, the dictates of his conscience. In proceeding along this path of moral righteousness, trustees may give different "reasons" for their interpretation of this role. First, the trustee's ideas, attitudes, or legislative objectives are in harmony with those of the represented. And because they are in harmony, he need not pay attention to instructions—for no instructions are forthcoming, and he can follow the dictates of his conscience. . . .

Secondly, the trustee claims that he must fall back on his own principles in making decisions because those from whom he might take cues—constituents, lobbyists, leaders, or colleagues—cannot be trusted. . . .

Finally, if the representative as a man of principle finds himself in conflict with the represented, he should not submit but try to persuade them to his convictions. The trustee here sees himself as a "mentor." He is not in agreement with his constituents, but he does not turn his back on them. Sticking to his ideas, he tries to bring others around to his point of view. . . .

There is also a judgmental conception of the role of trustee. The trustee is not bound by a mandate because his decisions are his own considered judgments based on an assessment of the facts in each decision, his understanding of all the problems and angles involved, his thoughtful appraisal of the sides at issue. . . .

Evidently, a great variety of conceptions of representation are involved in the role orientation of the trustee. In particular, it seems that this orientation derives not only from a normative definition of the role of the representative, but that it is also often grounded in interpersonal situations which make it functionally inevitable. The condition that the represented do not have the information necessary to give intelligent instructions, that the representative is unable to discover what his clientele may want, that preferences remain unexpressed, that there is no need for instructions because of an alleged harmony of interests between representative and represented—all of the circumstances may be acknowledged as sources of the role orientation of trustee, at times even forced on the representative against his own predilection for a mandate if that were possible.

Delegate. Just as the trustee role orientation involves a variety of conceptions of representation, so does the orientation of delegate. All delegates are agreed, of course, that they should not use their independent judgment or principled convictions as decision-making premises. But this does not mean that they feel equally committed to follow instructions, from whatever clientele. Some merely say that they try to inform themselves before making decisions by consulting their constituents or others; however, they seem to imply that such consultation has a mandatory effect on their behavior. . . .

Finally, there is the representative in the delegate role who not only feels that he should follow instructions, but who also believes that he should do so even if these instructions are explicitly counter to his own judgment or principles. . . .

Delegates, it seems, have a simpler, more mechanical conception of the political process and of the function of representation in legislative behavior. Perhaps most noticeable, in contrast to the trustee orientation, is the omission of delegates to raise the question of political responsibility under conditions of strict instructions. Apparently, the problem is ignored by the delegate precisely because he rejects the possibility of discretion in his decision making. It is a matter of speculation whether the role orientation of delegate is based on a conscious majoritarian bias which he could elaborate and defend if necessary, or whether it simply reflects lack of political articulation and sophistication. On the other hand, the fact that the delegate seems to have so little doubt about his role suggests that, whatever his reasons and regardless of whether his decisions are really in accord with the views of different groups among his clientele, he is likely to be characterized by a fairly high sense of personal effectiveness in his approach to lawmaking.

Politico. . . . The classical dichotomization of the concept of representation in terms of independent judgment and mandate was unlikely to exhaust the empirical possibilities of representational behavior. In particular, it would seem to be possible for a representative to act in line with both criteria. For roles and role orientations need not be mutually exclusive. Depending on circumstances, a representative may hold the orientation of trustee at one time, and the role orientation of delegate at another time. Or he might even seek to reconcile both orientations in terms of a third. In other words, the representational-role set comprises the extreme orientations of trustee and delegate and a third orientation, the politico, resulting from overlap of these two. Within the orientational range called politico, the trustee and delegate roles may be taken simultaneously, possibly making for role conflict, or they may be taken seriatim, one after another as legislative situations dictate.

Because our data do not permit us to discriminate too sharply between these two possibilities, we shall speak of legislators who express both orientations, either simultaneously or serially, as politicos. In other words, in contrast to either trustees or delegates as relatively "pure" types, representatives holding the role orientation of politico exhibit a certain amount of flexibility in their representational relationships. . . .

Both role orientations—that of trustee and that of delegate—may be held serially, depending on whether the legislator's focus of attention is centered in one clientele or another. For instance, he may see himself as a delegate in matters of local interest, and as a trustee in all other matters:

> As a member there are certain things you should do. First you have a specific responsibility to the people of your own constituency on matters of local interest. Second, you should use your own judgment on all matters pertaining to benefits for the people within the framework of governmental policy and should think of what's best for the state as a whole. It's not necessary to follow the will of the people always as you should decide what most benefits the present and future and hope history proves you right.

Or the legislator may feel that he must follow his party's instructions in political matters, though on others he can be a free agent:

> My conception of party responsibility—there's a responsibility to the party to vote with them, with respect to administration bills—there's responsibility to go along with the governor. On matters removed from the political category I would vote my convictions.

These comments suggest that both the trustee and delegate roles may be taken, depending on the character of the issue involved or the legislator's focus of attention. But no attempt is made to reconcile the two orientations. They coexist side by side and may be invoked as political circumstances require. These legislators do not seem to feel that they are facing a situation which makes for conflict of roles, largely because they succeed in avoiding conflict by not attempting to reconcile the two orientations. . . .

On the other hand, some legislators may be more sensitive to the potential conflict to which they may be exposed by the ambiguity of the representational relationship and seek to come to grips with it. These representatives are not only aware of the problem, but, instead of solving it by sometimes taking the trustee role, sometimes the delegate role, they seek to balance simultaneously the instructions or preferences of clienteles against their own judgment. . . .

In general, then, the politico as a representational-role taker differs from both the trustee and the delegate in that he seems to be more sensitive to conflicting alternatives, more flexible in the ways in which he tries to resolve the conflict among alternatives, and less dogmatic in his orientation towards legislative behavior as it is related to his representational role. Whether he is or can be successful in performing the role is a matter to which we shall turn later on.

Distribution of Representational-Role Orientations

. . . The exigencies of modern government, even on the relatively low level of state government, are exceedingly complex. Taxation and finance, education and public welfare, legal reform, licensing and regulatory problems, transportation, and so on are topics more often than not beyond the comprehension of the average citizen. Unable to understand their problems and helpless to cope with them, people are likely to entrust the affairs of government to the elected representatives who, presumably, are better informed than their constituents. Many of the comments made by trustees about their constituents articulated this set of reasoning. People themselves may pay lip service to the notion that a representative should not use his independent judgment,[2] but in fact they are unlikely to be able, or may not care, to give him instructions as was possibly the case at an earlier time when the tasks of government were comparatively simple. It is likely, therefore, that the representative has become less and less a delegate and more and more a trustee as the business of government has become more and more intricate and technical as well as less locally centered. Rather than being a "pious formula," the role orientation of trustee may be a functional necessity. We might expect, therefore, that it is held by state legislators more frequently today than the role orientation of delegate, with the politico orientation in a middle position.

Comparative analysis of the distribution of representational-role orientations in the four states seems to support these considerations. As Table 1 shows, the role orientation of trustee is held by greater proportions of legislators in all four states than either the politico or delegate orientations. Moreover, the politico appears somewhat more often in all four states than the delegate.

The trustee orientation, Table 1 indicates, appears more frequently in Tennessee than in the other three states, a fact that seems to contradict the proposition that the orientation of trustee varies with the complexity of governmental affairs. As Tennessee is less urbanized and industrialized than the other states, one might expect Tennessee legislators to be less often trustees and more often delegates than legislators in California, New Jersey, or Ohio. But it may be that "complexity" is a function of perceptions, regardless of the real situation. If so, then to Tennesseans the relatively less complex character of socio-economic life may appear more complex than it actually is, compared with the other states. The more frequent appearance of the trustee there may only by symptomatic of an even greater feeling of helplessness and inefficacy on the part of people vis-à-vis governmental problems, as it is perceived by their representatives. It may also be a reflection of the lower educational level in Tennessee. In all these cases, the political character of Tennessee constituencies would seem to make it very difficult for a legislator to be a delegate for his constituency, forcing him to act as either a trustee or a politico. But to demonstrate this is beyond the limits of this analysis. But the most surprising feature of Table 1 is the very small proportion of legislators in each state subscribing to the role orientation of delegate. If one assumes that the extent to which any role is taken is a function of its difficulty, it would seem that the role orientation of delegate is, indeed, most difficult to hold. We noted in the review of responses regarding different orientations made in the interviews that legislators repeatedly gave as a reason for their

T A B L E 1 . Distribution of Representational-Role Orientations

ROLE ORIENTATION	CALIF. $N = 49$	N.J. $N = 54$	OHIO $N = 114$	TENN. $N = 78$
Trustee	55%	61%	56%	81%
Politico	25	22	29	13
Delegate	20	17	15	6
Total	100%	100%	100%	100%

taking the role of trustee the fact that it was impossible to find out what people really wanted, and that, therefore, the delegate role was unrealistic. Whether realistic or not the data reveal that very few legislators took the delegate role. . . .

Conclusion

Three major role orientations—trustee, politico, and delegate—seem to be characteristic of the legislator's representational style, i.e., of how he relates himself to his decision-making behavior. The trustee claims to rely on his own conscience, on what he thinks is right, or on his considered judgment of the facts involved in the issue which he has to decide. The delegate claims that he seeks and follows instructions from his constituents or other clienteles. The politico claims that he will adopt one or the other orientation as conditions call for, and that he must balance one against the other.

Under modern conditions, the trustee orientation is probably more realistic. Given the complexity of governmental problems, on the one hand, and the difficulty of finding out what clienteles may want, the delegate orientation is probably least functional from the point of view of effective representation. In the four states, many more legislators take the role of trustee than the roles of politico or delegate. If extent of role taking is an indication of the degree of difficulty involved in a given role, it would seem that the trustee role is the easiest and the delegate role the most difficult to take. . . .

Notes

1. Edmund Burke, "Speech to the Electors of Bristol" (1774), *Works*, II, 12.
2. See Hadley Cantril, ed., *Public Opinion, 1935–1946* (Princeton, N.J.: Princeton University Press, 1951), p. 133.

22

Regulatory Commissioners and Party Politics
Stuart S. Nagel

In 1936, Pendleton Herring asked "Does party allegiance mean anything in the functioning of our commissions?" On the basis of his extensive knowledge of individual commissioners, he answered: "Nominal party allegiance conveys nothing in itself."[1] In 1955, Marver Bernstein stated, "there is little evidence that commissioners decide on major policy issues according to their party affiliations."[2] No systematic quantitative study, however, seems to have been made of the presence, direction, or degree of correlation between party affiliation and decision making on the seven major regulatory agencies. It is the purpose of this chapter to offer some data relevant to that matter.

The Research Design

The sample of commissioners involved in this study consists of all the commissioners who served in the CAB, FCC, FPC, FTC, ICC, NLRB, and SEC for the years 1936, 1946, and 1956, thereby provid-

Excerpt from *The Legal Process from a Behavioral Perspective*. Homewood, Ill.: The Dorsey Press, © 1969, pp. 237–249. Reprinted by permission of the author and publisher.

ing 20 groups of commissioners (there was no CAB in 1936) and 100 separate commissioners. Commissioners serving during more than one time period were used only for the first time period unless they sat on no nonunanimous adjudications in their first time period. Commissioners who served on only a small portion of the year's cases were excluded from the analysis. The seven agencies were chosen because of the high importance and large quantity of cases they adjudicate. The three time periods were chosen in order to have a substantial sample of commissioners, while minimizing overlap between time periods and maximizing the likelihood of diversity of appointers within each time period.

Information on the party affiliation, state from which appointed, appointer, and other characteristics of the commissioners was obtained from *Who's Who in America*, the *Government Organization Manuals*, and from correspondence with the agencies. Information on their decisional propensities was obtained from the hearing reports of the agencies for the years 1936, 1946, and 1956. Each commissioner was given a score, indicating whether he was above or below the average of his agency for the year involved with regard to the proportion of times he decided nonunanimous decisions in what might be considered a liberal direction.

Only nonunanimous decisions were used because (1) these are the most controversial decisions and thus generally the most important decisions in terms of the conflicting interests involved, (2) because only nonunanimous decisions provide differences to be accounted for, and (3) because unanimous decisions do not affect whether a commissioner is above or below the average of his agency. Only about 5 percent of the total agency decisions, however, were nonunanimous, although this figure varied substantially, depending on the agency, the year, and the type of cases involved. By liberal direction is meant a decision in favor of the consumer, shipper, or investor (rather than the seller, producer, transporter, or broker), in favor of labor (rather than management), in favor of a small business or increased competition (rather than a larger firm or decreased competition). Borderline decisions that could not be readily positioned as liberal or conservative were excluded from the analysis, as were decisions decided by less than the full agency for the year involved.

Party, Region, Appointer, and Liberalism

Table 1 shows the findings with regard to the relations between the party, region, appointer, and the decisions of the commissioners. The types within each group are arranged from the type of commis-

TABLE 1. Relations between Party, Region, Appointer, and the Direction of Commissioners' Decisions

TYPE OF COMMISSIONERS	NUMBER WITH BACKGROUND INFO.	NUMBER WITH BACKGROUND & LIBERALISM INFORMATION	PERCENT OF TYPE ABOVE THEIR AGENCY'S AVERAGE LIBERALISM SCORE
Party			
1 Democrats	54	37	57
2 Republicans	40	31	39
Region			
3 Northerners	64	50	54
4 Southerners	28	21	43
Party and region			
5 Dems. from the North	27	20	65
6 Dems. from the South	23	16	44
7 Reps. from the North	34	26	38
8 Reps. from the South	4	4	25
Appointer			
9 Appointed by Democrats	60	43	56
10 Appointed by Republicans	40	30	47
Party and appointer			
11 Dems. appointed by Democrats	39	26	54
12 Dems. appointed by Republicans	15	11	64
13 Reps. appointed by Democrats	16	13	46
14 Reps. appointed by Republicans	24	18	33
Party, region, and appointer			
15 Dems. from North apptd. within	19	13	69
16 Dems. from North apptd. across	6	5	80
17 Dems. from South apptd. within	15	11	46
18 Dems. from South apptd. across	8	5	40
19 Reps. from North apptd. across	15	12	42
20 Reps. from North apptd. within	18	13	31
21 Reps. from South apptd. across	0	0	—
22 Reps. from South apptd. within	4	4	25

sioners hypothesized to be most liberal down to the type of commissioner hypothesized to be least liberal. Lines 1 and 2 indicate that 54 of the 100 commissioners were Democrats and 40 were Republicans. The remaining six were independents. When the sum of the commissioners in a group of types does not total 100 in Tables 1 or 2, the remainder equals unknowns and inapplicables. Of the 54 Democratic Commissioners, 37 could be given liberalism scores (proportion of times deciding in a liberal direction), and 57 percent of these 37 were above their agency's average liberalism score. On the other hand, only 39 percent of the 31 scorable Republicans were above their agency's average liberalism score. This difference of 18 percentage points between 57 percent and 39 percent is larger than the corresponding differences in Table 1 between Northerners and Southerners and between Democratic-appointed and Republican-appointed commissioners, indicating that party is a better predictive or explanatory variable is than region or appointer. The Democratic-Republican difference is understandable in view of the history, urbanism, working-class orientation, and ethnic-group orientation of the Democratic Party relative to the Republican Party.

Lines 3 and 4 indicate that commissioners appointed from northern states are more likely to be found on the liberal side of split decisions than are commissioners appointed from southern states.[3] Similar decisional differences can be shown, although slightly less so if one uses region where born rather than region where appointed from for those few commissioners whose birthplace and appointment place differ. Much of the relative conservatism of the southern commissioners can probably be attributed to the effects of their relative ruralism, which places a greater emphasis on consumer and worker self-sufficiency and on face-to-face relations between consumers and sellers and between workers and employers.[4]

Lines 5 through 8 combine party and region. They reveal a difference of 40 percentage points between the percent of Democrats from the North who were above their agency's average liberalism score and the corresponding percentage for Republicans from the South. Democrats from the South and Republicans from the North had approximately equal propensities to be on the liberal side of split decisions with a slight edge to the southern Democrats. This near equality between southern Democrats and northern Republicans is probably due to the offsetting effects of combining liberal party affiliation with conservative regionalism and liberal regionalism with conservative party affiliation. As mentioned, however, party seems to be stronger than region in shaping commissioners' attitudes on these economic issues.

Lines 9 and 10 show that commissioners receiving their initial appointment from a Democratic president are more likely to be above their agency's average liberalism score than are commissioners receiving their initial appointment from a Republican president. A similar although less strong difference can also be shown if one uses the party of the most recent appointer for each commissioner rather than the party of his initial appointer. Possibly the difference is less strong because reappointments may be based more on inertia and less on ideological considerations than are initial appointments. The decisional differences attributable to the party of the appointers are accountable in terms of the same factors mentioned in accounting for the differences attributable to the party of the commissioners themselves. The appointer difference, however, is less than the party or regional difference, probably because Republican presidents so frequently appoint Democratic commissioners (15 out of 39 appointments as shown on lines 12 and 14) and because Democratic presidents so frequently appoint Republican commissioners (16 out of 55 appointments). The authorizing statutes of all seven agencies except the NLRB require some bipartisan appointments.

Lines 11 through 14 reveal a substantial difference of 21 percentage points (with regard to being above one's agency liberalism score) between Democratic commissioners appointed by Democratic presidents and Republican commissioners appointed by Republican presidents. Democratic commissioners appointed across party lines (generally by Eisenhower) seemed to be even more liberal than Democratic commissioners appointed within party lines. This strange difference may be partly due to post-1930 Republican presidential attempts to influence northern urban Democratic voters through regulatory appointments analogous to Eisenhower's appointment of Brennan and Hoover's appointment of Cardozo to the Supreme Court in contrast to Truman's appointments of Vinson, Clark, and Minton. Marver Bernstein states that "Franklin Roosevelt often appointed Republicans who were closer to the policy of his administration than many Democrats were."[5] The relatively small difference between the 64 percent on line 12 and the 54 percent on line 11 may also be due to chance, since relatively few scorable Democrats were appointed by Republicans in the sample of 100.

Lines 15 through 22 combine party, region, and appointer simultaneously. Forty-four percentage points separate the liberalism percentage for northern Democrats appointed within party lines from the southern Republicans appointed within party lines. The five northern Democrats appointed across party lines were again the only group deviating from the expected pattern. Southern Democrats and northern Republicans tend to occupy a middling to right-wing position on the economic decisional spectrum as do their counterparts in the congressional arena.

It is interesting to note that some background characteristics other than party, region, appointer, and urbanism had correlations with being above the average liberalism score of one's agency. Thus, commissioners who were nonlawyers were somewhat more likely to be found on the liberal side of split decisions, as were commissioners who had held other federal positions before becoming commissioners. Alumni of the higher tuition, more northeastern undergraduate schools were also more liberal. Whether or not a commissioner had been a former professor or had done corporate or business work did not make a difference. The role of the religious variable could not be determined, since 41 commissioners were listed as Protestants, only 4 as Catholics, and none as Jews in *Who's Who in America.*

Party, Ideology, Agency Domination, and the Propensity to Dissent

As indicated above, each one of the 100 commissioners was given a liberalism score equal to the proportion of times he voted in favor of the liberal position in the full-agency nonunanimous decisions he participated in. Likewise, each commissioner was given a dissenting score equal to the proportion of times he dissented in those same decisions. The dissenting scores for the members of each agency in each time period can be totaled and divided by the number of agency members to determine the agency's average dissenting score. Table 2 indicates the percent of commissioners of various types who were above their agency's average dissenting score.

The patterns revealed in Table 2 on dissenting are less clear than those in Table 1 on liberalism. Two variables, however, do seem to account for most of the dissenting variation among the commissioner types. If a commissioner is in the ideological minority on his agency, it is understandable that he would dissent more than his fellow commissioners who are in the ideological majority. A commissioner who is liberal (pro-consumer, pro-union) also tends to be more likely to dissent than is a commissioner who is conservative (pro-seller, pro-management) regardless of what ideology or party dominates the agency, possibly because liberals may be more innovative and nonconformist.

The types within each group in Table 2 are arranged from the type of commissioners hypothesized to be most likely to dissent down to the type of commissioners hypothesized to be least likely to dissent.

TABLE 2. Relations Between Party, Ideology, Agency Domination, and the Propensity to Dissent

TYPE OF COMMISSIONERS	NUMBER WITH BACKGROUND INFORMATION	NUMBER WITH BACKGROUND & DISSENT INFORMATION	PERCENT OF TYPE ABOVE THEIR AGENCY'S AVERAGE DISSENT SCORE
Party			
1 Democrats	54	37	57%
2 Republicans	40	31	35
Ideology			
3 Liberals	38	38	53
4 Conservatives	35	35	37
Ideology and party			
5 Liberal Democrats	21	21	67
6 Liberal Republicans	12	12	42
7 Conservative Democrats	16	16	44
8 Conservative Republicans	19	19	32
Party and agency domination			
9 Democrats on Rep. Agency	13	11	73
10 Democrats on Dem. Agency	39	26	50
11 Republicans on Dem. Agency	19	16	27
12 Republicans on Rep. Agency	19	16	44
Ideology and agency domination			
13 Liberals on Cons. Agency	13	13	92
14 Conservatives on Lib. Agency	12	12	50
15 Liberals on Liberal agency	23	23	35
16 Conservatives on Cons. Agency	21	21	24

Lines 1 and 2 indicate there is a substantial relationship between being a Democrat and being a dissenter, since 57 percent of the 37 positionable Democrats were above their agency's average dissenting score, whereas only 35 percent of the 31 positionable Republicans were. This difference is possibly due to the relative liberalism of the Democrats in general and to the fact that the dissenting Democrats represented an especially liberal minority, even among the agencies numerically dominated by the nominal Democrats.

Lines 3 and 4 show a significant difference in dissenting rates between relative conservatives (i.e., those below their agency's average liberalism score) and relative liberals (i.e., those above their agency's average liberalism score), although not so large as expected. Lines 5 through 8 show how the differences in dissenting can be sharpened by combining party and liberalism, since 35 percentage points separate the liberal Democrats from the conservative Republicans. The liberal Republicans did not dissent more than the conservative Democrats, partly because most of the liberal Republicans happened to be coincidentally on agencies numerically dominated by liberals.

Lines 9 through 12 indicate the effect of being in the minority party on being a dissenter. The Democrats on Republican agencies (i.e., agencies having more Republicans than Democrats) dissented more than Democrats on Democratic agencies, although Republicans on Democratic agencies did not dissent so much as Republicans on Republican agencies. The influence of liberalism is also shown on lines 9 through 12 by the fact that dissenting by the minority is stronger when the Democrats are the minority than when the Republicans are the minority, and, likewise, Democrats on Democratic agencies dissented more than Republican agencies.

Lines 13 through 16 reveal the clearest pattern in Table 2. Of the liberals on conservative agencies (i.e., agencies having more commissioners below the average liberalism score of their agency than above), 92 percent were above the average dissenting score of their agency. Likewise, 50 percent of the conservatives on liberal agencies were above the average dissenting score of their agency. On the other hand, only 35 percent of the liberals on liberal agencies were above on dissenting, and only 24 percent of the conservatives on conservative agencies were above.

Conclusions

Many important decisions of the regulatory agencies inherently involve value judgments correlated with party, region, and appointer. To offset the potentially biasing influence of these background factors, it does seem desirable that the authorizing statutes of nearly all the agencies currently require approximately equal party representation, with the odd seat going to the party occupying the Presidency. It also seems desirable to know that informal pressures and senatorial courtesy promote a roughly proportional representation among the major geographical regions. In addition, the present five- to seven-year terms for commissioners also seem desirable, since they are short enough to allow for a diversity of appointers without hampering the ability of the commissioners to obtain and apply valuable experience over time.

Notes

1. Herring, Federal Commissioners: A Study of their Careers and Qualifications 10-11 (1936).
2. Bernstein, Regulating Business by Regulatory Commissions 104 (1955).
3. The southern states consisted of Ala., Ark., Del., Fla., Ga., Ky., La., Md., Miss., Mo., N.C., Okla., S.C., Tenn., Texas, W. Va., and Va. The northern states consisted of the other 33. Two commissioners appointed from Washington, D.C., were excluded from the regional analysis.
4. Commissioners who were appointed from cities larger than 100,000 were disproportionately more likely to be above their agency's liberalism score, to be Democrats, and to be Northerners than were commissioners from cities smaller than or equal to 100,000 in population.
5. Bernstein, op. cit., supra note 2, at 104.

APPENDIX II:

LEGAL DOCUMENTS

Role Redefinitions

A. Equal Pay Act, 1963
B. Civil Rights Act (Title VII), 1964
C. Executive Order 11246—Equal Employment Opportunity, 1965
D. Age Discrimination Act, 1967

Status-Set Conflicts

E. Interested Persons Acting as Government Agents, 1948
F. Acts Affecting a Personal Financial Interest, 1962

Introduction

Defining and redefining the rights and duties of individuals performing diverse roles in a society is a significant, albeit taken-for-granted, function of law. In documents A through D in this Appendix, the Federal statutes in question redefine occupational roles. Thus, the Equal Pay Act of 1963 prohibits discriminatory wage differentials between men and women; under this law, men and women performing the same occupational roles must receive equal pay.

Title VII of the Civil Rights Act of 1964 prohibits employment discrimination on the basis of "race, color, religion, sex or national origin." This provision applies to employers in their hiring and discharging practices; to employment agencies in their referral decisions; to labor unions in their decisions to exclude, expel, or classify members; and to employers, unions, or joint labor–management committees in their decisions regarding training programs.

In 1965, one year following the passage of the Civil Rights Act, President Lyndon Johnson issued Executive Order 11246, which prohibits discrimination in employment because of "race, color, reli-

285

gion, sex, or national origin" in Federal employment and in firms holding contracts or subcontracts with the Federal government.

The Age Discrimination Act of 1967 prohibited yet another basis for employment discrimination. When passed, this statute applied to individuals who are "at least forty years of age but less than sixty-five years of age." In 1978 this law was amended raising the mandatory retirement age to seventy.

The role redefinitions enacted in these four statutes may be viewed as part of the civil rights movement to eradicate a variety of forms of discrimination practiced in everyday life. Questions of the extent to which such laws have been implemented and the nature of their social consequences are significant empirical problems for the sociology of law.

The fact that members of a society, including personnel of a legal system, concurrently occupy many roles gives rise to the problem of "status-set conflicts" or, in common parlance, "conflict of interest" situations (Evan and Levin, 1966). Documents E and F in this Appendix bear on this problem. In these documents, conflicts of interest involving officers or agents of the Federal government are proscribed. The 1948 statute prohibits an officer or an agent of the United States Government who is also an agent, an officer, or a member of a private business organization from participating in a transaction with that business organization. The 1962 statute (document F) is broader in scope in that it prohibits any employee of the Federal government from engaging in any action in which he/she has, directly or indirectly, a "financial interest." This statute covers judicial as well as other proceedings, and the employee's business-related as well as kin-related roles.

What additional mechanisms do you suppose a legal system could experiment with to reduce the potentially dysfunctional effects of status-set conflicts or conflicts of interest?

In the documents in Appendix II, role analysis is applied to changes in the law regarding *nonlegal roles*. The readings in Part IV, however, are concerned with the application of role analysis to *legal roles*. How would you apply role analysis to possible legal redefinitions of legal roles, e.g., changes in the length of tenure of judges, legislators, and administrative agency officials?

Reference

Evan, W. M. and E. G. Levin (1966). "Status-Set and Role-Set Conflicts of the Stockbroker." *Social Forces*, 45: 73–83.

Role Redefinitions

A—Equal Pay Act of 1963
Public Law 88–38
29 U.S.C. 206

Declaration of Purpose

Sec. 2 (a) The Congress hereby finds that the existence in industries engaged in commerce or in the production of goods for commerce of wage differentials based on sex—

(1) depresses wages and living standards for employees necessary for their health and efficiency;

(2) prevents the maximum utilization of the available labor resources;

(3) tends to cause labor disputes, thereby burdening, affecting, and obstructing commerce;

(4) burdens commerce and the free flow of goods in commerce; and

(5) constitutes an unfair method of competition.

(b) It is hereby declared to be the policy of this Act, through exercise by Congress of its power to regulate commerce among the several States and with foreign nations, to correct the conditions above referred to in such industries.

Sec. 3. Section 6 of the Fair Labor Standards Act of 1938, as amended (29 U.S.C. et seq.), is amended by adding thereto a new subsection (d) as follows:

"(d) (1) No employer having employees subject to any provisions of this section shall discriminate, within any establishment in which such employees are employed, between employees on the basis of sex by paying wages to employees in such establishment at a rate less than the rate at which he pays wages to employees of the opposite sex in such establishment for equal work on jobs the performance of which requires equal skill, effort, and responsibility, and which are performed under similar working conditions, except where such payment is made pursuant to (i) a seniority system; (ii) a merit system; (iii) a system which measures earnings by quantity or quality of production; or (iv) a differential based on any other factor other than sex: *Provided;* That an employer who is paying a wage rate differential in violation of this subsection shall not, in order to comply with the provisions of this subsection, reduce the wage rate of any employee.

"(2) No labor organization, or its agents, representing employees of an employer having employees subject to any provisions of this section shall cause or attempt to cause such an employer to discriminate against an employee in violation of paragraph (1) of this subsection.

B—Civil Rights Act of 1964
Title VII Equal Employment Opportunity
Public Law 88–352
42 U.S.C. Sections 2000e–2000e–17

Definitions

ʃ701,2000e. For the purposes of this title—

(a) The term "person" includes one or more individuals, governments, governmental agencies, political subdivisions, labor unions, partnerships, associations, corporations, legal representatives, mutual companies, joint-stock companies, trusts, unincorporated organizations, trustees, trustees in bankruptcy, or receivers. [As amended March 24, 1972, P.L. 92-261, Sec. 2.] . . .

Employer Practices

∫703, 2000e-2. (a) It shall be an unlawful employment practice for an employer—

(1) to fail or refuse to hire or to discharge any individual, or otherwise to discriminate against any individual with respect to his compensation, terms, conditions, or privileges of employment, because of such individual's race, color, religion, sex, or national origin; or

(2) to limit, segregate or classify his employees or applicants for employment in any way which would deprive or tend to deprive any individual of employment opportunities or otherwise adversely affect his status as an employee, because of such individual's race, color, religion, sex, or national origin. [As amended March 24, 1972, P.L. 92-261, Sec. 8.]

Employment Agency Practices

(b) It shall be an unlawful employment practice for an employment agency to fail or refuse to refer for employment, or otherwise to discriminate against, any individual because of his race, color, religion, sex, or national origin, or to classify or refer for employment any individual on the basis of his race, color, religion, sex, or national origin.

Labor Organization Practices

(c) It shall be an unlawful employment practice for a labor organization—

(1) to exclude or to expel from its membership, or otherwise to discriminate against, any individual because of his race, color, religion, sex, or national origin;

(2) to limit, segregate, or classify its membership or applicants for membership, or to classify or fail or refuse to refer for employment any individual, in any way which would deprive or tend to deprive any individual of employment opportunities, or would limit such employment opportunities or otherwise adversely affect his status as an employee or as an applicant for employment, because of such individual's race, color, religion, sex, or national origin; or

(3) to cause or attempt to cause an employer to discriminate against an individual in violation of this section. [As amended March 24, 1972, P.L. 92-261, Sec. 8.]

Training Programs

(d) It shall be an unlawful employment practice for any employer, labor organization, or joint labor-management committee controlling apprenticeship or other training or retraining, including on-the-job training programs to discriminate against any individual because of his race, color, religion, sex, or national origin in admission to or employment in, any program established to provide apprenticeship or other training. . . .

C—Executive Order 11246—Equal Employment Opportunity
30 Federal Register 12319
September 28, 1965

Part I. Non-discrimination in Government Employment

Sec. 101. It is the policy of the Government of the United States to provide equal opportunity in Federal employment for all qualified persons, to prohibit discrimination in employment because of race, color, religion, sex or national origin, and to promote the full realization of equal employment opportunity through a positive, continuing program in each executive department and agency. The policy of equal opportunity applies to every aspect of Federal employment policy and practice.

Sec. 102. The head of each executive department and agency shall establish and maintain a positive program of equal employment opportunity for all civilian employees and applicants for employment within his jurisdiction in accordance with the policy set forth in Section 101.

Sec. 103. The Civil Service Commission shall supervise and provide leadership and guidance in the conduct of equal employment opportunity programs for the civilian employees of and applications for employment within the executive departments and agencies and shall review agency program accomplishments periodically. In order to facilitate the achievement of a model program for equal employment opportunity in the Federal service, the Commission may consult from time to time with such individuals, groups, or organizations as may be of assistance in improving the Federal program and realizing the objectives of this Part.

Sec. 104. The Civil Service Commission shall provide for the prompt, fair, and impartial consideration of all complaints of discrimination in Federal employment on the basis of race, color, religion, sex or national origin. Procedures for the consideration of complaints shall include at least one impartial review within the executive department or agency and shall provide for appeal to the Civil Service Commission.

Sec. 105. The Civil Service Commission shall issue such regulations, orders, and instructions as it deems necessary and appropriate to carry out its responsibilities under this Part, and the head of each executive department and agency shall comply with the regulations, orders, and instructions issued by the Commission under this Part.

Part II. Non-discrimination in Employment by Government
Contractors and Subcontractors

Subpart A. Duties of the Secretary of Labor

Sec. 201. The Secretary of Labor shall be responsible for the administration of Parts II and III of this Order and shall adopt such rules and regulations and issue such orders as he deems necessary and appropriate to achieve the purposes thereof.

Subpart B. Contractor's Agreements

Sec. 202. Except in contracts exempted in accordance with Section 204 of this Order, all Government contracting agencies shall include in every Government contract hereafter entered into the following provisions:

"During the performance of this contract, the contractor agrees as follows:

"(1) The contractor will not discriminate against any employee or applicant for employment because of race, color, religion, sex or national origin. The contractor will take affirmative action to ensure that applicants are employed, and that employees are treated during employment, without regard to their race, color, religion, sex or national origin. Such action shall include, but not be limited to the following: employment, upgrading, demotion, or transfer; recruitment or recruitment advertising; layoff or termination; rates of pay or other forms of compensation; and selection for training, including apprenticeship. The contractor agrees to post in conspicuous places, available to employees and applicants for employment, notices to be provided by the contracting officer setting forth the provisions of this nondiscrimination clause.

"(2) The contractor will, in all solicitations or advertisements for employees placed by or on behalf of the contractor, state that all qualified applicants will receive consideration for employment without regard to race, color, religion, sex or national origin.

"(3) The contractor will send to each labor union or representative of workers with which he has a collective bargaining agreement or other contract or understanding, a notice, to be provided by the agency contracting officer, advising the labor union or workers' representative of the contractor's commitments under Section 202 of Executive Order No. 11246 of September 24, 1965, and shall post copies of the notice in conspicuous places available to employees and applicants for employment. . . .

"(6) In the event of the contractor's noncompliance with the nondiscrimination clauses of this contract or with any of such rules, regulations, or orders, this contract may be cancelled, terminated or suspended in whole or in part and the contractor may be declared ineligible for further Government contracts in accordance with procedures authorized in Executive Order No. 11246 of Sept. 24, 1965, and such other sanctions may be imposed and remedies invoked as provided in Executive Order No. 11246 of September 24, 1965, or by rule, regulation, or order of the Secretary of Labor, or as otherwise provided by law. . . .

Sec. 203. (a) Each contractor having a contract containing the provisions prescribed in Section 202 shall file, and shall cause each of his subcontractors to file, Compliance Reports with the contracting agency or the Secretary of Labor as may be directed. Compliance Reports shall be filed within such times and shall contain such information as to the practices, policies, programs, and employment policies, programs, and employment statistics of the contractor and each subcontractor, and shall be in such form, as the Secretary of Labor may prescribe. . . .

Sec. 204. The Secretary of Labor may, when he deems that special circumstances in the national interest so require, exempt a contracting agency from the requirement of including any or all of the provisions of Section 202 of this Order in any specific contract, subcontract, or purchase order. The Secretary of Labor may, by rule or regulation, also exempt certain classes of contracts, subcontracts, or purchase orders (1) whenever work is to be or has been performed outside the United States and no recruitment of workers within the limits of the United States is involved; (2) for standard commercial supplies or raw materials; (3) involving less than specified amounts of money or specified numbers of workers; or (4) to the extent that they involve subcontracts below a specified tier. . . .

Subpart D. Sanctions and Penalties

Sec. 209. (a) In accordance with such rules, regulations, or orders as the Secretary of Labor may issue or adopt, the Secretary or the appropriate contracting agency may:

(1) Publish, or cause to be published, the names of contractors or unions which it has concluded have complied or have failed to comply with the provisions of this Order or of the rules, regulations, and orders of the Secretary of Labor.

(2) Recommend to the Department of Justice that, in cases in which there is substantial or material violation or the threat of substantial or material violation of the contractual provisions set forth in Section 202 of this Order, appropriate proceedings be brought to enforce those provisions, including the enjoining, within the limitations of applicable law, of organizations, individuals, or groups who prevent directly or indirectly, or seek to prevent directly or indirectly, compliance with the provisions of this Order.

(3) Recommend to the Equal Employment Opportunity Commission or the Department of Justice that appropriate proceedings be instituted under Title VII of the Civil Rights Act of 1964.

(4) Recommend to the Department of Justice that criminal proceedings be brought for the furnishing of false information to any contracting agency or to the Secretary of Labor as the case may be.

(5) Cancel, terminate, suspend, or cause to be cancelled, terminated, or suspended, any contract, or any portion or portions thereof, for failure of the contractor or subcontractor to comply with the nondiscrimination provisions of the contract. Contracts may be cancelled, terminated, or suspended absolutely or continuance of contracts may be conditioned upon a program for future compliances approved by the contracting agency.

(6) Provide that any contracting agency shall refrain from entering into further contracts, or extensions or other modifications of existing contracts, with any noncomplying contractor, until such contractor has satisfied the Secretary of Labor that such contractor has established and will carry out personnel and employment policies in compliance with the provisions of this Order. . . .

Part III. Non-discrimination Provisions in Federally Assisted
      Construction Contracts

Sec. 301. Each executive department and agency which administers a program involving Federal financial assistance shall require as a condition for the approval of any grant, contract, loan, insurance, or guarantee thereunder, which may involve a construction contract, that the applicant for Federal assistance undertake and agree to incorporate, or cause to be incorporated, into all construction contracts paid for in whole or in part with funds obtained from the Federal Government or borrowed on the credit of the Federal Government pursuant to such grant, contract, loan, insurance, or guarantee, or undertaken pursuant to any Federal program involving such grant, contract, loan, insurance, or guarantee, the provisions prescribed for Government contracts by Section 202 of this Order or such modification thereof, preserving in substance the contractor's obligations thereunder, as may be approved by the Secretary of Labor, together with such additional provisions as the Secretary deems appropriate to establish and protect the interest of the United States in the enforcement of those obligations. . . .

D—Age Discrimination in Employment Act of 1967, as Amended 1978
Public Law 202
29 U.S.C. 621

Statement of Findings and Purpose

Sec. 2. (a) The Congress hereby finds and declares that—

(1) in the face of rising productivity and affluence, older workers find themselves disadvantaged in their efforts to retain employment, and especially to regain employment when displaced from jobs;

(2) the setting of arbitrary age limits regardless of potential for job performance has become a common practice, and certain otherwise desirable practices may work to the disadvantage of older persons;

(3) the incidence of unemployment, especially long-term unemployment with resultant deterioration of skill, morale, and employer acceptability is, relative to the younger ages, high among older workers; their numbers are great and growing; and their employment problems grave;

(4) the existence in industries affecting commerce, of arbitrary discrimination in employment because of age, burdens commerce and the free flow of goods in commerce.

(b) It is therefore the purpose of this Act to promote employment of older persons based on their ability rather than age; to prohibit arbitrary age discrimination in employment; to help employers and workers find ways of meeting problems arising from the impact of age on employment.

Prohibition of Age Discrimination

Sec. 4. (a) It shall be unlawful for an employer—

(1) to fail or refuse to hire or to discharge any individual or otherwise discriminate against any individual with respect to his compensation, terms, conditions, or privileges of employment, because of such individual's age;

(2) to limit, segregate, or classify his employees in any way which would de-

prive or tend to deprive any individual of employment opportunities or otherwise adversely affect his status as an employee, because of such individual's age; or

(3) to reduce the wage rate of any employee in order to comply with this Act.

(b) It shall be unlawful for an employment agency to fail or refuse to refer for employment, or otherwise to discriminate against, any individual because of such individual's age, or to classify or refer for employment any individual on the basis of such individual's age.

(c) It shall be unlawful for a labor organization—

(1) to exclude or to expel from its membership, or otherwise to discriminate against, any individual because of his age;

(2) to limit, segregate, or classify its membership, or to classify or fail or refuse to refer for employment any individual, in any way which would deprive or tend to deprive any individual of employment opportunities, or would limit such employment opportunities or otherwise adversely affect his status as an employee or as an applicant for employment, because of such individual's age;

(3) to cause or attempt to cause an employer to discriminate against an individual in violation of this section.

(d) It shall be unlawful for an employer to discriminate against any of his employees or applicants for employment, for an employment agency to discriminate against any individual, or for a labor organization to discriminate against any member thereof or applicant for membership, because such individual, member or applicant for membership has opposed any practice made unlawful by this section, or because such individual, member or applicant for membership has made a charge, testified, assisted, or participated in any manner in an investigation, proceeding, or litigation under this Act.

(e) It shall be unlawful for an employer, labor organization, or employment agency to print or publish, or cause to be printed or published, any notice or advertisement relating to employment by such an employer or membership in or any classification or referral for employment by such a labor organization, or relating to any classification or referral for employment by such an employment agency, indicating any preference, limitation, specification, or discrimination, based on age.

(f) It shall not be unlawful for an employer, employment agency, or labor organization—

(1) to take any action otherwise prohibited under subsections (a), (b), (c), or (e) of this section where age is a bona fide occupational qualification reasonably necessary to the normal operation of the particular business, or where the differentiation is based on reasonable factors other than age;

(2) to observe the terms of a bona fide seniority system or any bona fide employee benefit plan such as a retirement, pension, or insurance plan, which is not a subterfuge to evade the purposes of this chapter, except that no such employee benefit plan shall excuse the failure to hire any individual, and no such seniority system or employee benefit plan shall require or permit the involuntary retirement of any individual specified by section 631 (a) [or section 12] of this title because of the age of such individual; or

(3) to discharge or otherwise discipline an individual for good cause. . . .

Recordkeeping, Investigation, and Enforcement

Sec. 7. (a) The Secretary shall have the power to make investigations and require the keeping of records necessary or appropriate for the administration of this Act in accordance with the powers and procedures provided in sections 9 and 11 of the Fair Labor Standards Act of 1938, as amended (29 U.S.C. 209 and 211). . . .

(c) (1) Any person aggrieved may bring a civil action in any court of competent jurisdiction for such legal or equitable relief as will effectuate the purposes of this chapter: *Provided,* That the right of any person to bring such action shall terminate upon the commencement of an action by the Secretary to enforce the right of such employee under this chapter.

(2) In an action brought under paragraph (1) a person shall be entitled to a trial by jury of any issue of fact in any such action for recovery of amounts owing as a result of a violation of this chapter, regardless of whether equitable relief is sought by any party in such action. . . .

Criminal Penalties

Sec. 10. Whoever shall forcibly resist, oppose, impede, intimidate or interfere with a duly authorized representative of the Secretary while he is engaged in the performance of duties under this Act shall be punished by a fine of not more than $500 or by imprisonment for not more than one year, or both: *Provided, however,* That no person shall be imprisoned under this section except when there has been a prior conviction hereunder. . . .

Limitation

Sec. 12. (a) The prohibitions in this chapter shall be limited to individuals who are at least 40 years of age but less than 70 years of age. . . .

Status-Set Conflicts

E—Interested Persons Acting as Government Agents (1948)
18 U.S.C. 434

§434. Interested Persons Acting as Government Agents.

Whoever, being an officer, agent or member of, or directly or indirectly interested in the pecuniary profits or contracts of any corporation, joint-stock company, or association, or of any firm or partnership, or other business entity, is employed or acts as an officer or agent of the United States for the transaction of business with such business entity, shall be fined not more than $2,000 or imprisoned not more than two years, or both. . . .

F—Acts Affecting a Personal Financial Interest (1962) 18 U.S.C. 208

§208. Acts Affecting a Personal Financial Interest.

(a) Except as permitted by subsection (b) hereof, whoever, being an officer or employee of the executive branch of the United States Government, of any independent agency of the United States, or of the District of Columbia, including a special Government employee, participates personally and substantially as a Government officer or employee, through decision, approval, disapproval, recommendation, the rendering of advice, investigation, or otherwise, in a judicial or other preceeding, application, request for a ruling or other determination, contract, claim, controversy, charge, accusation, arrest, or other particular matter in which, to his knowledge, he, his spouse, minor child, partner, organization in which he is serving as officer, director, trustee, partner or employee, or any person or organization with whom he is negotiating or has any arrangement concerning prospective employment, has a financial interest—

Shall be fined not more than $10,000, or imprisoned not more than two years, or both.

(b) Subsection (a) hereof shall not apply (1) if the officer or employee first advises the Government official responsible for appointment to his position of the nature and circumstances of the judicial or other proceeding, application, request for a ruling or other determination, contract, claim, controversy, charge, accusation, arrest, or other particular matter and makes full disclosure of the financial interest and receives in advance a written determination made by such official that the interest is not so substantial as to be deemed likely to affect the integrity of the services which the Government may expect from such officer or employee, or (2) if, by general rule or regulation published in the Federal Register, the financial interest has been exempted from the requirements of clause (1) hereof as being too remote or too inconsequential to affect the integrity of Government officers' or employees' services. . . .

PART V

Social-Structural Theory of Law: Organizational Analysis

Even in the legal systems of nonliterate societies, it is possible to discern some organizational elements, e.g., a council of elders performing a judicial function. Organizational analysis, the third component of our social-structural theory of law, involves an analysis of values, norms, and roles as they affect the functioning of an organization within a legal system. In analyzing a court, a legislature, an administrative agency or some other organizational component of a legal system, it is important to attend to its structural design, i.e., its internal as well as external organizational relationships.

In the past two decades, the field of organization theory has devoted considerable effort to measuring internal structural variables of organizations (Pugh et al., 1968, 1969; Blau and Schoenherr, 1971). Only in recent years has research attention shifted to the problems of measuring interorganizational relationships (Evan, 1976a, 1976b). Both classes of variables need to be taken into account in an organizational analysis of a legal system problem (Evan, 1977). Another noteworthy trend in organization theory of considerable import for organizational research on legal systems is the concern with conceptualizing and measuring organizational effectiveness (Spray, 1976). Increasingly, researchers are inquiring into the relationships between internal and external structural variables, on the one hand, and various dimensions of organizational effectiveness, on the other.

Internally, an organization's norms, formal and informal, governing its functions permit the researcher to obtain a measure of its degree of formalization. Its role structure or division of labor yields a measure of its degree of role differentiation and specialization. The values, goals, or objectives of any organization, official as well as operative (Perrow, 1963), affect its authority structure and, in turn, its degree of centralization of decision making. These organizational variables also affect an organization's interorganizational design, viz., its boundary spanning units and personnel as well as its interaction with other organizations within and without the legal system (Evan, 1976b).

Some of the foregoing distinctions are illustrated in the three selections in Part V and in the legal documents in Appendix III. Lawrence Baum inquires into an important organizational problem of a court system: To what extent and under what circumstances are decisions of higher courts implemented by lower courts? Given the relatively low degree of centralization within the American judicial system, is it any wonder that there are problems in ensuring that higher court decisions are implemented by lower courts?

Froman identifies a set of organizational characteristics of the U.S. Congress—as regards its norms, its role structure, and its technology—that affect its legislative functioning. Of particular importance are various environing organizations representing different constituencies and interest groups as they impinge on the decision-making of legislators. This is further spelled out in the reading by Nader and Serber on administrative agencies. Because of the power that regulated industries exert on administrative agencies, the regulatory process frequently neither achieves its official purposes nor contributes to what Nader and Serber claim is a function of law, to wit, the "equalization of power" in society. In the legal documents in Appendix III there are several examples of the law's seeking to regulate interorganizational relations involving influence, power, and conflict.

What organizational mechanisms would you devise to increase the independence of organizations within legal systems, be they courts, legislatures, or administrative agencies? To what extent would such mechanisms be compatible with the principles of a democratic system of government?

References

Blau, P. and R. A. Schoenherr (1971). *The Structure of Organizations*. New York: Basic Books.

Evan, W. M. (1976a). *Organization Theory.* New York: John Wiley & Sons.

Evan, W. M., ed. (1976b). *Interorganizational Relations.* London: Penguin Books.

Evan, W. M. (1977). "Administrative Law and Organization Theory." *Journal of Legal Education,* 19: 106-125.

Perrow, C. (1963). "Goals and Power Structure: A Historical Case Study." Pp. 112-146 in E. Freidson, ed., *The Hospital in Modern Society.* New York: Free Press of Glencoe.

Pugh, D. S. *et al.* (1968). "Dimensions of Organization Structure." *Administrative Science Quarterly,* 13: 65-105.

Pugh, D. S. *et al.* (1969). "The Context of Organizational Structures." *Administrative Science Quarterly,* 14: 91-114.

Spray, S. L., ed. (1976). *Organizational Effectiveness.* Kent, Ohio: Kent State University, Comparative Administrative Research Institute.

COURTS

23

Implementation of Judicial Decisions
Lawrence Baum

Over the past two decades, students of the American judicial system have paid increasing attention to the process by which Supreme Court decisions are implemented (see Wasby, 1970; Becker and Feeley, 1973; and Shapiro, 1970). When the Court lays down rules which conflict with the existing policies of other government agencies, personnel of these agencies must decide whether and how they will alter their policies to conform to the Court's rules. Scholars have examined the response of policy makers to Supreme Court decisions which impinge upon their activities in a variety of policy areas: the most popular subjects of implementation studies have been the Court's rulings on school desegregation (McKay, 1956; Peltason, 1971), school religious practices (Dolbeare and Hammond, 1971; Muir, 1967), and police behavior (Milner, 1971; Medalie et al., 1968). This literature has provided considerable empirical information on policy responses to Supreme Court decisions. . . .

The treatment of Supreme Court decisions by other policy makers, one type of judicial impact, may best be understood as a form of

Excerpt from "Implementation of Judicial Decisions: An Organizational Analysis," *American Politics Quarterly* 4 (January 1976), pp. 86–114. Reprinted by permission of the publisher, Sage Publications, Inc.

policy implementation. The concept of implementation is narrower and more clearly delineated than that of impact. Its use also underlines the fact that response to judicial decisions is analogous to the implementation of nonjudicial policies. Awareness of this analogy facilitates comparison between what may be called "judicial implementation" and other processes of implementation within government; moreover, it indicates the relevance of a useful body of work on policy implementation for the study of response to court decisions (see Van Meter and Van Horn, 1975).

In contrast with the large body of empirical work on judicial implementation, there has been relatively little development of theory designed to explain and to order empirical findings. However, several scholars have offered analytic models which provide insight on the implementation process; these models borrow from such sources as sociological conceptions of power (Johnson, 1967; ch. 2), psychological conceptions of cognitive dissonance (Muir, 1967), and economic conceptions of utility (Brown and Stover, 1974). Still, there remains a great need for models which provide comprehensive and coherent frameworks for the analysis of judicial implementation.

Organizational analysis offers one promising approach to the development of such frameworks. If the relationship between a court issuing decisions and the agencies responding to those decisions is conceived as one between superior and subordinate officials within a complex organization, the process of implementation may be examined in organizational terms. Organization theory then can provide both a framework for analysis and a source of concepts and hypotheses to build an analytic scheme within this framework.

Students of judicial implementation have made little use of organization theory, in part because of an implicit assumption that relationships between courts and other policy makers do not fit easily into models of organizational hierarchy. Indeed, only where there is a clear element of hierarchy in the relationship between court and responding agencies is an organizational model of this type appropriate. Thus, a hierarchical framework would be of limited utility for the analysis of presidential or Congressional response to Supreme Court decisions[1] But this framework is highly appropriate for the study of the relationship between an appellate court and the courts below it in the judicial system, and a few students of the judicial implementation process have indicated the utility of an organizational perspective on the treatment of Supreme Court decisions by lower federal and state courts (Canon, 1974; Shapiro and Hobbs, 1974: 497-501). . . .

An Organizational Perspective

The judicial system[2] resembles other organizations in its stratified structure. The Supreme Court stands at the top of the system; below it are several levels of federal and state appellate courts, with the trial courts of the system at the bottom. As in other organizations, in each hierarchical relationship there is a division of labor between the higher and lower participants. The former issue policy directives, and the latter are responsible for executing these directives where they are relevant. As Simon (1957: 2-3) has suggested, the role of higher participants is basically one of influencing the behavior of lower participants who actually produce outputs.

The role of the Supreme Court exemplifies this division of labor. First, the Court seldom makes the final decision in a case; rather, if the Court disagrees with the decision below, it normally remands the case to the lower court with instructions for its reconsideration. . . . More important, the application of a Court ruling to other cases with similar issues is primarily the task of the courts below. The same is true of other appellate courts in relation to the courts below them. In the sense that nearly all final organizational decisions are made by the lower participants[3] in the system, the degree of delegation of responsibility in the judicial system is unusually great.

In a traditional Weberian model of rational organizations, delegation of the power to implement policies has no significant effect on organizational action, because subordinates carry out policies accurately and faithfully (Gerth and Mills, 1946: ch. 8). Many observers of the judicial implementation process have adopted a similar view, at least as a normative expectation. Yet students of complex organizations have shown that independent policy-making by subordinates is a standard quality of organizational behavior rather than an anomaly.[4] Such unlikely groups as maintenance workers in factories (Crozier, 1964: ch. 4) and attendants in mental hospitals (Scheff, 1961) may shape their organizations' outputs in fundamental ways, thereby establishing policies which deviate considerably from those desired by their superiors. Similarly, political scientists have found that subordinates in government bureaucracies may play a highly independent role in the implementation of policy (Riggs, 1967; Goodnow, 1964), even so-called totalitarian governments like that of the Soviet Union (Fainsod, 1967; Berliner, 1957; ch. 18).

The independent role of subordinates in policy-making stems chiefly from two general phenomena. The first is the difficulty which frequently attends the transmission of higher participants' desires to lower officials. This difficulty arises from problems both in formulating messages which clearly express the actions desired and in communicating those messages effectively and accurately to the intended receivers.

Second and more fundamentally, subordinates obtain the ability to shape policy through their very role as implementors. This role requires that superiors give to subordinates physical control over the actual production of outputs through activities like the fabrication of goods, the treatment of mental patients, or the making of judicial decisions. In performing the task of production, subordinates obtain the opportunity to shape the outputs which they produce.

This opportunity would be meaningless if subordinates lacked either the motivation or the ability to deviate from their superiors' directives. Neither condition, however, is common. A variety of motives for deviation may exist, ranging from disagreement about policy to a desire to make one's job easier. At the same time, factors such as inadequate feedback mechanisms, limitations on the supply of sanctions, and the possession of organizational power by lower participants generally ensure that the executors of policy retain freedom to take independent action. Thus, the notion of lower participants as slaves of their superiors is highly inaccurate. Closer to reality is the opposite view, as expressed by one sociologist (Mechanic, 1962: 351): "Organizations, in a sense, are continually at the mercy of their lower participants. . ." (see also Kaufman, 1973: 11–14).

In examining judicial implementation as an organizational process, then, we shall not begin with the assumption that any deviation from the policies of a superior court is aberrant. Rather, we shall view lower-court judges as independent actors, who will not follow the lead of higher courts unless conditions are favorable for their doing so. This perspective is a useful one not only because of its consistency with organizational reality. Equally important, it requires the analyst of implementation processes to search for the positive forces which may cause judges to take the actions indicated by their superiors. It is this approach which our analysis will take. . . .

The Implementation Process:
Transmission of Directives

For a superior who seeks to obtain certain policy behavior from subordinates, the first step is to issue and to communicate directives indicating the actions desired.[5] In the judicial system, an appellate court must issue one or more decisions, which then must be communicated to the lower courts for which they are relevant. The importance of this stage in the implementation process is clear. Congruence between the policies desired by an appellate court and those undertaken by lower courts depends in part on the effectiveness of communication downward in the system.

Clarity of Directives

All organizational superiors face difficulties in issuing clear directives to their subordinates, and the ambiguities which result from these difficulties may have serious consequences for the implementation of policy. . . . If this generalization is applied to the judicial system, we may hypothesize as follows:

H_1 : The greater the clarity with which appellate decisions define what subordinates are to do, the more faithful will be the implementation of those decisions.

Some students of judicial implementation have offered similar arguments (Johnson, 1967: 58–59; Wasby, 1973: 1102–1103). In contrast, Krislove (1972: 344) has suggested that under certain circumstances ambiguity might actually favor faithful implementation by providing lower-court judges with alternative paths to obedience. But in the great majority of situations ambiguity will work against effective implementation in two ways: by leaving loyal judges uncertain as to their superior's intent and by providing leeway which recalcitrant judges may use to evade obedience to a directive. . . .

This hypothesis is particularly important because appellate courts often face great problems in issuing clear directives; several constraints on their behavior foster decisional ambiguity. . . . Some of these constraints are self-imposed, stemming from well-established rules by which judges regulate their own policy-making. . . . Among these are the rule that cases are to be decided as narrowly as possible and the injunction that courts will deal only with issues properly before them. Rules like these encourage courts to issue narrow decisions whose implications for lower courts may be ambiguous.

Other constraints are practical in origin. One is the relatively small number of cases heard by appellate courts. Some courts . . . decide fewer than two hundred cases with opinion each year. As a result, they can develop and sustain a clear policy line on only a limited number of issues at any time (Frank, 1958: ch. 2). Another constraint is imposed by the plurality of membership on appellate courts, which makes policy-blurring compromise likely (Howard, 1968). On courts which divide into panels, this problem is aggravated by the fact that different groups of judges may decide successive cases concerned with a particular question (Richardson and Vines, 1970: 122–125; Atkins and Zavoina, 1974).

Many of these constraints are shared by superiors in other kinds of organizations, and the difference between appellate courts and other superiors in this respect is one of degree. In general, however, the constraints on appellate courts force on them relatively limited roles as effective policy makers, both in terms of the number of issues on which they speak and—more important for our concerns—the clarity of their messages concerning the issues on which they do speak.

Courts are not uniformly ambiguous in their messages to lower courts. On some issues, particularly those with a narrow scope, clear decisions may be relatively easy to achieve. On more difficult issues like standards of legislative apportionment a determined court can attain considerable clarity by issuing a series of decisions over time (see Dixon, 1968). Our hypothesis predicts that, all else being equal, the implementation of decisions will be relatively faithful when ambiguity is avoided.

Communication of Directives

Once a directive is issued, it must be communicated to subordinates. Communication represents a major source of potential problems in the implementation process. Messages which travel downward in a hierarchy frequently suffer distortion in the process of communication, both because of intentional alterations by intermediate officials and because of unintentional errors in transmission (Downs, 1967: 133–136). Any distortion which occurs will tend to limit the effective implementation of a policy by causing subordinates to be misinformed about what they are being asked to do. Moreover, communication channels may be so poor that subordinates do not become aware that a superior has issued a directive, thereby making implementation impossible. Hence, we may hypothesize:

H_2 : The greater the accuracy with which decisions are communicated to subordinates, the more faithful will be their implementation.

The communication of judicial decisions is formally structured so as to minimize the possibility of problems. Appellate opinions are written and collected in volumes, and most judges are trained to locate and to read opinions. As a result, we might expect that communication would present few of the difficulties commonly found in complex organizations.

However, the judiciary shares with other organizations the problem of inattention to messages. Few judges monitor directly the decisions of the courts above them (Frank, 1958: 22). Even judges on the federal courts of appeals, for instance, seldom read Supreme Court decisions as they are issued. Therefore, mechanisms must exist to direct judges to relevant decisions (Wasby, 1974: 1029).

In the higher levels of the judicial system, lawyers serve well as a communications channel. In presenting their cases, they inform judges of relevant appellate decisions which support their positions (Shapiro, 1970: 86–87). In the lower levels of the system, particularly state trial courts, this mechanism operates less effectively. Many litigants are unrepresented or poorly represented by counsel. Moreover, there frequently exists an atmosphere unfavorable to the intrusion of "law" into court proceedings, particularly in the routinized criminal courts which rely on rapid processing of cases (Blumberg, 1967; Downie, 1972; ch. 2; Foote, 1956). Because of these conditions, judges in the lower courts may not be informed of relevant appellate decisions.

Thus, the total blockage of messages may be a fairly common phenomenon. There may exist the problem of message distortion where the court issuing a decision is several steps removed in the hierarchy from the courts to which the decision is relevant. For example, lawyers and judges in state trial courts tend to use their own state's appellate courts as the primary source of legal precedent; the Supreme Court decisions will become known in trial courts only as they are cited and interpreted by state appellate courts, and in doing so these courts may distort the Court's message considerably (Canon, 1974). . . .

This discussion suggests the likelihood of serious communication problems in the judiciary, problems which increase with the organizational distance between issuing and receiving courts. It is doubtful, however, that the communication problems faced by appellate courts are significantly more serious than those which exist in most other organizations. The kinds of difficulties which we have described are found in all but the simplest and the most effectively functioning organizations. Appellate courts face special problems in issuing clear directives, but in communicating those directives they suffer from a near-universal organizational weakness.

The Implementation Process:
Responding to Directives

Once a directive has been issued and communicated to subordinates, they must choose their responses to it. As several students of judicial implementation have shown (Krislov, 1965; Rodgers and

Bullock, 1972; Brown and Stover, 1974), these responses may be analyzed in terms of utility theory. More specifically, subordinates can be expected to implement policies faithfully when they possess positive motivations to do so. Similarly, a subordinate will fail to carry out policies when he lacks adequate motivation to do so. We may posit three types of motivations for subordinates to respond positively to policy directives: personal advantage to be gained from implementation of a directive (interests); agreement with the policy embodied by a directive (policy preferences); and belief that one has an obligation to follow the directives issued by a superior (authority). This typology of motivations may be used to explain and to predict response to directives in any implementation process. . . .

Interests

The interests of subordinates represent perhaps the most significant motivational factor in most organizations. These interests may take a variety of forms, from monetary gain to evasion of responsibility. Crozier (1964) and other students of complex organizations have shown the fundamental effect of interests on the implementation process, an effect which is clear if we conceive of behavior as largely self-interested. . . . Thus,

H_3 : The more that subordinates' interests are favored by faithful implementation of appellate decisions, the more faithful
their implementation will be.

For two important reasons, subordinates' interests frequently will be opposed to implementation of the directives received from superiors. The first concerns the psychic and material costs of policy change, which increase with the magnitude of change required to implement a new policy. As particular ways of doing things become institutionalized within an organization, significant changes in these ways will be resisted. . . . Resistance will be all the greater when change requires additional expenditure of resources.

Second, subordinates working without direction from above will tend to adopt policies which maximize their interests (see Noll, 1971: 39-46). If they subsequently receive a directive demanding significant policy change, implementation of the directive will require abandoning the interest-maximizing policies, and it is likely to be resisted. For example, the Federal Bureau of Investigation developed cooperative relationships with Southern law enforcement officials to aid in performing its tasks effectively; when orders from above required that the FBI take a limited adversary stance toward these officials, its personnel understandably resisted (Navasky, 1971: ch. 3). . . .

Nevertheless, situations may exist in which judges have strong interests relevant to appellate decisions. Studies of these situations offer unsystematic but significant support for our hypothesis. In the desegregation controversy, the pressures on Southern judges from their environments created an interest in minimal implementation of the Supreme Court's decisions and seemed to have a significant effect on the behavior of many judges (Peltason, 1971; Friedman, 1965). Similarly, judges in many criminal trial courts develop strong interests in processing cases quickly, and appellate decisions whose establishment of procedural safeguards for defendants threaten this interest are resisted for that reason. Where judges' interests do become relevant, this limited evidence suggests that they can play a large role—and generally a negative one—in determining response to appellate decisions.

Policy Preferences

Subordinates' views about policy issues also may play a central role in determining their responses to directives. If a directive accords with a person's own values, he has reason to carry it out; similarly, one who disagrees with a directive will be disposed against it (see Pressman and Wildavsky, 1973: ch. 5). "The problem of noncompliance," Petrick writes, "arises from the fact that human groups find it difficult to carry out effectively acts for which they have no underlying beliefs" (1968: 7). It follows that:

> H_4 : The greater the consistency between an appellate decision and a subordinate's policy preferences, the more faithful will be his implementation of that decision.

Subordinates frequently lack strong preferences concerning the policies which are subjects of directives. This condition is particularly common in what Etzioni (1971: 31-39) calls utilitarian organizations, whose members participate primarily because of concrete benefits and who may have little interest in their organization's substantive policies. Accordingly, they will be indifferent to the values embodied in most directives.

In contrast, most judges are interested in the subject matter of their work and have strong opinions on many of the issues which come before them. On important and controversial issues like civil rights and the rights of criminal defendants, few judges will be indifferent. Moreover, the relative unimportance of interests in most situations gives greater weight to policy preferences as a motivational factor.

Like interests, policy preferences frequently will be opposed to faithful implementation of a directive in an organization like the judicial system. Prior to the issuance of an appellate decision on a policy question, lower-court judges may have established positions on that question. Unless dictated by earlier appellate rulings, these positions usually are based largely on judges' own preferences. Thus an appellate directive which calls for change in lower-court policies often will be asking judges to abandon their preferences. Yet this is not inevitably the case; an appellate ruling might call for a new policy which a subordinate judge favors but has not previously adopted, particularly where the appellate court advocates a policy which lower-court judges had overlooked or thought impossible.

Evidence on the relationship between judges' policy preferences and their implementation behavior is slim, perhaps because this relationship is taken for granted by many scholars. Thus, the significance of policy preferences stands as an implicit but untested premise in much of the empirical work on judicial implementation. Some relatively direct evidence of this significance is provided by studies of state-court resistance to the Supreme Court's criminal justice decisions, resistance which was related to disagreement with the Court's values (Canon, 1974; Neubauer, 1974: 174–176). Studies of administrative response to Court decisions also offer evidence supporting our hypothesis; in particular, they underline the effect of disagreement with the Court in limiting officials' willingness to carry out its policies (Birkby, 1966: 316–317; Way, 1968). . . .

Authority

A belief by subordinates that they have an obligation to implement directives handed down from above is a near-universal condition in organizations (Simon, 1957: 124–130). This acceptance of authority functions as a crucial centripetal force. Subordinates' interests and preferences often incline them against obedience to higher officials, but the authority which they attach to those officials' decisions tends to counteract these centrifugal tendencies and to provide an important motivation for faithful implementation. However, the strength of authority may vary tremendously. In normative organizations, the perceived legitimacy of superiors is the major force favoring acceptance of directives; in some kinds of coercive organizations, in contrast, authority may be very limited (Etzioni, 1971). Even within a particular organization, such as the court system, there may exist considerable differences in the authority ascribed to superiors' directives. Thus,

H_5 : The greater the authority attached to an appellate decision by subordinates, the more faithful will be their implementation of that decision.

. . . A few studies of judicial implementation, especially Peltason's study (1971) of district-court response to the desegregation decisions, suggest the significance of Supreme Court authority for some judges. But there has been no direct analysis of the effect of variation in appellate-court authority on the behavior of subordinate judges.

On a more general level, however, several scholars have debated the general strength of authority relationships in the judiciary (Petrick, 1968; Johnson, 1967: ch. 3; Levine and Becker, 1970). There is some basis to conclude that authority is unusually strong in this organization. The judicial system is a normative organization in which acceptance of the authority of higher courts is a central facet of the dominant ideology. Members of the legal profession are strongly socialized to believe in the legitimacy of appellate decisions for subordinate courts, and this socialization has considerable effect on their perspectives as judges. . . .

In no circumstances is the authority of an appellate court absolute. Indeed, judges share with other lower participants an ambivalence toward their superiors which serves to limit the strength of authority (Carp and Wheeler, 1972: 377-378). Rather, acceptance of authority represents one of several motivations which help to determine the treatment of appellate decisions. When neither interests nor policy preferences are strong, so that the judge's choice falls within his "zone of indifference," . . . the authority attached to a decision may induce almost automatic acceptance of it. Where there is conflict between appellate authority and these other motivations, a whole array of responses from total obedience . . . to complete intractability . . . may occur. In general, the existence of authority provides a powerful cement to the judicial system, one more potent than that which exists in most organizations.

Within this general situation, considerable variation in appellate authority may exist, variation which makes our hypothesis an important one. For instance, the authority of an appellate court varies according to the relationship between its directive and the case being decided by a subordinate judge. The authority of an order sent directly to a lower-court judge for the treatment of a particular case is highest. Somewhat more limited, though still considerable, is the authority of a decision determinative of the question faced by a subordinate judge but issued in another case. . . . Judges' feelings of obligation are weakest of all when a superior court has indicated a position or view relevant to a current case but has not ruled directly on the question involved. The kinds of implementation questions which have interested scholars fall primarily into the second category.

Authority also varies with the organizational distance between a court issuing a decision and a subordinate court receiving it. An appellate court's authority generally is greatest for the courts immediately below it. When two courts are separated by several tiers of intermediate courts, the authority relationship is attenuated by their lack of contact. Even the Supreme Court may suffer from considerably diluted authority in the lowest levels of the judicial system. . . .

Influencing Subordinates' Motivations

. . . Borrowing from Gamson (1968: 116–143), we may suggest that three mechanisms of influence are the most important within organizations. The first is insulation, selective hiring and firing of subordinates and the removal of recalcitrant subordinates from the implementation process. The second is sanctioning, the use of rewards and punishments to induce faithful implementation of directives. The third is persuasion, the creation of attitudes favorable to the implementation of directives. . . .

H_6 : The more powerful the mechanisms of influence utilized by appellate courts, the more favorable will be subordinates' motivations to implement decisions faithfully.

Insulation

The function of insulation is to ensure that those responsible for implementing organizational policies are individuals with motivations relatively favorable for doing so; in utilizing this mechanism, superiors change structure rather than the perspectives of subordinates. Each form of insulation is commonly employed in organizations. Subordinates are selected with concern for their willingness to follow superiors' lead. Recalcitrant subordinates may be removed from their positions. Where removal is impossible or undesirable, a subordinate's responsibilities may be changed to take him from a role in the implementation process. . . .

Appellate courts are relatively limited in powers of insulation. In general, courts do not hire and fire lower-court judges. Their formal powers over hiring are limited to the membership of some appellate judges on the commissions which select judges or approve their appointment in some states, . . . and only a few appellate judges (see Murphy, 1962) gain informal influence over lower-court appointments by other agencies. The firing power is limited to that of removing lower-court judges for misconduct, enjoyed by the supreme courts of some states. Appellate courts may take control of particular cases rather than remanding them to lower courts, . . . , and they possess some power to disengage lower-court judges from particular cases or even—in most unusual circumstances—from their entire dockets. . . . The utility of the firing and case-removal powers is limited by the general perception of them as extreme and their lack of legitimacy as broad mechanisms to obtain the implementation of appellate policies.

Sanctioning

Sanctions are designed to influence the interests of subordinates in a direction favorable to the implementation of superiors' policies. They may take a variety of forms, from physical coercion to the provision of monetary rewards. In most organizations, they provide a crucial means for superiors to overcome recalcitrance and to obtain desired behavior from subordinates. This fact is particularly clear in coercive and utilitarian organizations like the military and factories, but it is also true in some normative organizations like volunteer groups and "amateur" political parties (Clark and Wilson, 1961).

Appellate courts are conspicuously lacking in some powerful sanctions. They have little control over the tenure of judicial subordinates, as we have noted. Moreover, they possess almost no power over the promotion, remuneration, or working conditions of lower-court judges. Of the powers which they do possess, the most important is the ability to affirm or reverse a lower-court decision. . . .

Reversal may have practical effects when it requires that a court relitigate cases. The chief importance of affirmance and reversal, however, is symbolic. The frequency of reversal is the clearest indicator of a judge's ability to perform his job well, and judges believe strongly in its significance. According to one federal judge, "a decent trial judge ought to be affirmed about two-thirds of the time" (Wyzanski, 1965: 4). Others might disagree about the desired proportion, but there is strong consensus for the proposition that affirmances are a sign of a job done well (Schick, 1970: 141-153; Peltason, 1971: 10-11).

The significance of affirmance and reversal as sanctions are limited in some important ways. First, an appellate court may affirm or reverse only the decisions which it reviews on appeal, and in general it reviews only the decisions of its immediate subordinates. Thus, the Supreme Court has few opportunities to review federal district judges and almost none to review state trial judges. If these judges are to be affirmed or reversed according to their willingness to implement Supreme Court decisions, it will be by intermediate courts, and these courts themselves may not be willing to follow the Court's lead. Moreover, an appellate court can reverse the decisions of disobedient subordinates only when appropriate cases are appealed from these judges, and such appeals may not occur in instances of disobedience.

Second, one or even several reversals on an issue may constitute less than an overwhelming sanction for a judge. If he believes strongly in a course of action, he may decide to continue that action even if the cost is a decline in his "batting average." Certainly, this was the case with many federal district judges who opposed desegregation of Southern schools. Where reversal is accompanied by a rebuke of the lower-court judge, . . . the sanction is more powerful but still may be tolerable.

A more severe sanction is the power to hold a judge in contempt for violation of an appellate order. But direct orders play a relatively small part in the implementation process, and rarely do courts hold subordinate judges in contempt for their violations. The Supreme Court has never done so. . . . In practice, then, the contempt power is much less important than the power of reversal.

Sanctions can be effective only if a superior possesses sufficient information about subordinates' conduct to apply them appropriately. Communication problems deprive superiors of such information in many organizations. . . . These problems are relatively limited in the judicial system, because the process of appeal operates as a feedback mechanism informing appellate courts of deviation from their doctrines in lower courts. Since deviating decisions are not always appealed, however, this mechanism is an imperfect one.

The substantial power which lower participants possess in most organizations limits the utility of sanctions as mechanisms of influence. . . . If subordinates can retaliate for negative sanctions with sanctions of their own, such as the withholding of needed information, then superiors may be deterred from using these devices. This problem exists in the judiciary, in the form of judges' retaliation for reversals with increased efforts to sabotage the policy intent of these reversals. . . . But its effects are more significant in organizations which rely more heavily on sanctions as bases for securing faithful implementation of policies.

Persuasion

Persuasion is less tangible and probably less powerful than the other means of control which we have discussed, . . . but it may have a meaningful effect in some organizations. Persuasion is used to increase the motivation to implement directives by increasing the authority of superiors and by helping to create policy preferences favorable to their directives. An example of the former is the attempts of the military and of large companies to develop loyalty to the organization and its officials. The latter is exemplified by the use of written and oral communications to convince members of labor unions and of volunteer organizations of the wisdom of their leaders' policies.

Courts have relatively little opportunity to persuade subordinates, because of the absence of contact between judges at different levels of the judicial hierarchy. The most important means of persuasion are the opinions which appellate courts regularly issue in conjunction with their decisions. A major function of opinions is to convince a court's audience of the rightness of decisions. It is difficult to estimate the effects of opinions on lower-court judges, but it seems unlikely that the judge who feels strongly about an issue will abandon his position because of an appellate opinion. Whatever effect opinions do have is probably limited to judges who are indifferent about an issue.

Conclusions

. . . This model provides a general perspective on the implementation process, one that places judicial implementation within a broader conception of organizational hierarchy. The use of this conception allows comparison between the positions of appellate courts and of other organizational superiors. Our analysis has pointed to some features of the judicial implementation process which distinguish it from analogous processes in many other organizations, such as the relative weakness of sanctions in the court system. However, the similarities between the judiciary and other organizations are more notable than the differences; implementation is a general process which takes a common form in organizations of very different types. Most important, the difficulties involved in the implementation of judicial policies are far from unique. If problems of implementation are common in the judiciary, these problems are chiefly the result not of special conditions in the judicial system but of the universal weaknesses of organizational superiors. This fact is a crucial one for the understanding of judicial implementation.

References

Atkins, B. M. and W. Zavoina (1974). "Judicial leadership on the court of appeals: a probability analysis of panel assignment in race relations cases on the Fifth Circuit." *Amer. J. of Pol. Sci.* 4 (November): 701-711.

Becker, T. L. and M. M. Feeley, eds. (1973). *The Impact of Supreme Court Decisions.* New York: Oxford Univ. Press.

Berliner, J. S. (1957). *Factory and Manager in the USSR.* Cambridge: Harvard Univ. Press.

Birkby, R. (1966). "The Supreme Court and the Bible Belt: Tennessee reaction to the 'Schempp' decision." *Midwest J. of Pol. Sci.* 10 (August): 304-319.

Blumberg, A. (1967). *Criminal Justice.* Chicago: Quadragle.

Brown, D. W. and R. V. Stover (1974). "An economic approach to compliance with court decisions." Presented at the annual meeting of the American Political Science Association, Chicago, August-September.

Canon, B. C. (1974). "Organizational contumacy in the transmission of judicial policies: the Mapp, Escobedo, Miranda and Gault cases." *Villanova Law Rev.* 20 (November): 50-79.

Carp, R. and R. Wheeler (1972). "Sink or swim: the socialization of a federal district judge." *J. of Public Law* 21: 359-393.

Carrington, P. D. (1969). "Crowded dockets and the courts of appeals: the threat to the function of review and the national law." *Harvard Law Rev.* 82 (January): 542-617.

Clark, P. B. and J. Q. Wilson (1961). "Incentive systems: a theory of organizations." *Administrative Sci. Q.* 6 (September): 129-166.

Crozier, M. (1964). *The Bureaucratic Phenomenon.* Chicago: Univ. of Chicago Press.

Dahl, R. A. (1963). *Modern Political Analysis.* Englewood Cliffs, N.J.: Prentice-Hall.

Dixon, R. G. (1968). *Democratic Representation: Reapportionment in Law and Politics.* New York: Oxford Univ. Press.

Dolbeare, K. and P. E. Hammond (1971). *The School of Prayer Decisions: From Court Policy to Local Practice.* Chicago: Univ. of Chicago Press.

Downie, L. (1972). *Justice Denied: The Case for Reform of the Courts.* Baltimore: Penguin.

Downs, A. (1967). *Inside Bureaucracy.* Boston: Little, Brown.

Eisenstein, J. (1973). *Politics and the Legal Process.* New York: Harper & Row.

Etzioni, A. (1971). *A Comparative Analysis of Complex Organizations.* New York: Free Press.

Evan, W. M. (1966). "The organization-set: toward a theory of inter-organizational relations." Pp. 173-191 in J. D. Thompson, ed., *Approaches to Organizational Design.* Pittsburgh: Univ. of Pittsburgh Press.

Fainsod, M. (1967). "Bureaucracy and modernization: the Russian and Soviet case." Pp. 233-267 in J. La Palombara, ed., *Bureaucracy and Political Development.* Princeton, N.J., Princeton Univ. Press.

Foote, C. (1956). "Vagrancy-type law and its administration." *Pennsylvania Law Rev.* 104 (March): 603-650.

Frank, J. P. (1958). *Marble Palace: The Supreme Court in American Life.* New York: Alfred A. Knopf.

Friedman, L., ed. (1965). *Southern Justice.* Cleveland: World.

Gamson, W. (1968). *Power and Discontent.* Homewood, Ill.: Dorsey.

Gerth, H. H. and C. W. Mills, eds. (1946). *From Max Weber: Essays in Sociology.* New York: Oxford Univ. Press.

Goodnow, H. (1964). *The Civil Service of Pakistan.* New Haven, Conn.: Yale Univ. Press.

Hall, R. H. (1972). *Organizations: Structure and Process.* Englewood Cliffs, N.J.: Prentice-Hall.

Howard, J. W. (1968). "On the fluidity of judicial choice." *Amer. Pol. Sci. Rev.* 62 (March): 43–56.

Johnson, R. M. (1967). *The Dynamics of Compliance.* Evanston, Ill.: Northwestern Univ. Press.

Kaufman, H. (1973). *Administrative Feedback: Monitoring Subordinates' Behavior.* Washington: Brookings.

Krislov, S. (1972). "The perimeters of power: the concept of compliance as an approach to the study of the legal and political processes." Pp. 333–350 in S. Krislov et al., eds. *Compliance and the Law: A Multi-Disciplinary Approach.* Beverly Hills, Calif.: Sage.

—— (1965). *The Supreme Court in the Political Process.* New York: Macmillan.

Levine, J. P. and T. L. Becker (1970). "Toward and beyond a theory of Supreme Court impact." *Amer. Behavioral Scientist* 13 (March/April): 561–573.

McKay, R. B. (1956). "'With all deliberate speed': a study of school desegregation." *New York Univ. Law Rev.* 31 (June): 991–1090.

Mechanic, D. (1962). "Sources of power of lower participants in complex organizations." *Administrative Sci. Q.* 7 (December): 349–364.

Medalie, R. J., L. Zeitz, and P. Alexander (1968). "Custodial police interrogation in our nation's capital: the attempt to implement Miranda." *Michigan Law Rev.* 66 (May): 1347–1422.

Milner, N. (1971). *The Court and Local Law Enforcement: The Impact of Miranda.* Beverly Hills, Calif.: Sage.

Muir, W. K. (1967). *Prayer in the Public Schools: Law and Attitude Change.* Chicago: Univ. of Chicago Press.

Navasky, V. S. (1971). *Kennedy Justice.* New York: Atheneum.

Neubauer, D. W. (1974). *Criminal Justice in Middle America.* Morristown, N.J.: General Learning Press.

Noll, R. G. (1971). *Reforming Regulation: An Evaluation of the Ash Council Proposals.* Washington: Brookings.

Peltason, J. W. (1971). *Fifty-Eight Lonely Men: Southern Federal Judges and School Desegregation.* Urbana: Univ. of Illinois Press.

Petrick M. J. (1968). "The Supreme Court and authority acceptance." *Western Pol. Q.* 21 (March): 5–19.

Pressman, J. L. and A. Wildavsky (1973). *Implementation.* Berkeley: Univ. of California Press.

Richardson, R. J. and K. N. Vines (1970). *The Politics of Federal Courts.* Boston: Little, Brown.

Riggs, F. W. (1967). "Bureaucrats and political development: a paradoxical view." Pp. 120-167 in J. La Palombara, ed., *Bureaucracy and Political Development*, Princeton, N.J.: Princeton Univ. Press.

Rodgers, H. R. and C. S. Bullock (1972). *Law and Social Change: Civil Rights Laws and Their Consequences*. New York: McGraw Hill.

Scheff, T. J. (1961). "Control over policy by attendants in a mental hospital." *J. of Health and Human Behavior* 2: 93-105.

Schick, M. (1970). *Learned Hand's Court*. Baltimore: Johns Hopkins Press.

Shapiro, M. (1970). "The impact of the Supreme Court." *J. of Legal Education* 23: 77-89.

—— and D. S. Hobbs (1974). *The Politics of Constitutional Law*. Cambridge: Winthrop.

Simon, H. A. (1957). *Administrative Behavior*. New York: Macmillan.

Van Meter, D. S. and C. E. Van Horn (1975). "The policy implementation process: a conceptual framework." *Administration and Society* 6 (February): 445-488.

Wald, M. *et al.* (1967). "Interrogations in New Haven: the impact of Miranda." *Yale Law J.* 76 (July): 1519-1648.

Wasby, S. L. (1974). "The United States Supreme Courts' impact: broadening our focus." *Notre Dame Lawyer* 49 (June): 1023-1036.

—— (1973). "The communication of the Supreme Court's criminal procedure decisions: a preliminary mapping." *Villanova Law Rev.* 18 (June): 1086-1118.

—— (1970). *The Impact of the United States Supreme Court: Some Perspectives*. Homewood, Ill.: Dorsey.

Way, H. F. (1968). "Survey research on judicial decisions: the prayer and Bible reading cases." *Western Pol. Q.* 21 (June): 189-205.

Wyzanski, C. E. (1965). *Whereas—A Judge's Premises*. Boston: Little, Brown.

Yale Law Journal (1947). "State court evasion of United States Supreme Court mandates." 56 (February): 574-583.

Notes

1. However, other kinds of organizational models, such as those concerning interorganizational relationships (Evan, 1966; Hall, 1972: ch. 10), might be appropriate for analysis of these processes.

2. Of course, the federal and state judicial systems are largely separate, with interaction between the two relatively limited. However, because the Supreme Court is a direct superior of state supreme courts, a linkage exists which makes it possible to speak of a single hierarchical system.

3. All appellate courts except the Supreme Court stand in an intermediate situation, serving both as superiors and as subordinates in relationships with other courts. In referring to these courts as higher or lower participants, we will be speaking within the context of the particular relationship involved.

4. The discussion in the remainder of this section is heavily indebted to Mechanic (1962), Crozier (1964), and Downs (1967).

5. The analysis of judicial implementation in the remainder of the paper is based in part on the information obtained by the author from interviews with 21 federal judges concerning questions of judicial implementation. The interview data are reflected most in the sections on communication, authority and sanctioning.

24

Organization Theory and the Explanation of Important Characteristics of Congress
Lewis A. Froman, Jr.

By and large the Congress of the United States has been studied on its own terms, as a somewhat unique political institution. Studies of Congress are usually considered to be important simply because they shed light on an important institution in the American political system. It is true, of course, that Congress *is* an important policy-making body and does deserve study for that reason. But there is no reason why substantive importance cannot be combined with "importance" in another sense. It is also important, for example, to develop theory within any discipline which will help explain the phenomena under study. Trivial substantive problems can be made interesting because of the theory which they suggest. And because a problem may already be substantively important does not mean that it cannot be made even more significant by theoretical development.

As a result of this substantive focus, research on Congress has produced a very rich body of descriptive data on various components of the institution, including its members and leadership, group struc-

Excerpt from "Organization Theory and the Explanation of Important Characteristics of Congress," *American Political Science Review* 62 (June 1968), pp. 518–526, by permission of the author and publisher, American Political Science Association.

ture, committees, party systems, organization, and rules and procedures. Studies have also provided generalizations concerning such
things as the decentralized decision-making of Congress and the
effects of the seniority rule on the distribution of power within the
House and Senate. These descriptive data and generalizations may
serve as the content to be explained within the context of a theory.
As yet there has been very little effort at theory construction concerning Congress. The data are there—their organization and explication remain.

Characteristics of Congress

Although it is difficult to abstract *the* most important characteristics of Congress which have emerged from these studies, most close
observers would agree that the following thirteen accurately reflect
some of the more interesting and useful things which may be said
about Congress.

I.   Impact on Public Policy
    1. Congress is an important political decision-making body
       which, unlike legislatures in many other countries, makes a
       significant, independent contribution to public policy.
II. Organization
    2. Decision-making in Congress is highly decentralized, with
       power widely dispersed among committees, subcommittees,
       and the formal and party leadership.
    3. Each body has a well-developed system of formal and im-
       personal rules and procedures, with the rules of the House
       of Representatives more formal and impersonal than those
       of the Senate.
III. Members
    4. Members in each body may make large individual contribu-
       tions to public policy, although some members are more
       salient than others.
    5. Members of each house have a high commitment and loy-
       alty to the Congress.
IV. Group Structure
    6. There are many subgroups within each body, with the
       House having a larger number than the Senate.
    7. There is a highly developed specialization of labor and
       specificity of roles, and more so in the House than the
       Senate.
    8. Group cohesion in each body is relatively low.

9. The existence of an active group structure has important consequences for decision-making and public policy.
V. Leadership
10. Each house has a relatively elaborate and complex leadership structure.
11. Authority of leadership is relatively low.
VI. Processes
12. Internal communication within each body is relatively elaborate and complex.
13. A prevalent form of decision-making within each body is bargaining.

These thirteen generalizations about Congress are obviously not meant to be exhaustive of those which could be made in each category (as well as in additional categories). They are, however, among the more important propositions which aid in the understanding of the congressional process. As far as I know none are contradicted by any study, and most are supported extensively in the literature. These thirteen propositions, then, will be taken as "given," as true of Congress, and as important enough to be "explained."

Possible Explanatory Theories

. . . What is necessary . . . in order to "explain" certain salient features of Congress is to subsume the specific findings under a set of more general hypotheses or laws (whether the former or the latter will affect the *credibility* of the explanation). But to do so requires moving away from the view that Congress is a unique institution and treating it, instead, as an instance of a more general category. . . .

If we view Congress as a formal organization, and use the general propositions which have been stated, with more or less validity, about formal organizations, we will be able to avoid strictly ad hoc interpretations of Congressional phenomena and, in their place substitute a somewhat organized and consistent set of empirical generalizations which have been found to be true of other formal organizations. Such propositions, used in explanation, may be quite powerful and parsimonious and aid immeasurably in our understanding of why Congress is as it is. . . .

What follows, then, is an effort to explain the thirteen general characteristics of Congress concerning public policy, organization, members, group structure, leadership and processes, by subsuming these characteristics under general statements which have been drawn from organizations other than Congress. It is in this sense that Congress will be treated as a formal organization, subject to the same "laws" as other organizations, and unique only in the sense that there is only one Congress of the United States although there are many formal organizations. The major source of these propositions is an article by Stanley Udy, Jr., which is an effort to subsume the extant literature on comparative organizations by the formulation of somewhat abstract generalizations.[1] . . .

Explanation of Major Findings of Congress

The propositions about organizations from Udy and March and Simon may be placed in one of two categories, depending upon the reference of the independent variable: (1) propositions in which the environment of the organization is the independent variable, and (b) propositions in which either the organization itself or its membership is the independent variable. We will first consider three propositions which specify the environment or social setting as the independent variable. These three propositions help to explain seven of the descriptive statements about Congress enumerated at the beginning of this paper. The numbers in parentheses following each proposition refer to the descriptive statements (see above) being subsumed. We will then proceed to discuss four propositions in which organizational factors are the independent variables.

Environmental Determinants

1a. *The more highly differentiated the social setting, the more salient the organization itself.*[2]

Since outcomes of legislatures are public policies, this proposition asserts that although any setting undoubtedly affects an organization's output, the more differentiated and less unitary the setting the greater will be the effects of the organization itself in determining the organization's outcomes.

Applying this general proposition to Congress, it has often been suggested that Congress does not simply ratify the requests from its environment (including requests from the executive, interest groups, public opinion, political parties, etc.), but that the organization itself has a major impact on matters of public policy. It is even suggested that the American Congress is probably more powerful vis-à-vis the executive than are most other national legislatures. One explanation of this independence, as this first proposition suggests, is that the United States Congress may be classed with those formal organizations which face a relatively more differentiated environment. The social setting of the British Parliament, for example, is a good deal less highly differentiated given the fact that the diversity of interests which exist are already aggregated as a strong, cohesive, majority party which presents the bulk of requests. In Britain, of course, Parliament is not a highly salient political institution in terms of its independent impact on public policy. This observation may lead to a general hypothesis about legislatures: the independent influence which a legislature exerts will vary inversely with the centralization of other pressures. The French Assembly under the Fourth Republic could have a greater impact on public policy than the French Assembly in the Fifth Republic. In the former centralization of pressure was rather weak; in the latter it is relatively strong.

1b. *The more highly differentiated the social setting, the more decentralized the decisional apparatus, the greater the amount of internal communication and group interaction, and the greater the expectation of high commitment of members.* (2, 12, and 5)

Part b of this proposition asserts that not only will a diffuse and non-unitary environment make the organization more important as a determiner of its own decisions, but such an environment will also affect how the body is organized and how its members behave. An organization which faces a more unitary environment will be less likely to have an elaborate decentralized decision-making structure. It will also have less internal communication and less commitment of its members to the organization (which may, incidentally, also help to explain why a more centralized decision-structure is necessary).

The fact that Congress is subjected to a wide breadth and diffuseness of external pressures is documented without contradiction in the literature on Congress as well as in the relevant literatures on interest groups, political parties, public opinion, and public administration. The literature, of course, also supports the findings that Congress is highly decentralized, has a large amount of internal communication and interaction, and a high commitment of members to the organization.

It is also interesting to observe that propositions 1a. and 1b. are probably mutually reinforcing. That is, an organization which has an important independent influence on its own decisions is also an organization where one would expect the commitment of members to be high. Similarly, an organization where commitment of its members is low is much more likely to be hierarchically organized (in order to force compliance) than an organization where commitment is high.

The amount of differentiation in the social setting, then, affects four important variables, some of which also influence (or at least are consistent with) the others.

2. *The . . . greater the amount of pressure exerted on the organization from the social setting, the greater the emphasis on administration.* (10)

In this proposition "administration" may mean at least three things: (1) routine tasks, (2) elaborate rules and procedures, and (3) complexity of leadership structure. Although we are primarily interested in the latter, all three meanings of the term are consistent with congressional findings. Proposition 2, then, asserts that organizations will vary in amount of routine tasks, the elaboration of rules and procedures, and leadership complexity and that one of the factors affecting the extent of "administration" is the amount of pressure exerted on the organization from the environment.

Studies of Congress attest to the large amount of outside pressure which is exerted on its members (from interest groups, constituents, executive agencies, party leaders, etc.) and also to the large amount of time which is spent by Congressmen and Senators on routine tasks (answering the mail, going to meetings, "making a record," etc.), the rather elaborate rules and procedures in both bodies, and the relatively complicated leadership structure. As is suggested by the general proposition, the two sets of factors, amount of pressure and amount of administration, are related in organizations other than Congress as well.

Another way to state this proposition is in terms of work overload. Congressmen and Senators are literally deluged with requests, information, and "pressure." The three administrative responses of routine, rules, and role structure are efforts to cope with this overload.

3. *The greater the degree of conflict with the social setting, the greater the amount of authority exercised at all levels, and the more cohesive the group structure.* (11, 8)

Authority exercised by leaders in Congress is relatively small. Committee chairmen, the Speaker, the Majority and Minority Leaders, etc., are not able to command support although they do bargain for it. The literature suggests that leaders do have rewards and punishments to dispense, but all agree that the size of these resources is relatively small. Similarly, although the group structure in Congress is important and extensive it is not cohesive.

These features follow from the independent variable in the above proposition, that is, Congress as an organization is not in conflict with the social setting. Rather, one would more accurately describe the relationship as being *in league* with the social setting. This comes about in two ways. First, Congressmen and Senators have constituents to court and care for, and they in fact spend an enormous amount of time doing just that. Estimates of time spent on constituency affairs range as high as ninety percent. Congressmen and Senators may, in fact, be in conflict with certain segments of the population, but not a majority of their own constituents (at least not publicly).

Second, it has been pointed out numerous times that although in some senses the executive branch and Congress are in conflict, in most matters legislators work hand in glove with the administrative departments which they oversee. Of course, the amount of cooperation undoubtedly varies in the House and Senate from committee to committee, but by and large relations with executive agencies are cordial and friendly, not hostile.

Another aspect of these same phenomena of lack of strong authority and low cohesion is the fact that Congress exhibits a good deal of intraorganizational conflict, not only between the parties but within parties as well. It would also be expected that this would be true of other organizations which have non-conflictual environmental relations, a fact which might suggest that relationships between organizational variables in Congress might also be generalizable to other organizations.

These three environmental factors, extent of differentiation, amount of pressure, and degree of conflict help to explain a wide range of congressional phenomena in particular (statements 1, 2, 5, 8, 10, 11, and 12 in the list at the beginning of this paper), and organizational phenomena in general.

Organizational Determinants

In the previous three propositions the environment or social setting has been the major independent variable. In this section we will consider propositions in which the independent variable is intra-organizational.

4. *The more permanent the organization, the lower its turnover rate, and the less mechanized the technology, the higher the salience of its group structure.* (9).

One of the features of Congress which has intrigued several recent writers on Congress is the important role which informal groups and group norms have in affecting the way in which Congressmen do their work. It has long been known, since Woodrow Wilson's *Congressional Government*, [3] that committees and subcommittees play an all but overwhelming role in Congressional deliberations. But not only are these more formal groups now recognized as important cogs in the decision-making apparatus, but informal groups such as state delegations, voluntary clubs such as the Democratic Study Group in the House, informal groups of individuals within committees and subcommittees, and even larger groups such as the "conservative coalition," are being given increasingly more attention. Both the House and the Senate have a large number of informal groups as well as formal ones.

Causal proposition 4 asserts that the permanence of an organization, its relatively low turnover, and an unmechanized technology help to produce in organizations generally a highly salient group structure. Congress is certainly a permanent organization. Less well known, however, is the fact that turnover from Congress to Congress is relatively low, averaging about fifteen percent in the House of Representatives every two years.[4] That is, approximately eighty-five percent of all Congressmen remain in Congress from one election to the next. The turnover in leadership positions, of course, is even smaller. In addition Congress is noted for its resistance to mechanization. Even such simple things as the installation of electric voting devices have failed to attract much enthusiasm among Congressmen and Senators. Most members of Congress pick up their information about what is going on as a result of talking with others. Televising the proceedings in each chamber, with closed-circuit outlets in each office would certainly be an aid to the members in determining when their presence on the floor might be desired. Rather than this, however, reliance is placed on word of mouth, and such low mechanization items as the telephone.

In addition to the high salience of the group structure, or more likely as a consequence of it, a number of informal norms have developed which help to protect the members and preserve stability. In a body in which members will be in contact with one another over long periods of time, and in which the technology of the organization is almost entirely social, it is not surprising to find that informal ways of doing things grow up which help to avoid serious threats to the stability and functioning of the organization. The seniority rule, senatorial courtesy, restrained debate, and even the so-called "Senate type," are undoubtedly a product of this. No issue is worth the destruction of the institution—members will have to deal with other members over a wide range of issues and over long periods of time. Legislators are, in effect, socialized into rules which specify that one must not jeopardize his ability to play future games by seriously discombobulating other members.

5. *The greater the need for technical expertise, the more salient the membership.* (4)

Not only is Congress as an organization highly salient (essentially because of its highly differentiated environment), and groups within Congress important (causal proposition 4), but its members may also become significant figures in the development of public policy. Undoubtedly, as this proposition suggests, part of the reason why this is true is the importance attached to technical knowledge about very complicated matters of public policy. Such expertise may lie in a substantive field like housing or tax matters, or in parliamentary skills. In any event members may become influential by the amount of information about a topic which they have at their command.

This factor of technical expertise also helps to explain why some Congressmen are more important than others and why periods of apprenticeship are developed within the institution. A number of norms of behavior, in fact, revolve around the learning of technical expertise. Freshman members are expected not to participate extensively in debate, to speak only about what they know, and generally to watch and listen rather than participate. One source of power in the House and Senate is information and, like other technical skills, it must be learned. Additional support is given to this hypothesis by the deference which is paid to those who have information and skills. . . .

6. *The larger the size of the organization, the greater the number of subgroups in it; hence the greater the overall emphasis on formal and impersonal rules and specificity of roles.* (3, 6, 7)

This proposition helps us in two ways. First, both the House and Senate are relatively large organizations. For example, in 1960 more than ninety-five percent of the 4.7 million business organizations in the United States had less than one hundred employees. Even without counting the large supporting staffs in the House and Senate, each is larger than this figure. We would expect, then, that both houses of Congress would have a relatively large number of subgroups, formal and impersonal rules, and high specificity of roles.

But the fact that membership in the House is over four times that of the Senate would also suggest that the House, as compared with the Senate, would have a larger number of subgroups, a more complex and impersonal set of rules, and greater role specificity. The data indicate that each of these is true. Although the data on social groups is incomplete, in formal group structures the House in the Eighty-ninth Congress (1965–66) had 20 committees and 125 subcomittees, whereas the comparable figures for the Senate were 16 and 99. On the question of role specificity, Representatives are usually members of only one committee whereas Senators normally have three or more committee assignments. In addition fifty-one percent of Senate Democrats have two or more committee or subcommittee chairmanships whereas only twelve percent of House Democrats play such multiple roles. The data on rules and procedures is somewhat more difficult to summarize, but existing evidence supports the contention that House rules are more elaborate, formal, and impersonal than are Senate rules.

7. *The extent of use of analytic processes to resolve conflict is a function of the type of organizational conflict involved. The more organizational conflict represents individual rather than intergroup conflict, the greater the use of analytic procedures. The more organizational conflict represents intergroup differences, the greater the use of bargaining.* (13)

This proposition simply asserts that bargaining as a method of reaching agreement will be prevalent in organizations which have group conflict as opposed to analytic problem-solving devices in individual conflict. The processes of log-rolling, compromise, and side-payments are widely used to reach majority agreement in committees, subcommittees, and on the floor of both the House and Senate. The reasons for intergroup conflict in Congress are, of course, obvious. Disagreements in Congress reflect, generally, the cleavages within society. Such cleavages include ideological differences (e.g., over the role of the federal government), religion, race, region, social class, and many others. Small groups of Congressmen and Senators may think somewhat alike on such matters, but putting together a majority coalition with respect to any single policy which touches on one or more cleavages usually results in extensive bargaining.

These last four intraorganizational propositions, then, account for the remaining six descriptive statements about Congress (3, 4, 6, 7, 9, and 13).

Summary

We began this paper with thirteen major propositions about Congress. Each was subsumed under a more general empirical proposition about formal organizations derived independently of any data on Congress but which fit other formal organizations. We can now briefly summarize, diagrammatically, the major relationships (see Figure 1).

In each of the thirteen explanations there is no recourse to factors peculiar to Congress (and hence no problem in proving the validity of unique explanations). In addition several additional findings about Congress were cast in a more general language to suggest that they too may not be peculiar to only one formal organization. . . .

FIGURE 1. Summary relationships.

Independent Variables

Setting   *Organizational*

Congressional Dependent Variables

	Policy	*Organization*	*Members*	*Group Structure*	*Leadership*	*Process*

1. highly differentiated

2. amount of pressure

3. low conflict

4. high permanence
   low turnover
   low mechanization

5. high technical expertise

6. size

7. intergroup conflict

1. high salience of Congress

2. high decentralization

3. high formal and impersonal rules

4. high salience of members

5. high commitment

6. large number of subgroups

7. high specificity of roles

8. low cohesion

9. high salience of group structure

10. high complexity of leadership

11. low authority

12. higher internal communications

13. bargaining

329

Notes

1. Stanley H. Udy, Jr., "The Comparative Analysis of Organizations," in James G. March (ed.), *Handbook of Organizations* (Chicago: Rand McNally, 1965), pp. 678–709. Proposition seven comes from James G. March and Herbert A. Simon, *Organizations* (New York: Wiley, 1958), p. 130.
2. This part of proposition one is actually a deduction from two others: The more highly differentiated . . . the social setting, the less salient it will be; the less salient the social setting . . . the more salient the organization itself; therefore. . . . By "differentiated" is meant dispersed, heterogeneous, plural, non-unitary. By "salient" is meant important as an influence on the output of the organization.
3. (New York, Meridian Books, 1956.) This book was first published in 1885.
4. See Samuel P. Huntington, "Congressional Responses to the Twentieth Century," in David B. Truman (ed.), *The Congress and America's Future* (Englewood Cliffs: Prentice-Hall, 1965); Nelson W. Polsby, "The Institutionalization of the House of Representatives," paper delivered at the 1966 Annual Meeting of the American Political Science Association. . . .

25

Power as Process in Regulation
Laura Nader and David Serber

Law has been analyzed by scholars as a mechanism which maintains order in society. Whose order, however, is a question that is rarely asked. One observation that we illustrate in this paper is that powerful classes and groups shape the legal structure so that it serves their own narrow interests.

National law is a mechanism and a process which may be used to distribute or centralize power, or it may be used to legitimate and maintain power groups. In this paper our general concern is to improve our understanding of the direction and nature of controlling processes. This concern relates directly to the debate over the respective roles of formal government apparatus and informal controlling groups in ruling nation-states, and as well to the debate as to how change is best accomplished. Informal processes are often more important than formal processes in the shaping of the legal system. Knowledge of the formal and informal processes by which the powerful maintain control could enable the powerless to more effectively mobilize their resources to force a redistribution of power. Social scientists have an important role to play in obtaining and disseminating this information.

In the sociological literature on power attention has been paid to

Excerpt from "Law and the Distribution of Power" in Lewis A. Coser and Otto N. Larsen, eds., *The Uses of Controversy in Sociology*, New York: The Free Press, A Division of Macmillan Publishing Co., Inc., 1976, pp. 273–291.

legal structures and the way in which such structures have been used to maintain incipient or entrenched social stratification (see, e.g., Carlin et al., 1967; Sutherland, 1968). In the United States today there is a striking imbalance of power, if power is to be measured by accumulated capital and income. Yet we still know relatively little about the structures and processes which function either to equalize or redistribute power on the one hand, or to further increase and maintain an imbalance of power on the other. Nor is there any comprehensive understanding of law and the distribution of power in other parts of the world and in other kinds of societies which would help us to develop a model for legal development. We need to know whether national legal systems are performing similar functions independent of cultural difference, and whether these similar functions may be related to the larger framework of the world's economy. . . .

Much of the recent research on social structure in the United States concludes that the government tends to function in the interest of the corporate rather than the public sector (see Domhoff, 1970; Miliband, 1969; O'Connor, 1973). Power structure researchers have attempted to demonstrate "ruling class" control of various state institutions through network studies revealing consistent patterns of cross-cutting linkages between personnel in the monopoly segment of the economy and the government (see Domhoff, 1975). What we still have not documented, however, are the processes by which state policy and its administration is controlled or what the nature of that control is. However, researchers imply that the formal processes of courts, government agencies, and elected bodies may not be the loci of this control and that increased access by powerless people to the formal processes of the state is unlikely to affect power equalization (Galanter, 1974). For example, the formal process of selection of public officeholders in the United States is structured to equalize power. Theoretically, every citizen has equal access to the ballot box and no person's vote is weighted more than another's. Yet the informal process by which individuals are selected to seek public office tends to be dominated by those who either control the capital or have access to the capital necessary to run a successful election campaign.

"Power Equalizers"

State and federal regulatory agencies are the classic examples of state institutions which have been organized to function as "power equalizers," that is, their stated role is to protect consumer interests by regulating various aspects of big business. Yet, as with the legal system, this goal is merely rhetorical, as their practice serves the interests in the industry they are intended to regulate. It is common knowledge in the fields of political economy and public policy that regulatory agencies are substantially captured by the regulated.[1] But, as M. Bernstein has pointed out (1972: 21). "Our thinking about the regulatory process and the independent commissions, as much of our thinking about the state, remains impressionistic, and the need for empirical research is largely unfulfilled." In order to understand effective and ineffective responses to access and equalization we must understand the processes by which these agencies are captured.

The type of research Bernstein is discussing here goes beyond studying formal procedures, tracing complex linkages, or analyzing policy; he is implicitly proposing the study of informal process by which regulatory policy and practice are developed and carried out. It is a study of the processes of power in action, not simply the structure of power and the results of its influence. This type of research would involve not only firsthand field work among those who are active in the government agency and legislatures, but also field work among those industry representatives who are actually involved in persistently undermining the potential "power equalization" function of regulation.

Insurance Regulation

Insurance regulation in California epitomizes the actual and ideological patterns of the relationship between the industry, the state, and the public. The law originally mandating insurance regulation in California embodies the fundamental contradiction of government regulation. On the one hand, it outlines the duties of the insurance commissioner on behalf of the consuming public, and on the other hand, the duties of the commissioner on behalf of the private industry in adequately supervising and maintaining "the financial stability" of the insurance companies licensed in California. . . . In terms of the actual regulatory practice the term "financial stability" has become a euphemism for industry profit maximization. Despite the fact that more often than not public interests tend to be in conflict with the interests of maintaining "industry stability," the practice of the department is to "safeguard" consumer interests by promoting continued industry growth and profits.

Given this statutory mandate, let us examine examples of the actual process of insurance regulation in California and Pennsylvania. In both states there are two primary types of influence by which the industry becomes an active participant in the regulatory process (Serber, 1975). One consists of the building of long-term informal relationships with both the regulators and the legislators at all levels throughout the legislative and regulatory hierarchies. The effect of this type of influence is operative in the day-to-day regulatory and legislative activities. The relationship desired by industry is achieved through various types of collegial interaction and gift-giving by the industry. Many of the regulators are recruited from industry and/or have a promise of positions in industry—the delayed bribe, this is sometimes called.

On the level of the regulatory agency the regulators, excepting isolated instances, are not being "bought off" by the industry in the way that police may be by narcotics dealers or underworld syndicates. The mechanisms are more subtle and complex. The process by which this type of influence is established centers around making the regulators feel a privileged and personal part of the social milieu of industry rather than a part of the public, thereby negating the motivation to make the agency function as a power-equalizing institution working in the interests of the people.

Normal regulatory activities frequently involve industry representatives meeting with middle-level regulators. The social status of these civil servants is relatively low, and not only does their work tend to be boring and routinized, but there is little room for any type of professional autonomy, just as the hierarchy leaves little room for personal autonomy. . . . The industry representatives who deal with the departments, on the other hand, are of a relatively high status. The company presidents, vice-presidents, successful corporate attorneys, or professional lobbyists who come into the department consciously interact with the civil servants in a friendly, cordial, and respectful fashion, unlike the way these civil servants are so often treated by those higher up on the bureaucratic ladder. When a lobbyist and a few company vice-presidents take a supervisor, assistant supervisor, and an insurance officer out to lunch at an elegant restaurant they are not necessarily bribing them, they are attempting to make them feel important and to reaffirm their continuing relations. Many regulators come to measure their success as civil servants by the quality of their relationships with higher-status industry representatives:

> Formally I was quite successful in the Department of Insurance. I advanced quite quickly. But the real measure of success is informal. Informally, Jesus! I had a list of references, I mean fifteen company presidents. I'd say I was pretty successful. [A former attorney for the California Department of Insurance]

It is through this process that the industry is successfully transformed from an adversary to an esteemed reference group or a client in the consciousness of many regulators.

The establishment of long-term influence of an informal nature involves the general adoption of a set of expectations and attitudes by the regulators which are the basis for behavior in everyday regulatory practice. Despite the civil service system, acceptance of industry's sets of ideas and behaviors governs advancement of individuals within the bureaucracy. We can show how people lose their jobs when they do not follow this pattern (Nader, Petkaf, and Blackwell, 1972).

> Knowledge of the insurance code . . . is never tested in any exam administered to us. They pick out who they want and they put on a little show and pretend there is some authenticity and fairness. The criterion is being close to the Commissioner and his immediate assistants. And that always reflects their interpretation of the law and policy of regulation. Those people who know what companies and issues not to touch and do what the Commissioner and his assistants would like them to with a smile are those who advance. If you don't go along with their decisions with a smile you can forget it. The kind of people they want to advance are those who know the line. I mean this on many levels; socially, politically and regulatory. [California Department of Insurance Attorneys]

In this sense the rigid hierarchy and spurious meritocracy of the bureaucratic structure perpetuates informal industry influence within the regulatory agency.

This type of long-term influence establishes a firm social base for the second type of influence, which is instrumental in nature and involves the manipulation of specific regulatory activities and policies, and usually operates at the top levels of the agency. Without the access provided by the long-term yet nonspecific influence, direct instrumental control over the individual cases would be far more problematic for the industry. In this sense the establishment and maintenance of long-term informal influence is more critical for the industry than their effectiveness in determining the substance and direction of any one particular piece of legislation or agency regulation.

The maintenance of the staff–industry relationship may also function as an important protective barrier to change if the traditional network connections are severed at the top levels of the agency. In both California and Pennsylvania, as network-oriented research would suggest, the commissioner of insurance is either drafted from industry or is actively involved with industry representatives in social clubs or other informal settings. Yet occasionally a maverick who does not see himself as a member of that community is appointed and attempts to establish and maintain an adversarial relationship with the industry. This occurred in Pennsylvania between 1971 and early 1974. The commissioner, Herbert S. Denenberg, actively attempted to regulate in the interest of the public in order to end industry influence in the regulatory process. In effect Denenberg was attempting to transform the Department of Insurance into the power-equalizing institution the ideology would suggest it should be.

Denenberg's strategy to reform regulation was primarily composed of three aspects. The thrust of his approach was to publicize, through an extensive media campaign, the abuses of consumers by the insurance industry. The goals of this strategy were to bring public pressure on the insurance industry to reform some of its practices, to gain public support for Denenberg's regulatory policies, and to raise the level of public awareness of exploitation by industry. The second aspect was to increase public awareness of the problems of the Department of Insurance. The third aspect of the strategy was to sever the relationships previously existing between the regulators and the industry.

Denenberg maintained his extreme adversarial position throughout his term and increased public access to the formal insurance complaint remedies of the agency. However, he was unable to transform the agency itself. The relationship of the industry with the regulatory staff successfully functioned to maintain the perspective of industry in day-to-day regulation. Furthermore, civil service staff members successfully undermined attempts by the commissioner to implement proconsumer policies potentially damaging to the industry. Many of these programs had to be abandoned because of staff sabotage (Serber, forthcoming). The locus of the industry's instrumental influence in the regulatory agency was shifted from the commissioner to the civil service staff. New regulations specifically aimed at severing the informal relationships between the civil service staff and the industry were proposed by Denenberg, but were never implemented. The proposal to draft a formal regulation forbidding staff members to meet industry representatives for lunch (paid or unpaid) or to accept gifts encountered so much resistance by staff that Denenberg was forced to abandon the idea.

Not all civil service workers were unsympathetic to the attempted reforms of the administration, though the cynicism and passivity of these bureaucrats made them easily susceptible to the pressure which was exerted by the industry and those regulators closest to the industry. Furthermore, the staff was aware that Denenberg would not be reappointed (as industry promised) and that the next commissioner would seek to maintain a "better," more amicable relationship with industry. Fearing reprisals from industry and those higher up in the bureaucracy, even proreform civil service staff, continued to work closely with industry:

Part of the problem of reorganizing the Department of Insurance is that the staff fights you. When you try to regulate the industry they have an instinctive feeling that one way or another this is the only thing that could eventually cost them their job and any career possibilities in insurance they might have. And in most cases they are right. [An assistant to Commissioner Dennenberg]

Not only did Denenberg's own staff function to negate the attempts at reform but the legislature, where industry long-term and instrumental influence is strong, actively prevented any legal institutionalization of the attempted reforms. Not a single bill which was sponsored by Denenberg and strongly opposed by industry was passed by the Pennsylvania State Legislature during Denenberg's entire administration.

Denenberg's highly visible anti-insurance industry public relations program to gain public support may have created the illusion for vast numbers of people that the industry was now being regulated in the public interest, and that Denenberg had made the ideology of power equalization a reality. In effect Denenberg's attempted reform of insurance regulation in Pennsylvania may have strengthened the power relationships previously existing rather than equalizing power, and may also have strengthened the ideology of regulation, while industry's informal influence continued and continues to dominate insurance regulation in Pennsylvania.

In both the California and Pennsylvania cases we discover that the insurance industry does not dictate regulation in an instrumental fashion, except upon occasion. Rather industry's techniques of informal influence and the structure and subculture of the bureaucracy integrate the regulator into the industry, and as well integrate the industry into the regulatory process. Informal influence increases industry power which already exists in terms of the wealth and resources it commands as the second largest industry in the world.[2] However, such informal influence or control of an institution ideologically dedicated to power equalization permits the industry to continue its expansion while appearing to be regulated. Furthermore, such informal control has the built-in feature of *nearly* being reform-proof.

Informal Regulatory Process

Despite the apparent impermeability of industry influence, there is at least one potential conflict within the system of regulation itself which becomes apparent when studying the informal processes of regulation. The conflict lies in the experiences of workers in the regulatory agency. Being a public servant, yet not serving the public interest, but in fact having material success determined by how effectively the worker undermines the public interest, is a contradiction. A growing portion of employees are sensitive to this situation and would welcome a chance to work creatively in the interests of the public.

In the case presented here we have found that an analysis which focuses on leadership alone, or which concentrates on models of change which are uninformed of informal regulatory processes, is inadequate for understanding industry control of a regulatory agency. One must examine the social organization and subculture of the regulatory process. Such analyses have important implications in developing models of change or reform of such state institutions. Policy studies of administrative agencies and state regulatory commissions such as those produced by the Brookings Institution (Knolls, 1974) and the Ash Commission have developed models of change which are uninformed of informal regulatory process. As a result the model of change generated by these studies focuses on leadership, formal procedures, and public access rather than informal relationships between the state and industry which are a result of both the wealth and organization of the industry and the structure and subculture of the state bureaucracies.

There is a qualitative aspect to this process which can only be achieved through the qualitative type of research summarized above. It is inadequate to look at the question of power manipulation simply as a mechanical process. One cannot get at the actual social organization of the process by just looking at legal structures or formal relationships between legal structures, because, in fact, the social organization functions through sets of informal relationships based on individuals and their perception of their life chances. We cannot, either empirically or theoretically, entirely separate the actual power relations from how people feel about these relations. Without looking at how people interpret their own life chances, whether they are working in the courts, in Congress, in regulatory agencies, or in industry, we cannot adequately understand or demonstrate how power functions.

In the setting of the regulatory processes described above it is clear that people interpret their life chances in terms of their own private individual advancement and profit.

Ultimately, all you have to look forward to in Civil Service is promotion to the next job; incompetence won't bar you from that next job, but getting somebody in the industry really angry at you, getting involved in a real furor, will. And a civil servant knows that, you train a man, it's like training a puppy—you can tell him what you want him to do, but he knows that's not

what you want him to do. He has gotten his nose spanked with a newspaper
or has seen somebody else being spanked.

. . . there's the savagery of the inner office struggle in the Department to
get that next job, which results in more and more Machiavellian and Byzantine type people at each level up. The competition for the next job is murder-
ous. They're jockeying for attention and developing techniques for bypassing
your next superior and down-grading him if he's weak and getting the men
above him and brown-nosing him if he's strong. . . . [A former high-level
employee, California Department of Insurance]

In this cultural milieu the idea of power equalization is not taken
seriously by people at all levels. Returning to the question of models
of reform, the kind of data discussed here is indispensable in developing a model which may bring the ideology of power equalization in
line with practice. The current conceptual model of the state and its
regulatory agencies is based on the attempt to represent a collective
public by individual bureaucrats who are looking for private gains,
and is a contradiction which impedes reform of the sort based solely
on leadership, access, and formal procedures.

Law and Power

The degree to which law functions as a power equalizer will depend on a number of factors, such as who controls the courts, or
who controls the civil servants, or whether there is easy access to
adversarial representatives such as lawyers. There is in all societies
some contradiction between the ideology governing legal structures
and how such structures operate in reality. However, gross contradictions are most likely to appear in communities characterized by
social and cultural diversity. Scholars who theorize about the function of law (see Nader, 1965) speak to the function of the ideology
of law rather than to the functions of the law in action. Clearly, law
functions to equalize power, to insure fairness, and also to legitimize
the dominance relations of some cultures or subcultures over others.
One needs only to scan the cases decided on merit, to examine the
subject matter of public-interest litigation, or to see who it is that
sits in our jails to document these functions. In the examples given
in this chapter, however, the suggestion is being made that in isolated
indigenous societies a variety of functions may appear, but in industrialized and highly stratified countries characterized also by
cultural diversity the weight of law as equalizer appears light in
comparison to the power derived from the routine actions of law.
There is public-interest litigation that is addressing problems that
result from an imbalance in power. Nevertheless, unless government

provides plaintiffs as well as defendants with lawyers, unless the legislatures focus more on prevention, it is likely that increased industrialization and class stratification will make it improbable that legal structures will in the main be used for purposes of power distribution.

In isolated, homogeneous societies there is a kind of social control that stems from the fact that people in conflict know each other and share a broad range of interpersonal ties and consensus about power relations. Individuals are dependent on each other for their social welfare. In the United States there is a general absence of the kind of community social control so usual in isolated societies. Economics is crucial here. When individuals are no longer dependent on each other for their economic welfare the tendency is for the powerful to manipulate available legal means for exclusive advantage. The case of the United States illustrates the relation between economic conditions, the relative distribution of power, and the kinds of legal mechanisms used and outcome sought. Without community social control the lack of access to individual and class legal action is all the more striking. In the absence of the main avenues by which order is traditionally maintained in society, power is likely to be abused by the powerful and the response is likely to be self-help. Self-help can be negative, as with increased incidence of theft, or positive, as with the work of such groups as California Citizen Action Groups.

For many reasons Americans today tend to bypass the courts, which theoretically could be functioning as power equalizers. There are two different strategies used by people to deal positively with the lack of state responsiveness to their needs. The first is to mobilize their resources to obtain the influence of those occupying formal positions sufficiently high in the system to at least attempt to equalize power. Political machines such as that of Daley are built on such demands. Our analyses of consumer complaint letters show that increasingly people use strategies such as the carbon-copy strategy—sending letters of complaint, then building up a support group by sending copies of the complaint letter to individuals thought to be of the same or higher level of power as the person being complained about. Problems with government bureaucracies such as social security, workmen's compensation, taxation are taken increasingly to Congressmen. Other problems go to Action Lines, to volunteer consumer action groups, to consumer advocates, to attorney-generals' offices. The alternative strategy is to deal collectively with conflict, rather than individually with complaints. As people discover the difference between making a specific complaint and a general complaint that is preventative in orientation, People's Lobbies, tenants' unions, rank-and-file union caucuses, and other groups are organized.

Americans since 1960 are responding to their powerlessness and inventing mechanisms which are not embedded either in formal or codified law; rather, these extrajudicial mechanisms are part of a developing American customary law which is independent of but affected by our national law. We are in the early stages of building support groups to function as power equalizers, much in the way that the small isolated communities such as the Zapotec have done over the centuries. Such support groups need to be informed of the informal processes by which private interests manipulate institutions of the state if they are to be more effective than previous government responses to the need for reform, responses which accept as a norm industry power and the subculture of bureaucratic society. These developing efforts at community or consumer control, based on group rather than individual advancement, could provide a common focus for those currently isolated workers within the state bureaucracy whose role as public servant has become meaningless in the face of industry control of their work place.

Conclusion

Studies of power processes are extremely important in developing directions for change. For example, if rank-and-file workers wanted to make critical changes in established labor unions, it would be essential to understand not only who the leadership of the union was and their relationship to the bosses, but also what the conflicts and weak points of the system were and the process by which the needs of the rank and file are subjected to the demands of the company and the union bureaucracy. If citizens were organizing a controlling voice in a comprehensive national health care program, it would be critical to know not only what powerful interests are seeking to profit from the control of such a program (such as the insurance industry or the medical profession), but also the processes by which such control is sought. As anthropologists we believe our contribution in the study of power is not only in demonstrating that the public interest *is* undermined, but in laying out in detail *how* it is undermined, in order to help the understanding of those citizen groups who are working to transform vastly unequal power relations. . . .

In the past most social scientists who have been concerned with social policy have looked to those in power to make reforms. Yet it has been shown that reforms made by and through this homogeneous class of people, without the input of varied citizen groups, do not function in the public interest.

References

Bernstein, Marver (1972). "Independent regulatory agencies: A perspective on their reform." In Marver Bernstein (ed.), *The Government as Regulator. Annals of The American Academy of Political and Social Sciences*, vol. 400 (March).

Carlin, J. E., J. Howard, and S. L. Messinger (1967). *Civil justice and the poor. Issues for Sociological Research*. New York: Russell Sage.

Domhoff, G. William (1970). *The Higher Circles*. New York, Random House.

Domhoff, G. William (ed.) (1975). "New directions in power structure research." Special issue of *The Insurgent Sociologist* 5, no. 3 (Spring).

Galanter, M. (1974). "Why the 'haves' come out ahead." *Law and Society Review* 9, no. 1 (Fall): 95-160.

Green, Mark (ed.) (1973). *The Monopoly Makers*. New York: Grossman.

Knolls, Roger (1974). *Reforming Regulation*. Washington, D.C.: Brookings Institution.

Kolko, Gabriel (1963). *The Triumph of Conservatism*. New York: Free Press.

—— (1965). *Railroads and Regulation*. Princeton, N.J.: Princeton University Press.

Miliband, Ralph (1969). *The State in Capitalist Society*. New York: Basic Books.

Nader, Laura. (1965). "The anthropological study of law." In *The Ethnography of Law*. Special issue of *American Anthropologist* 67: 3-32.

Nader, Ralph, P. Petkaf, and K. Blackwell (1972). *Whistle Blowing: The Report of the Conference on Professional Responsibility*. New York: Grossman.

O'Connor, James (1973). *The Fiscal Crisis of the State*. New York: St. Martin's Press.

Serber, David (1975). "Regulating reform: The social organization of insurance regulation." In G. W. Domhoff (ed.), *New Directions in Power Structure Research*. Special issue of *The Insurgent Sociologist* 5, no. 3 (Spring).

Forthcoming "Assemblyline lawyers: The proletarianization of legal professionals in the California Department of Insurance." In Karen Michaelson (ed.), *The Anthropology of the Middle Class*.

Sutherland, Edwin H. (1968). "White-collar criminality." In G. Geis (ed.), *White Collar Criminal*. New York: Atherton.

Notes

1. See Bernstein, 1972, for an excellent summary of some of the academic literature concerning regulatory agencies. See Kolko, 1963, for a discussion of the development of economic regulation by the state; and Kolko, 1965. Also see Mark Green, 1973, which contains numerous references to the political science, law, and economics literature in the extensive footnotes, pp. 347-89.

2. The insurance industry and individual insurance companies transacting business in California are the institutions involved in disputes with one individual consumer. The assets of insurance companies operating in California were $226,262,231,000 in 1969. This figure is larger than the 1969 Gross National Product of any nation in the world except the U.S.A. . . .

APPENDIX III:

LEGAL DOCUMENTS

Organizational and Interorganizational Relationships

A. National Labor Relations Act, 1935, as amended, 1947 (National Labor Relations Board)
B. *J. P. Stevens and Co., Inc. and Textile Workers of America, AFL–CIO, 1975*
C. Civil Rights Act of 1964 (Equal Employment Opportunity Commission)
D. Reorganization Plan No. 1 of 1978 (Federal Equal Employment Activities)
E. Regulation of Lobbying (1946)

Introduction

A legal system has extensive effects on the organizations within and outside its boundaries. In the course of enacting laws, a legal system, especially in a complex industrialized society, often creates "administrative agencies" charged with implementing various laws. This has become so pervasive a phenomenon in the twentieth century that these agencies have been viewed as constituting a "fourth branch of government"—as distinct from the legislative, judicial, and executive branches (Evan, 1977).

The first and third documents in this Appendix set forth some of the provisions pertaining to two administrative agencies: the National Labor Relations Board (NLRB), the the Equal Employment Opportunity Commission (EEOC). As of 1978, no less than eighteen Federal administrative agencies were charged with the responsibility for enforcing statutes, executive orders, and administrative regulations pertaining to equal employment opportunity. To solve the organizational problems arising from such a high degree of decentralization of responsibilities for implementing fair employment laws, President Carter issued an Executive Order in 1978 (Appendix III-D), transferring all enforcement responsibilities to the Equal Employment Opportunity Commission.

In Appendix III-B, an NLRB administrative decision is presented concerning an embittered conflict between a textile manufacturing firm, J. P. Stevens and Company, and the Textile Workers Union of America. As this decision makes clear, the two organizations have been engaged in a protracted conflict over a unionization campaign, and the employer has been found guilty of repeatedly violating the "unfair labor practices" provisions of the National Labor Relations Act.

Appendix III-E illustrates the impact of the law on organizations outside the legal system, and, in turn, the potential effects of such organizations on the law. In the 1946 statute requiring the registration of lobbyists, an attempt was made to monitor the efforts of those organizations that seek to influence the Federal legislative process. Once again the question can be raised as to the effectiveness of such statutes. In principle, evaluation research can identify the obstacles to implementation and the limits of the law in regulating such organizational processes (see, for example, Ahart's "Evaluating Contract Compliance" and the readings in Parts IV and V).

Taking into account the case involving J. P. Stevens and Company and the Textile Workers Union of America, inquire into the organizational impact of judicial reviews of administration decisions.

Reference

Evan, W. M. (1977). "Administrative Law and Organization Theory." *Journal of Legal Education*, 19: 106–125.

Organizational Relationships

A—National Labor Relations Act, 1935, as Amended, 1947
29 U.S.C. 141

Title I—Amendment of National Labor Relations Act

Sec. 101. The National Labor Relations Act is hereby amended to read as follows:

Findings and Policies

Section 1. The denial by some employers of the right of employees to organize and the refusal by some employers to accept the procedure of collective bargaining lead to strikes and other forms of industrial strife or unrest, which have the intent or the necessary effect of burdening or obstructing commerce by (a) impairing the efficiency, safety, or operation of the instrumentalities of commerce; (b) occurring in the current of commerce; (c) materially affecting, restraining, or controlling the flow of raw materials or manufactured or processed goods from or into the channels of commerce, or the prices of such materials or goods in commerce; or (d) causing diminution of employment and wages in such volume as substantially to impair or disrupt the market for goods flowing from or into the channels of commerce.

The inequality of bargaining power between employees who do not possess full freedom of association or actual liberty of contract, and employers who are organized in the corporate or other forms of ownership association substantially burdens and affects the flow of commerce, and tends to aggravate recurrent business depressions, by depressing wage rates and the purchasing power of wage earners in industry and by preventing the stabilization of competitive wage rates and working conditions within and between industries.

Experience has proved the protection by law of the right of employees to organize and bargain collectively safeguards commerce from injury, impairment, or interruption, and promotes the flow of commerce by removing certain recognized sources of industrial strife and unrest, by encouraging practices fundamental to the friendly adjustment of industrial disputes arising out of differences as to wages, hours, or other working conditions, and by restoring equality of bargaining power between employers and employees.

Experience has further demonstrated that certain practices by some labor organizations, their officers, and members have the intent or the necessary effect of burdening or obstructing commerce by preventing the free flow of goods in such commerce through strikes and other forms of industrial unrest or through concerted activities which impair the interest of the public in the free flow of such commerce. The elimination of such practices is a necessary condition to the assurance of the rights herein guaranteed.

It is hereby declared to be the policy of the United States to eliminate the causes of certain substantial obstructions to the free flow of commerce and to mitigate and eliminate these obstructions when they have occurred by encouraging the practice and procedure of collective bargaining and by protecting the exercise by workers of full freedom of association, self-organization, and designation of representatives of their own choosing, for the purpose of negotiating the terms and conditions of their employment or other mutual aid or protection. . . .

National Labor Relations Board

Sec. 3. (a) The National Labor Relations Board (hereinafter called the "Board") created by this Act prior to its amendment by the Labor Management Relations Act, 1947, is hereby continued as an agency of the United States, except that the Board shall consist of five instead of three members, appointed by the President by and with the advice and consent of the Senate. Of the two additional members so provided for, one shall be appointed for a term of five years and the other for a term of two years. Their successors, and the successors of the other members, shall be appointed for terms of five years each, excepting that any individual chosen to fill a vacancy shall be appointed only for the unexpired term of the member whom he shall succeed. The President shall designate one member to serve as Chairman of the Board. Any member of the Board may be removed by the President, upon notice and hearing, for neglect of duty of malfeasance in office, but for no other cause.

(b) The Board is authorized to delegate to any group of three or more members any or all of the powers which it may itself exercise. The Board is also authorized to delegate to its regional directors its powers under section 9 to determine the unit appropriate for the purpose of collective bargaining, to investigate and provide for hearings, and determine whether a question of representation exists, and to direct an election or take a secret ballot under subsection (c) or (e) of section 9 and certify the results thereof, except that upon the filing of a request therefor with the Board by any interested person, the Board may review any action of a regional director delegated to him under this paragraph, but such a review shall not, unless specifically ordered by the Board, operate as a stay of any action taken by the regional director. A vacancy in the Board shall not impair the right of the remaining members to exercise all of the powers of the Board, except that two members shall constitute a quorum of any group designated pursuant to the first sentence hereof. The Board shall have an official seal which shall be judicially noticed. . . .

(d) There shall be a General Counsel of the Board who shall be appointed by the President, by and with the advice and consent of the Senate, for a term of four years. The General Counsel of the Board shall exercise general supervision over all attorneys employed by the Board (other than trial examiners and legal assistants to Board members) and over the officers and employees in the regional offices. He shall have final authority, on behalf of the Board, in respect of the investigation of charges and issuance of complaints under section 10, and in respect of the prosecution of such complaints before the Board, and shall have such other duties as the Board may prescribe or as may by provided by law. . . .

Rights of Employees

Sec. 7. Employees shall have the right to self-organization to form, join, or assist labor organizations, to bargain collectively through representatives of their own choosing, and to engage in other concerted activities for the purpose of collective bargaining or other mutual aid or protection, and shall also have the right to refrain from any or all of such activities except to the extent that such right may be affected by an agreement requiring membership in a labor organization as a condition of employment as authorized in section 8(a) (3).

Unfair Labor Practices

Sec. 8. (a) It shall be an unfair labor practice for an employer—

(1) to interfere with, restrain, or coerce employees in the exercise of the rights guaranteed in section 7;

(2) to dominate or interfere with the formation or administration of any labor organization or contribute financial or other support to it: *Provided,* That subject to rules and regulations made and published by the Board pursuant to section 6, an employer shall not be prohibited from permitting employees to confer with him during working hours without loss of time or pay;

(3) by discrimination in regard to hire or tenure of employment or any term or condition of employment to encourage or discourage membership in any labor organization: *Provided,* That nothing in this Act, or in any other statute of the United States, shall preclude an employer from making an agreement with a labor organization (not established, maintained, or assisted by any action defined in section 8(a) of this Act as an unfair labor practice) to require as a condition of employment membership therein on or after the thirtieth day following the beginning of such employment or the effective date of such agreement, whichever is the later, (i) if such labor organization is the representative of the employees as provided in section 9(a), in the appropriate collective-bargaining unit covered by such agreement when made, and (ii) unless following an election held as provided in section 9(e) within one year preceding the effective date of such agreement, the Board shall have certified that at least a majority of the employees eligible to vote in such election have voted to rescind the authority of such labor organization to make such an agreement: *Provided further,* That no employer shall justify any discrimination against an employee for nonmembership in a labor organization (A) if he has reasonable grounds for believing that such membership was not available to the employee on the same terms and conditions generally applicable to other members, or (b) if he has reasonable grounds for believing that membership was denied or terminated for reasons other than the failure of the employee to tender the periodic dues and the initiation fees uniformly required as a condition of acquiring or retaining membership;

(4) to discharge or otherwise discriminate against an employee because he has filed charges or given testimony under this Act:

(5) to refuse to bargain collectively with the representatives of his employees, subject to the provisions of section 9(a).

(b) It shall be an unfair labor practice for a labor organization or its agents—

(1) to restrain or coerce (A) employees in the exercise of the rights guaranteed in section 7: *Provided,* That this paragraph shall not impair the right of a labor organization to prescribe its own rules with respect to the acquisition or retention of membership therein; or (B) an employer in the selection of his representatives for the purposes of collective bargaining or the adjustment of grievances;

(2) to cause or attempt to cause an employer to discriminate against an employee in violation of subsection (a) (3) or to discriminate against an employee with respect to whom membership in such organization has been denied or terminated on some ground other than his failure to tender the periodic dues and the initiation fees uniformly required as a condition of acquiring or retaining membership:

(3) to refuse to bargain collectively with an employer, provided it is the representative of his employees subject to the provisions of section 9(a):

(4) (i) to engage in, or to induce or encourage any individual employed by any person engaged in commerce or in an industry affecting commerce to engage in,

a strike or a refusal in the course of his employment to use, manufacture, process, transport, or otherwise handle or work on any goods, articles, materials, or commodities or to perform any services: or (ii) to threaten, coerce, or restrain any person engaged in commerce or in an industry affecting commerce, where in either case an object thereof is:

(A) forcing or requiring any employer or self-employed person to join any labor or employer organization or to enter into any agreement which is prohibited by section 8(e):

(B)* forcing or requiring any person to cease using, selling, handling, transporting, or otherwise dealing in the products of any other producer, processor, or manufacturer, or to cease doing business with any other person, or forcing or requiring any other employer to recognize or bargain with a labor organization as the representative of his employees unless such labor organization has been certified as the representative of such employees under the provisions of section 9: *Provided*, That nothing contained in this clause (B) shall be construed to make unlawful, where not otherwise unlawful, any primary strike or primary picketing:

(C) forcing or requiring any employer to recognize or bargain with a particular labor organization as the representative of his employees if another labor organization has been certified as the representative of such employees under the provisions of section 9;

(D) forcing or requiring any employer to assign particular work to employees in a particular labor organization or in a particular trade, craft, or class rather than to employees in another labor organization or in another trade, craft, or class, unless such employer is failing to conform to an order or certification of the Board determining the bargaining representative for employees performing such work. . . .

(5) to require of employees covered by an agreement authorized under subsection (a) (3) the payment, as a condition precedent to becoming a member of such organization, of a fee in an amount which the Board finds excessive or discriminatory under all the circumstances. In making such a finding, the Board shall consider, among other relevant factors, the practices and customs of labor organizations in the particular industry, and the wages currently paid to the employees affected;

(6)† to cause or attempt to cause an employee to pay or deliver or agree to pay or deliver any money or other thing of value, in the nature of an exaction, for services which are not performed or not to be performed; and

(7) to picket or cause to be picketed, or threaten to picket or cause to be picketed, any employer where an object thereof is forcing or requiring an employer to recognize or bargain with a labor organization as the representative of his employees, or forcing or requiring the employees of an employer to accept or select such labor organization as their collective bargaining representative, unless such labor organization is currently certified as the representative of such employees:

(A) where the employer has lawfully recognized in accordance with this Act

Editor's note: Secondary boycott.
†*Editor's note:* Feather bedding.

any other labor organization and a question concerning representation may not appropriately be raised under section 9(c) of this Act,

(B) where within the preceding twelve months a valid election under section 9(c) of this Act has been conducted, or

(C) where such picketing has been conducted without a petition under section 9(c) being filed within a reasonable period of time not to exceed thirty days from the commencement of such picketing: *Provided*, That when such a petition has been filed the Board shall forthwith, without regard to the provisions of section 9(c) (1) or the absence of a showing of a substantial interest on the part of the labor organization, direct an election in such unit as the Board finds to be appropriate and shall certify the results thereof: *Provided further*, That nothing in this subparagraph (C) shall be construed to prohibit any picketing or other publicity for the purpose of truthfully advising the public (including consumers) that an employer does not employ members of, or have a contract with, a labor organization, unless an effect of such picketing is to induce any individual employed by any other person in the course of his employment, not to pick up, deliver or transport any goods or not to perform any services.

Nothing in this paragraph (7) shall be construed to permit any act which would otherwise be an unfair labor practice under this section 8(b). . . .

(d) For the purposes of this section, to bargain collectively is the performance of the mutual obligation of the employer and the representative of the employees to meet at reasonable times and confer in good faith with respect to wages, hours, and other terms and conditions of employment, or the negotiation of an agreement, or any question arising thereunder, and the execution of a written contract incorporating any agreement reached if requested by either party, but such obligation does not compel either party to agree to a proposal or require the making of a concession. . . .

Representatives and Elections

Sec. 9. (c) (1) Wherever a petition shall have been filed, in accordance with such regulations as may be prescribed by the Board—

(A) by an employee or group of employees or any individual or labor organization acting in their behalf alleging that a substantial number of employees (i) wish to be represented for collective bargaining and that their employer declines to recognize their representative as the representative defined in section 9(a), or (ii) assert that the individual or labor organization, which has been certified or is being currently recognized by their employer as the bargaining representative, is no longer a representative as defined in section 9(a): or

(B) by an employer, alleging that one or more individuals or labor organizations have presented to him a claim to be recognized as the representative defined in section 9(a); the Board shall investigate such petition and if it has reasonable cause to believe that a question of representation affecting commerce exists shall provide for an appropriate hearing upon due notice. Such hearing may be conducted by an officer or employee of the regional office, who shall not make any recommendations with respect thereto. If the Board finds upon the record of such hearing that such a question of representation exists, it shall direct an election by secret ballot and shall certify the results thereof. . . .

B—*J. P. Stevens and Co., Inc., and Textile
Workers of America, AFL–CIO*
220 NLRB No. 34 (1975)

Decision of Administrative Law Judge

Statement of the Case

Marvin Roth, Administrative Law Judge: This case was tried at Wilmington,
North Carolina, on March 26, 1975. The charge and amended charge were filed,
respectively, on November 22, 1974, and January 21, 1975, by Textile Workers
Union of America, AFL–CIO, herein called the Union. The complaint, which
issued on January 29, 1975, and was amended at the hearing, alleges that J. P.
Stevens & Co., Inc., herein called the Company or Respondent, violated Section
8(a)(1) of the National Labor Relations Act, as amended. The Company's answer
denies the commission of the alleged unfair labor practices.

Issues

The issues are:

1. Whether, during the course of an organizing campaign by the Union among
the Company's employees at its Carter plant in Wallace, North Carolina, the
Company, by its supervisor Roland Rivenbark, violated Section 8(a)(1) of the
Act by interrogating employee Faye Rogers as to how she felt about the Union
and by requesting her to report upon the union sympathies of other employees;
and

2. Whether a remedial order is warranted.

All parties were afforded full opportunity to participate, to present relevant
evidence, to examine and cross-examine witnesses, and to argue orally on the evidence and the law. The parties waived the filing of briefs. Upon careful consideration of the arguments of counsel, the entire record in the case, and from my
observation of the witnesses and their demeanor, I make the following:

Findings of Fact

I. THE BUSINESS OF RESPONDENT

The Company is a New York corporation engaged in the manufacture and distribution of textile products, with plants located in several States of the United
States, including plants located at Wallace, North Carolina. The Company
annually receives goods and raw materials at its Wallace plants directly from
points outside the State of North Carolina valued in excess of $50,000, and
annually manufactures at its Wallace plants and ships directly to points outside
of North Carolina products valued in excess of $50,000. The Board has in prior
cases asserted jurisdiction over the Company's operations. Upon these undis-
puted facts I find that the Company is an employer engaged in commerce within
the meaning of Section 2(6) and (7) of the Act and that it will effectuate the
policies of the Act to assert jurisdiction herein.

II. THE LABOR ORGANIZATION INVOLVED

The complaint alleges, the Company admits and I find that the Union is a labor
organization within the meaning of Section 2(5) of the Act.

III. THE ALLEGED UNFAIR LABOR PRACTICES

A. *Background: The Company's History of Unfair Labor Practices.* The Company has an extensive history of unfair labor practice litigation in the Board and courts. In *J. P. Stevens & Co.* v. *N.L.R.B.* . . . (known as *"Stevens I"*), the court of appeals affirmed the Board's findings . . . that the Company engaged in "massive violations" of Section 8(a)(1), (3), and (4) of the Act. Thereafter, in *"Stevens II"* . . . the same court affirmed the Board's findings . . . that the Company committed additional violations of Section 8(a)(1), (3), and (4). In *Stevens III and IV* . . . the Fourth Circuit Court of Appeals enforced, in substantial part, Board orders . . . based on findings of violations of Section 8(a)(1), (3), and (4). In *Stevens V* . . . and *Stevens VI* . . . the Fifth Circuit Court enforced Board orders against the Company, including a remedial bargaining order in *Stevens VI.* The court noted "Stevens" known predisposition to violate the law . . . unchastened by and impervious to judicial homilies" . . . and "the tenacity with which the Employer persists in the exercise of deep seated anti-union convictions." . . . Thereafter, the Fourth Circuit Court of Appeals declined to enforce a Board order relating to charged violations of Section 8(a)(1) and (3) at the Company's Roanoke Rapids, North Carolina plants . . . but enforced a Board order relating to violations of Section 8(a)(1) and (3) at company plants in Shelby and Hickory, North Carolina. . . .

On July 13, 1972, the Second Circuit Court found the Company to be in civil contempt of the decrees in *Stevens I and II*, by reason of the Company having engaged in conduct violative of Section 8(a)(1), (3), and (4) at several of its plants, including the Carter plant in Wallace, North Carolina, i.e., the plant here involved. . . . On the basis of its findings, the court subsequently adjudged the Company and several of its supervisors in civil contempt of court, directing that they take certain steps to purge themselves of civil contempt, and "reserve[d] jurisdiction to assess fines, issue writs of body attachment or take other appropriate action against any officer or agent of the Company and against any of the individual respondents responsible for noncompliance with the foregoing [purgation] provisions; of this order and the decrees of this Court." . . . There is also presently pending a second civil contempt proceeding before a special master of the same court, involving company plants in North and South Carolina.

At the outset of the instant hearing, General Counsel requested that I take judicial notice of the foregoing cases, and I have done so. . . . Supervisor Rivenbark, the Company's only witness, testified that the Company "was definitely against the Union" and that it was part of his duties to do what he legally could to keep the Union out. Whether, in this instance, the Company exceeded the bounds of legality is a matter which I have decided on the basis of the evidence adduced in this proceeding.

B. *The Union's Organizational Campaign and the Alleged Interrogation of Employee Rogers.* In the early fall of 1974, the Union commenced an organizational campaign among the approximately 1,200 employees at the Company's Carter plant. The Union distributed literature at plant entrances, and solicited signed authorization cards. This campaign promptly came to the attention of management.

Faye Rogers was and is, knitter on the third shift in the tricot department at the Carter plant. Rivenbark is her immediate supervisor. Rogers, General Counsel's only witness, testified that in early October, while Rivenbark was making his nightly rounds and coming by her machines, he apparently saw one Glisson, an employee in the tricot department, attempting to get her to sign a union card. Rogers testified that about 3 days later, Rivenbark summoned her alone to his office. Rivenbark first discussed certain defects in her work. Rogers testified that after pausing, Rivenbark asked her how she felt about the Union. Rogers answered that she didn't know because she had never worked under one. After pausing again, Rivenbark said "if you know of anybody that's for it, let me know." Rogers then got up and returned to work. Rogers testified that later that morning, Rivenbark approached her at her machines and said "if anything comes up, don't mention my name." Rogers testified that in November, she informed Union International Representative Pope of her conversation with Rivenbark, and that Pope told her "it was a violation." Rogers testified that prior to speaking with Pope she had "often wondered" why Rivenbark would tell her not to mention his name should anything come up.

On his direct examination Rivenbark denied seeing Glisson attempt to get Rogers to sign a union card. Rogers indicated that Rivenbark was about 45 feet from them at the time of the incident. I might have been inclined to question whether Rivenbark could have seen a union card at that distance, even if he had seen the two employees together. However, on cross-examination Rivenbark admitted that the incident occurred, but testified that he couldn't recall whether the incident occurred before or after Rogers allegedly told him that an unidentified employee had approached her with a "blue card" and asked her to sign it. I find that the incident occurred as testified to by Rogers.

Rivenbark categorically denied questioning Rogers about her attitude toward the Union or about union adherents. He admitted that he summoned her to his office to discuss her work, but denied that the Union was discussed in that meeting or in any other conversation between them. He testified that on one occasion, as he was making his nightly rounds, she approached him and said that she had been approached by an employee (otherwise unidentified) with a "blue card" who asked her to sign it, but that she would not sign it. Rivenbark testified that he did't know that a blue card meant a union card, but that he "had heard that there was union cards being passed out. And so I didn't say anything." However, Rivenbark readily identified, at a distance of about 10 feet, a blue union card as being the kind of card which "I received at the gate one morning when I went out." . . .

In this posture, the witnesses' relative candor and the quality of their testimony with respect to related matters is of particular significance. Here, I find Rogers to be the more credible witness. Her testimony was straightforward and consistent, even with respect to matters which might be considered adverse to her own interests. She candidly admitted that Rivenbark had good reason to criticize her work. I cannot, however, say the same for Rivenbark's testimony. The inconsistencies in his testimony have previously been noted. I find it difficult to believe his testimony that although he had only 21 employees, whom he knew well, under his supervision, and had an intense interest in learning about union activities, he could not remember the name of a single person under his supervision who was pushing for the Union, or who told him about Rogers' husband, or from whom he learned that union cards were being circulated, or in what month he saw union leaflets being passed out at the gate. Therefore, I credit Rogers' testimony that Rivenbark questioned her as to how she felt about the Union and requested her to report upon the union sympathies of other employees.

Rivenbark interrogated Rogers in "an atmosphere of 'unnatural formality.'" specifically, after she had been summoned from her work station to his office. Rivenbark's familiarity with the do's and don'ts of Section 8(a)(1), his pregnant pauses, and the circumstances described above which apparently led him to question Rogers, also lead me to believe that this was no mere casual conversation, but an intentional act on the part of the Company. Rivenbark had no legitimate reason to question Rogers as to the identity of union supporters or, indeed, as to her own views Rivenbark gave Rogers no assurance against reprisal; on the contrary, he admonished her not to mention his name "if anything comes up." Moreover, the interrogation was conducted in the context of the Company's known hostility to the Union, and past demonstrated proclivity to violate the Act. Therefore, I find that the circumstances of the present case substantially meet the standards set by the Board in *Blue Flash Express, Inc.*, 109 NLRB 591 (1954) for determining the coercive nature of interrogation. In light of the foregoing, I find that the interrogation here tended to interfere with, restrain, and coerce employees in the exercise of their right to support the Union's organizational effort, and thus violated Section 8(a)(1) of the Act.

IV. THE REMEDY

. . . One may question what useful purpose would be served by entering yet another Board order against the company. . . . However, viewing this case in the context of an unfair labor practice proceeding, I find that the issuance of a Board order and the posting of appropriate notices may have a salutary effect. Because of the Company's demonstrated proclivity to violate the Act, I am recommending that the Company be ordered to cease and desist not only from the specific unfair labor practices found, but also from in any manner interfering with, restraining, or coercing employees in the exercise of their rights guaranteed by Section 7 of the Act. However, I am recommending that the requirement for posting of notices be limited to the Carter plant, where the unfair labor practices occurred. See *J. P. Stevens & Co.*, 183 NLRB 25 (1970).

Conclusions of Law

1. The Company is an employer engaged in commerce within the meaning of Section 2(6) and (7) of the Act.

2. The Union is a labor organization within the meaning of Section 2(5) of the Act.

3. By coercively interrogating employee Faye Rogers concerning her own and other employees' union sympathies and activities, the Company has interfered with, restrained, and coerced its employees in the exercise of their rights guaranteed to them by Section 7 of the Act, in violation of Section 8(a)(1) of the Act.

4. The aforesaid unfair labor practices are unfair labor practices affecting commerce within the meaning of Section 2(6) and (7) of the Act.

5. An order requiring the Company to cease and desist from the unfair labor practices found herein, and to take appropriate affirmative action, is warranted and necessary to effectuate the policies of the Act.

Upon the foregoing findings of fact and conclusions of law, and upon the entire record, and pursuant to Section 10(c) of the Act, I hereby issue the following recommended:

Order

Respondent J. P. Stevens & Co., Inc., Wallace, North Carolina, its officers, agents, successors, and assigns, shall:

1. Cease and desist from:

(a) Interrogating employees concerning their own or other employees' membership in, activities on behalf of, or sympathy for Textile Workers Union of America, AFL–CIO, or any other labor organization.

(b) In any other manner interfering with, restraining, or coercing employees in the exercise of their rights guaranteed in Section 7 of the Act.

2. Take the following affirmative action necessary to effectuate the policies of the Act:

(a) Post at its Carter plant in Wallace, North Carolina copies of the attached notice marked "Appendix." Copies of the notice on forms provided by the Regional Director for Region 11, after being duly signed by Respondent's authorized representative, shall be posted by Respondent immediately upon receipt thereof, and be maintained by it for 60 consecutive days thereafter in conspicuous places, including all places where notices to employees are customarily posted. Reasonable steps shall be taken by Respondent to insure that said notices are not altered, defaced, or covered by any other material.

(b) Notify the Regional Director for Region 11, in writing, within 20 days from the date of this Order, what steps Respondent has taken to comply herewith.

Decision and Order
By Chairmain Murphy and Members Fanning
and Jenkins

On April 18, 1975, Administrative Law Judge Marvin Roth issued the attached Decision in this proceeding. Thereafter, the General Counsel and the Charging Party filed exceptions and supporting briefs.

Pursuant to the provisions of Section 3(b) of the National Labor Relations Act, as amended, the National Labor Relations Board has delegated its authority in this proceeding to a three-member panel.

The Board has considered the record and the attached Decision in light of the exceptions and briefs and has decided to affirm the rulings, findings, and conclusions of the Administrative Law Judge and to adopt his recommended Order, as modified herein.

We agree with the Administrative Law Judge's finding that Respondent violated Section 8(a)(1) of the Act by coercively interrogating an employee concerning her own and other employees' union sympathies and activities. The General Counsel and the Charging Party except to the omission of a specific remedy by the Administrative Law Judge for the Respondent's solicitation of the same employee to report to Respondent on the union activities of other employees. We agree.

The Administrative Law Judge credited the testimony of employee Rogers that her supervisor, Rivenbark, "requested her to report upon the union sympathies of other employees." No exception was filed by Respondent to that finding. Accordingly, we shall correct this omission by amending the conclusions of law and providing an appropriate remedy in our Order and in the notice.

The Charging Party also urges, in view of the extensive unfair labor practice history of the Respondent, that the Board should order extraordinary remedies in this case. The Charging Party requests that the Respondent be required to post the notices at all of Respondent's plants in North Carolina and South Carolina; that the union be given access for 1 year to the bulletin boards at Respondent's plants in North Carolina and South Carolina; and that Respondent be required, upon request, to furnish to the Union a list of the names and addresses of all of the employees at all of the Respondent's plants in North Carolina and South Carolina.

We have considered the numerous prior violations of the Act by this same Respondent at various locations. As set forth in the Decision of the Administrative Law Judge, the Respondent has an extraordinary history of unfair labor practice litigation before this Board and the courts. The Respondent has committed violations of the Act which are identical or similar to the violations found in this case on numerous other occasions. . . .

In view of the extensive history of unfair labor practice violations by this Respondent and the repeated violations of the Act which are similar to those found in this case, we find that employees of the Respondent at other plants must be assured of their rights under the Act and that other employees must be assured that they are protected against similar violations by this Respondent. Accordingly, we find it necessary in these circumstances to order that Respondent post the notice at all of its plants.

With regard to the additional remedies sought by the Charging Party, the Union seeks access to the plant bulletin boards and names and addresses of employees at plants in North Carolina and South Carolina. We are not persuaded that the nature and extent of the violations found in this case have significantly diminished the Union's ability to initiate communication with Respondent's employees. As the remedy provided is designed to eliminate Respondent's coercive interference with employee–union organizational activities, we shall not grant the request for additional extraordinary remedies in this case.

Amended Conclusions of Law

Delete Conclusions of Law 3 and substitute therefor the following:

"3. By coercively interrogating employee Faye Rogers concerning her own and other employees' union sympathies and activities and by soliciting Faye Rogers to report to Respondent on other employees' union activities, the Company has interfered with, restrained, and coerced its employees in the exercise of their rights guaranteed to them by Section 7 of the Act, in violation of Section 8(a)(1) of the Act."

Order

Pursuant to Section 10(c) of the National Labor Relations Act, as amended, the National Labor Relations Board adopts as its Order the recommended Order of the Administrative Law Judge as modified below and hereby orders that the Respondent, J. P. Stevens & Co., Inc., Wallace, North Carolina, its officers, agents, successors, and assigns, shall take the action set forth in the Administrative Law Judge's recommended Order, as so modified:

1. Add the following as paragraph 1(c):

"(c) Soliciting employees to report to Respondent on other employees' membership in, activities on behalf of, or sympathy for Textile Workers Union of America, AFL–CIO, or any other labor organization."

2. Substitute the following sentence for the first sentence in paragraph 2(a):

"(a) Post at all of its plants copies of the attached notice marked 'Appendix.'"

3. Substitute the attached notice for the Administrative Law Judge's notice.

Appendix

Notice to Employees
Posted by Order of the
National Labor Relations Board
An Agency of the United States Government

After a trial at which all sides had a chance to give evidence, the National Labor Relations Board has found that our Company at its Carter Plant, Wallace, North Carolina, violated the National Labor Relations Act and has ordered us to post this notice.

The National Labor Relations Act protects employees in their right to form, join, or assist labor unions or to refrain from such activity.

We will not interrogate employees concerning their own or other employees' membership in, activities on behalf of, or sympathy for Textile Workers Union of America, AFL–CIO, or any other labor organization.

We will not solicit employees to report to us on other employees' membership in, activities on behalf of, or sympathy for Textile Workers Union of America, AFL–CIO, or any other labor organization.

We will not in any other manner interfere with, restrain, or coerce our employees in the exercise of rights guaranteed them by Section 7 of the National Labor Relations Act, as amended.

J. P. Stevens & Co., Inc.

C—Civil Rights Act of 1964
Public Law 88–352
42 U.S.C. 2000e–4

Equal Employment Opportunity Commission

∫705, 2000e–4. (a) There is hereby created a Commission to be known as the Equal Employment Opportunity Commission, which shall be composed of five members, not more than three of whom shall be members of the same political party. Members of the Commission shall be appointed by the President by and with the advice and consent of the Senate for a term of five years. Any individual chosen to fill a vacancy shall be appointed only for the unexpired term of the member whom he shall succeed, and all members of the Commission shall continue to serve until their successors are appointed and qualified, except that no such member of the Commission shall continue to serve (1) for more than sixty days when the Congress is in session unless a nomination to fill such vacancy shall have been submitted to the Senate, or (2) after the adjournment sine die of the session of the Senate in which such nomination was submitted. The President shall designate one member to serve as Chairman of the Commission, and one member to serve as Vice Chairman. The Chairman shall be responsible on behalf of the Commission for the administrative operations of the Commission, and, except as provided in subsection (b), shall appoint, in accordance with the provisions of title 5, United States Code, governing appointments in the competitive service, such officers, agents, attorneys, hearing examiners, and employees as he deems necessary to assist it in the performance of its functions and to fix their compensation in accordance with the provisions of chapter 51 and subchapter III of chapter 53 of title 5, United States Code, relating to classification and General Schedule pay rates. . . .

Enforcement Provisions

∫706, 2000e-5. (a) The Commission is empowered, as hereinafter provided, to prevent any person from engaging in any unlawful employment practice as set forth in section 703 or 704 of this title. [As amended March 24, 1972, P.L. 92–261, Sec. 4.]

State or Local Enforcement Provisions

(b) Whenever a charge is filed by or on behalf of a person claiming to be aggrieved, or by a member of the Commission, alleging that an employer, employment agency, labor organization, or joint labor-management committee controlling apprenticeship or other training or retraining, including on-the-job training programs, has engaged in an unlawful employment practice, the Commission shall serve a notice of the charge (including the date, place and circumstances of the alleged unlawful employment practice) on such employer, employment agency, labor organization, or joint labor-management committee (hereinafter referred to as the "respondent") within ten days, and shall make an investigation thereof. . . . If the Commission determines after such investigation that there is not reasonable cause to believe that the charge is true, it shall dismiss the charge and promptly notify the person claiming to be aggrieved and the respondent of its action. . . . If the Commission determines after such investigation that there is reasonable cause to believe that the charge is true, the Commission shall endeavor to eliminate any such alleged unlawful employment practice by informal methods of conference, conciliation, and persuasion. Nothing said or done during and as a part of such informal endeavors may be made public by the Commission, its officers or employees, or used as evidence in a subsequent proceeding without the written consent of the persons concerned. Any person who makes public information in violation of this subsection shall be fined not more than $1,000 or imprisoned for not more than one year, or both. The commission shall make its determination on reasonable cause as promptly as possible and, so far as practicable, not later than one hundred and twenty days from the filing of the charge. . . .

Civil Action by Commission, Attorney General, or Person Aggrieved

(f) (1) If within thirty days after a charge is filed with the Commission . . . the Commission has been unable to secure from the respondent a conciliation agreement acceptable to the Commission, the Commission may bring a civil action against any respondent not a government, governmental agency, or political subdivision named in the charge. In the case of a respondent which is a government, governmental agency, or political subdivision, if the Commission has been unable to secure from the respondent a conciliation agreement acceptable to the Commission, the Commission shall take no further action and shall refer the case to the Attorney General who may bring a civil action against such respondent in the appropriate United States district court. The person or persons aggrieved shall have the right to intervene in a civil action brought by the Commission or the Attorney General in a case involving a government, governmental agency, or political subdivision. If a charge filed with the Commission pursuant to subsection (b) is dismissed by . . . the Commission, or the Attorney General in a case involving a government, governmental agency, or political subdivision, shall so notify the person aggrieved and within ninety days after the giving of such notice a civil action may be brought against the respondent named in the charge (A) by the person claiming to be aggrieved or (B) if such charge was filed by a member of the Commission, by any person whom the charge alleges was aggrieved by the alleged unlawful employment practice. . . .

(2) Whenever a charge is filed with the Commission and the Commission concludes on the basis of a preliminary investigation that prompt judicial action is necessary to carry out the purposes of this Act, the Commission, or the Attorney General in a case involving a government, governmental agency, or political subdivision, may bring an action for appropriate temporary or preliminary relief pending final disposition of such charge. . . .

(3) Each United States district court and each United States court of a place subject to the jurisdiction of the United States shall have jurisdiction of actions brought under this title. . . .

Injunctions; Appropriate Affirmative Action, Back Pay

(g) If the court finds that the respondent has intentionally engaged in or is intentionally engaging in an unlawful employment practice charged in the complaint, the court may enjoin the respondent from engaging in such unlawful employment practice, and order such affirmative action as may be appropriate, which may include, but is not limited to, reinstatement or hiring of employees, with or without back pay (payable by the employer, employment agency, or labor organization, as the case may be, responsible for the unlawful employment practice), or any other equitable relief as the court deems appropriate. Back pay liability shall not accrue from a date more than two years prior to the filing of a charge with the Commission. Interim earnings or amounts earnable with reasonable diligence by the person or persons discriminated against shall operate to reduce the back pay otherwise allowable. No order of the court shall require the admission or reinstatement of an individual as a member of a union, or the hiring, reinstatement, or promotion of an individual as an employee, or the payment to him of any back pay, if such individual was refused admission, suspended, or expelled, or was refused employment or advancement or was suspended or discharged for any reason other than discrimination on account of race, color, religion, sex, or national origin or in violation of section 704(a). [As amended March 24, 1972, P.L. 92-261, Sec. 4.]

Proceedings by Commission to Compel Compliance with Judicial Orders

(i) In any case in which an employer, employment agency, or labor organization fails to comply with an order of a court issued in a civil action brought under this section, the Commission may commence proceedings to compel compliance with such order. [As amended March 24, 1972, P.L. 92-261, Sec. 4.] . . .

D—Reorganization Plan No. 1 of 1978
Re: Federal Equal Employment Opportunity Activities
124 *Congressional Record* H 1457
(H. Doc. No. 95-295)

To the Congress of the United States:

. . . In 1940 President Roosevelt issued the first Executive Order forbidding discrimination in employment by the Federal government. Since that time the Congress, the courts and the Executive Branch—spurred by the courage and sacrifice of many people and organizations—have taken historic steps to extend equal employment opportunity protection throughout the private as well as public sector. But each new prohibition against discrimination unfortunately has brought with it a further dispersal of Federal equal employment opportunity responsibility. This fragmentation of authority among a number of Federal agencies has meant confusion and ineffective enforcement for employees, regulatory duplication and needless expense for employers.

Fair employment is too vital for haphazard enforcement. My Administration will aggressively enforce our civil rights laws. Although discrimination in any area has severe consequences, limiting economic opportunity affects access to education, housing and health care. I, therefore, ask you to join with me to reorganize administration of the civil rights laws and to begin that effort by reorganizing the enforcement of those laws which ensure an equal opportunity to a job.

Eighteen government units now exercise important responsibilities under statutes. Executive Orders and regulations relating to equal employment opportunity:

- The Equal Employment Opportunity Commission (EEOC) enforces Title VII of the Civil Rights Act of 1964, which bans employment discrimination based on race, national origin, sex or religion. The EEOC acts on individual complaints and also initiates private sector cases involving a "pattern or practice" of discrimination.
- The Department of Labor and 11 other agencies enforce Executive Order 11246. This prohibits discrimination in employment on the basis of race, national origin, sex, or religion and requires affirmative action by government contractors. While the Department now coordinates enforcement of this "contract compliance" program, it is actually administered by eleven other departments and agencies. The Department also administers those statutes requiring contractors to take affirmative action to employ handicapped people, disabled veterans and Vietnam veterans.

In addition, the Labor Department enforces the Equal Pay Act of 1963, which prohibits employers from paying unequal wages based on sex, and the Age Discrimination in Employment Act of 1967, which forbids age discrimination against persons between the ages of 40 and 65.

- The Department of Justice litigates Title VII cases involving public sector employers—State and local governments. The Department also represents the Federal government in lawsuits against Federal contractors and grant recipients who are in violation of Federal nondiscrimination prohibitions.
- The Civil Service Commission (CSC) enforces Title VII and all other nondiscrimination and affirmative action requirements for Federal employment. The CSC rules on complaints filed by individuals and monitors affirmative action plans submitted annually by other Federal agencies.
- The Equal Employment Opportunity Coordinating Council includes representatives from EEOC, Labor, Justice, CSC and the Civil Rights Commission. It is charged with coordinating the Federal equal employment opportunity enforcement effort and with eliminating overlap and inconsistent standards.
- In addition to these major government units, other agencies enforce various equal employment opportunity requirements which apply to specific grant programs. The Department of Treasury, for example, administers the antidiscrimination prohibitions applicable to recipients of revenue sharing funds.

These programs have had only limited success. Some of the past deficiencies include:

- inconsistent standards of compliance;
- duplicative, inconsistent paperwork requirements and investigative efforts;
- conflicts within agencies between their program responsibilities and their responsibility to enforce the civil rights laws;
- confusion on the part of workers about how and where to seek redress;
- lack of accountability.

I am proposing today a series of steps to bring coherence to the equal employment enforcement effort. These steps, to be accomplished by the Reorganization Plan and Executive Orders, constitute an important step toward consolidation of equal employment opportunity enforcement. They will be implemented over the next two years, so that the agencies involved may continue their internal reform.

Its experience and broad scope make the EEOC suitable for the role of principal Federal agency in fair employment enforcement. Located in the Executive Branch and responsible to the President, the EEOC has developed considerable expertise in the field of employment discrimination since Congress created it by the Civil Rights Act of 1964. The Commission has played a pioneer role in defining both employment discrimination and its appropriate remedies.

The Reorganization Plan I am submitting will accomplish the following:

- On July 1, 1978, abolish the Equal Employment Opportunity Coordinating Council (42 U.S.C. 2000e-14) and transfer its duties to the EEOC (no positions or funds shifted).
- On October 1, 1978, shift enforcement of equal employment opportunity for Federal employees from the CSC to the EEOC (100 positions and $6.5 million shifted).
- On July 1, 1979, shift responsibility for enforcing both the Equal Pay Act and the Age Discrimination in Employment Act from the Labor Depart-

ment to the EEOC (198 positions and $5.3 million shifted for Equal Pay; 119 positions and $3.5 million for Age Discrimination).

- Clarify the Attorney General's authority to initiate "pattern or practice" suits under Title VII in the public sector. . . .

By abolishing the Equal Employment Opportunity Coordinating Council and transferring its responsibilities to the EEOC, this plan places the Commission at the center of equal employment opportunity enforcement. With these new responsibilities, the EEOC can give coherence and direction to the government's efforts by developing strong uniform enforcement standards to apply throughout the government: standardized data collection procedures, joint training programs, programs to ensure the sharing of enforcement related data among agencies, and methods and priorities for complaint and compliance reviews. Such direction has been absent in the Equal Employment Opportunity Coordinating Council.

It should be stressed, however, that affected agencies will be consulted before EEOC takes any action. When the Plan has been approved, I intend to issue an Executive Order which will provide for consultation, as well as a procedure for reviewing major disputed issues within the Executive Office of the President. The Attorney General's responsibility to advise the Executive Branch on legal issues will also be preserved.

Transfer of the Civil Service Commission's equal employment opportunity responsibilities to EEOC is needed to ensure that: (1) Federal employees have the same rights and remedies as those in the private sector and in State and local government; (2) Federal agencies meet the same standards as are required of other employers; and (3) potential conflicts between an agency's equal employment opportunity and personnel management functions are minimized. The Federal government must not fall below the standard of performance it expects of private employers.

The Civil Service Commission has in the Past been lethargic in enforcing fair employment requirements within the Federal government. While the Chairman and other Commissioners I have appointed have already demonstrated their personal commitment to expanding equal employment opportunity, responsibility for ensuring fair employment for Federal employees should rest ultimately with the EEOC.

We must ensure that the transfer in no way undermines the important objectives of the comprehensive civil service reorganization which will be submitted to Congress in the near future. When the two plans take effect, I will direct the EEOC and the CSC to coordinate their procedures to prevent any duplication and overlap.

The Equal Pay Act, now administered by the Labor Department, prohibits employers from paying unequal wages based on sex. Title VII of the Civil Rights Act, which is enforced by EEOC, contains a broader ban on sex discrimination. The transfer of Equal Pay responsibility from the Labor Department to the EEOC will minimize overlap and centralize enforcement of statutory prohibitions against sex discrimination in employment.

The transfer will strengthen efforts to combat sex discrimination. Such efforts would be enhanced still further by passage of the legislation pending before you, which I support, that would prohibit employers from excluding women disabled by pregnancy from participating in disability programs.

The Plan I am submitting is moderate and measured. It gives the Equal Employment Opportunity Commission—an agency dedicated solely to this purpose—the primary Federal responsibility in the area of job discrimination, but it is designed to give this agency sufficient time to absorb its new responsibilities. This reorganization will produce consistent agency standards, as well as increased accountability. Combined with the intense commitment of those charged with these responsibilities, it will become possible for us to accelerate this nation's progress in ensuring equal job opportunities for all our people.

JIMMY CARTER

THE WHITE HOUSE
February 23, 1978

E—Regulation of Lobbying (1946)
  2 U.S.C. 261

§261. Definitions.

When used in this chapter—

(a) The term "contribution" includes a gift, subscription, loan, advance, or deposit of money or anything of value and includes a contract, promise, or agreement, whether or not legally enforceable, to make a contribution.

(b) The term "expenditure" includes a payment, distribution, loan, advance, deposit, or gift of money or anything of value, and includes a contract, promise, or agreement, whether or not legally enforceable, to make an expenditure.

(c) The term "person" includes an individual, partnership, committee, association, corporation, and any other organization or group of persons.

(d) The term "Clerk" means the Clerk of the House of Representatives of the United States.

(e) The term "legislation" means bills, resolutions, amendments, nominations, and other matters pending or proposed in either House of Congress, and includes any other matter which may be the subject of action by either House. . . .

§262. Detailed Accounts of Contributions; Retention of Receipted
       Bills of Expenditures.

(a) It shall be the duty of every person who shall in any manner solicit or receive a contribution to any organization or fund for the purposes hereinafter designated* to keep a detailed and exact account of—

(1) all contributions of any amount or of any value whatsoever;

(2) the name and address of every person making any such contribution of $500 or more and the date thereof;

(3) all expenditures made by or on behalf of such organization or fund; and

*Editor's note: See section 266.

(4) the name and address of every person to whom any such expenditure is made and the date thereof.

(b) It shall be the duty of such person to obtain and keep a receipted bill, stating the particulars, for every expenditure of such funds exceeding $10 in amount, and to preserve all receipted bills and accounts required to be kept by this section for a period of at least two years from the date of the filing of the statement containing such items. . . .

§264. Statements of Accounts Filed with Clerk of House.

(a) Every person receiving any contributions or expending any money for the purposes designated in subparagraph (a) or (b) of section 266 of this title shall file with the Clerk between the first and tenth day of each calendar quarter, a statement containing complete as of the day next preceding the date of filing—

(1) the name and address of each person who has made a contribution of $500 or more not mentioned in the preceding report; except that the first report filed pursuant to this chapter shall contain the name and address of each person who has made any contribution of $500 or more to such person since August 2, 1946;

(2) the total sum of the contributions made to or for such person during the calendar year and not stated under paragraph (1) of this subsection;

(3) the total sum of all contributions made to or for such person during the calendar year;

(4) the name and address of each person to whom an expenditure in one or more items of the aggregate amount or value, within the calendar year, of $10 or more has been made by or on behalf of such person, and the amount, date, and purpose of such expenditure;

(5) the total sum of all expenditures made by or on behalf of such person during the calendar year and not stated under paragraph (4) of this subsection;

(6) the total sum of expenditures made by or on behalf of such person during the calendar year.

(b) The statements required to be filed by subsection (a) of this section shall be cumulative during the calendar year to which they relate, but where there has been no change in an item reported in a previous statement only the amount need be carried forward. . . .

§266. Persons to Whom Chapter is Applicable.

The provisions of this chapter shall apply to any person (except a political committee as defined in the Federal Corrupt Practices Act, and duly organized State or local committees of a political party), who by himself, or through any agent or employee or other persons in any manner whatsoever, directly or indirectly, solicits, collects, or receives money or any other thing of value to be used principally to aid, or the principal purpose of which person is to aid, in the accomplishment of any of the following purposes:

(a) The passage or defeat of any legislation by the Congress of the United States.

(b) To influence, directly or indirectly, the passage or defeat of any legislation by the Congress of the United States. . . .

§267. Registration of Lobbyists with Secretary of the Senate and
Clerk of House; Compilation of Information.

(a) Any person who shall engage himself for pay or for any consideration for
the purpose of attempting to influence the passage or defeat of any legislation
by the Congress of the United States shall, before doing anything in furtherance
of such object, register with the Clerk of the House of Representatives and the
Secretary of the Senate and shall give to those officers in writing and under oath,
his name and business address, the name and address of the person by whom he
is employed, and in whose interest he appears or works, the duration of such employment, how much he is paid and is to receive, by whom he is paid or is to be
paid, how much he is to be paid for expenses, and what expenses are to be included. Each such person so registering shall, between the first and tenth day of
each calendar quarter, so long as his activity continues, file with the Clerk and
Secretary a detailed report under oath of all money received and expended by
him during the preceding calendar quarter in carrying on his work; to whom
paid; for what purposes; and the names of any papers, periodicals, magazines, or
other publications in which he has caused to be published any articles or editorials; and the proposed legislation he is employed to support or oppose. The
provisions of this section shall not apply to any person who merely appears
before a committee of the Congress of the United States in support of or opposition to legislation; nor to any public official acting in his official capacity; nor in
the case of any newspaper or other regularly published periodical (including any
individual who owns, publishes, or is employed by any such newspaper or periodical) which in the ordinary course of business publishes news items, editorials, or
other comments, or paid advertisements, which directly or indirectly urge the
passage or defeat of legislation, if such newspaper, periodical, or individual, engages in no further or other activities in connection with the passage or defeat of
such legislation, other than to appear before a committee of the Congress of the
United States in support of or in opposition to such legislation. . . .

§269. Penalties and Prohibitions.

(a) Any person who violates any of the provisions of this chapter, shall, upon
conviction, be guilty of a misdemeanor, and shall be punished by a fine of not
more than $5,000 or imprisonment for not more than twelve months, or by
both such fine and imprisonment.

(b) In addition to the penalties provided for in subsection (a) of this section,
any person convicted of the misdemeanor specified therein is prohibited, for a
period of three years from the date of such conviction, from attempting to influence, directly or indirectly, the passage or defeat of any proposed legislation or
from appearing before a committee of the Congress in support of or opposition
to proposed legislation; and any person who violates any provision of this subsection shall, upon conviction thereof, be guilty of a felony, and shall be punished by a fine of not more than $10,000, or imprisonment for not more than
five years, or by both such fine and imprisonment. . . .

PART VI

Social-Structural Theory of Law: Interinstitutional Analysis

The fourth component of our social-structural theory of law deals with interinstitutional analysis. This is, by definition, more complex than the other three components, because a system, subsystem, or institution in our theoretical approach is a composite of values, norms, roles, and organizations. From the vantage point of inter-institutional analysis, a legal system is at any point in time a function of its interaction with the particular configuration of nonlegal institutions in a given society. Since the configuration of institutions in a society changes over time and differs from one type of society to another, we should expect to observe corresponding differences in legal systems. Hence there is a need for a comparative as well as a historical perspective in the study of legal systems.

The opening selections in Part VI deal with two models of legal development: Weber's typology of lawmaking and lawfinding, with his underlying historical proposition concerning the trend toward formal rationality in legal systems; and Turner's application of Parsons's action theory as it bears on the interactions—over extended time periods—of legal and nonlegal institutions.

To illustrate some of the difficulties as well as potentialities in undertaking an interinstitutional analysis, six readings are presented relating law to different institutional frameworks. In the selection by Friedman and Ladinsky, the authors trace the development of tort law in the United States from the emergence of the fellow-servant rule in the 1830s, based on the principle of no liability without fault, to the new principle of liability regardless of fault as incorporated in the Workmen's Compensation Law in the first decade of the twentieth century. This shift in tort law is related to the development of the industrial economy, which in turn gave rise to a high rate of industrial accidents. The authors question the adequacy of Ogburn's theory of "cultural lag" in explaining the time delay of the legal system in adjusting itself to continuing changes in the industrial economy.

The delay of the legal system in adjusting its tort concept to the realities of industrialism is also observed in the case of the rapidly advancing technology which poses a threat to civil liberties. Westin's analysis of the dangers of public data banks raises complex policy issues for a society that prizes both individual freedom and information. It also dramatizes the contrasting role of law as a *reactive* institution—to the problems created by other societal institutions—versus law as a *proactive* institution, which presupposes a capacity to forecast and control dysfunctions generated by other social institutions.

That religion as an institution has had a profound effect on legal systems is made abundantly clear by Berman in his sketch of the development of Christianity. The emergence of canon law and ecclesiastical courts, thereby constituting "the first modern legal system of the West," stimulated secular authorities to create their own court system. In the centuries since the Protestant Reformation, the Church, though "delegalized," has influenced the development of the law of property and contract through its emphasis on individual will. According to Berman, the Church has succeeded in "Christianizing the law." In light of Berman's thesis, critically analyze the legal documents A to D in Appendix IV.

In the next two readings, Van Alstyne and Rheinstein trace the transformation of bodies of law regarding education and the family, respectively. The doctrine of due process was not deemed relevant in disciplinary actions against students in state-owned colleges and universities in the eighteenth and nineteenth centuries. Instead, the courts fell back on the doctrine of *in loco parentis*, thus granting the college or university a free hand in discipling its students. Toward the end of the nineteenth century this doctrine was superseded by the law of contract. In applying for admission to a college or a university, the courts argued that the student in effect agreed to abide by all the rules and regulations set forth in student handbooks and catalogs. In recent decades, Van Alstyne contends, the law of contract is giving way to constitutional safeguards of students' rights, including the application of concepts of due process.

In tracing the evolution of marriage from a legal standpoint, Rheinstein harks back to pre-Roman times, when people were free to establish and disestablish a family without legal sanction or constraint. With the rise of Christianity, marriage became a sacrament and hence was viewed as an indissoluble bond. Only in modern times, as religious institutions have waned, has the legal doctrine of marriage as a terminable contract come to the fore.

The last of the readings on interinstitutional relationships deals with the complex relationship between power and law. The political institutions of any society may be defined as those having a monopoly over the legitimate use of violence—in domestic as well as in foreign relations—through the control of police power, military power, and so forth. Power can be exercised in accordance with the rule of law—that is, the impersonal administration of universalistic legal norms—or in accordance with the particularistic wishes and interests of a dominant political party, social class, or powerful leader. In the analysis of law enforcement in Communist China from 1949 to 1970, Lung-sheng Tao analyzes the dominant role of the Communist Party. In the name of the "mass line," the Chinese Communist Party has succeeded in employing the courts to maintain its control over the society.

Clearly, the relationships between legal and nonlegal institutions illustrated in the foregoing readings depend upon the institutional configuration of a given society. This highlights the need for comparing legal systems in relation to the total social structures of societies. In Glendon's study of family law, we observe the impact of the emergence of the value of equality of the sexes on revisions of statutes and judicial decisions in four different legal systems: in two civil law countries (West Germany and France) and in two common law countries (England and the United States). In Evan's cross-national analysis of legal systems, in which seven indicators of legal systems are interrelated with ten indicators of nonlegal institutions, we note the effect of industrialization on selected attributes of legal systems. In particular, the four major families of legal systems—civil law, Anglo-Saxon law, socialist law, and Islamic law—differ significantly in the level of industrialization and in the level of education associated with them.

How would you apply an interinstitutional analysis in explaining the two U.S. Supreme Court decisions excerpted in Appendixes IV–E and IV–F?

26

Types of Lawmaking and Lawfinding
Max Weber

Categories of Legal Thought

A body of law can be "rational" in several different senses, depending on which of several possible courses legal thinking takes toward rationalization. Let us begin with the apparently most elementary thought process, viz., generalization, i.e., in our case, the reduction of the reasons relevant in the decision of concrete individual cases to one or more "principles," i.e., legal propositions. This process of reduction is normally conditional upon a prior or concurrent analysis of the facts of the case as to those ultimate components which are regarded as relevant in the juristic valuation. Conversely, the elaboration of ever more comprehensive "legal propositions" reacts upon the specification and delimitation of the potentially relevant characteristics of the facts. . . .

In our legal system the analytical derivation of "legal propositions" and the decision of specific cases go hand in hand with the synthetic work of "construction" of "legal relations" and "legal institutions," i.e., the determination of which aspects of a typical kind of communal or consensual action are to be regarded as *legally*

Excerpt from *Max Weber on Law in Economy and Society*, Max Rheinstein, translator and editor, Edward Shils, translator. Cambridge, Mass.: Harvard University Press, 1954, pp. 61-64, 303-308, 351-353, 355-356. Reprinted by permission of the publisher. Copyright © 1954 by the President and Fellows of Harvard College.

relevant, and in which logically consistent way these relevant components are to be regarded as *legally* coördinated, i.e., as being in "legal relationships." Although this latter process is closely related to the one previously described, it is nonetheless possible for a very high degree of sublimation in analysis to be correlated with a very low degree of constructional conceptualization of the legally relevant social relations. Conversely, the synthesis of a "legal relationship" may be achieved in a relatively satisfactory way despite a low degree of analysis, or occasionally just because of its limited cultivation. This contradiction is a result of the fact that analysis gives rise to a further logical task which, while it is compatible with synthetic construction, often turns out to be incompatible with it in fact. We refer to "systematization," which has never appeared but in late stages of legal modes of thought. To a youthful law, it is unknown. According to present modes of thought it represents an integration of all analytically derived legal propositions in such a way that they constitute a logically clear, internally consistent, and, at least in theory, gapless system of rules, under which, it is implied, all conceivable fact situations must be capable of being logically subsumed lest their order lack an effective guaranty. Even today not every body of law (e.g., English law) claims that it possesses the features of a system as defined above and, of course, the claim was even less frequently made by the legal systems of the past; where it was put forward at all, the degree of logical abstraction was often extremely low. In the main, the "system" has predominantly been an external scheme for the ordering of legal data and has been of only minor significance in the analytical derivation of legal propositions and in the construction of legal relationships. The specifically modern form of systematization, which developed out of Roman law, has its point of departure in the logical analysis of the meaning of the legal propositions as well as of the social actions. . . .

Both lawmaking and lawfinding may be either rational or irrational. They are "formally irrational" when one applies in lawmaking or lawfinding means which cannot be controlled by the intellect, for instance when recourse is had to oracles or substitutes therefor. Lawmaking and lawfinding are "substantively irrational" on the other hand to the extent that decision is influenced by concrete factors of the particular case as evaluated upon an ethical, emotional, or political basis rather than by general norms. "Rational" lawmaking and lawfinding may be of either a formal or a substantive kind. All formal law is, formally at least, relatively rational. Law, however, is "formal" to the extent that, in both substantive and procedural matters, only unambiguous general characteristics of the facts of the case are taken into account. This formalism can, again, be of two different kinds. It is possible that the legally relevant characteristics are of a tangible nature, i.e., that they are perceptible as sense data. This adherence to external characteristics of the facts, for instance, the utterance of certain words, the execution of a signature, or the performance of a certain symbolic act with a fixed meaning, represents the most rigorous type of legal formalism. The other type of formalistic law is found where the legally relevant characteristics of the facts are disclosed through the logical analysis of meaning and where, accordingly, definitely fixed legal concepts in the form of highly abstract rules are formulated and applied. This process of "logical rationality" diminishes the significance of extrinsic elements and thus softens the rigidity of concrete formalism. But the contrast to "substantive rationality" is sharpened, because the latter means that the decision of legal problems is influenced by norms different from those obtained through logical generalization of abstract interpretations of meaning. The norms to which substantive rationality accords predominance include ethical imperatives, utilitarian and other expediential rules, and political maxims, all of which diverge from the formalism of the "external characteristics" variety as well as from that which uses logical abstraction. However, the peculiarly professional, legalistic, and abstract approach to law in the modern sense is possible only in the measure that the law is formal in character. In so far as the absolute formalism of classification according to "sense-data characteristics" prevails, it exhausts itself in casuistry. Only that abstract method which employs the logical interpretation of meaning allows the execution of the specifically systematic task, i.e., the collection and rationalization by logical means of all the several rules recognized as legally valid into an internally consistent complex of abstract legal propositions. . . .

The Anti-Formalistic Tendencies of Modern Legal Development

From a theoretical point of view, the general development of law and procedure may be viewed as passing through the following stages: first, charismatic legal revelation through "law prophets"; second, empirical creation and finding of law by legal honoratiores, i.e., law creation through cautelary jurisprudence and adherence to precedent; third, imposition of law by secular or theocratic powers; fourth and finally, systematic elaboration of law and professionalized administration of justice by persons who have received their legal training in a learned and formally logical manner. From this perspective, the formal qualities of the law emerge as follows: arising in

primitive legal procedure from a combination of magically conditioned formalism and irrationality conditioned by revelation, they
proceed to increasingly specialized juridical and logical rationality
and systematization, passing through a stage of theocratically or
patrimonially conditioned substantive and informal expediency.
Finally, they assume, at least from an external viewpoint, an increasingly logical sublimation and deductive rigor and develop an
increasingly rational technique in procedure.

Since we are here only concerned with the most general lines of
development, we shall ignore the fact that in historical reality the
theoretically constructed stages of rationalization have not everywhere followed in the sequence which we have just outlined, even if
we ignore the world outside the Occident. We shall not be troubled
either by the multiplicity of causes of the particular type and degree
of rationalization that a given law has actually assumed. . . .

Only the Occident has witnessed the fully developed administration of justice of the folk-community . . . and the status group
stereotyped form of patrimonialism; and only the Occident has witnessed the rise of the rational economic system, whose agents first
allied themselves with the princely powers to overcome the estates
and then turned against them in revolution; and only the West has
known "Natural Law," and with it the complete elimination of the
system of personal laws and of the ancient maxim that special law
prevails over general law. Nowhere else, finally, has there occurred
any phenomenon resembling Roman law and anything like its reception. All these events have to a very large extent been caused by concrete political factors, which have only the remotest analogies
elsewhere in the world. For this reason, the stage of decisively shaping law by trained legal specialists has not been fully reached anywhere outside of the Occident. Economic conditions have, as we
have seen, everywhere played an important role, but they have
nowhere been decisive alone and by themselves. To the extent that
they contributed to the formation of the specifically modern features
of present-day occidental law, the direction in which they worked
has been by and large the following: To those who had interests
in the commodity market, the rationalization and systematization of
the law in general and, with certain reservations to be stated later,
the increasing calculability of the functioning of the legal process in
particular, constituted one of the most important conditions for the
existence of economic enterprise intended to function with stability
and, especially, of capitalistic enterprise, which cannot do without
legal security. Special forms of transactions and special procedures,
like the bill of exchange and the special procedure for its speedy

collection, serve this need for the purely formal certainty of the guaranty of legal enforcement.

On the other hand, the modern and, to a certain extent, the ancient Roman, legal developments have contained tendencies favorable to the dilution of legal formalism. At a first glance, the displacement of the formally bound law of evidence by the "free evaluation of proof" appears to be of a merely technical character. We have seen that the primitive system of magically bound proof was exploded through the rationalism of either the theocratic or the patrimonial kind, both of which postulated procedures for the disclosure of the real truth. Thus the new system clearly appears as a product of substantive rationalization. Today, however, the scope and limits of the free evaluation of proof are determined primarily by commercial interests, i.e., by economic factors. It is clear that, through the system of free evaluation of proof, a very considerable domain which was once subject to formal juristic thought is being increasingly withdrawn therefrom. But we are here more concerned with the corresponding trends in the sphere of substantive law. One such trend lies in the intrinsic necessities of legal thought. Its growing logical sublimation has meant everywhere the substitution for a dependence on externally tangible formal characteristics of an increasingly logical interpretation of meaning in relation to the legal norms themselves as well as in relation to legal transactions. In the doctrine of the continental "common law" this interpretation claimed that it would give effect to the "real" intentions of the parties; in precisely this manner it introduced an individualizing and relatively substantive factor into legal formalism. This kind of interpretation seeks to construct the relations of the parties to one another from the point of view of the "inner" kernel of their behavior, from the point of view of their mental "attitudes" (such as good faith or malice). Thus it relates legal consequences to informal elements of the situation and this treatment provides a telling parallel to that systematization of religious ethics which we have already considered previously. Much of the system of commodity exchange, in primitive as well as in technically differentiated patterns of trade, is possible only on the basis of far-reaching personal confidence and trust in the loyalty of others. Moreover, as commodity exchange increases in importance, the need in legal practice to guarantee or secure such trustworthy conduct becomes proportionally greater. But in the very nature of the case, we cannot, of course, define with formal certainty the legal tests according to which the new relations of trust and confidence are to be governed. Hence, through such ethical rationalization the courts have been helpful to powerful interests. Also, outside of the sphere of commodity exchange, the rationalization of the law has substituted attitude-evaluation as the significant element for assessment of events according to external criteria. In criminal law, legal rationalization has replaced the purely mechanistic remedy of vengeance by rational "ends of punishment" of an either ethical or utilitarian character, and has thereby introduced increasingly non-formal elements into legal practice. In the sphere of private law the concern for a party's mental attitude has quite generally entailed evaluation by the judge. "Good faith and fair dealing" or the "good" usage of trade or, in other words, ethical categories have become the test of what the parties are entitled to mean by their "intention." Yet, the reference to the "good" usage of trade implies in substance the recognition of such attitudes which are held by the average party concerned with the case, i.e., a general and purely business criterion of an essentially factual nature, such as the average expectation of the parties in a given transaction. It is this standard which the law has consequently to accept.

Now we have already seen that the expectations of parties will often be disappointed by the results of a strictly professional legal logic. Such disappointments are inevitable indeed where the facts of life are juridically "construed" in order to make them fit the abstract propositions of law and in accordance with the maxim that nothing can exist in the realm of law unless it can be "conceived" by the jurist in conformity with those "principles" which are revealed to him by juristic science. The expectations of the parties are oriented towards the economic and utilitarian meaning of a legal proposition. However, from the point of view of legal logic, this meaning is an "irrational" one. . . . To a large extent such conflicts rather are the inevitable consequence of the incompatibility that exists between the intrinsic necessities of logically consistent formal legal thinking and the fact that the legally relevant agreements and activities of private parties are aimed at economic results and oriented towards economically determined expectations. It is for this reason that we find the ever-recurrent protests against the professional legal method of thought as such, which are finding support even in the lawyers' own reflections on their work. But a "lawyers' law" has never been and never will be brought into conformity with lay expectation unless it totally renounce that formal character which is immanent in it. . . .

Rational and Irrational Administration of Justice

Rational adjudication on the basis of rigorously formal legal concepts is to be contrasted with a type of adjudication which is guided primarily by sacred traditions without finding therein a clear basis for the decision of concrete cases. It thus decides cases either as charismatic justice, i.e., by the concrete "revelations" of an oracle, a prophet's doom, or an ordeal; or as Khadi justice non-formalistically and in accordance with concrete ethical or other practical value-judgments; or as empirical justice, formalistically, but not by sub-sumption of the case under rational concepts but by the use of "analogies" and the reference to and interpretation of "precedents." The last two cases are particularly interesting for us here. In khadi justice, there are no "rational" bases of "judgment" at all, and in the pure form of empirical justice we do not find such rational bases, at least in that sense in which we are using the term. The concrete value-judgment aspect of khadi justice can be intensified until it leads to a prophetic break with all tradition, while empirical justice can be sublimated and rationalized into a veritable technique. Since the non-bureaucratic forms of authority exhibit a peculiar juxtaposi-tion of a sphere of rigorous subordination to tradition on the one hand and a sphere of free discretion and grace of the ruler on the other, combinations and marginal manifestations of both principles are frequent. In contemporary England, for instance, we still find a broad substratum of the legal system which is in substance khadi justice to an extent which cannot be easily visualized on the Con-tinent. Our own jury system, in which the reasons of the verdict are not pronounced, frequently operates in practice in the same way.[1] One should thus be careful not to assume that "democratic" prin-ciples of adjudication are identical with rational, i.e., formalistic, adjudication. The very opposite is the truth, as we have shown in another place. Even American and British justice in the great national courts still is to a large extent empirical adjudication, based on pre-cedent. The reason for the failure of all attempts to codify English law in a rational way as well as for the rejection of Roman law lay in the successful resistance of the great, centrally organized lawyers' guilds, a monopolistic stratum of honoratiores, who have produced from their ranks the judges of the great courts. They kept legal education as a highly developed empirical technique in their own hands and combated the menace to their social and material position which threatened to arise from the ecclesiastical courts and, for a time, also from the universities in their attempts to rationalize the legal system. The struggle of the common law lawyers against Roman and ecclesiastical law and against the power position of the church was to a large extent economically caused by their interest in fees, as was demonstrated by the royal intervention in this conflict. But their power position, which successfully withstood this conflict, was a result of political centralization. In Germany, there was lacking, for predominantly political reasons, any socially powerful estate of honoratiores who, like the English lawyers, could have been the bearers of a national legal tradition, could have developed the national law as a veritable art with an orderly doctrine, and could have resisted the invasion of the technically superior training of the jurists educated in Roman law. It was not the greater suitability of substantive Roman law to the needs of emerging capitalism which decided the victory here. As a matter of fact, the specific legal institutions of modern capitalism were unknown to Roman law and are of medieval origin. No, the victory of the Roman law was due to its rational form and the technical necessity of placing procedure in the hands of rationally trained specialists, i.e., the Roman law trained university graduates. The increasingly complicated nature of the cases arising out of the more and more rationalized economy was no longer satisfied with the old crude techniques of trial by ordeal or oath but required a rational technique of fact-finding such as the one in which these university men were trained. The factor of a changing economic structure operated, it is true, everywhere including England, where rational procedures of proof were introduced by the royal authority especially in the interest of the merchants. The main cause for the difference which nonetheless exists between the development of substantive law in England and Germany is not, as is already apparent, to be found here but rather in the autonomous tendencies of the two types of organization of authority. In England there was a centralized system of courts and, simultaneously, rule by honoratiores; in Germany there was no political centralization but yet there was bureaucracy. The first country of modern times to reach a high level of capitalistic development, i.e., England, thus preserved a less rational and less bureaucratic legal system. That capitalism could nevertheless make its way so well in England was largely because the court system and trial procedure amounted until well in the modern age to a denial of justice to the economically weaker groups. This fact and the cost in time and money of transfers of landed property, which was also influenced by the economic interests of the lawyers, influenced the structure of agrarian England in the direction of the accumulation and immobilization of landed property. . . .

The demands for "legal equality" and of guaranties against arbitrariness require formal rational objectivity in administration in contrast to personal free choice on the basis of grace, as characterized the older type of patrimonial authority. The democratic ethos, where it pervades the masses in connection with a concrete question, based as it is on the postulate of substantive justice in concrete cases for concrete individuals, inevitably comes into conflict with the formalism and the rule-bound, detached objectivity of bureaucratic administration. For this reason it must emotionally reject what is rationally demanded. The propertyless classes in particular are not served, in the way in which bourgeois are, by formal "legal equality" and "calculable" adjudication and administration. The propertyless demand that law and administration serve the equalization of economic and social opportunities vis-à-vis the propertied classes, and judges or administrators cannot perform this function unless they assume the substantively ethical and hence nonformalistic character of the Khadi. The rational course of justice and administration is interfered with not only by every form of "popular justice," which is little concerned with rational norms and reasons, but also by every type of intensive influencing of the course of administration by "public opinion," that is, in a mass democracy, that communal activity which is born of irrational "feelings" and which is normally instigated or guided by party leaders or the press. As a matter of fact, these interferences can be as disturbing as, or, under circumstances, even more disturbing than, those of the star chamber practices of an "absolute" monarch.

Note

1. Written before the unpopular jury system was replaced in Germany, in 1924, by the system of the mixed bench, consisting of a majority of laymen and a minority of professional career judges deliberating jointly on all aspects of the case. . . .

27

Legal System Evolution: An Analytical Model
Jonathan H. Turner

All legal systems reveal four basic elements: (1) a body of law, (2) law-enacting processes, (3) adjudicating procedures or courts, and (4) enforcement agencies (Hoebel, 1954; Davis et al., 1962; Lloyd, 1964). When one examines actual legal systems, however, these elements and their organization evidence enormous variability. For example, the laws, courts, lawmaking process, and enforcement capacities of the Trobriand Islanders (Malinowski, 1926) and Cheyenne Indians (Hoebel, 1960: 49–58) can be distinguished not only from each other but also from the legal systems of more developed and differentiated societies. To capture this variability at the empirical level, legal scholars initially tended to construct typologies of legal systems (Wigmore, 1936). More recent efforts, however, have involved the delineation of developmental typologies which seek to describe the "stages" of legal system evolution from simple to complex forms (Parsons, 1965; Schwartz and Miller, 1965; Carlston, 1956; Sawer, 1965). These developmental typologies have consider-

Excerpt from a revised version of "A Cybernetic Model of Legal Development," *Western Sociological Review* 5 (Summer 1974) pp. 3–16, by permission of the author and publisher.

able advantage over the older classificatory schemes, because they view legal systems as constantly in change and as influenced by the broader social structure of society (L. Friedman, 1959; W. Friedman, 1969, Parsons, 1962, 1965; Evan, 1968).

The developmental approach emphasizes several points: The increasing internal differentiation of the four basic elements of legal systems—law, enactment, courts, and enforcement—as they are influenced by the differentiation of institutions in the broader society (Bredemeier, 1962). And, since Weber's (1922) and Durkheim's (1893) early analyses, the emphasis has been on viewing legal system development as a response to the integrative "problems" created during the process of societal differentiation. For example, scholars such as Parsons (1962) have noted that as traditional forms of social control break down with the differentiation of such key institutions as economy, polity, kinship, and religion, structural elaboration of the legal system occurs as a "response" to the integrative problems posed by this differentiation. Moreover, in Parsons's (1965) view, the elaboration of the legal system under specified conditions can create a new set of institutional relations that accelerates development in the broader society.

The developmental view of law, then, focuses on the reciprocal relations between societal and legal differentiation. Societal differentiation is often facilitated by the elaboration of laws, lawmaking capacities, courts, and enforcement agencies, while the differentiation, elaboration, and internal integration of these basic elements is considered to be a response to integrative problems created by broader societal differentiation. The circularity of this argument is, to some degree, inherent in functionalist assumptions about structures meeting "needs" (Turner, 1974b, 1978), but it also points out an essential fact of social life: System relationships are reciprocal, and each mutually sets conditions for the other's structural change and elaboration. The problem with this "circular" argument is not its circularity but its vagueness. To posit that institutional change forces legal development, and vice versa, leaves unanswered many of the theoretically interesting questions: Why does this reciprocal relationship exist? Through what specific processes does this change occur? Which points of articulation between law and the broader institutional environment are most critical?

There are two general ways of approaching such questions. One involves analytical modeling of institutional linkages in societal systems, and the other seeks the discovery of abstract principles from which generalizations about societal and legal development can be deduced (Turner, 1978: 1-19). Both of these approaches have been employed in the analysis of legal systems, but neither has been used to its full potential. For example, implicit in the view of societies as having integrative "problems" or "requisites" that legal systems "resolve" or "meet" is an abstract theoretical principle that scholars from Durkheim to Parsons have implicitly employed but never made explicit. An explicit formulation of this principle can provide one kind of "explanation" as to why legal system development should occur. Abstract principles, however, do not specify what is typically of interest to sociologists: the causal connections among specified variables. For this reason, analytical modeling where key relations among structures are isolated has become the dominant mode of theoretical analysis in sociology. Yet, in the context of legal development, the current models reveal as much vagueness as the implicit laws underlying notions of "functional needs" and "integrative problems." Key structural linkages are often ignored; there is a tendency to place heavy emphasis on one variable, such as the economy, and ignore the impact of other variables in an effort to discover *the primary* cause of legal development. . . .

A Theory of Differentiation and Integration

It was Émile Durkheim in his *The Division of Labor in Society* (1893) who first clearly articulated the principles of structural differentiation and integration. Subsequent scholars such as Parsons have adopted Durkheim's notions but have often failed to state his insights as true theoretical principles. If one transcends Durkheim's specific concern with the division of labor and focuses on the more general question of social differentiation and integration, Durkheim can be credited with formulating four related laws:

1. The greater the size of a population in a system, the greater the volume of interaction, and the more likely its members' differentiation into diverse activities.
2. The more differentiated a social system, the less likely is that system to be integrated in terms of common cultural values.
3. The more differentiated a social system, the more likely is that system to be integrated in terms of structural interdependencies.
4. The more differentiated the system and the less its integration in terms of cultural values, the more likely is that system to differentiate specific integrative structures.

. . . In Durkheim's terms, the "collective conscience" becomes "enfeebled" with the growth of the division of labor, setting into motion a new form of social integration—"organic solidarity"—to replace the old "mechanical solidarity." To regularize interdependencies, specific structures from "contract law" to "occupational groups" emerge to specify normatively what is to occur in social transactions. And for Durkheim, systems that fail to develop such structures evidence "anomie" and will reveal high rates of deviance and conflict.

When examined more abstractly, these Durkheimian principles can apply to a wide variety of system referents, from a specific organization to an entire society or system of societies. When a society is the unit of analysis, the principles argue that differentiation increases the number of relations among diverse social units which, in turn, forces cultural values, in Parsons's terms, to "generalize" and have less capacity to regulate affairs. Without this regulation, rates of deviance and conflict will increase, creating pressures for the development, by design or chance, of regulative structures. One of the most important of these regulative structures to be differentiated and elaborated is the legal system.

While Durkheim's theory may be deficient on many points, it gives us a sense of why legal systems should become differentiated. It does not specify causal connections or provide specific information about actual historical events, but rather denotes certain generic properties of social structure and expresses these as a series of principles. As abstract principles, they provide insight into all differentiating systems, but for our purposes, they give us a sense of why, in terms of certain inherent features of social structure, legal development is likely to occur in societal social systems. Moreover, these principles capture the essence of the more functional argument about "integrative imperatives" without resorting to the troublesome vocabulary of functionalism. The principles simply argue that "selective pressures" in differentiating systems are initiated for the search for and adoption of integrative structures. They do not say that these structures must exist, since the historical record is filled with examples of systems that, for a variety of specific historical reasons, were not able to create adequate integrative substructures.

These structural principles, however, are devoid of specifics. They do not indicate *which* differentiating structures in a societal system create pressures for *what aspects* of legal evolution. Nor do they specify the specific processes through which legal systems and societal structures reciprocally influence each other. This kind of information be provided can only with an analytical model that "fills in" the causal connections unspecified by theoretical principles. . . . The remainder of this paper will seek to outline the broad contours of such an analytic model.

An Analytic Model of Legal Development

An analytical model accentuates certain features of actual empirical systems. In such models, it is not assumed that all facets and nuances of the empirical world are being depicted, nor is there any pretense that all the potential variations in the phenomena under study are being captured. . . .

In approaching such a task, we are immediately confronted with several problems. First, since we are concerned with legal development over time, it will be necessary to develop a model that describes historical systems. The historical data that can help construct a model and then "test" its plausibility will thus tend to be open to varying interpretations, since "reading" the historical "record" is always a controversial enterprise. Yet we must accept this limitation if we are to do more than develop a synchronic analysis of contemporary legal systems.

Second, we are confronted with the fact that relations between legal systems and their institutional environment are reciprocal. Our model will therefore need to address the "feedback" relations among structures. But in using the concept of "feedback" and in developing a model that can be seen as "cybernetic," we encounter a problem of definition. The concepts "cybernetics" and "feedback" have, with their infiltration into the general lexicon, lost much of their originally precise meaning. It is necessary, therefore, to clarify just how the concept of feedback will be employed in constructing this present model. The original conception of feedback involved an image of goal-directed systems which systematically sought information on the consequences of their actions in the environment. Such information was, initially at least, visualized as "feedback," which would allow the system to "correct" its actions so as to continue the pursuit of goals (Weiner, 1952). This vision of cybernetics has increasingly been seen as too limiting: It tends to stress only negative feedback and hence can be used only to describe systems that are rigidly programmed into predetermined goals and that can only engage in a process of self-correction. One extension of the concept of feedback involves the recognition that it can be "deviation amplifying" or "positive." That is, on the basis of positive signals from the environment, a system can alter or expand its goals and pursue lines of conduct that deviate considerably from its initial programming (Maruyama, 1963). Another extension of the concept involves the recognition that not all feedback systems are teleological—that is, they do not collect "information" on performance in relation to goals. Ecological systems, for example, cannot be considered to have "goals" in the same sense as a complex organization or thermostat, but they do seem to evidence patterns of self-correction and deviation amplification. Another complication is introduced by the fact that in human systems teleological decisions among individual units can have unanticipated and unintended consequences when viewed as a "collective decision"(Homans, 1975). For example, Boudon (1968) offers the illustration that as each individual family decides that a college education for its children is a goal that will increase income, the collective result of too many families' making this decision can be for a decrease in the economic value of college education as it becomes a less scarce commodity in the job market. It is hard to visualize such "collective decisions" as teleological; yet they will "feedback" and have an impact on families' explicitly teleological decisions to seek a college education.

These issues suggest the use of a broad definition of cybernetics, unless we wish to restrict its usage to only rigidly programmed goal-directed and decision-making systems. In the model to be developed here, the following definition will be employed: *Cybernetics* is a process whereby system outputs at one point in time generate consequences in the environment which "feedback" on the system and influence, at a subsequent point in time, the structure of the system and its outputs. *Negative feedback* is a situation where outputs generate consequences that restrain structural elaboration of a system and that maintain its present state of outputs. *Positive feedback* is a situation where outputs have consequences that encourage structural elaborations which alter outputs. These definitions allow us to visualize nonteleological and deviation-amplifying processes that often typify both the biotic and human world. . . .

In using this vision of cybernetics to examine legal system development, we must remember that the institutions of a society constitute the environment of the legal system and that, for certain analytical purposes, the legal system can be seen to represent the environment of other social institutions. Thus, outputs of the legal system that are in response to broader institutional pressures represent "feedback" to these institutions from their legal system "environment." Conversely, changes in any or all institutions that effect changes in the legal system represent "feedback" to the legal system.

These considerations raise a third problem: Which institutions represent the most important facet of the legal system's environment? If we conclude that all are important, we will fail to accentuate only the most important feedback relations between the legal system and its institutional environment. We need, therefore, some analytical criteria for selecting important linkages. . . . It is in this context that Parsons's notion of four universal needs for "adaptation," "goal attainment," "integration," and "latency" are most useful.[1] If we *assume* that the legal system is, to varying degrees in different empirical systems at different stages of development, primarily an "integrative" institution, then analysis turns to the examination of relations between the major "adaptive," "goal attainment," and "latency" institutions and the legal system. Moreover, if the development of the legal system meets integrative needs formerly met by other institutions, then analyses must explore the feedback relations between law and those institutions that it displaces. The concept of functional needs, then, can provide criteria for sorting out the crucial from less crucial cybernetic relations. Parsons's four functional needs do not explain *why* an institution exists, but they do provide a useful set of assumptions that allow us to cut through the complexity of the empirical world.

In sum then, a model of legal system development should (a) examine legal systems over long historical periods, (b) utilize the concepts of cybernetics and feedback to capture the reciprocal *relations* between law and its institutional environment, and (c) employ analytical criteria of what is important in social systems. . . .

Legal Development in Historical Societies

In terms of the Parsonian action theory, the economy is the main adaptive institution at the social level of social system organization; the polity is the principal goal-attainment institution; education and kinship are the primary latency institutions; and religion and law are the main integrative institutions. Thus, the dynamics of legal system development revolve around the feedback relations among economy, polity, education, kinship,[2] and religion on the one hand and the legal system on the other. It is around these feedback relations that the following historical model is constructed.

Economic and Legal Development

It can be assumed that the initial impetus behind legal development in historical societies came from the economy (Weber, 1922). As soon as economies have been capable of creating economic surplus beyond the needs of subsistence, extensive exchange of goods can occur. Just how to regulate these exchanges and assure the good faith of the parties involved probably led to the initial differentiation of *torts* from *crimes* in the body of law. It is no coincidence that torts apparently first emerged around 4000 B.C. in Egypt in response to the extensive trading activities among seminomadic groups of this region. By 2100 B.C., in the Codes of Hammurabi, torts were institutionalized in the legal system of this area (Davis, 1962: 81). In feudal Europe several thousand years later, the emergence of economic surplus and its exchange in the market similarly stimulated a body of torts, or "merchant laws," which while remaining unincorporated in the formal legal system were nevertheless binding on all parties.

The differentiation of torts from crimes was probably a result of the expansion in number and function of courts that arose to mediate disputes arising from new patterns of exchange. However, the enforcement of the law and of the court's decisions seems to have remained in the hands of the economic community, indicating that the initial emergence of a stable police force occurs less in response to economic pressures than in response to the needs of an emerging state bureaucracy—an occurrence that lags somewhat behind economic development by virtue of being dependent upon the existence of an economic surplus (Fried, 1967).

To the extent such torts and court structures could emerge in historical societies, economic development was greatly facilitated, since the regularization of exchange represents positive feedback to the productive sector of the economy (Turner, 1971). Later, with political development and the emergence of a stable police and a legislative body, the purview of torts could be greatly expanded, thus accelerating economic development. This crucial linkage between law and economic development in historical societies can be illustrated by China, which was as culturally and technologically developed as feudal Europe and yet did not industrialize until much later. Part of the explanation for this lack of economic development, as Weber emphasized (Weber, 1905, 1922), probably lay in the nature of the traditional Chinese legal system, which revolved around crimes rather than torts. The Imperial Code was primarily a criminal body of law and did not concern matters of trade, commerce, transaction, exchange, and contract. These matters were left to local customary law and hence did not become codified into a consistent, society-wide body of torts—thus serving as negative feedback to economic development.

To the extent that the emergence of torts and an expanded court system represented positive feedback to the economy, increased economic activity represented positive feedback to legal development, for economic growth creates conditions favorable to an expanded body of torts and court system, while allowing sufficient political development (see below), so that enforcement and legislative elements of the legal system can similarly expand. This process is represented diagrammatically in Figure 1.

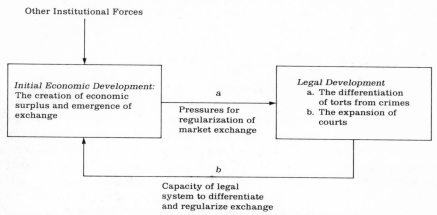

FIGURE 1. Economic and Legal Development in Historical Societies

In Figure 1 the amount of economic surplus and exchange that exists in a developing economy is denoted by arrow a. Arrow b represents the extent to which the differentiation of torts from crimes and the expansion of courts can result in increased trade, which in turn can lead to further legal development. Such legal development would then initiate this cycle again, thereby accelerating economic development. For example, if as in China the political structure was such as to inhibit the differentiation of a comprehensive body of torts from crimes, then arrow b would represent negative feedback on to economic development. Or, if alternative patterns of regulating exchange existed in a society (along kinship and community lines), then the weights assigned to arrow a would be low, indicating little economic pressure for legal development. Or, as Weber emphasized in his classic work on Protestantism and capitalism (1905), if the necessary structural conditions (technology, urbanism, the availability of capital, etc.) are not supplemented by a value system emphasizing accumulation, thrift, and expansion, then the weights for linkage a would be low.

Figure 1, like the other figures to follow, does not provide weights for the connections between the economy and legal system denoted by arrows a and b. What an analytical model does is accentuate key points of interchange; it cannot specify weights, since these vary from one empirical system to another. There is, of course, an implicit weighting of causal connections in view of the fact that legal development is initiated by economic changes. But so many unique empirical conditions can influence connections a and b that it is impossible to assign weights in the abstract. Indeed, a model that sought to assign weights would become an empirical description of a particular system and would thereby lose the advantages that come with abstraction.

Political and Legal Development

Political development involves the consolidation of society-wide power. Initially such consolidation occurred within kinship in historical societies as certain kin groups assumed dominance over other kin groups. However, the kinship basis of a polity eventually shifts to a less ascriptive and more bureaucratized form of political organization. As historical political systems increasingly consolidated power into a centralized state, they necessarily stimulated legal development. In turn, such development in the legal system allowed for the further consolidation of power in the hands of the state.

Power ultimately rests upon the capacity to use force, and thus a well-established police force must accompany the exercise of power. It is hypothesized that this political necessity of using force was the primary condition for the initial differentiation from kinship and community of a discrete and stable set of social control positions. The emergence of such a police force is crucial to legal development, for without a separate set of control statutes, enforcement of laws and court decisions must rest with kinship and community, thereby stalling legal development beyond the expansion of courts and the differentiation of torts that originally emerged under economic imperatives (see above). While the power of historical political systems was usually legitimated by religious symbols, some of these and other unifying cultural symbols were often codified in law as general legal postulates, thus initiating the process of legal legitimation of political processes evident in all modern societies. Accompanying these developments, the differentiation of *public* and *private* law became more clear-cut, as the state attempted to specify its relationship to the public, and vice versa, while defining what is properly the business of private parties. While this differentiation of public and private law is anticipated in the separation of crimes from torts, *public* law begins to specify noncriminal, administrative relationships between the state and public, thus initiating the incipient development of what is a vast body of administrative law in modern legal systems.

To institutionalize the relationships between the state and public, the political system typically expands the court system. Such expansion in historical systems was often a ploy by the political elite to buffer itself from the public by providing the appearance of a grievance mechanism. Yet, whatever the motives, this development greatly expanded the court system and initiated its centralization into a hierarchical system of courts, culminating in some form of supreme tribunal.

As the political system of a historical society consolidated power, it attempted to extend its sphere of control in all areas of social life. To do so, it often enacted through a nonrepresentative legislative structure comprehensive bodies of *civil* law. In the absence of a centralized state, *common* law precedents established in decentralized courts, tied to local markets and governments, will be the principal mechanism for expanding the body of law in a society. But with political development, civil law enactment begins to supplement, and eventually surpass, common law as the principal mechanism for expanding a society's body of law. With the institutionalization of civil law, a necessary condition for expanding the other elements of the legal system is met, since comprehensive enactment allows law to become systematized, internally consistent, and tied less to local territories. Furthermore, the legislative process can expand very rapidly the laws of a society and thereby necessitate expansion of the court system and enforcement agencies.

Thus, political development greatly accelerated legal development initiated under economic expansion in historical societies. In turn, such legal development represents positive feedback to the polity, allowing it to consolidate more power and extend its sphere of control. This consolidation of power and control eventually stimulates further pressures for legal development, creating a cyclical feedback process between the legal and political subsystems of a society. This process is represented diagrammatically in Figure 2.

Arrow c in Figure 2 denotes the strength of pressures for main-

FIGURE 2.   Political and Legal Development in Historical Societies

Other Institutional Forces

Political Development
Consolidation of power
into a centralized,
bureaucratized state

c

Imperatives for
regulating society-
wide activities

Legal Development
a. Stabilized enforcement
b. Legislature enactment
   of civil law
c. Further expansion of
   courts
d. Legitimation of polity

d

Capacity of legal
system to differentiate
and promote consolidation
of power

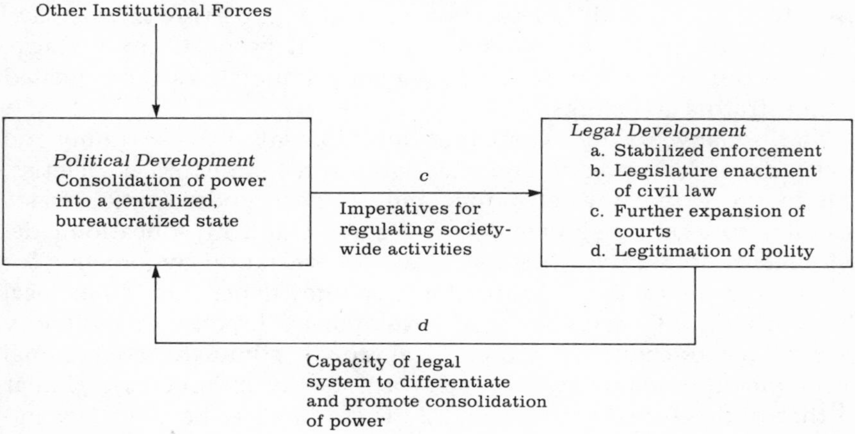

taining power and regulating society-wide activities by the emerging state bureaucracy. To the extent that such pressures become translated into a stable police force, legal postulates that codify unifying cultural symbols, a body of public law, an expanded court system, and legislative mechanisms for civil law enactment, they represent positive feedback to the political system, as is denoted by arrow d. As with linkages with the economy, broader societal conditions will affect the weights assigned to arrows c and d for any particular system. For example, the strength of kinship groups can greatly inhibit political unification into a state bureaucracy and hence the implementation of new legal processes. Or, the level of economic surplus in a society can limit the resources available to the polity for consolidation of power and expansion of law (Fried, 1967).

Education and Legal Development

While integrative problems created by the differentiation of the economy and polity initiated legal evolution in historical societies, continued expansion of legal systems was dependent upon educational development. To expand rapidly under civil law enactment, the political elite and its legislative body in historical societies tended to be dependent upon a group of scholars educated in a legal tradition. Without such expertise, law enactment would have been unsystematic and contradictory to previously established common-law precedents. For example, the early emergence of an extensive civil code in France under Napoleon can be attributed to a large group of educated legal scholars who advised the legislators. Eventually, the legislators themselves must become educated in at least the rudiments of law for continued extension of civil codes. Similarly, to operate an expanded court system requires that incumbents, especially lawyers and judges, possess some expertise in the law. Furthermore, as the courts and enforcement agencies grow in size, they become bureaucratized and generate imperatives for educated administrators and clerks.

Additionally, to the extent that development in the economy and polity depended upon an educated labor force in historical societies, and to the extent that economic and political modernization was a stimulus to legal development (see Figures 1 and 2), educational development indirectly influenced legal modernization by allowing for differentiation of those institutional spheres dependent upon legal differentiation. Conversely, legal development directly, or indirectly as it influences economic and political growth, stimulated educational development—thus initiating reciprocal feedback processes similar to that outlined in Figures 1 and 2. These linkages between law and education are represented in Figure 3.

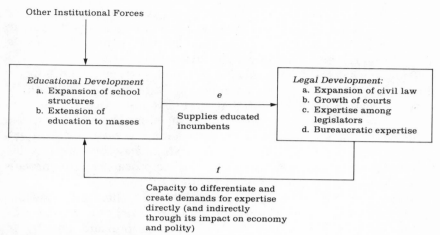

FIGURE 3. Legal and Educational Development

Arrow e in Figure 3 denotes the reliance of the legal system upon expertise supplied by the educational system. Arrow f represents the feedback, both direct and indirect, of legal development upon educational expansion. As for arrows a through d, the weights of the linkages represented by e and f are a function of the unique institutional configuration of a society. For example, should religious dogma and its institutionalization in a powerful church impede the development of a secularized educational system, then the weight assigned to linkage c would be low, as would that of f. Or, if economic and political development be impeded, imperatives for a large, educated labor pool, and hence expanded educational system, would not be met, thus lowering the weights for e and f.

Religion and Legal Development

With societal differentiation, religious beliefs and rituals become increasingly incapable of providing society-wide integration. Integrative problems within and among differentiating structures become too specific, secular, variable, and ever expanding for beliefs and rituals directed toward the supernatural to have much impact. Initially, common-law precedents set by local courts begin to proliferate in response to sources of malintegration that are not resolvable by religious doctrines. Eventually, the emerging state begins to enact bodies of civil law, while consolidating local courts and establishing a society-wide system of enforcement. It is at this stage that institutionalized religion can either inhibit or accelerate legal development. To the extent that religious elites permitted legal encroachment into what was traditionally a religious sphere, legal development was accelerated in historical systems. However, to the degree that these elite rejected new legal doctrines and the emerging court system, emphasizing instead doctrinal orthodoxy and ritual solutions to integrative problems, legal development was inhibited.

Thus, once legal development is initiated, a crucial condition for further development is the institutional segregation of religion. If such segregation could be initiated with little resistance, then expansion of the legal system occurred. In turn, expansion of law into the integrative sphere further segregated religion, decreasing the latter's capacity to provide society-wide integration and thus encouraging even more rapid legal development. This reciprocal feedback process is diagrammatically represented in Figure 4.

Arrow g in Figure 4 denotes the inability of religious institutions to provide society-wide integration. Linkage h denotes the capacity of the legal system to provide such integration, and thereby to segregate religion even further in a society.

In sum, the interrelationships specified in Figures 1 through 4 are believed to be the most critical in understanding legal evolution in historical societies. Such evolution is a reflection of forces in the institutional environment of law. However, once these forces initiate changes in the profile of law, the legal system generates feedbacks, as indicated by relationships b, d, f, and h, and accelerates those broader institutional forces, as represented by linkages a, c, e, and g, that eventually stimulate further legal development.

A model such as that outlined in Figures 1 through 4 provides clear leads for empirical inquiry. By focusing on the connections denoted by arrows a through g, crucial aspects of legal system devel-

FIGURE 4. Religious Segregation and Legal Development

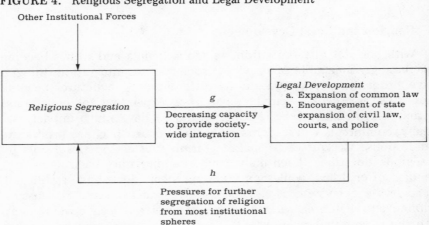

opment will be exposed. While the model does not provide operational indicators, it does make explicit the abstract class of variables that will require empirical exploration. The goal of such exploration should be to discover the weights of arrows a through g and thereby render a complete description of empirical systems. By assessing the degree to which the weights represent positive or negative feedback, understanding of why a concrete historical system experienced rapid or slow legal development should be possible.

Legal Development in Contemporary Societies

In addition to providing a means for understanding legal development in historical societies, the analytic model developed in Figures 1 through 4 can offer guidelines for examining legal systems in the present. Indeed, contemporary systems are the product of positive feedback relations between a differentiating institutional environment and expanding legal system. Since further legal development in the future of any contemporary society is likely to involve increased differentiation (as opposed to de-differentiation), the linkages outlined in arrows a through h in Figures 1 through 4 are still highly relevant to understanding both the present profile of contemporary systems and the causes of their future development. . . .

Drawing heavily from Parsons's and Smelser's (1956: 68) analysis of the interchanges between the integrative "sector" of a society on the one hand and the adaptive, goal-attainment, and latency sectors on the other, we can visualize the essential points of articulation between societal and legal development. . . .

Comparing the linkages of historical and modern legal systems with their respective institutional environments reveals an elaboration of trends evident during initial legal evolution. These linkages are summarized in Figure 5.

The profile of any modern legal system will be a reflection of the weights attached to these reciprocal relationships. Comparison of different modern legal systems will inevitably reveal differences in the pressures from the institutional environment. Furthermore, since the relationship between any particular institution and law is reciprocal, a mutual, positive feedback process can occur such that one feature of a legal system can develop at a disproportionate rate—thus accounting for much of the uniqueness of any particular legal system. Thus, for each concrete legal system the weights of these, and certainly the other linkages not delineated in this simple model, could be established and used to account for the particular profile of the legal system in question.

FIGURE 5. Institutional Exchanges between the Legal System and the Institutional Environment

Functional Imperative		Institutional Environment	Legal System
Adaptation	Economy	integrative demands entrepreneurship	Law: a. expanded torts and court system b. administrative tribunals c. regulatory agencies
Goal Attainment	Polity	financial resources; demands for society-wide power and legitimation legitimated administrative capacity to wield power	Law: a. proliferation of administrative law b. centralization of laws, courts, legislature, and enforcement c. bureaucratization of legal system at all levels
Latency	Education	expert incumbents; diffuse support of law institutionalization of mass education in law	Law: a. professionalization of legal roles b. increasing expertise at all levels of legal bureaucracy
Integration	Religion	diffuse symbolic support institutionalized segregation, subordination, and privilege	Law: a. church public law

The model outlined in Figure 5 is descriptive, since it provides a set of analytical criteria for comparing concrete empirical systems. It does, however, hold out the promise of a more mature, predictive model, since once the consequences of various combinations of weights on different linkages are assessed for a variety of empirical systems, then it should be possible to make predictions as to how events in a particular system will influence legal system development and how a particular pattern of such development will effect differentiation in the broader institutional environment.

Such predictions can supplement what I hope will be concurrent refinements in the primitive theoretical principles presented earlier on the relationship between differentiation and integrative processes. The simultaneous search for general structural principles and for specific models on particular facets of social systems will, I feel, provide sociology with the conceptual tools that will allow for the better realization of all three goals of mature theory: description, explanation, and prediction. . . .

Notes

1. "Adaptation" is the problem of securing resources from the environment, converting them into usable form, and distributing them to system units; "goal attainment" is the problem of formulating system goals and priorities among them as well as mobilizing and allocating resources for their attainment; "latency" is the dual problem of "managing tensions" among system units and of generating new units ("pattern maintenance"); and "integration" is the problem of coordinating relations among system units.
2. For reasons of parsimony, the relationship between kinship and law will not be analyzed, primarily because this relationship is not regarded to be as crucial for legal system development as that between education and law.

References

Boudon, R. (1968). *A quoi sert la notion de structure?* Paris: V. Gallimard.

Bredemeier, H. C. (1962). "Law as an Integrative Mechanism." In W. M. Evan (ed.), *Law and Sociology: Exploratory Essays*. New York: The Free Press, pp. 73-90.

Carlston, K. (1956). *Law and Structures of Social Action*. New York: Columbia University Press.

Davis, J. F., H. S. Foster, Jr., and C. R. Jeffery (1962). *Society and Law: New Meanings for an Old Profession*. New York: The Free Press.

Durkheim, E. (1893) *The Division of Labor in Society*. New York: Free Press (1933 edition).

Evan, W. M. (1968). "A Data Archive of Legal Systems: A Cross-national Analysis of Sample Data." *European Journal of Sociology* 9: 113-125.

Fried, M. H. (1967). *The Evolution of Political Society.* New York: Random House.

Friedman, L. M. (1969). "Legal Culture and Societal Development." *Law and Society Review* 4 (August): 29-44.

Friedman, W. (1959). *Law in a Changing Society.* Berkeley: University of California Press.

Hoebel, E. A. (1954). *The Law of Primitive Man.* New York: Atheneum Publishers.

—— (1960). *The Cheyennes.* New York: Holt.

Homans, G. C. (1975). "What Do We Mean by Social Structure?" In P. M. Blau (ed.), *Approaches to the Study of Social Structure.* New York: Free Press, pp. 53-65.

Lloyd, D. (1964). *The Idea of Law.* Baltimore: Penguin Books.

Malinowski, B. (1926). *Crime and Custom in Savage Society.* London: Routledge.

Maruyama, M. (1963). "The Second Cybernetics: Deviation-amplifying Mutual Causal Processes." *American Scientist* 51 (June): 164-179.

Parsons, T. (1962). "The Law and Social Control." In W. M. Evan (ed.), *Law and Sociology: Exploratory Essays.* New York: The Free Press, pp. 56-72.

—— (1965). *Societies: Evolutionary and Comparative Perspectives.* Englewood Cliffs, N.J.: Prentice-Hall.

Parsons, T., and N. J. Smelser (1956). *Economy and Society.* New York: Free Press.

Sawer, G. (1965). *Law in Society.* London: Oxford at the Clarendon Press.

Schwartz, R. D., and J. C. Miller (1965). "Legal Evolution and Societal Complexity." *American Journal of Sociology* 70 (August): 159-169.

Turner, J. H. (1971). "A Cybernetic Model of Economic Development." *The Sociological Quarterly* 17 (Summer): 191-204.

—— (1972). *Patterns of Social Organization.* New York: McGraw-Hill.

—— (1974a). "A Cybernetic Model of Legal Development." *Western Sociological Review* 5 (Summer): 3-16.

—— (1974b). *The Structure of Sociological Theory.* Homewood, Ill.: Dorsey.

—— (1978). *The Structure of Sociological Theory.* Revised edition. Homewood, Ill.: Dorsey.

Weber, M. (1905). *The Protestant Ethic and the Spirit of Capitalism.* New York: Scribner's (1958 edition).

—— (1922). *On Law in Economy and Society.* Cambridge, Mass.: Harvard University Press (1954 edition).

Weiner, N. (1952). *The Human Use of Human Beings.* Garden City, N.Y.: Doubleday.

Wigmore, L. A. (1936). *A Panorama of the World's Legal Systems.* Washington, D.C.: Washington Law Book Co.

28

Social Change and the Law of Industrial Accidents
Lawrence M. Friedman and
Jack Ladinsky

Sociologists recognize, in a general way, the essential role of legal institutions in the social order.[1] They concede, as well, the responsiveness of law to social change and have made important explorations of the interrelations involved.[2] Nevertheless, the role law plays in initiating—or reflecting—social change has never been fully explicated, either in theory or through research. The evolution of American industrial accident law from tort principles to compensation systems is an appropriate subject for a case-study on this subject. It is a topic that has been carefully treated by legal scholars,[3] and it is also recognized by sociologists to be a significant instance of social change.[4] This essay, using concepts drawn from both legal and sociological disciplines, aims at clarifying the concept of social change and illustrating its relationship to change in the law. . . .

Development of the Law of Industrial Accidents

Background of the Fellow-Servant Rule

At the dawn of the industrial revolution, the common law of torts afforded a remedy, as it still does, for those who had suffered injuries

Excerpt from "Social Change and the Law of Industrial Accidents," *Columbia Law Review* 67 (January 1967), pp. 50–82, by permission of the author and publisher.

at the hands of others. If a man injured another by direct action—by striking him, or slandering him, or by trespassing on his property—the victim could sue for his damages. Similarly, the victim of certain kinds of negligent behavior had a remedy at law. But tort law was not highly developed. Negligence in particular did not loom large in the reports and it was not prominently discussed in books of theory or practice. Indeed, no treatise on tort law appeared in America until Francis Hilliard's in 1859,[5] the first English treatise came out in 1860.[6] By this time, the field was rapidly developing. A third edition of Hilliard's book was published in 1866, only seven years after the first edition. The explosive growth of tort law was directly related to the rapidity of industrial development. The staple source of tort litigation was and is the impact of machines—railroad engines, then factory machines, then automobiles—on the human body. During the industrial revolution, the size of the factory labor force increased, the use of machinery in the production of goods became more widespread, and such accidents were inevitably more frequent. In Hilliard's pioneer treatise, railroads already played a major role in tort litigation—a role which he ascribed to their "great multiplication and constant activity; their necessary interference, in the act of construction, with the rights of property . . . the large number and various offices of their agents and servants; and the dangers, many of them of an entirely novel character, incident to their mode of operation. . . ."[7]

In theory, at least, recovery for industrial accidents might have been assimilated into the existing system of tort law. The fundamental principles were broad and simple. If a factory worker was injured through the negligence of another person—including his employer—an action for damages would lie. Although as a practical matter, servants did not usually sue their master nor workers their employers, in principle they had the right to do so.

In principle, too, a worker might have had an action against his employer for any injury caused by the negligence of any other employee. The doctrine of *respondeat superior* was familiar and fundamental law. A principal was liable for the negligent acts of his agent. . . .

Conceivably, then, one member of an industrial work force might sue his employer for injuries caused by the negligence of a fellow worker. A definitive body of doctrine was slow to develop, however. When it did, it rejected the broad principle of *respondeat superior* and took instead the form of the so-called fellow-servant rule. Under this rule, a servant (employee) could not sue his master (employer) for injuries caused by the negligence of another employee. The consequences of this doctrine were far reaching. An employee retained the right to sue the employer for injuries, provided they were caused by the employer's personal misconduct. But the factory system and corporate ownership of industry made this right virtually meaningless. The factory owner was likely to be a "soulless" legal entity; even if the owner was an individual entrepreneur, he was unlikely to concern himself physically with factory operations. In work accidents, then, legal fault would be ascribed to fellow employees, if anyone. But fellow employees were men without wealth or insurance. The fellow-servant rule was an instrument capable of relieving employers from almost all the legal consequences of industrial injuries. Moreover, the doctrine left an injured worker without any effective recourse but an empty action against his co-worker.

When labor developed a collective voice, it was bound to decry the rule as infamous, as a deliberate instrument of oppression—a sign that law served the interests of the rich and propertied, and denied the legitimate claims of the poor and the weak. The rule charged the "blood of the workingman" not to the state, the employer, or the consumer, but to the working man himself. Conventionally, then, the fellow-servant rule is explained as a deliberate or half-deliberate rejection of a well-settled principle of law in order to encourage enterprise by forcing workmen to bear the costs of industrial injury. And the overthrow of the rule is taken as a sign of a conquest by progressive forces. . . .

Birth and Acceptance of the Rule

The origin of the fellow-servant rule is usually ascribed to Lord Abinger's opinion in *Priestley v. Fowler*,[8] decided in 1837. Yet the case on its facts did not pose the question of the industrial accident, as later generations would understand it; rather, it concerned the employment relationships of tradesmen. The defendant, a butcher, instructed the plaintiff, his servant, to deliver goods which had been loaded on a van by another employee. The van, which had been overloaded, broke down, and plaintiff fractured his thigh in the accident. Lord Abinger, in his rather diffuse and unperceptive opinion, reached his holding that the servant had no cause of action by arguing from analogies drawn neither from industry nor from trade:

> If the master be liable to the servant in this action, the principle of that liability will . . . carry us to an alarming extent. . . . The footman . . . may have an action against his master for a defect in the carriage owing to the negligence of the coachmaker. . . . The master . . . would be liable to the servant for the negligence of the chambermaid, for putting him into a damp

bed; . . . for the negligence of the cook in not properly cleaning the copper vessels used in the kitchen. . . .[9]

These and similar passages in the opinion suggest that Abinger was worried about the disruptive effects of a master's liability upon his household staff. These considerations were perhaps irrelevant to the case at hand, the facts of which did not deal with the household of a nobleman, great landowner, or rich merchant; a fortiori the decision itself did not concern relationships within an industrial establishment. Certainly the opinion made extension of the rule to the factory setting somewhat easier to enunciate and formulate technically. But it did not justify the existence of an industrial fellow-servant rule. The case might have been totally forgotten—or overruled—had not the onrush of the industrial revolution put the question again and again to courts, each time more forcefully. Priestley v. Fowler and the doctrine of respondeat superior each stood for a broad principle. Whether the one or the other (or neither) would find a place in the law relative to industrial accidents depended upon needs felt and expressed by legal institutions in response to societal demands. Had there been no Priestley v. Fowler, it would have been necessary—and hardly difficult—to invent one.

In the United States, the leading case on the fellow-servant situation was Farwell v. Boston & Worcester Railroad Corp.,[10] decided by Massachusetts' highest court in 1842. The case arose out of a true industrial accident in a rapidly developing industrial state. Farwell was an engineer who lost a hand when his train ran off the track due to a switchman's negligence. As Chief Justice Shaw, writing for the court, saw it, the problem of Farwell was how best to apportion the risks of railroad accidents. In his view, it was superficial to analyze the problem according to the tort concepts of fault and negligence. His opinion spoke the language of contract, and employed the stern logic of nineteenth century economic thought. Some occupations are more dangerous than others. Other things being equal, a worker will choose the least dangerous occupation available. Hence, to get workers an employer will have to pay an additional wage for dangerous work. The market, therefore, has already made an adjustment in the wage rate to compensate for the possibility of accident, and a cost somewhat similar to an insurance cost has been allocated to the company. As Shaw put it, "he who engages in the employment of another for the performance of specified duties and services, for compensation, takes upon himself the natural and ordinary risks and perils incident to the performance of such services, and in legal presumption, the compensation is adjusted accordingly."[11] The worker, therefore, has assumed the risk of injury—for a price. The "implied contract of employment" between the worker and employer did not require the employer to bear any additional costs of injury (except for those caused by the employer's personal negligence).

In *Priestley v. Fowler* too, counsel had argued in terms of implied contract. But Lord Abinger had not framed his logic accordingly. Shaw did, and his opinion had great influence on subsequent judicial reasoning. The facts of the case were appropriate and timely, and Shaw saw the issue in clear economic terms. His decision helped convert the rules and concepts of the status-bound law of master and servant to the economic needs of the period, as he understood them.

Shaw's opinion makes extreme assumptions about behavior, justified only by a philosophy of economic individualism. Partly because of this, it has a certain heartlessness of tone. A disabled worker without resources was likely to be pauperized if he had no realistic right to damages. Unless his family could help him, he would have to fall back upon poor relief, the costs of which were borne by the public through taxation. The railroads and other industrial employers paid a share as taxpayers and, in addition, a kind of insurance cost as part of their wage rate—but no more. Additional damages had to be borne by the worker; if he could not bear them, society generally would pay the welfare costs. Thus the opinion expresses a preference for charging the welfare cost of industrial accidents to the public generally, rather than to the particular enterprise involved.

It is not surprising that such a preference was expressed. Shaw's generation placed an extremely high value on economic growth. As Willard Hurst has noted, that generation was thoroughly convinced it was "socially desirable that that there be broad opportunity for the release of creative human energy," particularly in the "realm of the economy."[12] . . .

Men like Shaw, the bearers of power and influence, might have conceded that the misfortunes of factory workers were real, but insecurity of economic position cursed the lot of all but the very rich. The problem was one of *general* insecurity.

Shaw and his generation placed their hopes of salvation on rapid economic growth. Perhaps they were anxious to see that the tort system of accident compensation did not add to the problems of new industry. Few people imagined that accidents would become so numerous as to create severe economic and social dislocation. On the contrary, rash extension of certain principles of tort law to industrial accidents might upset social progress by imposing extreme costs on business in its economic infancy. The 1840's and 1850's were a period of massive economic development in New England and the Midwest, a period of "take-off" (perhaps) into self-sustaining economic growth. Textiles, and then iron, spearheaded the industrial revolution; westward expansion and the railroads created new markets. Communities and states made a social contribution to the construction of railroads through cash subsidies, stock subscriptions, and tax exemptions. The courts, using the fellow-servant doctrine and the concepts of assumption of risk and contributory negligence, socialized the accident costs of building the roads. That these solutions represented the collective, if uneasy, consensus of those with authority and responsibility is supported by the fact that every court of the country, with but one transient exception,[13] reached the same conclusion in the years immediately following *Farwell*. Moreover, the fellow-servant rule was not abolished by any legislature in these early years. Although legislative inaction is not a necessary sign of acquiescence, it at least indicates lack of a major feeling of revulsion.

Weakening the Rule

A general pattern may be discerned which is common to the judicial history of many rules of law. The courts enunciate a rule, intending to "solve" a social problem—that is, they seek to lay down a stable and clear-cut principle by which men can govern their conduct or, alternatively, by which the legal system can govern men. If the rule comports with some kind of social consensus, it will in fact work a solution—that is, it will go unchallenged, or, if challenged, will prevail. Challenges will not usually continue, since the small chance of overturning the rule is not worth the cost of litigation. If, however, the rule is weakened—if courts engraft exceptions to it, for example—then fresh challenges probing new weaknesses will be encouraged. Even if the rule retains *some* support, it will no longer be efficient and clear-cut. Ultimately, the rule may no longer serve *anybody's* purposes. At this point, a fresh (perhaps wholly new) "solution" will be attempted.

The history of the fellow-servant rule rather neatly fits this scheme. Shaw wrote his *Farwell* opinion in 1842. During the latter part of the century, judges began to reject his reasoning. . . .

The rule was strong medicine, and it depended for its efficacy upon continued, relatively certain, and unswerving legal loyalty. Ideally, if the rule were strong and commanded nearly total respect from the various agencies of law, it would eliminate much of the mass of litigation that might otherwise arise. Undoubtedly, it did prevent countless thousands of law suits; but it did not succeed in choking off industrial accident litigation. For example, industrial accident litigation dominated the docket of the Wisconsin Supreme Court at the beginning of the age of workmen's compensation; far more cases arose under that heading than under any other single field of law. Undoubtedly, this appellate case-load was merely the visible portion of a vast iceberg of litigation. Thus, the rule did not command the respect required for efficient operation and hence, in the long run, survival.

One reason for the continued litigation may have been simply the great number of accidents that occurred. At the dawn of the industrial revolution, when Shaw wrote, the human consequences of that technological change were unforeseeable. In particular, the toll it would take of human life was unknown. But by the last quarter of the nineteenth century, the number of industrial accidents had grown enormously. After 1900, it is estimated, 35,000 deaths and 2,000,000 injuries occurred every year in the United States. One quarter of the injuries produced disabilities lasting more than one week. The railway injury rate doubled in the seventeen years between 1889 and 1906.

In addition to the sheer number of accidents, other reasons for the increasing number of challenges to the rule in the later nineteenth century are apparent. If the injury resulted in death or permanent disability, it broke off the employment relationship; the plaintiff or his family thereafter had nothing to lose except the costs of suit. The development of the contingent fee system provided the poor man with the means to hire a lawyer. . . .

The contingent fee system was no more than a mechanism, however. A losing plaintiff's lawyer receives no fee; that is the essence of the system. The fact is that plaintiffs won many of their lawsuits; in so doing, they not only weakened the fellow-servant rule, but they encouraged still more plaintiffs to try their hand, still more attorneys to make a living from personal injury work. . . .

Some weakening of the doctrine took place by means of the control exercised by trail court judge and jury over findings of fact. But sympathy for injured workers manifested itself also in changes in doctrine. On the appellate court level, a number of mitigations of the fellow-servant rule developed near the end of the nineteenth century. For example, it had always been conceded that the employer was liable if he was personally responsible (through his own negligence) for his worker's injury. Thus, in a Massachusetts case, a stable owner gave directions to his employee, who was driving a wagon, that caused an accident and injury to the driver (or so the jury found). The employer was held liable. Out of this simple proposition grew the so-called vice-principal rule, which allowed an employee to sue his employer where the negligent employee occupied a supervisory position such that he could more properly be said to be an alter ego of the principal than a mere fellow-servant. This was a substantial weakening of the fellow-servant doctrine. Yet some states never accepted the vice-principal rule; in those that did, it too spawned a bewildering multiplicity of decisions, sub-rules, and sub-sub-rules. . . .

There were scores of other "exceptions" to the fellow-servant rule, enunciated in one or more states. Some of them were of great importance. In general, an employer was said to have certain duties that were not "delegable"; these he must do or have done, and a failure to perform them laid him open to liability for personal injuries. Among these was the duty to furnish a safe place to work, safe tools, and safe appliances. Litigation on these points was enormous, and here too the cases cannot readily be summed up or even explained. . . .

So phrased, of course, the exception comes close to swallowing the rule. Had the courts been so inclined, they might have eliminated the fellow-servant rule without admitting it, simply by expanding the safe place and safe tool rules. They were never quite willing to go that far, and the safe tool doctrine was itself subject to numerous exceptions. . . .

Even though the exceptions did not go the length of obliterating the rule, and even though many (perhaps most) injured workers who had a possible cause of action did not or could not recover, the instability and unpredictability of operation of the common law rule was a significant fact.

The numerous judge-made exceptions reflected a good deal of uncertainty about underlying social policy. The same uncertainty was reflected in another sphere of legal activity—the legislature. Though the rule was not formally abrogated, it was weakened by statute in a number of jurisdictions. Liability statutes, as will be seen, were rudimentary and in many ways ineffective. This was partly because of genuine uncertainty about the proper attitude to take toward industrial accident costs—an uncertainty reflected in the cases as well. The early nineteenth century cannot be uncritically described as a period that accepted without question business values and practices. Rather, it accepted the ideal of economic growth, which certain kinds of enterprise seemed to hinder. Thus in the age of Jackson, as is well known, popular feeling ran high against financial institutions, chiefly the chartered banks. Banks were believed to have far too much economic power; they corrupted both the currency and the government. . . .

Later on, the railroads replaced the banks as popular bogeymen. By the 1850's some of the fear of excessive economic power was transferred to them. Disregard for safety was one more black mark against the railroads; farmers, small businessmen, and the emerging railroad unions might use the safety argument to enlist widespread support for general regulation of railroads, but the essential thrust of the movement was economic. The railroads were feared and hated because of their power over access to the market. They became "monopolistic" as the small local lines were gradually amalgamated into large groupings controlled by "robber barons." Interstate railroad nets were no longer subject to local political control—if anything, they controlled local politics, or so it plausibly appeared to much of the public. Farmers organized and fought back against what they identified as their economic enemy. It is not coincidental that the earliest derogations from the strictness of the fellow-servant rule applied *only* to railroads. For example, the first statutory modification, passed in Georgia in 1856, allowed railroad employees to recover for injuries caused by the acts of fellow-servants, provided they themselves were free from negligence. A similar act was passed in Iowa in 1862. Other statutes were passed in Wyoming (1869) and Kansas (1874). The chronology suggests—though direct evidence is lacking—that some of these statutes were connected with the general revolt of farmers against the power of the railroad companies, a revolt associated with the Granger movement, which achieved its maximum power in the 1870's. Wisconsin in 1875 abolished the fellow-servant rule for railroads; in 1880, however, when more conservative forces regained control of the legislature, the act was repealed. . . .

The Federal Employers' Liability Act of 1908[14] went much further; it abolished the fellow-servant rule for railroads and greatly reduced the strength of contributory negligence and assumption of risk as defenses. Once the employers had been stripped of these potent weapons, the relative probability of recovery by injured railroad employees was high enough so that workmen's compensation never seemed as essential for the railroads as for industry generally. The highly modified FELA tort system survives (in amended form) to this day for the railroads. It is an anachronism, but one which apparently grants some modest satisfaction to both sides. Labor and management both express discontent with FELA, but neither side has been so firmly in favor of a change to workmen's compensation as to make it a major issue.

FELA shows one of many possible outcomes of the decline in efficacy of the fellow-servant rule. Under it, the rule was eliminated, and the law turned to a "pure" tort system—pure in the sense that the proclivities of juries were not interfered with by doctrines designed to limit the chances of a worker's recovery. But the railroads were a special case. Aside from the special history of regulation, the interstate character of the major railroads made them subject to national safety standards and control by a single national authority. For other industrial employers, the FELA route was not taken;

instead, workmen's compensation acts were passed. In either case, however, the fellow-servant rule was abolished, or virtually so. Either course reflects, we can assume, some kind of general agreement that the costs of the rule outweighed its benefits.

Rising Pressures for Change

The common law doctrines were designed to preserve a certain economic balance in the community. When the courts and legislatures created numerous exceptions, the rules lost much of their efficiency as a limitation on the liability of businessmen. The rules prevented many plaintiffs from recovering, but not all; a few plaintiffs recovered large verdicts. There were costs of settlements, costs of liability insurance, costs of administration, legal fees and the salaries of staff lawyers. These costs rose steadily, at the very time when American business, especially big business, was striving to rationalize and bureaucratize its operations. It was desirable to be able to predict costs and insure against fluctuating, unpredictable risks. The costs of industrial accident liability were not easily predictable, partly because legal consequences of accidents were not predictable. Insurance, though available, was expensive.

In addition, industry faced a serious problem of labor unrest. Workers and their unions were dissatisfied with many aspects of factory life. The lack of compensation for industrial accidents was one obvious weakness. Relatively few injured workers received compensation. Under primitive state employers' liability statutes, the issue of liability and the amount awarded still depended upon court rulings and jury verdicts. Furthermore, the employer and the insurance carrier might contest a claim or otherwise delay settlement in hopes of bringing the employee to terms. The New York Employers' Liability Commission, in 1910, reported that delay ran from six months to six years. . . .

When an employee did recover, the amount was usually small. The New York Commission found that of forty-eight fatal cases studied in Manhattan, eighteen families received no compensation; only four received over $2,000; most received less than $500. The deceased workers had averaged $15.22 a week in wages; only eight families recovered as much as three times their average yearly earnings. The same inadequacies turned up in Wisconsin in 1907. Of fifty-one fatal injuries studied, thirty-four received settlements under $500; only eight received over $1,000. . . .

A large fraction of the disbursed payments, about one-third, went to attorneys who accepted the cases on a contingent basis.

These figures on the inadequacy of recoveries are usually cited to show how little the workers received for their pains. But what did these figures mean to employers? Assuming that employers, as rational men, were anxious to pay as little compensation as was necessary to preserve industrial peace and maintain a healthy workforce, the better course might be to pay a higher *net* amount direct to employees. Employers had little or nothing to gain from their big payments to insurance companies, lawyers, and court officials. Perhaps at some unmeasurable point of time, the existing tort system crossed an invisible line and thereafter, purely in economic terms, represented on balance a net loss to the industrial establishment. From that point on, the success of a movement for change in the system was certain, provided that businessmen could be convinced that indeed their self-interest lay in the direction of reform and that a change in compensation systems did not drag with it other unknowable and harmful consequences.

As on many issues of reform, the legal profession did not speak with one voice. Certainly, many lawyers and judges were dissatisfied with the status quo. . . . Justice Roujet D. Marshall propagandized for workmen's compensation in his judicial opinions. He claimed in his autobiography "to have been largely the exciting cause of the establishment of the workmen's compensation law" in Wisconsin.[15] He also wrote part of the governor's message to the 1909 legislature appealing for a workmen's compensation statute, and he helped induce the Republican Party to back a workmen's compensation plan in its 1910 platform. Legal writers and law teachers also spoke out against the common law and in favor of a compensation system. . . .

When considerations of politics were added to those of business economics and industrial peace, it was not surprising to find that businessmen gradually withdrew their veto against workmen's compensation statutes. They began to say that a reformed system was inevitable—and even desirable. A guaranteed, insurable cost—one which could be computed in advance on the basis of accident experience—would, in the long run, cost business less than the existing system. In 1910, the president of the National Association of Manufacturers (NAM) appointed a committee to study the possibility of compensating injured workmen without time-consuming and expensive litigation, and the convention that year heard a speaker tell them that no one was satisfied with the present state of the law— that the employers' liability system was "antagonistic to harmonious relations between employers and wage workers."[16] By 1911 the NAM appeared convinced that a compensation system was inevitable and that prudence dictated that business play a positive role in shaping the design of the law—otherwise the law would be "settled for us by the demagogue, and agitator and the socialist with a vengeance."[17] Business would benefit economically and politically from a compensation system, but only if certain conditions were present. Business, therefore, had an interest in pressing for a specific kind of program, and turned its attention to the details of the new system. For example, it was imperative that the new system be in fact as actuarially predictable as business demanded; it was important that the costs of the program be fair and equal in their impact upon particular industries, so that no competitive advantage or disadvantage flowed from the scheme. Consequently the old tort actions had to be eliminated, along with the old defenses of the company. In exchange for certainty of recovery by the worker, the companies were prepared to demand certainty and predictability of loss—that is, limitation of recovery. The jury's caprice had to be dispensed with. In short, when workmen's compensation became law, as a solution to the industrial accident problem, it did so on terms acceptable to industry. Other pressures were there to be sure, but when workmen's compensation was enacted, businessmen had come to look on it as a positive benefit rather than as a threat to their sector of the economy.

The Emergence of Workmen's Compensation Statutes

The change of the businessman's, the judge's, and the general public's attitudes toward industrial injuries was accelerated by the availability of fresh information on the extent of accidents and their cost to both management and workers. By 1900, industrial accidents and the shortcomings of the fellow-servant rule were widely perceived as *problems* that had to be solved. After 1900, state legislatures began to look for a "solution" by setting up commissions to gather statistics, to investigate possible new systems, and to recommend legislation. . . .

From the information collected, the commissions were able to calculate the costs of workmen's compensation systems and compare them with costs under employers' liability. Most of the commissions concluded that a compensation system would be no more expensive than the existing method, and most of them recommended adoption, in one form or another, of workmen's compensation. In spite of wide variations in the systems proposed, there was agreement on one point: workmen's compensation must fix liability upon the employer regardless of fault.

Between 1910 and 1920 the method of compensating employees injured on the job was fundamentally altered in the United States. In brief, workmen's compensation statutes eliminated (or tried to eliminate) the process of fixing civil liability for industrial accidents through litigation in common law courts. Under the statutes, compensation was based on statutory schedules, and the responsibility for initial determination of employee claims was taken from the courts and given to an administrative agency. Finally, the statutes abolished the fellow-servant rule and the defenses of assumption of risk and contributory negligence. Wisconsin's law, passed in 1911, was the first general compensation act to survive a court test. Mississippi, the last state in the Union to adopt a compensation law, did so in 1948.

Compensation systems varied from state to state, but they had many features in common. The original Wisconsin law was representative of the earlier group of statutes. It set up a voluntary system—a response to the fact that New York's courts had held a compulsory scheme unconstitutional on due process grounds. Wisconsin abolished the fellow-servant rule and the defense of assumption of risk for employers of four or more employees. In turn, the compensation scheme, for employers who elected to come under it, was made the "exclusive remedy" for an employee injured accidentally on the job. The element of "fault" or "negligence" was eliminated, and the mere fact of injury at work "proximately caused by accident," and not the result of "wilful misconduct," made the employer liable to pay compensation but exempt from ordinary tort liability. The state aimed to make it expensive for employers to stay out of the system. Any employer who did so was liable to suit by injured employees and the employer was denied the common law defenses. . . .

In essence, then, workmen's compensation was designed to replace a highly unsatisfactory system with a rational, actuarial one. It should not be viewed as the replacement of a fault-oriented compensation system with one unconcerned with fault. It should not be viewed as a victory of employees over employers. In its initial stages, the fellow-servant rule was not concerned with fault, either, but with establishing a clear-cut, workable, and predictable rule, one which substantively placed much of the risk (if not all) on the worker. Industrial accidents were not seen as a social problem—at most as an economic problem. As value perceptions changed, the rule weakened; it developed exceptions and lost its efficiency. The exceptions and counter-exceptions can be looked at as a series of brief, ad hoc, and unstable compromises between the clashing interests of labor and management. When both sides became convinced that the game was mutually unprofitable, a compensation system became possible. But this system was itself a compromise: an attempt at a new, workable, and predictable mode of handling accident liability which neatly balanced the interests of labor and management.

The Law of Industrial Accidents and Social Theory: Three Aspects of Social Change

This case study, devoted to the rise and fall of the fellow-servant rule, utilizes and supports a view of social change as a complex chain of group bargains—economic in the sense of a continuous exchange of perceived equivalents, though not economic in the sense of crude money bargains. It also provides a useful setting for evaluating three additional popular explanations of the origin or rate of social change. First, the apparently slow development of workmen's compensation is the classic example of what Ogburn called "cultural lag." Second, since German and English statutes were enacted prior to the American laws, the establishment of compensation schemes in America can be viewed as a case of cross-cultural influence. Third, the active role of particular participants (in Wisconsin, for example, Judge Marshall and John R. Commons) may substantiate the theory which advances the causal influence of "great men" in the process of social change. A thorough examination of these theories is not contemplated here. Students both of law and of sociology, however, may profit from a brief discussion of these theories in the context of the social change embodied in workmen's compensation statutes.

The Concept of Cultural Lag

. . . In a famous book written in 1922, the sociologist William Fielding Ogburn used the example of workmen's compensation and the fifty-year period of fumbling to verify his "hypothesis of cultural lag."[18] "Where one part of culture changes first," said Ogburn, "through some discovery or invention, and occasions changes in some part of culture dependent upon it, there frequently is a delay. . . . The extent of this lag will vary . . . but may exist for . . . years, during which time there may be said to be a maladjustment."[19] In the case of workmen's compensation, the lag period was from the time when industrial accidents became numerous until the time when workmen's compensation laws were passed, "about a half-century, from 1850–70 to 1915." During this period, "the old adaptive culture, the common law of employers' liability, hung over after the material conditions had changed."[20] . . .

The lesson of industrial accident law, as here described, may be quite the opposite of the lesson that Ogburn drew. In a purely objective (nonteleological) sense, social processes—and the legal system—cannot aptly be described through use of the idea of lag. When, in the face of changed technology and new problems, a social arrangement stubbornly persists, there are *social* reasons why this is so; there are explanations why no change or slow change occurs. The legal system is a part of the total culture; it is not a self-operating machine. The rate of response to a call for change is slow or fast in the law depending upon who issues the call and who (if anybody) resists it. "Progress" or "catching up" is not inevitable or predictable. Legal change, like social change, is a change in behavior of individuals and groups in interaction. The rate of change depends upon the kind of interaction. To say that institutions lag is usually to say no more than that they are slow to make changes of a particular type. But why are they slow? Often the answer rests on the fact that these institutions are controlled by or respond to groups or individuals who are opposed to the specific change. This is lag only if we feel we can confidently state that thes groups or individuals are wrong as to their own self-interest as well as that of society. Of course, people *are* often wrong about their own self-interest; they can be and are short-sighted, ignorant, maladroit. But ignorance of this kind exists among progressives as well as among conservatives—among those who want change as well as among those who oppose it. Resistance to change is "lag" only if there is only one "true" definition of a problem—and one "true" solution.

There were important reasons why fifty years elapsed before workmen's compensation became part of the law. Under the impact of industrial conditions Americans were changing their views about individual security and social welfare. Dean Pound has remarked that the twentieth century accepts the idea of insuring those unable to bear economic loss, at the expense of the nearest person at hand who can bear the loss. This conception was relatively unknown and unacceptable to judges of the nineteenth century. The fellow-servant rule could not be replaced until economic affluence, business conditions, and the state of safety technology made feasible a more social solution. Labor unions of the mid-nineteenth century did not call for a compensation plan; they were concerned with more basic (and practical) issues such as wages and hours. Note the form that the argument for workmen's compensation took, after 1900, in the following quotation; few Americans reasoned this way fifty years earlier. . . . Social insurance, as much as private insurance, requires standardization and rationalization of business, predictability of risk, and reliability and financial responsibility of economic institutions. These were present in 1909, but not in 1850.

Prior to workmen's compensation, the legal system reflected existing conflicts of value quite clearly; the manifold exceptions to the fellow-servant rule and the primitive liability statutes bear witness to this fact. These were no symptoms of "lag"; rather, they were a measure of the constant adjustments that inevitably take place within a legal system that is not insulated from the larger society but an integral part of it. To be sure, the courts frequently reflected values of the business community and so did the legislatures, but populist expressions can easily be found in the work of judges, legislatures, and juries. In the absence of a sophisticated measuring-rod of past public opinion—and sophisticated concepts of the role of public opinion in nineteenth century society—who is to say that the legal system "lagged" behind some hypothetical general will of the public or some hypothetically correct solution?

The concept of lag may also be employed in the criticism of the courts' use of judicial review to retard the efficacy of social welfare legislation. In 1911, the New York Court of Appeals declared the state's compulsory workmen's compensation act unconstitutional. As a result of this holding, the state constitution had to be amended— two years later—before workmen's compensation was legally possible in New York. Because of the New York experience, six states also amended their constitutions and others enacted voluntary plans. The issue was not finally settled until 1917, when the United States Supreme Court held both compulsory and elective plans to be constitutional. But it adds little to an understanding of social process to describe this delay in terms of the concept of cultural lag. Courts do not act on their own initiative. Each case of judicial review was instigated by a litigant who represented a group in society which was fighting for its interests as it perceived them; these were current, real interests, not interests of sentiment or inertia. This is completely apart from consideration of what social interests the courts thought they were serving in deciding these cases—interests which hindsight condemns as futile or wrong, but which were living issues and interests of the day.

Conflicts of value also arose in the legislatures when they began to consider compensation laws. The Massachusetts investigating commission of 1903 reported a workmen's compensation bill to the legislature, but the bill was killed in committee on the ground that Massachusetts could not afford to increase the production costs of commodities manufactured in the state. Once more, the emergence of compensation depended upon a perception of inevitability—which could cancel the business detriment to particular states which enacted compensation laws—and of general economic gain from the new system. It is not enough to sense that a social problem exists. Rational collective action demands relatively precise and detailed information about the problem, and clear placement of responsibility for proposing and implementing a solution. For many years legislatures simply did not consider it their responsibility to do anything about industrial injuries. Since they did not view accidents as a major social problem, and since state legislatures were weak political structures, they were content at first to leave accidents to tort law and the courts. Moreover, state agencies were not delegated the task of collecting information on the nature and extent of industrial accidents until relatively late. . . .

What appears to some as an era of "lag" was actually a period in which issues were collectively defined and alternative solutions posed, and during which interest groups bargained for favorable formulations of law. It was a period of "false starts"—unstable compromise formulations by decision makers armed with few facts, lacking organizational machinery, and facing great, often contradictory, demands from many publics. There was no easy and suitable solution, in the light of the problem and the alignment of powers. Indeed, workmen's compensation—which today appears to be a stable solution—was only a compromise, an answer acceptable to enough people and interest groups to endure over a reasonably long period of time.

Part of what is later called "lag," then, is this period of false starts—the inadequate compromises by decision makers faced with contradictory interest groups pressing inconsistent solutions. There may not *be* a "solution" in light of the alignment of interests and powers with respect to the problem at any given point in time. Perhaps only a compromise "solution" is possible. What later appears to be the final answer is in fact itself a compromise—one which is stable over some significant period of time. Sociologically, that is what a "solution" to a problem is: nothing more than a stable compromise acceptable to enough people and interest groups to maintain itself over a significant period of time. Theoretically, of course, total victory by one competing interest and total defeat of another is possible. But in a functioning democratic society, total victories and defeats are uncommon. Total defeat would mean that a losing group was so utterly powerless that it could exert no bargaining pressure whatsoever; total victory similarly would imply unlimited power. In the struggle over industrial accident legislation, none of the interests could be so described. Different perceptions of the problem, based at least in part on different economic and social stakes, led to different views of existing and potential law. When these views collided, compromises were hammered out. Workmen's compensation took form not because it was (or is) perfect, but because it represented a solution acceptable enough to enough interests to outweigh the costs of additional struggle and bargaining. If there was "lag" in the process, it consisted of acquiescence in presently acceptable solutions which turned out not to be adequate or stable in the long run. "Lag" therefore at most means present-minded pragmatism rather than long-term rational planning.

Cross-Cultural Borrowing

The adoption of workmen's compensation in America does represent an instance of what can be called conscious cross-cultural borrowing. Workmen's compensation was not an American innovation; there were numerous European antecedents. Switzerland passed a workmen's compensation act in 1881; Germany followed in 1884 with a more inclusive scheme. By 1900 compensation laws had spread to most European countries. In 1891 the United States Bureau of Labor commissioned John Graham Brooks to study and appraise the German system. His report, published in 1893, was widely distributed and successfully exposed some American opinion-leaders to the existence of the European programs. Most of the state investigating commissions also inquired into the European experience, and a number of early bills were modeled after the German and British systems.

Though workmen's compensation can therefore be viewed as an example of cross-cultural borrowing, care must be exercised in employing the concept. Successful legal solutions to social problems are often borrowed across state and national lines but this borrowing must not be confused with the actual "influence" of one legal system over another. "Influence" carries with it an implication of power or, at the least, of cultural dominance. The forces that led to a demand for workmen's compensation were entirely domestic, as this study has argued. The fact that European solutions to similar problems were studied and, to an extent, adopted here shows not dominance but an attempt to economize time, skill, and effort by borrowing an appropriate model. It would be quite wrong to detect European legal "influence" in this process. The existence of the European compensation plans was not a cause of similar American statutes. Rather, the interest shown in the foreign experiences was a response to American dissatisfaction with existing industrial accident law. . . .

Great Men and Social Change

Sociologists are fond of pointing out the inaccuracy of the "great-man theory of history," which holds that particular persons play irreplaceably decisive roles in determining the path of social change. The influence of single individuals, they say, is hardly as critical as historians would have us believe. The role of outstanding persons in bringing about workmen's compensation acts seems on one level quite clear. In Wisconsin, Roujet Marshall excoriated the existing system from the bench; off the bench he was a vigorous champion of the new law and, indeed, helped draft it. John R. Commons worked tirelessly for passage of the act, and served on the first Industrial Commission whose obligation it was to administer the law. His writings and teachings helped mobilize informed public opinion and virtually created a lobby of academicians for workmen's compensation. Political figures, businessmen, union leaders, and others played active roles in the passsage of the law. It is quite tempting to say that the Wisconsin law would be unthinkable but for the work of Marshall, or Commons, or LaFollette and the Progressive tradition in the state, or the craftsmanship of Wisconsin's pioneering legislative reference service under the skilled leadership of Charles McCarthy. Reformers and academicians served as important middlemen in mediating between interest groups and working out compromises. Their arguments legitimated the act; their zeal enlisted support of middle-class neutrals. They were willing to do the spadework of research, drafting, and propagandizing necessary for a viable law. . . .

The great-man hypothesis is not susceptible of proof or disproof. But the course of events underlying workmen's compensation at least suggests that social scientists are properly suspicious of placing too much reliance on a great-man view. If the view here expressed is correct, then economic, social, political and legal forces made workmen's compensation (or some alternative, such as FELA) virtually inevitable by the end of the nineteenth century. Outstanding men may be necessary in general for the implementation of social change; someone must take the lead in creating the intellectual basis for a change in perception. Nonetheless, when a certain pattern of demand exists in society, more than one person may be capable of filling that role. Particular individuals are normally not indispensable. The need is for talent—men with extraordinary ability, perseverance, and personal influence, men who can surmount barriers and accomplish significant results. Obviously, the absence of outstanding persons interested in a particular cause can delay problem solving or lead to inept, shoddy administration. The appearance of truly exceptional persons at the proper moment in history is undoubtedly not automatic. But talent, if not genius, may well be a constant in society; and the social order determines whether and in what direction existing talent will be exerted.

Thus, it would be foolish to deny that specific individuals exert great influence upon the development of social events, and equally foolish to conclude that other persons could not have done the job as well (or better) if given the opportunity. "Great men," however, must be in the right place, which means that society must have properly provided for the training and initiative of outstanding persons and for their recruitment into critical offices when needed. In difficult times, great businessmen, political leaders, musicians, or physicists will emerge. "Great men" appear "when the time is ripe"— but only insofar as society has created the conditions for a pool of creative manpower dedicated to the particular line of endeavor in which their greatness lies. . . .

Notes

1. *See, e.g.*, T. Parsons, Structure and Process in Modern Society 190–92 (1960).
2. *See, e.g.*, J. Willard Hurst, Law and Social Process in United States History (1960).
3. *See generally* C. Auerbach, L. Garrison, W. Hurst & S. Mermin, The Legal Process (1961) [hereinafter cited as Auerbach].
4. *See, e.g.*, W. Ogburn, Social Change With Respect to Culture and Original Nature 213–36 (Viking ed, 1950).
5. F. Hilliard, The Law of Torts (1st ed. 1859); *see* C. Warren, History of the American Bar 450 (1911).
6. C. Addison, Wrongs and Their Remedies (1st ed. 1860).
7. 2 F. Hilliard, The Law of Torts 339 (3rd ed. 1866).
8. 150 Eng. R. 1030 (Ex. 1837).
9. *Id.* at 1032.
10. 45 Mass. (4 Met.) 49 (1842). . . .
11. *Farwell v. Boston* & W. R. R., 45 Mass. (4 Met.) 49, 57 (1842) (emphasis added).
12. J. Willard Hurst, Law and the Conditions of Freedom in the Nineteenth Century United States 5–6 passim (1956).
13. Wisconsin, in Chamberlain v. Milwaukee & M. R. R., 11 Wis. 248 (1860), rejected the fellow-servant rule, but one year later, in *Moseley v. Chamberlain*, 18 Wis. 700 (1861), the court reversed itself and adopted the rule which was "sustained by the almost unanimous judgments of all the courts both of England and this country . . . [an] unbroken current of judicial opinion." *Id.* at 736.
14. 35 Stat. 65 (1908).
15. 2 Autobiography of Roujet D. Marshall 53 (Glasier ed. 1931).
16. National Association of Manufacturers, Proceedings of the Fifteenth Annual Convention 280 (1910).
17. National Association of Manufacturers, Proceedings of the Sixteenth Annual Convention 106 (1911) (remarks of Mr. Schwedtman).
18. W. Ogburn, Social Change With Respect to Culture and Original Nature 200 (Viking ed. 1950). *See generally id.* at 199–280. In the book cultural lag was offered as a hypothesis; in later writing Ogburn referred to it as a theory.
19. *Id.* at 201.
20. *Id.* at 236.

29

Civil Liberties Issues in Public Data Banks
Alan F. Westin

From the earliest days of the American Republic, our legal and political system has been devoted to placing limits on the powers of surveillance that authorities can conduct over the lives of individuals and private groups. This tradition of limiting surveillance goes back to a stream of development in Western history that begins at least as early as the democratic Greek city-state and represented one of the keystones of the American Constitution.

Physical and Psychological Surveillance

When the Framers wrote, physical surveillance over individuals and groups was possible only in terms of actual entry onto property, eavesdropping on conversations by ear, and overlooking individuals. To place limits on these forms of surveillance, the American Constitution required that searches and seizures by government be "reasonable," describing specifically the places to be searched and the persons or things to be seized. Reasonableness was determined by a judicial inquiry in which law enforcement officers had to establish probable cause and were examined by a judge about the scope and conduct of the enquiry.

When the Framers wrote, psychological surveillance over individuals was possible only by torture to extract information or beliefs, or proceedings to compel individuals to testify against themselves. To meet these threats to psychological security, the American Constitution forbade torture and self-incrimination.

The other remaining form of surveillance known to eighteenth-century life was the record and dossier system maintained by European monarchies to control the movement of population and the activities of "disloyal" groups. In the United States, the openness and mobility of our frontier system and the deliberate refusal to employ a passport and dossier system of police control guaranteed that the American citizen would be free from these means of surveillance over his life.

Until the late nineteenth century, this legal framework was thoroughly adequate. The reasonable search and seizure principle allowed the balance to be struck by the courts and legislatures between the individual and group claims to privacy on the one hand and the needs of law enforcement and government information systems on the other. Then, late in the nineteenth century and accelerating rapidly during the first half of the twentieth century, technological developments began to erode the legal system for guaranteeing a libertarian balance of privacy. The invention of the telephone in the late 1880's meant that conversations were now projected outside the home and a network of wires, conduits, and central offices contained the speech that originated in one private place and was meant for reception in another. Telephone tapping by police and private adventurers began virtually simultaneously with the installation of telephone systems in the United States, just as telegraph tapping had begun in the 1850's when the telegraph first became an important means of communication. At about the same time, in the 1890's, the microphone was developed and quickly applied to the problem of monitoring speech through surreptitious devices. The law enforcement agencies and the Pinkerton Detective Agency made "dictaphone detection" a by-word of the late 1890's and the pre-World War I era. With these developments, the erosion of physical boundaries on which the reasonable search and seizure concept of the Constitution had been based began to create stress in the application of Constitutional protections to privacy from physical surveillance. During the same period, advances in techniques of psychological surveillance also grew. The polygraph, developed in the 1920's, provided means of measuring the physical states and emotional responses of individuals under stress, and this was picked up both by law enforcement agencies for questioning suspects and by private employers for investigating business employees and business crimes. Paralleling the polygraph development was the spread of deeply probing psychological tests of personality. . . . On the whole, American law drew a simple line in these areas—it forbade the use of polygraph or personality test results as legal evidence in courts but did not interfere in any way in the use of such tests for personnel selection and other non-judicial decision-making by authorities.

Data Surveillance

In the area of data surveillance, American society began the expansion of records and information-keeping in the period between World War I and World War II, events which represented the natural outcome of an industrial society with a growing regulatory and welfare function by government and an increasingly large bureaucratic structure in private organizational life. For the most part, American law dealt with this problem by setting general standards of confidentiality for information given to government agencies under compulsion of law (such as census data, social security information, and income tax records). However, the prime protection in this area remained the inability of government agencies and private authorities to use the mountains of information they had secured in anything like a centralized and efficient fashion.

Now, the contemporary era of electronics and computers has provided the final coup de grace to the technological premises on which the classic American law of privacy has been based. Microminiaturization, advanced circuitry, radar, the laser, television optics, and related developments have shifted the balance of power from those who seek to protect their conversations and actions against surveillance to those who have access to the new devices. What was once Orwell's science fiction is now current engineering. . . .

The area which has undergone the greatest leap forward in technological capacity, however, is not physical or psychological surveillance, but data surveillance. The impact of data processing by computer is altering, in a way so profound that we are only barely aware of it as yet, the relation between individual spontaneity and social control in our society. As computers have made possible the collection, storage, manipulation, and use of billions of bits of information, at quite cheap prices and through operations done at incredible speeds, ours has become the greatest data-collecting society in human history. Government agencies, corporations, universities, churches, labor unions, and a host of other organizations now handle more volumes of personal data than they ever did before. More organizations exchange information from their files than ever took place before. More centralized records are growing up to collect information according to certain functional aspects of individual life—education records, employment records, military service records, medical records, security clearance records, and many others. At the same time, the pressure to move from our present cash and check economy, with its relatively small-scale credit card sector, to a money-less transaction system, based on a computerized flow of credits and debits to central bank accounts for each individual (and fingerprint, voiceprint measures for unique identification) represents the most far-reaching utilization of computer capability, yet many experts in banking, government, and corporate life state confidently that such an automated transaction system is on the way. Finally, as government has had to deal with its increased responsibilities in social welfare, law enforcement, civil rights compliance, economic regulation and forecasting, and national security, the pressures have mounted for centralized information systems that would apply large-scale data analysis on both a statistical and personal dossier basis.

Of course, the collection and storage in computers of vast amounts of personal data about individuals and private data about groups does not mean that we currently possess the technology to make all the comparisons, syntheses, and retrievals that proponents of computer information systems sometimes claim or their critics sometimes envisage. . . .

This brief sketch of the interaction between technology, law, and social values in American society during nearly two centuries suggests in the briefest possible way the revolutionary character of the situation we are facing today. An enormous leap forward has been made in the power of public and private authorities to place individuals and private groups under close surveillance. In reaction, American society has stirred in alarm over the "Big Brother" prospects presented by these developments and has mounted an energetic campaign to either outlaw or control the techniques that have outstepped classic legal and social restraints. Among thoughtful segments of the American public and the law-making community, the search now is for a whole new framework for defining privacy in a technological age. . . .

American Law and Technological Threats to Privacy

In many ways American law is in the worst possible shape to deal with information processing and privacy, much worse than the task of modernizing its concepts in the fields of physical and psychological surveillance. In the physical and psychological areas, American law has clear-cut concepts to build from—ideas such as trespass, intrusion, physical rights of property, etc.—but consider the difficulties of applying constitutional standards to the information process. First, American law has no clear cut definition of personal information as a precious commodity. It has well-developed notions of proprietary information, corporate records, and similar business information, derived from medieval law on the secrets of trades and professions and codified in the American patent system. But when information is not needed to make a profit, when it involves the flow of disclosure about the individual among those he comes in contact with and those who exercise authority over him, American law has had no general theory of value, no set of rights and duties to apply as a general norm. Second, American law has had no general system for dealing with the flow of information which government agencies and other levels of government control, apart from a few examples such as census data (which has been closed to any additional circulation) and income tax (which has been given a set of additional areas of circulation controlled by statute or executive order). On the one hand, we have traditions of free circulation of information that arise in our credit investigation and public opinion collection processes. On the other hand, we have traditions of confidentiality and classified-secrecy which mark the other boundary. How information can circulate between these two poles and what to do with information systems that are likely to contain all of these types of information are problems that American law has not considered. Third, American law has not developed institutional procedures to protect against improper collection of information, storage of inadequate or false data, and intra-organizational use of such information for reaching decisions about individuals outside or inside the organization. Again, we have been most creative where tangible property rights have been involved. The Federal Administrative Procedure Act of 1946 assured businessmen facing federal regulatory agencies that they would know what information about them was going into the records in certain key types of government hearings, that they would have opportunities to present other information to challenge or modify this data, and that the record produced by such a procedure would be subject to review through higher administrative and judicial processes. The development of such a theory of information and government action was set back badly during the late 1940's and 1950's, when the loyalty-security problem produced large-scale information collection about individuals without open hearings which provided full due process. Without the opportunity to know what was in the record, to cross-examine those who had given the information, and to challenge the evaluation put on the information by government security officials, individuals were left without effective protection in their personal reputations and job rights. It is important to note that American law never came to a final resolution of this dilemma. Supreme Court decisions limited the scope of the loyalty-security process in government to truly sensitive agencies and trimmed back its application in various marginal areas such as the granting of passports. But it has never been held by the courts that an individual has a right to full due process in loyalty-security matters and thus one model for information challenge that still exists is a model which rejects the obligation of government to give individuals whose loyalty has been questioned the kinds of remedies that are available to businessmen when property rights are involved.

Finally, American law is seriously challenged by some of the technological aspects of computer information systems which tend to work against the kinds of reasonableness standards that the law tries to apply where balancing is necessary among privacy, disclosure, and surveillance. If, for example, there were ways to assure that statistical data banks, such as the proposed Federal Data Center, could be set up so that they could not be transformed by those who run the system into a means of obtaining various sets of information about known individuals, American law could well set carefully differentiated standards for data banks and intelligence systems. But the clear message of the technological specialists involved is that identifying names or numbers must be left attached to statistical data if information from various sources is to be put together for statistical purposes and if longitudinal studies are to be made of specific individuals through time. When this is the case, American law must confront the possibility that data banks might become intelligence systems and it is this hard dilemma that is now deeply troubling the congressional committees and legal writers concerned with the first wave of data-pool systems for federal and state governments.

Alternative Legal Safeguards

This short summary of the ways in which American law is not well prepared for developing new doctrines to control mis-use of information collection does not mean that the future is gloomy. What it does mean is that the same kind of imaginative thinking and systematic programming and planning must be applied to this problem as went into the development of the technology for the information systems themselves. This is a job in which the most fruitful discussions can take place among the computer scientists, lawyers, social scientists, and public officials. The sharing of expertise, the recognition of needs and values, and the setting of new balances are the key developments. To suggest the kind of approach that I think American society should take to information systems, let me sketch the response that I think sets these balances most sensitively. At the outset, I would have the courts and legislatures adopt as their guiding principle the concept that an individual's right to limit the circulation of personal information about himself is a vital ingredient of his right to privacy and this should not be infringed without the showing of strong social need and the satisfaction of requirements for protective safeguards. The First Amendment to the American Constitution which guarantees our rights to freedom of speech, press, and association must have as its necessary corollary the fact that we have a right not to communicate. It must also mean that we have the right to choose those to whom we communicate and the terms on which we do so. Any action by government that "turns us on" without that consent violates the right to silence that the Framers intended to give in the First Amendment just as much as the right to communicate. I would predict that this principle will come to be the guiding constitutional approach of the United States Supreme Court in dealing with the areas of physical, psychological, and data surveillance. Following this approach, when government takes information from an individual for one purpose (such as income taxation, social security, government licensing and employment) and uses it to influence, regulate, or prosecute the individual on unrelated matters, this raises a question about violation of the confidence under which the information was originally given. The more that centralized information pools on individuals are assembled, the more serious the unrestricted flow of information becomes. This suggests that we need in our legal system some procedure for classifying information into various categories and distinguishing the rights to use of such information according to such classifications. For example, personal information could be divided into matters of public record that are expected to be open to virtually everyone; confidential information that is given in trust to certain individuals or agencies with the expectation of limited use; and security information which is either given under the expectation of complete non-circulation or which contains derogatory information about individuals that has been obtained by physical and psychological surveillance. Different standards must be set for the receipt, storage, and circulation of such different classes of information. This could be done by federal and state legislation, by administrative rules, and by the way in which information systems are technologically related to one another.

With these general proposals established, our policy-making would turn to the technological safeguards that could limit the capacities for mis-use of information systems. It is important to realize that storing data in computers rather than on pieces of paper in metal files allows us to create far more technological protection for sensitive information than in the era of written records and physical manipulation. For example, information "bits" in the memory banks could be locked so that only one or several persons who have special passwords could get to it. Computers could be programmed to reject requests for statistical data about "groups" which are really attempts to get information on specific individuals or organizations. A data system could be set up so that a permanent record was made of all inquiries and the "audit trail" could be subject to annual review by the management of the information center, independent "watchdog" commissions of public officials and private citizens, and legislative committees.

Although many other ways to set system controls on information systems could be discussed, the fact remains that the system could still be "beaten" by those in charge of it, from the programmers who run it and mechanics who repair breakdowns to those who are in charge of the enterprise and know all the passwords. This means that a network of legal controls is absolutely essential. For example, a federal statute could specify that the data put into a statistical center is to be used solely for statistical purposes. It could forbid all other uses of the data to influence, regulate, or prosecute anyone, making such use a crime, and excluding all such data from use as evidence in judicial or governmental proceedings. It could forbid all persons other than data center employees to have access to the files, and the data could be specifically exempted from subpoena. An Inspector General or Ombudsman-type official could be set up to hear complaints about alleged misuse, and judicial review for such complaints could be provided for.

A far more extensive set of safeguards are required when intelligence systems are involved. These must deal with which individuals go into the system at all, which public officials have access to the information, what classes of information are completely excluded and what safeguards are provided for challenging both the information collected and the use made of it. Regulations for mis-use of the information by the intelligence system personnel and by agencies which use the information would have to be provided and, again, some form of outside review of the system would be required, preferably by both an independent executive agency and legislative committees.

At the moment, American society is barely entering the beginning stage of this debate over data surveillance. We can see that three quite different approaches are already appearing. One position, reflected by the initial views of many newspaper editors, civil liberties groups, and congressional spokesmen is to oppose creation of data centers and intelligence systems completely. The need for better statistics for policy analysis or of richer information systems for criminal justice purposes is seen as inadequate when weighed against the increase in government power and fears of invasion of privacy that such systems might bring.

A second view, reflected in the initial thinking of many executive agency officials and computer scientists, assumes that traditional administrative and legal safeguards, plus the expected self-restraint of those who would manage such systems, are enough to protect the citizen's privacy. The more reflective spokesmen in this group would add that a large-scale decrease in the kind of personal privacy we have through inefficiency of information collection may well be on its way out, but that this would be something individuals could adjust to and would not seriously threaten the operations of a democratic society.

The third position, which I have tried to describe in my earlier discussion, assumes that neither the "total ban" nor the "traditional restraints" positions represent desirable alternatives. What is called for is a new legal approach to the processing of personal information by authorities in a free society and a new set of legal, administrative, and system protections to accomplish this objective. The fact is that American society wants both better information analysis *and* privacy. Ever since the Constitution was written, our efforts to have both order and liberty have succeeded because we found ways to grant authority to government but to tie it down with the clear standards, operating procedures, and review mechanisms that protected individual rights. A free society should not have to choose between more rational use of authority and personal privacy if our talents for democratic government are brought to bear on the task. The most precious commodity we have now is the few years of lead-time before this problem grows beyond our capacity for control. If we act now, and act wisely, we can balance the conflicting demands in the area of data surveillance in this same tradition of democratic, rational solutions.

30

Influence of Christianity on Western Law
Harold J. Berman

. . . Every legal system shares with religion certain elements—ritual, tradition, authority, and universality—which are needed to symbolize and educate men's legal emotions. Otherwise law degenerates into legalism. Similarly, every religion has within it legal elements, without which it degenerates into private religiosity. . . .

Historical Jurisprudence in a Christian Perspective

For Judaism, the center of gravity of human history is the history of the Jewish people and of the Judaic law that binds it to God and its members to each other; whereas for Christianity, the church from the time of St. Paul, though conceived to be a historical continuation of the Jewish people, was intended to embrace all other peoples as well, each with its own law. Therefore a new law was required within the church itself, as a religious community, to govern its relationships with God as well as the relationships of its members with each other; also new attitudes and policies were required with respect to the secular law by which individual Christians were governed in their nonreligious activities and by which the church as a whole was governed in its relationships with "the world."

Excerpt from *The Interaction of Law and Religion*. Nashville, Tenn.: Abingdon Press, 1974, pp. 47, 52-66, by permission of the author.

In the first age of the church, the most striking fact about the secular law—the law of the Roman Empire—was that it altogether prohibited Christian worship. The church was illegal: to survive, it had to go underground—literally—into the catacombs. Thus the first principle of Christian jurisprudence, established by historical experience, was the principle of civil disobedience: laws that conflict with Christian faith are not binding in conscience. This had had its counterpart in Jewish history as well—for example, in the resistance to the worship of Baal, the story of Daniel's disobedience to King Darius, and refusals to place statues of the Roman emperors in the synagogues. There was, however, a difference: as Roman citizens, disobedient Christians were defying the laws of their own people. This fact had a considerable significance for the future, when the Christian church became part of the political establishment and individual Christians were confronted with unconscionable laws enacted by their own, not pagan but Christian, rulers—laws that were often imposed in the name of the church itself. People could not forget that the Christian era began with the assertion of a moral right—indeed, a duty—to violate a law that conflicts with God's will. This right and duty, reasserted in our own time by such men as Martin Luther King and the Berrigan brothers, is one of the foundations of our constitutional law of freedom of speech.

With the conversion of the Roman emperors to Christianity in the fourth century, the church came to operate within the power structure. Now it faced a quite different aspect of the question of the relationship between law and religion—namely, whether the emperor's acceptance of the Christian faith had anything positive to contribute to his role as a legislator. The answer given by history was that the Christian emperors of Byzantium considered it their Christian responsibility to revise the laws, as they put it, "in the direction of greater humanity."[1] Under the influence of Christianity, the Roman law of the postclassical period reformed family law, giving the wife a position of greater equality before the law, requiring mutual consent of both spouses for the validity of a marriage, making divorce more difficult (which at that time was a step toward women's liberation!), and abolishing the father's power of life or death over his children; reformed the law of slavery, giving a slave the right to appeal to a magistrate if his master abused his powers and even, in some cases, the right to freedom if the master exercised cruelty, multiplying modes of manumission of slaves, and permitting slaves to acquire rights by kinship with freemen; and introduced a concept of equity into legal rights and duties generally, thereby tempering the strictness of general prescriptions. Also the great collections of laws compiled by Justinian and his successors in the sixth, seventh, and eighth centuries were inspired in part by the belief that Christianity required that the law be systematized as a necessary step in its humanization. These various reforms were, of course, attributable not only to Christianity, but Christianity gave an important impetus to them as well as providing the main ideological justification. Like civil disobedience, law reform "in the direction of greater humanity" remains a basic principle of Christian jurisprudence derived from the early experience of the church.

In contrast to the Byzantine emperors, who inherited the great legal tradition of pagan Rome, the rulers of the Germanic, Slavic, and other peoples of Europe during roughly the same era (from the fifth to the tenth centuries) presided over a legal regime consisting chiefly of primitive tribal customs and rules of the blood feud. It is more than coincidence that the rulers of many of the major tribal peoples, from Anglo-Saxon England to Kievan Russia, after their conversion to Christianity promulgated written collections of tribal laws and introduced various reforms, particularly in connection with family law, slavery, and protection of the poor and oppressed, as well as in connection with church property and the rights of clergy.[2] The Laws of Alfred (about A.D. 890) start with a recitation of the Ten Commandments and excerpts from the Mosaic law; and in restating and revising the native Anglo-Saxon laws Alfred includes such great principles as: "Doom [i.e., judge] very evenly; doom not one doom to the rich, another to the poor; nor doom one to your friend, another to your foe."

The church in those centuries, subordinate as it was to emperors, kings, and barons, sought to limit violence by establishing rules to control blood feuds; and in the tenth and eleventh centuries the great Abbey of Cluny, with its branches all over Europe, even had some success in establishing the so-called Peace of God, which exempted from warfare not only the clergy but also the peasantry, and the so-called Truce of God, which prohibitied warfare on the weekends.[3] Here, too, are influences of religion on law that have bearing for our time.

Nevertheless, despite the reforms and innovations of Christian kings and emperors, the prevailing law of the West remained—prior to the twelfth century—the law of the blood feud, and of trial by battle, and by ordeals of fire and water, and by ritual oaths. There were no professional judges, no professional lawyers, no law books, either royal or ecclesiastical. Custom reigned—tribal custom, local custom, feudal custom. In the households of kings and in the monasteries there was civilization to a degree; but without a system of law it was extremely difficult to transmit civilization from the centers to the localities. To take one example: the church preached that marriage is a sacrament which cannot be performed without the consent of the spouses, but there was no effective system of law by which the church could overcome the widespread practice of arranging marriages between infants. And not only were civilized values crushed by a hostile environment, but the church itself was under the domination of the same environment: lucrative and influential clerical offices were bought and sold by feudal lords, who appointed brothers and cousins to be bishops and priests.

In the latter part of the eleventh and first part of the twelfth century, there took place in the West a great revolution which resulted in the formation of a visible, corporate, hierarchical church, a legal entity independent of emperors, kings, and feudal lords, and subordinate to the absolute monarchical authority of the bishop of Rome. This was the Papal Revolution, of whose enormous significance medieval historians both inside and outside the Catholic Church are becoming increasingly aware.[4] It led to the creation of a new kind of law for the church as well as new kinds of law for the various secular kingdoms.

Previously the relationship between the spiritual and secular realms had been one of overlapping authorities, with emperors and kings (Charlemagne and William the Conqueror, for example) calling church councils and promulgating new theological doctrine and ecclesiastical law, and wtih popes, archbishops, bishops, and priests being invested in their offices by emperors, kings, and lords. In 1075, however, Pope Gregory VII proclaimed the complete political and legal independence of the church and at the same time proclaimed his own supreme political and legal authority over the entire clergy of Western Christendom.[5] It took forty-five years of warfare between the papal and the imperial parties—the Wars of Investiture—and in England it took the martyrdom of Thomas Becket before the papal claims were established (albeit with some substantial compromises).

The now visible, hierarchical, corporate Roman Catholic Church needed a systematic body of law, and in the twelfth and thirteenth centuries this was produced—first in a great treatise written about 1140 by the Italian monk Gratian and eighty years later, after a succession of jurist-popes had promulgated hundreds of new laws, by Pope Gregory IX in his Decretals of 1234. The Decretals remained the basic law of the Roman Church until 1917.

Of course there had been ecclesiastical canons long before Gratian, but they consisted of miscellaneous scattered decisions, decrees, teachings, etc., mostly of a theological nature, pronounced by various church councils and individual bishops, and occasionally gathered in chronologically arranged collections. There were also traditional procedures in ecclesiastical tribunals. However, there was no systematized body of ecclesiastical law, criminal law, family law, inheritance law, property law, or contract law, such as was created by the canonists of the twelfth and thirteenth centuries. The canon law of the later Middle Ages, which only today, eight centuries later, is being called into question by some leading Roman Catholics themselves,[6] was the first modern legal system of the West, and it prevailed in every country of Europe. The canon law governed virtually all aspects of the lives of the church's own army of priests and monks and also a great many aspects of the lives of the laity. The new hierarchy of church courts had exclusive jurisdiction over laymen in matters of family law, inheritance, and various types of spiritual crimes, and in addition it had concurrent jurisdiction with secular courts over contracts (whenever the parties made a "pledge of faith"), property (whenever ecclesiastical property was involved—and the church owned one-fourth to one-third of the land of Europe), and many other matters.

The canon law did not prevail alone, however, Alongside it there emerged various types of secular law, which just at this very time, in the twelfth and thirteenth centuries, began to be rationalized and systematized. In about 1100, the Roman law of Justinian, which had been virtually forgotten in the West for five centuries, was rediscovered. This rediscovery played an important part in the development of the canon law, but it also was seized upon by secular rulers who resisted the new claims of the papacy. And so in emulation of the canon law, diverse bodies of secular law came to be created by emperors, kings, great feudal lords, and also eventually in the cities and boroughs that emerged in Europe in the twelfth and thirteenth centuries, as well as among merchants trading in the great international fairs. The success of the canon law stimulated secular authorities to create their own professional courts and a professional legal literature, to transform tribal, local, and feudal custom, and to create their own rival legal systems to govern feudal property relations, crimes of violence, mercantile transactions, and many other matters.

Thus it was the church that first taught Western man what a modern legal system is like. The church first taught that conflicting customs, statutes, cases, and doctrines may be reconciled by analysis and synthesis. This was the method of Abelard's famous *Sic et Non* (*Yes and No*), which lined up contradictory texts of Holy Scriptures—the method reflected in the title of Gratian's *Concordance of Discordant Canons.* By this method the church, in reviving the study of the obsolete Roman law, transformed it by transmuting its complex categories and classifications into abstract legal concepts. These techniques were derived from *the principle of reason* as understood by the theologians and philosophers of the twelfth centry as well as by the lawyers.

The church also taught *the principle of conscience*—in the corporate sense of that term, not the modern individualist sense: that the law is to be found not only in scholastic reason but also in the heart of the lawgiver or judge. The principle of conscience in adjudication was first stated in an eleventh-century tract which declared that the judge must judge himself before he may judge the accused, that he must, in other words, identify himself with the accused, since thereby (it was said) he will know more about the crime than the criminal himself knows. A new science of pleading and procedure was created in the church courts, and later in secular courts as well (for example, the English Chancery), "for informing the conscience of the judge." Procedural formalism was attacked. (In 1215 the Fourth Lateran Council effectively abolished trials by ordeal throughout Europe by forbidding clergy to participate in them.) The right to direct legal representation by professional lawyers and the procedure for interrogation by the judge according to carefully worked out rules were among the new institutions created to implement the principle of conscience. Conscience was associated with the idea of the equality of the law, since in conscience all litigants are equal; and from this came equity—the protection of the poor and helpless against the rich and powerful, the enforcement of relations of trust and confidence, and the granting of so-called personal remedies such as injunctions. Equity, as we noted earlier, had been part of the postclassical Roman law as well, but it was now for the first time made systematic, and special procedures were devised for invoking and applying it.

And so the church sought both to legalize morality and to moralize legality; it took legal jurisdiction over sins, and it influenced the secular law to conform to moral principles. As in ancient Israel, the distinction between law and morality was minimized. On the one hand, standards of right and wrong were reinforced by legal procedures and legal sanctions; on the other hand, a divine righteousness was attributed to legal standards which they by no means always had. Universal celibacy of the priesthood, for example, was made a legal requirement in the eleventh century in order to insulate the clergy from clan and feudal politics, but it acquired an aura of sanctity that made it survive long after it had ceased to be necessary. The law of heresy is another example of the evil of confusing immorality with illegality. Excommunication for disobedience to ecclesiastical authority was a legal remedy which could deprive a person of his entire moral security.

There was, however, an important difference between medieval Christendom and ancient Israel in this regard: in medieval Christendom there was a conflict of jurisdictions between church and state, a coexistence and rivalry and diverse legal systems within each nation and a coexistence and rivalry of diverse nations within the church. The sanctity which a visible, hierarchical, corporate church could give to its law was challenged by the fact that each person in Christendom lived not only under church law but also under several secular legal systems—royal law, feudal law, local law, merchant law, and others. Each of the secular legal systems also claimed sanctity, and that sanctity, too, was challenged—by the other secular legal systems as well as by ecclesiastical law. This pluralism of legal systems has remained a dominant feature of Western law, despite the inroads of nationalism and of positivism since the Protestant Reformation. In all countries of the West today, including the United States, every person lives under more than one legal system. We live not only under national law but also under international law; and we may invoke international legal custom as well as treaties and conventions and even declarations of the United Nations to challenge the acts of our national authorities. Also, we in America live under both state and federal law, and may run from one to the other for protection; we live under both statute law and constitutional law and may invoke concepts of "due process" and "equal protection" to oppose the will of the legislature; we live under both strict law and equity— under the rule and under the discretion to depart from the rule in exceptional cases. The coexistence of diverse legal systems within the same polity gives a legal foundation to the concept of the supremacy of law; political power is always subject to legal challenge, unless the ruler has seized control of *all* the available legal systems.

The medieval church also taught *the principle of the growth of the law*—that legal doctrines and legal institutions are to be consciously based on past authority and yet are to be consciously adapted to the needs of the present and future. The canon lawyers worked out new rules and doctrines on the basis of Justinian, the Bible, the church fathers, Aristotle, Germanic customs; they revered the authoritative texts, but they glossed them and then glossed the glosses. The concept of organic growth helped to reconcile stability with flexibility. Just as the great Gothic cathedrals were built over centuries and had budgets projected for a thousand years, so the great law texts were constructed and reconstructed with eyes both to the past and to the future. And indeed they have survived: the reforms now taking place in the Roman Catholic Church are in part an effort to build once again on the legal foundations of the twelfth and thirteenth centuries. But more than that, the canon laws—of marriage, of inheritance, of torts, of crime, of contracts, of property, of equity, of procedure—have entered into the secular legal systems of the West, as has the principle of growth itself, with the result that there has in fact been created a common language of Western law, a Western legal tradition capable or organic development.

The Lutheran Reformation broke the medieval dualism of two kinds of official hierarchy, two kinds of official legal systems—that of the church and that of the secular authorities—by delegalizing the church. Where Lutheranism succeeded, the church came to be conceived as invisible, apolitical, alegal; and the only sovereignty, the only law (in the political sense), was that of the secular kingdom or principality. It was just before this time, in fact, that Machiavelli invented the word "state" to apply to the purely secular political order. The Protestant reformers were in one sense Machiavellians in that they were skeptical of man's power to create a human law which would reflect eternal law, and they explicitly denied that it is the task of the church as such to develop human law. This Protestant skepticism made possible the emergence of a theory of law—legal positivism—which treats the law of the state as morally neutral, a means and not an end, a device for manifesting the policy of the sovereign and for securing obedience to it. But the secularization of law and the emergence of a positivist theory of law are only one side of the story of the contribution of the Protestant Reformation to the Western legal tradition. The other side is equally important: by freeing law from theological doctrine and from direct ecclesiastical influence, the Reformation enabled it to undergo a new and brilliant development. In the words of the great German jurist and historian Rudolf Sohm, "Luther's Reformation was a renewal not only of faith but also of the world: both the world of spiritual life and the world of law."[7]

The key to the renewal of law in the West from the sixteenth century on was the Protestant concept of the power of the individual, by God's grace, to change nature and to create new social relations through the exercise of his will. The Protestant concept of the individual will became central to the development of the modern law of property and contract. Nature became property. Economic relations became contract. Conscience became will and intent. The last testament, which in the earlier Catholic tradition had been a means of saving souls by charitable gifts, became a means of controlling social and economic relations. By the naked expression of their will, their intent, testators could dispose of their property after death and entrepreneurs could arrange their business relations by contract. The property and contract rights so created were held to be sacred and inviolable, so long as they did not contravene conscience. Conscience gave them their sanctity. And so the secularization of the state, in the restricted sense of the removal of ecclesiastical controls from it, was accompanied by a spiritualization, and even a sanctification, of property and contract.

It is not true, therefore, that Protestantism placed no limits upon the political power of the absolute monarchs that ruled Europe in the sixteenth century. The development of positive law was conceived to rest ultimately upon the prince alone, but it was presupposed that in exercising his will he would respect the individual consciences of his subjects, and that meant respecting also their property and contract rights. This presupposition rested—precariously, to be sure—upon four centuries of history in which the church had succeeded in Christianizing law to a remarkable extent (given the level of the cultural life of the Germanic peoples to begin with). Thus a Protestant positivism which separates law from morals, denies the lawmaking role of the church, and finds the ultimate sanction of law in political coercion nevertheless assumes the existence of a Christian conscience among the people and a state governed by Christian rulers.

We have spoken thus far of Protestantism primarily in its Lutheran form. A later form, Calvinism, has also had profound effects upon the development of Western law, and especially upon American law. The Puritans carried forward the Lutheran concept of the sanctity of the individual conscience and also, in law, the sanctity of the individual will as reflected in property and contract rights. But they added two new elements: first, a belief in the duty of Christians to reform the world—indeed, "reforming the world" was a specifically Puritan slogan;[8] and second, a belief in the local congregation, under its elected minister and elders, as the seat of truth—a "fellowship of active believers" higher than any political authority.[9] The active Puritan, bent on reforming the world, was ready to defy the highest powers of church and of state in asserting his faith, and he did so on grounds of individual conscience, also appealing to divine law, to the Mosaic law of the Old Testament, and to natural-law concepts embodied in the medieval legal tradition. As the early Christian martyrs founded the church by their disobedience to Roman law, so the seventeenth-century Puritans, including men like Hampden, Lilburne, Udall, William Penn, and others, by their open disobedience to English law laid the foundations for the English and American law of civil rights and civil liberties as expressed in our respective Constitutions: freedom of speech and press, free exercise of religion, the privilege against self-incrimination, the independence of the jury from judicial dictation, the right not to be imprisoned without cause, and many other such rights and freedoms. We also owe to Calvinist congregationalism the religious basis of our concepts of social contract and government by consent of the governed.[10] . . .

Notes

1. See the Preamble of the *Ecloga* (a collection of laws promulgated by the Byzantine emperors in about A.D. 740), Edwin H. Freshfield, *A Manual of Roman Law, the Ecloga* (Cambridge, Mass., 1926). The opening paragraph states: "A selection of laws arranged in compendious form by Leo and Constantine, the wise and pious Emperors, taken from the Institutes, the Digests, the Code, and the Novels of the Great Justinian, and revised in the direction of greater humanity, promulgated in the month of March, Ninth Indiction in the year of the world 6234."

2. Examples include the Lex Salica of the Frankish King Clovis (about A.D. 511), the laws of the Anglo-Saxon King Ethelbert (about A.D. 600), and the *Russkaia Pravda* of the Kievan Prince Yaroslav (about A.D. 1030).

3. The Peace of God (*pax Dei*, also called *pax ecclesiae*, Peace of the Church), which originated at synods in France in 990, also forbade acts of private warfare against ecclesiastical property. Enforcement was weak, being vested in the bishop or count on whose lands violations occurred. The Truce of God (*treuga Dei*) originated at a synod of 1027. It was more successful, especially in the twelfth century when fighting was—in principle—outlawed during nearly three-fourths of the year.

4. The view that the Great Reform championed by Pope Gregory VII was the first of the Great Revolutions of European history was pioneered by Eugen Rosenstock-Huessy in *Die Europaeischen Revolutionen* (Jena, 1931). See also Eugen Rosenstock-Huessy, *Out of Revolution: The Autobiography of Western Man* (New York, 1938), and *The Driving Power of Western Civilization: The Christian Revolution of the Middle Ages* (Boston, 1949). Although Gregory is still viewed as a traditionalist and even a reactionary by a few historians, virtually none now deny that it was in his time that the Roman Catholic Church took its modern form as a legal institution. Cf. Schafer Williams, ed., *The Gregorian Epoch: Reformation, Revolution, Reaction?* (Boston, 1964); Brian Tierney, *The Crisis of Church & State 1050–1300* (Englewood Cliffs, N.J., 1964). . . .

5. The text of Gregory VII's *Dictatus papae* (Dictates of the Pope) of 1075 may be found in Ernest F. Henderson, *Select Historical Documents of the Middle Ages* (New York, 1968), pp. 366–67, and Frederic A. Ogg, *A Source Book of Medieval History* (New York, 1972), pp. 262–64. It reflected papal claims of supremacy over both the ecclesiastical and the secular realms. Some of the claims with respect to the secular realm had to be abandoned, but papal autocracy within the church has survived to this day. Among the most radical provisions of the *Dictatus* were the following:
    "That the Roman bishop alone . . . has the power to depose bishops and reinstate them. . . . That he has the power to dispose emperors. . . . That he may, if necessity require, transfer bishops from one see to another. . . . That

he has power to ordain a clerk of any church he may wish. . . . That he can be judged by no man. . . . That no one shall dare to condemn a person who appeals to the apostolic see. . . . That to the latter should be referred the more important cases of every church. . . . That the Roman Church has never erred, nor ever, by the testimony of Scripture, shall err, to all eternity. . . . That no one can be considered Catholic who does not agree with the Roman Church. . . . That he [the pope] has the power to absolve the subjects of unjust rulers from their oath of fidelity."

6. A considerable discussion has resolved around the proposal to revise the Code of Canon Law, which in 1917 replaced the Decretals of Pope Gregory IX. The Second Vatican Council proposed that the code be thoroughly revised, and a commission has been constituted to prepare such a revision. The discussion of its revision has included arguments to the effect that law should be wholly eliminated from the life of the church.

7. Rudolf Sohm, *Weltliches und geistliches Recht* (Munich and Leipzig, 1914), p. 69.

8. Cf. Gerrard Winstanley, *Platform of the Law of Freedom:* "The spirit of the whole creation was about the reformation of the world." Quoted in Rosenstock-Huessy, *Out of Revolution* p. 291. Cf. Thomas Case, sermon preached before the House of Commons in 1641: "Reformation must be universal. Reform all places, all persons and callings; reform the benches of judgment, the inferior magistrates. . . . Reform the universities, reform the cities, reform the countries, reform inferior schools of learning, reform the Sabbath, reform the ordinances, the worship of God. Every plant which my heavenly father hath not planted shall be rooted up." Quoted in Michael Walzer, *The Revolution of the Saints: A Study in the Origins of Radical Politics* (Cambridge, Mass., 1965), pp. 10–11. . . .

9. Cf. A. D. Lindsay, *The Modern Democratic State* (New York, 1962), pp. 117–18; David Little, *Religion, Order, and Law: A Study in Pre-Revolutionary England* (New York, 1969), p. 230.

10. This point is usually overlooked; instead, the theory of social contract is generally traced to seventeenth-century philosophers such as John Locke and Thomas Hobbes. But a century earlier, Calvin had asked the entire people of Geneva to accept the confession of faith and to take an oath to obey the Ten Commandments, as well as to swear loyalty to the city. People were summoned in groups by the police to participate in the covenant. Cf. J. T. McNeill, *The History and Character of Calvinism* (New York, 1957), p. 142. . . .

31

From Free to Indissoluble to Terminable Marriage
Max Rheinstein

To the student of comparative law it is an impressive experience to realize how little the private law systems of the world differ from one another. Wide divergencies exist in public law, between democratic and authoritarian countries, between private enterprise countries and socialist countries. In the latter, the field of private law is narrower than in the former, but insofar as private law exists, it is of striking similarity, irrespective of whether the country is one of free enterprise or of socialist planning, whether it is democratic or authoritarian. Differences exist with respect to commercial and other contractual transactions; they can be annoying in international transactions, but they relate to matters of detail. In the field of property, especially property in land, the differences appear to be larger than they actually are. They lie more in the conceptual structure of the legal rules and institutions than in practical results. But in one field of private law diversity is glaring, namely, in that of divorce.

Diversity of Divorce Laws

No divorce at all is permitted in Andorra, Argentina, Brazil, Chile, Colombia, Eire, Paraguay, the Philippine Republic, or Spain; it is not

Excerpt from *Marriage Stability, Divorce and the Law*. Chicago, Ill.: University of Chicago Press, 1972, pp. 6–27 and 201–202, by permission of the publisher.

available to Roman Catholics in Liechtenstein or Portugal. But in Japan it may be obtained upon mutual consent. Until 1970, in England, a divorce could be had only upon the grounds of adultery, cruelty, or desertion, i.e., of grave marital misconduct (and, in addition, upon the ground of the other spouse's incurable insanity), while in Switzerland a marriage may be terminated when it is found to be incurably disrupted for any reason.

We do not even have to go outside of the United States to find diversity of divorce laws, at least as they appear on the statute books. Until 1949, no divorce at all was obtainable in South Carolina. In New York adultery was the only ground until 1967. But in Alaska, Kansas, Nevada, New Mexico, Oklahoma, and the Virgin Islands, a marriage may be terminated upon the mere ground of incompatibility of temperament, in Illinois upon the ground of mental cruelty, whatever that may mean, in over half the jurisdictions simply upon the fact that the parties have lived separate and apart from each other for a certain period of time, which varies from one year in the District of Columbia to ten years in Rhode Island. But basically divorce law in the United States is similar to what it was in England until 1970: a divorce can be granted upon the ground of one spouse's grave marital misconduct, especially adultery, cruelty, or desertion for a certain length of time, provided the petitioner himself is not guilty too.

Variety also exists with respect to the mode in which a divorce is brought about. In the United States as in most other countries of Christian tradition, a marriage cannot be terminated, except by death, in any way other than by the decree of a court. In the Soviet Union, until 1968 even two courts had to act, first the people's court and then the appellate court. In some Oriental countries the court is not, as with us, a secular court of the state, but it is, as it was in England and, into our own century, in eastern European countries, a religious body which applies the law of its faith rather than any secular law of the state. In Lebanon, for instance, the divorce law is different for every one of the nineteen religious groups, of which each has its own court. In Denmark, Norway, and Iceland marriages are, at least normally, terminated by administrative agencies rather than by courts. In countries which for Moslems still uphold the classical law of Islam, such as Afghanistan, Pakistan, or Saudi Arabia, a divorce, or we should rather say, a repudiation, is brought about by the extrajudicial, unilateral declaration of the husband. In Japan, as we have seen, a marriage may be terminated by the mutual agreement of the parties and the notification of the registrar of civil status. In ancient Rome at the period of the principate a marriage was dissolved simply by the parties' mutual consent or by the repudiation formlessly declared by one of them. . . .

Truly, in the field of divorce, we find a bewildering variety, in the substantive laws, in procedures, and in actual practices. Why is it that here we do not find the measure of uniformity so conspicuous in other fields of private law?

The answer lies, of course, in the diversity of social factors by which the patterns of the various societies are determined. Among these factors ethical and religious value judgments are as important as, or even more than, objective facts of social, economic, and political development. These value judgments are widely held without conscious reflection or rational deliberation. They may be felt deeply or professed superficially. Upon the living they have been implanted in that process of acculturation which has shaped the civilization of those successive generations by which civilizations have been built and developed.

In Western civilizations two trends can be traced, two sets of drives, ideas, and ideals which have shaped our present institution of monogamous marriage including divorce. The struggle between and intermingling of these two trends has brought about results which have varied from time to time and which now vary from place to place. One of these two trends has prevailed for centuries. In recent decades the pendulum has come to swing in the direction of the other, but there has not been a completel reversal of the ideas that have been dominant for the last fifteen hundred years.

The two competing ideologies may be called the Christian-conservative and the eudemonistic-liberal. When carried out consistently, the Christian-conservative principle implies that marriage is indissoluble save by death. Its consistent opposite implies that marriage may be terminated by either party at any time. The former principle is that of Roman Catholic canon law. The latter principle prevailed in ancient Rome in the time of the principate; in modern times it does not seem to have been fully adopted anywhere, at least not in official law.

Christianity and the Principle of Indissoluble Marriage

Marriage as we know it is a product of centuries of Christianity. From Judaism, Christianity took over the commandment of strict premarital and extramarital chastity. Sexual intercourse is permitted only in marriage. It is by this commandment that Judaism differed from the religions of the surrounding world. Time and again the Jews were reminded of it by the prophets, who were horrified by the constantly recurring temptation presented to God's people by the licentiousness of neighboring peoples with their orgiastic religious rites. Out of Jewish and older Roman ideals the Christian church fathers fashioned the rule of strict monogamy. Firm bounds were set to the sex drive. Intercourse was to be permissible only between one man and one woman, and between them only if they were united by the bond of Christian marriage. Even then sexual activity was to be carried on only in the "natural" way apt to result in the procreation of issue.

Christianity's new idea was that marriage is to be indissoluble, that it is to last for the duration of the joint lives of the partners. Marriage is to be the fullest community of life. Sexual intercourse is to take place only between partners who are united in this complete union. It is not to be indulged for its own sake, not even between partners living together without the marital intent of permanency. Married partners, between whom alone intercourse is not sinful, ought to be able to rely upon each other in all ups and downs of life; and in past centuries, especially in those of early Christianity, life was full of risk to a degree which it is hard for us today to imagine. Intercourse was also restricted to those who would be united not only by physical attraction or material considerations but by their common faith and the bond of common responsibility before God, a responsibility, above all, to raise their offspring in the faith in Christ and in the discipline of Christian morals. But even beyond this responsibility for the future generation and thus for the permanency of human society as God's creation, husband and wife themselves were to strengthen each other in the faith and thus to be *one* not only in the flesh but in spirit. In the symbolism of the time, this ideal was expressed through the doctrine of marriage being a sacrament, i.e., a vessel of divine grace. Significantly, this sacrament is not administered to the parties by the priest; it is mutually administered to each other by the parties. Man's most animalistic act is thus elevated to the highest bond of spirituality. The idea is sublime. That the high demands of Christian sex morals have never been fulfilled completely, the church itself recognizes. It is aware of the sinful nature of man, and in the sacrament of penance, as combined with the institution of confession, the church has fashioned the way in which the commands of the morality of perfection can be combined with the imperfection of man. . . .

The new ethics of sex and marriage constituted part and parcel of that reaction against the hedonistic latitude which had been characteristic of the Hellenistic society of imperial Rome. Austerity, strictness, and renunciation came to be the new values; asceticism, carried to extremes by the anchorites of the desert and the stylites of the East, became the ideal of the religious virtuosi.

Much time was needed for the new ideology to make its way in the core region of the Roman empire and in the lands of mission, inhabited by Germanic tribes who, in the storms of the great invasions, overran and conquered the western parts of the empire. Their conversion to Christianity did not imply the immediate acceptance of the Christian sex ethics, which were as new to them as they had been to the Hellenist and Oriental peoples of the eastern parts.

The Principle of Terminable Marriage

The new order of ideas made necessary a far-reaching change in the method of social regulation of marriage. Nowhere, of course, were the matters of sex and marriage free of all social regulation. Incest taboos were universal and social norms were recognized everywhere as to propriety of marriage age, choice of partners, and the legitimacy of offspring. Mostly these norms belonged to the spheres of religion, convention, and morality. That means that the sanction of contrary behavior was expected to be supernatural retribution, or would consist in unorganized social disapproval or in the internal discomfort of pangs of conscience. The law, i.e., the norm structure enforced by politically organized society, had little concern for matters of marriage and the family. In Rome in particular the head of a "house," the *paterfamilias*, had, so to speak, sovereign power over all its members, except, in later times, his wife. Indeed, nobody but a *paterfamilias* could own any property or could be bound by contractual obligations. For torts committed by any member of the house, the head, and only the head, was financially responsible. The law, i.e., the regulatory power of the state, did not seek to penetrate into the internal structure of the houses of which the body politic was composed. Roman law, at least Roman private law, was a law dealing with relations between houses as represented by their heads. As for the houses themselves, the law could content itself with the establishment of rules determining membership. Such rules were, of course, indispensable. Strangely enough, however, for the determination of the initiation and termination of marriage, i.e., of that relationship which is basic for the creation of house membership, especially of offspring, Roman law contented itself with a reference to the norms of religion and convention. In early times marriage was, at least among the leading class of patricians, initiated by a religious ceremony (*confarretio*) or by *coemptio*. These rituals became obsolete in later republican times, when it became customary to marry simply by starting life in common, provided both parties had the intention thereby to become husband and wife. But no ritual, religious or secular, was prescribed by the law. The state simply accepted as a marriage what was recognized as such by the mores. In the same way, the state treated a marriage as dissolved when it was treated as such by the mores, under which it was sufficient that the parties separated, or that one terminated the community of marital life and so informed the other. Attempts to limit freedom of divorce by such agreements as can still today be found in circles subject to Islamic or Jewish law were frustrated by the rule of their invalidity.

Initiation of a marriage presupposed, of course, that no taboo existed. In addition to the incest taboos, there were strictly religious ones, such as the one against marriage of a Vestal Virgin, and, above all, the political taboo against marriage outside the circle of *conubium*. A Roman citizen could not, and here the law entered, marry a noncitizen, unless the latter belonged to that privileged group of allies upon whom *conubium* had been expressly conferred. That no marriage was possible between a free person and a slave, or among slaves, was self-evident. Through legislation of Augustus, the scope of legal regulation of marriage was somewhat extended by the attempt to reconfirm the old Roman virtues by discouraging hypogamy of members of senatorial and other upper-class houses.

Full freedom to terminate a marriage was a rule so firmly rooted in the mores that it took centuries of Christian effort to replace it by the new principle of indissolubility. Even when this new doctrine had begun to be settled in the teaching of the church, and Christianity had become the established religion of the Roman state, the emperors, who were the heads of both the political and the religious side of the church–state empire, did no more than threaten with punishment a husband who would repudiate his wife without justification or a wife who would abandon the marital bond without good cause. The legislation, which started with Constantine, wavered a great deal. Generally, repudiation by the husband was treated as justified in the case of a wife's behavior that would raise the suspicion of adultery, making an attempt upon the spouse's life, or committing such a serious crime as preparing poison, desecrating sepulchres, or treason. The punishment for unjustified repudiation or abandonment consisted in forfeiture of certain rights of marital property, confiscation of property, deportation, or imprisonment in a monastery. Generally women were treated more harshly than men. They were also prohibited from remarrying before the expiration of five years so as to make sure that the repudiation would not be motivated by "cupidity." . . .

Role of Canon Law

Marriage did not become indissoluble until jurisdiction in marital causes was firmly established to lie with the courts of the church. The establishment of that jurisdiction extended over centuries of struggle between church and state, in the Byzantine empire and in the Germanic kingdoms of the west. In matrimonial matters, exercise of jurisdiction by any kind of court, ecclesiastical or secular, constituted for the most part an innovation. Matters of marriage, as we have observed, had been largely outside the sphere of law. That the church, once it had organized itself on a bureaucratic–hierarchical pattern, headed by the Bishop of Rome, would develop lawlike norms on matters of internal organization and discipline and would establish for these matters a court system of its own, was but natural. . . .

With the establishment of a court system of its own, the church also had to develop a procedural and substantive law that could be applied in its courts. Thus there grew up that peculiar body of law known as canon law. It is law in the sense that its norms are formalized and expressed in that conceptualistic way in which Roman law came to be formalized in its later stage of development. It is "law" also in the sense that it is administered in courts, the structure and procedure of which are patterned on those of the late Roman empire. It is different from law in the strict sense of the word in that its sanction is not the action of some officer of politically organized society who inflicts upon the violator of the law some act of physical force such as imprisonment, death, or forced seizure of property. The sanction of canon law is the same as that of religion, namely, the fear of supranatural retribution. But in the framework of the church this sanction is set to work by the formal act of an officer of the church, ordinarily a bishop, such as excommunication or the imposition of penance. The fact that in the medieval framework of society the imposition by the ecclesiastical authority of spiritual punishment might be the occasion for the imposition by the secular authority of secular punishment strengthened the force of the canon law. Such cooperation was especially effective in the field of marriage, where ecclesiastical judgments of nullity or separation could be accompanied by property detriments to be suffered in the secular forum.

Canon law constitutes a unique case of juridification of religious tenets and commands. A close combination of law and religion exists in Judaism and Islam and, to some extent, in Hinduism. But what has occurred there is the opposite of what occurred in Christianity. The law, instead of including religion, was swallowed up by religion. The sacred books, in Judaism the Torah as expounded in the Talmud, in Islam the Koran together, in Sunnite view, with the tradition of the Prophet, covers all and every aspect of life. But Christianity found itself compelled, besides the realm of the Lord, also to recognize that of Caesar. In its canon law the church has adopted the method of Caesar for the formulation and enforcement of the commands of its own realm. In the Jewish and Islamic view there is no realm of Caesar; there is only that of God, and that realm includes those affairs in which Caesar, i.e., the khalif, is interested. This view has resulted in the theologification of the law. Legal learning coincides with theological. This fact accounts for that peculiar climate of Jewish and Islamic law which Max Weber calls "substantive rationality" and which now tends to invade our secular law, since it has begun to be forged by the new religion of humanitarianism. The rules of law are developed so as to give expression to religious tenets and religiously inspired commands of ethics.

In that method of "formalistic rationality" which was characteristic of revived Roman law as well as of later nineteenth-century civil law and common law, the rules of law, which in the last resort constitute expressions of moral value judgments based to a considerable extent upon configurations of political power, have tended to be formalized and thus stabilized by the use of concepts of some abstract character. This tendency of secular law has invaded canon law in general and its marriage part in particular. . . .

Only the canon law background renders understandable . . . the present learning about nullity and voidability of marriages and about actions for declaration of nullity and annulment. Only the canon law background explains why a party's restoration to the freedom of remarriage depends on the spouse's having committed adultery or some other marital offense, and why, under the doctrine of recrimination, a marriage, while it may be dissolved when it has been disrupted by the misconduct of one party, may not be dissolved when it is so thoroughly confounded that both parties have been guilty of marital misconduct.

But we have run ahead of our story. We left it at the point when the church had ultimately established the jurisdiction of its courts in matrimonial causes and had thus been enabled consistently to enforce its doctrine of indissolubility of marriage. The effects of that doctrine were mitigated by the theological learning that was developed, in a manner of continuous refinement, about validity and invalidity of marriages and thus about the possibility of a marriage being declared null and void, with the resulting freedom of remarriage of the parties.

Probably the development of such rules was due more to the

necessity of intrinsic logic than to practical regard for human nature. When it became established that a marriage once concluded was to be indissoluble, it became necessary to work out clear criteria for determining whether or not a marriage had been concluded. It was the merit of the canonists that they, following Roman tradition, made the conclusion of a marriage primarily dependent upon the will of the parties. . . . Their mutual consent, even without any ceremony, was to suffice for the conclusion of a marriage. But then it became necessary to prevent a marriage from being concluded without consent, and to see to it that consent, on general principle, be serious, real, and free of coercion or fraud. In the long run, it is true, the vitiating—or shall we rather say, the liberating—effects of coercion and fraud were restricted to the cases in which they would relate to "the essentials of the marriage relationship" and that concept was so considerably narrowed that a great many forced marriages or marriages induced by fraud have come to be held valid and so to be indissoluble. . . .

The concept of consent came to be so refined that it meant only the consent to enter upon a marriage in the sense of an indissoluble union including carnal knowledge apt to procreate issue. Mental reservation to maintain the relationship for a limited time only, for instance as long as love should persist, or a secret intention not to engage in marital intercourse, or not in "natural" intercourse, would prevent the conclusion of a valid marriage. There have been ups and downs as to the mode in which such a mental reservation might be proved. After a period of remarkable liberality around the turn of the last century, the requirements of proof have recently been tightened.

Even when the consent was valid on the part of both spouses, a marriage could still be shown to be invalid because of the existence of such an objective impediment as holy orders, solemn vow of chastity, existing prior marriage, pre-contract, impotency, blood relationship, affinity, and spiritual relationship within the prohibited degrees. In the later Middle Ages these last-named concepts were broadened enormously. Considering the limited travel opportunities of the time and its rigid class structure—circumstances which very much limited the range of marriageable partners—it would seem that in any unsuccessful marriage the parties might well be proved to be related to each other in some way that would invalidate their marriage. To what extent nullity proceedings were actually used as a substitute for divorce, we do not know. The proceedings were lengthy and expensive, and resort to them may also have been discouraged by the mores for those who were anxious to maintain respectability. For those who were not, there was another substitute of which we shall still have to speak, namely, the ease with which one could disappear in a society without registration and without services for the tracing of missing persons.

In addition to nullity proceedings, canon law provided proceedings for judicial separation. Such a decree did not open up the possibility of remarriage. The marriage tie remained unaffected. But the concepts which were worked out for cases of separation and the procedural forms which were used continued to be applied when, beginning with the Protestant Reformation and steadily gaining impetus from the eighteenth century on, divorce, in the modern sense of dissolution of the tie of an existing marriage, began to be admitted, first in Protestant theology and then in the secular laws.

Impact of Protestant Reformation

The resurrection of divorce marks the resurgence of that great trend which, since the days of Martin Luther, has been the antagonist of the Catholic doctrine of indissolubility of marriage and which has been constantly gaining ground at the expense of the latter. Martin Luther was the originator of a new idea which was to have far-reaching consequences. Marriage, he said, is not a sacrament but "a worldly thing." Its regulation belongs to the sphere of Caesar rather than that of God. But Caesar, being under God, in shaping his law of marriage has to do it in the right Christian way, which means that he has to conform to the words of the Lord as reported in the Gospel. Taking Matthew more literally than the canonists of the Roman church, Luther found in it the permission for the secular lawgiver to permit a husband to put away his wife if she has committed adultery.

In the rejection of complete indissolubility Luther was joined by Zwingli and Calvin. They were equally anxious to condemn all kinds of lewdness and sexual impurity, but only Calvin expressly equated a married man's to a married woman's adultery as a ground for the other spouse to treat the marriage as broken. That only the innocent party was free to remarry was self-evident. Finding a scriptural basis in 1 Corinthians 7:15, Zwingli and Calvin also regarded remarriage permissible for a spouse who had been definitely abandoned by his partner. Other grounds were added in practice.

The regulations were mostly contained in ordinances of the secular powers, but, as the bases were found in scripture, the resuscitated institution of divorce was conceived in analogy to the ancient institution of repudiation modified as it had been under the Christian emperors of Rome as retribution for grave marital misconduct. The new institution of divorce was thus started on the path of that principle of marital offense by which it is still dominated in the major part of the United States and in a great many other parts of the world of Christian tradition.

Soon the new institution also came to be burdened with that other feature which has fatefully determined the course of divorce law, namely, the idea that divorce was to be a matter of adversary civil procedure. In the early years of the Reformation, repudiation was a private act, as it had been in Rome. When the repudiating party wished to remarry, the minister had to determine whether the repudiation was so justified that the former marriage bond was dissolved. As this task turned out to be too difficult for ministers, judicial bodies were established, mostly by secular authority, to relieve the ministers of the delicate task. If, following the practice of the Reformers, divorce was to be treated as a punishment of the guilty spouse and a privilege for the innocent, it was to be expected that a wife whose husband sought to put her away, conceivably without support, would resist, just as, later, a husband could be expected to resist his wife's attempt to put him away and simultaneously saddle him with a duty to pay alimony. It was no wonder either that the procedure to be followed in such cases would be patterned upon the model of separation and nullity proceedings of the ecclesiastical courts of the old church. After all, both institutions had been called divorce, limited or absolute. . . .

The one country in which, in spite of its involvement in the Reformist movement, divorce did not take hold, was England. The Church of England never gave up its claim of continuing the Catholic tradition. . . . In the time immediately following the breach with Rome it looked as if the Church of England might follow the example of the Protestants of the Continent and admit the possibility of divorce at least in the case of a wife's adultery. But in the reign of the Virgin Queen it was, after some hesitation, settled that marriage would remain indissoluble, at least for the common man. Since the king in Parliament was the head of both the state and the church, he could, as a matter of special privilege, dissolve indissoluble marriages. From the late seventeenth century on, parliamentary divorce developed into a regular practice. But the proceedings were so cumbersome and expensive that they were available only to the most affluent. The number of parliamentary divorces thus remained low, one to three a year. Under the general law of the land, marriage remained indissoluble, even though in the middle of the eighteenth century grounds and procedure came to be matters of settled routine. Not until 1858 was divorce admitted in the modern sense, as a dissolution of the tie of marriage obtainable in a secular court as a matter of law rather than of grace, but even then adultery was to be the only ground, and that only if in the case of a husband's adultery it was accompanied by such aggravating circumstances as bigamy, rape, cruelty, or desertion for at least two years.

The reinterpretation of the Gospel by the Protestant Reformers started a movement that was in the long run to bear fruits which they had hardly desired and which were slow in ripening. For a century and a half the situation remained as it was shaped by Reformation and Counter-Reformation: no divorce at all in Roman Catholic regions and in England, divorce available in comparatively rare cases and conceived as punishment for grave marital misconduct in Protestant territories. But with Reformation, Renaissance, and humanism new trains of thought had been set in motion, thought which moved away from the bases of scripture and church, which came to be secular and to find its sole base in human reason and nature. The intense concern of the educated with the documents of ancient Greece and Rome acquainted them with a social system in which marriage had been regarded as a secular affair, a contract, that, like any other, was 'concluded by the consent of the parties and that could be terminated even more easily than a commercial contract, namely, by the will of just one of the participants. Thinkers of the persuasion of rationalistic natural law and of the philosophy of the Enlightenment conceived of marriage as one of the avenues open to man in his pursuit of happiness, and man's right to pursue happiness was one of those inalienable rights which no government ought to be able to block. What greater sources of happiness could be found than a harmonious marriage; what greater misery could there be than being caught in an unhappy one? If a marriage turned out to be unsuccessful, well, then each spouse ought to be free to put an end to it and seek happiness in a new marital venture.

This new notion of marriage, enthusiastically received by the sophisticated, was, of course, too radically opposed to tradition to be readily accepted by society in general or by legislators. But in an age in which legislation lay in the hands of absolute monarchs, the way was open to an enlightened prince to impose upon his people the new set of ideas, however strange they might appear to those who did not belong to the small but influential circle of the Illuminati. An eighteenth-century monarch took the lead, King Frederick II, later called the Great, of Prussia.

The Prussian General Code

Frederick appears to have been the first European ruler to pour the new ideas about divorce into the mold of legislation, first by an edict of 1751 and then in the great codification that was inspired by him but did not become law until 1794, eight years after his death. Under the Prussian General Code, marriages could be dissolved, not only for cause as under traditional Protestant law, but also by the mutual consent of both parties, provided the marriage was "utterly child-less," or even upon the unilateral application of one party who would allege and prove "through relevant facts the existence of so violent and deeply rooted an aversion that no hope remains for a reconciliation and the achievement of the ends of the marital state." Those two new possibilities of divorce were, to be sure, hedged in by cumbersome and time-consuming formalities, but—and this was essential—they were given recognition in the legislative scheme of a leading prince of the time.

The model of the Prussian General Code played a major role in future developments in Germany as well as in other countries, especially France and, it seems, in part of the United States. In the see-sawing struggle between the two orders of ideas about divorce, the liberal provisions of the Prussian Law of 1791/94 were later repealed by German legislation of 1896, but the ideas expressed by them have continued to live and to combine with those of conservatism in the much criticized but inevitable compromise of judicial toleration of consent divorce brought about by the collusive allegation and "proof" of some official ground for divorce.

The French Law of 1792

In France a spectacular course of events was set in motion by the revolutionary upheaval of 1789. Down to the very end of the *ancien régime* France, since the repeal of the Edict of Nantes in 1685 again a purely Catholic state, adhered to the traditional system of Catholic territories, save for some inroads into the idea of purely ecclesiastical regulation of marriage by that peculiar claim of limited secular jurisdiction in church matters known as Gallicanism. Apart from some royal ordinances concerning registration, marriage remained a domain of ecclesiastical regulation and jurisdiction. Ecclesiastical decrees of nullity and separation from bed and board could thus be obtained, but a divorce *a vinculo* remained unobtainable, whatever the *philosophes* and the men of the *Encyclopédie* might say about the "irrationality, cruelty, and unnaturalness" of the system. But with the collapse of the old order came the triumph of the new ideas. In the sequel of the stormy events of 1789 many a Frenchman and many a French woman simply shook off the fetters of an unhappy marriage, walked out on, or separated from, the old spouse and united with a new one in some form of secular ceremony or with no formality at all. Soon the situation became so confused that the new legislature, the National Convention, found it necessary to step in. The famous Law of 1792 anticipated later developments in France and elsewhere. Its intentions and its effects have been controversial among contemporaries and in later generations. . . .

The enactment of the Law of 1792 had been preceded by the solemn pronouncement in the revolutionary Constitution of 1791, that the law regarded marriage merely as a civil contract. The principal features of the new law were these:

1. Divorce in the sense of termination of the bond of marriage was to be permitted only upon those grounds which were enumerated in the statute. Two of these grounds were broad enough: mutual consent and incompatibility of temper. But the two grounds were hedged in by cumbersome and time-consuming formalities.

In addition the Act enumerated eight specific situations in which the termination of a marrage might be procured. Five were formulated upon the model of the ancient institution of judicial separation, which, it will be remembered, was obtainable in cases of grave misconduct of one spouse against the other. Slightly broadened in the new secular law, these grounds were cruelty, desertion for two years or more, notoriously dissolute conduct of life. The idea of guilt and misconduct was also implied in the ground of conviction of infamous crime. A political note underlay the provision under which a divorce was to be available to persons whose spouse had emigrated from France. In the time of internal revolution and external war, an emigrant was, of course, an enemy of the people. The spirit of individualistic enlightenment found expression in the availability of divorce in the case of a spouse's absence without news for at least two years, and in that of a spouse's incurable insanity. In contrast to modern laws, adultery, it will be observed, was not separately cited as a ground for divorce. Apparently, a man's simple adultery was not regarded as sufficiently serious, and that of a women to be so delicate as to require it to be hidden behind the facade of a less scandalous ground.

2. The ancient remedy of judicial separation, with its characteristic feature of continuance of the marriage bond and thus of continuing disability to remarry, was abolished. In cases in which a judicial separation had been pronounced prior to the law of 1792, either party could unilaterally have it transformed into a divorce.

3. As a general rule matters of divorce did not have to be brought before a judicial tribunal. The marriage bond was ended when, upon proof of observance of the formalities and delays prescribed by the Law, the divorce was registered by an administrative officer.

4. Disputed matters of partition of property, alimony, child custody, and child support were to be adjusted by family arbitrators.

The Law of 1792 clearly constituted a radical break with the pre-revolutionary past. In accordance with the postulates of the Enlightenment, marriage was proclaimed a secular institution designed to serve individual human beings in their pursuit of happiness. . . .

32

Due Process and College Students

William Van Alstyne

Due process for college students consists of the rights and procedural guarantees which protect these students from the arbitrary exercise of authority by college administrators. Colloquially, it may include any rule which limits or qualifies the power of a college to exclude or to discipline students. In its more formal aspect, it is identified with the due process and equal protection clauses of the Fourteenth Amendment to the federal Constitution, which impose general limitations on the exercise of governmental power.

The judicial application of these constitutional norms in behalf of student claims is a relatively recent development. Indeed, until the early 1960's the phrase "student due process" had no particular established usage or identifiable content.

"In Loco Parentis"

Since colonial times, three different legal models have been used to determine the disciplinary relationship between students and colleges. The earliest of these models analogized the authority of a college over its students to that of a parent disciplining his own children. The model developed from the common law doctrine *in loco parentis*, applicable in the law of torts to the adjudication of disputes

Reprinted from "Due Process," *Encyclopedia of Education*, vol. 2. New York: Macmillan Company, 1971, pp. 238-241, by permission of the author and the publisher.

between pupils and tutors. In occasional suits brought in behalf of minors seeking money damages from tutors for assault and battery, the tutor was held to enjoy an implied parental agency which permitted him to discipline the refractory pupil by all means allowed to a parent. As long as the tutor used no more force than a parent was privileged to use at home and the use of force was related to the maintenance of discipline within the tutor's professional responsibility, he was allowed a defense against the pupil's suit on the ground that he was acting *in loco parentis*.

Originally developed in this limited context, the doctrine became more generalized as a legal model against which the overall authority of colleges vis-à-vis students might be judicially reviewed. Thus, the validity of college rules prohibiting students from spending time or money in certain ways, going to or living in certain places, or associating with certain people came to be tested by analogy: Could a parent have maintained a similar rule in the supervision of his offspring at home? The disciplinary procedures of colleges were reviewed by the same narrow standard: Did a parent have an enforceable legal obligation to provide his offspring with any sort of hearing before determining his guilt? Must a parent publish a set of rules to enforce discipline? Therefore, courts almost always sided with colleges, and students were largely without legal protection against wide-ranging, unilateral college authority. State supreme court decisions, in Kentucky in 1913 and in Florida in 1925, illustrate this legal position:

> College authorities stand in loco parentis concerning the physical and moral welfare, and mental training of the pupils, and we are unable to see why to that end they may not make any rules or regulations for the government or betterment of their pupils that a parent could for the same purpose. Whether the rules or regulations are wise, or their aims worthy, is a matter left solely to the discretion of the authorities, or parents, as the case may be. (*Gott* v. *Berea College*, 156 Ky. 376 at 379, 161 S.W. 204 at 206)

As to mental training, moral and physical discipline, and welfare of the pupils, college authorities stand *in loco parentis* and in their discretion may make any regulation for their government which a parent could make for the same purpose. . . . [C]ourts have no more authority to interfere than they have to control the domestic discipline of a father in his family. (*Stetson University* v. *Hunt*, 88 Fla. 510 at 516, 102 So. 637 at 640)

Changing Circumstances

By the middle of the twentieth century the altered environment of college life led to abandonment of the family model and the *in loco parentis* rationale. Institutions had become so large (some having more than 30,000 students) that few could preserve the charm of domestic intimacy or the tempering personalism of parental affection in the administration of rules. Many had assumed large-scale research and service functions and were drawing on students to assist in professional and subprofessional capacities. Most institutions had lost their local coloration; their administrations, faculties, and student bodies had become so heterogeneous that any claim of similarity to a close family of like-minded people was implausible. Moreover, of the 7 million students enrolled in American colleges and universities, more were over 30 years old than under 18. By 1960 the average age of American college students was 21, the age at which even parents' disciplinary prerogatives are no longer privileged at common law. Perhaps equally important, the personal and economic consequences of suspension or expulsion from college had increased significantly.

Because of the modifications in the character and functions of higher education and the enhanced importance of a university degree, courts gradually abandoned use of the *in loco parentis* rationale for not reviewing college decisions. It may still be relevant in cases involving the dwindling number of small, residential, private, denominational colleges (there have been no recent cases involving such institutions), but generally it no longer accurately reflects judicial thinking.

Several cases illustrate this change. In 1968 a federal district court stated in *Buttny* v. *Smiley* (281 F. Supp. 280 at 286): "We agree with the students that the doctrine of *in loco parentis* is no longer tenable in a university community." One year earlier, in *Goldberg* v. *Regents of the University of California* (57 Cal. Rptr. 463 at 469), a state court had decided that "the better approach . . . recognizes that state universities should no longer stand *in loco parentis* in relation to their students." It was the view of an Alabama federal district court in the 1968 case of *Moore* v. *Student Affairs Committee of Troy State University* (284 F. Supp. 725 at 729) that the "college does not stand, strictly speaking, *in loco parentis* to its students."

Contract Doctrine

Toward the end of the nineteenth century, first as a complementary perspective to *in loco parentis* and then as an independent legal model (still influenced in interpretations favorable to colleges, however, by vestiges of *in loco parentis*), the common law of contracts was applied to student-college relations. Accordingly, a student's freedom became circumscribed by all college rules in existence at the time of his initial matriculation and all subsequent college rules added pursuant to an express or implied reservation of authority . The student's continuing to observe the rules was a condition of the college's continuing to furnish educational services. The question in each case was largely one of deciding whether there was a rule in point and whether the student had observed it, the burden of proof usually being on the student. Thus, in *Stetson University* v. *Hunt* (88 Fla. 510 at 517, 102 So. 637 at 638) the Florida supreme court stated, as an alternative to basing the decision on the *in loco parentis* doctrine, that the "relation between a student and an institution of learning . . . is solely contractual in character and there is an implied condition that the student knows and will conform to the rules and regulations of the institution, and for breach of which he may be suspended or expelled." Similarly, in 1928 the New York court of appeals, in *Anthony* v. *Syracuse University* (224 App. Div. 487 at 489–490, 231 N.Y.S. 435 at 438), noted that "under ordinary circumstances a person matriculating at a university establishes a contractual relationship under which, upon compliance with all reasonable regulations as to scholastic standing, attendance, deportment, payment of tuition, and otherwise, he is entitled to pursue his selected course to completion." As late as 1958, assiduous research into the cases led a student writer to conclude:

> Courts generally agree that the relation between a private university and its students is contractual: As soon as a student has commenced a course of study, the university is bound to provide instruction during the balance of the course and to confer the appropriate credentials signifying completion. The university's duty of performance is conditioned upon compliance by the student with academic and disciplinary standards. ("A Student's Right to Hearing . . ." 1958, p. 746)

In the movement toward determining students' rights by contract rather than by status (*in loco parentis*), students gained very little in terms of either personal freedom from institutional control or participation in institutional government.To be sure colleges could not act against students without having some rule, but assisted by counsel they could develop rules (to which a student impliedly agreed) flexible enough to leave the practical situation substantially unaltered. Residing on campus for a specified, limited time, students lacked the continuity necessary to organize for collective bargaining purposes, and they also lacked the individual authority necessary to negotiate personalized contracts. Therefore, they had little choice but to adhere to whatever rules each college might unilaterally impose, sometimes learning the ultimate terms of their contracts by belatedly encountering standard rules in standard handbooks incorporated by reference into standard matriculation contracts.

Thus, Bryn Mawr College could successfully rest a defense for expelling a student on the following clause, upheld in litigation in 1923: "[T]he college reserves the right to exclude at any time students whose conduct or academic standing it regards as undesirable" (*Barker* v. *Trustees of Bryn Mawr College*, 278 Pa. 121 at 122). Five years later Syracuse University relied on the following provision in expelling a student for conduct unbecoming a typical Syracuse girl: "[T]he university reserves the right and the student concedes the right to require the withdrawal of any student at any time for any reason deemed sufficient to it, and no reason for requiring such withdrawal need be given" (*Anthony* v. *Syracuse University*, 224 App. Div. 487 at 489).

Accordingly, students were expelled from various colleges, often after only the faintest semblance of a hearing, for eating in forbidden restaurants, failing to attend chapel, participating in disfavored (albeit peaceful and lawful) political rallies, writing letters critical of the college administration, or marrying in a civil ceremony. Given the similarity of provisions in most college handbooks, students lacked even the indirect power to influence the scope of institutional authority by changing schools.

These conditions still essentially characterize the technical legal relationship of students to many private colleges in the United States, but they are being modified. The courts are beginning to apply equitable and legal doctrines of conscionability and interpretation to mitigate the rigor of some college contracts, a development surprisingly late in comparison with its emergence in other areas of contract law. In addition, a number of private colleges have willingly committed some administrative authority to student courts, councils, or boards and some rule-making authority to student legislative groups. More important is the application of overriding constitutional law principles to student-college relations in public universities. A number of private colleges have moved in the same direction as the public universities, not so much from fear that they could not otherwise continue to draw students as from a combination of embarrassment at appearing less enlightened and of simple inability to explain to their students why they cannot pursue constitutional freedoms open to their public university counterparts.

Constitutional Rights

The majority of American college students today are enrolled in public, not private, institutions. Moreover, the percentage of college students enrolled in public institutions is increasing. This trend is significant, since federal constitutional limitations have recently been applied to curtail the control of public colleges and universities over certain aspects of student freedom.

The watershed decision, *Dixon* v. *Alabama State Board of Education* (294 F. 2d. 150), appeared in 1961. In that case the U.S. Court of Appeals for the Fifth Circuit revived a federal civil rights statute of the Reconstruction period to order the reinstatement of students dismissed from a state college without a written specification of charges or a hearing.

In later cases, the applicability of procedural due process to college decisions has been erratically enlarged to protect students from summary proceedings. For example, in the 1969 case *Stricklin* v. *Regents of the University of Wisconsin* (297 F. Supp. 416) a federal district court ruled that the Fourteenth Amendment prohibits a public university from suspending students, even on an interim basis to protect institutional safety, in the absence of prompt informal review. The Fourteenth Amendment was also held to bar a public university from expelling a student after a hearing if the student's retained counsel was excluded from that hearing (*French* v. *Bashful*, 303 F. Supp. 1333 [1969]).

Simultaneously, substantive constitutional rights of speech, association, and assembly have been applied in behalf of state college and university students to mitigate institutional disciplinary powers. An advancing line of federal court decisions now shelters students at public institutions from rules forbidding or limiting peaceful expression on campus (*Tinker* v. *Des Moines School District*, 393 U.S. 503 [1969]), access to controversial outside speakers (*Brooks v. Auburn University*, 296 F. Supp. 188, affirmed 412 F. 2d. 1171 [1969]), freedom to criticize the institution in the student press (*Dickey* v. *Alabama State Board of Education*, 273 F. Supp. 613 [1967]), and the freedom of male students to wear long hair (*Richards* v. *Thurston*, 304 F. Supp. 449 [1969]). Other federal decisions have protected the students' right of privacy in dormitory rooms and freedom in manner of dress.

The extent to which freedom of speech and association, procedural due process, equal protection, the right of privacy, and other constitutional norms may be extended remains uncertain, and it also remains unclear how far these freedoms may be extended laterally into the private colleges. It is clear, however, that student due process has achieved a substantial measure of recognition on American campuses, ensuring college students a larger measure of personal freedom and procedural fairness. . . .

33

Politics and Law Enforcement in China: 1949-1970
Lung-Sheng Tao

Law enforcement and politics are interwoven in any country, but while Western conception tends to stress judicial independence and dismiss political interference or control, a Marxist government often explicitly acknowledges the political nature of legal work. In the People's Republic of China, for example, law enforcement has been put under the guidance of what the Communist Party (CCP) calls the "mass line." This article is a study of politics and law enforcement in China, with a view to understanding the interrelations between the practice of the "mass line" and the functioning of what the Chinese refer to as the political-legal work (*chen-fa kung-tso*).

Before investigating the development of law enforcement in China, it is important to point out the connotation of the "mass line." It is characterized by the notion of "coming from the masses and going to the masses."[1] It consists of two aspects. First, it points to the creativity of the masses and demands that officials keep themselves in constant contact with them. Officials should never assume an attitude of aloofness or superiority toward the masses. This aspect, however, merely outlines the general style of work which officials should adopt. The second aspect suggests a process of obtaining the views of the masses, systematizing them into policy decisions, and taking those decisions back to the masses for implementation. This aspect of the mass line underlies the political process in China and assumes a specific content of the desirable work style. The problems in putting the mass line into practice have called for a number of formulations of legal policy in China in the past two decades.

During the period between 1949 and 1970 there were essentially three models of law enforcement in China. The first model is characterized by mass campaigns during 1949-1953, and is tentatively called the "mass campaign" model. An essential feature of this model was the mass trials against the political enemy of the regime. It represented contingent measures adopted by the Communists in seizing and consolidating their national political power. There was a lack of a well-structured legal system as the basis upon which the Communists exercised their political control. Large-scale mass campaigns were launched to wipe out the political enemy and solidify public order. The political-legal apparatus was used as a "weapon" for furthering the political ends. Because of the lack of legal norms upon which political-legal work was to operate, the Party's guidance was essential. The mass line facilitated the political campaigns, and political-legal work was to operate, the Party's guidance was essential. The mass line facilitated the political campaigns, and political-legal work was a spearhead for carrying out the mass line.

The second model may be called the "legal bureaucracy" model which prevailed during 1954-1957. This model was built on the notions that the political-legal apparatus was to exercise proletarian dictatorship in China and, as such, sought to protect the collective interests of the people as defined by the Party. Organizationally, the apparatus was to operate on the formal legal system prescribed by certain basic documents of the regime, particularly the 1954 Constitution. Essentially it was a specialized branch of the government bureaucracy, with the authority flowing vertically through the administrative hierarchies of the "system." The mass line, as implemented by the political-legal apparatus, required the cadres to protect the interests of the people against enemies, resolve disputes among individuals, and provide a uniform standard of behavior for the society. In performing these duties they were to listen to the people, understand their problems and demands, and at the same time rely on the masses for assistance and cooperation. The model portrayed two separate entities, the political-legal apparatus and the masses as a whole, and acted as a channel for communication and interaction between the two. Through the mass line it was expected that political-legal cadres could effectively implement Party policies among the masses, while transmitting the needs and interests of the people to the leadership.

The third model may be referred to as the "field work" model, which prevailed after 1957–1958, when a rigorous rectification campaign was launched against the "rightist" lawyers and public security cadres. Vitalized by the rigors of the Great Leap Forward, the model required that political-legal cadres leave their offices, go down to the masses, live with them, and work together for production. Law enforcement was to be carried out during productive field work. Political-legal cadres were to listen to the masses, feel their way of life and coordinate closely with the party committees. They should handle as many cases as possible, in the fastest manner, yet do the work correctly and save the time of the people. . . . This model dispensed with the image of the political-legal bureaucracy as a separate, specialized entity, but portrayed numerous political-legal work teams laboring among the masses under the leadership of the Party committees.

The three models presuppose different organizations, functions and work styles. This study is an attempt to describe the details of the three models, trace the reasons for the adoption of each of them in China, and discuss the problems each has posed for the Communist regime. The focus will be on the three most important events in China's political-legal work, the 1952–1953 Judicial Reform Movement in, the 1958 rectification, and the Cultural Revolution. [Our] thesis is that each of these events has shaped a distinctive pattern of political-legal work in China, and prescribed a model for political-legal work.

The "Mass Campaign" Model: 1949–1953

Consolidation of Power and Nation-Building

During 1949–1953 the Communists were faced with the tasks of consolidating their power in China. Political-legal work was placed in this political context. . . . To "safeguard the fruits of revolution," political-legal cadres were called upon to conduct mass trials and struggle meetings. Two important purposes were served by the trials. They punished the political enemy, and solidified the masses by awakening their political consciousness and rallying their support for the regime.

. . . The Communist regime was to "suppress all counter-revolutionary activities and punish severely all Kuomintang war criminals and other leading incorrigible counter-revolutionary elements who collude with imperialism, betray the fatherland, and oppose the cause of the people's democracy."[2] . This presupposed an important role to be played by the political-legal units. . . . . Where the political-legal offices were not set up, the Military Control Committees and the Public Security Forces of the People's Liberation Army (PLA) discharged law enforcement functions. The mass trials (*jen min kung shen*) based upon the policy of the mass line characterized the administration of the law during this time.

A policy decision first had to be made by the CCP. With a critical shortage of political-legal cadres for law enforcement on a national scale, would it be desirable to retain the originally Nationalist officials in the political-legal positions? While retaining these people in the courts, the procuracy, and the police was clearly hazardous to the regime, the Communists practically had no other choice. Yet to carry out the political objectives of the mass campaigns, it was necessary to rely on the police and the courts. A way out was to establish *ad hoc* people's tribunals . . . to conduct mass trials. The organization and functions of these tribunals will be discussed later. The widespread use of the people's tribunals is of interest for a number of reasons. The mass trials in the early years of the People's Republic in many ways resembled those carried out in the Kiangsi and Yenan periods. In a sense, the people's tribunal was but a continuation of the tribunal the Communists had used in previous years. However, the practical situation in China in 1949–1953 necessitated the use of *ad hoc* tribunals directly under the control of the Party and the PLA forces. To perform immediately and effectively the political tasks of consolidating their power in China, the Communists had to bypass the existing political-legal apparatus which included many holdover Nationalists and resort to the irregular yet efficient tribunals. Finally, the mood of the mass campaigns during this period was not consistent with the notion of law enforcement by regular courts on standard procedures. The mass line demanded that political-legal work be geared to rallying the support of the masses and agitating them against the political enemy.

Features of the Mass Trials. During 1949–1953 efforts were made to set up a formal legal system in China, based upon the experience in Kiangsi and Yenan, and patterned on Soviet precedent. Yet efforts along this direction did not yield practical results until 1954. Meanwhile, law enforcement was carried out largely outside the regular offices. . . .

Usually three steps were involved in a mass trial. After law enforcement officials had singled out certain political offenders and collected incriminating evidence, they called a small-scale meeting attended by the representatives of the masses. During the meeting the evidence would be discussed and the representatives would give their opinion on what ought to be done with the criminals. The second step would then be a mass meeting, where the guilty behavior of the offenders, the evidence against them, and the policy towards these kinds of persons were announced to the masses. Enthusiastic response was expected from the spectators, who were encouraged to raise more accusations. At the peak of the meeting, the cadres would announce the punishment meted out in advance, and also make a political speech on the meaning of the trial.

There is no doubt that the mass line underscored the establishment of the people's tribunals. As one contemporary Soviet observer pointed out, these tribunals "consolidated the ties between the legal organs and the masses and served as a guarantee of the justness and soundness of a legal decision made by a tribunal of such composition."[3]

Emergence of a Formal Legal System

While law enforcement in China during 1949–1953 was featured by mass trials and struggle meetings, efforts were also made to create a more elaborate legal system. An examination of these efforts suggests that the Chinese leadership did not intend permanently to use the "mass campaign" model of political-legal work to rule the country. It was to cope with political reality that they had to resort to excessive violence and to wage large-scale movements in the early years. . . .

Under the policy of the mass line there were, during this period of time, the "people's procuracy correspondents," "denunciation boxes," and reception offices for the purpose of mobilizing the masses to aid in the work of detection and prosecution of crimes. It was reported that in 1952 the authorities in East and Northwest China received through these devices 56,488 letters from the masses exposing bureaucratism among the cadres and illegal activities in general.

Public security bureaus, which emerged as soon as the Communists took power, penetrated into the grass-roots level of society. While in the early years the bureaus worked closely together with the Public Security Forces of the PLA, by 1954 the Chinese viewed them as an integral part of the general law enforcement apparatus.

Concomitant with the emergence of a law enforcement system was the promulgation of a number of basic regulations, including the organizational laws for the judiciary and the procuracy, anti-counter-revolutionary statutes, anti-corruption laws, the land reform law and the New Marriage Law. There seemed clear signs that the leadership intended to enact more laws in the future as the basis of the legal system. . . .

The emergence of a formal legal system and promulgation of basic laws suggest the rational side of the "mass campaign" period. Law enforcement should implement central policies. When the leadership's primary concerns were consolidation of power and rallying mass support, the "mass campaign" model of law enforcement best served those ends. When the primary concerns became nation-building and economic development, an elaborate legal system based upon a division of functions and standardization of procedures would seem better suited. Yet before a new political-legal network was to operate, the Party considered it imperative to cleanse the law enforcement apparatus to ensure its loyalty and create a correct work style.

Judicial Reform and the Mass Line

. . . The Judicial Reform began in August 1952 and ended the following April. During the movement, criticism from the masses was encouraged and accepted with prudence. Many holdover law enforcement cadres were removed from the offices on the basis of such criticism. In Shanghai more than 70% of the holdover cadres were found to be "corrupt elements" largely on the basis of information supplied by the masses and also investigation by the Party. 80% of the law enforcement officials in Kwangtung Province and in the city of T'aiyuan, Shansi, were branded "counter-revolutionaries." Information on most of them was reportedly provided, directly or indirectly, by the masses. Thus, the Judicial Reform not only sought to establish the mass line as the fundamental policy for law enforcement, but invited the masses to participate in crushing the retained elite and cleansing the law enforcement personnel.

By April 1953 the Reform is said to have successfully liquidated most of the undesirable elements from law enforcement positions, and thus purified the system. Because of the mass participation in the Reform, the movement was praised as having complied entirely with the mass demands concerning what a socialist legal system ought to be. It may be said that before giving way to a new pattern of work, the "mass campaign" model swept over the law enforcement apparatus to make sure that it followed faithfully the steps of the Party and was predicated upon the mass line policy.

But the efforts were not entirely successful. Despite the determination to overhaul the law enforcement apparatus, the regime found it impossible to eliminate all of the "holdover" personnel due to the critical shortage of competent persons to fill the vacancies. One of the results of the Reform was that by the end of 1953 the law enforcement system was seriously stagnant, as the courts were over-burdened with cases. The situation demanded that those undergoing "thought reform" who showed progress be placed back in office. By 1954, 2,369 retained cadres who had undergone "thought reform," among them 1,142 judges, had been so reinstated. . . .

The "Legal Bureaucracy" Model: 1954–1957

Organizational Aspects

Under the scheme provided for by the 1954 Constitution a complex legal system was established consisting of three branches: the judiciary, the procuracy and the public security office. The system was far more sophisticated than the previous one under the 1949 Common Program. It is noteworthy that unlike the previous system the post-1954 system was substantially put into practice in China for the next few years to come. . . . It is sufficient to note that the setting up of the "people's courts" was said to be demanded by the mass line. Public trials were held in these courts and the masses were encouraged, but not required, to attend the public trials in the courts, as spectators rather than participants. The masses were supposed to "supervise" the courts' behavior. Active participation in regular court work was only made possible by the "people's assessors" system.

The courts were given a separate identity in that they were not constituent parts of the local government. But they were "responsible to the local people's congresses at corresponding levels" and were to "report to them." There is no doubt that the political authorities could easily control the courts by exercising, or threatening to exercise, their power of removing judges from their offices. Since practically the Party controlled the local political organs, its influence on the courts was beyond question. Yet the Constitution made it very clear that the law enforcement offices, while under the direction of the Party, should handle and decide cases by themselves. The reason the Constitution allowed "independence" to the judges and failed to spell out the Party's role in law enforcement work was perhaps that the Chinese leadership, after the Judicial Reform, presumed the reliability of law enforcement cadres. Given the political control over the courts by local organs, the unquestioned leading role of the CCP in defining national priorities and policies, and the "supervisory" power of the procuracy over judicial administration, there was not much need to declare explicitly how much the Party could control law enforcement work. Moreover, after the Judicial Reform the leadership apparently was willing to delegate a rather complete authority to the law enforcement cadres in handling concrete cases.

Under the 1954 Constitution, the procuracy system was also made formally independent of the rest of the government machinery without lateral lines of administrative control. The Constitution explicitly provides that the people's procuracy works solely under the overall leadership of the highest procuracy office at Peking, the Supreme People's Procuracy. Thus, a vertical rule was established. The main functions of the procuracy were to prosecute criminal acts and to preserve the people's interests by "supervising" the work of the police and the courts. While the "procuracy correspondents" had reportedly been widely used in collective farms, mines, factories and enterprises to facilitate the detection of crimes, they were basically outposts for the procuracy office at the county level. Cases were to be reported to the procuracy office and not handled and disposed of on the spot by these outposts. In other words, the procuracy hierarchy in China was clearly predicated upon a notion of the mass line which was different from that underlying the previous "mass campaign" model. The new content called upon the procuracy not only to prosecute crimes, but to safeguard people's interests against arbitrariness by the other branches of the government.

Under the mass line policy, the public security system penetrated deep into the smallest social units in the country. Since 1952 security defense committees have been set up in factories, enterprises, schools, streets, villages, communes and production brigades. The committee consists of three to eleven officers and is subject to the direction of the city or county public security bureau. These committees have been the instrument through which the regime mobilizes the masses for executing policies, preserving public order and eliminating class enemies. However, it is important to note that the power of these committees was limited during 1954-1957. They could dispose of minor criminal cases and mediate civil disputes, but they had to transfer all important cases to the country or city public security bureau. In fact, the security defense committees functioned as a medium between the public security bureau, which is usually located in a county seat or city, and the masses who live in the remote rural areas.

Above the security defense committees are public security bureaus of the county or municipality and the provincial levels, all under the vertical rule of the Ministry of Public Security at Peking. While available evidence indicates that most public security officers were Party cadres during the mid-1950's, the apparatus itself, administratively and organizationallly, was not directly and avowedly under the control of the local Party committees.

The above sketchy description of the organization of the law enforcement apparatus in China during 1954–1957 suggests a few general observations. First, in terms of organization, the law enforcement system was a rather independent hierarchy. The existing laws and regulations did not explicitly specify the role and control of the Party over its work. This absence of legislative clarity does not, of course, imply that the Party played no part in law enforcement. To the contrary, it is the Party that provided the basic directives for the cadres. As law enforcement officials repeatedly stated, their work was to carry out the central tasks handed down by the Party. In fact, the very policy of the mass line was clearly recognized as a fundamental Party policy. However, the lack of explicitness about the role of the local Party committees did give rise to an understanding among some law enforcement cadres that as long as they prudently followed the general Party policies, they were not subject to the administrative control of local committees. Indeed, the Constitution and its related regulations provided a framework for a division of labor among the police, the procuracy and the judiciary. For the avowed purpose of protecting the people's interests, each branch was to impose checks and balances on the others. While low level enforcement offices were told to clear important cases with the local Party committees, the trend was clearly that law enforcement cadres could use their discretion in handling most concrete cases without having to consult with the Party committees. Up to the summer of 1957 a number of law enforcement cadres began to resist what they called the "outside interference" from local committees, and in certain places the Party members also acquiesced in the increasing professionalization of the law enforcement offices. It should be added that this trend was not considered undesirable by the Chinese leadership at this time.

Second, the mass line was understood after 1954 to call for the establishment of a law enforcement apparatus network all over the country. Hence, security defense committees and procuracy correspondents were set up in the smallest social and administrative units. All offices were open to the masses and made accessible to their views and opinions. The masses were encouraged to attend public trials, participate in investigation of crime under the guidance of the police and the procurator, and expose illegal activities to the authorities. Yet specialization was emphasized in law enforcement work, and there was a clear distinction between what the masses could contribute and what remained in the professional domain of the law enforcement cadres. So while the mass line called for the establishment of a law enforcement network in every local area for the purpose of safeguarding the people's interests and preserving public order, the model presupposed an efficient bureaucracy responsive to the mass demands but relying upon its own professional judgment in handling cases.

Third, after 1953 the *ad hoc* tribunals waned, or at least were not used on a national scale. As the Judicial Reform had supposedly cleansed the law enforcement apparatus, the principal responsibility for law enforcement was placed on the emerging legal bureaucracy. While the mass line continued to be the basic policy, there was a shift in its content. Law enforcement matters began to be regularized, and emphasis came to be put on stability. . . .

Functional Aspects

While the law enforcement apparatus pursued the mass line, it did so on the assumption that expertise was the basis for its work. Special legal training was widely held for law enforcement cadres, and there was a division of labor between the judiciary, the public security office and the procuracy. The law enforcement apparatus viewed itself as a highly specialized agency for implementing Government policies. The masses were relied upon only to the extent that efficient law enforcement needed their cooperation. Investigation of crime, for example, demanded a supply of information from the people. But indictment and trial were clearly in the domain of the law enforcement specialists. People were allowed to attend court sessions but were not permitted to participate in the proceedings. In short, education increasingly became the primary function of the mass line in law enforcement. Certainly this assumed that the cadres knew much which the masses did not know. The result was a distinctive, specialized law enforcement bureaucracy which relied upon the masses in performing its duties, guided the people in legal matters, and purported to protect the people's interests against political enemies and official encroachments. Yet it was not a basic policy to allow the lay population to guide or participate in the rather complex and highly specialized law enforcement work. The situation also tended to preclude intervention from local Party committees in individual cases. The mass line policy did not delineate a clear line between what the law enforcement offices should handle alone and what they should consult or clear with the Party committees. The ambiguity and the growing complexity of law enforcement matters gave rise to a wide variety of practices damaging the relationship between Party committees and the law enforcement offices. Since professionalism was obviously allowed by Peking during 1954–1957 the trend seemed to be in favor of leaving the legal bureaucracy alone, rather than subjecting it to daily influence and supervision by local Party members.

Problems in Law Enforcement: 1954–1957

Commandism

Deviations from the "Legal Bureaucracy" model gave rise to a number of problems. The first was "commandism." As revealed in law enforcement practices, commandism referred to two different types of behavior. One was over-emphasis on law enforcement at the expense of popular sentiment. In one case a cadre arrested and detained an individual for fighting. The individual had indeed been in a fight over a debt, but they had reached a conciliation. Nevertheless the cadre had him arrested, and as a result of his indignation the person committed suicide in the detention house. The cadre received severe criticism for "commandism."

A second type of "commandism" involved ignoring the restraints of the law. Law enforcement cadres were criticised or even punished for disobeying the law, although some of them were engaged in the performance of duties. In a number of cases, this kind of commandism took place when a public security cadre made arbitrary arrests or inflicted corporal punishment, or when a court denied a defendant the opportunity to argue his case. . . .

Subjectivism

Another type of improper behavior was "subjectivism." In May-June 1955, a meeting was held among the cadres of the Ministry of Justice and the Supreme People's Court to discuss this subject. One manifestation of this incorrect work style on the part of law enforcement officials was "presumption of the guilt of an accused." . . .

A second manifestation of subjectivism involved exclusive reliance on accusations from the masses. Because there was still a small percentage of reactionaries among the masses, sometimes accusations were unfounded. Even among loyal people false accusations were sometimes made for personal motives. Law enforcement cadres were not to be prejudiced by these false accusations. They were taught to avoid this kind of subjectivism by emphasizing the need for evidence. Again, the underlying value was fairness and justice in accordance with the professional judgment of cadres.

Bureaucratism

By the end of 1957, however, some things which had previously been considered desirable became sins. The breakdown of the "legal bureaucracy" model resulted in the exposure of "bureaucratism" among law enforcement cadres. As seen in 1958, bureaucratism manifested itself in a number of forms. The first was "closed-doorism." A worker's negligence in a coal mine, resulting in property damage, was referred to the procurator's office. The defendant was arrested on 5 September 1956, but the trial was not held until three months later. During this time neither the procurator nor the public security cadres conducted an investigation of evidence on the scene. The trial was allegedly held behind closed doors. After the judgment was announced, neither the local Party committee nor the worker were satisfied. They aired severe attacks against the local law enforcement offices during the Hundred Flowers Movement, charging them with deviations from the mass line.

Another type of bureaucratism was "formalism," manifested, e.g., by the refusal by public security units to detain criminal suspects caught and taken to them by the masses, due to lack of "written material" and sufficient evidence. Also, procurators were said to have departed from the mass line when they emphasized compliance with "legal process." . . .

A third practice was administering law enforcement matters "away from the masses." . . . This criticism suggests the extent to which law enforcement cadres during 1954–57 viewed their offices as a separate entity, apart from the masses, and their understanding of the mass line in contrast to that underlying the previous "mass campaign" model.

Another type of bureaucratism was the reluctance to carry out "on-the-spot investigation." Certain law enforcement cadres handled cases on the basis of information flowing to their offices, but never went down to the masses to investigate. When a directive from the center instructed them to eliminate unfavorable elements, they mopped up everyone they considered to be unreliable in one stroke, without even investigating their class status or actual behavior.

Finally, but most significantly, an increasing number of law enforcement cadres during 1954–57 were convinced that "judicial independence" was guaranteed by the Constitution and would be in the best interests of the masses. These cadres handled cases on their own initiatives and seldom consulted with local Party committees. This attitude became a sin in 1957–1958, and the leadership sought to rectify it during the anti-rightist movement. Law enforcement cadres were criticized for this "judicial independence," for believing "that they were a privileged group who possessed exclusive knowledge on law." Relying upon their own judgments, these cadres were increasingly isolated not only from the masses but from local Party committees as well.

The Search for An Independent Bureaucracy

During the Hundred Flowers, a number of leading law enforcement officials expressed dissatisfaction with the Party's policy toward the legal system. They leveled attacks on almost every aspect of the existing system and the Party leadership. These attacks can be summed up along the following general lines.

Some law enforcement officials complained that there was no law to follow, and that the situation in China had been "no law and no justice" (*Wu-fa wu-tien*). The assumption was that Party policies were not laws: "The Party realizes its leadership in judicial work through the enactment of laws. Since the law represents the will of the people as well as that of the Party, a judge who obeys the law in effect obeys the leadership of the Party."

Another criticism was directed against the quality of law enforcement. Many cadres, it was argued, were incompetent. They could not distinguish among concepts and regarded the Party directives as "golden rules and jade laws." As a result, miscarriage of justice was widespread. . . .

A further line of thought expressed by some law enforcement officials was an emphasis on expertise—that the law was a "special science" understood only by experts and hence should not be influenced by politics. Implicit in this view was a demand that judicial work be granted independence from "outside" interference. Interference from Party committees should be prevented because the committees "did not know the law or the circumstances of individual cases. Their leadership therefore may not be correct." As some officials claimed, "All a judge needs to do is to obey the law; there is no need for any more guidance from the Party." One judge went so far as to call for the complete elimination of control by local Party committees.

The Question of Party Leadership

The Party, of course, was surprised that "bourgeois legal thought" had permeated the law enforcement agencies. Its liquidation was essential. However, the question remained to what extent the Party leadership had acquiesced or encouraged the "legal bureaucracy model."

Evidence suggests that until 1958 the Party had accepted the trend toward regularization. In 1956 Tung Pi-wu had openly announced that codification of the law was under way. In the same year Liu Shao-ch'i stated that "a complete legal system becomes an absolute necessity."[4] Concrete actions were taken to draft new laws. Shih Liang, the Minister of Justice, announced in June 1957 that procedural laws were taking shape. Yet when rectification erupted in 1958, these leaders denounced all these efforts, placing blame on the jurists drafting the new laws. . . .

All this suggests that prior to 1958 the ideal functioning of law enforcement allowed for some role, although circumscribed, for the local Party committees, but that in practice there was a trend toward an independent legal bureaucracy subjected to a minimum of outside interference. The real cause for the tension was the ambivalent attitude of the central leadership toward the distribution of power between lower-level law enforcement offices and local Party committees. . . .

It should also be noted that the CCP was not opposed to regularization and professionalism of the law enforcement apparatus. Prior to 1957, law schools and short-term training classes increased markedly and the cadres received special professional training before taking a job. The demand of expertise was accepted by most local Party committee members, whose educational level was relatively low. Thus, in consultation, the law enforcement cadre's view might well prevail. As a result, "Party bureaucrats themselves appear to have been ambivalent and divided about the desirability of Party interference in individual cases."

Yet the emergence of what appeared to be a clear division of functions between local Party committees and law enforcement units became undesirable and alarming to the central leadership. The situation was worsened by the severe criticism of the Party leadership and the call for an administratively independent legal system during the Hundred Flowers. Moreover, by late 1957 a crucial step in the political development was taking place—the inception of the Great Leap Forward. The economic upsurge and its concomitant political developments in 1957–1958, both in the law enforcement field as well as in the country generally, reversed the model of the mass line which had been in use for the past few years and created a new model with emphasis on Party leadership and the face-to-face relationship between the cadre and the people.

The "Field Work" Model: Post-1958

Organizational Aspects

. . . Although the basic organization of the law enforcement apparatus was left intact, important measures were taken to strengthen "coordination" among the judge, the procurator, the police and the Party committee. The following is an example of the style that characterized the post-1958 law enforcement in China.

A joint meeting was first held between the public security bureau, the procuracy, and the court. The Officials reached a resolution proposed by a Party directive, that "cases must be handled on the spot." They then organized a circuit tribunal, consisting of three divisions represented, respectively, by a public security cadre, a procurator and a judge. This work team was called the "three chiefs." They left their offices, and went down to the countryside. They traveled to a coal mine where a theft and a sabotage case had occurred but was not resolved. Since the law enforcement cadres were not familiar with the technological aspects of the case, they obtained approval from the Party committee in charge of the mine, and proceeded to learn skills from the mine workers. They went down into the mine and learned mining skills while listening to the workers' opinions about the case under investigation. While the cadres were working in the mine, they learned that there was an one-hour break each day. They considered this the best time to adjudicate the criminal case. After obtaining the Party committee's consent, the cadres arrested a suspect on the basis of evidence collected from the mine workers. They took the suspect to an office where a secret preliminary hearing was conducted, with interrogation of the suspect. After this hearing the cadres went out to search for further evidence and to find corroborative witnesses. When adequate evidence was collected and the witnesses found, the cadres returned to the office and worked on the transcripts of the case, drafting the police recommendation to prosecute, the procurator's indictment and the court verdict. Having finished all this, the cadres then held a mass meeting during the one-hour break in the mine, where the defendant was tried in public. Because they had carefully prepared the case, the cadres were persuasive and the indictment and verdict received enthusiastic support from the workers. In announcing the verdict, the judge also lectured on Party policies on safeguarding socialist construction and eliminating reactionaries. The trial was then adjourned, the entire proceedings having taken only eighty minutes.

This case illustrates a new functional model. . . . It also signifies a change in organization. This style of work was aimed at correcting one of the past errors—that law enforcement agencies "did not have a purified thought; they could not coordinate closely, and in handling cases each agency managed its own business." Now, under the Party leadership and the mass line, cadres would work together in administering the law, but in investigating, processing and deciding a case, the joint work group would consult with the local Party committee and follow its direction. A member of the Party committee was often formally made a leading component of the joint work group. The basic units for law enforcement were callled "work teams" or the "three chiefs," whereby the heads of the local police, procuracy and court undertook "united action" in disposing of cases. Again, they followed the advice of the Party committee, and cleared important cases with it. . . .

Functional Aspects

A number of functional features of law enforcement stand out after 1958. First of all, instead of waiting for the people to bring in accusations, officials would now go down to the masses and carry out on-the-spot adjudications. During 1954–1957 cadres were supposed to conduct field investigation and rely upon concrete evidence flowing from the investigation. After the trip to the scene of a crime or a civil dispute the cadres would go back to the offices and handle the cases in accordance with legal procedures. Thus "go down to the masses" was a means of ensuring correctness in adjudication. After 1958 the mass line demanded a different behavior. Field work was now the central feature of law enforcement, and the entire process of handling a case was supposed to be conducted among the masses. Three principles underlay the new practices: "five goes," "three on-the-spots," and "four services." The "five goes" consisted of going to factories, to mines, to communes, to streets and to markets. The "three on-the-spots" referred to investigation, mediation and trial, and sentence on the spot. The "four services" meant "to serve politics, the center, production, and the masses." Two purposes were envisaged by these principles. First, law enforcement cadres were expected to improve the quality of their work. Second, they would form closer ties with the masses.

A second feature of post-1958 law enforcement was the integration of law enforcement with productive labor. The Great Leap Forward not only demanded that all cadres "leap" in their own fields, but sent them out to join the productive forces as a method of increasing industrial and agricultural production. Law enforcement cadres were to live, eat and labor with the masses, and to take a direct and active part in economic production. Several purposes were served by this policy. First, working closely with the masses would purify the thought of the cadres, helping them to dispense thoroughly with whatever "bourgeois" notions they still had. It should be recalled that during 1954–1957 law enforcement cadres themselves carried out the educational function of the mass line. The new model now demanded that *they* be educated by the masses. Second, it would strengthen the ties between the cadre and the masses, making easier the cadre's duties of law enforcement. Third, through direct participation in productive labor, the CCP expected to create useful cadres who would be both Red and expert.

The new model of law enforcement was aimed at halting the increasing bureaucratization of the law enforcement apparatus and putting it under Party control. The entire system was sufficiently decentralized, and to a considerable extent re-organized, ensuring Party leadership at every level of the hierarchy. Clearly this was but a part of a general CCP policy of decentralization of the administrative system during the Great Leap Forward. Legal expertise in the traditional sense was looked down upon, and law enforcement officials were required to learn from the masses, both by listening to them and by working with them in economic production. The new model completely broke the style of work practiced in the past. It now called upon the cadres to bring files with them, go down to the countryside, and administer justice on the spot.

The Style of Work

. . . Despite the waning of the Great Leap Forward after 1960, the work style hailed by the CCP during the movement continued to characterize law enforcement in China. While information on the administration of justice on the Chinese mainland was scanty by 1964, there is sufficient evidence to suggest the continuation of the "field work" model down to 1966. As noted earlier, one important aspect of the model was to strengthen the leadership of local Party committees in the day-to-day handling of individual cases. The law enforcement bureaucracy was largely placed under the control of the Party committees. A second aspect was the pursuit of the mass line to the point of substituting popular demands for professional judgments, and of integrating law enforcement with economic and social tasks. The following are but a few examples indicating the practice on the eve of the Cultural Revolution. . . .

In 1962 Chou En-lai reiterated the importance of the mass line, and stated that law enforcement cadres "should constantly make on-the-spot investigation, develop a work style characterized by seeking truth from facts and adhering to the mass line."[5] . . .

While the Great Leap Forward ended early in the 1960's, the model of law enforcement it created remained in use during a large part of the decade until the eruption of the Cultural Revolution. To be sure, the Great Leap approach was based upon the central nature of Party leadership and the decentralization of the administrative system. Yet absolute Party leadership was not confined to the movement; it was considered necessary even after the collapse of the Great Leap Forward. Apparently the spirit of politics in China prior to 1958 was fundamentally different from that after the Great Leap. Prior to 1958 the central leadership emphasized the process of orderly nation-building. This policy allowed specialization and regularization in government work. After the Great Leap, however, the approach focused upon integrating government functions with mass activities under the leadership of the Party. Revival of the revolutionary spirit was one of the principal purposes of this policy. This approach featured Party control and the mass line.

The Cultural Revolution: Strains on Party Leadership

One thesis of this study has been that since 1958 Party leadership over the law enforcement apparatus was strengthened. This was accomplished in two different but related ways. Through organizational innovations the Party assumed the leadership in the basic law enforcement units. The use of the "three chiefs" and the "joint work groups," and the division of small-scale jurisdictions among the teams, were designed to facilitate Party control over law enforcement operations. Organizationally, unreliable or unenthusiastic cadres were removed from office, with Party cadres and members of the Youth League filling the vacancies. The public security system is a good example of the latter approach.

Functionally, Party control over law enforcement was tightened. The public security units assumed an increased importance in handling cases. They now played an important role in prosecution and adjudication. They were also given increased discretion whether or not subject a person to reform through labor, without the need of going through the formal legal process. Moreover, Party secretaries and public security officers often decided cases on their own initiative, without consulting the procurator or the judge. Finally, a large number of Party members, mostly retired PLA cadres, were recruited into the public security system. Through these organizational and functional devices the law enforcement apparatus was considered completely under Party control.

This structure and practice were clearly based on the assumption

that public security cadres were the most reliable among the law enforcement cadres. That this is not absolutely true is shown by the
Party's criticism of the incorrect style of work and of certain disobedience to Party leadership during the 1957–1958 rectification. Yet
apparently the anti-rightist movement was believed to have purified
the system. As a result of recruiting a large number of the retired
PLA members into public security units, these offices seemed to have
less "retained" cadres and were predominantly composed of Party
cadres. The problem of work style was perhaps of secondary importance since the reinforcement of the mass line would hopefully help
to correct whatever errors the public security cadres might commit.

Party control and discipline, however, did not completely ensure
the "purity" of even the public security units. During the Cultural
Revolution, they were accused of being aligned with anti-Mao
groups. Under the leadership of P'eng Chen, who had supposedly
taken control of the police forces in Peking, and Lo Jui-ch'ing, who
for years had been Minister of Public Security, the public security
apparatus was accused by the Red Guards of "not carrying out all
things according to Mao Tse-tung's thought." "The thought of
Chairman Mao has not yet established its dominance and absolute
authority" in the apparatus, which became a primary target of attack
during the Cultural Revolution.

The mass line continued to be the basic criterion to measure law
enforcement work. The mass line as expounded by the Red Guards
during the Cultural Revolution did not seem different, in essence,
from that underlying the "field work" model. But law enforcement
prior to 1968 revealed a number of organizational and functional
changes.

The foremost change was, of course, the entry of revolutionary
mass organizations into law enforcement work. In certain areas Red
Guards themselves took over the work. Prior to 1968 they conducted investigations, made arrests and held mass trials against political enemies. While in most cases law enforcement cadres continued
to work with the Red Guards, their role was nominal. In Peking, for
example, "representatives" took the place of the people's judges
adjudicating cases in mass trials.

By the time the Cultural Revolution was launched, Mao was convinced of the desirability of a leading role by Party committees in
law enforcement work. As he said in one of his "latest instructions,"
". . . public security work can only be under the direct leadership
of the Party committee and cannot be under the vertical leadership
of the relevant government departments." He seemed to suggest a
hierarchy of the public security system under the sole leadership of
local and central Party offices.

With the onset of the Cultural Revolution, however, Mao seemed to have doubts about his earlier approach. Distrust in the law enforcement apparatus, for example, led Chiang Ch'ing, Mao's wife, to declare that "the public security organs, procuracies and the courts must be completely smashed." Local Red Guards, however, tore down the law enforcement system for different reasons. Some considered the seizure of these organs a necessary step to seize power in the local area. Clearly, law enforcement offices were rightly viewed as a part of the Government and Party bureaucracies which sought to preserve the *status quo*. Other Red Guards smashed the law enforcement offices because the cadres inhibited the radicalism of the Red Guards, placing more value on public order than on revolution. . . .

The attacks on the law enforcement apparatus during the Cultural Revolution show how the Party cadres who were injected into the apparatus after 1958 themselves became bureaucrats.

Under the Cultural Revolution, efforts were made to "smash" the law enforcement offices. Mao thought it necessary to use one "important weapon" for proletarian dictatorship, the Army, to override the other "weapon," the public security forces. It appears likely that the Cultural Revolution has successfully reoriented law enforcement work towards Mao's principles. It remains to be seen what kind of mass line model will emerge in consequence.

Conclusion

Since the end of the Cultural Revolution (1969), legal activity in China seems to have fallen into oblivion. Legal publications are no longer available, at least to outsiders. It is likely that the semi-official organization for Chinese jurists, the Political-Legal Association, no longer functions. But directly relevant to this study is the fact that many courts, at the local and provincial levels, have reportedly been dissolved. The directories of Chinese officials, and other documents issued by foreign countries as well as by Peking, no longer carry the names of any judges. The fact that provincial governance is currently exercised by the Revolutionary Committees suggests that the courts were still not functioning at the time this study was completed.

The functioning of law enforcement agencies, particularly the courts, was apparently disrupted during the Cultural Revolution. It was, to be sure, part of a political turmoil in which coercion was resorted to by different political groups in what was basically a power struggle. However, even though it appears that "normalcy" has been restored in China after 1969, there has been no report that the courts have resumed their previous functions. In fact, the structure of the present Chinese political system (based on a coalition of the Army, the Maoist group and a loyal group of Party bureaucrats) does not seem to assign a prominent place to the law enforcement units as they existed prior to the Cultural Revolution.

If one is struck by the changes in the directions of law enforcement in China, the fact should not be overlooked that the entire Chinese political system has experienced upheavals, shake-ups and power conflicts during the same period of time. What is remarkable is the fact that the judiciary, not to mention the public security forces, were not immune from the impact of changes and cleavages in the political system. Perhaps this reflects a tendency in the Chinese society, traditional as well as contemporary, to regard the administration of the law as part of the executive function of the Government. The traditional trend of mixing the judicial sector of government with the administrative sector has been reinforced by the CCP's policy of injecting the mass line into legal policies. The result has been that law enforcement in China, in the past twenty-five years has been heavily dependent on stability and change in the top Party leadership. The law enforcement agencies have thus easily fallen victim to power struggles in the political system.

In conclusion, it would be appropriate to return to the opening statement of this article. Perhaps judicial independence is not a meaningful notion in a political system based not upon a separation of powers but upon a unified administrative apparatus designed to preserve collective interests and achieve collective goals. And it certainly has not been an important part of political reality in China which has explicitly and proudly proclaimed that in all aspects of life "politics would be in command" (*Chen-chih kua-shuai*).

Notes

1. "On Methods of Leadership," Mao, *Selected Works* vol. 4, p. 111–14.
2. Art. 7, the Common Program in 1 *Chung-yang jen-ming cheng-fu faling hui-pen* (Compendium of the laws and regulations of the Central People's Government, hereafter "*Compendium*") 17 (1949–50).
3. Gudoshinikov "Legal Organs of the People's Republic of China," *Joint Publications Research Service* no. 1689–N, 88–89 (1959).
4. See *Eighth National Congress of the Communist Party of China* vol. 1, p. 81–82.
5. Chou En-lai, *Peking Review* 20 April 1961, p. 6–7.

34

Power and Authority in the Family
Mary Ann Glendon

Discussions of legal equality of the sexes usually begin or end with the recognition that full equality will not be achieved until there is change in the ideas widely held in society about sex roles. Stereotyped sex roles which result in social and economic disabilities are as inimical to equality as are laws and practices which directly discriminate against women. Family law, especially, has traditionally embodied ideas of separate spheres of activity appropriate for women and men. It has carried the image of the woman as housewife, the man as breadwinner, and of a family authority structure dominated by the husband and father.

Behavioral scientists however have been telling us for some time that in modern industrial societies ideas about sex roles and marriage have changed. Housewife-marriage, while still widespread, is only one of many current marriage patterns. At the same time the authority structure of the family has become less hierarchical and more democratic. Decision-making and division of labor within the family tend to follow a joint rather than a segregated role pattern. Boundaries between the roles of husband and wife are becoming blurred.

On the ideological plane contemporary society is a museum of

Excerpt from "Power and Authority in the Family: New Legal Patterns as Reflections of Changing Ideologies" *American Journal of Comparative Law* 23 (1975), pp. 1–33. Copyright © 1975 by The American Association for the Comparative Study of Law, Inc. Reprinted by permission.

various conceptions of marriage. Christians who believe in the sacramental nature of marriage see it as an indissoluble tie through which each partner, already responsible for his own salvation takes on the heavy additional responsibility for the salvation of the other. Engels saw this Christian ideal of marriage as supplanted by bourgeois marriage in which economic considerations make every marriage a marriage of convenience and a form of prostitution; modern Marxists see the bourgeois marriage of Engels' time, organized around production, as being supplanted today by bourgeois marriage organized around consumption. The idea that marriage exists primarily for the personal fulfillment of the individual spouses and should last only so long as it performs this function is also in vogue.

Recently there has been a little-noticed upheaval in family law as expressions of changing ideas and behavior have found their way into the legal system and have been cast as new legal norms. This can be seen most clearly in the continental European systems where such changes have occurred in the codes and are highly visible. But the formulation of new symbolic statements about ideal behavior can also be discerned in Anglo-American law.

The change in the ideology expressed in the law is profound. Reflecting in part, as it does, processes which are already well underway in society itself, it constitutes official recognition of the waning of housewife marriage as the dominant norm and of other sex-role stereotypes. At the same time new norms, ideals and symbolic expressions are being ensconced in the law. To some extent these seem to reflect what is going on in society. In other cases the new norms seem to be those of influential bodies of opinion whose ideas are different from those held by the majority of men and women in the society. Finally, with the establishment of new, egalitarian and democratic norms much direct legal sex discrimination withers away through repeal or disuse.

The above assertions, amounting as they do to a thesis that a process which many persons think is only beginning is so far advanced that even the legal system has come to reflect it, need to be supported. It is believed that a comparative analysis of the legal rules which purport to affect powers of decision within the family in Anglo-American, French and West German law will amply document the thesis. Therefore this article will analyze how changing marriage and sex-role behavior and ideology have found their way into American, English, French and West German legal authority patterns and how changing legal norms have in turn provoked further changes in specific legal rules. Finally, it will be seen that there are contradictions and unresolved problems within the new normative systems because ultimately the social goals of sex equality and individual liberty are in tension with other important social goals such as the nurture of future citizens and the promotion of family stability. The tension is a dynamic one however which may result in better child care and more stable family life than presently exist.

Two Approaches

Legal systems have developed two basic approaches to family politics. Laws of the continental European type plunge directly into the question of whether one spouse should predominate in the decision-making process of the family. Anglo-American common law on the other hand traditionally stays away from interspousal disputes unless and until they reach the divorce court.

The legal rules evolved by French and German law look more like exhortations to a certain ideal way of life than specific rules of conduct.[1] For example a hierarchical model was described in the French Civil Code of 1804: "The husband owes protection to his wife, the wife obedience to her husband."[2] The West German code describes an ideal of *Lebensgemeinschaft*:[3] "The spouses are obliged to live together in a matrimonial community of life." Not many systems have gone so far as the Imperial Russian Code which commanded the wife to love her husband, a rule which the French courts have found unrealistic, if not absurd.

In practice one generally does not discover what the consequences are of violating these symbolic norms of the continental systems until the spouses are before the court in a marital breakdown situation. Then divorce or support decisions may be affected by the fact that one spouse has been guilty of "fault" through failing to live up to the obligation to live in community or through failing to "protect" or "obey." Thus in both the continental European and the Anglo-American systems the search for legal authority patterns eventually leads to the interstices of the divorce law. This poses certain difficulties for comparative legal analysis if we are attempting to discern what content, if any beyond the symbolic, these legal rules may have.

In all the systems under consideration few divorces are denied. Furthermore, only a small percentage of divorces is contested and among those contested an even smaller percentage is litigated beyond the first instance. The question of interspousal decision-making powers may be presented in a contested case but will inevitably be distorted by the fact that regardless of who is "right" about that particular issue the principal issue for the court in reality is whether or not to grant the divorce, or to whom a divorce should be granted.

In deciding that issue the court will take other factors into consideration including, probably, the mutual behavior of the spouses over the whole course of the marriage.

With respect to decisions about children and property the situation is different, in that specific controversies about these matters are brought before courts more often than personal interspousal decisions, which tend to be reviewed by courts only in the context of divorce proceedings. Though the divorce proceedings themselves tend to overshadow the importance of any particular decision, in the case of disputes over decisions affecting children or property the only issue presented will often be the decision itself: Was the mother justified in removing the child from a religious school and placing it in a public school; Can the husband sell the matrimonial home without the consent of his wife? The rules which are pertinent to the resolution of this kind of dispute have definite legal as well as symbolic content. . . .

The continental approach is more revealing of the process of change that is occurring in the legal norms than the Anglo-American "hands off" system. But it will appear that as French and German legal norms have become more pluralistic the systems themselves have begun to move to a posture of noninterference with family authority structures even in areas where the courts traditionally were active.

The Decline of Family Harmony by Fiat

Changing Legal Authority Patterns in Matters
Affecting the Spouses Alone

The impossibility of providing a definitive answer to the question whether one spouse should predominate in the family decision-making process has not impeded heroic efforts to settle the matter once for all by legislative edict or executive decree. . . .

French and German law traditionally dealt elaborately with the allocation of powers of decision in matters of family life between husband and wife. From 1804 until 1938 Art. 213 of the French Civil Code read: "The husband owes protection to his wife, the wife obedience to her husband." In 1938 this language was repealed but from 1938 to 1970 revised Art. 213 referred to the husband as "head of the family." Little by little up to 1970 the husband's actual powers as head of the family were eroded by legislative reforms giving powers to children and married women, but his symbolic title remained. Indeed as late as 1965 attempts to remove this language were successfully defeated. The original draft by the Commission for the Reform of the Civil Code of the new matrimonial property law, which took effect in 1966, deposed the husband as the head of the family; but the opposition to this draft was such that the symbolic leadership of the husband was retained out of fear that the whole reform project would fail otherwise.

Then in 1967 another draft of Art. 213 was formulated with the approval of the Conseil d'État. This draft would have provided that in the case of an impasse between husband and wife the husband would make a decision in conformity with the interest of the household and the children. In 1970 this proposal was rejected. The 1970 legislature for a time considered retaining the provision so far as decision-making with respect to the children was concerned but finally rejected it even there.

In the Law of 4 June 1970 the historic principle "The husband is head of the family" was eliminated from Art. 213 of the Civil Code and the following statement was substituted: "The spouses together assure the moral and material direction of the family." Since most of the legal incidents of the husband's headship had already been eliminated from the law the chief importance of this change was symbolic. The hierarchical principle which at one time had organized French family law was casually swept away and Art. 215 was amended to include what may be the new organizing principle: "The spouses are mutually bound to a community of life." The unsettling effect on French society of the worker-student revolts of May–June 1968 probably explains why this reform which provoked such controversy in 1965 drew scarcely any attention in 1970.

German law too has undergone a legal and symbolic transformation. The German Civil Code of 1896 (effective 1900) emphasized the unity of the spouses and the predominance of the husband. The division of labor and of decision-making power within the family was clear so far as the law was concerned. Art. 1354 gave the husband the right to "decide all matters of matrimonial life." Other provisions of the code gave him a qualified right to give notice of termination to his wife's employer and to manage his wife's property. This traditional hierarchical structure of German family law was overturned by the West German Constitution of 1949 which proclaimed the principle of equality of the sexes. But the Constitution of 1949 also proclaimed that "Marriage and the family enjoy the special protection of the state." Can these two ideals be fully implemented without coming into conflict? This may depend on what is meant by "marriage" and "the family."

A certain equivocation has characterized West German efforts to implement the equality principle. The Constitution of 1949 provided for a delay of four years before the equality provision would become self-executing. This delay was supposed to give the legislature plenty of time to make the necessary adaptations. However four years passed with no action on the part of the legislature and the courts were faced with the task, starting on 31 March 1953, of implementing the equality rule. Four more years passed during which the courts struck down provision after provision of the old law. Finally in 1957 the Equality Law, the *Gleichberechtigungsgesetz*, was passed to implement the constitution and to amend the old law.

At the present time most of the legal provisions giving preeminence to the husband have been repealed or declared unconstitutional, but the Code continues to emphasize the community aspect of marriage in Art. 1353 which still states that "husband and wife are obliged to live with each other in marital community of life." But if marriage is to be viewed as a community of life, even though at the same time a union between two free and equal individuals, there will continue to be difficult situations where the law is asked to deal with a conflict between the community of the two spouses and the autonomy of the individual spouse.

The 1957 Equality Law itself was ambivalent. It gave the father the final right to make decisions in the event of disagreement between the spouses on the exercise of parental authority. This was promptly struck down as a violation of the equality principle but the equality principle has not been applied to strike down other provisions of the BGB which seem to give a dominant position to the husband and to enshrine housewife-marriage as the cultural ideal. For example Art. 1356.I. begins with the significant symbolic statement "The wife's responsibility is to run the household." Then it provides that the wife is authorized to work outside the home so long as this is compatible with her marital and family duties. Thus it seems that the wife does not have an equal right to independent work outside the home although it is hard to see how this is compatible with the equality principle. . . .

In the Social Democratic government's draft of a new marriage and divorce law now before the Bundesrat, the law is no longer organized around the image of *Hausfrauenehe* (housewife-marriage) but rather around the idea of marriage as a partnership of workers pursuing their chosen occupations whatever these may be. Art. 1356.I. has been eliminated. When and if the reform proposals are adopted German law will come to reflect not only the principle of equality but an entirely changed concept of marriage—a community of life in which the partners work out their own roles. This will be the "marriage" which according to the Constitution enjoys the "special protection of the State."

In the Anglo-American systems spouses have by and large been left to work out their roles, to make their decisions and to divide their labor by themselves so long as the marriage is functioning. . . .

Judicial handling of recent cases brought by husbands asserting a right to participate in the decision whether or not to have an abortion has been consistent with traditional American reluctance to intervene in marital decision-making. The Massachusetts Supreme Judicial Court, declining to recognize such a right in the husband, said: "Except in cases involving divorce or separation, our law has not in general undertaken to resolve the many delicate questions inherent in the marriage relationship. . . . Some things must be left to private agreement."[4] While the legislatures of a few states have not been so reticent and have enacted statutes requiring the husband's consent under some circumstances such statutes so far have been struck down by the courts as unconstitutional.

In American cases in which divorces are sought on grounds of mental cruelty, irreconcilable differences or other grounds used when marriages have broken down, and in some cases of desertion, one sees fact patterns which the French and German systems formerly described as problems of decision-making powers and which today those systems see as problems of the community of life of the spouses.

In England, although the situation is now similar to that in the United States, it was not always the case that the law remained aloof from the personal relationship of the spouses. The idea of matrimonial community of life in the English common law is embodied in the concept of *consortium*, the right of the spouses to the society and services of each other; but at one time only the husband was viewed as having this right. Until the middle of the 19th century it was thought that the husband's right to consortium might under certain circumstances be enforced by physically confining his wife. It was not until 1891 that it was finally held, where a wife who had failed to comply with a decree for restitution of marital rights was seized by her husband and confined to his residence, that the husband was not allowed to use force to restrain his wife's personal liberty. Even in that case two judges left open the question of whether a husband could still physically restrain his wife to protect his honor if, e.g., she was in the act of going to meet her paramour. Since that time however statutory changes have equated the rights of the spouses to the point that the position today with respect to consortium is, in the words of one authority, that "both spouses are the joint, co-equal heads of the family."[5] A recent English case illustrates that a corollary of the loss of the husband's right to compel the wife to cohabit is that the wife cannot compel the husband to receive her in his residence. In *Nanda v. Nanda* it was held that a husband who had deserted his wife was entitled to an injunction to prevent her from installing herself in the flat which he was sharing with another woman.[6]

Thus the present situation in England seems to be that consortium, the duty to cohabit, exists as a symbol of the community aspect of marriage but is legally unenforceable. It may however lead to other consequences such as divorce, judicial separation or the cessation of the duty to support.

Although the trend toward equality in decision-making and toward noninterference by courts in those disputes which do not result in marriage breakdown is clear there are still some instances in both French and American law where the husband is given legal dominance in decision-making. This is notably true in the matter of choice of residence. In matters affecting the children one can likewise find instances where the father is given a certain legal dominance. And in one area of French law and most American community property law the husband is given legal dominance in a matter of great practical importance—the management of community funds. All of these areas, though, are currently in flux.

Where choice of residence is concerned, since the husband was typically the spouse primarily responsible for the support of the family this choice was traditionally his. The French Code provided in former Art. 215: "The choice of the family residence belongs to the husband: the wife is obliged to live with him and he is bound to receive her." But in 1970 Art. 215 was changed to read: "The spouses are mutually bound to a community of life. The residence of the family is at the place which they choose by common accord."

In the very next line however the ambivalence which characterizes law reform in this area reasserts itself and the change is rendered more symbolic than substantive by the addition of the words: "In the absence of accord, in the place chosen by the husband." Then, so as not entirely to deprive the reform of substance, the legislature of 1970 added: "However, if the residence chosen by the husband presents serious inconvenience for the family, the wife may obtain authorization from the court for a separate residence." . . .

A similar development has taken place in American law. By case law or statute in many American states a husband was given the right to designate the place of the family's residence and a wife's refusal to follow her husband to a new home chosen by him was considered desertion, a ground for divorce. While sometimes this right seemed to belong to the husband just because he was the husband the cases for many years related it to the husband's duty to support the family. American case law, like French law, has developed some limitations on the husband's power to select the family residence. The wife's duty to follow her husband to a residence does not extend to situations where the new residence is manifestly unsuitable from the point of view of health, safety or physical comfort of the family. . . . Nevertheless the rule at the present time retains considerable vigor. As recently as 1965 a divorce was granted in Illinois on grounds of desertion against a wife who refused to follow her husband from Atlanta, Georgia to Chicago, Illinois even though the move would have required the wife to give up her tenure and pension rights in the Atlanta school system where she had been teaching since 1932.[7] The facts of the case strongly suggest that the marriage of this childless couple in their fifties had in fact broken down. But marriage breakdown is not a ground for divorce in most states whereas desertion is. Thus the Illinois Appellate Court decided the case on the basis that a wife has a duty to follow her husband when he chooses to change residence except where "special circumstances" exist. The wife's strong professional motivation to remain in Atlanta did not in the view of the court amount to "special circumstances."

Signs of erosion of the rule are appearing however in cases where the courts feel the need to justify the application of the rule on some ground other than the fact that the husband is entitled, as husband, to decide; and also in cases where the courts have found the reason for the rule absent under the circumstances. For example in a 1952 Maryland case a husband was refused a divorce on grounds of desertion, the court saying that where the wife contributed more financially to the household than did the husband the reason for the rule permitting the husband to choose the family residence was absent.[8]

In England equality seems to have been achieved in this area by the application on a case-by-case basis of the rule that neither spouse has an absolute right to designate the residence of the couple but that where the spouses disagree a divorce on grounds of desertion will be granted only if one spouse can be said to have acted unreasonably under all the circumstances. In situations where neither spouse clearly has right on his or her side, desertion will not be available as a ground of divorce. The older view that the husband as husband is entitled to make the decision seems not to have been expressed since 1940. In Germany former article 1354 of the BGB giving the husband the power to choose the family's place of residence did not survive the Equality Law of 1957.

Changing Legal Authority Patterns in Matters Affecting the Children

The law concerning decisions involving a married couple's children has been profoundly influenced not only by the changing status of women but also by increasing concern for the rights of children. Thus while one can discern a well-established trend toward sharing of parental rights and obligations equally between mother and father, at the same time there is a trend toward diminution of the rights of both. As equality between mother and father becomes the rule in the area of decisions about the children, mechanisms have had to be developed to deal with the situation where the parents are at an impasse. If equality is to be maintained at all costs this may mean that at some point the state as a third party in the form of a court or agency will have to step in as the final arbiter of such disputes. The trend seems however to be toward increased state involvement where the rights of children are concerned in general, but a pulling-back of the law from involvement in inter-spousal disputes concerning the care of the child's person, education or property.

An examination of recent developments in French, West German and American law is instructive.

Under the family structure envisioned by the German Civil Code of 1896, parental authority over minor children was exercised by the father with only a few specific rights given to the mother. In this area as in the realm of purely inter-spousal decisions the old provisions of the BGB would not stand after the equality provisions of the West German Constitution of 1949 became effective. Not only did the 1949 constitution provide for equality of the sexes, it specifically provided that the care and education of children was a basic right vested in both parents.

But as has already been pointed out above the Equality Law of 1957 was more equivocal than the 1949 constitution. It provided that in the case of disagreement between the spouses with respect to a decision concerning the care of the person or property of the child the father would have the final say. It also provided that the right to act as statutory representative on behalf of the child belonged to the father alone. When these provisions reached the courts both were held unconstitutional.

At present the right to decide about the child's education, place of residence and discipline; the right to act as the child's representative; and the right to care for the child's property are exercised by the parents jointly subject to statutory guidelines established for the protection of the child. Rather specific rules are laid down for the question of a child's religious education in a law dating back to 1921. Under this law the religious instruction of a child up to age 14 is determined by the parents jointly. In the case of disagreement the child is brought up in the religious denomination common to the parents at the time of their marriage; but if the parents had no common religious denomination at the time the religious instruction of the child is decided by the guardianship court. The law provides further that the religious denomination of a child over 12 cannot be changed against the child's will and that a child over 14 can determine his religious denomination for himself.

Disagreements concerning the exercise of parental authority are no longer resolved by the legal imposition of the decision of the father; rather, if the matter cannot be worked out by the spouses jointly the only recourse is to the guardianship court. But under the scheme of the Civil Code, after Arts. 1628 and 1629.I were held unconstitutional, the guardianship court is authorized to decide matters itself only in certain instances, e.g., where the child is being neglected or harmed by the parents or where the parents are divorced or separated. With these limitations on the power of the court to take specific measures it seems that in other disputes between parents the most it can do is authorize one spouse to make the decision alone.

The draftsmen of the statutes which fundamentally changed the law of family politics concerning children in France in 1970 were aware of and influenced by the German law but did not go so far toward equality between father and mother.

In the area of decision-making powers in matters affecting children, the father retains a certain dominance in France even under the new law of 4 June 1970. This law had as its principal object the complete reform of Title Nine of the Civil Code dealing with the father's power over the person and the property of his children, the *puissance paternelle*. Title Nine was renamed *De l'autorité parentale* and the new principle was established that the mother and the father exercise the parental authority in common. Under the prior law while parental power belonged to the mother and father it was exercised by the father in his capacity as head of the family. The change from "power" to "authority" is as significant as the change from "paternal" to "parental." *Puissance* came from the Roman *potestas* and signified dominion over the children which the father exercised as head of the family. *Autorité* on the other hand signifies under the new law a complex of rights and duties. For not only was the 1970 law a landmark in the development of legal equality of the sexes in France, it was also a landmark, indeed the culmination, of a steady trend to modify the degree and kind of control to which children are subjected.

The changes wrought by the 1970 law were so widely acclaimed by diverse groups in French society that the Minister of Justice claimed that the new law was a reflection of an evolution of mores and family practices in France. But it can hardly be doubted that the events of 1968 had an effect in causing the legislature so resistant to change only five years earlier to recognize this evolution, if it has indeed taken place.

It does seem clear that by 1970 circumstances had changed so much since similar reforms were proposed in 1945 and again in 1965 that the old arguments which were used successfully to resist change in the past did not sound the same any more: "Every human society must have a head;" "The elimination of the head of the family will hasten the dissolution of the family;" "The husband should be the head because he is better able to support the family;" "Disagreements between spouses will have to be resolved by the courts;" "More and more couples will seek judicial intervention and this will lead to marriage breakdown;" "The new marriage will be a *ménage à trois* of husband, wife and judge." . . . Indeed the prevailing conception of marriage in French society is probably more traditional than the conception which is now symbolically enshrined in the law; but it seems to have been the view of many of those responsible for the law that the law in this area should be "educational" or hortatory, encouraging couples to conform to an ideal of shared rather than hierarchical authority. . . .

Far-reaching as the symbolic and legal changes of 1970 were with respect to parental authority, they stopped short of establishing full equality between father and mother concerning the child's property. In this matter parental authority encompasses a duty to administer the property and a right to enjoy the revenues of the property (*administration légale and jouissance légale*).

With respect to these rights and duties the 1970 law retains the distinction made by the old law between the existence of a right and its exercise. Art. 382 of the Civil Code now provides that the mother and father "have" the administration and enjoyment of the property of the child "under the following conditions." Where both parents are living and not divorced or separated these conditions include that the father alone exercises the power of administration, subject however to the requirement that he consult the mother concerning acts of administration and obtain her consent for acts of disposition (C.C. Arts. 383, 389). The right to enjoy the child's property is linked to the exercise of administration. Thus despite general language of Art. 382 that the mother and father have the right to enjoyment and administration, Art. 383 provides that the right to enjoyment belongs to the parent who has charge of the administration. Normally of course this will be the father.

Unlike French and German law, parental authority in common law does not confer upon the parent any right to title, possession or control of the child's property. Unless such authority is conferred by statute it is the theory of the common law that a guardian to manage such property must be appointed by the court. Traditionally the father was preferred as guardian of the child's property but now statutes in many states treat the mother and father equally as joint guardians in the care and management of their children's property. Correlative to the parents' duty to support their child during minority is their right at common law to a minor child's services and earnings. To the extent that the duty of support has come to fall equally on the father and mother, and that statutes equalize the rights and duties of the parents in other respects, this right is now enjoyed by both parents.

Just as American law is characterized by its unwillingness to interfere with the interspousal decision-making process on matters concerning the spouses alone, so it does not step into marital disputes concerning children unless and until it must in the context of working out child custody problems in a divorce or separation or problems of neglect, abuse or delinquency. Then and only then it seems will American courts settle such disputes—and then not on the basis of which spouse's decision should prevail but on the basis of the "best interests of the child."

Thus in the United States one may say that the judges have so far declined to participate in the *ménage à trois* which some French writers feared would result from giving equality to spouses in decision-making. There seems to be no clamor for involving the state in these decisions, so one might tentatively conclude that a system which leaves these decisions entirely in the private order is a feasible alternative to permitting and thereby perhaps encouraging recourse to courts.

In England, if a spouse wishes to bring a matter concerning the care, custody, education or control of a child before the court without taking any other matrimonial proceedings he must proceed under the Guardianship of Minors Act or must apply to have the child made a ward of the court. Since an order under the Guardianship of Minors Act is unenforceable so long as the spouses are residing together and since jurisdiction to make a child a ward of the court is based on the necessity of protecting the child, the situation in England appears in fact to be much the same as in the United States—the law will not interfere with the decision-making processes of a functioning family unit.

Changing Legal Authority Patterns in Matters Affecting Property

In the search for legal techniques to implement the new policy of equality, legislators have found particular difficulties in one area—

that of providing for management of the family property be it owned in common, separately or by the children. Equality in decision-making on matters involving the couple or the children can be achieved by doing nothing, as in the common law, or by providing for an appeal to a court, as in some civil law systems. But in systems where much of a couple's property is regarded as jointly owned it has long been argued that complete equality would be unworkable and that a court cannot be looked to for the settlement of everyday business decisions. There has been much talk of two captains on one ship, two-headed families and other monstrosities.

In France these difficulties prevented the reforms of 1965 and 1970 from implementing full equality between husband and wife. While the 1970 law deposed the husband from his symbolic position as head of the family it did not affect his legal position as head of the community. Under new Art. 1421 of the Civil Code the husband still manages the community property by himself subject to the requirement of the wife's consent for certain important transactions. Thus significant legal distinctions remain between husband and wife so far as property is concerned. The law of 1970 did however take some important steps toward approximating the legal position of the wife to that of the husband.

Yet many systems do function with the husband and wife sharing equal powers with respect to property. In the separate property systems of the common law husbands and wives frequently acquire property in their joint names. Their contractual arrangements or the law in force typically require in the case of real property that the consent of both is needed for any disposition, or in the case of personal property such as bank accounts that either spouse may perform any act with respect to the property without the consent of the other.

In the hybrid communities of the German and Swedish type the spouses are free to act as they wish with respect to property of the type which would be part of the common fund at the end of the marriage, subject only to restraints on certain important transactions—e.g. in Germany, the transfer of the bulk of a spouse's goods or the transfer of household articles. Even these minimal restraints are being questioned in Sweden and Germany where marital property law reform efforts are putting more emphasis on the autonomy of the spouses than on sharing.

The socialist communities of acquests have long functioned with complete equality between husband and wife and since 1967 five of the eight American community property states have provided for equality between husband and wife in the management of the community. The system developed in Arizona, California and Washington permits either spouse acting alone to deal with community property, joinder of both spouses being required only for certain important transactions. The Texas system on the other hand closely resembles the German and Scandinavian systems. New Mexico, like Germany in 1957, has tried to implement its constitutional equality principle while providing continuity with its "four hundred year tradition of husband headship of the community."[9] . . .

The Rise of Pluralism

In mid-20th century, one can observe marked change on both the substantive and symbolic levels. In law and in fact in the United States, England, France and West Germany one can say that husband and wife are nearly equal so far as decision-making powers are concerned. The trend furthermore seems to be toward the abolition of the remaining distinctions. There is a general tendency for the law to pull away from the area of interspousal relationships altogether, and the new ideology of marriage expressed in the laws emphasizes equality and cooperation rather than hierarchy within the family. These trends are related to a number of social and economic phenomena which sociologists collect under the heading "modernization." In part they are due to worldwide trend toward equality. In Western countries technology and affluence have made it possible for more and more spouses to be concerned with such matters as personal development and fulfillment, which to the extent that they are different concerns from the economic welfare of the family unit would have been impossible luxuries in previous times for all but a few. Also to the extent that diversity of ideology is increasingly recognized the attempt to impose a single ideal of marriage becomes more and more futile. Added factors are a growing concern for individual and family privacy and the idea that internal affairs of a family should be free from state interference. In the United States this principle has been articulated at the constitutional level in the Supreme Court decision striking down birth control laws.[10] In view of and in addition to all these factors the law, in pulling back from the internal affairs of spouses, may simply be recognizing the running commentary made by folklore upon the law to the effect that the area is one which is difficult to affect through legislation or edict. Withdrawal of regulation may represent acceptance of the fact that where marriage stability is seen as a social goal, giving legal dominance to one partner in case of disputes will not necessarily advance that goal. As a practical matter, if husband and wife are unable to agree on a decision the future of the marriage is no more in danger if their *status quo* is maintained than if the law gave one spouse in these circumstances the power to impose his decision on the other. . . .

Tensions and Contradictions in the New Ideology of Tolerance

French and German law provide interesting examples of how law and symbolism have changed and how new symbols have generated new legal problems. As has been observed, in addition to setting forth legal norms they described a model or ideal of marriage in the particular society. It is doubtful whether in pluralistic American society a single ideology of marriage could ever have been articulated. We have seen that as ideologies of marriage are universally in the process of transformation many of the old *Leitbilder* have disappeared from the European codes. Legal norms about decision-making powers in European laws, to the extent that they still exist, seem rarely to be the subject of litigation. Rather, as in the United States, one sees disputes involving decision-making powers in the divorce courts, where the question will be whether one spouse has committed "fault" justifying the other in terminating the marriage or whether the marriage has factually broken down. . . .

In modern times, as divorce becomes increasingly available and couples become less reluctant to resort to divorce, there will probably be less use of courts as arbiters of marital disputes. The American attitude of noninterference with a functioning marriage seems to be compatible not only with pluralism in society but also with the principle of equality of husband and wife and the modern view of marriage as a free union of two individuals. Current notions of pluralism, privacy, individual liberty and equality all come together here and remain in equipoise for the moment.

To the extent that modern laws, while getting out of the marriage regulation business, have attempted to announce new *Leitbilder*, they have encountered a new set of problems arising from the contradiction between the modern vision of marriage as involving cooperation and community of interest on one hand and marriage as a vehicle for the fullest self-expression of the individual on the other.

These two ideas are always in tension. In a functioning marriage they will be for the most part in equilibrium. But in some marriages the autonomy of the spouses may manifest itself in such a way as to destroy the marital community. Recent cases involving a spouse's exercise of a religion illustrate this dilemma.

Although equality of the sexes has not been established at the constitutional level in France, the development of French statutory and case law demonstrates the emergence of the ideas of equality and individuality of each spouse and the difficulty of accommodating these ideas to the idea that marriage is a community of life involving some reciprocal obligations on the part of the spouses.

When controversies between the spouses concerning the power to make decisions come before the French courts in the context of divorce proceedings one can observe situations where the independent individuality of one spouse is claimed so to interfere with the community of life that is marriage that it constitutes an *injure grave* entitling the other spouse to divorce. It would be unrealistic to pretend that these divorce cases give an exact picture of the tension between community and individuality in French law or French marriages since the result of affirming the principle of individual liberty in these circumstances would be to deny a divorce, which judges may understandably be reluctant to do. Nevertheless the cases are instructive. . . .

French writers see in the case law an increasing recognition of the individual liberty of the spouses. As the writer of one of the leading treatises on French civil law put it "Same bed, different dreams."[11] The author of a recent article in a major journal goes further and finds that there is a new idea of marriage being expressed in French law: the idea of marriage as a means to the fullest possible development of the individual. From this he argues that the next step will be a unilateral right to divorce. He thinks the country is almost ready for a return to the spirit of the short-lived revolutionary law of 20 September 1792 which began "The right to divorce is a necessary consequence of individual liberty which would be lost through an indissoluble undertaking." Today, he says, it is repugnant to current views of individual liberty that a person should be forced to remain bound to a marriage which he or she no longer accepts and which has become intolerable to him or her. He claims that in practice unilateral divorce has already been accepted—fault divorce is really divorce by mutual consent; many divorces by mutual consent are in fact unilateral divorces because the consent of one spouse is so often purchased or forced in one way or another by the spouse who wants to be free of the marriage. . . .

German law is similar. The spouses are obliged by Art. 1353 to live together in marital community. To the extent that this obligation is anything more than an expression of an ideal it seems to impose some limit on the freedom of each spouse to act. Thus while each spouse has the power to decide personal matters for himself he may not thereby impair the matrimonial community of life. In making personal decisions concerning religious affiliation, dress, reading, smoking, etc. each spouse must have regard for the other.

Conversion to a new religious faith does not release one from one's duties toward one's family. The American treatment of these matters appears to be exactly the same. . . .

In addition to the tension just described between the ideal of community of life and the ideal of individual liberty there are other sources of movement and change which indicate that the trends here described toward legal recognition of sex equality, individual freedom and diverse ideologies of marriage are not irreversible or at least not moving in a straight line. Just as social and economic factors have been determinative in bringing the law to its present state, so will they be determinative in its future direction. . . .

In the long run it is possible that liberty of the individual and tolerance of diversity will be seen as phenomena of affluence. Perhaps they have reached their maximum development as affluence seems to have reached its peak. . . . Socrates thought that democracies "spangled with the manners and characters of mankind," "full of variety and disorder, and dispensing a sort of equality to equals and unequals alike" might seem to some men to be the fairest of states but were actually the prelude to disorder and tyranny.[12]

One need not be this pessimistic to reflect that as we adjust to a world of dwindling resources and expanding population, where it seems that there will never be enough of the necessities to go around, we may come to search in family law as elsewhere for mechanisms and models through which people can learn to live in community. New understanding of the meanings of equality and liberty may have to be found or old learning recalled.

Notes

1. The hortatory aspect of the current East German Family Code is explicitly recognized in Eberhardt, "Property Provisions in the GDR Family Code," *Law and Legis, in the GDR* 45 (1969) where the statement is made that the Family Code is "not only . . . an instrument in the hands of lawyers, but, over and beyond and even in the first place, a manual for the married citizen who looks for and actually finds orientation and advice for his personal conduct."
2. Former Art. 213 of the Code Civil (Text of 1804). Henceforth the French Code Civil will be cited as C.C.
3. Art. 1353.I of the German Civil Code, the *Bürgerliches Gesetzbuch*, which will be cited henceforth as BGB.
4. *Doe v. Doe*, 314 N.E.2d 128, 132 (Mass. 1974).
5. Bromley, *Family Law* 94 (4th ed. 1971).
6. [1968] P. 351.
7. Martin v. Martin, 210 N.E.2d 590 (Ill. App. 1965); See also, Motykowski v. Motykowski, 282 N.E.2d 458 (Ill. App. 1972).

8. *Blair v. Blair*, 85 A.2d 442 (Md. 1952).

9. N.M. Stat. Ann. § 57-4A-7, 57-4A-7.1, 57-4A-8 (Supp. 1973).

10. Griswold v. Connecticut, 381 U.S. 479 (1965).

11. II Carbonnier, *Droit Civil* 72 (8th ed. 1969).

12. Plato, *Republic*, Book VIII 558,562.

35

A Cross-National
Analysis of
Legal Systems
William M. Evan

Comparative research on legal systems has for many years been virtually the exclusive domain of comparative legal scholars. The range of scholarship of comparatists is indeed wide. At one extreme, some concentrate on specific problems in a limited number of legal systems, such as the dismissal of civil servants in the United States, Britain and France.[1] At the opposite extreme, some scholars undertake encyclopedic analyses of legal systems, as represented in the work of Wigmore[2] and David.[3] One of the virtues of comparative law, as Kahn-Freund recently observed in his inaugural address at Oxford, is that "it allows a scholar to place himself outside the labyrinth of minutiae in which legal thinking so easily loses its way and to see the great contours of the law and its dominant characteristic."[4]

Sociology and Comparative Law

From a sociological perspective much of the research in comparative law is concerned exclusively with legal doctrine, is descriptive in

Excerpt from "A Data Archive of Legal Systems: A Cross-national Analysis of Sample of Data," *European Journal of Sociology*, 9 (1968), pp. 113–125, by permission of the publisher.

nature, or is insufficiently oriented to the interplay of legal institutions with other institutions in society. Thus far, however, few sociologists or other social scientists have ventured into the field of comparative law. Some notable exceptions are Hoebel's comparison of the legal systems of five pre-literate societies,[5] Rose's study of the impact of law on voluntary associations in the United States, France and Italy,[6] and Rabinowitz's implicit comparative analysis of the legal profession in Japan and in Western countries.[7]

All comparative lawyers, except for those with a sociological orientation, would probably dismiss any social science study that purports to supplement the extant approaches in their field. It is, therefore, incumbent upon the sociological trespasser to indicate what he expects to contribute to cross-national research on law.

The sociologist attracted to this type of comparative research can bring to bear some of his distinctive theoretical and methodological biases. Theoretically, the sociologist might wish to investigate, for example, the differing role of law in social change as a function of the degree of bureaucratization, the degree of rigidity of the social stratification system, and the degree of social system integration. Because law pervades all the other institutional subsystems of society, a macro-sociological approach which takes into account the aggregate characteristics of a legal system would illuminate the relationships law has with other subsystems of society.

Methodologically, the sociologist would be interested in systematically collecting data on a sufficiently large number of societies to test propositions of theoretical and/or practical interest. He might even wish to test some propositions formulated by comparative lawyers. For example, Kahn-Freund recently advanced the tantalizing, if somewhat ambiguous, proposition that "under similar social, economic, cultural pressures in similar societies the law is apt to change by means of sometimes radically different technique."[8] Assuming this proposition were operationalized, the sociologist would put it to a systematic and quantitative test rather than resort to the case method often employed by legal scholars.

Proposal for a Data Archive

With presuppositions such as these in mind, I proposed in 1964 at a meeting of the Research Committee on the Sociology of Law of the International Sociological Association that a data archive of legal systems be developed.[9]

To be sure, the bookkeeping systems of nation-states, the United Nations, and various international organizations yield vast quantities of statistics. For example, the United Nations publishes data on mortality, fertility, manufacturing, newspaper circulation, etc.; the International Labor Organization publishes statistics on unemployment, number of man-hours lost from strikes, etc. However, the bulk of available data provides surprisingly little grist for the mill of the sociologist interested in cross-national research on legal systems. This is true even if one construes the concept of a legal system in very broad terms, as I have done, namely, as "a set of institutions comprising norms, roles, and patterns of behavior pertaining to judicial, legislative, executive, and administrative processes of a society."[10]

Translating this broad conception of a legal system into a set of quantitative indicators to permit cross-national comparisons is in itself a complex undertaking.[11] There is a strong temptation to focus only on those attributes of legal systems that readily lend themselves to quantification, such as the number of lawyers and judges, and ignore qualitative phenomena that require quantification and may even be more important, such as the degree to which norms of procedural due process are institutionalized[12] and govern judicial decision making.

An even more serious obstacle to developing a set of indicators is the diversity of meaning and behavior associated with seemingly unequivocal terms such as lawyer, policeman, and homicide. Lawyers differ substantially in professional training and function, with some countries making a distinction between a barrister and a solicitor while others do not. A policeman may be a local, regional, or national official; he may be known or unknown to the public; and he may perform a predominantly law-enforcement function or a political function.[13] As for the meaning of homicide, the United Nations has for some years wrestled with problems of defining major criminal offenses in order to make possible the collection, analysis and presentation of international criminal statistics.[14]

The problems of developing cross-national definitions of terms and comparable quantitative indicators pose a formidable intellectual challenge. This is evident when one examines the provisional list of 36 quantitative indicators included in the proposal that gave rise to the present study.[15] This list of items may give the impression of an aimless endeavor. However, though a data archive must have some theoretical underpinnings, it must also lend itself to the multiple purposes of various potential users if it is to be a useful archive.

Exploratory Analysis of Illustrative Data

By way of illustrating, rather than demonstrating, the feasibility and utility of such a data archive, a small body of data has been compiled from United Nations sources, from a document by the World Peace Through Law Center[16] and from several other sources. The legal indicators are quantitative as well as qualitative in nature. Among the quantitative indicators are law schools per 1,000 population, law professors per 1,000 population, lawyers per 1,000 population, legislators per 1,000 population, divorce rate, suicide rate, and illegitimacy ratio. Among the qualitative indicators are role of police—whether a predominantly political or law-enforcement function, and a classification of legal systems often used by comparatists, namely, civil law, common law, socialist law, and Moslem law.[17]

In order to explore the interrelationships of legal institutions and other institutions or social processes, some data on as large a number of nations as possible were collected, principally from United Nations sources and from the handbook of the Yale Political Data Program.[18] Ten quantitative indicators of non-legal institutions were selected: (1) level of industrialization, which consists of an average rank on three highly intercorrelated variables, namely, GNP per capita, energy consumption per capita, and percentage of labor force engaged in agriculture; (2) degree of urbanization, as measured by the percentage of population living in cities of over 20,000; (3) level of education, which consists of an average rank on three highly intercorrelated variables, namely, students enrolled in higher education per 100,000 population, primary and secondary school pupils as a percentage of the population aged 5–19, and percentage literate of population over 15 years of age; (4) date of political independence; (5) age of marriage as measured by the median age of grooms; (6) percentage of Christians in the population; (7) percentage of Moslems in the population; (8) degree of professionalization of the labor force, as measured by the percentage of professionals and technical personnel in the labor force; (9) degree of bureaucratization of the labor force, as measured by the percentage of administrative, executive and managerial personnel in the labor force; and, (10) the size of the military establishment as a percentage of the population aged 15–64.

All the data in this exploratory analysis, the 9 indicators of legal systems and the 10 indicators of other sub-systems of society, are cross-sectional in character. This precludes the possibility of measuring time lags and tracing feedback effects. Hence, I shall follow the general sociological assumption of regarding the indicators of the legal systems as *dependent* variables and the other indicators as *independent* variables, without, however, dismissing the possibility of feedback effects occurring over time.

As a first step in the analysis of the data, a matrix of Pearson product-moment correlations is presented in Table 1 for a "sample" of nations varying from 20 to 97, depending on the availability of each nation's data for a particular pair of variables. Inasmuch as this

TABLE 1. Pearson Product-Moment Correlation Coefficients of Indicators of Legal and Nonlegal Institutions of Selected Nations.†

Variable	Variable No.	Law Schools per 1,000 population 1	Law Professors per 1,000 population 2	Lawyers per 1,000 population 3	Legislators per 1,000 population 4	Divorce rate 5	Suicide rate 6	Illegitimacy ratio 7	Industrialization 8
Law Schools per 1,000 population	1								
Law Professors per 1,000 population	2	.45***							
Lawyers per 1,000 population	3	.42***	.46***						
Legislators per 1,000 population	4	.74***	.18	.20					
Divorce rate	5	.03	-.09	.24	.04				
Suicide rate	6	-.03	-.19	.06	.03	.61***			
Illegitimacy ratio	7	.00	.06	-.14	.04	-.52***	-.44***		
Industrialization	8	.16	.00	.47**	.37*	.26	.53**	-.46**	
Urbanization	9	.21	.17	.54***	.25	.26	.35	-.27	.81***
Bureaucratization	10	.44*	.07	.45	-.19	.24	.12	-.27	.59**

	Variable No.	Urban- ization 9	Bureau- crati- zation 10	Profession- alization 11	Level of Education 12	Date of Political Independence 13	Age of grooms 14	% of Christians 15	% of Moslems 16	Military as % of popula- tion 17
Law Schools per 1,000 population	1									
Law Professors per 1,000 population	2									
Lawyers per 1,000 population	3									
Legislators per 1,000 population	4									
Divorce rate	5									
Suicide rate	6									
Illegitimacy ratio	7									
Industrialization	8									
Urbanization	9									
Bureaucratization	10	.49**								

*Significant at the .05 level
**Significant at the .01 level
***Significant at or lower than the .001 level
†The size of the N varies from one pair of variables to another, the largest being 97 nations and the smallest, 20.

TABLE 1. Continued

Variable	Variable No.	Law Schools per 1,000 population (1)	Law Professors per 1,000 population (2)	Lawyers per 1,000 population (3)	Legislators per 1,000 population (4)	Divorce rate (5)	Suicide rate (6)	Illegitimacy ratio (7)	Industrialization (8)
Professionalization	11	.22	.06	.47*	.37	.36	.48**	-.44	.91***
Level of Education	12	.22	.28	.55***	.22	.43**	.59***	-.48***	.90***
Date of Political Independence	13	.13	.27*	.30**	.04	-.02	.32*	.06	.49***
Age of grooms	14	-.14	-.14	-.08	.00	-.31	-.19	.60***	-.29
% of Christians	15	.35***	.49***	.52***	.24	.08	.23	.33	.52***
% of Moslems	16	-.24*	-.37**	-.36**	-.08	.02	-.31	-.18	-.54***
Military as % of population	17	-.15	-.11	.16	.28	.37**	.07	-.50	.31

	Variable No.	Urbanization 9	Bureaucratization 10	Professionalization 11	Level of Education 12	Date of Political Independence 13	Age of grooms 14	% of Christians 15	% of Moslems 16	Military as % of population 17
Professionalization	11	.80***	.60***							
Level of Education	12	.75***	.61***	.91***						
Date of Political Independence	13	.40***	-.26	-.27	.44***					
Age of grooms	14	-.12	-.58***	-.50***	-.31*	.06				
% of Christians	15	.51***	.26	.42*	.58***	-.51	.11			
% of Moslems	16	-.35	-.31	-.43*	-.62***	-.35***	.00	-.65**		
Military as % of population	17	.32**	.02	.51*	.40***	-.12	.39**	.02	.00	

*Significant at the .05 level
**Significant at the .01 level
***Significant at or lower than the .001 level
†The size of the N varies from one pair of variables to another, the largest being 97 nations and the smallest, 20.

is an exploratory analysis, a 2-tail probability test is used in deciding which of the correlation coefficients to regard as statistically significant.

To begin with, it should be noted that of the 136 possible correlation coefficients among the 17 variables (7 quantitative indicators of legal systems and 10 quantitative indicators of non-legal systems), 61 are statistically significant, whereas on the basis of chance alone we would expect only 7 significant coefficients. Of the wealth of information in Table 1, a few findings are salient. It is surely not surprising that the variables pertaining to law schools, law professors, and lawyers are mutually interrelated. If they were not, we would have grounds for doubting the validity of the data. It is noteworthy, however, that there is a high positive correlation between the number of law schools and the number of legislators. This is consistent with the findings of several studies of the disproportionate representation of lawyers in legislatures and in other branches of government. Also noteworthy is the correlation between bureaucratization and the number of law schools. As the proportion of bureaucratic personnel in the labor force increases, more legally-educated personnel are required which stimulates the development of law schools. In turn, as the pool of available graduates of law schools increases it raises the level of bureaucratization of the labor force, as is also suggested by the high positive correlation between bureaucratization and the number of lawyers.

Apart from the impact of bureaucratization on the number of law schools and lawyers in a country, the other highly positive correlates are the major social trends of industrialization, urbanization, and professionalization. A scattergram of the correlation coefficient of .47 of industrialization and number of lawyers per 1,000 population in 42 nations is presented in Figure 1. This finding is related to Nagel's more inclusive observation that "The disproportionate presence of professional judges, jurors, lawyers, promulgating bodies, and appellate courts among manufacturing societies can probably be partially explained by the fact that increased industrialization bring increased specialization within the economic system of a society which carries over into the political and adjudicative systems."[19]

The general hypothesis that industrialization has a significant impact, directly or indirectly, on the legal system appears to be confirmed by the findings in Figure 1 as well as by several correlations in Table 1. Under the circumstances it seemed reasonable to assume that some of the zero-order correlation coefficients in Table 1 are due to the effects of industrialization. Thus a partial correlation analysis, controlling for the effects of industrialization, seemed advisable. As shown in Table 2, when the effects of industrialization are

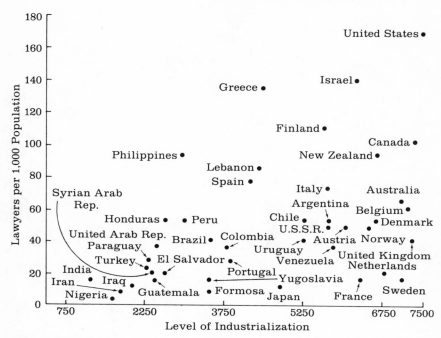

FIGURE 1. Scattergram of correlation between level of industrialization and lawyers per 1,000 population for 42 nations.

removed only 15 of the original 61 zero-order correlation coefficients are statistically significant. Among these are some of the salient findings noted above.

The impact of industrialization and attendant social processes on the legal system is also discernible when we examine the findings on the role of the policeman in various countries. In their highly innovative study in comparative social systems, Banks and Textor categorized the role of the policeman in 115 nations as to whether it entails a predominantly law-enforcement function or a political function.[20] Using their categorization, a statistical comparison was made of the 10 indicators of non-legal systems. On 5 of these indicators, as Table 3 shows, the *t* tests yielded significant mean differences. As important as statistically significant differences, however, is the pattern of consistency in the results: countries in which the role of the policeman is predominantly law-enforcement in nature have higher levels of industrialization, urbanization, education, professionalization, and bureaucratization than countries in which the role of the policeman is principally political in character. Evidently, when the function of the policeman is confined to law-enforcement, the principles of legality and rationality are prized, and such values appear to be consistent

TABLE 2. Partial Correlation Coefficients of Indicators of Legal and Nonlegal Institutions of Selected Nations, Controlling for the Effects of Industrialization†

Variable	Variable No.	Law Schools per 1,000 population 1	Law Professors per 1,000 population 2	Lawyers per 1,000 population 3	Legislators per 1,000 population 4	Divorce rate 5	Suicide rate 6	Illegitimacy ratio 7	Industrialization 8
Law Schools per 1,000 population	1								
Law Professors per 1,000 population	2	.63***							
Lawyers per 1,000 population	3	.42**	.37						
Legislators per 1,000 population	4	.02	.26	.07					
Divorce rate	5	-.82	-.18	.15	-.13				
Suicide rate	6	-.24	-.25	-.28	-.01	.36			
Illegitimacy ratio	7	-.01	.05	-.13	-.11	-.26	-.10		
Industrialization	8								
Urbanization	9	-.01	-.04	.10	-.08	.26	-.02	-.17	
Bureaucratization	10	.41*	.03	.21	-.63**	.17	-.18	.01	

506

	Variable No.	Urban-ization 9	Bureau-crati-zation 10	Profession-alization 11	Level of Education 12	Date of Political Independence 13	Age of grooms 14	% of Christians 15	% of Moslems 16	Military as % of popula-tion 17
Law Schools per 1,000 population	1									
Law Professors per 1,000 population	2									
Lawyers per 1,000 population	3									
Legislators per 1,000 population	4									
Divorce rate	5									
Suicide rate	6									
Illegitimacy ratio	7									
Industrialization	8									
Urbanization	9									
Bureaucratization	10	-.08								

*Significant at the .05 level
**Significant at the .01 level
***Significant at or lower than the .001 level
†The size of the N varies from one pair of variables to another, the largest being 97 nations and the smallest, 20.

TABLE 2. Continued

Variable	Variable No.	Law Schools per 1,000 population 1	Law Professors per 1,000 population 2	Lawyers per 1,000 population 3	Legislators per 1,000 population 4	Divorce rate 5	Suicide rate 6	Illegitimacy ratio 7	Industrialization 8
Professionalization	11	.12	.00	.07	.21	.36	.12	.07	
Level of Education	12	.28	.33	.08	.07	.21	.21	.36*	
Date of Political Independence	13	.19	.02	.42**	.16	.11	-.29	-.25	
Age of grooms	14	-.27	-.31	-.07	.37	-.10	-.13	.44*	
% of Christians	15	.25	.38	.01	.13	-.33	-.21	.49**	
% of Moslems	16	-.22	-.40*	-.05	.04	.47*	-.12	-.51**	
Military as % of population	17	-.18	-.18	.13	.03	.24	-.10	-.39*	

	Variable No.	Urban-ization 9	Bureau-crati-zation 10	Profession-alization 11	Level of Education 12	Date of Political Independence 13	Age of grooms 14	% of Christians 15	% of Moslems 16	Military as % of popula-tion 17
Professionalization	11	.11	.13							
Level of Education	12	.07	.19	.11						
Date of Political Independence	13	.04	.05	.40	.03					
Age of grooms	14	.03	-.43	-.18	-.34	-.13				
% of Christians	15	-.41**	-.13	-.49*	-.12	-.22	.22			
% of Moslems	16	.31	.06	.27	-.11	-.01	-.02	-.54***		
Military as % of population	17	.23	-.37	.29	.11	-.10	-.20	-.26	.33	

*Significant at the .05 level
**Significant at the .01 level
***Significant at or lower than the .001 level
†The size of the N varies from one pair of variables to another, the largest being 97 nations and the smallest, 20.

TABLE 3. Comparison of Means on Five Variables for Selected Nations Differing in Their Role of the Policeman

VARIABLE	MEAN FOR NATIONS WITH A POLITICAL POLICEMAN ROLE	MEAN FOR NATIONS WITH A LAW-ENFORCEMENT POLICEMAN ROLE	D.F.	T-VALUE	SIGNIFICANCE LEVEL
Industrialization	32.22 (n = 22)	56.70 (n = 23)	43	5.56	.0000
Urbanization	16.67 (n = 60)	36.53 (n = 30)	41	5.08	.0000
Level of Education	43.24 (n = 47)	70.66 (n = 32)	64	5.03	.0000
Professionalization	3.02 (n = 14)	7.50 (n = 16)	24	4.88	.0000
Bureaucratization	.68 (n = 14)	2.80 (n = 16)	17	3.38	.0035

with the five major social processes, listed in Table 3, that differentiate nations in the role their policemen perform.

Thus far, our exploratory analysis of some data on legal systems has probably failed to pique the curiosity of the comparative legal scholar. He is so oriented to the normative content of legal systems that role structures and organizational structures of legal systems,[21] which we have principally dealt with, probably hold little interest for him. Therefore, a modest effort will now be made to meet the comparative lawyer on his own grounds by examining some statistical differences associated with the traditional normative classification of legal systems, namely, civil law, common law, socialist law, and Moslem law.

A review of the interrelations of the various quantitative indicators and the classification of legal systems pointed to the importance of three variables: level of industrialization, level of education, and number of lawyers per 1,000 population. The largest differences in mean level of industrialization, as shown in Table 4, are between Moslem and civil law systems, on the one hand, and Moslem and common law systems, on the other. Civil and socialist law systems are virtually identical in mean level of industrialization. Although common law systems are noticeably higher than socialist law systems in their mean level of industrialization, the difference between them is not statistically significant. These findings raise the interesting question of what are the probable long-term effects of a leveling of industrialization on legal systems.

The second variable in Table 4, level of education, yields even more significant mean differences among the four types of legal systems. The lowest mean level of education is found among Moslem law countries and the highest mean among socialist and common law systems, which have virtually identical mean levels. Thus the significant mean differences occur between Moslem law systems and each of the other three types, with the only other significant difference between civil and socialist law systems. The import of these differences in level of education for knowledge of the law, compliance with the law, and the development of a "sense of justice" is probably considerable. Social science research on these questions is still in its infancy, though some notable progress has recently been made by Scandinavian sociologists and legal scholars.[22]

The third and last variable in Table 4 of significance for types of legal systems is the number of lawyers per 1,000 population. The highest mean occurs among common law systems and the lowest among Moslem law systems. And the significant differences in mean number of lawyers are between Moslem and civil law systems and between Moslem and common law systems. The fact that common law

TABLE 4. Comparison of Means on Three Variables for Selected Nations Differing in Type of Legal System

VARIABLE	MEAN FOR NATIONS WITH MOSLEM LAW	MEAN FOR NATIONS WITH CIVIL LAW	MEAN FOR NATIONS WITH SOCIALIST LAW	MEAN FOR NATIONS WITH COMMON LAW	t-TEST COMPARISON	D.F.	t-VALUE	SIGNIF-ICANCE LEVEL
Industrial-ization	24.86 (n = 6)	42.69 (n = 23)	46.33 (n = 2)	61.53 (n = 6)	Mos. vs. Civ.	12	3.46	.0046
					Mos. vs. Soc.	2	1.82	.2101
					Mos. vs. Comm.	8	3.48	.0083
					Civ. vs. Soc.	1	.32	.8030
					Civ. vs. Comm.	6	1.87	.1111
					Soc. vs. Comm.	5	1.04	.3467
Level of Education	28.53 (n = 11)	57.24 (n = 30)	69.87 (n = 8)	68.13 (n = 10)	Mos. vs. Civ.	22	4.68	.0001
					Mos. vs. Soc.	16	7.11	.0000
					Mos. vs. Comm.	16	4.07	.0008
					Civ. vs. Soc.	32	2.82	.0082
					Civ. vs. Comm.	13	1.21	.2474
					Soc. vs. Comm.	12	.20	.8460
Lawyers per 1,000 popula-tion	.18 (n = 12)	.44 (n = 29)	.38 (n = 7)	.57 (n = 10)	Mos. vs. Civ.	29	3.03	.0051
					Mos. vs. Soc.	13	1.72	.1082
					Mos. vs. Comm.	13	2.35	.0352
					Civ. vs. Soc.	12	.52	.6115
					Civ. vs. Comm.	12	.81	.4336
					Soc. vs. Comm.	16	1.05	.3101

and civil law systems have a higher mean number of lawyers than Moslem of socialist law systems suggests a correspondingly higher degree of reliance on legal institutions as mechanisms for resolving conflicts. More problems are probably perceived within these legal systems as likely candidates for judicial decision making for which the availability of an adequate supply of lawyers is necessary. How different legal systems are in their institutionalized use of legal mechanisms for conflict resolution and the sources of these differences are additional frontier problems for a comparative sociology of law.

Some Unsolved Problems

Our exploratory analysis of a small body of data may have demonstrated the heuristic value of a data archive of legal systems by identifying some relationships as well as some unsolved problems. Among the unsolved problems pertaining to the development of such an archive, at least three bear mentioning. The first is the general question of the nature of a "legal variable." More particularly, how do we conceptualize the content of legal norms, legal roles and organizational structures of the legal system to make cross-national research possible? The second problem is how do we gather data on legal systems which are currently not routinely collected by either governments or international organizations? The use of mail questionnaires to special informants is one promising technique.[23] The organization of world-wide teams of legal scholars and sociologists is another. To further complicate the data-gathering problems is the need to develop time series if we are to make any progress in testing propositions about sources of structural change in legal and non-legal sub-systems of society.

A third unsolved problem is the relevance of some organizational mechanism for accelerating progress in developing a data archive of legal system. The fact that there is a growing interest in developing a variety of data archives in social science[24] may well reduce the magnitude of the burden of developing a data archive of legal systems.

Conclusion

Mapping the legal systems of the world is a mammoth undertaking that will require the collaboration of sociologists and legal scholars in various countries for many years to come. Such an effort is not unrelated to the extensive work for many years of comparative legal scholars and others to internationalize and unify legal rules and thus contribute to the "common core of legal systems."[25] The very co-operation entailed in implementing the proposal to develop a data archive of legal system would contribute to the growth of a "global sociology."[26] The intellectual challenge is indeed worthy of the members of the relatively new but fast-growing field of the sociology of law and of the relatively old and well-established field of comparative law.

Notes

1. Mark R. Joelson, Legal Problems in the Dismissal of Civil Servants in the U.S., Britain and France, *American Journal of Comparative Law*, XII (1963), 147–171.
2. John Henry Wigmore, *A Panorama of the World's Legal Systems* (St. Paul, Minnesota, West Publishing Company, 1928), 3 vols.
3. René David, *Les grands systèmes de droit contemporains* (Paris, Dalloz, 1964).
4. O. Kahn-Freund, Comparative Law as an Academic Subject, *Law Quarterly Review*, LXXXII (1966), p. 40.
5. E. Adamson Hoebel, *The Law of Primitive Man* (Cambridge, Harvard University Press, 1954).
6. Arnold M. Rose, *Theory and Method in the Social Sciences* (Minneapolis, University of Minnesota Press, 1954), pp. 72–115; On Individualism and Social Responsibility, *European Journal of Sociology* II (1961), 163–169.
7. R. W. Rabinowitz, The Historical Development of the Japanese Bar, *Harvard Law Review*, LXX (1956), 61–81.
8. Kahn-Freund, *op. cit.* p. 45.
9. Cf. William M. Evan, Toward a Sociological Almanac of Legal Systems, *International Social Science Journal*, XVII (1965), 335–338.
10. *Ibid.* p. 336.
11. Raymond A. Bauer (ed.), *Social Indicators* (Cambridge, M.I.T. Press, 1966).
12. Cf. William M. Evan, Due Process of Law in Military and Industrial Organizations, *Administrative Science Quarterly*, VII (1962), pp. 203–207.
13. Cf. Arthur S. Banks and Robert B. Textor, *A Cross-Polity Survey* (Cambridge, M.I.T. Press, 1963), pp. 114–115.
14. Cf. Marc Ancel, Observations on the International Comparison of Criminal Statistics, *International Review of Criminal Policy*, I (1952), 41–48; U.N. Economic and Social Council, Report by the Secretariat, *Criminal Statistics: Standard Classification of Offenses*, E/CN 5/357, March 1959 (Mimeo).
15. Evan, Toward a Sociological Almanac of Legal Systems, *op. cit.* pp. 337–338.
16. Cf. World Peace Through Law Center, *Law and Judicial Systems of Nations* (Washington, World Peace Through Law Center, 1965).
17. See, for example, David, *op. cit.*
18. Bruce M. Russett, *et al.*, *World Handbook of Political and Social Indicators* (New Haven, Yale University Press, 1964); Karl W. Deutsch, Harold D. Lasswell, Richard L. Merritt, and Bruce M. Russett, The Yale Political Data Program, *in* Richard L. Merritt and Stein Rokkan, (eds.), *Comparing Na-*

tions: The Use of Quantitative Data in Cross-National Research (New Haven, Yale University Press, 1966), pp. 81–94.

19. Stuart S. Nagel, Culture Patterns and Judicial Systems, *Vanderbilt Law Review*, XVI (1962), pp. 151–152.

20. Banks and Textor, *op. cit.*

21. Cf. William M. Evan, Introduction: Some Approaches to the Sociology of Law, in William M. Evan (ed.), *Law and Sociology: Exploratory Essays* (New York, The Free Press of Glencoe, 1962), pp. 1–11.

22. Berl Kutschinsky, Law and Education: Some Aspects of Scandinavian Studies into "The General Sense of Justice", *Acta Sociologica*, X (1966), 21–41; Klaus Makela, Public Sense of Justice and Judicial Practice, *Acta Sociologica*, X (1966), 42–67.

23. Cf. William A. Glaser, International Mail Surveys of Informants, *Human Organization*, XXV (1966), 78–86.

24. Cf. Stein Rokkan, *Comparative Cross-National Research: The Context of Currents Efforts;* Merritt and Rokkan, *op. cit.* pp. 3–25; Ralph L. Bisco, Social Science Data Archives, *American Political Science Review*, LX (1966), 93–109; William A. Glaser and Ralph L. Bisco, Plans of the Council of Social Science Data Archives, *Social Science Information*, V (1966), 71–96; David Nasatir, Social Science Data Libraries, *American Sociologist*, II (1967), 207–12.

25. Cf. Rudolf B. Schlesinger, The Common Core of Legal Systems: An Emergent Subject of Comparative Study, *in* Kurt H. Nadelman, Arthur T. von Mehren and John N. Hazard (eds.), *XXth Century Comparative and Conflicts Law: Legal Essays in Honor of Hessel E. Yntema* (Leyden, A. W. Sythoff, 1961), pp. 65–79.

26. Cf. Wilbert E. Moore, Global Sociology: The World as a Singular System, *American Journal of Sociology*, LXXI (1966), 475–482.

APPENDIX IV:

LEGAL DOCUMENTS

Interinstitutional Relationships

A. *School District of Abington Township, Pa.* v. *Schempp et al.* (1963)
B. *Cleveland* v. *United States* (1946)

Evolution of Law and the Transformation of Social Systems

C. An Act to Restrain People from Labor on the First Day of the Week (1705)
D. Sunday Trading (1973)
E. *Bradwell* v. *State* (1873)
F. *Frontiero* v. *Richardson* (1972)

Introduction

As a generalized mechanism of social control, law interacts with each of the other social institutions or subsystems of a society. This interinstitutional function of law, as is evident from the readings in Part VI, is manifested in a variety of respects depending upon the configuration of social institutions in a society.

The United States, unlike some other societies, has a substantial separation of church and state, enshrined in the First Amendment. This was the rationale for the Supreme Court's decision in *School District of Abington Township, Pa.* v. *Schempp, et al.*, prohibiting reading of the Bible and recitation of the Lord's Prayer in the public schools. In this case, the law is regulating not only public school education but also the interplay of religious and educational institutions.

In *Cleveland* v. *United States*, the law, in exercising its control over a Fundamentalist Mormon sect that believes in and practices polygamy, is simultaneously protecting monogamy. Transporting a woman across state lines for the purpose of making her a plural

516

wife or cohabiting with her, although founded on religious belief, was deemed by the U.S. Supreme Court to be in violation of the Mann Act. In his dissenting opinion, Justice Murphy chastises the Court for its ethnocentric view of polygyny, a form of marriage involving multiple wives:

> We must recognize, then, that polygyny, like other forms of marriage, is basically a cultural institution rooted deeply in the religious beliefs and social mores of those societies in which it appears. It is equally true that the beliefs and mores of the dominant culture of the contemporary world condemn the practice as immoral and substitute monogamy in its place. To those beliefs and mores I subscribe, but that does not alter the fact that polygyny is a form of marriage built upon a set of social and moral principles. It must be recognized and treated as such.
>
> The Court states that polygamy is "a notorious example of promiscuity." The important fact, however, is that, despite the differences that may exist between polygamy and monogamy, such differences do not place polygamy in the same category as prostitution or debauchery. When we use those terms we are speaking of acts of an entirely different nature, having no relation whatever to the various forms of marriage. . . .
>
> The Court's failure to recognize this vital distinction and its insistence that polygyny is "in the same genus" as prostitution and debauchery do violence to the anthropological factors involved.

If Justice Murphy had succeeded in persuading a majority of his colleagues on the Supreme Court, what impact do you suppose this case would have had on the Fundamentalist Mormon sect, in particular, and on family institutions in the United States in general?

The last four documents in this Appendix illustrate a complex relationship between law and society that is still poorly understoood, namely, how laws undergo change over an extended period of time and how such change relates to ongoing societal change. Do laws change in reaction to the transformations in one or another of the social institutions constituting a society? Do they change as a means of transforming one or another social institution? Or is there an interaction over time between these two opposite mechanisms of societal transformation?

The two statutes on the Sunday "blue laws" in Pennsylvania, spanning 268 years, may be interpreted as reflecting a process of secularization of American society from the colonial period to the present. The very titles of the two statutes reflect this change. In 1705, when church and state were fused, even in Pennsylvania, which prided itself on its religious liberty, the title of the Sunday law read "An Act to Restrain People From Labor on the First Day of the Week." In 1973, on the other hand, the comparable Pennsylvania statute is entitled "Sunday Trading." The religious purpose of the act in the colonial period was explicitly stated:

> To the end that all people within this province may with the greater freedom devote themselves to religious and pious exercises . . . all people shall abstain from toil and labor, that . . . they may the better dispose themselves to read and hear the Holy Scriptures of truth at home, and frequent such meetings of religious worship abroad, as may best suit their respective persuasions.

The 1973 statute omits any reference to an objective; it merely enumerates those types of employment and business activities that are prohibited and those that are not. Both statutes specify sanctions in event of violation of the statute. In the colonial era, at least in Pennsylvania, violating the Sunday laws was evidently a misdemeanor punishable by a fine: "for every offense forfeit the sum of twenty shillings" after being "prosecuted within ten days after the offense [is] committed." By contrast, desecration of the Sabbath in Virginia and Massachusetts in the seventeenth century was much more severely punished; and it was a capital offense if the sin were committed three times in Virginia and if it were committed "proudly, presumptuously and with a high hand" in Massachusetts (Blakely and Colcord, 1970: 33–37). In the 1973 Pennsylvania statute, violating any of the enumerated prohibitions on Sunday is defined as a "summary offense." Without systematic research into legal history it is not possible to ascertain what specific mechanisms intervened during the 268 years to account for the overall secularization reflected in these two statutes.*

Another dramatic change in the law is reflected in the two U.S. Supreme Court decisions reproduced in Appendixes IV–E and IV–F. In *Bradwell* v. *State*, a case decided in 1872, a lawyer was denied admission to the bar on the grounds of her sex and her marital status. The Supreme Court of Illinois claimed that, as a married woman, Mrs. Bradwell could not enter into any binding contract with her clients without the consent of her husband. In interpreting the statute on qualifications for admission to the bar, the Illinois Court asserted that

> . . . God designed the sexes to occupy different spheres of action, and that it belonged to men to make, apply, and execute the laws, was regarded as an almost axiomatic truth.

---

* An even higher level of secularization was reached in 1978 when the Supreme Court of Pennsylvania struck down all of the state's "blue laws" as violating the equal protection guarantees of the Pennsylvania Constitution in *The Kroger Co.* v. *O'Hara Township, McCandless Township, et al.*, 481, Pa. 101 392 A. 2d 266 (filed October 5, 1978).

In view of these facts, we are certainly warranted in saying that when the legislature gave to this court the power of granting licenses to practice law, it was with not the slightest expectation that this privilege would be extended to women.

The U.S. Supreme Court affirmed the decision of the Illinois Court that the provisions of the statute on the qualifications for admission to the bar did not violate the Fourteenth Amendment. Justice Bradley, concurring with the opinion of the court, articulated his belief in the differences between the sexes:

. . . [C]ivil law, as well as nature herself, has always recognized a wide difference in the respective spheres and destinies of man and woman. Man is, or should be, woman's protector and defender. The natural and proper timidity and delicacy which belongs to the female sex evidently unfits it for many of the occupations of civil life. The constitution of the family organization, which is founded in the divine ordinance, as well as in the nature of things, indicates the domestic sphere as that which properly belongs to the domain and functions of womanhood. The harmony, not to say identity, of interests and views which belong, or should belong, to the family institution is repugnant to the idea of a woman adopting a distinct and independent career from that of her husband. So firmly fixed was this sentiment in the founders of the common law that it became a maxim of that system of jurisprudence that a woman had no legal existence separate from her husband, who was regarded as her head and representative in the social state.

A century later in *Frontiero* v. *Richardson* the Court reflected a quite different conception of the status of women, concluding that any statutory distinctions based on sex are "inherently suspect, and must . . . be subjected to strict judicial scrutiny." Frontiero, a servicewoman in the Air Force, applied for increased benefits for her husband as a "dependent," as provided in a relevant Federal statute. Her application was denied because she failed to demonstrate that her husband was a dependent. Contending that the statute in question discriminated against servicewomen in that a serviceman would not have had to demonstrate the dependence of his wife to obtain increased benefits, Frontiero appealed the decision of the U.S. District Court to the Supreme Court on the ground that the statute violated the Due Process Clause of the Fifth Amendment. Justice Brennan, in the Court's opinion, agreed that the statute was discriminatory and reversed the District Court's decision. In justifying his decision, Justice Brennan tellingly observed:

[O]ur statute books gradually became laden with gross, stereotyped distinctions between the sexes and, indeed, throughout much of the 19th century the position of women in our society was, in many respects, comparable to that of blacks under the pre-Civil War slave codes. Neither slaves nor women could hold office, serve on juries, or bring suit in their own names, and married women traditionally were denied the legal capacity to hold or convey property or to serve as legal guardians of their own children. . . . And although blacks were guaranteed the right to vote in 1870, women were denied even that right—which is itself "preservative of other basic civil and political rights"—until adoption of the Nineteenth Amendment half a century later.

In the century intervening between *Bradwell* v. *State* and *Frontiero* v. *Richardson*, the status of women in the family and in society as a whole has undergone significant changes. Apart from being granted suffrage, women in increasing proportions have been admitted to the labor force, to institutions of higher learning, and to the professions. In addition, systematic patterns of sex discrimination in employment and in other social roles have been declared illegal, as the documents in Appendix II make plain. Again, a sociologically informed legal historian would seek to explain why, as late as the nineteenth century, the law assigned virtually chattel status to women and why the movement for equal citizenship status has gained momentum in the twentieth century.

Reference

Blakely, W. A. and W. A. Colcord, eds. (1970). *American State Papers Bearing on Sunday Legislation.* New York: Da Capo Press.

Interinstitutional Relationships

A—*School District of Abington Township,
Pa.* v. *Schempp et al.* 374 U.S. 203 (1963)

Mr. Justice CLARK delivered the opinion of the Court.

Once again we are called upon to consider the scope of the provision of the First Amendment to the United States Constitution which declares that "Congress shall make no law respecting an establishment of religion, or prohibiting the free exercise thereof * * *." These companion cases present the issues in the context of state action requiring that schools begin each day with readings from the Bible. While raising the basic questions under slightly different factual situations, the cases permit of joint treatment. In light of the history of the First Amendment and of our cases interpreting and applying its requirements, we hold that the practices at issue and the laws requiring them are unconstitutional under the Establishment Clause, as applied to the States through the Fourteenth Amendment.

I

The Facts in Each Case

No. 142. The Commonwealth of Pennsylvania by law, 24 Pa.Stat. § 15–1516, as amended, Pub.Law 1928 (Supp.1960) Dec. 17, 1959, requires that "At least ten verses from the Holy Bible shall be read, without comment, at the opening of each public school on each school day. Any child shall be excused from such Bible reading, or attending such Bible reading, upon the written request of his parent or guardian." The Schempp family, husband and wife and two of their three children, brought suit to enjoin enforcement of the statute, contending that their rights under the Fourteenth Amendment to the Constitution of the United States are, have been, and will continue to be violated unless this statute be declared unconstitutional as violative of these provisions of the First Amendment. They sought to enjoin the appellant school district, wherein the Schempp children attend school, and its officers and the Superintendent of Public Instruction of the Commonwealth from continuing to conduct such readings and recitation of the Lord's Prayer in the public schools of the district pursuant to the statute. A three-judge statutory District Court for the Eastern District of Pennsylvania held that the statute is violative of the Establishment Clause of the First Amendment as applied to the States by the Due Process Clause of the Fourteenth Amendment and directed that appropriate injunctive relief issue. D.C., 201 F.Supp. 815. On appeal by the District, its officials and the Superintendent, under 28 U.S.C. § 1253, we noted probable jurisdiction. 371 U.S. 807, 83 S.Ct. 25, 9 L.Ed.2d 52.

The appellees Edward Lewis Schempp, his wife Sidney, and their children, Roger and Donna, are of the Unitarian faith and are members of the Unitarian Church in Germantown, Philadelphia, Pennsylvania, where they, as well as another son, Ellory, regularly attend religious services. The latter was originally a party but having graduated from the school system *pendente lite* was voluntarily dismissed from the action. The other children attend the Abington Senior High School, which is a public school operated by appellant district.

On each school day at the Abington Senior High School between 8:15 and 8:30 a.m., while the pupils are attending their home rooms or advisory sections, opening exercises are conducted pursuant to the statute. The exercises are broadcast into each room in the school building through an intercommunications system and are conducted under the supervision of a teacher by students attending the school's radio and television workshop. Selected students from this course gather each morning in the school's workshop studio for the exercises, which include readings by one of the students of 10 verses of the Holy Bible, broadcast to each room in the building. This is followed by the recitation of the Lord's Prayer, likewise over the intercommunications system, but also by the students in the various classrooms, who are asked to stand and join in repeating the prayer in unison. The exercises are closed with the flag salute and such pertinent announcements as are of interest to the students. Participation in the opening exercises, as directed by the statute, is voluntary. The student reading the verses from the Bible may select the passages and read from any version he chooses, although the only copies furnished by the school are the King James version, copies of which were circulated to each teacher by the school district. During the period in which the exercises have been conducted the King James, the Douay and the Revised Standard versions of the Bible have been used, as well as the Jewish Holy Scriptures. There are no prefatory statements, no questions asked or solicited, no comments or explanations made and no interpretations given at or during the exercises. The students and parents are advised that the student may absent himself from the classroom or, should he elect to remain, not participate in the exercises. . . .

The trial court, in striking down the practices and the statute requiring them, made specific findings of fact that the children's attendance at Abington Senior High School is compulsory and that the practice of reading 10 verses from the Bible is also compelled by law. It also found that:

The reading of the verses, even without comment, possesses a devotional and religious character and constitutes in effect a religious observance. The devotional and religious nature of the morning exercises is made all the more apparent by the fact that the Bible reading is followed immediately by a recital in unison by the pupils of the Lord's Prayer. The fact that some pupils, or theoretically all pupils, might be excused from attendance at the exercises does not mitigate the obligatory nature of the ceremony for * * * Section 1516 * * * unequivocally requires the exercises to be held every school day in every school in the Commonwealth. The exercises are held in the school buildings and perforce are conducted by and under the authority of the local school authorities and during school sessions. Since the statute requires the reading of the "Holy Bible," a Christian document, the practice * * * prefers the Christian religion. The record demonstrates that it was the intention of * * * the Commonwealth * * * to introduce a religious ceremony into the public schools of the Commonwealth [201 F.Supp., at 819].

No. 119. In 1905 the Board of School Commissioners of Baltimore City adopted a rule pursuant to Art. 77, § 202 of the Annotated Code of Maryland.

The rule provided for the holding of opening exercises in the schools of the city, consisting primarily of the "reading, without comment, of a chapter in the Holy Bible and/or the use of the Lord's Prayer." The petitioners, Mrs. Madalyn Murray and her son, William J. Murray III, are both professed atheists. Following unsuccessful attempts to have the respondent school board rescind the rule, this suit was filed for mandamus to compel its rescission and cancellation. It was alleged that William was a student in a public school of the city and Mrs. Murray, his mother, was a taxpayer therein; that it was the practice under the rule to have a reading on each school morning from the King James version of the Bible; that at petitioners' insistence the rule was amended to permit children to be excused from the exercise on request of the parent and that William had been excused pursuant thereto; that nevertheless the rule as amended was in violation of the petitioners' rights "to freedom of religion under the First and Fourteenth Amendments" and in violation of "the principle of separation between church and state, contained therein. * * *" The petition particularized the petitioners' atheistic beliefs and stated that the rule, as practiced, violated their rights

in that it threatens their religious liberty by placing a premium on belief as against non-belief and subjects their freedom of conscience to the rule of the majority; it pronounces belief in God as the source of all moral and spiritual values, equating these values with religious values, and thereby renders sinister, alien and suspect the beliefs and ideals of your Petitioners, promoting doubt and question of their morality, good citizenship and good faith.

The respondents demurred and the trial court, recognizing that the demurrer admitted all facts well pleaded, sustained it without leave to amend. The Maryland Court of Appeals affirmed, the majority of four justices holding the exercise not in violation of the First and Fourteenth Amendments, with three justices dissenting. 228 Md. 239, 179 A.2d 698. We granted certiorari. 371 U.S. 809, 83 S.Ct. 21, 9 L.Ed.2d 52. . . .

III

Almost a hundred years ago in Minor v. Board of Education of Cincinnati, Judge Alphonso Taft, father of the revered Chief Justice, in an unpublished opinion stated the ideal of our people as to religious freedom as one of absolute equality before the law, of all religious opinions and sects * * *.

The government is neutral, and, while protecting all, it prefers none, and it *disparages* none. . . .

V

The wholesome "neutrality" of which this Court's cases speak . . . stems from a recognition of the teachings of history that powerful sects or groups might bring about a fusion of governmental and religious functions or a concert or dependency of one upon the other to the end that official support of the State or Federal Government would be placed behind the tenets of one or of all orthodoxies. This the Establishment Clause prohibits. And a further reason for neutrality is found in the Free Exercise Clause, which recognizes the value of religious training, teaching and observance and, more particularly, the right of every person to freely choose his own course with reference thereto, free of any compulsion from the state. This the Free Exercise Clause guarantees. Thus, as we have seen, the two clauses may overlap. As we have indicated, the Establishment Clause has been directly considered by this Court eight times in the past score of years and, with only one Justice dissenting on the point, it has consistently held that the clause withdrew all legislative power respecting religious belief or the expression thereof. The test may be stated as follows: what are the purpose and the primary effect of the enactment? If either is the advancement or inhibition of religion then the enactment exceeds the scope of legislative power as circumscribed by the Constitution. That is to say that to withstand the strictures of the Establishment Clause there must be a secular legislative purpose and a primary effect that neither advances nor inhibits religion. . . . The Free Exercise Clause, likewise considered many times here, withdraws from legislative power, state and federal, the exertion of any restraint on the free exercise of religion. Its purpose is to secure religious liberty in the individual by prohibiting any invasions thereof by civil authority. Hence it is necessary in a free exercise case for one to show the coercive effect of the enactment as it operates against him in the practice of his religion. The distinction between the two clauses is apparent—a violation of the Free Exercise Clause is predicated on coercion while the Establishment Clause violation need not be so attended.

Applying the Establishment Clause principles to the cases at bar we find that the States are requiring the selection and reading at the opening of the school day of verses from the Holy Bible and the recitation of the Lord's Prayer by the students in unison. These exercises are prescribed as part of the curricular activities of students who are required by law to attend school. They are held in the school buildings under the supervision and with the participation of teachers employed in those schools. None of these factors, other than compulsory school attendance, was present in the program upheld in Zorach v. Clauson. The trial court in No. 142 has found that such an opening exercise is a religious ceremony and was intended by the State to be so. We agree with the trial court's finding as to the religious character of the exercises. Given that finding, the exercises and the law requiring them are in violation of the Establishment Clause.

There is no such specific finding as to the religious character of the exercises in No. 119, and the State contends (as does the State in No. 142) that the program is an effort to extend its benefits to all public school children without regard to their religious belief. Included within its secular purposes, it says, are the promotion of moral values, the contradiction to the materialistic trends of our times, the perpetuation of our institutions and the teaching of literature. The case came up on demurer, of course, to a petition which alleged that the uniform practice under the rule had been to read from the King James version of the Bible and that the exercise was sectarian. The short answer, therefore, is that the religious character of the exercise was admitted by the State. But even if its purpose is not strictly religious, it is sought to be accomplished through readings, without comment, from the Bible. Surely the place of the Bible as an instrument of religion cannot be gainsaid, and the State's recognition of the pervading religious character of the ceremony is evident from the rule's specific permission of the alternative use of the Catholic Douay version as well as the recent amendment permitting nonattendance at the exercises. None of these factors is consistent with the contention that the Bible is here used either as an instrument for nonreligious moral inspiration or as a reference for the teaching of secular subjects.

The conclusion follows that in both cases the laws require religious exercises and such exercises are being conducted in direct violation of the rights of the appellees and petitioners. Nor are these required exercises mitigated by the fact that individual students may absent themselves upon parental request, for that fact furnishes no defense to a claim of unconstitutionality under the Establishment Clause. . . . Further, it is no defense to urge that the religious practices here may be relatively minor encroachments on the First Amendment. The breach of neutrality that is today a trickling stream may all too soon become a raging torrent and, in the words of Madison, "it is proper to take alarm at the first experiment on our liberties." . . .

It is insisted that unless these religious exercises are permitted a "religion of secularism" is established in the schools. We agree of course that the State may not establish a "religion of secularism" in the sense of affirmatively opposing or showing hostility to religion, thus "preferring those who believe in no religion over those who do believe." . . . We do not agree, however, that this decision in any sense has that effect. In addition, it might well be said that one's education is not complete without a study of comparative religion or the history of religion and its relationship to the advancement of civilization. It certainly may be said that the Bible is worthy of study for its literary and historic qualities. Nothing we have said here indicates that such study of the Bible or of religion, when presented objectively as part of a secular program of education, may not be effected consistently with the First Amendment. But the exercises here do not fall into those categories. They are religious exercises, required by the States in violation of the command of the First Amendment that the Government maintain strict neutrality, neither aiding nor opposing religion.

Finally, we cannot accept that the concept of neutrality, which does not permit a State to require a religious exercise even with the consent of the majority of those affected, collides with the majority's right to free exercise of religion. While the Free Exercise Clause clearly prohibits the use of state action to deny the rights of free exercise to *anyone*, it has never meant that a majority could use the machinery of the State to practice its beliefs. Such a contention was effectively answered by Mr. Justice Jackson for the Court in *West Virginia Board of Education* v. *Barnette*, 319 U.S. 624, 638, 63 S.Ct. 1178, 1185, 87 L.Ed. 1628 (1943):

The very purpose of a Bill of Rights was to withdraw certain subjects from the vicissitudes of political controversy, to place them beyond the reach of majorities and officials and to establish them as legal principles to be applied by the courts. One's right to * * * freedom of worship * * * and other fundamental rights may not be submitted to vote; they depend on the outcome of no elections.

The place of religion in our society is an exalted one, achieved through a long tradition of reliance on the home, the church and the inviolable citadel of the individual heart and mind. We have come to recognize through bitter experience that it is not within the power of government to invade that citadel, whether its purpose or effect be to aid or oppose, to advance or retard. In the relationship between man and religion, the State is firmly committed to a position of neutrality. Though the application of that rule requires interpretation of a delicate sort, the rule itself is clearly and concisely stated in the words of the First Amendment. Applying that rule to the facts of these cases, we affirm the judgment in No. 142.

In No. 119, the judgment is reversed and the cause remanded to the Maryland Court of Appeals for further proceedings consistent with this opinion.

It is so ordered.

Judgment in No. 142 affirmed; judgment in No. 119 reversed and cause remanded with directions.

B—*Cleveland* v. *United States*
329 U.S. 14 (1946)

Mr. Justice Douglas delivered the opinion of the Court.

Petitioners are members of a Mormon sect, known as Fundamentalists. They not only believe in polygamy; unlike other Mormons,[1] they practice it. Each of petitioners, except Stubbs, has, in addition to his lawful wife, one or more plural wives. Each transported at least one plural wife across state lines,[2] either for the purpose of cohabiting with her, or for the purpose of aiding another member of the cult in such a project. They were convicted of violating the Mann Act (36 Stat. 825, 18 U.S.C. § 398) on a trial to the court, a jury having been waived. 56 F. Supp. 890. The judgments of conviction were affirmed on appeal. 146 F. 2d 730. The cases are here on petitions for certiorari which we granted in view of the asserted conflict between the decision below and *Mortensen* v. *United States*, 322 U.S. 369.

The Act makes an offense the transportation in interstate commerce of "any woman or girl for the purpose of prostitution or debauchery, or for any other immoral purpose." The decision turns on the meaning of the latter phrase, "for any other immoral purpose."

United States v. *Bitty*, 208 U.S. 393, involved a prosecution under a federal statute making it a crime to import an alien woman "for the purpose of prostitution or for any other immoral purpose." The act was construed to cover a case where a man imported an alien woman so that she should live with him as his concubine. Two years later the Mann Act was passed. Because of the similarity of the language used in the two acts, the *Bitty* case became a forceful precedent for the construction of the Mann Act. Thus one who transported a woman in interstate commerce so that she should become his mistress or concubine was held to have transported her for an "immoral purpose" within the meaning of the Mann Act. *Caminetti* v. *United States*, 242 U.S. 470.

It is argued that the *Caminetti* decision gave too wide a sweep to the Act; that the Act was designed to cover only the white slave business and related vices; that it was not designed to cover voluntary actions bereft of sex commercialism; and that in any event it should not be construed to embrace polygamy which is a form of marriage and, unlike prostitution or debauchery or the concubinage involved in the *Caminetti* case, has as its object parenthood and the creation and maintenance of family life. In support of that interpretation an exhaustive legislative history is submitted which, it is said, gives no indication that the Act was aimed at polygamous practices.

While *Mortensen* v. *United States, supra*, p. 377, rightly indicated that the Act was aimed "primarily" at the use of interstate commerce for the conduct of the white slave business, we find no indication that a profit motive is a *sine qua non* to its application. Prostitution, to be sure, normally suggests sexual relations for hire. But debauchery has no such implied limitation. In common understanding the indulgence which that term suggests may be motivated solely by lust. And so we start with words which by their natural import embrace more than commercialized sex. What follows is "any other immoral purpose." Under the *ejusdem generis** rule of construction the general words are confined to the class and may not be used to enlarge it. But we could not give the words a faithful interpretation if we confined them more narrowly than the class of which they are a part.

That was the view taken by the Court in the *Bitty* and *Caminetti* cases. We do not stop to reexamine the *Caminetti* case to determine whether the Act was properly applied to the facts there presented. But we adhere to its holding, which has been in force for almost thirty years, that the Act, while primarily aimed at the use of interstate commerce for the purposes of commercialized sex, is not restricted to that end.

We conclude, moreover, that polygamous practices are not excluded from the Act. They have long been outlawed in our society. As stated in *Reynolds* v. *United States*, 98 U.S. 145, 164:

> Polygamy has always been odious among the northern and western nations of Europe, and, until the establishment of the Mormon Church, was almost exclusively a feature of the life of Asiatic and of African people. At common law, the second marriage was always void (2 Kent, Com. 79), and from the earliest history of England polygamy has been treated as an offence against society.

As subsequently stated in *Mormon Church* v. *United States*, 136 U.S. 1, 49, "The organization of a community for the spread and practice of polygamy is, in a measure, a return to barbarism. It is contrary to the spirit of Christianity and of the civilization which Christianity has produced in the Western world." And see *Davis* v. *Beason*, 133 U.S. 333. Polygamy is a practice with far more pervasive influences in society than the casual, isolated transgressions involved in the *Caminetti* case. The establishment or maintenance of polygamous households is a notorious example of promiscuity. The permanent advertisement of their existence is an example of the sharp repercussions which they have in the community. We could conclude that Congress excluded these practices from the Act only if it were clear that the Act is confined to commercialized sexual vice.

*Editor's note: Of the same kind, class, or nature.

Since we cannot say it is, we see no way by which the present transgressions can be excluded. These polygamous practices have long been branded as immoral in the law. Though they have different ramifications, they are in the same genus as the other immoral practices covered by the Act. . . .

Petitioners' second line of defense is that the requisite purpose was lacking. It is said that those petitioners who already had plural wives did not transport them in interstate commerce for an immoral purpose. The test laid down in the *Mortensen* case was whether the transportation was in fact "the use of interstate commerce as a calculated means for effectuating sexual immorality." 322 U.S. p. 375. There was evidence that this group of petitioners in order to cohabit with their plural wives found it necessary or convenient to transport them in interstate commerce and that the unlawful purpose was the dominant motive. In one case the woman was transported for the purpose of entering into a plural marriage. After a night with this petitioner she refused to continue the plural marriage relationship. But guilt under the Mann Act turns on the purpose which motivates the transportation, not on its accomplishment. . . .

It is also urged that the requisite criminal intent was lacking since petitioners were motivated by a religious belief. That defense claims too much. If upheld, it would place beyond the law any act done under claim of religious sanction. But it has long been held that the fact that polygamy is supported by a religious creed affords no defense in a prosecution for bigamy. *Reynolds* v. *United States*, *supra*. Whether an act is immoral within the meaning of the statute is not to be determined by the accused's concepts of morality. Congress has provided the standard. The offense is complete if the accused intended to perform, and did in fact perform, the act which the statute condemns, viz., the transportation of a woman for the purpose of making her his plural wife or cohabiting with her as such.

We have considered the remaining objections raised and find them without merit.

Affirmed.

Mr. Justice Murphy, dissenting.

Today another unfortunate chapter is added to the troubled history of the White Slave Traffic Act. It is a chapter written in terms that misapply the statutory language and that disregard the intention of the legislative framers. It results in the imprisonment of individuals whose actions have none of the earmarks of white slavery, whatever else may be said of their conduct. I am accordingly forced to dissent.

The statute in so many words refers to transportation of women and girls across state lines "for the purpose of prostitution or debauchery, or for any other immoral purpose." The issue here is whether the act of taking polygamous or plural wives across state lines, or taking girls across state borders for the purpose of entering into plural marriage, constitutes transportation "for any other immoral purpose" so as to come within the interdict of the statute.

The Court holds, and I agree, that under the *ejusdem generis* rule of statutory construction the phrase "any other immoral purpose" must be confined to the same class of unlawful sexual immoralities as that to which prostitution and debauchery belong. But I disagree with the conclusion that polygamy is "in the same genus" as prostitution and debauchery and hence within the phrase "any other immoral purpose" simply because it has sexual connotations and has "long been branded as immoral in the law" of this nation. Such reasoning ignores reality and results in an unfair application of the statutory words.

It is not my purpose to defend the practice of polygamy or to claim that it is morally the equivalent of monogamy. But it is essential to understand what it is, as well as what it is not. Only in that way can we intelligently decide whether it falls within the same genus as prostitution or debauchery.

There are four fundamental forms of marriage: (1) monogamy; (2) polygyny, or one man with several wives; (3) polyandry, or one woman with several husbands; and (4) group marriage. The term "polygamy" covers both polygyny and polyandry. Thus we are dealing here with polygyny, one of the basic forms of marriage. Historically, its use has far exceeded that of any other form. It was quite common among ancient civilizations and was referred to many times by the writers of the Old Testament; even today it is to be found frequently among certain pagan and non-Christian peoples of the world. We must recognize, then, that polygyny, like other forms of marriage, is basically a cultural institution rooted deeply in the religious beliefs and social mores of those societies in which it appears. It is equally true that the beliefs and mores of the dominant culture of the contemporary world condemn the practice as immoral and substitute monogamy in its place. To those beliefs and mores I subscribe, but that does not alter the fact that polygyny is a form of marriage built upon a set of social and moral principles. It must be recognized and treated as such.

The Court states that polygamy is "a notorious example of promiscuity." The important fact, however, is that, despite the differences that may exist between polygamy and monogamy, such differences do not place polygamy in the same category as prostitution or debauchery. When we use those terms we are speaking of acts of an entirely different nature, having no relation whatever to the various forms of marriage. It takes no elaboration here to point out that marriage, even when it occurs in a form of which we disapprove, is not to be compared with prostitution or debauchery or other immoralities of that character.

The Court's failure to recognize this vital distinction and its insistence that polygyny is "in the same genus" as prostitution and debauchery do violence to the anthropological factors involved. Even etymologically, the words "polygyny" and "polygamy" are quite distinct from "prostitution," "debauchery" and words of that ilk. There is thus no basis in fact for including polygyny within the phrase "any other immoral purpose" as used in this statute.

Notes

1. The Church of Jesus Christ of Latter-Day Saints has forbidden plural marriages since 1800. See *Toncray* v. *Budge*, 14 Ida. 621, 654–55, 95 P. 26.
2. Petitioners' activities extended into Arizona, California, Colorado, Idaho, Utah and Wyoming.

Evolution of Law and the Transformation of Social Systems

C—An Act to Restrain People from Labor on the First Day of the Week (1705)
Laws of Pennsylvania, 1700–1714, at 35

To the end that all people within this province may with the greater freedom devote themselves to religious and pious exercises, be it enacted, etc., that according to the example of the primitive Christians, and for the ease of the creation, every first day of the week, commonly called Sunday, all people shall abstain from toil and labor, that whether masters, parents, children, servants or others, they may the better dispose themselves to read and hear the Holy Scriptures of truth at home, and frequent such meetings of religious worship abroad, as may best suit their respective persuasions. And that no tradesman, artificer, workman, laborer, or other person whatsoever, shall do or exercise any worldly business or work of their ordinary callings, on the first day, or any part thereof (works of necessity and charity only excepted) upon pain that every person so offending shall for every offense forfeit the sum of twenty shillings. . . . Provided always, that nothing in this act contained shall extend to prohibit the dressing of victuals in families, cook shops or victualing-houses, or to watermen landing their passengers on the first day of the week, nor to butchers their killing and selling of meat, or fishermen from selling fish on the first day of the week in the fourth, fifth, and sixth months, called June, July, and August; nor to the crying of milk before nine of the clock in the morning, or after five in the afternoon. Provided also, that no person shall be impeached, presented or molested for any offense before mentioned in this act unless he, or they, be prosecuted for the same within ten days after the offense committed.

And be it further enacted, that all persons who are found drinking and tippling in ale-houses, taverns, or other public house or place on the first day of the week, commonly called Sunday, or any part thereof, shall for every offense forfeit and pay one shilling and sixpence to any constable that shall demand the same, to the use of the poor; and all constables are hereby empowered, and by virtue of their office, required to search public houses and places suspected to entertain such tipplers, and then, when found, quietly to disperse; but in case of refusal, to bring the persons so refusing before the next justice of the peace, who may commit such offenders to the stocks, and bind them to their good behaviour, as to him shall seem requisite.

D—Sunday Trading (1973)
18 *Consolidated Pennsylvania Statutes Annotated,* 7361

§7361. Worldly Employment or Business

(a) **Offense defined.**—A person is guilty of a summary offense if he does or performs any worldly employment or business whatsoever on Sunday (works of necessity, charity and wholesome recreation expected). Fines collected for violations of this section shall be for the use of the Commonwealth.

(b) **Exception.**—Subsection (a) of this section shall not prohibit:

(1) The dressing of victuals in private families, bake-houses, lodging-

houses, inns and other houses of entertainment for the use of sojourners, travellers or strangers.

(2) The sale of newspapers.

(3) Watermen from landing their passengers, or ferrymen from carrying over the water travellers.

(4) Work in connection with the rendering of service by a public utility as defined in the Public Utility Law.

(5) Persons removing with their families.

(6) The delivery of milk or the necessaries of life, before nine o'clock antemeridian, nor after five o'clock postmeridian.

(7) The production and performance of drama and civic light opera for an admission charge by nonprofit corporations in cities of the second class, between the hours of two o'clock postmeridian and 12 o'clock midnight.

(8) The conducting, staging, managing, operating, performing or engaging in basketball, ice shows and ice hockey for an admission charge in cities of the first and second class, between the hours of two o'clock postmeridian and 12 o'clock midnight.

(c) **Definition.**—As used in this section "wholesome recreation" means golf, tennis, boating, swimming, bowling, basketball, picnicking, shooting at inanimate targets and similar healthful or recreational exercises and activities.

§7362. Trading in Motor Vehicles and Trailers

(a) **Offense defined.**—A person is guilty of a summary offense if he engages in the business of buying, selling, exchanging, trading, or otherwise dealing in new or used motor vehicles or trailers, on Sunday.

(b) **Limitation of action.**—Information charging violations of this section may be brought within 72 hours after the commission of the alleged offense and not thereafter.

(c) **Repeated offense penalty.**—A person who commits a second or any subsequent offense within one year after conviction for the first offense, shall be sentenced to pay a fine not exceeding $200.

(d) **Definitions.**—As used in this section the following words and phrases shall have the meanings given to them in this subsection:

"Motor vehicle." Every self-propelled device in, upon or by which any person or property is or may be transported or drawn on a public highway.

"Trailer." Every vehicle, without motor power, designed to carry property or passengers or designed and used exclusively for living quarters wholly on its own structure, and to be drawn by a motor vehicle.

§7363. Selling Certain Personal Property

(a) **Offense defined.**—A person is guilty of a summary offense if he engages on Sunday in the business of selling, or sells or offers for sale, on such day, at retail, clothing and wearing apparel, clothing accessories, furniture, housewares, home, business or office furnishings, household, business or office appliances, hardware, tools, paints, building and lumber supply materials, jewelry, silverware, watches, clocks, luggage, musical instruments and recordings, or toys.

(b) **Separate offenses.**—Each separate sale or offer to sell shall constitute a separate offense.

(c) **Exceptions.**—

(1) Subsection (a) of this section shall not apply to novelties, souvenirs and antiques.

(2) No individual who by reason of his religious conviction observes a day other than Sunday as his day of rest and actually refrains from labor or secular business on that day shall be prohibited from selling on Sunday in a business establishment which is closed on such other day the articles specified in subsection (a) of this section.

(d) **Limitation of action.**—Information charging violations of this section shall be brought within 72 hours after the commission of the alleged offense and not thereafter.

(e) **Repeated offense penalty.**—A person who commits a second or any subsequent offense within one year after conviction for the first offense shall be sentenced to pay a fine of not exceeding $200.

(f) **Definitions.**—As used in this section the following words and phrases shall have the meanings given to them in this subsection:

"A day other than Sunday." Any consecutive 24 hour period.

"Antique." An item over 100 years old, or ethnographic objects made in traditional aboriginal styles and made at least 50 years prior to their sale.

§7364. Selling or Otherwise Dealing in Fresh Meats, Produce and Groceries

(a) **Offense defined.**—A person is guilty of a summary offense if he engages in the business of selling or otherwise dealing at retail in fresh meats, produce and groceries on Sunday.

(b) **Separate offenses.**—Each separate sale, or offer to sell, shall constitute a separate offense.

(c) **Exceptions.**—Subsection (a) of this section shall not apply to any retail establishment:

(1) employing less than ten persons;

(2) where fresh meats, produce and groceries are offered or sold by the proprietor or members of his immediate family; or

(3) where food is prepared on the premises for human consumption.

(d) **Limitation of action.**—Information charging violations of this section shall be brought within 72 hours after the commission of the alleged offense and not thereafter.

(e) **Repeated offense penalty.**—A person who commits a second or any subsequent offense within one year after conviction for the first offense shall be sentenced to pay a fine not exceeding $200.

E—*Bradwell* v. *State*
16 Wall, 130 (1873)

Case Reporter's Statement of the Case

Mrs. Myra Bradwell, residing in the State of Illinois, made application to the judges of the Supreme Court of that State for a license to practice law. She accompanied her petition with the usual certificate from an inferior court of her good character, and that on due examination she had been found to possess the requisite qualifications. Pending this application she also filed an affidavit, to the effect "that she was born in the State of Vermont; that she was (had been) a citizen of that State; that she is now a citizen of the United States, and has been for many years past a resident of the city of Chicago, in the State of Illinois." And with this affidavit she also filed a paper asserting that, under the foregoing facts, she was entitled to the license prayed for by virtue of the second section of the fourth article of the Constitution of the United States, and of the fourteenth article of amendment of that instrument.

The statute of Illinois on the subject of admissions to the bar, enacts that no person shall be permitted to practice as an attorney or counsellor-at-law, or to commence, conduct, or defend any action, suit, or plaint, in which he is not a party concerned, in any court of record within the State, either by using or subscribing his own name or the name of any other person, without having previously obtained a license for that purpose from some two of the justices of the Supreme Court, which license shall constitute the person receiving the same an attorney and counsellor-at-law, and shall authorize him to appear in all the courts of record within the State, and there to practice as an attorney and counsellor-at-law, according to the laws and customs thereof.

On Mrs. Bradwell's application first coming before the court, the license was refused, and it was stated as a sufficient reason that under the decisions of the Supreme Court of Illinois, the applicant—"as a married woman would be bound neither by her express contracts nor by those implied contracts which it is the policy of the law to create between attorney and client." After the announcement of this decision, Mrs. Bradwell, admitting that she was a married woman— though she expressed her belief that such fact did not appear in the record—filed a printed argument in which her right to admission, notwithstanding that fact, was earnestly and ably maintained. The court thereupon gave an opinion in writing. Extracts are here given:

> Our statute provides that no person shall be permitted to practice as an attorney or counsellor at law without having previously obtained a license for that purpose from two of the justices of the Supreme Court. By the second section of the act, it is provided that no person shall be entitled to receive a license until he shall have obtained a certificate from the court of some county of his good moral character, and this is the only express limitation upon the exercise of the power thus intrusted to this court. In all other respects it is left to our discretion to establish the rules by which admission to this office shall be determined. But this discretion is not an arbitrary one, and must be held subject to at least two limitations. One is, that the court should establish such terms of admission as will promote the proper administration of justice; the second, that it should not admit any persons or class of persons who are not intended by the legislature to be admitted, even though their exclusion is not expressly required by the statute.
>
> The substance of the last limitation is simply that this important trust reposed in us should be exercised in conformity with the designs of the power creating it.
>
> Whether, in the existing social relations between men and women, it would promote the proper administration of justice, and the general well-being of

society, to permit women to engage in the trial of cases at the bar, is a question opening a wide field of discussion, upon which it is not necessary for us to enter. It is sufficient to say that, in our opinion, the other implied limitation upon our power, to which we have above referred, must operate to prevent our admitting women to the office of attorney at law. If we were to admit them, we should be exercising the authority conferred upon us in a manner which, we are fully satisfied, was never contemplated by the legislature.

It is to be remembered that at the time this statute was enacted we had, by express provision, adopted the common law of England, and, with three exceptions, the statutes of that country passed prior to the fourth year of James the First, so far as they were applicable to our condition.

It is to be also remembered that female attorneys at law were unknown in England, and a proposition that a woman should enter the courts of Westminster Hall in the capacity, or as a barrister, would have created hardly less astonishment than one that she should ascend the bench of bishops, or be elected to a seat in the House of Commons.

It is to be further remembered, that when our act was passed, that school of reform which claims for women participation in the making and administering of the laws had not then arisen, or, if here and there a writer had advanced such theories, they were regarded rather as abstract speculations than as an actual basis for action.

That God designed the sexes to occupy different spheres of action, and that it belonged to men to make, apply, and execute the laws, was regarded as an almost axiomatic truth.

In view of these facts, we are certainly warranted in saying that when the legislature gave to this court the power of granting licenses to practice law, it was with not the slightest expectation that this privilege would be extended to women.

The court having thus denied the application, Mrs. Bradwell brought the case here. . . .

Mr. Justice MILLER delivered the opinion of the court.

The record in this case is not very perfect, but it may be fairly taken that the plaintiff asserted her right to a license on the grounds, among others, that she was a citizen of the United States, and that having been a citizen of Vermont at one time, she was, in the State of Illinois, entitled to any right granted to citizens of the latter State.

The court having overruled these claims of right founded in the clauses of the Federal Constitution before referred to, those propositions may be considered as properly before this court.

As regards the provision of the Constitution that citizens of each State shall be entitled to all the privileges and immunities of citizens in the several States, the plaintiff in her affidavit has stated very clearly a case to which it is inapplicable.

The protection designed by that clause, as has been repeatedly held, has no application to a citizen of the State whose laws are complained of. If the plaintiff was a citizen of the State of Illinois, that provision of the Constitution gave her no protection against its courts or its legislation.

The plaintiff seems to have seen this difficulty, and attempts to avoid it by stating that she was born in Vermont.

While she remained in Vermont that circumstance made her a citizen of that State. But she states, at the same time, that she is a citizen of the United States, and that she is now, and has been for many years past, a resident of Chicago, in the State of Illinois.

The fourteenth amendment declares that citizens of the United States are citizens of the State within which they reside; therefore the plaintiff was, at the time of making her application, a citizen of the United States and a citizen of the State of Illinois.

We do not here mean to say that there may not be a temporary residence in one State, with intent to return to another, which will not create citizenship in the former. But the plaintiff states nothing to take her case out of the definition of citizenship of a State as defined by the first section of the fourteenth amendment.

In regard to that amendment counsel for the plaintiff in this court truly says that there are certain privileges and immunities which belong to a citizen of the United States as such; otherwise it would be nonsense for the fourteenth amendment to prohibit a State from abridging them, and he proceeds to argue that admission to the bar of a State of a person who possesses the requisite learning and character is one of those which a State may not deny.

In this latter proposition we are not able to concur with counsel. We agree with him that there are privileges and immunities belonging to citizens of the United States, in that relation and character, and that it is these and these alone which a State is forbidden to abridge. But the right to admission to practice in the courts of a State is not one of them. This right in no sense depends on citizenship of the United States. It has not, as far as we know, ever been made in any State, or in any case, to depend on citizenship at all. Certainly many prominent and distinguished lawyers have been admitted to practice, both in the State and Federal courts, who were not citizens of the United States or of any State. But, on whatever basis this right may be placed, so far as it can have any relation to citizenship at all, it would seem that, as to the courts of a State, it would relate to citizenship of the State, and as to Federal courts, it would relate to citizenship of the United States. . . .

Mr. Justice BRADLEY:

I concur in the judgment of the court in this case, by which the judgment of the Supreme Court of Illinois is affirmed, but not for the reasons specified in the opinion just read. . . .

The claim that that, under the fourteenth amendment of the Constitution, which declares that no State shall make or enforce any law which shall abridge the privileges and immunities of citizens of the United States, the statute law of Illinois, or the common law prevailing in that State, can no longer be set up as a barrier against the right of females to pursue any lawful employment for a livelihood (the practice of law included), assumes that it is one of the privileges and immunities of women as citizens to engage in any and every profession, occupation, or employment in civil life.

It certainly cannot be affirmed, as an historical fact, that this has ever been established as one of the fundamental privileges and immunities of the sex. On the contrary, the civil law, as well as nature herself, has always recognized a wide difference in the respective spheres and destinies of man and woman. Man is, or should be, woman's protector and defender. The natural and proper timidity and delicacy which belongs to the female sex evidently unfits it for many of the occupations of civil life. The constitution of the family organization, which is founded in the divine ordinance, as well as in the nature of things, indicates the domestic sphere as that which properly belongs to the domain and functions of womanhood. The harmony, not to say identity, of interests and views which belong, or should belong, to the family institution is repugnant to the idea of a woman adopting a distinct and independent career from that of her husband. So firmly fixed was this sentiment in the founders of the common law that it became a maxim of that system of jurisprudence that a woman had no legal existence separate from her husband, who was regarded as her head and representative in the social state; and, notwithstanding some recent modifications of this civil status, many of the special rules of law flowing from and dependent upon this cardinal principle still exist in full force in most States. One of these is, that a married woman is incapable, without her husband's consent, of making contracts which shall be binding on her or him. This very incapacity was one circumstance which the Supreme Court of Illinois deemed important in rendering a married woman incompetent fully to perform the duties and trusts that belong to the office of an attorney and counsellor.

It is true that many women are unmarried and not affected by any of the duties, complications, and incapacities arising out of the married state, but these are exceptions to the general rule. The paramount destiny and mission of woman are to fulfil the noble and benign offices of wife and mother. This is the law of the Creator. And the rules of civil society must be adapted to the general constitution of things, and cannot be based upon exceptional cases.

The humane movements of modern society, which have for their object the multiplication of avenues for woman's advancement, and of occupations adapted to her condition and sex, have my heartiest concurrence. But I am not prepared to say that it is one of her fundamental rights and privileges to be admitted into every office and position, including those which require highly special qualifications and demanding special responsibilities. In the nature of things it is not every citizen of every age, sex, and condition that is qualified for every calling and position. It is the prerogative of the legislator to prescribe regulations founded on nature, reason, and experience for the due admission of qualified persons to professions and callings demanding special skill and confidence. This fairly belongs to the police power of the State; and, in my opinion, in view of the peculiar characteristics, destiny, and mission of woman, it is within the province of the legislature to ordain what offices, positions, and callings shall be filled and discharged by men, and shall receive the benefit of those energies and responsibilities, and that decision and firmness which are presumed to predominate in the sterner sex.

For these reasons I think that the laws of Illinois now complained of are not obnoxious to the charge of abridging any of the privileges and immunities of citizens of the United States. . . .

F—*Frontiero* v. *Richardson*
    676 U.S. (1972)

MR. JUSTICE BRENNAN announced the judgment of the Court and an opinion in which Mr. Justice Douglas, Mr. Justice White, and Mr. Justice Marshall join.

The question before us concerns the right of a female member of the uniformed services[1] to claim her spouse as a "dependent" for the purposes of obtaining increased quarters allowances and medical and dental benefits under 37 U.S.C. §§401, 403, and 10 U.S.C. §§1072, 1076, on an equal footing with male members. Under these statutes, a serviceman may claim his wife as a "dependent" without regard to whether she is in fact dependent upon him for any part of her support. 37 U.S.C. §401(1); 10 U.S.C. §1072(2)(A). A servicewoman, on the other hand, may not claim her husband as a "dependent" under these programs unless he is in fact dependent upon her for over one-half of his support. 37 U.S.C. §401; 10 U.S.C. §1072(2)(C). Thus, the question for decision is whether this difference in treatment constitutes an unconstitutional discrimination against servicewomen in violation of the Due Process Clause of the Fifth Amendment. A three-judge District Court for the Middle District of Alabama, one judge dissenting, rejected this contention and sustained the constitutionality of the provisions of the statutes making this distinction. 341 F. Supp. 201 (1972). We noted probable jurisdiction. 409 U.S. 840 (1972). We reverse.

I

In an effort to attract career personnel through reenlistment, Congress established, in 37 U.S.C. §401 *et seq.*, and 10 U.S.C. §1071 *et seq.*, a scheme for the provision of fringe benefits to members of the uniformed services on a competitive basis with business and industry. Thus, under 37 U.S.C. §403, a member of the uniformed services with dependents is entitled to an increased "basic allowance for quarters" and, under 10 U.S.C. §1076, a member's dependents are provided comprehensive medical and dental care.

Appellant Sharron Frontiero, a lieutenant in the United States Air Force, sought increased quarters allowances, and housing and medical benefits for her husband, appellant Joseph Frontiero, on the ground that he was her "dependent." Although such benefits would automatically have been granted with respect to the wife of a male member of the uniformed services, appellant's application was denied because she failed to demonstrate that her husband was dependent on her for more than one-half of his support.[2] Appellants then commenced this suit, contending that, by making this distinction, the statutes unreasonably discriminate on the basis of sex in violation of the Due Process Clause of the Fifth Amendment.[3] In essence, appellants asserted that the discriminatory impact of the statutes is twofold: first, as a procedural matter, a female member is required to demonstrate her spouse's dependency, while no such burden is imposed upon male members; and, second, as a substantive matter, a male member who does not provide more than one-half of his wife's support receives benefits, while a similarly situated female member is denied such benefits. Appellants therefore sought a permanent injunction against the continued enforcement of these statutes and an order directing the appellees to provide Lieutenant Frontiero with the same housing and medical benefits that a similarly situated male member would receive.

Although the legislative history of these statutes sheds virtually no light on the purposes underlying the differential treatment accorded male and female members, a majority of the three-judge District Court surmised that Congress might reasonably have concluded that, since the husband in our society is generally the

"breadwinner" in the family—and the wife typically the "dependent" partner—
"it would be more economical to require married female members claiming
husbands to prove actual dependency than to extend the presumption of dependency to such members." 341 F. Supp., at 207. Indeed, given the fact that approximately 99% of all members of the uniformed services are male, the District
Court speculated that such differential treatment might conceivably lead to a
"considerable saving of administrative expense and manpower."

II

At the outset, appellants contend that classifications based upon sex, like classifications based upon race, alienage, and national origin, are inherently suspect
and must therefore be subjected to close judicial scrutiny. We agree. . . .

There can be no doubt that our Nation has had a long and unfortunate history
of sex discrimination.[4] Traditionally, such discrimination was rationalized by an
attitude of "romantic paternalism" which, in practical effect, put women, not
on a pedestal, but in a cage. . . .

As a result . . . our statute books gradually became laden with gross, stereotyped distinctions between the sexes and, indeed, throughout much of the 19th
century the position of women in our society was, in many respects, comparable
to that of blacks under the pre-Civil War slave codes. Neither slaves nor women
could hold office, serve on juries, or bring suit in their own names, and married
women traditionally were denied the legal capacity to hold or convey property
or to serve as legal guardians of their own children. . . . And although blacks
were guaranteed the right to vote in 1870, women were denied even that right—
which is itself "preservative of other basic civil and political rights"—until adoption of the Nineteenth Amendment half a century later.

It is true, of course, that the position of women in America has improved
markedly in recent decades.

Nevertheless, it can hardly be doubted that, in part because of the high visibil-
ity of the sex characteristic, women still face pervasive, although at times more
subtle, discrimination in our educational institutions, in the job market and, perhaps most conspicuously, the the political arena.[5] . . .

Moreover, since sex, like race and national origin, is an immutable characteristic determined solely by the accident of birth, the imposition of special disabilities upon the members of a particular sex because of their sex would seem to
violate "the basic concept of our system that legal burdens should bear some
relationship to individual responsibility. . . ." Weber v. Aetna Casualty & Surety
Co., 406 U.S. 164, 175 (1972). And what differentiates sex from such nonsus-
pect statuses as intelligence or physical disability, and aligns it with the recognized suspect criteria, is that the sex characteristic frequently bears no relation
to ability to perform or contribute to society. As a result, statutory distinctions
between the sexes often have the effect of invidiously relegating the entire class
of females to inferior legal status without regard to the actual capabilities of its
individual members.

With these considerations in mind, we can only conclude that classifications
based upon sex, like classifications based upon race, alienage, or national origin,
are inherently suspect, and must therefore be subjected to strict judicial scrutiny.

Applying the analysis mandated by that stricter standard of review, it is clear that the statutory scheme now before us is constitutionally invalid.

III

The sole basis of the classification established in the challenged statutes is the sex of the individuals involved. Thus, under 37 U.S.C. §§401, 403, and 10 U.S.C. §§1072, 1076, a female member of the uniformed services seeking to obtain housing and medical benefits for her spouse must prove his dependency in fact, whereas no such burden is imposed upon male members. In addition, the statutes operate so as to deny benefits to a female member, such as appellant Sharron Frontiero who provides less than one-half of her spouse's support, while at the same time granting such benefits to a male member who likewise provides less than one-half of his spouse's support. Thus, to this extent at least, it may fairly be said that these statutes command "dissimilar treatment for men and women who are . . . similarly situated." *Reed* v. *Reed*, 404 U.S., at 77.

Moreover, the Government concedes that the differential treatment accorded men and women under these statutes serves no purpose other than mere "administrative convenience." In essence, the Government maintains that, as an empirical matter, wives in our society frequently are dependent upon their husbands, while husbands rarely are dependent upon their wives. Thus, the Government argues that Congress might reasonably have concluded that it would be both cheaper and easier simply conclusively to presume that wives of male members are financially dependent upon their husbands, while burdening female members with the task of establishing dependency in fact.

The Government offers no concrete evidence, however, tending to support its view that such differential treatment in fact saves the Government any money. In order to satisfy the demands of strict judicial scrutiny, the Government must demonstrate, for example, that it is actually cheaper to grant increased benefits with respect to *all* male members, than it is to determine which male members are in fact entitled to such benefits and to grant increased benefits only to those members whose wives actually meet the dependency requirement. Here, however, there is substantial evidence that, if put to the test, many of the wives of male members would fail to qualify for benefits. And in light of the fact that the dependency determination with respect to the husbands of female members is presently made solely on the basis of affidavits, rather than through the more costly hearing process, the Government's explanation of the statutory scheme is, to say the least, questionable.

In any case, our prior decisions make clear that, although efficacious administration of governmental programs is not without some importance, "the Constitution recognizes higher values than speed and efficiency." *Stanley* v. *Illinois*, 405 U.S. 645, 656 (1972). And when we enter the realm of "strict judicial scrutiny," there can be no doubt that "administrative convenience" is not a shibboleth, the mere recitation of which dictates constitutionality. See *Shapiro* v. *Thompson*, 394 U.S. 618 (1969); *Carrington* v. *Rash*, 380 U.S. 89 (1965). On the contrary, any statutory scheme which draws a sharp line between the sexes, *solely* for the purpose of achieving administrative convenience, necessarily commands "dissimilar treatment for men and women who are . . . similarly situated," and therefore involves the "very kind of arbitrary legislative choice forbidden by the [Constitution]. . . ." *Reed* v. *Reed*, 404 U.S., at 77, 76. We therefore conclude that, by according differential treatment to male and female members of the uniformed services for the sole purpose of achieving administrative convenience, the challenged statutes violate the Due Process Clause of the Fifth Amendment insofar as they require a female member to prove the dependency of her husband.

Reversed.

Notes

1. The "uniformed services" include the Army, Navy, Air Force, Marine Corps, Coast Guard, Environmental Science Services Administration, and Public Health Service. 37 U.S.C. §101(3); 10 U.S.C. §1072(1).
2. Appellant Joseph Frontiero is a full-time student at Huntingdon College in Montgomery, Alabama. According to the agreed stipulation of facts, his living expenses, including his share of the household expenses, total approximately $354 per month. Since he receives $205 per month in veterans' benefits, it is clear that he is not dependent upon appellant Sharron Frontiero for more than one-half of his support.
3. [W]hile the Fifth Amendment contains no equal protection clause, it does forbid discrimination that is so unjustifiable as to be violative of due process.'" *Schneider* v. *Rusk*, 377 U.S. 163, 168 (1964); see *Shapiro* v. *Thompson*, 394 U.S. 618, 641-642 (1969); *Bolling* v. *Sharpe*, 347 U.S. 497 (1954).
4. Indeed, the position of women in this country at its inception is reflected in the view expressed by Thomas Jefferson that women should be neither seen nor heard in society's decisionmaking councils. See M. Gruberg, Women in American Politics 4 (1968). See also 2 A. de Tocqueville, Democracy in America (Reeves trans. 1948).
5. It is true, of course, that when viewed in the abstract, women do not constitute a small and powerless minority. Nevertheless, in part because of past discrimination, women are vastly underrepresented in this Nation's decisionmaking councils. There has never been a female President, nor a female member of this Court. Not a single woman present sits in the United States Senate, and only 14 women hold seats in the House of Representatives. And, as appellants point out, this underrepresentation is present throughout all levels of our State and Federal Government. . . .

PART VII

Legal System Failures and Planned Social Change

A legal system, whether of a given society or of the international system as a whole, can fail—and does fail—to achieve its purposes because of internal as well as external structural features. Internally, a legal system may suffer from various defects in its configuration of values, norms, roles, and organizations; its norms may be inconsistent, imprecise, and unsupported by any relevant sanctions; its structure of roles of legal personnel may be inappropriate; its role occupants may not be adequately socialized into pertinent values and hence highly vulnerable to corruption; its organizations may be ineffectively designed, etc. Externally, a legal system may be constrained to such a degree by one or more nonlegal social institutions in a society as to lose any semblance of a relatively autonomous institution seeking to generate universalistic norms and to apply them in a disinterested manner in regulating the behavior of the citizenry.

In systems-theoretic terms, a legal system is vulnerable to a variety of failures because of its inability to develop "closed-loop systems" to assess the effectiveness of its outputs. In the absence of appropriate regulatory mechanisms to ensure compliance with the law on the part of legal personnel as well as rank-and-file citizenry, a legal system will not show "negative feedback" responses, that is, self-corrective reactions; instead, there is a tendency for "positive feedback" of a detrimental nature to accumulate (Laszlo, Levine, and Milsum, 1974).

More specifically, there are many ways in which a legal system can fail: through the persistence of defects within a legal system; through its inability to cope with dysfunctional and unanticipated consequences of legal decisions; through the exercise of uncontrolled discretion on the part of judges and administrative and law-enforcement officials; and through its unresponsiveness to a society's urgent problems. Other examples of legal system failures include a tendency for law to lag behind changes in nonlegal institutions, with resulting maladjustments entailing considerable social costs; a tendency for "group interest" laws to be enacted instead of "social interest" laws, which may eventually undermine the confidence of the citizenry in the impartiality, legality, and independence of the law; inefficiency in enforcing some laws because of limited resources; and the failure of a legal system to promote the "double institutionalization" of some beneficial customs that have low normative salience among the citizenry.

The cumulative effect of legal system failures over time is a progressive decline in the perceived legitimacy of the legal system, leading to a withdrawal of support from the legal system. Short of a total collapse of a legal system suffering from a multitude of failures, a legal system may be progressively by-passed by subgroups in society through the use of two contrasting strategies: (1) extralegal mechanisms to manage societal conflicts, such as the use of labor and commercial arbitration in the United States; and (2) recourse to violence, involving a violation of the rule of law, either by legal personnel, by rank-and-file citizenry, or by both (Evan, 1978).

Among the variety of examples of legal system failures, perhaps the most dramatic as well as the most dangerous is the widespread lawlessness in the international system. In the first reading in Part VII, Levi points to the dilemmas of law versus politics and the frequent recourse to violence among nation-states. The predisposition of nation-states to resort to force in defense of perceived national self-interests makes it especially difficult to build durable and effective conflict-management mechanisms in the international system. Some significant advances in international law have been made in establishing various principles and conventions pertaining, for example, to war, the high seas, outer space, nuclear testing, human rights, and so forth. However, the implementation of such legal norms is very uncertain and erratic, in part because of the absence of adequate structural provisions for enforcement and in part because of the lack of consensus among the sovereign states regarding the values underlying the various legal norms. From this vantage point, Appendixes I-C, I-D and I-E merit rereading.

The multiplicity of legal system failures generates societal dysfunctions, which eventually result in pressures for social change. A common response to such pressures is the use of law as a deliberate instrument of social change. In Evan's analysis of the relation of law to social change, seven prerequisites are identified for the effective use of law in planned social change. Ascertaining the "limits of effective legal action" (Pound, 1917) is a significant and challenging problem in the sociology of law as well as in jurisprudence (Jones, 1969; Evan, 1979).

To what extent does a legal system make use of relevant knowledge *prior* to making new legal policies? Sharon Collins provides an answer to this question in her assessment of the use of social science research by American courts. Once a legal policy decision is made, whether by legislative enactment, judicial decision, administrative action, or other, it is important to undertake post-policy research to ascertain its consequences. In the legal documents in Appendix V, there is evidence of a growing awareness of the need for pre-policy as well as post-policy research in legislative, judicial, and administrative decisional contexts.

Ross's analysis of a legal reform to discourage drunken driving in Great Britain is of considerable interest substantively as well as methodologically. The law in question was successful for a period of time, after which its effectiveness faded. When law-enforcement officials reinstituted a program of law enforcement, Ross found—as a result of applying the technique of "interrupted time series analysis"—that the law's effectiveness was restored. By contrast, Galanter, in his study of the "Untouchability Offences Act" in India, documents the failure of this law. The persistent and widespread discrimination against Untouchables is due to several factors: defects in the provisions of the law itself, inadequate enforcement resources, incompatible value orientations toward the law by legal personnel and by rank-and-file citizens, and the impediments of cultural traditions and religious beliefs.

Clearly, if a legal system is to learn from both its successes and its failures, thereby upgrading its regulatory capabilities and enhancing its legitimacy, it is essential for legal personnel—and sociologists of law as well—to develop an *experimental* perspective toward the law rather than view the law as a set of commandments engraved in stone (Cowan, 1948, 1951; Campbell, 1970).

Bearing in mind the readings in Part VII and the legal documents in Appendix V, reexamine the theses of Black and Nonet in Part II. What arguments pro and con would you adduce for policy-related research in the sociology of law?

References

Campbell, D. (1970). "Legal Reforms as Experiments." *Journal of Legal Education*, 23: 212–239.

Cowan, T. A. (1948). "The Relation of Law to Experimental Social Science." *University of Pennsylvania Law Review*, 96: 484–502.

Cowan, T. A. (1951). "A Postulate Set for Experimental Jurisprudence." *Philosophy of Science*, 18: 1–5.

Evan, W. M. (1978). "Systems Theory and the Sociology of Law." Presented at the Ninth World Congress of Sociology in Uppsala, Sweden, August 1978 (to appear in my forthcoming book *Law and Social Structure*).

Evan, W. M. (1979). "Organizations and the 'Limits of Effective Legal Action': A Comparative Study," presented at a symposium on "Organizatorische Bedingungen des Gesetzesrollzugs," University of Oldenburg, May 24–26, 1979.

Jones, H. W. (1969). *The Efficacy of Law*. Evanston, Ill.: Northwestern University Press.

Laszlo, C. A., M. D. Levine, and J. H. Milsum (1974). "A General Systems Framework for Social Systems." *Behavioral Science*, 19: 79–92.

Pound, Roscoe (1917). "The Limits of Effective Legal Action." *The American Bar Association Journal*, 3: 55–70.

36

Law and Politics in the International Society
Werner Levi

. . . In the international society, in the absence of an acknowledged common welfare, each state caters to its own needs and must have a power potential for doing so. Power is exclusively possessed and exercised by states, an arrangement which the law sanctions through sovereignty. There is no authority above the states either for limiting their power potential or for regulating the manner of its use. Such limitation and regulation are matters of agreement among states and enforceable only by each individually.

This arrangement gives power a totally different role, or at least makes the power factor considerably more important. Essentially and simply, states must be preoccupied with building up a power potential as a significant and in some cases vital guarantee of their very existence. Several consequences arise for international law. The first is that states are not likely to accept laws in the first place which will prevent them from developing the power potential they consider necessary. The second is that as soon as states experience legal commitments as a hindrance in the fulfillment of important national interests, they will seek a release or escape from them. The

Excerpt from *Law and Politics in the International Society* (Sage Library of Social Research, vol. 32). Beverly Hills, Calif.: Sage Publications, 1976, pp. 52–62. Copyright © 1976 by Sage Publications, Inc. Reprinted by permission of the author and publisher.

third is that the costliness of building a power potential, the inability of many states to develop a power potential at all, or the effort of mobilizing an existing potential will lead states into attempts to restrain the role of power. The fourth is that the nature of power and of the international society diminishes the chances for such restraint. These consequences and their effect upon international law will now be examined.

The Struggle for Power

When a political decision is to be made about which state is to get what, when, and how, a trial of power is normally involved because there is no other way of discovering which state has the superior power to obtain a favorable decision. When there is conflict, the interests of the state with a preponderance of power prevail. Hence the enormous incentive for states to develop a power potential. Its elements are legion because influence can be exerted in a number of ways. What elements of its power potential a state will employ in the pursuit of its interests—whether, for instance, persuasion or violence—will depend upon the importance assigned to the interests, upon how much the conflicting interests may be matched by shared interests, and a host of other mostly subjective considerations. This is exactly the situation making the possession of a power potential vital. No state can ever predict with certainty when it may want to mobilize its power or how much of it, either to enforce its own political decision or to resist the enforcement of another state's decision.

This uncertainty is enhanced by the additional uncertainty regarding the magnitude of the power potential and its possible effectiveness. The reason for this lies in the manner in which power achieves its results. Power is a psychological relationship. Each government is trying to influence the other to act in a certain manner. The minds of those responsible for the behavior of a state are the targets of the application of power. What their reaction will be is generally unpredictable and the applied power cannot be measured. Moreover, several elements of power are also unmeasurable, such as the stamina or morale of a people, the prestige of a nation, and the effectiveness of a weapon. Governments can never be sure how much effective power is at their disposal to enforce or oppose decisions. The temptation and, indeed, the tendency are to "maximize" the power potential within the limits of a state's will and capacity. But as power cannot be measured the "maximum" cannot be determined. The enterprise can only mean adding forever increment upon increment of something states hope will increase their power potential. Thus the competition and struggle for power become prominent activities in international politics.

The effect of this situation upon international law is impressive—whatever one's theory is regarding the role of power in international politics. Inevitably under the conditions of the international society all states must be in quest of some power potential and international law is affected thereby, mainly unfavorably.

This quest for power and the application of power may take place within the legal framework. Ethical convictions of a government—genuine or pretended—may, for example, keep them there. Obedience to law can improve a state's reputation, and a good reputation is itself an element in the power potential. But states also use their power for unilaterally making and enforcing their interpretation of the law or for altogether extra- or illegal purposes. They can do so owing to the manner in which they have organized the (non)management of power. They will use it so when they judge the defense of the national interest to require an extra-legal use, although they may well be apologetic or defensive about such practice. For states prefer to remain within the legal framework but also, to facilitate this endeavor, to subject themselves to as few legal restraints as possible.

This wish of states to behave legally, on the one hand, and the need under all circumstances to build a power potential, on the other hand, leads states to keep the volume of legal rules low. They are quick to interpret every legal restraint upon building a power potential as an inhibition of their self-protection, and every restraint upon applying it as a virtual invitation to national suicide. There are situations when states feel more secure by relying upon their own power potential than upon the obedience to law by other states. They want to preserve their freedom to apply their power especially in such situations, and of necessity therefore to develop their power potential.

The connection between the quest for power and international law could appear at first sight to affect only that segment of a state's behavior devoted to building a power potential. But the elements of the power potential are legion, so that this segment becomes practically coterminous with the international behavior of states. There is hardly a limit to the items useful in "power politics" so that everything—things and actions, ideas and processes—can add to the power potential. Almost everything at some point can be useful for one state to influence the behavior of another. Virtually everything can become part of the state's power potential, from an atom bomb to a ping-pong team. Governments therefore routinely scrutinize everything for its relevance to the power potential—even though power may not be the obsessive concern of a particular government. This approach also affects international law.

States are reluctant to commit themselves. They are hesitant to grant legally binding force to general resolutions of international organizations or to be bound to broad concepts such as ."international cooperation." The Australian government stated the principle typically when it declared that "a General Assembly declaration of legal principles cannot itself be creative of legal duties" (Friedman et al., 1969: 98). Once they bind themselves, they are inclined to define their obligations as narrowly as possible. International tribunals have consistently held that when there is doubt about the meaning of a treaty "that interpretation should be adopted which is the most favorable to the freedom of States. The "domestic affairs" or "internal affairs" clause has consistently been used by states to withhold much subject matter from international jurisdiction (see, e.g., United Nations, 1954: 453–478). This limitation has been broadened by the "Connally Amendment." This amendment introduced a reservation when the United States accepted the so-called compulsory jurisdiction of the International Court of Justice. It stipulated that disputes were excluded relating to matters essentially within the domestic jurisdiction of the United States "as determined by the United States of America." Not only has this reservation been adopted by many other states, but as a type of "subjective" formulation it has also been introduced to narrow many other kinds of international obligations.

Generally, the wish to reserve freedom of action encourages "political" behavior, by which states understand behavior controlled essentially by power relationships. It discourages "legal" behavior, by which they understand behavior in conformity with pre-established rules, making their respective power potential in theory irrelevant. The net effect is to reduce the area of behavior subject to legal controls.

Power Versus Legal Control

The ambivalent attitude of states toward behavior within the law and freedom for accumulating and applying power has produced their practice of building into the body of law rules allowing them to escape legitimately from the bonds of law into the freedom of "political" behavior. Sovereignty is, of course, the main exit from obligatory behavior. But there are many smaller exits as well. The main function of these releases from legal obligation is to prevent binding the behavior of states beyond what they may consider non-essential to their own existence. The dilemma is the wish to tame power but also to exercise it. It has been solved, rather unsatisfactorily, by making the release not so easy as to threaten anarchy in the society, yet easy enough to serve the purpose. In general, the arrangements for limiting legal obligations have been vaguely defined and their use has been made sufficiently risky for social order to make states hesitant in taking advantage of them.

One of these arrangements is the classic "national honor and vital interests" clause. It was in vogue until about 1928. It could be found mostly in arbitration treaties for the exemption of disputes touching the vital interests of a state—if one of the parties made such a claim. In such a case the dispute was to be solved politically, i.e., by a trial of power.

In more recent practice, states distinguish between "legal," hence "justiciable" disputes, and "political," hence "nonjusticiable" disputes. States feeling that the settlement of a dispute by means of their power potential would be of advantage will try to evade any settlement on the basis of law by declaring a dispute political. The distinction between the two types of disputes has been recognized by the International Court. It can also be found in numerous treaties. Most prominent among these is the Locarno Pact of 1925 in which the parties agree to submit to judicial decision all questions "as to their respective rights"; and the United Nations Charter which, in Article 36, instructs the Security Council to refer "legal disputes" as a rule to the International Court of Justice. The same distinction has now been introduced also in regard to treaties. . . .

A novel and unambiguous release from a treaty obligation was introduced by the United States and the Soviet Union in their Nuclear Atmospheric Test Ban Treaty of 1963. "Each Party shall in exercising its national sovereignty have the right to withdraw from the Treaty if it decides that extraordinary events, relating to the subject matter of this Treaty, have jeopardized the supreme interests of its country."

A very rare, old, and dubious arrangement is the unilateral declaration by a state of a "state of necessity." It can exist when the vital interests or the existence of a country are at stake. It differs from the concept of legitimate self-defense and of military necessity in that the state of necessity need not be brought about by an illegal act of some other country. For instance, a country whose population is starving could seize a foreign ship loaded with foodstuffs and give this act legality by claiming a state of necessity. The principle is that a country, finding itself in such a situation may break a legal obligation to the extent necessary for the protection of its vital interests, although it must presumably do so without hurting vital interests of another country.

When all else fails, states can invoke the *clausula rebus sic stanti-*

bus. This clause entitles them to suspend or denounce a treaty if the circumstances prevailing at the conclusion of the treaty have very much changed against the state invoking the clause. As a tool for coping with social change, this clause caters to a real need. . . . It can render service as a safety valve in an age of rapid social change. . . . But the invention and use of this doctrine is another illustration of turning law into a handmaiden of politics. There is no objective way in the international system of determininig when the conditions for the application of the *clausula* are fulfilled, making its invocation by a party to the treaty a political act. Moreover, by definition, the reasons for involing the *clausula* are external to the law, possibly political, but in any case not legal (e.g., changes in the international power constellation, an improved bargaining position of one of the parties, basic alterations in national interests). Also, the conditions under which the clause may be invoked are not determinable by legal doctrine. They are located in the political arena, just as the reasons for concluding the treaty were located there. In other words, the *clausula rebus sic stantibus* is a legal cover for a political solution to a problem. . . .

Legal Restraints Upon the Use of Power

The preference of many states for a regulated rather than an arbitrary use of power has led to the call for a separation of politics from law.[1] Proposals have been made that politics should be neutralized by the development of a comprehensive set of laws for all occasions. . . . During the first year of the International Law Commission, Georges Scelle (United Nations, 1949: 38) defined the Commission's task as distinguishing what was legal even in the most political questions and as endeavoring "to enlarge the field of international law at the expense of that of politics." The Colombian delegate (United Nations, 1949: 38), agreeing with M. Scelle, suggested that the Commission "should avoid introducing politics into its work." In the course of time, many delegates to committees dealing with international law prided themselves in maintaining an "atmosphere of serenity" (e.g., United Nations, 1964d: 15; 1972: 305) as opposed, by implication, to the atmosphere of "dirty politics." Other delegates, however, presumably more aware of the different and necessary functions of both politics and law and of law's dependency upon politics, pointed out that the International Law Commission "was not a scientific body with purely academic terms of reference but a subsidiary organ of the General Assembly, itself a political body" (United Nations, 1949: 17, see also 21, 56; and 1947: 9; 1967: 5; 1963: 53).

Legal restraints upon a state's use of its power potential are generated more by modern developments than by national wills. The existence of collective goods (biosphere) or undistributed goods (marine resources) necessitates an integrated approach for their handling. And integration could be the objective part of a community, favoring a more positive role of law. The increasing overlapping of interests among states causing more confrontations but also more cooperation (pluralism) again enhances the role of law while reducing the usefulness of arbitrary power application. A very similar effect is produced by the changing importance of the elements of power, with economic factors, prestige, and status matching that of physical force. There is, finally and still most importantly, the limit set to the arbitrary use of power by the existence of countervailing power. A balance of power toward which most states are striving makes states amenable to creating and obeying a legal regulation of given situations. Lassa Oppenheim (1912 I: 193) and other international lawyers (Geiger, 1964: 351, 353; Huber, 1910: 63; Scelle, 1932 I: 24; Stone, 1959: 39–40; Schwarzenberger, 1939: 75) argue that the balance of power was "an indispensable condition of the very existence of international law," with Theodor Geiger expanding the argument to all kinds of law.

The balance of power as a main guarantor of international law fits into the diffusion of power in the international system. But the law so guaranteed shares the weaknesses of the balance of power. In particular, the reliance of law upon the balance of power for effectiveness could be self-defeating. . . . The consequence of an unending competition for a power potential (e.g., the armaments race) often causes a neglect of the law in the name of the national interest. A paradox arises. Under the very favorable assumption that states aim at a balance of power as a sound foundation for international law, they are ignoring that law in the process of constructing such a foundation.

The scant success so far in harnessing the use of power to international law consistently is explained by the nature of power and its international organization. States can hardly be expected to provide for their existence under legal restraints whose enforcement is unreliable. Hitler (1938: 104) confirmed that when a state "is in danger of oppression or annihilation, the question of legality plays a subordinate role." Dean Acheson (1963: 13-14) stated more radically that "The survival of states is not a matter of law."

Limits to Legal Restraint on Power

Legal restraints upon the use of power are most difficult under the best of circumstances. The usefulness of everything to the power potential of states creates an almost impossible task for the lawmaker. He could not know what to regulate, or how. One and the same matter could serve a multitude of purposes. Regulating it for one purpose would then mean unwanted regulation also for other purposes. The problem is very acute in regard to the sources of nuclear energy, for instance, which states want to regulate when they are to be used for warlike purposes, but not for peaceful purposes. The complications get worse in regard to the imponderable elements of power. Is the stimulation of nationalism in many newer states a device for strengthening the country for future aggression or for turning it into a nation? . . .

Yet another reason for the inability of law to contain power effectively is that the struggle for power (and also the application of power) is cause and effect of international tensions. Tensions stem from historic memories about the behavior of states in general. Fear, distrust, suspicion, and hostility are some of its ingredients. They escape legal regulation. Not tension, but only some of its symptoms, especially concrete conflicts, can be handled by law. But the settlement of conflicts through legal measures, while helpful, could not settle the underlying tension. Tension could find expression in an unending number of conflicts, minor in themselves, but assuming important proportions as symptoms of the tension. An Israeli official stated convincingly (United Nations, 1969: 296) that in the absence of a will for friendly relations and in the presence of grave tensions, the "operation of normal procedures" for the settlement of disputes was impaired. Legal processes "would at best superficially and formally solve certain technical problems without significantly contributing to the elimination of the real source of the dispute." One remedy would be the growth of a community in which fears, suspicions, and mistrust as the components of tension could be overcome, or where these factors could at least be balanced by common interests and loyalties to the group.

Fundamentally and ultimately, the absence of a community on the international scene is responsible for the role of power making the political system inadequate to perform its normal function of maintaining social order. . . . Moreover, the weakness . . . of other social controls in the international society, places an intolerable burden upon the control function of international law.

Note

1. Communist states are frank about the political nature of international law. In general, it is their theory, of course, that law is class law, hence political law. In specific instances they point this out expressly to weaken or reject rules they dislike. Starushenko (1969: 95) stated "International law is a sphere of relentless political struggle. . . ." At the Third Conference on the Law of the Sea at Caracas, the Chinese delegate stated that "The essence of the law of the sea was the struggle to defend sovereign security and natural resources of many medium-sized and small countries, and hence a serious political struggle" (United Nations, 1974d: 109).

References

Acheson, D. G. (1963). "Remarks on Cuban quarantine." Proceedings of the American Society of International Law, fifty-seventh meeting. Washington, D.C.

Friedmann, W., O. J. Lissitzyn, and R. C. Pugh (1969). *Cases and Materials on International Law*. St. Paul, Minn.: West.

Geiger, T. (1964). *Vorstudien zu einer Soziologie des Rechts*. Neuwied am Rhein: Hermann Luchterhand.

Hitler, A. (1938). *Mein Kampf*. London: Hurst & Blackett.

Huber, M. (1910). "Beitrage zur Kenntnis der soziologischen Grundlagen des Völkerrechts and der Staatengesellschaft." Pp. 56–134 in *Jahrbuch des öffentlichen Rechts der Gegenwart* 4.

Oppenheim, L. (1912). *International Law: A Treatise*. London: Longmans, Green.

Scelle, G. (1932 I). *Precis de droit des gens*. Paris: Recueil Sirey.

Schwarzenberger, G. (1939), "The Rule of Law and the Disintegration of the International Society," *American Journal of International Law* 33 (January): 56–77.

Stone, J. (1959). *Legal Controls of International Conflict*. New York: Rinehart.

United Nations:

—— (1972). A/C.6/SR.1364.

—— (1969). A/Conf. 39/aa/Add. 1.

—— (1967). The Work of the International Law Commission.

—— (1964). A/AC.119/SR.23.

—— (1963). A/C.6/SR. 791.

—— (1954). ST/PSCA/1 Repertoire of the Practice of the Security Council 1946-1951.

—— (1949). A/CN.4/Ser.A.

—— (1947). A/C.6/SR.38.

37

Law as an Instrument of Social Change
William M. Evan

In imaginary societies, such as some authors of utopias have depicted, there is such a high degree of social harmony and tranquility that no law is necessary—and no lawyers either. Such societies enjoy a perfect state of social equilibrium because there is a perfect degree of congruence between the ideal prescriptions and proscriptions of behavior and actual behavior. The free and frictionless association among all citizens makes the state superfluous as the source of law and as an instrument of social control.

In all real societies, whether "primitive" or "civilized," such an ideal state is not to be found. In fact, we can argue that in principle it is impossible for human beings ever to attain that blissful state of equilibrium which would not require law or some form of legal system. Disequilibrating forces are generated from both outside and inside a society. These pressures for change stem in part from the impossibility of achieving perfect congruence between the ideal cultural blueprint of a society and the actual social reality. A certain amount of social deviance occurs in all societies, if only because the socialization process through childhood as well as through the rest of the life cycle can not possibly be uniform and perfectly successful. As a consequence, in all societies of any appreciable size, there is a tendency for law to emerge distinct from "the cake of custom."

Reprinted from Alvin W. Gouldner and S. M. Miller, eds., *Applied Sociology: Opportunities and Problems*, New York: The Free Press, 1965, pp. 285-293.

Law in this context does not necessarily refer to a written statement of a rule of conduct, since in nonliterate societies this cannot occur, but rather to a particular social status—such as that of a tribal chieftain or a judge—the incumbent of which has the authority to assert a norm, resolve conflicts, and bring to bear the coercive power of the community against those guilty of violating a norm.

Contrasting Conceptions of the Function of Law

Law emerges not only to *codify* existing customs, morals, or mores, but also to *modify* the behavior and the values presently existing in a particular society. The conception of law as a codification of existing customs, morals, or mores implies a relatively passive function. On the other hand, the conception of law as a means of social change, i.e., as a potential for modifying behavior and beliefs, implies a relatively active function.[1]

The passive law, namely, that one cannot legislate mores and people's behavior, is rooted in the 19th century philosophies of Social Darwinism and historical jurisprudence. At the turn of the century, William Graham Sumner articulated this conception of the law. It assumes that law is a passive, rather than an active social force, which gradually emerges into a formal or codified state only after it has taken root in the behavior of the members of a society. Whenever an effort is made to enact a law in contradiction to existing folkways and mores, conflicts arise which result in the eventual undoing of the law. Since Sumner claims there is a "strain toward a consistency of the mores," he concludes, in effect, that "stateways cannot change folkways." An implicit assumption of this view is that the exclusive function of law is to reinforce the mores and to provide a uniform and predictable procedure for the evaluation and punishment of deviance. That is to say, the function of law is social control and the major problem is one of designing legal sanctions to minimize deviance and maintain social stability.

A contrary view is that law is not merely a reflection of existing customs, morals or codes, but also a potentially independent social force which can influence behavior and beliefs. As an instrument of social change, law entails two interrelated processes: the institutionalization and the internalization of patterns of behavior. In this context, institutionalization of a pattern of behavior means the establishment of a norm with provisions for its enforcement,[2] and internalization of a pattern of behavior means the incorporation of the value or values implicit in a law.[3] Law, as has been noted by others, can affect behavior directly only through the process of institutionalization; if, however, the institutionalization process is successful, it, in turn, facilitates the internalization of attitudes or beliefs.[4]

A Continuum of Resistance to Law

These opposing views of the function of law suggest a hypothetical continuum of the amount of potential resistance to the enactment of a new law. When there is likely to be zero per cent resistance to a law, one would obviously question the need for it, since complete agreement between the behavior required by the law and the existing customs or morals apparently exists. In this situation, there would be no need to codify the mores into law. At the other extreme, when there is likely to be 100 per cent resistance to a law, one would expect the law to be totally ineffective, because nobody would enforce it and the authority of the lawmaker would be undermined.[5]

No law would ever emerge if these two extremes existed at all times. Between these ends of our continuum, there are evidently two important thresholds involved in lawmaking. Somewhere at the lower end of our hypothetical continuum of resistance, where a certain degree of nonconformity or deviance from existing mores is reached, society acts to control it by codifying mores. What this threshold of nonconformity is for different societies, we do not yet know. Similarly, somewhere at the higher end of our continuum there is a threshold of such massive resistance to a new law that enforcement is impossible. At what point on this continuum a new law provokes the overwhelming majority of the citizenry to violate it so as to nullify it, we also do not know. Civil wars and revolutions approximate this form of massive resistance to law culminating in its "decodification". Thus, in considering the social functions of law, we have to focus on the intermediate portion of our hypothetical continuum of resistance to law.

Whenever a law is enacted in the face of any appreciable resistance, that is to say, whenever it falls somewhere in the middle of our hypothetical continuum, the legal system becomes involved in an educational as well as in a social control task. If the educational task is not accomplished, a situation exists in which individuals are obligated to obey a law at the threat of punishment, while, in fact, not believing in it. This situation produces what Festinger calls "forced compliance": viz., a discrepancy between public behavior and private belief.[6] So long as behavior involves forced compliance, there is no internalization of the values implicit or explicit in a new law. The resulting tension may lead to disobedience of the law, depending on the nature of the sanctions and the consistency and efficiency of enforcement. If law is to perform an educational function, it is necessary to convert *forced* compliance into *voluntary* compliance.

Necessary Conditions for Law Performing an Educational Function

Under what conditions can law succeed, not only in institutionalizing a new pattern of conduct, but also in generating the internalization of new attitudes implicit in the conduct required by the new law? The failure to specify these conditions leaves the theoretical problems of the relation of law to social change unanswered. It also leaves unsolved the administrative problems of the conscious use of law as an agent of social change. As a first approximation to an answer to this problem, we shall consider seven necessary, though perhaps not sufficient, conditions for law to perform an educational function.

The first condition is that the source of the new law be authoritative and prestigeful. This condition may at first appear to be trivial, since law, by definition, connotes an authoritative or legitimate action. There are, in fact, four authoritative lawmaking sources in our society: legislative, executive, administrative, and judicial. It is hypothesized that they differ not only in their reputed authoritativeness and prestige in exercising a lawmaking function, but also in their effectiveness in performing an educational function. A law enacted by a legislature—rather than issued as a decision by a court or an administrative agency, or as an executive order—probably lends itself more readily to performing an educational function. For, in the minds of the average citizens, legislatures—whether at the local, state or federal level—are probably perceived to be the proper and legitimate forums for the enactment of new laws. This perception may be due to the fact that legislatures are more sensitive to public pressures and sentiments than are the other sources of lawmaking.[7] Second in the perceived rank order to authoritativeness and prestige are probably executive orders, followed by the decisions of administrative agencies; and lastly, in all likelihood, are the decisions of the courts.

This hypothesis about the differential in perceived authoritativeness and prestige of lawmaking sources lead us, in turn, to the hypothesis that the more drastic the social change to be effected by law, i.e., the higher the proportion of potential resistance on our hypothetical scale, the more authoritative and prestigeful the lawmaking agency should be to effect the change. In other words, when there is a low degree of consensus regarding the norms involved in a law, "legislative lawmaking"—the most authoritative and prestigeful source of law—is apt to be more effective than "judicial lawmaking," the least authoritative and prestigeful source of law.[8]

The Supreme Court's decision to desegregate the public school system is generally acknowledged as representing an effort to effect a drastic social change. Consequently, we venture to suggest—in light of the hypothesis stated above—that Congress would have been a more effective lawmaking source in this instance. To be sure, had the Supreme Court in 1954 declined the opportunity to revise its 1896 doctrine of "separate but equal" treatment, enunciated in *Plessy* v. *Ferguson*, it might have taken many years for Congress to enact a desegregation law in view of the monumental resistance of the Southern pressure group.

The second condition is that the rationale of a new law clarify its continuity and compatibility with existing institutionalized values.[9] The fulfillment of this condition helps to overcome possible objections to a new law and establishes its legitimacy in the eyes of the citizenry. Such a rationale is readily imaginable in the desegregation decision. The Thirteenth and Fourteenth Amendments, as well as the Declaration of Independence and various judicial decisions in the preceding decade, clearly establish the rights of all citizens of this country to equal treatment by the law, including agencies of the state, such as the public school system. Thus, a legislative enactment of school desegregation could have drawn on prior legal support, quite apart from general cultural and historical justifications.

The third necessary condition for making law an educational force is the use of models or reference groups for compliance. This could involve several possible actions by a lawmaking body. It might single out a group or a community in which the proposed pattern of behavior already exists without any observable adverse effects. Thus, for instance, it would have been possible in our hypothetical "legislative law" on public school desegregation to have included statements that in various countries with which we identify politically, desegregated schools operate smoothly. Moreover, it would have been possible to point to any number of communities in this country where desegregation has been in effect for many years without any known untoward effects on either whites or Negroes. Also relevant would have been a reference to the successful desegregation in the armed services in both Northern and Southern installations. The examples cited of models for compliance may not have proved adequate for the law in question. The idea, however, of deliberately upholding a pragmatic model which is visible and the likely object of admiration by potential recalcitrants might contribute to overcoming resistance to a proposed change.

The fourth condition is that law make a conscious use of the element of time in introducing a new pattern of behavior. This is essential for breaking an old pattern and instituting a new one. To be sure, the Supreme Court took the time element into consideration when it resorted to the intentionally ambiguous phrase "with all deliberate speed" in its desegregation decision.

It may be hypothesized that if a significant pattern of social behavior is to be changed, the less the transition time, the easier—rather than the harder—the adaptation to the change.[10] The rationale for this proposition is that the reduction of time delay minimizes the chances for the growth of organized or unorganized resistance to the projected legal change. The possible validity of this hypothesis depends on at least two conditions, to which we now turn.

The first of these, our fifth condition, is that the enforcement agents must themselves be committed to the behavior required by the law, even if not to the values implicit in it. Any evidence of hypocrisy or corruptibility on the part of the personnel of the legal system, whose task it is to implement the law, undermines the chances of its being effectuated. One of the major reasons for the failure of the Prohibition Amendment was the disrespect for the law evidenced by enforcement agents, particularly local police, on whom the major task of enforcement devolved.[11]

The sixth condition, which also bears on the time factor mentioned earlier, is that as resistance to a new law increases, positive sanctions are probably as important as negative ones.[12] Legal sanctions are almost invariably negative in character, e.g., fines and/or imprisonment. As the severity of the punishment increases, compliance does not necessarily increase.[13] Severe punishment often affords people the opportunity to neutralize any guilt experienced for their wrong-doing with what feels like justified resentment against punishment. To encourage the learning of a new pattern of behavior and a new attitude, some positive reinforcement is required, as learning theorists have found experimentally. We would speculate that as the proportion of potential resistance to a new law increases, the need for including some positive sanctions or rewards for compliance also increases. In the case of the school desegregation decision, such rewards might have consisted of a special Federal school subsidy for teachers' salaries and school construction, and possibly even a rebate on Federal income tax for a given length of time for the people in those communities complying with the law. Although the Anglo-Saxon legal system generally does not provide for positive sanctions, there is no reason to doubt their value when law is used as an instrument of social change, particularly of a significant magnitude.

The seventh and final condition under which law performs an educational function is that effective protection be provided for the rights of those persons who would suffer if the law were evaded or violated. If an individual is required, because of the legal doctrine of "standing" in court, to vindicate his rights against those of an organized entity, public or private, whose resources are infinitely greater, his rights are, in fact, unprotected. Only if the law should provide that he have the aid of a public organization, such as an administrative agency charged with the enforcement of the law, or the aid of a private organization of his own choosing, does he stand a chance to obtain justice.

In the case of our hypothetical "legislative law" on public school desegregation, parents of Negro children who are barred from admission to white schools should not have to fight boards of education alone; rather, they should, if they wish, have the support of either a public agency, such as the Civil Rights Commission, or of private organizations. In the latter case, such organizations should not run the risk of being accused of the crime of barratry, as has occurred in recent legal conflicts in the South.[14] Adequate provisions to protect the rights of those affected by a law presuppose that special and suitable efforts be expended to inform people of their rights under a new law. The problem of informing people of their legal rights appears to be endemic in all known legal systems; appreciably more effort is devoted to informing people of their duties than of their rights.[15]

Conclusion

In short, we are suggesting that law can potentially act as an educational force in changing people's behavior, even in the presence of appreciable opposition to the projected change implied by the law, if it meets the following seven conditions:

1. The source of the law is perceived to be authoritative and prestigeful.

2. The rationale for the new law is articulated in terms of legal, as well as historical and cultural continuity and compatibility.

3. Pragmatic models for compliance are identified.

4. A relevant use of time is made to overcome potential resistance.

5. The enforcement agents are themselves committed to the be-

havior required by the law, at least to the extent of according it legitimacy if not to the extent of internalizing the values implicit in it.

6. Positive, as well as negative, sanctions are employed to buttress the law.

7. Effective protection is provided for the rights of those persons who would suffer from evasion or violation of the law.

In our large and heterogeneous society, laws are designed with an educational as well as a social control function. The existence of many organized groups devoting considerable resources to promoting or obstructing new laws means that an appreciable portion of the population will resist a new law if it conflicts with their interests and values.[16] Hence, of necessity, laws of this character must have built-in provisions for performing the educational function which we have been concerned with in this paper. In other words, it is necessary to institutionalize a new pattern of conduct so as to maximize the chances for the internalization of values implicit in it.

Resistance to law, organized and unorganized, is the price we must often be prepared to pay for living in a pluralistic and rapidly changing society. Greater knowledge of the means of overcoming resistance to laws seeking to effect social change will probably increase the chance of law performing an educational, rather than merely a social control function.

As Morroe Berger has put it, law is "one of the great movers and changers of basic institutions of all kinds, and helps in establishing the conditions which favor group equality in a free society."[17]

Notes

1. Cf. Arnold M. Rose, "Sociological Factors in the Effectiveness of Projected Legal Remedies," *Journal of Legal Education*, 11, 4 (1959), pp. 470–481; Will Maslow, "The Uses of Law in the Struggle for Equality," *Social Research*, 22 (Autumn, 1955), pp. 297–314; Robert M. Hutchins, "The Corporation and Education, Ethics, and Power," in Melvin Anshen and George Leland Bach, eds., *Management and Corporations, 1985*, New York: McGraw-Hill Book Co., 1960, pp. 183–196.
2. Ernst Borinski, "The Litigation Curve and the Litigation Filibuster in Civil Rights Cases," *Social Forces*, 37 (December, 1958), pp. 142–147.
3. Cf. Herbert C. Kelman, "Compliance, Identification, and Internalization: Three Processes of Attitude Change," *Journal of Conflict Resolution*, 2 (March, 1958), pp. 51–60. For an analysis using the concepts of institutionalization of norms as well as internalization of norms, see William M. Evan, "Due Process of Law in Military and Industrial Organizations," *Administrative Science Quarterly*. 7 (September, 1962), pp. 187–207. . . .
4. See, for example, Morroe Berger, *Equality by Statute*, New York: Columbia

University, 1948, pp. 170 ff.; Kenneth B. Clark, "Desegregation: An Appraisal of the Evidence," *Journal of Social Issues*, 9, 4 (1953), pp. 72-6.

5. Cf. Berger, *op. cit.*, p. 4.

6. Leon Festinger; "An Analysis of Compliant Behavior," in M. Sherif and M. O. Wilson, eds., *Group Relations at the Crossroads*, New York: Harper & Bros., 1953, pp. 232-256; *A Theory of Cognitive Dissonance*, Evanston, Ill.: Row, Peterson and Co., 1957, pp. 84-122.

7. Cf. John C. Wahlke and Heinz Eulau, eds., *Legislative Behavior: A Reader in Theory and Research*, Glencoe, Ill.: The Free Press, 1959, p. 6.

8. Cf. Robert A. Leflar, "Law of the Land," in Don Shoemaker ed., *With All Deliberate Speed*, New York: Harper & Bros., 1957, p. 1.

9. Cf. H. G. Barnett, *Innovation: The Basis of Cultural Change*, New York: McGraw-Hill, 1953, pp. 329 ff.

10. Clark, *op. cit.*, pp. 44-7.

11. Cf. Clark Warburton, "Prohibition," *Encyclopedia of the Social Sciences*, New York: Macmillan, 1933, p. 505.

12. Rose, *op. cit.*, p. 472.

13. See, for example, Frederick K. Beutel, *Some Potentialities of Experimental Jurisprudence*, Lincoln, Neb.: University of Nebraska Press, 1957, pp. 400-401.

14. Borinski, *op. cit.*, p. 145.

15. Cf. Evan, "Due Process of Law in Military and Industrial Organizations," *op. cit.*

16. Cf. William M. Evan and Mildred A. Schwartz, "Law and the Emergence of Formal Organizations," *Sociology and Social Research*, 48 (1964), pp. 270-280.

17. Berger, *op. cit.*, p. 186.

38

The Use of Social Research in the Courts

Sharon M. Collins

. . . This paper deals with the present relationship of social science to the law, and specifically the extent to which the courts are using social science research. Ranked according to use, the four types of social research and development most commonly incorporated into legal cases are: (1) expert testimony, (2) results of existing studies, (3) public opinion polls, and (4) results of studies conducted specifically for the case at hand. Social research used within the legal system is primarily either evaluative or predictive. Of the two, more weight has been accorded to the former.

Legal input from particular social science disciplines ranges widely. At one extreme, economics is used relatively intensively; at the other, anthropology is seldom used. Psychological and sociological research, although frequently relevant, is more controversial, and thus engenders a higher degree of skepticism; its use lies between the two extremes. . . .

Excerpt from "The Use of Social Research in the Courts" in Laurence E. Lynn, Jr., ed., *Knowledge and Policy: The Uncertain Connection.* Washington, D.C.: National Academy of Sciences, 1978, pp. 147, 167-176, 178-182, by permission of the author and publisher.

Sociological and Social Psychological Research

Exclusive use of sociological evidence is rare; more frequently, it is used in conjunction with psychological evidence. And in light of the controversial nature of social science research, this is an altogether logical approach. Psychology, a more scientific discipline dealing with individual behavior, when placed in a sociological context will yield more comprehensive and more credible evidence. As may be expected, social psychological evidence exhibits the most extensive range of input to court cases. First used to expose the detrimental personality effects of segregation and later to prove discrimination, sociological research has in the past 20 years successfully laid the basis for many arguments of equal protection. Indeed, the National Association for the Advancement of Colored People (NAACP), which consistently incorporated sociological evidence in substantiation of its allegations of Fourteenth Amendment violations, has been its most loyal and most successful advocate.

The Brown Decision

In the area of segregation, *Brown* v. *Board of Education* (347 U.S. 483 [1954] ; consolidated with *Briggs* v. *Elliot, Davis* v. *County School Board of Prince Edward County*, and *Gebhart v. Belton*) is considered a landmark for two reasons. First, it laid the legal foundation for a national integration policy. Second, it stands, particularly in the eyes of many social scientists, as one of the first examples of social theory that found its way into formal law. The famed footnote 11 to the majority opinion, which relied heavily on the research of psychologist Kenneth Clark, stands as the most widely renowned legal use of social research (347 U.S. 483 at 494, n. 11).[1] In fact, it is widely believed within the social science community that, due to their legitimizing effects, sociological and psychological studies beginning with *Brown* acted as catalysts for the social changes of the past two decades. Since *Brown*, when the contact theory became an officially sanctioned policy model, social science research "has been inextricably interwoven with policy decisions" (Armour 1972, p. 93). Ironically, close examination of the validity of the social science evidence in *Brown*, its role in the Court's decision, and its impact on the overall process of desegregation exposes many fallacies that both the social science community and the public accepted. (See Cahn 1955 for criticism of the Clark data.)

Clark's research allegedly demonstrated the harmful effects of racial discrimination on the personalities of black children and, subsequently, on society. In his experiments, he presented black children with two dolls, identical except for skin color. One was white; the other was black. After ascertaining that the child had a clear concept of the meaning of colored, he asked which doll they preferred, or which was the "nice" doll. Two-thirds of the children tested preferred the white doll, considered it nice, and rejected the brown doll. All of these children gave spontaneous explanations of their choices, which, when categorized, reflected existing stereotypes about Negroes. The brown doll was dirty, it was going to fight, or, quite simply, it was bad. Finally Clark asked them to show him the doll they resembled. Despite their knowledge that the brown doll was colored, many said they believed themselves to be like the white doll (Clinard 1951). Others were more disturbed. In his testimony in *Davis v. County School Board of Prince Edward County* (347 U.S. 483 [1954], Clark reported:

[A] great many of the children react as if I were the devil in hell, myself, when I ask this final question. Some of them break down and leave the testing station; they cry. Particularly this is true of children in the north. It is as if I had tricked them. We were all friendly before, . . . and then I put them on the spot. . . . The explosion . . . [is] the degree to which this method . . . puts its finger upon the flagrant damage to the self esteem . . . of the Negro child (*Davis v. County School Board of Prince Edward County*, Transcript of Record at 252, filed July 12, 1952, case consolidated with *Brown v. Board of Education* on appeal to Supreme Court).

Clark interpreted these results as indicative of the basic distorting personality effect of prejudice, discrimination, and segregation. He acknowledged that a number of factors, such as security, social class, and parental education level, would affect the child's reaction. But he attributed to segregation the basic conflict between the children's concepts of themselves as blacks and their self images as individuals. (*Davis v. County School Board of Prince Edward County*, Record at 252; testimony in *Briggs v. Elliot*, 347 U.S. 497). Although many believe his conclusions today, at the time his subjective method and apparent lack of sophistication in technique cast doubt upon the technical validity of his research. . . .

Strictly from a legal point of view, the Clark data bore no direct relevance to the case at hand. As pointed out by Cahn (1955), Clark's study did not purport to measure the effects of school segregation; rather, it measured the impact of segregation in general. At best this still remained subjective and not amenable to precise measurement. Isolation of the impact of school segregation from the general effects of societal conditions is difficult if not impossible, and, considering the ages of the children tested, school segregation might reasonably be assumed to be the weaker factor. Indeed, Clark testified that the unexpected, fascinating result of his research was the realization that the ego damage occurred so early. This early detection points to sources outside the schools. Granted, school segregation would reinforce and perpetuate the damage, but that aspect was not the ostensible point of the research.

Regardless of its direct relevance, the Clark research was persuasive and only the extent of its influence is left to speculation. One thing is clear. Although it was used to support the conclusions that "separate educational facilities are inherently unequal" (347 U.S. at 498), social science research was not the prime determinant in the outcome of the case. The majority opinion in *Brown v. Board of Education* explicitly states that the decision was based on grounds of equal protection afforded by the Fourteenth Amendment (347 U.S. at 495). At most, social research in the *Brown* case was used to buttress, not to formulate, the overturn of the separate-but-equal doctrine.   •

Theories abound as to the exact purpose of the use of the Clark research in *Brown,* but the secrecy that cloaks Supreme Court actions precludes the determination of any definite role. Quite plausibly, the social research could have served as a political placebo. Passed off as an objective basis for such a revolutionary decision, the Court could have merely injected the research to soothe the public mind and remove part of the blame from the Court. Alternatively, the changes in the Court between the initial argument of *Brown* in 1952 and its reargument one year later may yield a clue. Within this time span, the character of the Court had shifted. Chief Justice Vinson had died; Earl Warren had succeeded him. And the Court by a very narrow margin had assumed a more liberal position. In this perspective, it is possible that the social research influenced the swing vote—if not by its content, by its potential public role as justifier.

Finally, the legal precedents involved, coupled with the carefully developed strategy of the NAACP, shed an interesting light on the role of the research. Not only did the *Brown* decision overrule the separate-but-equal doctrine, but it gave the use of social science research in legal cases its big splash. Both results were the culmination of carefully developed trends; neither was without historical precedent. Many have argued that the social research was superfluous to the actual decision; others have proposed that it provided the final push needed for the overruling of *Plessy v. Ferguson* (163 U.S. 537 [1896]). In fact, it was both the nature of the Clark information and its timing that provided the final impetus for reform.

Investigation of the precedents to *Brown* reveals a carefully constructed foundation that at first glance would condemn social research as unnecessary. *Missouri ex rel. Gaines v. Canada* (305 U.S. 337 [1938]) dealt with the inferiority of a state-supported black law school. The briefs presented strictly legal equal-protection arguments; no social science data was cited. The Court held that, regardless of whether it was separate, the state of Missouri must furnish legal education to blacks equal to that provided to whites. Ten years later, Sipuel, a black, applied to the all-white state law school and was rejected. In *Sipuel v. Board of Regents of Oklahoma* (332 U.S. 631 [1948]), the Court held that this rejection from the only available school was in violation of equal protection. Again, there was no use of social science research.

However, further inspection reveals that, beginning with *McLaurin v. Oklahoma State Regents* (339 U.S. 637 [1950]) and *Sweatt v. Painter* (339 U.S. 629 [1950]), social science evidence was an important factor. In both of these cases, although a separate black school existed, it was inferior to the white school. Blacks who were denied admission to the white schools refused to enter the black school and sued. Expert social science evidence supporting their arguments in *Sweatt* asserted that there was no scientific evidence of intellectual inferiority determined by race, thus racial classification for educational purposes was arbitrary (*Sweatt v. Painter*, Brief for Petitioner at 24). Second, segregation prevented both black and white students from obtaining full knowledge of the separated group and consequently stimulated mutual hostility. Third, prejudice was not a congenital instinct; thus it was the very act of segregation that perpetuated group isolation and undercut social stability (Brief at 26). Fourth, segregation accentuated the imagined differences between blacks and whites, creating an atmosphere unfavorable to proper education and stifling the black child's motivation to learn. "A definitive study of the scientific works of contemporary sociologists, historians, and anthropologists conclusively document[s] the proposition that the intent and result of [segregation is] . . . the establishment of an inferior status" (Brief for Petitioner at 28). Asserting that this status was neither valid, necessary, nor societally advantageous, the petitioners argued that it should be eliminated. The Court accepted their propositions holding that, since the education offered by the black law school was substantially inferior, the Fourteenth Amendment required that blacks be admitted to the white law school. On its face, the *Sweatt* evidence appears strong enough to have supported the *Brown* decision, perhaps stronger than the Clark data actually used. Assuming the strength of the *Sweatt* precedent, the Clark data of *Brown* appears to be more a justifying than a persuasive factor.

Whether the intended role of social science research in the school segregation cases was to buttress or to exert influence on its own merits, its deliberate presence cannot be denied. Clearly, the NAACP had laid a careful foundation for *Brown*. They had struggled for 16 years to convince the Supreme Court that segregation was in violation of the Fourteenth Amendment; precedents to *Brown* contained both legal and social science arguments.

In the years following *Brown*, the courts probed the area of segregation; accordingly, the scope of segregation litigation expanded. Cases progressed from ruling against segregation in schools per se (*Brown v. Board of Education*) to upholding school busing programs (*Keyes v. School District No. 1*, 413 U.S. 189 [1973]), contesting the unfair educational consequences of school tracking systems (*Hobson v. Hansen*, 269 F. Supp. 401, 495 (D.D.C. 1967), *aff'd sub nom. Smuck v. Hobson*, 408 F.2d 175 [D.C. Cir. 1969]), standardized testing (*Chance v. Board of Examiners*, 330 F. Supp. 203 [S.D.N.Y. 1971]), and reevaluating school financing procedures (*Serrano v. Priest*, 5 Cal. 3d 584, 487 P.2d 1241, 96 Cal. Rptr. 601 [1971], 45 U.S.L.W. 2340, June 30, 1976). Moreover, the controversy sparked by the *Brown* decision generated its own demand for research. Consequently, relying on the *Brown* precedent and the ensuing boom in research, the arguments in cases after *Brown* frequently cited social science studies.

The Coleman Report

In the early 1960s, Congress commissioned the U.S. Office of Education to conduct a survey concerning the lack of public educational opportunities due to race, color, religion, or national origin. Known as the Coleman Report (Coleman *et al.* 1966), the report stressed two main points. First, the single greatest determinant of a child's academic performance is family background. And, second, if a minority pupil from a home lacking educational strength studies with schoolmates having strong educational backgrounds, the minority child's achievement level will improve—without effecting a negative response in the performance of the other children. Thus, increasing contact between white and minority students, from a purely educational viewpoint, was not a zero-sum operation. Coleman's "contact theory" predicted that the achievements and aspirations of black students should improve in direct proportion to the increased contact between black and white students, and the performance of white children would not suffer.

The publication of the Coleman Report in 1966 gave fresh impetus to the desegregation drive, which had been stymied by years of southern intransigence (Ravitch 1975). In particular, civil rights groups seized on Coleman's second point in advocating integration through the busing of school children. As a result, the Coleman Report strongly influenced the issuance of the federal busing order of 1970 and was persuasive in subsequent litigation (see *Keyes v. School District No. 1*, 413 U.S. 189 [1973]; *Swann v. Board of Education*, 402 U.S. 1 [1970]. . . .

However, the busing experiment has not achieved the success that the Coleman research projected. At present, there are widespread doubts regarding its overall effectiveness. The current debate turns on two particular issues: whether busing stimulates white flight from city public schools to suburbs and private schools, and whether it has educational value for black pupils. It is now apparent that the research on which the busing actions relied so heavily suffered from a far too limited scope, focusing solely on the positive impact on children but abstracting the potentially negative reactions of adults. . . .

Educational Tracking

By the 1970s social research had finally come into its own; it was no longer uncommon to have social science evidence supporting the arguments of both parties to a lawsuit. *Hobson v. Hansen*, one of the first educational tracking cases, was such a case. The briefs of both sides incorporated extensive social science research dealing with the segregative and educational impacts of tracking. The issues raised required the court not only to resolve the question of equal protection but, more significantly, to evaluate the scientific competence of the tracking system. Holding against tracking, the opinion stated that, although ability grouping is an accepted educational practice, the IQ tests upon which it was based did not reliably measure the innate abilities of minority students. Since IQ tests were standardized on white middle-class children, disadvantaged minority children were unfairly relegated to lower tracks. Thus, they received an education inferior to that of whites in violation of their Fourteenth Amendment rights (see also *Johnson v. San Francisco Unified School District*, 339 F. Supp. 1315 [N.D. Cal. 1971]).

Larry P. v. Riles (343 F. Supp. 1306 [N.D. Cal. 1972]) went a step further, challenging the teaching misclassification of black children as educably mentally retarded. Relying on the findings of *Hobson* and socio-psychological evidence of a statistical racial imbalance in IQ testing, the brief for Larry P. alleged that the IQ tests that were a substantial factor in placement yielded a disproportionate classification of black children as mentally retarded. And, introducing the "null hypothesis of special education," it proposed that failure to prove a relationship between race and intelligence requires the assumption that no relationship exists. On this basis, the court held that the disproportionate classification of blacks as educably mentally retarded was unconstitutionally discriminatory.

Standardized Testing for Employment

The case against standardized testing was carried into the employment arena in the early 1970s. Again, social science played a role in resolving the validity of these tests. Unlike the education cases, which involved allegations of deprivations of constitutional rights, employment discrimination cases required statutory interpretation as well. Title VII § 703 of the Civil Rights Act of 1964 forbids an employer to classify or segregate employees or limit their production to deprive them of employment opportunities or adversely affect their status because of race, color, religion, sex, or national origin. But § 703(h) authorizes the use of any professionally developed employee aptitude test provided it is not designed, intended, or used to discriminate. . . .

The leading case on this topic was *Griggs v. Duke Power Company* (401 U.S. 424 [1971]). Relying on a statistical study, the plaintiffs convinced the court that standardized tests used as an employment criterion failed to predict job success or measure job-related abilities and placed blacks at a marked disadvantage in the labor market. The Court held that employment tests must indicate a "demonstrably reasonable measure of job performance" (401 U.S. 436). Thus, any employment practice excluding blacks that cannot be shown to be related to job performance was prohibited, notwithstanding the employer's lack of discriminatory intent. . . .

School Financing

In the landmark decision of *Serrano v. Priest*, The Supreme Court of California relied on the statistical and socioeconomic research of Coons, Clune, and Sugarman in striking down the traditional means of support for local school systems—local property taxes (see, 57 Cal. L. Rev. 388). Following an analysis of the total assessed valuation of real estate, amount of money spent per pupil, local variations in property tax rates, and state contributions to student costs, the court concluded that regional variations in income and property values, as identified, yielded regional fluctuation in the quality of education. The subsequent inability of poorer districts to sustain an educational level comparable to that of the more wealthy districts was a denial of equal protection. Thus, the court concluded that:

> [T]he California public school financing system, with its substantial dependence on local property taxes and resultant wide disparities in school revenue, violates the equal protection clause of the Fourteenth Amendment. . . . [T]his funding scheme invidiously discriminates against the poor because it makes the quality of a child's education a function of the wealth of his parents and neighbors (5 Cal. 3d at 589, 96 Cal. Rptr. 601 at 604).

Serrano marked the start of a national trend eliminating state reliance on local property taxes as the principal means of financing public schools. Since the *Serrano* decision, 19 states have legislated major school financing reforms. Eight others have assumed larger shares of the burden of education. And persuaded by *Serrano*, state courts in New Jersey, Washington, and Connecticut have held state property tax financing systems unconstitutional because of the inequities created between rich and poor districts. Each court delegated the responsibility for developing a replacement system to the state legislatures. To date, only the New Jersey legislature, which passed a state income tax for school financing in 1976, has completed its reform measures (Sullivan, N.Y.T., April 20, 1976; see N.J. Stat. Ann. 18A:7A-2, -4 [Supp. 1976]).

But the battle stopped at the Supreme Court. Faced with analogous contentions and presented with similar supporting social science data, the United States Supreme Court arrived at a conclusion opposite to *Serrano*. In *Rodriquez v. San Antonio Independent School District* (411 U.S. 1 [1973]), the court dismissed the equal protection contention on the grounds that there was no fundamental right to education. Thus, only absolute denial of educational opportunities would trigger the protection of the Fourteenth Amendment. But there was no "interference with fundamental rights where only relative differences in spending levels [were] . . . involved and where . . . no charge fairly could be made that the system fails to provide each child with an opportunity to acquire the basic minimal skills necessary for the enjoyment of the rights of speech and of full participation in the political process" (411 U.S. at 37). . . . The Court retreated to an absolutist position in deference to more pervasive constitutional standards—irrespective of any supra-legal proof that might compel a contrary holding. It stated that to hold otherwise would require the Court to "intrude in an area which it has traditionally deferred to state legislature (411 U.S. at 40)" and assume a role for which the Court lacks both authority and competence (411 U.S. at 54). . . .

Forces Affecting the Growth of Sociolegal Cooperation

The application of social science research to legal problems has gained a strong foothold throughout the course of this century. Particularly in the last decade, the use of sociolegal research has intensified and branched out into more controversial, less quantifiable topics. Attorneys and judges have begun to view legal issues neither in isolation nor in a vacuum, but in the more comprehensive framework of conditions revealed by the social sciences. In perspective, however, this development represents only the first step. Upon analysis, three forces appear to be the major hindrances to social science-legal cooperation. Foremost is the intellectual strain between lawyers and social scientists. More subtle are the political context within which social science and the law must interact and the time lag between the results of research by social scientists and their effects on the attitudes of society.

Apprehension of the Legal Profession

Above all, the profound differences in perspective between social scientists and lawyers have laid an unstable foundation for the alliance between social science and law. The legal focus on remedies for individual clients presents both a strength and a weakness. "The strength is . . . individualized justice. . . . The weakness is that they sometimes treat only part of the problem and do not touch more basic issues" (Handler 1971, pp. 346, 347). Indeed, both in research and in resolution, the legal approach is much narrower than the scientific. Ideally, cooperation with social science would expand this relatively narrow scope.

There still remains a skepticism verging on hostility that pervades the legal attitude toward social science—a condition that in turn frustrates attempts to use social science research. It has been suggested that the single most important barrier to the use of social science evidence is ignorance (Lochner 1973). In practice, this contention gains merit. As most lawyers lack social science training, they are frequently incapable of evaluating sophisticated social science research. Consequently, their attitudes range from highly skeptical to uncritically receptive, although on the whole the skepticism prevails. But there are dangers inherent to either position. The skeptics, who substantiate their criticism with examples of unreliable research such as the misrepresentation of the *Brown* evidence . . . tend to discount the validity of the social science evidence automatically or disregard it entirely. At the other extreme, those who blindly use evidence without bothering to evaluate it critically risk perpetuating unsound research. If research is not scrutinized upon its initial use, mistakes that survived the first evaluation may survive each successive use, since previously used studies tend to receive only cursory legal review.

The recent inception of social science programs in many law schools is beginning to solve this problem. As a result, some new lawyers now enter the profession equipped with the analytical skills of the social sciences, particularly economics, in addition to those of law. But the skepticism of social science that pervades the legal profession reaches down to the ranks of the students as well, retarding the positive effect of their training. Morever, this positive effect will cut both ways. More thorough understanding of social science analysis will erase some of the inherent prejudice against social science, but it will also expose the analytical and methodological problems in the research.

Generally, the skepticism of the legal profession stems not from analytical handicaps but from sheer mistrust. In part this is a sensible reaction. Lawyers are skeptical, frequently justifiably, of the alleged "extravagant claims of . . . psychiatrists that every criminal is simply a sick individual who, given psychiatric treatment would be made sane . . . [or of] sociologists that every criminal is simply a product of his environment and if you will change this environment, you will have an honest, law abiding citizen" (Gibbons 1971, p. 151).

Moreover, many lawyers frequently condemn social science as overly dependent on value judgments and empirically and unverifiable. Critical of the malleability of social science evidence, they question its accuracy and doubt the integrity of a methodology that derives general observations from samples. Many believe that "shrewd resourceful lawyers can put together a Brandeis brief in support of almost any conceivable exercise of legislative judgment" (Geis 1962, p. 573). And some maintain that the social sciences will become useful to the legal profession only when they "achieve the rigor of the most advanced of the physical sciences" (Donnelly 1959, p. 83). But the focus of the social sciences and the very nature of the subject matter renders such an achievement virtually impossible.

In addition, many lawyers are wary of the dissension among social scientists, believing that it reflects deep-seated defects in the social science disciplines themselves. From the time of the first uses of social science evidence, this belief has prevailed:

> [W]hile courts will go a long way in admitting expert testimony deduced from a well-recognized scientific principle or discovery, the thing from which the deduction is made must be sufficiently established to have gained general acceptance in the particular field in which it belongs (*Frye v. United States*, 293 F. 1013, 1014 [D.C. Cir. 1923]).

As a result, they fear that the use of evidence as controversial and as impermanent as much of the social science research has proven to be would leave the determination of the law in an extremely uncertain state. They ask, "Can we afford, can we undertake every generation . . . to rewrite our statutes and our legislation when the sociological or psychiatric or medical theory changes?" (Kramer 1959, p. 568).

It has been alleged that part of the hostility toward social science evidence stems from territorial protectiveness—a defense against the increasing encroachment of the social sciences upon legal preserves. But the case against social science is not limited to subjective reactions. To a large degree, the antagonism of lawyers toward the social sciences springs from the inability of these sciences to provide pragmatic information directly relevant to the practice of law. Indeed, social research is most effective in those areas of law that affect a substantial portion of society, such as school segregation. In contrast, social research is much less valuable in cases that directly affect a limited number of individuals, such as cases determining criminality. Since the former category constitutes only a segment of the legal spectrum, social research can claim only a limited jurisdiction.

Judicial Reaction

Not only have attorneys used social science evidence to convince judges and juries, but, on occasion, judges have incorporated results of social science research into their opinions to convince the public as well. It is a logical assumption that the actual role of social science research has been not in directing court actions but in supporting them. In fact, in controversial cases when opinions relating to social issues have broken with precedent, social science evidence has often been cited, quite plausibly, to buttress the opinion of the court, lend legitimacy to a result decided on other grounds, and counteract the emotional reaction of the public (see *Brown v. Board of Education*).

However, even when the social research is well presented, judicial apprehension remains an uncertain factor. On the Supreme Court, five judges who are impressed with the social science research are frequently balanced by four who are not. In the lower courts, the variations are more extreme. And this uncertainty holds no promise of becoming clearer in the future. "We shall not know to what extent judges are significantly influenced by social science testimony until they tell us, and this is not customary, expedient, nor even wise from the standpoint of their relation to the public and to the losing party" (Rose 1955, p. 214).

Conclusion

Whatever the purpose in using the research, the impact of social science on the law is an identifiable factor that will grow as the cooperation of social science and the law further develops. . . .

References

Allport, F. (1953). The effects of segregation and the consequences of desegregation: a social science statement. Appendix to appellant's brief in *Davis v. County School Board*. 1952. 37 *Minn. L. Rev.* 427.

Armour, D. (1972). The evidence on busing. *The Public Interest*, Summer, pp. 90–126.

Cahn, E. (1955). Jurisprudence. *New York University Law Review* 30: 150.

Clinard, M. (1951). Sociologists and American criminology. *Journal of Criminal Law* 41: 549–77.

Coleman, J. S., *et al.* (1966). *Equality of Education Opportunity.* U.S. Department of Health, Education, and Welfare. Washington, D.C.: U.S. Government Printing Office.

Donnelly, R. C. (1959). Some comments upon the law and behavioral science program at Yale. *Journal of Legal Education* 12: 83.

Geis, G. (1962). Social science and the law. *Washburn Law Journal* 1: 569–86.

Gibbons, H. (1971). Law in an age of social change. *American Bar Association Journal* 57: 151.

Handler, J. F. (1971). Field research strategies in urban legal studies. *Law and Society Review* 5: 345.

Kramer, R. (1959). Some observations on law and interdisciplinary research. *Duke Law Journal*, Fall, p. 563.

Lochner, P. R., Jr. (1973). Some limits on the application of social science research in the legal process. *Law and Social Order* (1973): 815–48.

Ravitch, D. (1975). Busing: the solution that has failed to solve. *New York Times News of the Week in Review*, December 21, p. 3.

Rose, A. M. (1955). The social scientist as an expert witness. *Minnesota Law Review* 40: 205.

Note

1. See Allport 1953 for the appendix to the appellant's briefs in the school segregation cases prepared by psychiatrists and social scientists regarding the harmful effects of segregation on Negro school children.

39

Deterrence Regained: The Cheshire Constabulary's "Breathalyser Blitz"
H. Laurence Ross

The competence of law as a social tool in the control of drinking and driving has been firmly demonstrated in only one major case: the British Road Safety Act of 1967, the "breathalyser" law. Unfortunately, from the viewpoint of social engineering, evidence has been accumulating that the reductions in crashes, injuries and lives lost produced by this legislation were temporary, and that the effect of the law on a national scale has vanished. This paper reports a recapture of the deterrent effect of the breathalyser law occasioned by a police-initiated enforcement campaign in the county of Cheshire. The experiences gained in this little-known campaign aid in understanding the limited effectiveness of the "breathalyser" law and of deterrence-oriented legislation in general.

Legal Background

The "breathalyser blitz" was a local enforcement campaign based on the British Road Safety Act of 1967. That legislation replaced

Reprinted from "Deterrence Regained: The Cheshire Constabulary's "Breathalyser Blitz," *Journal of Legal Studies* 6 (January 1977), pp. 241–249, by permission of the author and publisher, The University of Chicago Law School.

the prior "classical" definition of illegal drinking and driving (impairment" of the ability to drive properly) with the quantitative one of driving with a blood alcohol level exceeding a prescribed limit. It provided a procedure based on scientific breath and blood tests for demonstration of the offense. In response to libertarian fears of police abuses the legislation limited the ability of the police to request these tests to situations in which a driver was involved in an accident or a traffic law violation, as well as situations in which the police suspected a driver of having consumed alcohol. The penalty for the offense was a mandatory year's license suspension, barring "special circumstances." The law was accompanied by considerable publicity at its inception in the form of government-sponsored campaigns as well as extensive press commentary, some of it negative and based on fears of police abuse.

When the Road Safety Act came into effect in October of 1967, crash rates in Britain declined precipitously, offering impressive evidence of deterrence of drinking and driving by the new law.[1] However, the initial success of the Act in mitigating the problem of drinking and driving on a national scale proved not to be maintained over time. A significant measure of the extent of alcohol involvement in fatal crashes—the percentage of killed drivers with illegal blood alcohol levels—which initially declined from 25 percent to 15 percent in 1967–1968, showed a steady increase and reached 35 percent by 1974.[2] Official dismay concerning the fate of the legislation led to the appointment by the Department of the Environment of an investigative committee chaired by Frank Blennerhassett, Q.C., which confirmed the loss of effectiveness of the Act and reported recommendations for revisions in the spring of 1976. The two major factors cited by Blennerhassett as causes for the declining effectiveness of the Road Safety Act were the "growing abuse of alcohol" and the fact of "the drinking driver's growing appreciation that the real risk of being detected and convicted, though higher than before, remains low."[3]

The "Blitz" in Cheshire

Although British police are a more coordinated organization than the congeries of local forces that exists in the United States, the Chief Constable of each provincial constabulary retains considerable discretion in setting enforcement priorities. As stated by the reporter for the Blennerhassett Committee, "Parliament tells the police what they may do, the Government gives resources, but the Chief Constables decide what use to make of their powers and means."[4] It was thus within the power of individual Chief Constables to place greater or less stress on the enforcement of the Road Safety Act. In early 1975 William Kelsall, the Chief Constable of Cheshire, became concerned about the problem of drinking and driving in the county for which he was responsible, and issued orders for stricter enforcement of the existing legislation:

> Last year, we found the number of accidents occurring after ten o'clock at night to be totally unacceptable. It could not be explained by the number of motorists, inclement weather, or other such factors. We thought that perhaps part of it might be due to light conditions, and part perhaps due to drinking and driving. We determined to experiment, to go as far as we could within the law to breathalyse all people driving between 10 at night and 2 in the morning. . . . We did this by eliminating all discretion for the officers: a breath test was to be done for every moving offence and every accident.[5]

Initially the effort was confined to a single week in July of 1975, with no publicity outside of the police force. During this week breath tests numbered 284 compared with 31 in the same week of 1974. Seemingly, the increase in breath tests more than doubled the number of drivers found guilty of violating the Road Safety Act—38 in the week of the enforcement campaign compared with 13 in the same week one year earlier. The program of maximum enforcement suggested that a significant number of impaired drivers had been overlooked when the request for a breath test was left to the discretion of the police officer.

The enforcement program was intended to be exploratory, to see whether a "campaign" was in fact needed. Prior to undertaking such a campaign, it was determined to repeat the enforcement effort on a somewhat larger scale, from September 1 to September 28, 1975, again without publicity, to assure the generalizability of the July results. Orders were given to require a breath test of drivers experiencing accidents and violations within the extended hours of 9 P.M. to 4 A.M. and also 2 P.M. to 5 P.M.

Contrary to the intentions of the Chief Constable, news of the enforcement program for September leaked to the press and soon the program became a controversial political question in Cheshire. Allegations were made by representatives of the Automobile Association and the Royal Automobile Club that the program was similar to random breath testing of drivers, which was considered abusive and which had been vehemently opposed in the origination of the Road Safety Act. The charge was taken up by a member of the Cheshire County Council, but Kelsall stoutly defended his actions, threatening resignation if there were any official criticism, and the program was in the end strongly backed by the supervising Police Committee and by most of the local press.

The effect of the publicity was to convert Kelsall's experiment in enforcement into a campaign. As in the early months of the Road Safety Act of 1967 there were reports in the press of complaints by pub owners of a great loss of business. And as in 1967 there were official claims of accidents reduced and lives saved. In a circular distributed following the termination of the program, Chief Constable Kelsall claimed:

> During [the program] between the hours of 9 P.M. and 4 A.M. the number of accidents was reduced from 153 in 1974 to 94 in 1975, and . . . the number of fatal accidents reduced from 13 to 8 . . . The result of all this has been that the campaign which we would have conducted after the exercise is now no longer necessary since the general motorists in Cheshire are well aware of the position and the need to exercise more care in the amount of alcohol consumed and the manner of driving. . . . All in all, I think the exercise has been worthwhile and that the beneficial effects might well be felt for some time.[6]

Interrupted Time-Series Analysis

The literature of quasi-experimental analysis asserts that causal conclusions based only on the comparison of conditions subsequent to a supposed cause with those prior to the cause are subject to a wide variety of rival alternative explanations. The differences noted by Kelsall might in the absence of other evidence be attributed for example to such matters as a possible general decline in miles driven due to some extraneous cause, to changes in drinking patterns unrelated to the "blitz", to changes in recordkeeping, to publicity acting without reference to the law enforcement, or to statistical artifacts of one kind or another.[7] More information is needed to furnish a scientifically acceptable basis for the impression of cause and effect noted in official statements. Fortunately, routinely published data on various kinds of accidents in Cheshire permit the application of interrupted time-series analysis to test and in general confirm the Chief Constable's conclusions.

Figure 1 presents a monthly time series of accidents causing serious and fatal injuries for the two years from April 1974 through March 1976.[8] It can be seen that in September 1975, the month of the campaign, the curve declined sharply. The drop is statistically significant, and accords with the interpretation that the "blitz", rather than the other factors mentioned, caused the reduction in accidents.[9] Further evidence appears in Figure 2, which graphs total accidents during the "drinking" hours of 10 P.M. to 4 P.M. over the same time period as Figure 1. The curve should be compared with that in Figure 3, which graphs accidents occurring during the "nondrinking" hours of 7 A.M. to 10 A.M. and 4 P.M. to 5 P.M. The for-

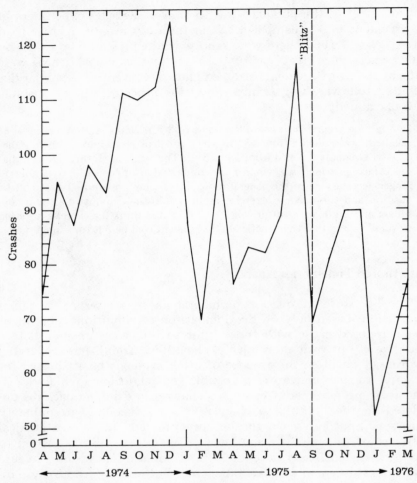

FIGURE 1. Crashes Producing Serious or Fatal Injuries in Chesire, England

mer figure shows a sharp decline which verges on statistical significance despite the very small data base, whereas the latter shows an increase rather than a decline in September of 1975. This comparison is consistent with the interpretation that accidents were affected by a factor that operates in "drinking" hours but not in "nondrinking" hours, and it is reasonable to suppose that this factor was the "breathalyser blitz."

As noted previously, the Road Safety Act of 1967 provided that police could at their discretion require breath tests for alcohol from drivers involved in accidents or law violations, or who were suspected by an officer of having alcohol in their blood. The Act permitted,

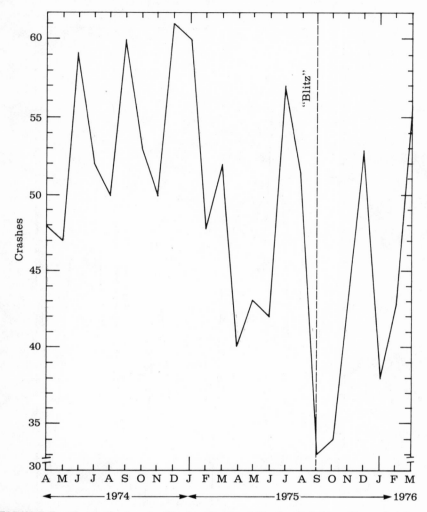

FIGURE 2. Total Crashes in Chesire, England During Drinking Hours (10 P.M. to 4 A.M. Daily)

but did not require, these tests. By requiring testing in all permissible situations, the Cheshire "blitz" was able to enlighten the pattern of *de facto* enforcement that had existed in the routine application of the Road Safety Act.

Table 1 compares the numbers of tests demanded during the "blitz" with those demanded during the same month of the previous year, when enforcement was routine. The demands are grouped into categories depending on the authorizing condition: accident (with or

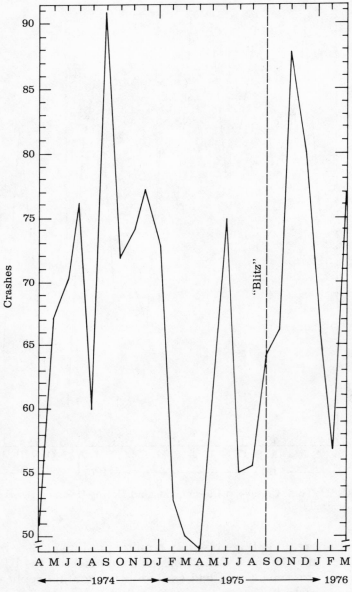

FIGURE 3. Total Crashes in Chesire, England During Non-Drinking Hours (7-10 A.M. & 4-5 P.M. Daily)

T A B L E 1 . Reasons Supporting Demands for Breath Tests by
Police in Cheshire

REASON	NUMBER IN SEPTEMBER 1975	NUMBER IN SEPTEMBER 1974	RATIO
Traffic law violation	970	62	15.6
Accident (no injury)	131	15	8.7
Accident (injury)	137	41	3.3
Suspicion of alcohol	387	35	14.1
Total	1625	153	10.6

without injury), violation, or suspicion of alcohol. It can be seen that
the greatest increase in breath tests occurred for drivers involved in
traffic law violations, and the least increase occurred for drivers
involved in accidents, especially where injury was involved. From
these facts it can be deduced that in routine enforcement conditions
police were more likely to use their discretion to test accident-
involved drivers than drivers committing traffic law infractions.[10]

Of further interest is the fact that occasions of suspicion of alcohol in the blood mounted considerably during the "blitz" despite the
absence of instructions on this matter. It would appear that police
officers perceived their mandate as an enforcement campaign against
drinking and driving and that they became more alert to cues apart
from violations and accidents that would warrant requesting a breath
test.

Discussion

Application of interrupted time-series methodology to data surrounding the time of the "breathalyser blitz" in Cheshire shows that
the initial effectiveness of the Road Safety Act of 1967 was retrieved
by a publicized local enforcement campaign. It is of particular interest to note that the series in question do not show any important
reactions of the crash curves to the July program, which was unpubli-
cized. The deterrent consequence is linked to a publicized enforcement effort, as commonsense expectations would predict.

The "blitz" was limited in time, with a known terminal date following which discretion in the matter of breath testing a driver was
returned to the police patrolmen. There is evidence of some residual
effect on decisions to require a breath test. Total tests were running
between 100 and 250 per month through 1974 and early 1975; they
reached nearly 450 in July of 1975, the month of the initial one-

week enforcement program, and more than 1600 during September. From October 1975 through March 1976 the level of tests, though down from the September peak, remained higher than before, varying from about 250 to 350 per month.

It is harder to say whether Kelsall was right in his assertion that a beneficial effect on the rate of crashes would continue for some time. The crash figures for October 1975 do appear to be close to the reduced level of September, but the figures for subsequent months suggest a return to normal. Such a restoration of the *status quo ante* seems expectable if the reason for the reduction in crashes was simple deterrence, that is, a reaction to the threat of punishment inherent in the enforcement campaign. In the absence of other data, this interpretation seems adequate to the facts at hand.

The termination of the "breathalyser blitz" makes it impossible to judge whether the level of enforcement obtained in Cheshire was sufficiently high to furnish permanent credibility and thus deterrence over the long run for the threat posed by the Road Safety Act. The level of breath testing achieved during the "blitz" was roughly six times the national figure on a per capita basis, and it would have been most interesting to know whether such a level of enforcement over a longer time would have had permanent or at least longer-run deterrent effects.

The Cheshire "breathalyser blitz" demonstrates important deterrent results for increased enforcement of a modern drinking-and-driving statute in a short-term and well-publicized campaign. It suggests both the possibilities for social engineering inherent in simple deterrence and the large number of unknown parameters that surely limit these possibilities. The need is evident and urgent to explore both the possibilities and the limitations suggested here.

Notes

1. H. Laurence Ross, Law, Science and Accidents: The British Road Safety Act of 1976, 2 *J. Leg. Studies* 1 (1973). It might be noted that this study stands virtually alone in furnishing scientifically convincing evidence of legal effectiveness controlling drinking and driving. Compare H. Laurence Ross, The Scandinavian Myth: The Effectiveness of Drinking-and-Driving Legislation in Sweden and Norway, 4 *J. Leg. Studies* 285 (1975); Brian R. Carr, H. Goldberg and C. M. L. Farbar, The Canadian Breathalizer Legislation: An Inferential Evaluation, in Alcohol, Drugs, and Traffic Safety 679–88 (Proc. 6th Int'l Conf. on Alcohol, Drugs and Traffic Safety, Toronto, Sept. 8–13, 1974; S. Israelstam & S. Lambert eds. 1975).
2. P. J. Codling, Road Casualties since the 'Drinking and Driving' Legislation (Transport & Road Research Laboratory Supp. Report 134 UC (1975).

3. Gt. Brit. Dep't of the Environment, Drinking and Driving: Report of the Departmental Committee 1 (1976).

4. Private communication to the author from Dennis Baldry, July 9, 1976.

5. Interview with Chief Constable William Kelsall, Chester, England, May 10, 1976.

6. Circular Letter distributed by Chief Constable William Kelsall, October 24, 1975.

7. Donald T. Campbell, Reforms as Experiments, 24 Am. Psych. 409 (1969), and H. Laurence Ross, Donald T. Campbell and Gene V. Glass, "Determining the Social Effects of a Legal Reform," *American Behavioral Scientist* 13 (March–April 1970): 493–509.

8. Data for the County of Cheshire are limited in extent and refinement. The County extends for approximately 900 square miles, and population is approximately 900,000. This is a very small jurisdiction for the accumulation of monthly traffic accident data. The small data base produces considerable instability in the series and no seasonal trends are evident, probably for the same reason.

9. The significance level is .05 (one-tailed test).

10. A possible explanation, not verifiable from presently available data, is that accident-involved drivers more frequently have elevated blood alcohol levels.

40

Untouchability and the Law
Marc Galanter

. . . In 1950 when the Constitution came into force, the exclusion of Untouchables from public facilities and Hindu temples, previously recognized and to some extent enforceable as law, had been transformed into statutory offenses throughout most of India. The Constitution itself carried the prohibition on this conduct a step further, by entrenching freedom from such disabilities as a fundamental right.

The Constitution of 1950 enacts as justiciable fundamental rights a battery of provisions designed to eliminate caste discrimination on the part of governmental bodies. Most of the Fundamental Rights conferred by the Constitution are restrictions solely on the actions of the state.[1] But several provisions, including those concerning untouchability, go beyond this to regulate private as well as official behavior. Article 17 provides that:

> "Untouchability" is abolished and its practice in any form is forbidden. The enforcement of any disability in arising out of "Untouchability" shall be an offense punishable in accordance with law.[2]

It is further provided in Article 15(2) that:

> (2) No citizen shall, on grounds only of religion, race, caste, sex, place of birth

Excerpt from "The Abolition of Disabilities—Untouchability and the Law," in J. Michael Mahar, ed., *The Untouchables in Contemporary India*. Tucson, Arizona: University of Arizona Press, 1972, pp. 241–291. Reprinted by permission of the author and publisher.

or any of them, be subject to any disability, liability, restriction or condition with regard to

a. access to shops, public restaurants, hotels and places of public entertainment; or

b. the use of wells, tanks, bathing ghats, roads and places of public resort maintained wholly or partly out of State funds or dedicated to the use of the general public.

Article 29(2) forbids persons in charge of "any educational institution . . . receiving aid out of state funds" to deny admission to an applicant "on grounds only of religion, race, caste, language or any of them." Article 23 prohibits *begar* and forced labor.

Article 25, which guarantees freedom to profess, practice and propagate religion is specifically made subject to the other fundamental rights provisions and is explicitly qualified by the proviso that:

(2) Nothing in this article shall affect the operation of any existing law or prevent the State from making any law . . .

    (b) providing for social welfare or reform or the throwing open of Hindu religious institutions of a public character to all classes and sections of Hindus.

Thus a broad range of disabilities is directly outlawed and government is empowered to take corrective action.

Article 17 not only forbids the practice of "untouchability" but declares that "enforcement of disabilities arising out of 'Untouchability' shall be an offense punishable in accordance with law." Article 35 provides that "Parliament shall have, and the Legislature of a State shall not have, power to make laws . . . prescribing punishment for those acts which are declared to be offenses under this Part." . . .

In 1955 Parliament exercised this exclusive power and passed the Untouchability (Offences) Act, which remains the culmination of anti-disabilities legislation to the early 1970s. The UOA outlaws the enforcement of disabilities "on the ground of untouchability" in regard to, inter alia, entrance and worship at temples, access to shops and restaurants, the practice of occupations and trades, use of water sources, places of public resort and accommodation, public conveyances, hospitals, educational institutions, construction and occupation of residential premises, holding of religious ceremonies and processions, use of jewelry and finery. The imposition of disabilities is made a crime punishable by fine of up to Rs. 500, imprisonment for up to six months, cancellation or suspension of licenses and of public grants.

The power of civil courts to enforce any claim or recognize any custom, usage or right which would result in the enforcement of any disability is withdrawn. The previous provincial enactments had also withdrawn all governmental sanction, but they did not venture into the area of "caste autonomy" or behavior indirectly supporting the practice of untouchability. But the UOA punishes not only the enforcement of disabilities, but indirect social support of untouchability. The use of social boycotts against persons who exercise rights under the Act, the use of sanctions, including excommunication, against persons who refuse to practice untouchability, and the instigation of the practice of untouchability in any form are likewise prohibited and penalized. The Act contains one further novel and notable feature: it provides that where any of the forbidden practices "is committed in relation to a member of a Scheduled Caste . . ." the Court shall presume, unless the contrary is proved, that such act was committed on the ground of "untouchability."

The Untouchability (Offences) Act in the Higher Courts

. . . No case involving the UOA has reached the Supreme Court and, since few petty criminal appeals do, it is not likely that the Supreme Court will play a significant role in interpreting the UOA. It seems fair to say that the UOA has not fared well in the High Courts, in contrast with the earlier state legislation, which generally received favorable interpretations from these courts. A very crude measure of the shift of judicial response is provided by Table 1, which compares the outcomes of High Court cases involving the UOA and the earlier state legislation. This unfavorable reception by the High Courts seems to involve three problem areas: the requirement that the forbidden act be committed "on the ground of untouchability"; the uncertainty

T A B L E 1 .   Disposition by High Courts of Appeals Concerning Temple-entry and Anti-disabilities Legislation

| | DECISION | |
LEGISLATION	IN FAVOR OF UNTOUCHABLES' RIGHTS	AGAINST UNTOUCHABLES' RIGHTS
State Acts	12	6
UOA	2	9

Note: This table includes all cases which could be found in the more prominent Indian law reports and in the local reports available to me, and two unreported judgments in my possession. Each case has been treated as a unit and scored as favoring the Untouchables' rights if the overall result is in their favor (i.e., conviction affirmed, act held applicable, relief granted) even where there are elements in the case that detract from the result, as, e.g., acquittal of some parties, reduction of fine, etc.

about coverage of private property; and the limitation of rights to those enjoyed by members of the same religious denomination.

The "Ground of 'Untouchability'" Problem

The principal substantive sections of the UOA forbid the denial of facilities and services "on the ground of 'untouchability.'" This requirement of specific intent makes it difficult to secure convictions, since states of mind are difficult to prove. The drafters of the UOA attempted to obviate this difficulty by reversing the onus of proof; the Act provides that where any of the forbidden practices "is committed in relation to a member of a Scheduled Caste . . . the court shall presume, unless the contrary is proved, that such act was committed on the ground of 'untouchability'."

Even accompanied by this presumption, the "ground of untouchability" requirement restricts the operation of the UOA to instances in which the accused's act proceeds from or is accompanied by a specific mental state. However . . . the nature of this mental state is far from clear. Neither the Constitution nor the UOA defines untouchability; judges required to define it find it no easy matter. Government, the legislature and the courts all tend to define it denotatively—by pointing to well-known examples of its practice rather than connotatively by specifying boundary criteria. How then can the judge as trier of fact decide whether this complex and obscure notion of untouchability was a component of the mental state of the accused at the time of the purported offense? States of mind can only be inferred from observed behavior. And observed behavior may involve a complex admixture of motives: economic, religious, social and psychological. Making this imponderable mental state a part of the offense makes it difficult to deal with those patterns of discriminatory conduct whose incidence does not correspond precisely and directly with the touchable-untouchable distinction. . . .

The Private Property Problem

A second weakness in the UOA is the equivocation in its coverage of facilities which are used by the "public" but are not, technically, public. In *Benudhar Sahu* v. *State*, two Pano boys were prevented from drawing water from a privately owned well used by most villagers.[3] The High Court reversed the conviction of the owner of the well on the ground that the boys had no right to use the well. The Court was unwilling to measure their access to the well by the access of other villagers, but insisted that it be shown they had a right to use the well.

Merely because he was permitting other people to draw water from his well, it cannot be said that every villager had a right [to use] . . . the well. The prosecution must affirmatively establish that the public had a right [to use] the well in question before the offence . . . is established.[4]

It is not clear here that this conclusion is required by § 4 (iv) of the UOA, which provides:

Whoever on the ground of "untouchability" enforces against any person any disability with regard to
(iv) the use of, or access to, any river, stream, spring, well . . . which other members of the public have a right to use or have access to. . . .

. . . In any event, this seems to leave the Untouchable with a remedy only against exclusion from places used by the public as of right. Since there is no exact correspondence between facilities ordinarily used for public life in villages and those which the public has an enforceable right to enter, Untouchables are left with restricted rights. . . .

The "Same Denomination" Problem

Crucial sections of the UOA provide that an Untouchable can enter and use premises open to other persons "professing the same religion or belonging to the same religious denomination or any section thereof." Section 3 of the UOA provides that:

Whoever on the ground of "untouchability" prevents any person:
(i) from entering any place of public worship which is open to other persons professing the same religion or belonging to the same religious denomination or any section thereof, as such person; or
(ii) from worshipping or offering prayers or performing any religious service in any place of public worship, or bathing in, or using the waters of any sacred tank, well, spring or water course, in the same manner and to the same extent as is permissible to other persons professing the same religion or belonging to the same religious denomination or any section thereof, as such person;
shall be punishable with imprisonment which may extend to six months, or with fine which may extend to five hundred rupees or with both.

The scope of the rights conferred by this provision (and other crucial sections of the Act) depends on the meaning of the qualifying phrases, "the same religion or the same religious denomination or section thereof." The lawmakers, presumably for the purpose of clarifying these terms, added an explanation that:

persons professing the Buddhist, Sikh, or Jaina religion or persons professing the Hindu religion in any of its forms or developments including Virashaivas,

Lingayats, Adivasis, followers of Brahmo, Prarthara, Arya Samaj and the Swaminarayan Sampradaya shall be deemed to be Hindus.

In spite of this explanation, the courts have resisted the implication that temple-entry provisions obviate denominational and sectarian distinctions. In *State* v. *Puranchand* it was held that denial to Untouchables of entry to Jain temples is not a violation of Section 3 of the UOA, since those excluded are not of the "same religion" as those admitted. The UOA, according to the Court, does not abolish the distinction between Hindus and Jains, nor does it create any new right—either in Untouchables or in caste Hindus—to enter Jain temples. It only puts the rights of Untouchables on a parity with the right of "others of the same religion"; i.e., Untouchables have the same rights to enter a Jain temple that were previously enjoyed by caste Hindus. If the temple was not open to the latter before, it is no offense to exclude Untouchables from it now. Jain Untouchables, if there are any, would of course now have the right to enter Jain temples since the latter are open to persons of the "same religion."

This interpretation of the temple-entry provisions is supported by the absence in the UOA of any evidence of intent to confer any new rights on non-Untouchables. The Act penalizes exclusion only "on grounds of untouchability," not on grounds of caste or sectarian exclusiveness. It would be, as the High Court points out, anomalous if Untouchables were given rights of entry more extensive than those enjoyed by their high-caste co-religionists. . . .

It appears, then, that the Court has read the explanation right out of the UOA. But the result would not be much different if it were taken in its most direct and plausible meaning—as lumping all of the named groups into the "same religion." For the "same religion" qualification is followed by the further requirement that the excluded persons belong to the "same religious denomination or section thereof" as those admitted. Even if all of the different faiths and sects mentioned in the explanation are deemed to be the "same religion" they would still remain distinct denominations or sections within it. And these denominational lines would set the boundary of the rights conferred by the UOA . . .

The acceptance by the courts of denominational lines within Hinduism as limiting the operation of temple-entry provisions may produce some unanticipated results. For the "religion" and "denomination" qualifiers also appear in other provisions of the UOA relating to: use of utensils and other articles kept in restaurants, hotels, etc.; use of wells, water sources, bathing ghats, cremation grounds; the use of "places used for a public or charitable purpose"; the enjoyment of benefits of a charitable trust; and the use of dharmasalas, sarais and musafirkhanas. Given the reading of "religion" and "denomination" generated by judicial solicitude for sectarian prerogatives, the rights granted by some of the central and crucial provisions of the UOA seem to be seriously limited.

There is thus a wide gap between the extent of the power conferred by Article 25(2)b, as interpreted by the Supreme Court in the *Venkataramana Devaru* case and the exercise of this power in the UOA, as interpreted by the High Courts. The UOA, as interpreted, uses only part of the power conferred by the Constitution, for it recognizes denominational and sectarian differences as limiting the extent of rights of entry. . . .

Aware of the denominational limitations of the UOA and also troubled by the anomalous situation that while it is an offense to exclude Untouchables from temples, classes of touchable Hindus could be excluded with impunity, several states have enacted supplementary legislation. . . . These laws apparently utilize the full ambit of the constitutional power regarding temples. They extend protection to non-Untouchables and they overcome the sectarian and denominational limitations which the courts read into the UOA. Although the states are limited in their power to legislate directly on untouchability, this legislation will substantially broaden the rights of Untouchables as well. For the rights of the latter under the UOA are automatically elevated to a parity with the new rights which the state legislation confers on caste-Hindus. . . .

The Effectiveness of Anti-disabilities Legislation

. . . Assessment of the impact of anti-disabilities legislation is rendered exceedingly difficult by the absence of any reliable measure of recent changes in the condition of the Untouchables. Some notable advances are evident. Untouchables have succeeded in participating in public life to an extent unimaginable a few decades ago. Increasing numbers of Untouchables have succeeded in securing employment in the higher reaches of government and in attaining political office. There has been a marked increase in the number of Untouchables receiving education at all levels. But the vast majority of Untouchables remain poor, rural, landless, uneducated, indebted and dependent.

There is reason to believe that there has been some decline in the level of disabilities suffered by Untouchables. . . . Although the decline in disabilities varies from locality to locality and from one aspect of untouchability to another, a few generalizations may be tendered on the basis of scattered reports. Disabilities have, it seems, declined more in urban than in rural areas; they have declined more in public and occupational life than in social and family matters; they have declined more among the educated than among the uneducated; more among men than among women. The highest castes are, it seems, generally more accepting of change than the middle groups. The higher groups among the Untouchables are the greatest beneficiaries of these changes; their disabilities have declined more than those of the lower groups, especially the sweepers.

Official reports almost invariably overstate the progress that has been made. . . . Occasionally a note of frankness obtrudes, as when the Chief Secretary of Uttar Pradesh wrote to all magistrates in 1959 that there had been:

> no appreciable improvement in the treatment given by members of the so-called higher castes to the persons belonging to the Scheduled Castes. The practice of untouchability continues unabated. . . . The provisions of the Untouchability (Offences) Act are being disregarded on a large scale.

From a variety of sources, we may conclude that most Untouchables continue to suffer under disabilities which are both onerous in themselves and which severely restrict their life chances. The public disabilities most often reported are exclusion from restaurants and hotels (and restrictions on the use of utensils), restrictions on the use of wells and other water sources, denial of services by barbers, *dhobis*, etc. and, in rural areas, denial of equality in seating arrangements, and exclusion from accommodation. Exclusion from schools and government offices is rarely reported of late and entry into Hindu temples is common, although restrictions within temples are not unusual. All of this exists against a background of widespread harassment of those who assert their right to equality and a pervasive discrimination which bars even the more fortunate urban and educated Untouchables from full social acceptance and full participation in society. . . .

The Incidence of Anti-disabilities Litigation

The official reports do not usually record the subject matter of anti-disabilities cases. However, there are some scattered breakdowns by subject matter which give us a rough indication of the kinds of situations in which these acts are invoked. . . .

The preponderance of cases are directed against restaurants, tea shops, hotels and similar places. Smaller but appreciable groups of cases concern wells (and other water sources) and temples; only a scattering are directed at other forms of disabilities. . . . It appears, then, that the Act has been used mostly to deal with exclusion from commercial establishments and less with invidious treatment in looser settings. It appears that exclusion from such prominent and delimited establishments lends itself more readily to bringing of cases, since these establishments can be more readily exposed to the social workers or other outsiders who are, as we shall see, often involved in the invocation of the Act. Also, these opponents may be less likely than fellow villagers to have at their disposal formidable counter-sanctions.

Although reports are far from complete, it is possible to make an informed estimate as to the prevalence of cases under the UOA and the predecessor state acts, which covered most of India by 1949. In the early 1950s there were probably more than four hundred cases registered each year under these state acts. . . .

The Untouchability (Offenses) Act came into force on June 1, 1955. It made more things punishable; it made all offenses cognizable; it extended throughout India. It provided heavier penalties and contained a presumption designed to make proof easier. It was accompanied by a great deal of publicity. One would then expect that there would be more enforcement activity on the basis of this stronger and more extensive statute. This was anticipated both by its proponents and by critics who considered it too far-reaching and harsh.

During the first few years that the UOA was in force, there was a slight increase in the number of prosecutions registered, but this tapered off in the early 1960s. By a rough projection from the data available, we arrive at an average of approximately 520 cases a year during 1956–64. This is probably a slight overstatement, since it does not take into account the decline in recent years. But for the moment we may take this figure as representing roughly the level of use of the Act. Most of the "increase" in reported cases over the period 1952–55 is accounted for by the inclusion of Rajasthan, which had no earlier state act. Population increases more than offset the remainder of the increase. So we may conclude that, contrary to expectations, the UOA does not have a significantly higher level of use than did the predecessor state acts. In those areas covered by the state acts, there were more anti-disabilities prosecutions in the early 1950s than in the early 1960s. . . .

The decline in anti-disabilities prosecutions . . . emerges even more clearly upon inspection in the course of affairs in any of the states with sizable numbers of cases (e.g., Bombay, Rajasthan, Madhya Pradesh). It is sometimes claimed that the decline in prosecutions reflects the success of the UOA in eradicating disabilities, a claim labelled "fantastic" by the Commissioner of Scheduled Castes and Schedules Tribes. If there is any merit at all to the "success" explanation it is only a partial explanation of the decline. . . .

The "success" hypothesis rests on the assumption that the number of cases is directly related to the quantum of disabilities. This assumption is improbable, first, because such a minute fraction of instances of disabilities eventuate in cases. Whatever progress has been made in eliminating disabilities, there is no doubt that there are more offenses against the UOA in a good-sized village in a week than there are UOA prosecutions in all of India in an entire year. Second, the nature of the UOA makes it unlikely that the relationship would be direct. Because of its level of penalties, the UOA is addressed only to what we might call the middle range of imposition of disabilities, between the subtle and covert on the one hand and the violent and repressive on the other. The latter impinge on the legal system in the major crime categories, if at all. Thus the most serious cases having to do with the imposition of disabilities come up in other forms than UOA cases, e.g., in prosecutions for rioting, assault, arson or murder that may ensue when new rights are exercised by Untouchables. The UOA is, in effect, aimed at a low level of resistance and use of the UOA may be taken as an indication that resistance is relatively mild. A rise in UOA cases may reflect not an increase in disabilities but a decrease in the severity of repression. Conversely a decline in UOA cases might indicate not the disappearance of disabilities, but that resistance to the assertion of Untouchables' rights is either more subtle or more violent. Third, since the bringing of cases requires an expenditure of resources on the part of an Untouchable complainant and of the police, variations in the number of cases may involve changes in available resources or in judgments about their best use.

An alternative to the "success" hypothesis might be called the "initial impetus" explanation of the decline. In this view, the factors which induced the bringing of cases during the early years of the statute's life have waned with time. The state anti-disabilities acts and later the UOA were passed with a great deal of attendant publicity and public excitement. In the initial years there was a backlog of ready complainants and vulnerable targets. News of the Act might be expected to hearten potential complainants and impress them with a sense of the possibility of change. Police would be responsive to the exhortations of their superiors who urged them to enforce the Act vigorously. In the initial impetus view, public excitement faded, the backlog got used up, potential complainants were uninspired by the results of prosecutions, and new contenders would have stronger call on police efforts. . . .

The Disposition of Cases

During the period when the state anti-disabilities acts were in force, about 80 percent of all the cases registered were challaned* by the police. Fully half of those challaned ended in conviction. There were few compounded** cases and even fewer acquittals (see Table 2). During the first eight years of the UOA, the percentage of registered cases challaned by the police rose slightly (to about 86 percent). But there has been a drastic shift in the pattern of dispositions. The percentage of cases ending in conviction has dropped steadily: from 70.8 percent in 1952–55 (under the state Acts) to 42.8 percent during the first three and a half years of the UOA's operation, to a mere 31.1 percent during the next four years. The number of cases compounded increased with the coming of the UOA and has grown slightly since. The percentage of cases ending in acquittal has grown steadily larger.

Thus, in the early 1950s the conviction rate in anti-disabilities cases was close to the average rate of convictions for all criminal trials in India. But by the early 1960s the convictions in anti-disabilities cases fell to less than half of the former rate. In part this decrease represents an increase in the number of cases compounded. But we may view this as a sharp decline in the number of cases in which the outcome is successful for the Untouchable complainant. . . .

The Logistics of UOA Litigation

Although the Untouchability (Offences) Act is a central law, responsibility for its enforcement, like that of virtually all central laws, lies with the states. There is no separate central enforcement apparatus for this or (typically) for other national policies. Nor is there any central agency which actively coordinates or directs enforcement activity in the various states. Within each state, the same decentralized pattern is replicated. There is no special agency or staff for the enforcement of these laws or coordination of the enforcement activities of local officials. There is not at any level any agency which systematically gathers information about the problems and policies of enforcement. Thus, initiative is extremely decentralized.

The total expenditure of law enforcement resources on anti-disabilities enforcement is minuscule compared, e.g., with prohibition. For example, in Bombay from 1946–54 there were over 100,000 prohibition cases registered (and over 44,000 convictions obtained). . . . There were far less than 1,000 anti-disabilities prosecutions during the comparable period. While dry states typically have

*Editor's note: formally pursued.
**Editor's note: compromised.

TABLE 2. Disposition of Cases Under State Anti-disabilities Acts and UOA

LEGISLATION	TIME	TOTAL DISPOSALS	DISPOSALS		
			CONVICTED	COMPOUNDED	ACQUITTED
State Acts (41 mos.)	Jan. 1952— May 1955	508	360(70.9%)	58(11.4%)	90(17.7%)
U.O.A. (55 mos.)	June 1955— Dec. 1959	1,281	548(42.8%)	427(33.3%)	306(23.9%)
U.O.A. (48 mos.)	1960— 1963	1,124	350(31.1%)	421(37.5%)	353(31.4%)

SOURCES: Derived from information found in Reports for Commissioner for Scheduled Cases and Scheduled Tribes. . . .

special squads, task forces, coordinating officers and intelligence bureaus for prohibition enforcement, there are no special squads or staffs for enforcing laws against Untouchability.

There are no non-governmental organizations which systematically undertake a purposeful role in the development of anti-disabilities legislation or in its enforcement. There is no group (like, for example the American Civil Liberties Union or the legal staff of the National Association for the Advancement of Colored People) which concerns itself with the strategy or tactics of anti-disabilities litigation. . . . There are no lawyers with specialized expertise in such matters. Untouchable lawyers, particularly those in politics, are involved in some UOA cases. But again, there is no coordinated program of action nor are there any channels for sharing of experience. It should of course be added that opposition to anti-disabilities laws appears if anything more unorganized. Except in a few disputes involving major temples, there has been no organizational support to defendants in such cases. . . .

Anti-disabilities prosecutions depend on the initiative of the local police and the sympathy of local magistrates, both of whom have obvious reason to be disinclined to antagonize the dominant elements of the local community. If they are not themselves members of the latter, they are heavily dependent upon their cooperation in order to do their jobs and gain promotions. (As an Untouchable Ph.D. succinctly put it, "law means police and police means higher caste people.") Police are often uninformed of the provisions of the UOA— or even of its existence. The vast majority of potential cases that come to the attention of the police are ignored or at best "compromised" without being registered. Even if the police were sympathetic—and they often are not—limited resources and career pressures would keep them from expending much effort on this unrewarding line of activity.

Initiative then must be supplied by the Untouchable to press his claim for police time and resources. Complainants and the witnesses they need to prove their cases are extremely vulnerable to intimidation and reprisal. Very often they are economically dependent upon the higher castes. They may face social boycott or reprisal in the form of eviction or denial of grazing rights, when they do not meet with physical coercion in the form of beatings, house burnings or worse. Except in cases where outsiders are involved, witnesses other than their caste fellows are not ordinarily forthcoming. . . .

Once the case is presented to the court there are formidable obstacles due to the ambiguities and loopholes of the Act. These defects are, as we have seen, difficult to overcome in the High Courts where there is a higher level of skill, more time for preparation and greater insulation from local pressures. It may be surmised that in the magistrates' courts the tendency of the Act's ambiguities and of the difficulties of proof to reduce chances of conviction are amplified. It is, simply, very hard to win one of these cases. . . .

Even if a conviction is secured, the penalties imposed are so light as to have little deterrent effect (and to generate little favorable publicity). "Ludicrously low" fines of only three or four rupees are not uncommon. In the event of an appeal, there is a high probability that a conviction will be reversed. . . .

In view of the trouble and expense, often accompanied by economic hazard and physical danger, the uncertainty of securing a conviction and the tiny effect of such a conviction, it is not difficult to see why few Untouchables would feel that there is anything to be gained by instituting a case under the UOA. It is sometimes suggested that the failure to invoke the Act or to abide by its provisions is due to lack of awareness of its provisions. There would seem to be little merit to this explanation. The Act has been widely publicized. . . . There can be no doubt that vast numbers of Untouchables are aware of the UOA. It is not unawareness of its existence that inhibits its use, but awareness of its hazards and weaknesses. Untouchables are, quite sensibly, more deterred by the formidable difficulties of using the UOA than caste Hindus are deterred by the remote and mild penalties that it threatens them with. . . .

The question, then, is not why so few cases are brought, but rather why any cases are brought! Probably very few are brought without the intervention of some "outsider" to the local situation—usually political leaders, social workers or religious reformers. . . . This intervention tends to concentrate on certain kinds of facilities. Temple-entry has often, particularly in the early years of anti-disabilities legislation, involved political sponsorship. Social workers tend to concentrate on public accommodations like tea shops, hotels and barbers. Such conspicuous and fixed establishments appear to be most vulnerable to anti-disabilities litigation. The identifiable offender with a fixed establishment and a public license cannot melt away like the crowd at the village well or return later to intimidate the complainant. Where, however, disabilities are supported by self-help of coherent social groups it is unlikely that they will be deterred by the UOA, even when the presence of transient intervenors increases the probability that it will be invoked. In these settings, the problem is not that the UOA depends on outside intervention for its invocation, but rather that it is such a poor vehicle for getting intervention of the requisite strength and tenacity. It leaves Untouchables vulnerable to itinerant reformers who often cannot deliver the goods that they promise, after Untouchables have risked their well-being. . . .

The Impact of Anti-Disabilities Legislation

The impact of anti-disabilities legislation is not to be measured merely by the few cases that are brought. The aim of such laws is not to prosecute offenders, but to promote new patterns of behavior. Undoubtedly the total effect of the UOA as propaganda, as threat and as leverage for securing external intervention outweighs its direct effect as an instrument for the prosecution of offenders. To some extent, however, its effectiveness as an educational device and as a political weapon depends upon its efficacy as a penal provision. The power of the law to elicit widespread compliance depends in part on its ability to deal with obvious cases of non-compliance. A law that permits effective prosecution of offenders may, of course, not succeed in inducing widespread compliance, but surely a statute which fails to enable effective prosecution is less likely to secure general compliance.

This is especially so in the case of laws like the UOA. For successful legal regulation depends upon what might be called the "halo-effect"—the general aura of legal efficacy that leads those who are not directly the targets of enforcement activities to obey the law. The "halo" may be generated by self-interest, approval of the measure, generalized respect for the law-making authority, the momentum of existing social patterns, expectation of enforcement—or a combination of these. In the case of anti-disabilities legislation which runs counter to the sentiments and established behavior patterns of wide sectors of the public, the "halo" of efficacy depends very heavily on the expectation of enforcement. By this measure, the UOA appears an unwieldly and ineffective instrument; its shortcomings as a penal provision vitiate its capacity to secure general compliance.

However, even where there are massive inputs of governmental enforcement, the other components of compliance (approval, self-interest, momentum of existing patterns) must be successfully mobilized to some extent. In the case of the UOA, there is little in the way of these other components, except for generalized respect for government. The law goes counter to perceived self-interest and valued sentiments and deeply ingrained behavioral patterns. Thus the difficulties of securing general compliance in the case of anti-disabilities legislation are so formidable that to measure the Act in these terms sets too high a standard. A more modest approach would be to ask how the Act stands as an enabling measure. First, to what extent does it enable Untouchables to improve their position vis-à-vis disabilities? Does it provide useful leverage for those willing to expend their resources and take risks? Second, does the level of enablement sustain itself? Is the Act effective enough so that its use as an enabling measure is cumulative and self-reinforcing?

Perhaps the greatest "enabling" feature of anti-disabilities legislation is its general symbolic output. This legislation has an effect on the morale and self-image of Untouchables, who perceive government action on their behalf as legitimating their claims to be free of invidious treatment. By providing an authoritative model of public behavior that they have a right to demand, it educates their aspirations. More generally, such legislation promotes awareness of an era of change in caste relations. Specifically it provides an alternative model of behavior; it puts the imprimatur of prestigious official authority upon a set of values which are alternative to prevailing practice. . . .

Although mere knowledge of the existence of such legislation does not in itself bring about changes, there are instances in which these laws have contributed to "widespread change in daily behavior." For at least some groups the Act provided leverage for securing favorable changes. However, this successful use did not lead to widespread use of the legislation. . . .

The present situation, then, is characterized by a wide gap between the law on the books and the law in operation. As in many other areas, the government's commitment to change greatly outruns its power to effect it. This disparity between aspiration and performance, between great commitments of principle and small deployment of resources, itself transforms the symbolic as well as the practical uses of anti-disabilities legislation. Symbolically, it blurs what the Government's commitment is. The law's equivocation is institutionalized: in the ceremonial character that attends the admission of Untouchables to many facilities; in the fact that anti-disabilities measures become leverage for increasing separate facilities for Untouchables; and, generally, in the law's provision of remedies without relieving the dependence which prevents them from being used. . . .

The ineffectiveness of the law means that the new national norms are not conveyed—or rather, tolerance of their violation is communicated at the same time that they are espoused. . . .

At the same time, the law's equivocation serves to disillusion reformers and Untouchables who are convinced that the law is totally useless and without effect. While the complacent look only to the law on the books, overlooking that its performance in practice falls far short of its promise, the cynical focus on the modest results of the law in operation and tend to dismiss it as mere lip service, overlooking the pressure that this law might exert on local practice. Both the complacent and the cynical concur in equating the present legal accomplishments with the law's potential. There is widespread agreement that all that might be done by law has been done and that only a "change of heart" can secure further gains to the Untouchables. . . .

This estimate of the law's potential is sustained by a number of features of the current Indian scene. One is the absence of controversy about the working of anti-disabilities laws: all of the laws (if not all of the law's enforcers) are on the "side" of the Untouchables. There is no articulate public opposition to these laws, and Untouchables do not exert much pressure for their enforcement or their improvement, preferring to divert their efforts into search for tangible gains through protective discrimination. All of this takes place in a milieu which puts great store on the symbolic aspects of the law and where a tradition of conceptualistic legal thinking is shared by lawyers and the educated public, who are both equally innocent of any tradition of looking at legal institutions empirically.

The notion that untouchability cannot be dealt with by legislation, but must await a change of heart on the part of its perpetrators, comports with a great deal of evidence on the difficulty of inducing social change by penal regulation. The dangers of law becoming ineffective when it moves too far from prevailing public opinion are well known.[5] It may be even more difficult to induce change in behavior which is not merely instrumental but is invested with deep expressive meanings for those concerned.[6]

The ultimate argument against the efficacy of law in changing relations between groups is that law cannot affect the deepest values and attitudes of the target group. However, this assumes that there is a direct relationship between the "prejudiced" attitudes of the target group and their discriminatory behavior. But there is evidence (from other settings) that the relationship is not direct; that specified behaviors can be changed without waiting for change in underlying attitudes, and that legal regulations can be effective in changing these behaviors in the field of intergroup relations.[7]

The problem of a "change of heart" is not one of waiting upon a wave of moral edification, but rather of changing specific behaviors that have their roots in a variety of attitudes about pollution, hierarchical grading, indignity of manual labor, etc. The problem is how the law might be used to induce changes in these behaviors. There is no reason to conclude that patterns of caste interaction are exempt from the general human capacity for acting at variance from belief. Also, there is evidence of great pliability in caste behaviors in the past and at present. If caste will not break, it is known to bend. The question is: How can law be used to induce it to bend more quickly and without inordinate cost?

Prospects and Options

The picture we have drawn of the working of the anti-disabilities legislation shows that it is of limited effect in eliminating disabilities. We have argued that this is not because the legislation has reached the utmost limits of effective legal action, but because it stops far short of these limits. One would be foolish indeed to believe that legal measures alone could secure the elimination of untouchability from society, but it is possible to envision a policy of anti-disabilities legislation and enforcement which might contribute more effectively to this end.

The improvement or upgrading of anti-disabilities law can be analyzed into four stages of increasing difficulty and increasing significance. First there is the task of closing the loopholes and eliminating the ambiguities that plague the UOA. This is a job that does not lie beyond the present capabilities of the draftsman's art. Such redrafting might eliminate throughout the UOA the requirement that the accused be proved to have acted "on grounds of untouchability. . . .

Similarly, the provisions describing the coverage of the Act could be re-drafted to insure that the scope of the rights granted by the Act is not measured by an artificial rigor. Thus it could be made clear that the Act applies to any property, by whomsoever owned, which is used by the public—not only to property that the public has a legal right to use. Regarding religious places, the Act could be extended along the lines of the legislation now in force in several states to cover places which are used by any section of the Hindu public. This could be accomplished simply by replacing the "same religion or same religious denomination thereof" language on the order of "open to Hindus in general or any section thereof."

These changes would extend the scope of the rights conferred by the Act, making ordinary usage rather than enforceable rights the measure of their scope. . . .

Secondly, there are a number of improvements possible in the enforcement of the UOA. Changes of this kind would require greater and continuous inputs of administrative attention, and willingness to divert some resources. These might include measures for reducing delay, either by priority on court calendars or by appointing special magistrates to try offenses; redress of any disparity of legal talent by deputing public prosecutors to prosecute these cases (or, perhaps, generous legal aid to attract high-level legal talent); making outcomes more visible by making anti-disabilities offenses non-compoundable; provision of mandatory higher fines or prison sentences; providing

exceedingly heavy penalties for interfering with complainants or witnesses in UOA cases. Such measures would not solve the fundamental
problems of the Act, but they would go some way to reduce the cost
and risk is not entirely negligible.

Third, the effect of these improvements might be greatly aug-
mented by the establishment of machinery to guide and coordinate
enforcement activity. Such an establishment might gather and disseminate information on enforcement problems and techniques; it
might develop coordinated strategies of enforcement, using both the
UOA and other legal provisions now largely unused. (E.g., writ
petitions, civil suits, preventive police action, etc.) By assigning priorities, providing continuity and encouraging development of specialized skills in this area, such a coordinating body could promote the
best use of resources allocated to enforcement.

But even these improvements in the clarity, scope and rigor of the
UOA would not touch the major weaknesses of the UOA—for
these flow from the very nature of the remedy it provides. The simple
penal sanction, dependent upon detection and investigation by the
regular police, trial by the regular magistrate, and punishment by
fine or imprisonment of guilty individuals is probably not capable
of delivering the goods.

The effectiveness of ordinary penal sanctions is dependent upon
several conditions which typically do not obtain in the case of anti-
disabilities measures. These conditions are, first, that the victim of
the offense will have widespread community sympathy—or at worst
indifference—and that he (and those who cooperate with him) will
be able to invoke the law without being subject to community sanctions. Second, that the offender will be an identifiable and isolable
individual who will, as a result of his infraction, be subject to community censure and isolated from community support. Third, that
the enforcing officials will be independent of the accused and his
supporters and that the total outcome for the enforcing official will
be positive. (The sort of situation in which the UOA is most frequently invoked is one which approximates these conditions; the
offender is an identifiable and relatively isolated tea shop or cinema
owner, not the villagers as the well; and outside support reduces the
likelihood of reprisal and increases the cost to the police of inaction.)
What is needed then is a way to build these favorable conditions—or
surrogates for them—into the enforcement machinery. In order to do
this, it is necessary to move away from the ordinary penal law
process.

One way to do this would be by means of an administrative
agency . . . which could, on its own ititiative, depute examiners to investigate suspected cases of persistent imposition of disabilities. The
purpose of the investigation would be to determine the existence of

patterns of discrimination, not to establish individual instances. . . .
Violations of its order might be punished by the contempt power, by
resumption of government grants to the village, etc. The agency
might devise penalties which would mobilize the leverage of caste discipline and village solidarity against the continuance of disabilities,
rather than in support of them—e.g., disqualifications for government
service or contracting. The agency might undertake periodic checks
to see that compliance was permanent.

Such an administrative remedy would conform more closely to the
conditions of effectiveness than do the present remedies. It would
place the burden of initiative on someone other than the local Untouchables or the police. Initiative would lie with those immune to
retaliation or pressure and whose careers would be helped, not hin-
dered, by enforcement. The agency would have a continuing interest
and would be able to exercise continuing scrutiny, affording outside
support of a persistence not available at present. As such a body it
could develop expertise and might articulate anti-disabilities enforcement with other measures for the welfare of the Untouchables. Were
such an administrative procedure to prove effective, it might be possible for investigators to operate principally by arranging settlements,
with formal undertakings by responsible village parties and periodic
re-checking by the investigatory staff.

Just how much could be accomplished even by such an amplified
machinery for enforcement depends on things beyond enforcement
itself, that is, to what extent government programs for distributing
resources and opportunities succeed in liberating Untouchables from
economic dependence on higher castes. Surely, though, there are
even now at least some groups of Untouchables who are in a position
to use the leverage of amplified enforcement to improve their position, and there are some villagers who would modify their behavior
when faced with this kind of enforcement.

It may be argued that a higher level of enforcement in such a
sensitive area would lead to negative results by provoking greater
resistance, more circumvention, more pressure on Untouchables. On
the other hand, there is the opposite danger that if the law moves too
slowly and is too solicitous of those who resist, it will lose its ability
to secure compliance from those who are not themselves the direct
targets of enforcement activities. . . .

Author's 1978 Addendum

The mid-70s saw a dramatic reversal of the public inattention to
untouchability that prevailed when this essay was written. From
1972 on, there was a dramatic increase in the number of cases

brought under the UOA. Untouchability is indeed a very troubling and prominent issue in the late 1970s. One consequence of the new attention is that the UOA was finally amended in 1976 and renamed the Protection of Civil Rights Act. The amendments incorporate some changes along the lines suggested here, but not all of them.

Notes

1. Article 15(1) forbids discrimination by the State on grounds of caste. Other provisions deal with specific areas of governmental activity: Art. 16(2) with government employment; Art. 23(2) with compulsory public service; Art. 29(2) with admission to state-aided educational institutions. Cf. Art. 325 which forbids separate electorates for Parliament or State legislatures on caste lines.

     The restrictions on state use of these forbidden classifications are qualified to allow special provision in favor of women (Art. 15[3]) and Backward Classes, Scheduled Castes and Scheduled Tribes (Art. 15[4], cf. Art. 46). . . .

2. Only two other provisions in the Fundamental Rights section of the Constitution regulate private as well as public conduct: Art. 24, which forbids child labor in hazardous employment; and Art. 18(2) which prohibits acceptance of titles from foreign states.

3. India Law Reports 1962 Cuttack 256.

4. Id., at 258.

5. The classic formulation is by Sumner 1960. The most dramatic evidence of legal inefficacy is drawn from two areas: "crimes without victims" (i.e., penal prohibition of commodities and practices which are not disapproved by their purchasers, such as liquor, drugs and abortion) and family law. For recent and vivid documentation, see Schur 1965; Massell 1968. The analogy of these areas with the regulation of intergroup relations is not, however, conclusive. Unlike "crimes without victims" the proscription of untouchability has a class of beneficiaries who have a tangible interest in enforcement. And, unlike family law, the beneficiaries are coherent social groups capable of coordinated action, protection and support in the use of such legal advantages.

6. Dror 1959 suggests that laws have more difficulty in changing expressive and evaluative areas of activity than emotionally neutral and instrumental ones. Chambliss 1967 suggests that the effectiveness of deterrence varies with the expressive nature of the act and the degree of commitment to "crime" as a way of life. Untouchability offenses would seem to rank high on both counts. For the villager there would seem to be high commitment to a way of life that puts a positive value on the proscribed conduct and which provides group support for it. For the tea shop keeper, cinema owner or school principal there may be less expressiveness and less commitment, which clearly comports with the greater effectiveness of the UOA in these settings than in dealing with wells and housing.

7. Berger 1952: chap. V; Raab and Lipset 1959. Cf. Mayhew's (1968) finding of greater impact of an anti-discrimination law in the field of housing than in the field of employment (in spite of greater opposing sentiment in the hous-

ing area), suggesting that institutional features may be more important than sentiment in determining the effectiveness of anti-discrimination legislation.

References

Berger, Morroe (1952). *Equality by Statute: Legal Controls Over Group Discrimination.* New York: Columbia University Press.

Chambliss, William J. (1967). Types of Deviance and the Effectiveness of Legal Sanctions. *Wisconsin Law Review* 1967: 703-19.

Dror, Yehezkel (1959). Law and Social Change. *Tulane Law Review* 33: 787-802.

Massell, Gregory J. (1968). Law as an Instrument of Revolutionary Change in a Traditional Milieu: the Case of Soviet Central Asia. *Law and Society Review* 2: 178-228.

Mayhew, Leon (1968). *Law and Equal Opportunity: A Study of the Massachusetts Commission Against Discrimination.* Cambridge: Harvard University Press.

Raab, Earl and Seymour Martin Lipset (1959). *The Prejudiced Society.* New York: Anti-Defamation League of B'nai B'rith.

Schur, Edwin M. (1965). *Crimes Without Victims: Deviant Behavior and Public Policy.* Englewood Cliffs, N.J.: Prentice-Hall.

Sumner, William Graham (1960). *Folkways: A Study of the Sociological Importance of Usages, Manners, Customs, Mores, and Morals.* New York: New American Library.

APPENDIX V:

LEGAL DOCUMENTS

Introduction

Legislative Acknowledgment of the Need for Policy Research

A. Civil Rights Act (Title IV), 1964
B. Age Discrimination Act (1967), Amendment 1978
C. National Environmental Policy Act of 1969
D. Technology Assessment Act, 1972

Judicial Acknowledgment of the Need for Policy Research

E. *Brown et al.* v. *Board of Education of Topeka et al.* (1954)
F. *Schmidt* v. *United States* (2nd cir. 1949)

Administrative Agency Acknowledgment of the Need for Policy Research

G. *Shopping Kart Food Market, Inc.* (Apr. 8, 1977)
H. *Chelsea Neighborhood Association* v. *U.S. Postal Service* (2nd Cir. 1975)

Introduction

The enactment of law, whether in the course of legislation, judicial decision making, administrative action, or executive decision making, can be guided by research-based knowledge. Typically, however, it is not: "Conventional wisdom" and intuition are all too often the bases of policy decisions. For example, Cohen, Robson, and Bates (1958) have pointedly drawn attention to the court's frequent reliance on the "moral sense" or "common conscience" without any systematic

608

scientific inquiry into its content:

> Despite lip service to the need to treat the moral sense as an observable da-
> tum; and despite exhortations to employ "the spirit of science" in the task of
> observation, judicial law-makers have relied mainly upon intuitive hunch, on
> the vagaries of "judicial notice," on the predilections of the groups identified
> with the social origin of the law-makers, on crude personal observation, on a
> "best guess," or some such other esoteric method for divining the *Zeitgeist*. It
> is not that there is an unawareness of the unreliability of these methods. Mr.
> Justice Cardozo's observation that "In every court there are likely to be as
> many estimates of the *'Zeitgeist'* as there are judges on its bench," and Judge
> Frank's wry remark that "Usually a person who talks of 'opinion of the world
> at large' is really referring to the 'few people with whom I happened to con-
> verse,'" evidence a lively alertness to the problem [pp. 7-8].

Almost as uncommon is an appreciation of the importance of empirically assessing the consequences of a legal enactment in order to discover whether the implicit or explicit purposes of a law have been
fulfilled.

In this Appendix several examples of the acknowledgment of the
need for pre-policy and post-policy research are presented. These
examples are drawn from legislative, judicial, and administrative
decisional contexts.

Appendixes V-A through V-D pertain to the actions of the U.S.
Congress. Section 402 of Title IV of the Civil Rights Act of 1964
requires a post-policy study to be reported to the President and the
Congress "within two years of the enactment of this title, concerning
the lack of availability of equal educational opportunities for individuals by reason of race, color, religion, or national origin in public
educational institutions at all levels in the United States, its territories and possessions and the District of Columbia". This provision
paved the way for the evaluation study entitled *Equality of Educational Opportunity* (Coleman *et al.*, 1966).

The 1978 amendment to the Age Discrimination Act of 1967, extending involuntary retirement from sixty-five to seventy years of
age, stipulates that the Secretary of the Department of Labor shall
undertake a study of the consequences of this policy for executives
in industry and officials in government.

Unlike the two foregoing laws, the Technology Assessment Act of
1972 is concerned with providing Congress with relevant knowledge
prior to the enactment of laws involving the application of new technology. Acknowledging the possibility that technological applications can have beneficial as well as detrimental effects, Congress
recognized the need for pre-policy studies as an aid to the legislative
process. With the passage of this law, the Office of Technology Assessment was established with a mission "to provide early indications

of the probable beneficial and adverse impacts of the applications of technology and to develop other coordinate information which may assist Congress." The underlying assumption of this act is that the legislative branch can channel technology for the benefit of society instead of assuming that law can perform only a reactive function with respect to technology. What are some of the obstacles to the law's performing a *proactive* instead of a *reactive* function in society (Tribe, 1973)?

Perhaps the clearest example of pre-policy research in federal administrative agencies is the institutionalization of environmental impact analysis and the resulting document known as an "environmental impact statement" (EIS). The National Environmental Policy Act (NEPA), which was signed into law in 1970, requires that each federal agency, before proceeding with any major action, recommendation, or report on proposals for legislation, undertake a study of the probable changes in the various socioeconomic and biophysical characteristics of the environment that may result from the proposed action. To develop guidelines for the preparation of environmental impact statements and to review and appraise the environmental impact statements of the various agencies, NEPA created the Council on Environmental Quality.

Since environmental impact analysis is a complex undertaking that deals with problems that fall into the domain of different disciplines, Section 102(2)A required that a "systematic and interdisciplinary approach" be used to ensure the integrated use of social, natural, and environmental sciences in planning and decision making.

In judicial "lawmaking," "judicial notice" takes account of relevant past research findings justifying an opinion and occasionally points to the desirability of post-policy research. In the landmark school desegregation decision, *Brown* v. *Board of Education* (Appendix V-E), declaring separate but equal schools unconstitutional, footnote 11 cited various social science studies supporting the assertion that racially segregated schools impair the self-image and learning capacity of black children.

In the naturalization case of *Schmidt* v. *United States* (Appendix V-F), which involves a statutory standard of good "moral character," Judge Learned Hand acknowledges the need to consult the "moral feelings now prevalent in the country" instead of relying on his own subjective feelings. And yet he reluctantly concluded that there is no practicable way to undertake a pre-policy study to guide judicial decision making in such cases:

> Even though we could take a poll [on the "common conscience"] it would not be enough merely to count heads, without an appraisal of the voters. A majority of the votes of those in prisons and brothels for instance ought

scarcely to outweigh all accredited churchgoers. Nor can we see any reason to suppose that the opinion of clergymen would be a more reliable estimate than our own.

Do you agree or disagree with the way Judge Hand resolved this dilemma? In either case, how would you justify your position on this matter?

In theory, since regulatory agencies are repositories of expertise, one would expect them to be more receptive to pre-policy as well as post-policy research than the legislature or the judiciary. In practice this is not so, possibly because of their confidence in their expertise. Structurally, most regulatory agencies do not have the budgetary resources, the personnel, or the mandate to conduct systematic research on underlying issues being adjudicated. In the case of the NLRB, Samoff (1957), in a pioneering study, has cogently argued for the need for post-policy research. And in *Getman* v. *N.L.R.B.*, 450 F. 2d 670(1971), Judge Wright takes the Board to task for failing to undertake research on the assumptions and effects of its own policies:

> [T]he Board's position suffers from the obvious self-justifying tendency of an institution which in over 30 years has itself never engaged in the kind of much needed systematic empirical effort to determine the dynamics of an election campaign or the type of conduct which actually has a coercive impact. The public interest need for such an empirical investigation into the assumptions underlying the Board's regulation of campaign tactics has for some time been recognized by labor law scholars.

In the *Shopping Kart Food Market* case (Appendix V-G), which involves a representative election issue, the majority opinion of the NLRB draws on the research findings of a study by Getman, Goldberg, and Herman (1976). The minority opinion of the Board challenges this study on evidentiary grounds. This is an example of a federal agency's use of pre-policy research in the course of reaching an administrative decision.

In the last document, Appendix V-H, we have another instance of an administrative decision based on pre-policy research in the form of an environmental impact statement (EIS), which was eventually challenged in a lawsuit. The U.S. Postal Service proposed the construction of a vehicle maintenance facility in combination with a multistory public housing project. The plaintiff, a community organization, challenged the adequacy of the EIS, contending that the social as well as physical effects of the proposed project were inadequately assessed. The Circuit Court of Appeals decided in favor of the plaintiff, agreeing that the EIS filed by the U.S. Postal Service was inadequate.

Can the EIS provisions of the National Environmental Policy Act serve as a model for pre-policy as well as post-policy research throughout the legal system?

References

Cohen, J. R., A. H. Robson, and A. Bates (1958). *Parental Authority*. New Brunswick, N.J.: Rutgers University Press.

Coleman, J. S. *et al.* (1966). *Equality of Educational Opportunity*, Washington, D.C.: U.S. Government Printing Office.

Getman, J. G. *et al.* (1976). *Union Representation Elections: Law and Reality*. New York: Russell Sage Foundation.

Samoff, B. (1957). "Research on the Results and Impact of NLRB Decisions." *Labor Law Journal*, 8: 235–238, 283–288.

Tribe, L. H. (1973). *Channeling Technology Through Law*. Chicago: Bracton Press.

Legislative Acknowledgment of the Need for Policy Research

A—Civil Rights Act (Title IV), 1964
42 U.S.C. 2000c-6

Title IV—Desegregation of Public Education

Definitions

Sec. 401. As used in this title—(a) "Commissioner" means the Commissioner of Education, (b) "Desegregation" means the assignment of students to public schools and within such schools without regard to their race, color, religion, or national origin, but "desegregation" shall not mean the assignment of students to public schools in order to overcome racial imbalance.

Survey and Report of Educational Opportunities

Sec. 402. The Commissioner shall conduct a survey and make a report to the President and the Congress, within two years of the enactment of this title, concerning the lack of availability of equal educational opportunities for individuals by reason of race, color, religion, or national origin in public educational institutions at all levels in the United States, its territories and possessions, and the District of Columbia.

Suits by the Attorney General

Sec. 407. (a) Whenever the Attorney General receives a complaint in writing—
(1) signed by a parent or group of parents to the effect that his or their minor children, as members of a class of persons similarly situated, are being deprived by a school board of the equal protection of the laws, or
(2) signed by an individual, or his parent, to the effect that he has been denied admission to or not permitted to continue in attendance at a public college by reason of race, color, religion, or national origin,
and the Attorney General believes the complaint is meritorious and certifies that the signer or signers of such complaint are unable, in his judgment, to initiate and maintain appropriate legal proceedings for relief and that the institution of an action will materially further the orderly achievement of desegregation in public education, the Attorney General is authorized, after giving notice of such complaint to the appropriate school board or college authority and after certifying that he is satisfied that such board or authority has had a reasonable time to adjust the conditions alleged in such complaint, to institute for or in the name of the United States a civil action in any appropriate district court of the United States against such parties and for such relief as may be appropriate. . . .

B—Age Discrimination Act (1967), Amendment 1978
29 U.S.C. 621

§ 624. Study by Secretary of Labor; reports to President and Congress; scope of study; implementation of study; transmittal date of reports

(a) (1) The Secretary of Labor is directed to undertake an appropriate study of institutional and other arrangements giving rise to involuntary retirement, and report his findings and any appropriate legislative recommendations to the President and to the Congress. Such study shall include—

(A) an examination of the effect of the amendment made by section 3(a) of the Age Discrimination in Employment Act Amendments of 1978 in raising the upper age limitation established by section 631(a) of this title to 70 years of age;

(B) a determination of the feasibility of eliminating such limitation;

(C) a determination of the feasibility of raising such limitation above 70 years of age; and

(D) an examination of the effect of the exemption contained in section 631(c) of this title, relating to certain executive employees, and the exemption contained in section 631(d) of this title, relating to tenured teaching personnel.

(2) The Secretary may undertake the study required by paragraph (1) of this subsection directly or by contract or other arrangement.

(b) The report required by subsection (a) of this section shall be transmitted to the President and to the Congress as an interim report not later than January 1, 1981, and in final form not later than January 1, 1982. . . .

C—National Environmental Policy Act of 1969
42 U.S.C. 4321

§ 4321. Congressional Declaration of Purpose

The purposes of this chapter are: To declare a national policy which will encourage productive and enjoyable harmony between man and his environment; to promote efforts which will prevent or eliminate damage to the environment and biosphere and stimulate the health and welfare of man; to enrich the understanding of the ecological systems and natural resources important to the Nation; and to establish a Council on Environmental Quality.

Subchapter I—Policies and Goals

§ 4331. Congressional Declaration of National Environmental Policy

Creation and Maintenance of Conditions Under Which Man and Nature Can Exist in Productive Harmony

(a) The Congress, recognizing the profound impact of man's activity on the interrelations of all components of the natural environment, particularly the profound influences of population growth, high-density urbanization, industrial expansion, resource exploitation, and new and expanding technological advances and recognizing further the critical importance of restoring and maintaining environmental quality to the overall welfare and development of man, declares that it is the continuing policy of the Federal Government, in cooperation with State and local governments, and other concerned public and private organizations, to use all practicable means and measures, including financial and technical assistance, in a manner calculated to foster and promote the general welfare, to create and maintain conditions under which man and nature can exist in productive harmony, and fulfill the social, economic, and other requirements of present and future generations of Americans.

Continuing Responsibility of Federal Government to Use All Practicable Means to Improve and Coordinate Federal Plans, Functions, Programs, and Resources

(b) In order to carry out the policy set forth in this chapter, it is the continuing responsibility of the Federal Government to use all practicable means, consistent with other essential considerations of national policy, to improve and coordinate Federal plans, functions, programs, and resources to the end that the Nation may—

(1) fulfill the responsibilities of each generation as trustee of the environment for succeeding generations;

(2) assure for all Americans safe, healthful, productive, and esthetically and culturally pleasing surroundings;

(3) attain the widest range of beneficial uses of the environment without degradation, risk to health or safety, or other undesirable and unintended consequences;

(4) preserve important historic, cultural, and natural aspects of our national heritage, and maintain, wherever possible, an environment which supports diversity and variety of individual choice;

(5) achieve a balance between population and resource use which will permit high standards of living and a wide sharing of life's amenities; and

(6) enhance the quality of renewable resources and approach the maximum attainable recycling of depletable resources.

Responsibility of Each Person to Contribute to Preservation and Enhancement of Environment

(c) The Congress recognizes that each person should enjoy a healthful environment and that each person has a responsibility to contribute to the preservation and enhancement of the environment.

§ 4332. Cooperation of Agencies; Reports; Availability of Information; Recommendations; International and National Coordination of Efforts

The Congress authorizes and directs that, to the fullest extent possible: (1) the policies, regulations, and public laws of the United States shall be interpreted and administered in accordance with the policies set forth in this chapter, and (2) all agencies of the Federal Government shall—

(A) utilize a systematic, interdisciplinary approach which will insure the integrated use of the natural and social sciences and the environmental design arts in planning and in decisionmaking which may have an impact on man's environment;

(B) identify and develop methods and procedures, in consultation with the Council on Environmental Quality established by subchapter II of this chapter, which will insure that presently unquantified environmental amenities and values may be given appropriate consideration in decisionmaking along with economic and technical considerations;

(C) include in every recommendation or report on proposals for legislation and other major Federal actions significantly affecting the quality of the human environment, a detailed statement by the responsible official on—

(i) the environmental impact of the proposed action,

(ii) any adverse environmental effects which cannot be avoided should the proposal be implemented,

(iii) alternatives to the proposed action,

(iv) the relationship between local short-term uses of man's environment and the maintenance and enhancement of long-term productivity, and

(v) any irreversible and irretrievable commitments of resources which would be involved in the proposed action should it be implemented.

Prior to making any detailed statement, the responsible Federal official shall consult with and obtain the comments of any Federal agency which has jurisdiction by law or special expertise with respect to any environmental impact involved. Copies of such statement and the comments and views of the appropriate Federal, State, and local agencies, which are authorized to develop and enforce environmental standards, shall be made available to the President, the Council on Environmental Quality and to the public as provided by section 552 of Title 5, and shall accompany the proposal through the existing agency review processes;

(D) Any detailed statement required under subparagraph (C) after January 1, 1970, for any major Federal action funded under a program of grants to States shall not be deemed to be legally insufficient solely by reason of having been prepared by a State agency or official, if:

(i) the State agency or official has statewide jurisdiction and has the responsibility for such action,

(ii) the responsible Federal official furnishes guidance and participates in such preparation,

(iii) the responsible Federal official independently evaluates such statement prior to its approval and adoption, and

(iv) after January 1, 1976, the responsible Federal official provides early notification to, and solicits the views of, any other State or any Federal land management entity of any action or any alternative thereto which may have significant impacts upon such State or affected Federal land management entity and, if there is any disagreement on such impacts, prepares a written assessment of such impacts and views for incorporation into such detailed statement.

The procedures in this subparagraph shall not relieve the Federal official of his responsibilities for the scope, objectivity, and content of the entire statement or of any other responsibility under this chapter; and further, this subparagraph does not affect the legal sufficiency of statements prepared by State agencies with less than statewide jurisdiction.

(E) study, develop, and describe appropriate alternatives to recommended courses of action in any proposal which involves unresolved conflicts concerning alternative uses of available resources;

(F) recognize the worldwide and long-range character of environmental problems and, where consistent with the foreign policy of the United States, lend appropriate support to initiatives, resolutions, and programs designed to maximize international cooperation in anticipating and preventing a decline in the quality of mankind's world environment;

(G) make available to States, counties, municipalities, institutions, and individuals, advice and information useful in restoring, maintaining, and enhancing the quality of the environment;

(H) initiate and utilize ecological information in the planning and development of resource-oriented projects; and

(I) assist the Council on Environmental Quality established by subchapter II of this chapter. . . .

D—Technology Assessment Act, 1972
2 U.S.C. 471

An Act

To establish an Office of Technology Assessment for the Congress as an aid in the identification and consideration of existing and probable impacts of technological application; to amend the National Science Foundation Act of 1950; and for other purposes.

Findings and Declaration of Purpose

Sec. 2. The Congress hereby finds and declares that:

(a) As technology continues to change and expand rapidly, its applications are—

(1) large and growing in scale; and

(2) increasingly extensive, pervasive, and critical in their impact, beneficial and adverse, on the natural and social environment.

(b) Therefore, it is essential that, to the fullest extent possible, the consequences of technological applications be anticipated, understood, and considered in determination of public policy on existing and emerging national problems.

(c) The Congress further finds that:

(1) the Federal agencies presently responsible directly to the Congress are not designed to provide the legislative branch with adequate and timely information, independently developed, relating to the potential impact of technological applications, and

(2) the present mechanisms of the Congress do not and are not designed to provide the legislative branch with such information.

(d) Accordingly, it is necessary for the Congress to—

(1) equip itself with new and effective means for securing competent, unbiased information concerning the physical, biological, economic, social, and political effects of such applications; and

(2) utilize this information, whenever appropriate, as one factor in the legislative assessment of matters pending before the Congress, particularly in those instances where the Federal Government may be called upon to consider support for, or management or regulation of, technological applications.

Sec. 3. (a) In accordance with the findings and declaration of purpose in section 2, there is hereby created the Office of Technology Assessment (hereinafter referred to as the "Office") which shall be within and responsible to the legislative branch of the Government.

(b) The Office shall consist of a Technology Assessment Board (hereinafter referred to as the "Board") which shall formulate and promulgate the policies of the Office, and a Director who shall carry out such policies and administer the operations of the Office.

(c) The basic function of the Office shall be to provide early indications of the probable beneficial and adverse impacts of the applications of technology and to develop other coordinate information which may assist the Congress. In carrying out such function, the Office shall:

(1) identify existing or probable impacts of technology or technological programs;

(2) where possible, ascertain cause-and-effect relationships;

(3) identify alternative technological methods of implementing specific programs;

(4) identify alternative programs for achieving requisite goals;

(5) make estimates and comparisons of the impacts of alternative methods and programs;

(6) present findings of completed analyses to the appropriate legislative authorities;

(7) identify areas where additional research or data collection is required to provide adequate support for the assessments and estimates described in paragraph (1) through (5) of this subsection; and

(8) undertake such additional associated activities as the appropriate authorities specified under subsection (d) may direct.

(d) Assessment activities undertaken by the Office may be initiated upon the request of:

(1) the chairman of any standing, special, or select committee of either House of the Congress, or of any joint committee of the Congress, acting for himself or at the request of the ranking minority member or a majority of the committee members;

(2) the Board; or

(3) the Director, in consultation with the Board.

(e) Assessments made by the Office, including information, surveys, studies, reports, and findings related thereto, shall be made available to the initiating committee or other appropriate committees of the Congress. In addition, any such information, surveys, studies, reports, and findings produced by the Office may be made available to the public except where—

(1) to do so would violate security statutes; or

(2) the Board considers it necessary or advisable to withhold such information in accordance with one or more of the numbered paragraphs in section 552 (b) of title 5, United States Code.

Sec. 7. (a) The Office shall establish a Technology Assessment Advisory Council (hereinafter referred to as the "Council"). The Council shall be composed of the following twelve members:

(1) ten members from the public, to be appointed by the Board, who shall be persons eminent in one or more fields of the physical, biological, or social sciences or engineering or experienced in the administration of technological activities, or who may be judged qualified on the basis of contributions made to educational or public activities;

(2) the Comptroller General; and

(3) the Director of the Congressional Research Service of the Library of Congress.

(b) The Council, upon request by the Board, shall—

(1) review and make recommendations to the Board on activities undertaken by the Office or on the initiation thereof in accordance with section 3 (d);

(2) review and make recommendations to the Board on the findings of any assessment made by or for the Office; and

(3) undertake such additional related tasks as the Board may direct.

Sec. 10. (a) The Office shall maintain a continuing liaison with the National Science Foundation with respect to—

(1) grants and contracts formulated or activated by the Foundation which are for purposes of technology assessment; and

(2) the promotion of coordination in areas of technology assessment, and the avoidance of unnecessary duplication or overlapping of research activities in the development of technology assessment techniques and programs.

(b) Section 3 (b) of the National Science Foundation Act of 1950, as amended (42 U.S.C. 1862(b)), is amended to read as follows:

"(b) The Foundation is authorized to initiate and support specific scientific activities in connection with matters relating to international cooperation, national security, and the effects of scientific applications upon society by making contracts or other arrangements (including grants, loans, and other forms of assistance) for the conduct of such activities. When initiated or supported pursuant to requests made by any other Federal department or agency, including the Office of Technology Assessment, such activities shall be financed whenever feasible from funds transferred to the Foundation by the requesting official . . . and any such activities shall be unclassified and shall be identified by the Foundation as being undertaken at the request of the appropriate official."

Sec. 11. The Office shall submit to the Congress an annual report which shall include, but not be limited to, an evaluation of technology assessment techniques and identification, insofar as may be feasible, of technological areas and programs requiring future analysis. Such report shall be submitted not later than March 15 of each year. . . .

Judicial Acknowledgment of the Need for Policy Research

E—*Brown, et al.* v. *Board of Education of Topeka, et al.* 347 U.S. 483 (1954).

Mr. Chief Justice Warren delivered the opinion of the Court.

These cases come to us from the States of Kansas, South Carolina, Virginia, and Delaware. They are premised on different facts and different local conditions, but a common legal question justifies their consideration together in this consolidated opinion.

In each of the cases, minors of the Negro race, through their legal representatives, seek the aid of the courts in obtaining admission to the public schools of their community on a nonsegregated basis. In each instance, they had been denied admission to schools attended by white children under laws requiring or permitting segregation according to race. This segregation was alleged to deprive the plaintiffs of the equal protection of the laws under the Fourteenth Amendment. In each of the cases other than the Delaware case, a three-judge federal district court denied relief to the plaintiffs on the so-called "separate but equal" doctrine announced by this Court in *Plessy* v. *Ferguson*, 163 U.S. 537. . . .

The plaintiffs contend that segregated public schools are not "equal" and cannot be made "equal," and that hence they are deprived of the equal protection of the laws.

In the instant cases, that question is directly presented. Here, unlike *Sweatt* v. *Painter*, there are findings below that the Negro and white schools involved have been equalized, with respect to buildings, curricula, qualifications and salaries of teachers, and other "tangible" factors. Our decision, therefore, cannot turn on merely a comparison of these tangible factors in the Negro and white schools involved in each of the cases. We must look instead to the effect of segregation itself on public education.

In approaching this problem, we cannot turn the clock back to 1868 when the Amendment was adopted, or even to 1896 when *Plessy* v. *Ferguson* was written. We must consider public education in the light of its full development and its present place in American life throughout the Nation. Only in this way can it be determined if segregation in public schools deprives these plaintiffs of the equal protection of the laws.

Today, education is perhaps the most important function of state and local governments. Compulsory school attendance laws and the great expenditures for education both demonstrate our recognition of the importance of education to our democratic society. It is required in the performance of our most basic public responsibilities, even service in the armed forces. It is the very foundation of good citizenship. Today it is a principal instrument in awakening the child to cultural values, in preparing him for later professional training, and in helping him to adjust normally to his environment. In these days, it is doubtful that any child may reasonably be expected to succeed in life if he is denied the opportunity of an education. Such an opportunity, where the state has undertaken to provide it, is a right which must be made available to all on equal terms.

We come then to the question presented: Does segregation of children in public schools solely on the basis of race, even though the physical facilities and other "tangible" factors may be equal, deprive the children of the minority group of equal educational opportunities? We believe that it does.

In *Sweatt* v. *Painter* . . . in finding that a segregated law school for Negroes could not provide them equal educational opportunities, this Court relied in large part on "those qualities which are incapable of objective measurement but which make for greatness in a law school." In *McLaurin* v. *Oklahoma State Regents* . . . the Court, in requiring that a Negro admitted to a white graduate school be treated like all other students, again resorted to intangible considerations: ". . . his ability to study, to engage in discussions and exchange views with other students, and, in general, to learn his profession." Such considerations apply with added force to children in grade and high schools. To separate them from others of similar age and qualifications solely because of their race generates a feeling of inferiority as to their status in the community that may affect their hearts and minds in a way unlikely ever to be undone. The effect of this separation on their educational opportunities was well stated by a finding in the

Kansas case by a court which nevertheless felt compelled to rule against the Negro plaintiffs:

"Segregation of white and colored children in public schools has a detrimental effect upon the colored children. The impact is greater when it has the sanction of the law; for the policy of separating the races is usually interpreted as denoting the inferiority of the negro group. A sense of inferiority affects the motivation of a child to learn. Segregation with the sanction of law, therefore, has a tendency to [retard] the educational and mental development of negro children and to deprive them of some of the benefits they would receive in a racial[ly] integrated school system."[10]

Whatever may have been the extent of psychological knowledge at the time of *Plessy* v. *Ferguson*, this finding is amply supported by modern authority.[11] Any language in *Plessy* v. *Ferguson* contrary to this finding is rejected.

We conclude that in the field of public education the doctrine of "separate but equal" has no place. Separate educational facilities are inherently unequal. Therefore, we hold that the plaintiffs and others similarly situated for whom the actions have been brought are, by reason of the segregation complained of, deprived of the equal protection of the laws guaranteed by the Fourteenth Amendment. This disposition makes unnecessary any discussion whether such segregation also violates the Due Process Clause of the Fourteenth Amendment. . . .

Notes

10. A similar finding was made in the Delaware case: "I conclude from the testimony that in our Delaware society, State-imposed segregation in education itself results in the Negro children, as a class, receiving educational opportunities which are substantially inferior to those available to white children otherwise similarly situated." 87 A. 2d 862, 865 (*Editor's note:* Actual reference numbers are used here rather than numbers adjusted for deleted portions, as elsewhere).

11. K. B. Clark, Effect of Prejudice and Discrimination on Personality Development (Midcentury White House Conference on Children and Youth, 1950); Witmer and Kotinsky, Personality in the Making (1952), c. VI; Deutscher and Chein, The Psychological Effects of Enforced Segregation: A Survey of Social Science Opinion, 26 J. Psychol. 259 (1948); Chein, What are the Psychological Effects of Segregation Under Conditions of Equal Facilities?, 3 Int. J. Opinion and Attitude Res. 229 (1949); Brameld, Educational Costs, in Discrimination and National Welfare (MacIver, ed., 1949), 44–48; Frazier, The Negro in the United States (1949), 674–681. And see generally Myrdal, An American Dilemma (1944).

F—*Schmidt* v. *United States* 177 F.2d
    450 (2nd Cir. 1949).

L. Hand, Chief Judge.
The petitioner has appealed from an order denying his petition for naturalization on the ground that he had failed to establish that he was a person of "good

moral character" for the five years preceding the filing of the petition on July 5, 1944. He was a native of Germany, at that time thirty-nine years old, who had been admitted to the United States for permanent residence on January 17, 1939. He was a teacher of French and German in the College of the City of New York and was in every way qualified as a citizen, except that in a moment of what may have been unnecessary frankness, he verified an affidavit before the examiner, which contained the following passage. "Now and then I engaged in an act in sexual intercourse with women. These women have been single and unmarried women. As to the frequency of these acts I can only state that they occurred now and then. My last such act took place about half a year ago with an unmarried woman." The only question in the case is whether by this admission the alien showed that he was not a person of "good moral character."

In United States ex rel. Iorio v. Day, a deportation case where the Commissioner of Immigration had held that a violation of the Prohibition Law was "a crime involving moral turpitude", we said that it was "impossible to decide at all without some estimate, necessarily based on conjecture, as to what people generally feel." The phrase, "good moral character", in the Naturalization Law 8 U.S.C.A. § 155 is of the same kind, and makes the same demand. It is true that in Estrin v. United States we held that a single act of adultery, unexplained and unpalliated, was alone enough to prevent the alien's naturalization; but we refused to say whether under the "common standards of morality" there might not be "extenuating circumstances" for such a single lapse. In Petitions of Rudder et al, the question arose as to what those circumstances might be. Each of several aliens had been living for years with a single woman in an adulterous union, which apparently had not been concupiscent. Either the alien or the woman had been unable, for one reason or another, to get a divorce. We admitted them all because we did not "believe that the present sentiment of the community views as morally reprehensible such faithful and long continued relationships under the circumstances here disclosed." In United States v. Rubia, the alien was admitted upon substantially the same facts, save that he had had a good war record. In United States v. Francioso, we admitted an alien who had married, and was living with his niece under circumstances where we thought that "the moral feelings, now prevalent generally in this country" would not "be outraged because Francioso continued to live" with his wife and with four children whom he had had by her. The last case in which we passed on the clause was Repouille v. United States where the alien, in order to relieve his family of crushing expense, had killed his child who was a hopeless bed-ridden idiot. We thought that such conduct did not conform to "the generally accepted moral conventions current at the time"; but we added: "Left at large as we are, without means of verifying our conclusion, and without authority to substitute our individual beliefs, the outcome must needs be tentative; and not much is gained by discussion." In two very recent cases the Third Circuit by an equally divided court of all six judges, affirmed orders admitting two aliens in the following circumstances. In the first case, an unmarried man admitted that he had had occasional meretricious relations with a single woman for pay; in the second case, the facts were the same, except that the alien had a wife and children in Italy, from whom he had apparently not been legally separated.

The foregoing are the only cases that we have discovered in Courts of Appeal which touch nearly enough upon the case at bar to be important; and it must be owned that the law upon the subject is not free from doubt. We do not see how we can get any help from outside. It would not be practicable—even if the parties had asked for it, which they did not—to conduct an inquiry as to what is the common conscience on the point. Even though we could take a poll, it would not be enough merely to count heads, without any appraisal of the voters. A majority of the votes of those in prisons and brothels, for instance, ought scarcely to outweigh the votes of accredited churchgoers. Nor can we see any reason to suppose that the opinion of clergymen would be a more reliable estimate than our own. The situation is one in which to proceed by any available method would not be more likely to satisfy the impalpable standard, deliberately chosen, than that we adopted in the foregoing cases; that is, to resort to our own conjecture, fallible as we recognize it to be. It is true that recent investigations have attempted to throw light upon the actual habits of men in the petitioner's position, and they have disclosed—what few people would have doubted in any event—that his practice is far from uncommon; but it does not follow that on this point common practice may not have diverged as much from precept as it often does. We have answered in the negative the question whether an unmarried man must live completely celibate, or forfeit his claim to a "good moral character"; but, as we have said, those were cases of continuous, though adulterous, union. We have now to say whether it makes a critical difference that the alien's lapses are casual, concupiscent and promiscuous, but not adulterous. We do not believe that discussion will make our conclusion more persuasive; but, so far as we can divine anything so tenebrous and impalpable as the common conscience, these added features do not make a critical difference.

Order reversed; petition granted.

Administrative Agency Acknowledgment of the Need for Policy Research

G—*Shopping Kart Food Market, Inc.*
     228 NLRB N. 190 (April 8, 1977)

. . . During a meeting on the evening of June 19, 1974. Petitioner's vice president and business representative, Roger W. Deason, told the employees that the Employer had profits of $500,000 during the past year. The uncontroverted evidence establishes that the Employer's profits during this period amounted to approximately $50,000. The election was conducted the next day, June 20, 1974, between the hours of 3 and 4 p.m. Deason did not explain to the assembled employees how he arrived at the $500,000 figure.

Relying on *Cumberland Wood and Chair Corp.*, the Regional Director concluded that the Petitioner's statement did not constitute a material misrepresentation within the *Hollywood Ceramics* rule[1] because there was no evidence that Deason either had or could reasonably be perceived to have had knowledge concerning the Employer's profits. Accordingly, he overruled the Employer's objection and certified the Petitioner.

We agree with the Regional Director that the alleged misrepresentation does not warrant setting aside the election, but so find for the reasons set forth in Member Penello's dissenting opinions in *Medical Ancillary Services, Inc.*, and *Ereno Lewis*. In sum, we decide today that the Board will no longer probe into the truth or falsity of the parties' campaign statements. Accordingly, we hereby overrule *Hollywood Ceramics*.

As an initial matter, we understand this judgment to be one which the Board is clearly authorized to make. Thus, the Supreme Court has long recognized that the Board possesses a "wide degree of discretion" in performing its function of establishing policies and procedures to safeguard the conduct of representation elections. Most significant, in the recent *Weingarten* decision, the Court held that the exercise of our administrative discretion in the decisionmaking process necessarily includes the authority to revise or modify principles previously adopted. The Court stated its holding in the following emphatic terms:

> The use by an administrative agency of the evolutional approach is particularly fitting. To hold that the Board's earlier decisions froze the development of this important aspect of the national labor law would misconceive the nature of administrative decisionmaking. "'Cumulative experience' begets understanding and insight by which judgments . . . are validated or qualified or invalidated. The constant process of trial and error, on a wider and fuller scale than a single adversary litigation permits, differentiates perhaps more than anything else the administrative from the judicial process." [Citation omitted.]

. . . Our more than 20 years' experience with the rule of *Hollywood Ceramics* and its progenitor, *The Gummed Products Company*, 112 NLRB 1092 (1955), has revealed that although its adoption was premised on assuring employee free choice its administration has in fact tended to impede the attainment of that goal. The ill effects of the rule include extensive analysis of campaign propaganda, restriction of free speech, variance in application as between the Board and the courts, increasing litigation, and a resulting decrease in the finality of election results. As has been thoughtfully examined in several scholarly studies of this subject, to a large degree the source of these difficulties lies in the very nature of the standards we have formulated and sought to administer. Thus, Professor Bok, in his classic treatise on Board election procedures,[2] stated: "If a standard of truth and accuracy could actually provide an administrable norm, something might be said for adopting such a view. But this possibility tends to dissolve on more careful analysis. In the welter of words exchanged during a heated campaign, it is plainly impractical to intervene upon every misstatement made by the agents of the union or the employer. Thus, judges and administrators have long recognized that inaccurate or misleading assertions should be proscribed only under certain conditions. These qualifications, however, immediately began to blur the line between the licit and illicit." Professor Bok concluded that restrictions on the content of campaign propaganda requiring truthful and accurate statements "resist every effort at clear formulation and tend inexorably to give rise to vague and inconsistent rulings which baffle the parties and provoke litigation." . . .

Despite the many difficulties in administering the *Hollywood Ceramics* rule, we, too, would nevertheless choose to continue to adhere to it if we shared the belief that employees needed our "protection" from campaign misrepresentations. However, we do not find this to be the case. For our fundamental disagreement with past Board regulation in this area lies in our unwillingness to embrace the completely unverified assumption that misleading campaign propaganda will interfere with employees' freedom of choice. Implicit in such an assumption is a view of employees as naive and unworldly whose decision on as critical an issue as union representation is easily altered by the self-serving campaign claims of the parties. If these postulates had any validity 20 years ago at the time of *Gummed Products*, they are surely anachronisms today. We decline to join those who would continue to regulate on the basis of such assumptions notwithstanding "improvements in our educational processes, and despite the fact that our elections have now become almost commonplace in the industrial world so that the degree of employee sophistication in these matters has doubtless risen substantially during the years of this Act's existence. . . ." Rather, we believe that Board rules in this area must be based on a view of employees as mature individuals who are capable of recognizing campaign propaganda for what it is and discounting it.

The recently published results of an empirical study of NLRB elections suggest that ours is the more accurate model of employee behavior.[3] In this study, Professors Getman and Goldberg interviewed over 1,000 employees in 31 elections conducted in five States. The data cast doubt on the assumption that employees are unsophisticated about labor relations and are therefore easily swayed by campaign assertions, as 43 percent of the study's respondents had been union members elsewhere and 30 percent had voted in previous Board elections. Perhaps the study's most significant finding was that the votes of 81 percent of the employees could be correctly predicted from their *precampaign* intent and their attitudes toward working conditions and unions in general. Thus, the campaign did not influence the majority of employees to vote contrary to their predispositions for or against union representation. Rather, the choices of these employees appear to be a product of attitudes formed on the basis of their everyday experiences in the industrial world. This conclusion is supported by other data indicating that employees are generally inattentive to the campaign.[4] Concerning the remaining employees who voted contrary to their original intent or were undecided at the outset of the campaign, only the 5 percent of the total sample who either switched to the union or were originally undecided and ultimately voted for the union could be said to have been influenced by the campaign of the party for which they voted.

Based on assumptions of employee behavior which we find dubious at best and productive of a host of ill effects, we believe that on balance the *Hollywood Ceramics* rule operates more to frustrate free choice than to further it and that the purposes of the Act would be better served by its demise. Accordingly, we decide today that we will no longer set elections aside on the basis of misleading campaign statements. However, Board intervention will continue to occur in instances where a party has engaged in such deceptive campaign practices as improperly involving the Board and its processes, or the use of forged documents which render the voters unable to recognize the propaganda for what it is. While the former standard represents no change in Board law, by our adoption of the latter we choose to revert to our earlier policy of setting an election aside not on the basis of the *substance* of the representation, but the deceptive *manner* in which it was made. The essential difference lies in the fact that, while employees are able to evaluate mere propaganda claims, there is simply no way any person could recognize a forged document "for what it is" from its face since, by definition, it has been altered to appear to be that which it is not.

Retention of this standard is fully consonant both with our view of employees as intelligent voters and with our duty to insure the integrity of our election process. We shall, of course, continue our policy of overseeing other campaign conduct which interferes with employee free choice outside the area of misrepresentations which had been objectionable only under the *Hollywood Ceramics* rule.

Accordingly, as the Employer's objection has been overruled, and as the revised tally of ballots shows that the Petitioner has received a majority of the valid ballots cast in the election, we shall certify it as the exclusive bargaining representative of the employees in the appropriate unit. . . .

MEMBERS FANNING AND JENKINS, dissenting in part:

Our colleagues are today departing from long-established Board precedent concerning the treatment of substantial misrepresentations in campaign rhetoric incident to employee opportunity to elect a bargaining representative. This Board will "no longer probe into the truth or falsity of the parties' campaign statements." . . .

Now . . . a majority of this Board has come to the conclusion that there is no need to protect employee voters; that, if there ever was a need, the passage of time has made employees so sophisticated as to negate such need. Our colleagues suggest that we have considered employees "naive," "unworldly," and easily swayed by a self-serving campaign. In *some* cases, we have had such concerns. Overall we would characterize our concern as stemming from the desirability of maintaining election standards that call a halt to misrepresentation considerably short of fraud. It is well for the parties to have a minimum of lingering doubt as to the fairness of the election if bargaining ensues. Stability of the bargaining relationship and, hence, industrial peace are encouraged if that doubt is minimized.

In rationalizing their policy shift, our colleagues rely upon studies whose authors essentially conclude that employees do not attend closely to preelection campaigns, and that employee voting predilections are not easily changed by campaign information. Therefore, say our colleagues, the *Hollywood Ceramics* rule has done no more than protect free choice in a few. That, we sincerely question. We are aware of these studies and of the fact, as well, that our Nation is given to opinion polling, a technique much used in political campaigns, partly as a guide to tailoring campaign content. In the recent study on "Behavioral Assumptions," the poll consisted of postelection interviews in a five-state area of the Midwest and Upper South, made within a few days after the elections. To our colleagues it is significant that it appears that 81 percent of the employee vote could have been accurately predicted from individual precampaign intent, as recalled postelection. Not commented upon from the same study is the apparent fact that 50 percent of the employees were aware of union claims concerning wages elsewhere, though the precise amount (within 10 percent of the actual claim) was recalled by only 22 percent. We are not prepared to view 22-percent "precise" recall as insignificant. Even the 5 percent of voters who appear to have admitted changing their minds due to the campaign are not insignificant in our view. Highly significant is awareness by *half* the voters of the wages-elsewhere issue. In such circumstances, if substantially inaccurate wage claims were made at the last minute and the employees themselves had no basis for evaluation, we consider it desirable for this Board to rivet attention on a correction by holding a second election. If the result, as here, is not to hold a second election, the parties are nevertheless made aware of the principle—that misleading matter has been considered. An appropriate standard is thereby maintained.

In 1974, the year the authors of "Behavioral Assumptions" made their study, objections of all kinds were filed in only 11 percent of the 9,000 or more elections conducted by the Board. Board elections held per year now top 10,000. The General Counsel's statistics for the last 6 years show that objections based on misrepresentation averaged between 3 and 4-½ percent:

ALLEGED UNION MISPREPRESENTATIONS	PERCENT SUSTAINED
1971—174	1.7
1972—176	9.1
1973—240	3.8
1974—142	10.6
1975—245	4.1
1976—223	3.6
ALLEGED EMPLOYER MISREPRESENTATIONS	
1971—205	10.7
1972—150	11.3
1973—210	10.0
1974—104	15.4
1975—207	7.2
1976—84	21.4

Thus the Board considers some 300 to 400 cases per year on the issue. Considering its importance, this seems to us an excellent investment in maintaining our election standards. The number of second elections run as a result can hardly be viewed as burdensome. For the above figures show that second elections are directed in 7 percent (25 to 27 second elections per year) of the cases in which misrepresentation objections are filed under *Hollywood Ceramics*.

These figures demonstrate two facts of considerable importance to our decision in this case. First, they refute the argument of critics of the *Hollywood Ceramics* policy, adopted by our colleagues, that the losing parties "will object routinely" to their opponent's campaign statements. Objections there may be; routinely filed, no. Secondly, these figures also refute our colleagues' view that the rule guaranteeing investigation and resolution of misrepresentation objections "operates more to frustrate free choice than to further it and that the purposes of the Act would be better served by its demise." For the significance of these numbers lies not in the fact that so few elections are set aside under *Hollywood Ceramics*, but that in over 95 percent of the more than 10,000 elections conducted each year the employees can cast their ballots after responsibly conducted campaigns. Indeed, even if one were inclined to accept the view that the 31 elections studied by the authors of "Behavioral Assumptions" constitute a statistically significant sample—a dubious proposition at best—and the resultant conclusion that precampaign intent can predict the result in 29 out of 31 cases, its validity is surely limited to campaigns conducted in accordance with *Hollywood Ceramics* standards. Were those standards to be relaxed—to the "almost anything goes" standard proposed by our colleagues—one result can be fairly predicted. Campaign charges and countercharges would surely escalate. For the parties will campaign, and they will campaign on the assumption that what they say may make the difference. As "bad money drives out the good," so misrepresentation, if allowed to take the field unchallengeable as to its impact, will tend to drive out the responsible statement.

Our colleagues seek to eliminate the delay in resolving objections under the present system and we agree with them—and with those who thoughtfully follow Board decisions and discuss them, often in published writings—that this delay is a haunting problem to us. This case in particular is egregious in its postponement of election results. However, in view of the consensus not to set aside, it is most unfortunate that this case was not allowed to issue and a more timely one chosen as the vehicle. Perhaps that is inevitable in reevaluations. . . .

Thus, we are unimpressed by the mirage of ill effects our colleagues see in the *Hollywood Ceramics* policy. In our view, proof is entirely lacking that administration of the rule has tended to impede informed free will exercise of voter franchise. Rather, in untold numbers of uncontested elections, it has encouraged that objective.

MEMBER JENKINS, dissenting further:

The majority, in deciding that misrepresentations in an election campaign are of no importance, relies extensively, indeed perhaps solely, on a law review article which the writers have since expanded into a book.[5] In evaluating this conclusion and where it might lead, it is appropriate to examine the latest and most complete expression of the writers' methods, rationale, logic, and conclusions. Such examination leads me to substantial reservations on all points.

These writers conclude (pp. 120-121) that potential union supporters are unaffected by what they perceive as an employer's unlawful campaigning. They base this on their finding that, among the initial union supporters, those who ultimately voted against the union did not report unlawful campaigning in a greater percentage of cases than those who voted for the union. Yet, the most that can be drawn from this "fact" appears to me to be that the depth of conviction regarding union support varies with individuals, and some of them can be turned around while others cannot.

Using the same sort of "fact" and logic, the writers conclude that discharges perceived as discriminatory similarly have no effect in influencing employees' votes (p. 126).

They also conclude that interrogation does not affect employee attitudes, because "it was rarely reported by employers as a campaign tactic" (p. 149). Yet, the writers did not ask directly whether interrogation had taken place and, nevertheless, 20 employees volunteered that it had occurred in (seemingly) 16 of the 31 elections examined. This appears to me to indicate that interrogation made a substantial impression on the employees. The writers further support their conclusion by the facts that 43 percent of the union voters believed the employer knew their views, and 76 percent of these had voluntarily disclosed their views to the employer. Obviously, interrogation of these hardy souls, 33 percent of the voters, would be unimportant and indeed needless—it is the other two-thirds that concern us, and about whom the writers tell us nothing.

They find that union authorization cards are sufficiently reliable indicators of union support that elections are really not needed (pp. 135, 153), but then conclude that elections are preferable to recognition on the basis of cards in order to allow the employer to present his campaign (pp. 136, 153), and they concede, contrary to what one would expect from their willingness to ignore all election campaign misconduct, that such campaigns are effective in switching the position of the voters (p. 145).

With this sort of nonprobative factual data and *non sequitur* logic, these writers find it easy to conclude that discharges, other reprisals, grants of benefits, threats, promises, interrogation, and misrepresentations should be eliminated as grounds for setting aside elections (pp. 147-152). It is these uncertain guides the majority is here following with regard to misrepresentations. There is no reason to think the same course will not lead them to disregarding threats, promises, discharges, other reprisals, grants of benefits, and interrogation. The number of *Gissel* bargaining orders[6] issued on the basis of card majorities after unions have lost elections tainted by unlawful conduct shows that something is causing voters to switch. It is this inescapable fact which my majority colleagues, in reliance on these writers, ignore.

Notes

1. *Hollywood Ceramics Company, Inc.* 140 NLRB 221 (1962).
2. "The Regulation of Campaign Tactics in Representation Elections Under the National Labor Relations Act," 78 Harv. L. Rev. 38, 85 (1964).
3. Getman and Goldberg, "The Behavioral Assumptions Underlying NLRB Regulation of Campaign Misrepresentations: An Empirical Evaluation," 28 Stanford L. Rev. 263 (1976).
4. *Id.* at 276-279. This conclusion is also in accord with that of an earlier study of NLRB elections. See Brotslaw, "Attitude of Retail Workers Toward Union Organization," 18 Lab. L.J. 149 (1967).
5. "Union Representation Elections: Law and Reality." Getman, Goldberg and Herman (Russell Sage Foundation, New York, 1976).
6. *N.L.R.B.* v. *Gissel Packing Co., Inc.*, 395 U.S. 575 (1969).

H—*Chelsea Neighborhood Association* v. *U.S. Postal Service* 516 F.2d 378 (2nd Cir. 1975)

Feinberg, Circuit Judge:

The United States Postal Service (the Service) appeals from a decision of the United States District Court for the Southern District of New York, Robert J. Ward, J., enjoining it "from entering into any contract for, or proceeding in any way with, the construction of the U.S. Postal Service Vehicle Maintenance Facility" in the Chelsea neighborhood of Manhattan "pending final determination of this action or alternatively, pending . . . [the district] court's determination that there has been compliance with NEPA, 42 U.S.C. § 4332(2)(C)." The preliminary injunction was granted upon the motion of plaintiffs, a group of Chelsea neighborhood associations and individuals residing in the area. We affirm the order of the district court.

I. Background

In 1968, the then Post Office Department acquired a square-block site next to the Morgan Station postal facility in New York City. Subsequently, it was proposed that the ground levels be used for a Vehicle Maintenance Facility (VMF) and the air space be granted to New York City for public housing. An apartment complex was to be built on the roof of the VMF. This was agreed upon in 1972, and the New York District Army Corps of Engineers commenced preparing an Environmental Impact Statement (EIS) for the project. The first draft of the EIS was released to the public in January 1973. Another draft was prepared and circulated. The final Statement, dated March 26, 1974, was submitted to the Council on Environmental Quality, which published its receipt on April 8, 1974, in the Federal Register. 39 Fed.Reg. 12783 (1974). The EIS described the subject matter of this lawsuit as the construction

> of a major U.S. Postal Service vehicle maintenance facility (VMF) in combination with a multi-story housing project in the lower West Side of the Borough of Manhattan, New York City. The project will occupy an entire city block, presently vacant, adjacent to the Morgan Station mail processing center. Features of the proposed action are a multi-story VMF, a housing project of approximately 860 units utilizing air rights space above the VMF, and the closure of 29th Street between Ninth and Tenth Avenues to non-postal traffic, except during the evening rush period.

Plaintiffs characterize the VMF as a huge garage with space for over 900 vehicles. Its concrete walls would rise directly from the sidewalk for approximately 80 feet, on top of which would be a flat platform with housing extending upward from there. Noting that approximately 2,200 truck movements in and out of the VMF are anticipated daily, plaintiffs contend that the impact of the garage would devastate their community. The Service points out that many of the trucks would travel to and from the adjacent Morgan Station in any event; the Service also minimizes the impact of the VMF, asserting that it is not located in the Chelsea residential area, but rather on the border between Chelsea and a commercial district. According to the Service, the VMF will actually act as a buffer against further commercial encroachment and help stabilize the area. Nevertheless, plaintiffs clearly do not want the VMF in or near Chelsea. In July 1974, they requested the Service in writing to abandon the VMF and convey the site to the city for strictly residential purposes. Plaintiffs suggested that another site, the Yale Express garage located ten blocks away, be considered. The Service rejected the demand and this action followed. Plaintiffs sought to enjoin the project until the provisions of the National Environmental Policy Act of 1969 (NEPA), 42 U.S.C. § 4321 et seq., and the Clean Air Act, 42 U.S.C. § 1857 et seq., had been fully complied with, and asked for a mandate directing the Service to reconsider the VMF in light of the availability of the Yale Express garage. Thereafter, the Service solicited and obtained bids for construction of the VMF alone. Upon plaintiffs' motion, Judge Ward granted a preliminary injunction, finding that the Service was subject to NEPA, and that the EIS already prepared was inadequate. The Clean Air Act and Yale Express allegations were not considered. The judge also denied without prejudice the Service's motion to dismiss or for summary judgment on the Clean Air Act claims.

On appeal, the Service contends, as it did below, that it is exempt from NEPA. If it is not exempt, the Service argues that the EIS already filed was sufficient. Finally, the Service asks us to dismiss plaintiffs' Clean Air Act claims even though they were not reached below. . . .*

III. Adequacy of the Environmental Impact Statement

Having decided that the Service must comply with NEPA, we turn to the Environmental Impact Statement actually filed. The adequacy of an EIS can only be considered in light of its purpose. "The primary purpose of the impact statement is to compel federal agencies to give serious weight to environmental factors in making discretionary choices." Monroe County Conservation Council, Inc. v. Volpe, 472 F.2d 693, 697 (2d Cir. 1972). NEPA, in effect, requires a broadly defined cost-benefit analysis of major federal activities. It seeks to insure that more than economic costs alone are considered.

"Environmental amenities" will often be in conflict with "economic and technical considerations." To "consider" the former "along with" the latter must involve a balancing process. In some instances environmental costs may outweigh economic and technical benefits and in other instances they may not. But NEPA mandates a rather finely tuned and "systematic" balancing analysis in each instance.

. . . NEPA is, "at the very least, 'an environmental full disclosure law.'" *Monroe County*, supra, 472 F.2d at 697.

The EIS in this case describes the "Proposed Action," as already noted, as "a major U.S. Postal Service vehicle maintenance facility (VMF) in combination with a multi-story housing project." The EIS is a sizeable document whose very bulk is impressive.[1] Unfortunately for the Service, however, Judge Ward was not sufficiently impressed with its substance, finding it lacking in three respects.[2] These were the failure of the EIS to discuss sufficiently (1) the impact of the proposed housing; (2) the possibility that no housing would ever be erected; and (3) alternatives to the proposed construction.

Turning to the first of these alleged inadequacies, the judge found that one shortcoming of the EIS lay in using the housing portion of the project as a virtue, while ignoring many of its associated disadvantages. There is no doubt that the air-rights housing was a chief "selling point" for the entire project. In the "Assessment of Trade-Offs" section of the EIS, the paragraph concerning beneficial consequences ends as follows:

Most importantly, the proposed project is a response to a pressing local housing need, to which the community readily admits.

And the ultimate finding is:

It is the conclusion of this Statement that the *net effect* of the project development is positive, as it represents an improvement of Postal Service opera-

Editor's Note: The court found that the Postal Service is subject to NEPA.

tions as well as a much needed source of low- and moderate-income housing for the Chelsea-Clinton community. [Emphasis in the original.]

EIS at III-35-36. The summary portion of the EIS, in the section concerning impacts, notes: "The most significant impact of the project is the positive response to a pressing and obvious need for low- and moderate-income housing in the area." EIS at 3. And there are other instances where the project is justified on the basis of the housing.

Yet the EIS does not contain a comprehensive analysis of the environmental impact of the housing. There is brief mention of possible overcrowding at a local elementary school, the need for future expansion of local health services, and the effect on park usage. But the report does not treat the effect of the housing with anywhere near the thoroughness accorded the VMF. For example, the VMF will require closing 29th Street for most of the day and diversion of traffic onto adjacent streets. The EIS states that tightened parking enforcement on those streets will help keep the extra volume of traffic flowing. But the statement does not consider where those parked cars will go; nor does it discuss what will be done with the automobiles of the residents of the proposed 860 apartments in the air-rights housing or the automobiles of the 1,500 drivers and employees of the VMF. The required support services for the housing are not adequately discussed. Garbage collection is disposed of by a single paragraph stating, in effect, that it will all be trucked away. What will be the expected noise and air pollution contribution from those trucks is not adequately discussed.

A possibly more serious shortcoming of the housing analysis lies in the social, not physical, sciences. What effect will living at the top of an 80-foot plateau have on the residents of the air-rights housing? Will there be an emotional as well as physical isolation from the community? Will that isolation exacerbate the predicted rise in crime due to the increase in population density? That an EIS must consider these human factors is well established. . . . The EIS gives scant attention to these serious questions. It acknowledges that "project size, height and design and the incidence of crime" are all related. EIS at III-31. But the only response is to suggest that "[p]roject design should reflect this emerging body of research to the extent practicable." Id. This is not enough. We do not know whether informed social scientists would conclude that the top of the VMF would likely become a human jungle, unsafe at night and unappealing during the day. The question must be faced, however, by those who plan the project.[3]

In short, we agree with Judge Ward that the impact of the housing was not accorded the "full consideration" required by NEPA. See Calvert Cliffs', 449 F.2d at 1128. The Service argues that since the housing portion of the project is speculative it cannot be required to assess the unknowable or to postpone the VMF indefinitely. We agree that the Service can only do the possible, but the total number of apartment units has been approximated and an evaluation of probable environmental impact need not await final detailed design. . . .

The judgment of the district court is affirmed. The appeal from that portion of the order denying the Service's motion to dismiss or for summary judgment on the Clean Air Act claims is dismissed.

Notes

1. The EIS contains over 250 pages.
2. While the court did not make explicit the standard of review it applied to the sufficiency of the EIS, we believe it applied the proper test: Was the agency's consideration of the factors listed in 42 U.S.C. § 4332(2)(C) arbitrary, capricious, or an abuse of discretion? Hanly v. Kleindienst, 471 F.2d 823, 829 (2d Cir. 1972), cert. denied, 412 U.S. 908, 93 S.Ct. 2290, 36 L.Ed.2d 974 (1973); Citizens to Preserve Overton Park, Inc. v. Volpe, 401 U.S. 402, 413-14, 91 S.Ct. 814, 28 L.Ed.2d 136 (1971); Committee for Nuclear Responsibility, Inc. v. Seaborg, 149 U.S.App.D.C. 380, 463 F.2d 783, 787 (1971).
3. The Senate Committee Report accompanying NEPA states:

   Using an interdisciplinary approach . . . would result in better planning and better projects. Too often planning is the exclusive province of the engineer and cost analyst.

   S. Rep.No. 91-296, supra, at 20. The treatment in the EIS of the social impact of the housing suggests that the narrow approach feared by the drafters occurred.

Author Index

Subject Index

641